★ ★

NATIONAL GRANGE

BICENTENNIAL YEAR
COOKBOOK

★ ★

Dear Patrons and Friends:

How many times have you heard people say, "Do you remember Grandma's homemade bread and her wonderful strawberry preserves?" Haven't you often wished that you could put your hands on some of those old and really good-tasting "receipts" of yesteryear?

This National Grange Bicentennial Year Cookbook is an attempt to thoughtfully reminisce about the good old days and bring back the nutritious and flavorful cooking of our mothers and grandmothers.

We received thousands of recipes from Grange members and friends to use in the cookbook. I truly wish we could have used them all, but the cost factor in printing a larger book was prohibitive. We also wanted to keep the cost down so the sale price to you would be reasonable.

All of the recipes in this book are family tested and selected from many personal recipe collections. We are also proud to include recipes from the wives of both the President and Vice President as well as many other government and Congressional leaders and friends of Grange members.

Grange women and men are renowned for their culinary skills and we know this cookbook will be an appropriate Bicentennial project for the women's activities department. No doubt, in years to come, it will be a very valuable souvenir of the Bicentennial celebration.

This project was first conceived because someone had faith in the women of the Grange to make it a success. The Grange has always been far ahead of its time where women are concerned. It was the very first organization in the country to give women an equal vote with men. Consequently, because of the foresight of our Founders, the Grange has stayed alive and vital and continues to play a leading role in the development of rural America and remains dedicated to the prosperity of farmers and rural citizens everywhere.

A project of this nature is not done overnight. We are indeed indebted to many who have helped in the development and production of this book. A particular note of appreciation is due the personnel at Favorite Recipes Press in Montgomery, Alabama, for their enthusiastic support, encouragement and cooperation.

We are hopeful this cookbook will focus attention on agriculture and further promote the use of American agricultural products and that you and your families and friends will enjoy it.

With all good wishes for a world of happy and nutritious eating,

Fraternally and sincerely,

Jenny Grobusky

Mrs. Jenny Grobusky
Director of Women's Activities

©Favorite Recipes Press MCMLXXV
Post Office Box 3396, Montgomery, Alabama 36109
Library of Congress Cataloging in Publication Data
Main entry under title:
National Grange Bicentennial Year Cookbook.
Compiled by the National Grange of the Patrons of
Husbandry Cookbook Committee.
Includes index.
1. Cookery.   I. Patrons of Husbandry.
National Grange. Cookbook Committee.
TX715.N328   641.5   75-30860
ISBN 0-87197-100-3

National Grange Headquarters
Washington, D.C.

Board of Advisors

Cookbook Committee

Coordinator
Mrs. Judy Taylor Massabny
Director of Information and Public Relations

Contributing Editors

Mrs. John (Dorothy) Scott
Wife, National Master

Mrs. Robert (Mary) Proctor
Wife, National Secretary

Mrs. Herschel (Blanche) Newsom
Wife, Past National Master

Staff Assistants

Mrs. Lorena Stigers
Mrs. Suellen Meyer
Miss Cheryl Overbeck
Miss Denise Field

Contents

Special Recipes from Friends in the Nation's Capitol

Washington, D.C., the home of our nation's capital, is also the home of many of our country's highest officials. It is a city in which senators, representatives and department heads from every state in the union work to keep the government of the United States of America "of the people, by the people and for the people."

Entertaining has long been an important part of political life. Statesmen's wives are always looking for new ways to add a special flair to their frequent dinner parties. Throughout the years, their personal recipe files have grown to include some of the most appetizing and varied dishes ever prepared. Because these women have chosen to share their favorites with the members of Grange, this is the most unique category presented in the National Grange Bicentennial Year Cookbook.

Just as our representatives in Washington are a reflection of the great diversity of people and customs in our nation, these recipes present a panorama of our nation's history and eating pleasures. Their wide variety is indicative of the great abundance which we enjoy in our country. Many recipes use products which are locally available in each statesman's district and reflect the foods that are preferred there. Thumbing through this section is almost like taking a condensed tour of the country.

Evolving from the simple methods of the past to the elaborate procedures of the present, American cooking has undergone as many changes in the past 200 years as has our nation. While many of these recipes are original, treasured heirlooms, others have been revised from the basic dishes served in homes years ago. All are truly delicious and deserve to be preserved for future generations.

Experience the delight of serving a dish that has been enjoyed by some of the most distinguished guests in the nation.

★ ★

RUBY RED GRAPEFRUIT-CHICKEN

2 ruby red grapefruit
1/2 c. whole cranberry sauce
1 tbsp. honey
1/4 tsp. cloves
1/4 tsp. salt
1 fryer, disjointed
3 tbsp. butter

Peel and section grapefruit, squeezing all juice from membranes into saucepan. Add cranberry sauce, honey, cloves and salt, mixing well, then bring to a boil. Stir in grapefruit sections. Brown chicken in butter in frypan, then place in shallow baking dish. Baste with grapefruit sauce. Bake in 350-degree oven for about 45 minutes, basting frequently. Serve chicken with remaining grapefruit sauce. Yield: 4 servings.

Mrs. Gerald R. Ford
Wife of President of United States

NEW YORK STATE FLAT APPLE PIE

1/2 c. butter
1/2 c. margarine
2 c. flour
3 to 4 tbsp. ice water
11 or 12 med. New York State Apples
1 c. sugar
1 tbsp. cinnamon
Juice of 1/2 lemon
1/2 c. New York State maple syrup
New York State sharp cheese, sliced

Cut the butter and margarine into the flour with knife or pastry blender until like cornmeal. Add ice water gradually, and work in just enough to hold together. Roll out on lightly floured board or marble slab until one inch thick. Place in refrigerator for 20 minutes. Remove; roll again until 1/8 inch. Place pastry on 15 x 10-inch flat pan or baking sheet. Peel, core and cut each apple into 6 sections. Arrange in 1 layer on pastry in pan. Mix sugar and cinnamon; sprinkle over apples. Sprinkle with lemon juice. Bake in preheated 450-degree oven for 20 minutes. Reduce oven temperature to 350 degrees; bake for 30 minutes longer. Remove from oven; drizzle with maple syrup. Serve while warm with generous slice of cheese.

Mrs. Nelson A. Rockefeller
Wife of Vice President of United States

FAVORITE ROLLS

4 c. sifted flour
1 tsp. baking powder
1/2 tsp. soda
1/2 c. sugar
1 tsp. salt
1/2 c. shortening
1 cake yeast
2 c. buttermilk

Sift dry ingredients together; cut in shortening. Dissolve yeast in buttermilk; add to flour mixture, mixing

by hand. Place in refrigerator until ready to use. This dough will be very soft. Make rolls into small balls, using heavily floured fingers. Place balls close together in 2 greased 9-inch cake pans. Cover; let rise for about 2 hours. Bake in preheated 350-degree oven until done. Serve very hot.

Mrs. Earl L. Butz
Wife of Secretary of Agriculture
Washington, D.C.

SHRIMP CREOLE
(Recipe 25 years old)

3 tbsp. butter
1 lb. fresh or frozen shrimp
2 c. cooked rice
1 c. light cream sauce
1/2 c. tomato sauce
1/2 tsp. salt
1 med. onion, grated
1/2 tsp. celery salt

Melt butter; add shrimp and simmer for 3 minutes. Add rice, cream sauce, tomato sauce, salt, onion and celery salt; mix well. Bring to a boil; turn into a casserole. Bake in preheated 350-degree oven for 30 minutes. Yield: 6 servings.

Mrs. John T. Dunlap
Wife of Secretary of Labor
Washington, D.C.

COUNTRY-FRIED STEAK

Flour
8 cubed or minute steaks
Salt and pepper to taste
Butter
1 med. can sliced mushrooms, drained
1 lg. onion, coarsely chopped
Garlic powder to taste
Worcestershire sauce to taste
Soy sauce to taste
Oregano to taste
Tabasco sauce to taste

Sprinkle generous amount of flour on large platter. Season each steak with salt and pepper. Turn steaks over and over in flour, rubbing flour into steaks with fingers until coated and no more flour will adhere. Melt enough butter in deep, heavy aluminum or iron skillet to more than cover bottom. Cook steaks, 2 or 3 at a time, over medium heat until brown, adding butter as each batch is cooked and placing steaks in Pyrex dish. Add more butter to skillet. Add mushrooms and onion; cook over medium heat, stirring, until onion is lightly browned. Add garlic powder, Worcestershire sauce, soy sauce, oregano and Tabasco sauce, then stir in flour remaining on platter. Place steaks on onion mixture in layers; pour enough very hot or boiling water into skillet to just cover steaks. Stir around bottom of skillet with cooking spoon, moving steaks around to mix water with onion mixture. Reduce heat to very low; cover skillet tightly. Cook for about 2

★ ★

hours or until steaks are very tender and gravy is thick, stirring occasionally and moving bottom steaks to top to cook all equally. Serve with rice or mashed potatoes.

Mrs. James B. Allen
Wife of Senator from Alabama
Washington, D.C.

GRANDMOTHER FRASIER'S HAGGIS

(Recipe about 100 years old)

2 lb. beef or lamb heart
2 lb. calves liver, scalded
1 lb. lean pork
2 tbsp. minced beef suet
1 c. coarse oatmeal
1 c. cooked pearl barley
Salt to taste
Pepper to taste
Chopped onion to taste
2 tsp. allspice
Scotch whisky

Put meats through coarse blade of food grinder. Combine meats with remaining ingredients except whisky in large saucepan. Cook until all red color disappears, stirring down constantly. Line 4-quart bowl with cheesecloth; pack in meat mixture. Tie up ends of cheesecloth to form closed bag. Place in upper part of steamer. Cover; steam for 2 hours. Uncover; remove cheesecloth. Flame with Scotch whisky.

Haggis is said to be enjoyed in proportion to amount of Scotch drunk with it, and/or poured over it. Haggis is the national dish of Scotland, the only country where this unique dish is appreciated. The stomach of a sheep is filled with seasoned stuffing of minced heart, liver, lung, oatmeal and chopped suet, then boiled like a pudding. Pot haggis is more easily appreciated by non-Scots as it is a simpler version.

Mrs. Caspar W. Weinberger
Wife of Past Secretary of HEW
Washington, D.C.

JELLIED VEAL

4 1/2 lb. veal on the bone, leg, shoulder
  or neck
3 1/2 pt. water
1 tbsp. salt
10 white peppercorns
5 allspice
1 bay leaf
2 whole cloves
1 onion
White pepper
1 tbsp. vinegar
1 env. unflavored gelatin, soaked in
  1/4 c. cold water

Trim the veal; place in saucepan. Pour in water; bring to a boil. Add remaining ingredients except gelatin. Cover; simmer for about 1 hour and 30 minutes or until veal is tender. Lift veal from liquid; let cool. Do

not waste any of the liquid. Cut the veal into cubes or mince. Return the bones to liquid; bring to a boil. Continue to boil to get rich stock. Strain, then pour stock back into saucepan. Add veal; bring to a boil. Add more seasoning if needed; stir in gelatin. Boil for several minutes longer. Pour into molds; refrigerate until set. This amount makes about 2 pounds of jellied veal. Do not freeze.

This is an old Swedish recipe, always prepared for the Christmas Holidays, but is served at any time of the year. Use as a first course or with a buffet.

Mrs. Warren E. Burger
Wife of Chief Justice of the United States
Supreme Court
Washington, D.C.

CRAB CASSEROLE

8 slices bread
2 c. crab
1/2 c. mayonnaise
1 onion, chopped
1 green pepper, chopped
1 c. chopped celery
3/4 c. milk
1 egg
1 1/4 c. thick white sauce with mushrooms
Grated cheese
Paprika

Dice half the bread. Mix crab, mayonnaise, onion, pepper and celery; spread on bread. Trim remaining bread; arrange over crab mixture. Combine milk and egg; mix well. Pour over all. Bake at 325 degrees for 15 minutes. Remove from oven; pour mushroom sauce over top. Sprinkle with cheese and paprika; bake for 1 hour longer. Yield: 8 servings.

Mrs. Ted Stevens
Wife of Senator from Alaska
Washington, D.C.

ARIZONA CHILI

1 lb. dried pinto beans
1 lb. coarsely ground beef
2 c. chopped onions
1 6-oz. can tomato puree
3 tbsp. chili powder
Salt to taste
1 tbsp. cumin

Cook beans in boiling water until tender. Saute beef in skillet until lightly browned; drain off excess fat. Add onions, puree and beans. Mix chili powder, salt and cumin; add to beef mixture. Bring to a boil; reduce heat to low. Cook until flavors are well blended. Beans may be soaked overnight and added without precooking; chili must cook long enough for beans to be tender.

Mrs. Paul J. Fannin
Wife of Senator from Arizona
Washington, D.C.

★ ★

PEGGY'S RANCH-STYLE FRIJOLES

    2 lb. pinto beans
    2 tsp. salt
    2 lg. onions
    4 cloves of garlic
    1 can roasted green chilies
    1/2 tsp. pepper
    1 can taco sauce
    1/2 tsp. cumino seed
    1 can tomatoes

Soak pinto beans in cold water overnight. Drain and rinse; cover with about 2 inches of water. Add salt; boil over moderate heat for about 1 hour, adding water as needed. Dice onions and garlic. Chop green chilies. Combine garlic, onions, chilies, pepper, taco sauce, cumino seed and tomatoes. Stir tomato mixture into beans. Cook over low heat for 1 hour and 30 minutes or until beans are tender. Add 1 to 2 teaspoons of red chili powder for spicier beans. Beans may be reheated with a small amount of water or tomato sauce added. Stir to prevent burning.

Mrs. Barry M. Goldwater
Wife of Senator from Arizona
Washington, D.C.

MARGARET CHILES' FRIED CORN
(Recipe 100 years old)

    10 ears fresh corn
    10 slices bacon
    Salt and pepper to taste

Shuck corn; remove silk. Place large end of ear on board; hold perpendicular to board with other hand. Slice outer edge of kernels off with sharp knife, then scrape cream out of remaining part of kernels. Fry bacon; set aside. Pour corn into hot bacon drippings; fry for 4 minutes. Season with salt and pepper. Milk may be added if corn is not creamy enough.

Mrs. Lawton Chiles
Wife of Senator from Florida
Washington, D.C.

BAKED COUNTRY-CURED HAM

    1 country-cured ham
    Whole cloves
    Brown sugar
    Honey
    Apple cider
    Brandy Sauce

Wash ham thoroughly; place in roasting pan, fat side up. Pour 2 inches water into pan. Wine, ginger ale, apple cider, orange juice, pineapple juice, peach pickle juice, Coca-Cola or champagne may be used instead of water, if desired. Cover roasting pan. Bake ham in preheated 350-degree oven for about 20 minutes per pound or until done, basting frequently. Remove ham from oven; uncover. Increase oven temperature to 450 degrees. Remove rind from ham; trim off some of the fat. Score fat in diamond shapes; stud each diamond with 1 clove. Cover ham with brown sugar, then honey. Add desired amount of apple cider to roasting pan. Bake until ham is glazed, basting frequently. Serve with Brandy Sauce. Ham may be soaked in cool water for 12 to 24 hours for milder flavor, if desired.

BRANDY SAUCE

    1 1-lb. box brown sugar
    6 whole cloves
    Juice of 2 oranges
    2 oz. brandy

Mix sugar, cloves and orange juice in saucepan; bring to a boil. Remove from heat; stir in brandy.

Mrs. Herman Eugene Talmadge
Wife of Senator from Georgia
Washington, D.C.

PEKING DUCK

    1 4 to 6-lb. Long Island duckling
    Salt
    6 to 7 green onions
    1 sm. piece of gingerroot
    2 tbsp. dry sherry
    1/4 c. Hoisin sauce
    2 tbsp. honey
    2 tbsp. shoyu sauce

Wash and clean duckling. Rub salt on skin and cavity; let stand for 30 minutes. Wash and clean onions and gingerroot; crush together. Combine crushed mixture, sherry, Hoisin sauce, honey and shoyu sauce in small bowl; let stand for about 10 minutes. Pour sauce over and inside duckling; let marinate for at least 1 hour. Bake in 375-degree oven for 30 minutes. Reduce oven temperature to 250 degrees; bake for 1 hour. Increase oven temperature to 400 degrees; bake for 30 minutes. Coals should be red hot with vents slightly open if duckling is cooked in a charcoal fire drum. Hang duck in drum; roast for 1 hour or until tender.

Mrs. Hiram L. Fong
Wife of Senator from Hawaii
Washington, D.C.

SUET PUDDING
(Recipe 75 years old)

    2 3/4 c. flour
    1 tsp. soda
    1 tsp. salt
    1 tsp. cinnamon
    1 tsp. nutmeg
    1/4 tsp. allspice
    1/4 tsp. cloves
    1/2 c. sugar
    1 c. coarsely ground suet
    1 c. chopped nuts
    1 c. ground raisins
    1/2 c. molasses
    1/2 c. dark corn syrup
    1 c. hot water

★ ★ ★ ★ ★★★★★★★★★★★★★★★★★★★★★★★★★★★★★★★★★★★★★★ ★ ★ ★ ★

Sift flour, soda, salt, cinnamon, nutmeg, allspice, cloves and sugar together into bowl. Mix suet, nuts and raisins in bowl. Add enough flour mixture to coat all ingredients; mix well. Add molasses, corn syrup and hot water to remaining flour mixture; mix well. Add suet mixture; stir until mixed. Pour into greased and sugared 8-cup pudding mold or 9 x 5-inch loaf pan; cover tightly. Place on trivet or rack in heavy kettle; add 1 inch boiling water. Cover kettle tightly. Bring to a boil over high heat. Reduce heat to low; cook for 3 hours, adding boiling water, if needed. Remove lid; cool before unmolding. Yield: 12-14 servings.

Mrs. Jim McClure
Wife of Senator from Idaho
Washington, D.C.

BASQUE CHICKEN

4 whole chicken breasts, cut in halves
Flour
4 tbsp. corn oil
1 med. onion, thinly sliced
1 c. fresh mushrooms, sliced
Thyme and bay leaf to taste
Coarsely ground pepper and salt to taste
1 No. 2 can tomatoes
1 green pepper, thinly sliced
1/4 c. stuffed green olives

Dust chicken lightly with flour. Cook in 2 tablespoons corn oil in skillet until golden brown. Place in casserole. Brown onion and mushrooms in remaining 2 tablespoons corn oil; add thyme, bay leaf, pepper and salt. Add tomatoes; simmer until part of the liquid has evaporated. Add green pepper and olives; mix well. Pour over chicken. Bake in preheated 300-degree oven for 1 hour. Serve over rice. One fryer, disjointed, may be substituted for chicken breasts. One can mushroom stems and pieces may be used instead of fresh mushrooms. Yield: 4-8 servings.

Mrs. Frank Church
Wife of Senator from Idaho
Washington, D.C.

SPAGHETTI AND MEATBALLS

1 onion, chopped
2 cloves of garlic, chopped
1 can Italian tomato paste
3 tomato paste cans water
Salt and pepper to taste
1/4 c. (or more) sugar
2 bay leaves
1 lb. ground beef
4 slices bread moistened with water
2 eggs
1/2 c. grated cheese
1/4 c. chopped parsley
Spaghetti

Fry onion and 1 clove of garlic in hot oil in skillet until brown. Add tomato paste; cook and stir with fork for 3 minutes. Add water, salt, pepper, sugar and

bay leaves. Simmer for 1 hour and 30 minutes. Combine ground beef, moistened bread, eggs, cheese, parsley, remaining garlic, salt and pepper in large bowl; mix well. Dampen hands; roll ground beef mixture in small balls. Fry in another skillet until brown all over. Transfer meatballs to skillet with sauce; simmer for 1 hour or longer. Meatballs and sauce may be prepared ahead. Allow 3/4 pound spaghetti per person; cook in large amount of boiling salted water according to package directions. Cook spaghetti just before serving time. Meatballs and sauce may be reheated to serve with spaghetti.

Mrs. Vance Hartke
Wife of Senator from Indiana
Washington, D.C.

YELLOW ANGEL FOOD CAKE

5 eggs, separated
1 1/2 c. cold water
1 1/2 c. sugar
1 1/2 c. flour
1/2 tsp. baking powder
1/4 tsp. salt
1 tsp. vanilla extract
3/4 tsp. cream of tartar

Beat egg yolks well; beat cold water into eggs. Add sugar; beat well. Sift flour, baking powder and salt into egg yolk mixture. Add vanilla; mix well. Beat egg whites until stiff; beat in cream of tartar. Add to flour mixture, folding carefully. Place in tube pan. Bake in preheated 300-degree oven for 15 minutes. Increase temperature to 350 degrees; bake for 1 hour longer.

Mrs. Birch Bayh
Wife of Senator from Indiana
Washington, D.C.

GRANOLA

5 c. rolled oats
1 c. wheat germ
1 c. soy flour
1 c. powdered milk
1 c. sesame seeds
1 c. sunflower nuts
1 c. chopped mixed nuts
1 c. honey
1 c. vegetable oil or peanut oil

Mix all dry ingredients in a large roasting pan. Mix honey and oil in a bowl. Add to dry ingredients; mix until all dry ingredients are coated. Bake in 350-degree oven for about 30 minutes, stirring several times. Store in airtight jars or containers. Make sure all ingredients are natural ingredients with no chemicals, preservatives or additives.

Dick Clark
Senator from Iowa
Washington, D.C.

★ ★

CHEESE NUGGETS

1/4 c. soft butter
1 c. sharp Cracker Barrel cheese, softened
3/4 c. flour
1/8 tsp. salt
1/2 tsp. paprika
Stuffed green olives or cocktail onions

Blend butter with cheese. Sift in flour, salt and paprika; mix well. Shape dough around olives; place on ungreased cookie sheet. Bake in preheated 400-degree oven for 10 to 15 minutes. May be made ahead and refrigerated or frozen; may be served hot or cold.

Mrs. John Culver
Wife of Senator from Iowa
Washington, D.C.

JAM CAKE
(Recipe over 100 years old)

1 c. butter
1 1/2 c. sugar
4 eggs, separated
1 c. blackberry jam
3 c. all-purpose flour
1 tsp. (or more) cinnamon
1 tsp. nutmeg
1 tsp. allspice
1 tbsp. soda
1 c. buttermilk
1/2 c. finely chopped black walnuts (opt.)

Cream butter and sugar; add slightly beaten egg yolks. Add jam; mix well. Sift flour and spices together; mix soda and buttermilk. Add flour mixture to creamed mixture alternately with buttermilk mixture. Fold in stiffly beaten egg whites. Dredge walnuts with small amount of additional flour; fold into batter. Line 3 layer pans with waxed paper; pour batter into pans. Bake in preheated 350-degree oven for 35 to 40 minutes or until straw inserted in center comes out clean. Cool for 10 minutes; remove from pan. Cool.

FILLING

2 1/2 c. sugar
2 eggs, beaten
1 1/2 c. milk or cream
1/2 c. flour
1 pkg. figs, chopped
1 pkg. dates, chopped
1 c. dark seeded raisins
3/4 c. black walnuts or pecans
1 tbsp. vanilla extract

Mix all ingredients in saucepan; cook until very thick, stirring to keep from sticking. May be cooked in double boiler. Frost cake with Filling; decorate with nuts and green and red candied pineapple. One and 1/4 cups brown sugar may be substituted for half the sugar; 1/2 cup white raisins may be substituted for half the dark raisins.

Mrs. Wendell Ford
Wife of Senator from Kentucky
Washington, D.C.

SHRIMP REMOULADE

1/2 c. tarragon vinegar
2 tbsp. tomato catsup
4 tbsp. creole mustard
1 tbsp. paprika
1 tsp. salt
1/2 tsp. cayenne pepper
1 clove of garlic, pulverized
1 c. salad oil
1/2 c. minced green onions with tops
1/2 c. minced celery
4 lb. cooked and cleaned shrimp

Mix vinegar, catsup, mustard, paprika, salt, pepper and garlic in small bowl. Add oil gradually. Stir in green onions and celery. Place vinegar, catsup, mustard, paprika, salt, pepper and garlic in blender container, if desired; blend for 17 seconds. Pour oil gradually through center opening while blender is running; blend until well mixed. Pour sauce over shrimp; marinate in refrigerator for 4 to 5 hours. Place 6 marinated shrimp on shredded lettuce for each serving. Yield: 16 servings.

Mrs. Russell B. Long
Wife of Senator from Louisiana
Washington, D.C.

JANE MUSKIE'S NEW ENGLAND DINNER

4 to 5 lb. corned beef brisket
1/2 bay leaf
5 peppercorns
Basil to taste
Thyme to taste
Parsley to taste
6 white or yellow turnips, peeled
    and sliced
8 carrots, pared
4 parsnips, peeled
10 sm. onions, peeled
8 med. potatoes, peeled
1 green cabbage, cored and cut in wedges

Place beef in deep kettle; cover with cold water. Add herbs, but no salt. Bring water to a boil, skimming off fat. Cover and simmer for 3 to 4 hours. Add all vegetables except cabbage; cook for about 20 minutes. Add cabbage; cook for about 25 minutes longer or until all vegetables are tender. Place beef on hot platter; surround with vegetables.
The Muskie family likes New England dinner with horseradish, mustard pickle and hot buttered bread, then fresh fruit and brownies for dessert.

Mrs. Edmund S. Muskie
Wife of Senator from Maine
Washington, D.C.

SEMI-FREDDO

1 tsp. vanilla extract
6 egg yolks, beaten

★ ★

1 tsp. grated lemon rind
10 tbsp. sugar
6 tbsp. flour
4 c. milk, scalded
2 sq. cooking chocolate, grated
1/3 c. rum
3 3-oz. packages ladyfingers
Whipped cream flavored with vanilla

Combine vanilla, egg yolks, lemon rind, 6 tablespoons sugar and flour in saucepan; mix well. Add milk slowly, beating constantly with rotary beater. Cook over low heat, stirring constantly with wooden spoon, until mixture comes to a boil. Cook for 4 minutes, stirring constantly; remove from heat. Pour half the pudding into bowl; set aside to cool, stirring occasionally to prevent film from forming on top. Add chocolate to remaining hot pudding. Cook for 1 minute longer or until chocolate is melted, stirring constantly; cool. Line 10 x 5-inch deep baking pan or dish with waxed paper, leaving overlap of waxed paper. Mix 1/3 cup water, remaining 4 tablespoons sugar and rum in small bowl. Dip ladyfingers lightly in rum mixture; line bottom and sides of the baking pan with ladyfingers. Pour half the chocolate pudding over ladyfingers; cover with layer of dipped ladyfingers. Pour half the vanilla pudding over ladyfingers; cover with layer of dipped ladyfingers. Repeat layers, ending with vanilla pudding; chill until cold. Unmold onto serving platter; remove waxed paper. Frost with whipped cream. Garnish with maraschino cherries and additional grated chocolate. May substitute 1 package prepared chocolate pudding mix flavored with almond and vanilla extracts and 1 package prepared vanilla pudding mix flavored with almond extract and grated lemon rind for cooked pudding in recipe. Yield: About 12 servings.

Mrs. Edward W. Brooke
Wife of Senator from Massachusetts
Washington, D.C.

CHICKEN MURIEL

1 fryer
2 c. milk
Salt
1/4 c. butter
Lime or lemon juice
Pepper
1 pkg. long grain and wild rice mixture
1 c. sour cream
1 bouillon cube, dissolved (opt.)
1/4 c. chopped chives
Pinch of oregano or Season-All
1/4 to 1/2 c. dry California white
wine (opt.)

Cut fryer into serving pieces. Mix milk and 1 teaspoon salt in bowl. Add chicken; marinate for about 2 hours. Drain chicken; reserve milk mixture. Cook chicken in butter in skillet until lightly browned. Sprinkle lightly with lime juice; add salt and pepper to taste. Prepare rice mixture according to package directions; place in casserole. Place chicken over rice. Mix sour cream with

1/2 cup reserved milk mixture. Add 1/4 teaspoon salt, 1/8 teaspoon pepper, 1/2 teaspoon lime juice and bouillon; stir in chives, oregano and wine. Pour over chicken; cover. Bake in preheated 375-degree oven for 1 hour and 40 minutes. Uncover; bake for 20 minutes longer. May be baked at 400 degrees for 1 hour, then temperature reduced to 325 degrees until ready to serve.

Mrs. Hubert H. Humphrey
Wife of Senator from Minnesota
Washington, D.C.

PUMPKIN BREAD

1 1/2 c. sugar
1 tsp. soda
1/4 tsp. baking powder
3/4 tsp. salt
1/2 tsp. cloves
1/2 tsp. nutmeg
1/2 tsp. cinnamon
1 2/3 c. flour
2 eggs
1/2 c. oil
1 c. canned pumpkin
1/2 c. water
1/2 c. chopped nuts
1/2 c. chopped dates

Sift sugar, soda, baking powder, salt, spices and flour together into large bowl. Add eggs, oil, pumpkin and water to dry mixture; beat with electric mixer until well mixed. Stir in nuts and dates. Turn into two 9 x 5-inch pans. Bake in 350-degree oven for 1 hour and 30 minutes.

Mrs. Walter F. Mondale
Wife of Senator from Minnesota
Washington, D.C.

MISSISSIPPI BANANA CAKE

1/2 c. butter
1/2 c. Wesson oil
2 c. sugar
4 eggs, well beaten
3 c. flour
1 1/2 tsp. cloves or allspice
2 tsp. cinnamon
1 1/2 tsp. soda
1/2 tsp. salt
5 or 6 ripe bananas, well mashed
2 c. chopped pecans
2 c. halved candied cherries

Cream butter, Wesson oil and sugar in bowl. Add eggs; mix well. Sift flour, cloves, cinnamon, soda and salt together 3 times. Add to butter mixture alternately with bananas; fold in pecans and cherries. Place in greased tube pan. Bake in preheated 300-degree oven for 1 hour and 30 minutes.

Mrs. John C. Stennis
Wife of Senator from Mississippi
Washington, D.C.

★ ★

CHOCOLATE CAKE

    3 c. sifted flour
    2 c. sugar
    6 tbsp. cocoa
    2 tsp. soda
    1 tsp. salt
    3/4 c. cooking oil
    2 tbsp. vinegar
    2 tsp. vanilla extract
    2 c. water

Sift flour, sugar, cocoa, soda and salt into mixing bowl. Add oil, vinegar, vanilla and water; beat until smooth. Pour into greased and floured 13 x 9 1/2 x 2-inch baking pan. Bake in preheated 350-degree oven for 25 to 30 minutes; cool. Top with desired frosting.

Thomas F. Eagleton
Senator from Missouri
Washington, D.C.

MARMALADE PUDDING
(Recipe about 50 years old)

    3 eggs, separated
    Sugar
    2 tbsp. orange marmalade
    1/2 tsp. orange extract
    Butter
    1 c. whipping cream
    Vanilla extract to taste

Beat egg whites until stiff; add 3 tablespoons sugar and marmalade slowly. Fold in orange extract. Butter top of double boiler generously. Add egg white mixture; cook over boiling water for 45 minutes to 1 hour or until firm. Beat egg yolks until lemon colored. Beat cream until stiff, adding sugar to taste and vanilla. Fold egg yolks into whipped cream until just combined; serve with Marmalade Pudding. Yield: 4 servings.

Wife of Senator from Montana
Washington, D.C.

POTATO SOUP

    5 med. potatoes
    3 med. onions
    3 stalks celery with tops
    1 1/2 tsp. salt
    1 1/4 c. water
    1 qt. scalded milk
    Salt and pepper to taste

Pare and dice potatoes. Chop onions and celery. Combine potatoes, onions, celery, salt and water in large saucepan; cover. Cook until vegetables are soft. Mash until pureed; add milk. Season with salt and pepper. Simmer for 10 minutes, beating occasionally with rotary beater. Serve hot or cold. Flavor improves on second day.

Mrs. Clifford Case
Wife of Senator from New Jersey
Washington, D.C.

YEAST DUMPLINGS

    2 c. milk
    1 cake yeast
    1 tsp. sugar
    1 1/2 tsp. salt
    2 eggs, beaten
    5 2/3 to 6 c. flour
    2 slices stale bread

Scald milk; cool to lukewarm. Crumble yeast into milk; add sugar and 1/2 teaspoon salt. Add eggs; mix well. Stir in 4 cups flour gradually. Let rise in warm place until doubled in bulk. Toast bread; cut into small cubes. Add to dough; add 1 cup flour. Work with spoon until dough is elastic. Place on board; knead remaining flour into dough, then knead until dough is very elastic. Divide into 6 even portions; form into oblong shapes. Let rise until doubled in bulk. Fill 8-quart kettle with water; add remaining 1 teaspoon salt. Bring to a boil. Add dumplings; cover. Cook for about 7 minutes on each side or until cake tester inserted in center comes out clean. Remove to board; cut each dumpling with string or thread into 6 slices.

Mrs. Roman L. Hruska
Wife of Senator from Nebraska
Washington, D.C.

CHICKEN BREASTS WITH GRAPES

    8 chicken breast halves or thighs, boned
    Flour
    1 tbsp. butter
    Seasoned salt and pepper to taste
    1 tsp. mace
    1/2 c. chopped green onions
    1 clove of garlic, crushed (opt.)
    1 c. dry white wine
    1/2 c. water
    1 c. seedless grapes

Sprinkle chicken pieces with flour. Saute in butter in skillet until brown on both sides, seasoning each side with salt, pepper and mace. Add onions and garlic; transfer all ingredients to casserole. Add wine and water to skillet; stir to remove browned particles. Pour over chicken. Chicken may be refrigerated and baked later. Bake, covered, in preheated 400-degree oven for 40 minutes or until chicken is done. Add grapes; cover. Bake until grapes are heated through. Yield: 4 servings.

Mrs. Howard W. Cannon
Wife of Senator from Nevada
Washington, D.C.

WILD RICE CASSEROLE

    1 lb. veal, cut in 1-in. cubes
    1 tbsp. melted butter
    1 tsp. salt
    1 c. wild rice
    1 1/4 c. thick white sauce with mushrooms
    1/4 c. chopped onions
    1/2 c. chopped celery
    1/2 tsp. Worcestershire sauce

★ ★

2 tbsp. sherry
1/4 c. grated cheese

Cook and stir veal in butter until brown; season with salt. Cook rice according to package directions. Combine veal, rice, mushroom sauce, onions, celery, Worcestershire sauce and sherry; mix well. Pour into greased 1 1/2-quart casserole; sprinkle cheese on top. Bake in 350-degree oven for 50 minutes. Yield: 4 servings.

Mrs. Harrison A. Williams, Jr.
Wife of Senator from New Jersey
Washington, D.C.

CHILI CON QUESO

1 c. American cheese
1/2 c. cheddar cheese
1/4 c. evaporated milk
1 fresh tomato, peeled and finely chopped
1 (or more) green chili, chopped
1/8 tsp. garlic powder

Melt cheeses together over low heat. Add milk, stirring constantly. Add chopped tomato, chopped green chili and garlic powder. Stir to blend all flavors. Add more milk, if desired. Serve warm with tostados or potato chips.

Mrs. Joseph M. Montoya
Wife of Senator from New Mexico
Washington, D.C.

MAMA'S SPAGHETTI SAUCE
(Recipe 35 years old)

6 lb. good hamburger
3 lb. ground pork
2 onions, chopped
3 carrots
4 stalks celery
Dash of nutmeg
Dash of allspice
3 family-size cans tomato paste
3 lg. cans tomato sauce
3 lg. cans tomatoes
1 tbsp. sugar
4 to 6 qt. water
Salt and pepper to taste

Cook meat in oil until brown. Add onions, carrots, celery, nutmeg and allspice. Add tomato paste; cook for 10 minutes. Blend and add the remaining ingredients; simmer for 3 to 4 hours. Sauce freezes well in plastic containers. Yield: 14 servings.

Pete V. Domenici
Senator from New Mexico
Washington, D.C.

EASY GOULASH

1 lb. ground beef
Cooking oil
1 No. 2 can tomatoes

1 med. onion, diced
1 c. cooked rice
Salt and pepper to taste
Grated sharp cheese

Cook ground beef in skillet in small amount of cooking oil until brown. Cook tomatoes and onion in saucepan until onion is tender. Mix beef, tomato mixture, and rice; season with salt and pepper. Place in casserole; cover with cheese. Bake in preheated 350-degree oven for 30 minutes.

Mrs. Jesse Helms
Wife of Senator from North Carolina
Washington, D.C.

VENISON SAUERBRATEN

2 c. red wine
1 stalk celery, chopped
1 carrot, chopped
1 onion, chopped
1 bay leaf
Several peppercorns
Salt to taste
Pinch of thyme
1 venison roast
Crushed gingersnaps
Sour cream to taste

Combine wine, chopped vegetables, bay leaf, peppercorns, salt and thyme in glass dish or bowl. Add venison; marinate for 3 days, turning each morning and evening. Drain and wipe dry. Cook in small amount of butter until browned. Strain marinade; add to roast. Bring to a boil, then reduce heat. Simmer until tender. Add enough gingersnaps to pan juices to thicken for gravy. Add sour cream just before serving. Serve with noodles or German potato dumplings.

Mrs. Milton R. Young
Wife of Senator from North Dakota
Washington, D.C.

DELICIOUS HAM LOAF

1 lb. cured ham, ground
1/2 lb. fresh ham, ground
1 1/2 c. dry bread crumbs
2 eggs
3/4 c. milk
Pepper to taste
1/2 c. water
1/4 c. vinegar
1/4 c. sugar
1 tbsp. mustard

Mix first 6 ingredients in bowl; form into loaf. Place in baking pan. Mix water, vinegar, sugar and mustard; pour over loaf. Bake in preheated 350-degree oven for 1 hour and 30 minutes, basting frequently.

Mrs. John Glenn
Wife of Senator from Ohio
Washington, D.C.

★ ★

PEANUT BRITTLE

2 c. sugar
1/2 c. water
1 c. light corn syrup
2 c. shelled peanuts
Dash of salt
1 tsp. (heaping) soda
1 tsp. vanilla extract

Combine sugar, water and corn syrup in large, heavy saucepan; cook to hard-ball stage. Remove from heat; add peanuts and salt. Mixture will be quite thick. Return to heat; boil until mixture is golden brown and peanuts done. Remove from heat; stir in soda and vanilla. Pour out onto well-buttered surface; smooth until of desired thickness. Cool; break into pieces.

Mrs. Henry Bellmon
Wife of Senator from Oklahoma
Washington, D.C.

GOUGERE

1 c. water
1/2 c. butter
1 tsp. salt
1/8 tsp. pepper
Dash of nutmeg
1 c. sifted flour
5 eggs
2 c. grated Gruyere cheese

Pour water into saucepan; add butter, salt, pepper and nutmeg. Bring to a boil; reduce heat. Simmer until the butter has melted; remove from heat. Add all the flour at once; beat vigorously with electric hand mixer until thoroughly blended. Beat over moderately high heat for 1 or 2 minutes or until mixture leaves side of pan and forms ball. Remove saucepan from heat; add 4 eggs, one at a time, beating after each addition until egg is thoroughly mixed. Beat for 1 minute longer after last egg is added. Add cheese; mix well. Place mounds the size of a walnut 1 inch apart on greased sheet. Beat remaining egg with 1 teaspoon water; brush over mounds. Bake in preheated 425-degree oven for about 20 minutes; cool on rack.

Mrs. Mark O. Hatfield
Wife of Senator from Oregon
Washington, D.C.

PENNSYLVANIA DUTCH SHOOFLY PIE

1 tsp. soda
1 1/2 c. boiling water
1 1/2 c. blackstrap or barrel molasses
3 c. flour
1 c. (packed) brown sugar
1/2 c. shortening
1 tsp. salt
2 unbaked 9-in. pie crusts

Dissolve soda in boiling water; combine with molasses. Combine flour, sugar, shortening and salt until texture of cornmeal. Pour molasses mixture into pie crusts;

sprinkle flour mixture over molasses mixture. Bake in preheated 350-degree oven for 45 minutes.

Mrs. Richard S. Schweiker
Wife of Senator from Pennsylvania
Washington, D.C.

MEAT ROLL STEW

1/4 tsp. pepper
1/2 tsp. salt
1/8 tsp. garlic salt
1/2 c. bread crumbs
1 tbsp. grated cheese
1 tsp. chopped parsley
4 thinly sliced bottom round steaks
2 tbsp. oil
2 tbsp. wine (opt.)
1 c. water
4 peeled potatoes
4 peeled onions
4 pared carrots
1 stalk celery, diced

Mix pepper, salt, garlic salt, bread crumbs, cheese and parsley in bowl; spread on steaks. Roll each steak as for jelly roll; tie with string. Cook in deep pan in oil, turning to brown all sides; add wine and water. Place vegetables on steak rolls; do not turn vegetables. Add more salt and pepper to taste, if desired. Cover pan. Cook over low heat for 1 hour or until potatoes are done. Remove string from steaks before serving. Yield: 4 servings.

Mrs. John O. Pastore
Wife of Senator from Rhode Island
Washington, D.C.

CURRY SOUP

1 8-oz. package cream cheese
1 can consomme
2 tbsp. tomato paste
1 tbsp. curry
1 clove of garlic

Let cream cheese soften at room temperature. Combine cream cheese, consomme, tomato paste, curry and garlic in blender container. Blend until well combined. Chill before serving. Yield: 4 servings.

Mrs. Claiborne Pell
Wife of Senator from Rhode Island
Washington, D.C.

HOBO BREAD

2 c. raisins
2 c. boiling water
4 tsp. soda
2 c. sugar
2 tbsp. oil
4 c. flour

Combine raisins, boiling water and soda in large bowl; let stand overnight. Add sugar, oil and flour; mix well.

★ ★ ★ ★ ★★★★★★★★★★★★★★★★★★★★★★★★★★★★★★★★★★★★★★

Fill well-greased cans or pans 1/2 full. Bake in 350-degree oven for about 1 hour or until bread tests done.

Mrs. James Abourezk
Wife of Senator from South Dakota
Washington, D.C.

FRENCH SILK CHOCOLATE PIE

3/4 c. butter
3/4 c. sugar
1 1/2 oz. bitter chocolate, melted
1 tsp. vanilla extract
2 eggs
1 baked 8-in. pie shell
Whipped cream

Place butter in mixing bowl; beat with electric mixer at medium speed until creamed. Add sugar gradually, beating thoroughly. Blend in cooled chocolate; add vanilla. Add eggs, one at a time, beating for 5 minutes after each addition; pour into pie shell. Chill. Top with whipped cream before serving.

Mrs. Strom Thurmond
Wife of Senator from South Carolina
Washington, D.C.

TEXAS CHILI

3 lb. chili meat
1   15-oz. can tomato sauce
1 c. water
1 tsp. Tabasco sauce
3 (heaping) tbsp. chili powder
1 (heaping) tbsp. oregano
1 (heaping) tsp. cumino powder
2 onions, chopped
Garlic to taste
1 tsp. salt
1 tsp. paprika
12 red peppers
4 to 5 chili pods
2 (heaping) tbsp. flour

Cook meat over high heat, stirring constantly, until gray. Stir in tomato sauce and water, then add seasonings. Simmer for 1 hour and 15 minutes. Make a paste with flour and enough water to blend; add to thicken. Simmer for 30 minutes longer. Grind fresh chili peppers for chili powder.

John G. Tower
Senator from Texas
Washington, D.C.

BAKED CRAB IN SHELL

1 c. diced onions
2 c. diced celery
1 green pepper, diced
Butter
1 c. cracker crumbs

1 c. cream
Tabasco sauce to taste
Worcestershire sauce to taste
Lemon juice to taste
Minced parsley to taste
1 lb. lump crab
Paprika

Saute onions, celery and green pepper in small amount of butter until golden. Combine cracker crumbs, cream and seasonings in bowl; add sauteed mixture and crab. Mix well. Fill crab shells; sprinkle tops with paprika. Bake in preheated 350-degree oven for 40 minutes. Garnish with lemon to serve.

Lloyd Bentsen
Senator from Texas
Washington, D.C.

COLD OVEN POUND CAKE

1/2 c. shortening
1 c. butter
3 c. sugar
5 eggs
3 c. cake flour, sifted
1 lg. can evaporated milk
1 tsp. vanilla extract
1 tsp. baking powder

Cream shortening and butter in large bowl. Add sugar, small amount at a time, beating well after each addition. Add eggs, one at a time, beating vigorously after each addition. Add flour alternately with milk; beat well. Add vanilla; beat well. Add baking powder; beat well. Pour into greased and floured stem pan; place in cold stove. Bake in 350-degree oven for 1 hour and 15 minutes. Remove from oven immediately; remove from pan.

Mrs. William L. Scott
Wife of Senator from Virginia
Washington, D.C.

BAKED CRUSTY PINEAPPLE
(Recipe 35 years old)

8 slices pineapple
1/4 c. pineapple syrup
1 tsp. cinnamon
1/3 c. (packed) brown sugar
1 tsp. butter
1/3 c. graham cracker crumbs
Vanilla ice cream

Place pineapple slices in shallow pan; add pineapple syrup. Sprinkle slices with cinnamon. Cream sugar and butter; stir in cracker crumbs. Sprinkle crumb mixture on slices. Bake in preheated 400-degree oven for about 25 minutes. Serve each slice with scoop of ice cream. Yield: 8 servings.

Mrs. Gale McGee
Wife of Senator from Wyoming
Washington, D.C.

★ ★

BAKED CHICKEN SALAD

2 c. diced cooked chicken
1 c. diced celery
1/2 c. grated onion
1 1/4 c. thick white sauce with mushrooms
1/2 c. mayonnaise
1 tbsp. soy sauce
1/4 tsp. white pepper
1 c. slivered almonds

Combine chicken, celery and onion in large bowl. Combine sauce, mayonnaise, soy sauce and pepper; add to chicken mixture. Mix well. Arrange almonds on top. Bake in 350-degree oven for 35 to 40 minutes. Serve with hot rice.

Mrs. Gaylord Nelson
Wife of Senator from Wisconsin
Washington, D.C.

MEAT LOAF

1 1/2 lb. ground beef
1 c. bread crumbs
1 tsp. grated onions or onion salt
1 egg, beaten
1 1/2 tsp. salt
1/4 tsp. pepper
2 sm. cans tomato sauce
1/2 c. water
3 tbsp. vinegar
3 tbsp. brown sugar
2 tbsp. mustard
2 tsp. Worcestershire sauce
Bacon strips

Blend ground beef, bread crumbs, onions, egg, salt, pepper, and 1/2 cup tomato sauce. Form into loaf; place in shallow pan. Mix remaining tomato sauce, water, vinegar, brown sugar, mustard and Worcestershire sauce together in bowl. Place bacon strips on top of meat loaf. Pour tomato sauce mixture over loaf. Bake in 350-degree oven for 1 hour and 15 minutes.

Mrs. Jennings Randolph
Wife of Senator from West Virginia
Washington, D.C.

GRANDMA'S DROP COOKIES

1 c. butter
1 c. sugar
3 eggs, beaten
1/2 c. molasses
3 c. (about) flour
1 tsp. soda
1 tsp. cinnamon
1 tsp. cloves
1 tsp. nutmeg
1/2 c. sour milk
1/2 c. nutmeats
1/2 c. raisins

Cream butter and sugar until fluffy. Add eggs and molasses; mix well. Sift flour, soda and spices to-gether. Add flour mixture to molasses mixture alter-nately with sour milk; mix well after each addition. Stir in nutmeats and raisins. Drop by teaspoonfuls on greased baking sheet. Bake at 350 degrees for about 20 minutes.

Mrs. Clifford Hansen
Wife of Senator from Wyoming
Washington, D.C.

MATHIS FAMILY CHRISTMAS FRUITCAKE

1 lb. butter
2 c. sugar
6 eggs, beaten
4 c. all-purpose flour
1 tsp. baking powder
1/4 tsp. salt
2/3 tsp. vanilla extract
1 tsp. lemon extract
1/2 lb. candied cherries, cut in sm. pieces
1/2 lb. candied pineapple, cut in sm. pieces
1 qt. chopped pecans

Cream butter and sugar together until light. Add eggs; beat well. Combine 3 cups flour with baking powder and salt. Add flour mixture gradually to butter mix-ture, mixing well. Blend in vanilla and lemon extracts. Mix remaining 1 cup flour with candied fruits and pecans until well coated. Add fruit mixture to batter, stirring until well blended. Turn into a greased and floured 10 x 4 1/4-inch loaf pan. Bake in a preheated 250-degree oven for 3 hours.

Mrs. Patricia Mathis
Wife of Representative from Georgia
Washington, D.C.

FRESH APPLE SALAD

Red and golden Delicious apples
Lemon juice
1 c. diced celery
1 c. diced oranges
1 c. diced pineapple
1/2 c. green seedless grapes, halved
1/2 c. currants, raisins or dates
1/2 c. chopped pecans or walnuts
Sliced bananas to taste
Cream Cheese Dressing

Core apples but do not peel red ones; dice enough apples to make 4 cups. Sprinkle with lemon juice to prevent discoloring. Add celery, oranges, pineapple, grapes, currants, pecans and bananas, tossing to mix well. Add enough Cream Cheese Dressing to coat well, just before serving. Canned oranges and pineapple may be used, if desired.

CREAM CHEESE DRESSING

1   3-oz. package cream cheese, softened
2 to 3 tbsp. pineapple juice

★ ★ ★ ★ ★★ ★ ★ ★ ★

1 c. whipping cream, whipped
Confectioners' sugar to taste, (opt.)

Beat cream cheese until fluffy; beat in juice. Fold in whipped cream and small amount of sugar, if desired. Will keep for several days in refrigerator.

Mrs. Steven D. Symms
Wife of Representative from Idaho
Washington, D.C.

IRISH STEW

4 1/2 lb. lamb neck chunks
2 tbsp. butter
2 1/2 c. water
2 tsp. salt
1/4 tsp. pepper
1/4 tsp. thyme
3 med. potatoes
6 sm. white onions
1 pkg. frozen green peas
1/4 lb. fresh or canned sliced mushrooms
1 c. light cream or milk
1/4 c. flour

Brown lamb in butter in large Dutch oven or kettle. Add water and seasonings; cover and simmer for 45 minutes. Peel potatoes; cut into medium-sized chunks. Skim excess fat from top of kettle. Add potatoes and onions. Simmer, covered, for 15 minutes. Add peas and mushrooms; simmer, covered, for 15 minutes longer or until lamb and vegetables are tender. Blend cream into flour, stirring until well mixed. Pour flour mixture into bubbling stew; boil for 1 minute, stirring constantly. Add more seasoning, if desired. Yield: 6 servings.

Tom Harkin
Representative from Iowa
Washington, D.C.

WATERMELON RIND PICKLES
(Recipe 50 years old)

7 lb. watermelon rind
Lime
4 1/2 lb. sugar
1 qt. vinegar
1 tbsp. whole cloves
1 tbsp. allspice
1 tbsp. stick cinnamon
1 tbsp. ginger

Peel and cut rind into small pieces. Prepare lime water by mixing 1 heaping tablespoon lime and 1 gallon water in portion large enough to cover watermelon rind. Pour lime water over rind in large glass or enameled container; let soak overnight. Drain and rinse thoroughly with cold water. Cover rind with clear water; cook until rind can be pierced with straw. Drain, then add sugar, vinegar and spices and water to cover. Cook until rind is clear and thick syrup forms. Pack rind in sterilized jars up to 1/2 inch from top. Cover with boiling syrup, leaving 1/2-inch headspace. Place lids and rings on jars. Process in boiling water bath for 10 minutes.

Mrs. Charles G. Rose
Wife of Representative from North Carolina
Washington, D.C.

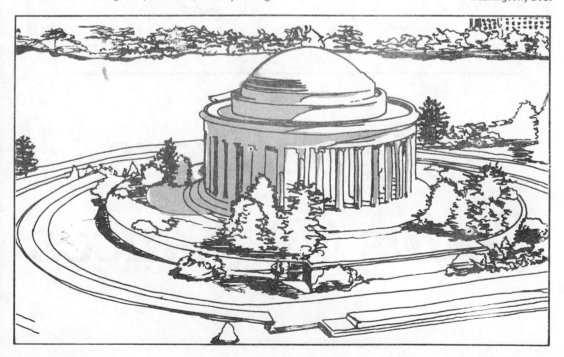

Appetizers, Soups & Sauces

Appetizers not only lend a hint of good food to come later and get the appetite ready, but also make nourishing snacks and nibbles for after school, television viewing, parties and meetings. They are also a thrifty way to use cheese, vegetable and meat leftovers in a fresh, taste-pleasing way. The numerous variations of mayonnaise and sour cream-based dips make an endless source of mix and match flavors for appetizers.

Soups can serve as an appetizer, or make an entire meal. One of the best qualities about soup is that it can be made from the most expensive, fresh ingredients or the most common of leftovers and can be as light or as filling as desired and still be a nutritious and satisfying dish. Think of a hearty, thick soup served with crusty bread on a cold, wintery day! It is as nutritious and satisfying for us today as it was for our forefathers during the early years of settling this country. As the recipes in this section suggest, the ingredients that comprise a soup are as varied as what nature has to offer. Some of the ingredients, like squirrel, pumpkin and oatmeal, have been used in soups and stews for hundreds of years. The vegetable and meat combinations for soups are limitless, and it is important to remember that the addition of potatoes, dumplings and noodles can extend and fortify even the plainest broth.

Sauces, although one of the easiest ways to add a special touch to a dish, are probably one of the most neglected areas of American cooking. From the most basic white sauce or pan gravy to the spiciest of barbecue or seafood sauces, there is hardly a better way to top vegetables, meats and appetizers.

All the recipes in this section point to ways in which you can add extra touches to and make the most use of the foods on your menu, as well as stretch the food budget. This is as important to homemakers today as it was to the settlers in times when even the basics were often hard to come by.

★ ★

ARTICHOKE FRITATA
(Recipe 50 years old)

1/2 c. melba toast crumbs
1/2 c. milk
1 tbsp. oil
1 med. onion, chopped
2 c. cooked chopped artichoke hearts
1 lg. clove of garlic, pressed
2 tbsp. minced parsley
1/2 c. grated Parmesan cheese
4 eggs, beaten
1 tsp. Accent
1/2 tsp. thyme
Salt and pepper to taste

Place crumbs in large bowl. Pour milk over crumbs; let stand until crumbs are moistened. Heat oil in saucepan. Add onion; cook, stirring, until tender. Add to crumbs mixture. Add remaining ingredients in order listed, mixing well after each addition; place in oiled square baking dish or large pie plate. Bake in preheated 350 to 400-degree oven for about 25 minutes or until set. Broil until brown; cool. May be served hot for entree.

Neola Kreiss
Pescadero Grange, No. 793
Pescadero, California

To prevent Lamp-wicks from Smoking: Soak them in vinegar and then dry them thoroughly.

CREAM CHEESE-STUFFED CELERY

1 3-oz. package cream cheese
2 tbsp. grated carrot
2 tbsp. chopped parsley
2 tbsp. chopped green pepper
2 tbsp. chopped chives or green onion
Short lengths of celery stalks

Mix first 5 ingredients thoroughly. Stuff celery with cream cheese mixture.

Myrtle Buckmaster
Rio Linda Grange, No. 403
Highlands, California

CHEESE PUFFS

2 c. grated sharp American cheese
1/2 c. soft butter
1 c. sifted flour
1/2 tsp. salt
1 tsp. paprika
48 stuffed olives, drained

Blend cheese with butter in mixing bowl; stir in flour, salt and paprika. Wrap 1 teaspoon cheese mixture

around each olive, covering completely; arrange on baking sheet. Bake in preheated 400-degree oven for 15 minutes; serve warm. May be made ahead and frozen before baking; bake as needed.

Dorothy Tobey
Fair Harbor Grange, No. 1129
Grapeview, Washington

COTTAGE CHEESE-STUFFED CELERY

3 tbsp. sour cream
1/4 lb. cottage cheese
7 radishes, chopped
2 tbsp. chopped chives or scallions
Salt and pepper to taste
Paprika to taste
Celery stalks

Mix sour cream with cottage cheese; stir in radishes and chives. Sprinkle with salt, pepper and paprika; mix well. Fill celery with cheese mixture.

Mrs. Margaret Colson
Jefferson Grange, No. 2019
Sharpsville, Pennsylvania

CHEESE PLEASERS

4 eggs
1/2 c. cream
1 loaf sliced sandwich bread
Melted butter
Grated Parmesan cheese

Place eggs and cream in bowl; beat until mixed. Cut crusts off entire loaf of bread. Dip 1 slice bread in egg mixture until soggy; drain. Place on top of a dry slice; place another dry slice on top, making 3-slice sandwich. Repeat with remaining slices of bread. Cut each sandwich into 9 cubes; place on cookie sheet. Place in freezer until frozen. Place in plastic bags; freeze. Dip each cube in melted butter, then roll in Parmesan cheese when ready to serve. Place on cookie sheet. Bake in preheated 400-degree oven for 8 to 10 minutes or until brown, watching carefully.

Jerrine May
Goldendale Grange
Goldendale, Washington

PECAN-CHEESE BALL

1 8-oz. package cream cheese
1 oz. bleu cheese, grated
1/2 c. softened butter
Chopped tops of green onions to taste
Chopped black olives to taste
Chopped pimentos to taste
Chopped pecans

Soften cream cheese in mixing bowl. Add bleu cheese and butter; mix with electric mixer until combined. Stir in onions, olives and pimentos; refrigerate for

★ ★

about 1 hour and 30 minutes. Shape into ball; roll in pecans. Serve with assorted crackers.

Cheryl Breckenridge Day
Lincoln Grange, No. 295
Oklahoma City, Oklahoma

GOLDEN CHEESE SANDWICH SPREAD

2 c. shredded Cheddar cheese
1 3-oz. package cream cheese, softened
1/4 c. mayonnaise or salad dressing
1/2 tsp. Worcestershire sauce
1/8 tsp. onion salt
1/8 tsp. garlic salt
1/8 tsp. celery salt

Place all ingredients in large bowl; stir until well mixed. Yield: About 1 1/2 cups.

Charlene Panter
Bandon Grange, No. 702
Bandon, Oregon

DILLWEED DIP

2/3 c. salad dressing
2/3 c. sour cream
1 tsp. garlic salt
1 tsp. celery salt
2 tsp. dillweed
1 tsp. parsley flakes
1 tsp. onion flakes
1 tsp. Beau Monde seasoning

Mix all ingredients in bowl; chill. Serve with fresh vegetable plate.

Molly Krueger
Trentwood Grange, No. 1056
Spokane, Washington

GERRY'S DIP

1 8-oz. package cream cheese
1/4 c. salad dressing
1/4 c. catsup
1/4 tsp. mustard
1 tsp. prepared horseradish
1/2 tsp. Worcestershire sauce
1/4 c. sweet pickles
1 onion
1 green pepper
1/4 c. stuffed olives

Place cream cheese, salad dressing, catsup, mustard, horseradish and Worcestershire sauce in large bowl; mash with fork. Beat until creamy. Grind pickles, onion, green pepper and olives through fine blade of meat grinder; drain well. Fold into cream cheese mixture.

Mrs. Geraldine Laursen
Stow Grange, No. 103
Stow, Massachusetts

SAUERKRAUT BALLS
(Recipe 25 years old)

3 tbsp. butter
1 onion, finely chopped
1 c. finely chopped ham
1 c. finely chopped corned beef
Flour
1 egg, beaten
2 c. drained sauerkraut, ground
Dash of Lawry's seasoned salt
Dash of Accent
Dash of Worcestershire sauce
1 tsp. minced parsley
1/2 c. beef stock
Dash of garlic salt
2 c. milk
Fine bread crumbs

Melt butter in saucepan. Add onion; saute until tender. Add ham and corned beef; cook until well done. Stir in 6 tablespoons flour and egg; cook, stirring, until well blended. Add sauerkraut and remaining ingredients except milk and bread crumbs; cook until thick. Spread on platter to cool. Form into balls, using 1 heaping teaspoon sauerkraut mixture for each. Mix milk and 2 1/2 cups flour. Dip balls in milk mixture, then roll in bread crumbs. Fry in deep 375-degree fat until well browned; drain. Balls may be frozen until ready to use, then dipped in batter and bread crumbs and fried as directed.

Mrs. James Hanawalt
Rainsboro Grange, No. 2653
Washington Court House, Ohio

MUSHROOMS ROYALE

1 lb. medium fresh mushrooms
4 tbsp. butter
1/4 c. finely chopped green pepper
1/4 c. finely chopped onion
1 1/2 c. soft bread crumbs
1/2 tsp. salt
1/2 tsp. thyme
1/4 tsp. turmeric
1/4 tsp. pepper

Wash and dry mushrooms; remove stems. Chop enough stems to measure 1/3 cup. Melt 3 tablespoons butter in skillet. Add mushroom stems, green pepper and onion; saute for about 5 minutes or until tender. Remove from heat; stir in remaining ingredients except mushroom caps and remaining 1 tablespoon butter. Melt remaining butter in shallow baking dish. Fill mushroom caps with stuffing mixture; place, filled side up, in baking dish. Bake in preheated 350-degree oven for 15 minutes, then broil 3 to 4 inches from heat for about 2 minutes. Yield: 3 dozen.

Lela Riffle
Tallmadge Grange, No. 2589
Akron, Ohio

★ ★

STUFFED CLAMS

1 onion, minced
1 clove of garlic, pressed
1 tsp. olive oil
1 c. minced clams with liquid
1 c. bread crumbs
1 tsp. lemon juice
2 tbsp. white wine
1/4 c. grated Parmesan cheese
1 tbsp. minced parsley
1 tsp. oregano
Salt and pepper to taste

Saute onion and garlic in oil in saucepan until golden. Add remaining ingredients; mix well. Stuff into clam shells; place on baking sheet. Bake in preheated 350-degree oven for 10 minutes; serve hot in shells. May add hot sausage for variety, if desired.

Doris S. White, P.M.
Chequesset Grange, No. 372
Wellfleet, Massachusetts

SWEET AND SOUR SALMON

Fresh salmon
1 lg. onion, sliced
1 sm. jar sweet pickle relish
1 sm. bottle catsup

Cut desired amount of salmon into small chunks; place in saucepan. Add onion, relish and catsup; mix well. Boil for 20 minutes, stirring gently with wooden spoon; cool. Chill for 24 hours. Serve on crackers. May use canned salmon. Boil onion, relish and catsup, then add salmon and heat through.

Helen E. Moore
Upper Sound Grange, No. 705
Vaughn, Washington

TUNA TEASERS
(Recipe 20 to 25 years old)

1   7-oz. can tuna
1 tbsp. grated onion
1/4 tsp. salt
1   3-oz. package cream cheese, softened
1/4 tsp. garlic salt
Dash of Tabasco sauce

Drain tuna; remove bones. Place tuna in bowl; flake. Stir in remaining ingredients; chill. Shape into 1/2-inch balls; roll in minced parsley or chives, if desired. Chill. Serve on toothpicks. Tuna mixture may be spread on thin cucumber slices and chilled. Yield: 36 balls.

Mrs. Arthur Short
Smyrna Grange, No. 21
Smyrna, Delaware

ANDERSEN'S SPLIT PEA SOUP
(Recipe at least 50 years old)

2 qt. water
2 c. split peas

4 stalks celery
2 carrots
1 onion
1/2 tsp. thyme
Pinch of cayenne pepper
1 bay leaf
Salt and pepper to taste

Pour water into saucepan; add remaining ingredients. Bring to a boil; boil for 20 minutes. Reduce heat; simmer until peas are well done. Pour through colander into kettle; press vegetables through to make puree. Reheat soup. Soup may be cooled and all ingredients processed in blender until pureed. Serve with crackers or bread. Yield: 6 to 8 servings.

Frances McElhinney, CWA Chm.
San Luis Obispo Grange, No. 639
San Luis Obispo, California

CREAMY FRENCH ONION SOUP

3/4 c. butter
7 c. sliced onions
2 tbsp. all-purpose flour
1 tsp. salt
4 c. water
3 tbsp. beef stock base
4 c. milk
1 sm. clove of garlic, crushed
8 slices French bread, cut 1 in. thick
2 c. shredded Swiss cheese

Melt 1/4 cup butter in 4-quart saucepan; saute onions in butter for about 15 minutes or until tender. Stir in

★ ★

flour and salt; add water and beef stock base. Bring to a boil; reduce heat. Cover; simmer for 30 to 40 minutes. Stir in milk; heat to serving temperature. Do not boil. Melt remaining 1/2 cup butter in saucepan; stir in garlic. Dip both sides of bread in butter mixture; place on jelly roll pan. Toast in preheated 325-degree oven for 10 minutes. Turn; toast for 5 minutes or until lightly browned. Place soup in 8 ovenproof soup bowls; top each with 1 croute and 1/4 cup Swiss cheese. Place in oven for 10 minutes or until cheese melts. Twelve bouillon cubes may be substituted for beef stock base. Yield: 8 servings.

Photograph for this recipe on page 24.

CORN AND POTATO CHOWDER
(Recipe about 83 years old)

2 tbsp. diced salt pork
1 onion, chopped
4 c. diced potatoes
2 c. boiling water
2 c. canned corn
1 pt. milk
Salt and pepper to taste

Fry salt pork and onion in skillet for 2 minutes. Boil potatoes in boiling water in large saucepan for 15 minutes. Add pork mixture and corn; cook until potatoes are tender. Add milk; season with salt and pepper. Bring to boiling point. Yield: 6 servings.

Marie Rice
San Dimas Grange, No. 658
San Dimas, California

BEAN SOUP

1 to 2 lb. small navy beans
1 lg. hambone with meat
Celery leaves to taste
1 onion, quartered
1/2 tsp. garlic
2 tsp. pepper
2 tbsp. salt
Several bay leaves

Soak beans overnight in large pot of cold water; remove bad beans. Place remaining ingredients in another large pot; cover with water. Bring to a boil; cover. Reduce heat to medium; cook for about 2 hours. Add beans; reduce heat to low. Cover; cook for 4 to 6 hours or until beans are tender. Ham hocks may be substituted for hambone. Yield: 12 servings.

Suellen Meyer
Potomac Grange, No. 1
Washington, D.C.

CABBAGE SOUP
(Recipe over 100 years old)

2 c. finely chopped cabbage
Salt to taste

4 c. milk
Butter to taste
Salt and pepper to taste

Combine cabbage, salt and enough water to cover in kettle; bring to a boil. Reduce heat; simmer for 30 minutes or until tender. Press through food mill; return to the kettle. Add milk, butter, salt and pepper; bring to boiling point. Serve hot with oyster crackers. Yield: 4 servings.
This recipe was in an 1860 cookbook.

Sunbeam Duncan
Ash Valley Grange, No. 1436
Rozel, Kansas

CHICKEN-CORN SOUP
(Recipe at least 50 years old)

1 4-lb. chicken
1 tsp. salt
10 ears of sweet corn
1 onion, chopped fine
1/2 c. chopped celery and leaves
1/4 tsp. pepper
2 hard-boiled eggs, chopped
1 tbsp. chopped parsley

Disjoint chicken; place in kettle. Add 4 quarts cold water; bring to a boil. Reduce heat; simmer until chicken is tender, adding salt during last 30 minutes of cooking. Remove chicken from broth; cool. Strain broth through fine sieve; pour back into kettle. Remove chicken from bones; add to broth. Cut corn from cob; add to broth. Add onion, celery and pepper; cook until corn is tender. Add eggs and parsley; simmer for 8 minutes.

Mrs. T. Gilpin Cooke
Eureka Grange, No. 1915
Dillsburg, Pennsylvania

ASPARAGUS SOUP SUPREME
(Recipe over 100 years old)

1 lg. bunch asparagus
2 lg. potatoes, diced
Salt to taste
1/4 c. butter
1 1/2 qt. milk
1 tbsp. flour

Cut asparagus into small pieces; place in large saucepan. Add potatoes and enough water to cover; bring to a boil. Add salt; reduce heat. Cook until tender. Add butter, then add milk. Add enough milk mixture to flour to moisten; stir into soup. Cook, stirring, until thickened. Yield: 4 servings.

Della Fox, Women's Activities Chm.
Emerson Grange, No. 1426
Adena, Ohio

★ ★

CHICKEN-NOODLE SOUP

3 lb. chicken necks and backs
1 1-lb. can whole tomatoes
1/4 c. chopped celery and leaves
1/2 tsp. thyme
2 tbsp. chopped parsley
1 1/2 tsp. salt
1/8 tsp. pepper
1 med. onion, thinly sliced
2 lg. carrots, thinly sliced
1/4 lb. fresh mushrooms, sliced
1 c. noodles or macaroni
1/2 c. Chablis or white dinner wine (opt.)

Place chicken in kettle; add 3 quarts water. Add remaining ingredients except noodles and Chablis; bring
to boiling point. Reduce heat; simmer for about 2
hours. Remove chicken from soup; cool enough to
remove chicken from bones. Add chicken to soup;
simmer for about 40 minutes. Add noodles and
Chablis; add more seasonings, if needed. Simmer for
20 minutes longer or until noodles are tender. May be
cooked in crock pot on low temperature for 10 to 12
hours; add Chablis just before serving. Yield: 10 to 12
servings.

Mrs. Verna B. Mortensen
Sequim Prairie Grange
Sequim, Washington

AMBER SOUP
(Recipe more than 50 years old)

1 2-lb. soupbone
1 chicken
1 sm. slice ham
1 onion
3 whole cloves
2 sprigs of parsley
1/2 sm. carrot
1/2 sm. parsnip
1/2 stalk celery
Salt and pepper to taste
Beaten egg whites and crushed shells of
    2 eggs
1 tbsp. Caramel Coloring

Place soupbone, chicken and ham in kettle; add 1 gallon cold water. Bring to a boil; reduce heat. Simmer
for 4 hours. Stud the onion with cloves; cook in small
amount of fat until golden. Add to kettle. Tie parsley,
carrot, parsnip and celery together; add to kettle. Season with salt and pepper; bring to a boil. Reduce heat;
simmer for 1 hour. Strain broth into large bowl; chill
overnight. Remove fat from top; pour jellied broth
into kettle, leaving settlement in bottom of bowl. Stir
in egg whites and shells; bring to a rapid boil. Boil for
30 seconds; remove from heat. Skim off all scum and
egg whites from top of soup carefully, not stirring
soup itself. Pour soup through jelly bag, cheesecloth or
muslin; soup should be clear. Stir in Caramel Coloring;
serve. Soup may be set aside and reheated just before

serving, then stir in Caramel Coloring. Yield: 12
servings.

CARAMEL COLORING

1 c. sugar
Dash of salt

Mix sugar and 1 tablespoon water in heavy saucepan.
Cook over low heat, stirring constantly, until sugar is
dissolved and dark brown. Add 1 cup water and salt;
bring to a boil. Boil for several seconds; cool and
strain. Pour into bottle; seal with cork.

Mrs. John Roll
Union Grange, No. 1450
New Philadelphia, Ohio

MRS. RANDALL'S COUNTRY POTATO SOUP

3 c. diced pared Idaho potatoes
1/2 c. diced celery
1/2 c. diced onion
1 1/2 c. water
2 chicken bouillon cubes
1/2 tsp. salt
2 c. milk
1 c. sour cream
2 tbsp. flour
1 tbsp. chopped chives

Combine potatoes, celery, onion, water, bouillon
cubes and salt in a large saucepan. Cover; cook for
about 20 minutes or until potatoes are just tender, not
mushy. Add 1 cup milk; heat. Mix sour cream, flour,
chives and remaining 1 cup milk in medium bowl. Stir
sour cream mixture into soup base gradually. Cook
over low heat, stirring constantly, until thickened.
Yield: 6 cups.

Photograph for this recipe on page 272.

CORN AND TOMATO CHOWDER
(Recipe 50 years old)

1/4 lb. diced bacon
1 med. onion, sliced
1 qt. tomatoes
1 pt. whole-kernel corn
3 c. water
Salt and pepper to taste
1 8-oz. package noodles
1 tbsp. chopped parsley (opt.)

Fry bacon in skillet until crisp; remove from skillet
and drain. Crumble. Discard all but 1 tablespoon of fat
from skillet. Saute onion in remaining fat until tender.
Heat tomatoes, corn and water in large saucepan. Add
bacon, onion and seasonings; bring to a brisk boil.
Add noodles, several at a time, stirring as added. Simmer until noodles are tender; stir in parsley. Dried

★ ★

homemade noodles may be substituted for packaged noodles. Yield: 8 servings.

Laura V. Reeher
West Salem Grange, No. 1607
Greenville, Pennsylvania

HAM AND POTATO SOUP

1/4 c. butter
1/4 c. flour
1 tsp. salt
1/4 tsp. pepper
2 c. milk
5 lg. potatoes, cubed
1 1/2 c. diced ham

Melt butter in saucepan over low heat. Add flour, salt and pepper; cook, stirring, until smooth. Remove from heat. Stir in milk gradually; return to heat. Cook, stirring constantly, until thickened. Cook potatoes in boiling water until tender; drain. Add ham and potatoes to white sauce; simmer until hot. Yield: 4 servings.

Mrs. Don Beck
Spring Creek Grange
Reardan, Washington

MILK RIFFLES
(Recipe 150 years old)

1 c. flour
1 egg
1/2 tsp. salt
2 c. milk

Place flour in small bowl. Add egg and salt; mix with fork until small flakes form. Pour 2 cups salted water into heavy kettle; bring to a boil. Stir flour mixture into boiling water; cook until transparent and thickened. Add milk; heat through. Serve in bowls. May be eaten as prepared or with cream or milk and sugar. Yield: 4 servings.
In the olden days the cooks scraped their rolling pins and boards after making noodles, pie, biscuits, etc. into a jar. When they had enough they'd make Milk Riffles. Some people called this Lumps.

Mrs. Jess L. Walter
Camas Valley Grange
Springdale, Washington

OATMEAL SOUP
(Recipe over 100 years old)

1 c. oatmeal
1 tsp. salt
Dash of pepper
1/8 tsp. nutmeg

Pour enough bacon drippings into 2-quart saucepan to coat bottom of pan. Add oatmeal; cook, stirring constantly, until oatmeal is lightly browned. Add enough boiling water to fill saucepan 1/2 full; add salt, pepper and nutmeg. Cook for about 10 minutes or until oatmeal is tender, stirring frequently.
This recipe was handed down from my great grandfather. He used to make this soup for us and we still like it. Recipe came from Switzerland.

Nick Martell
Washington Grange, No. 82
Vancouver, Washington

OLD-FASHIONED VEGETABLE SOUP
(Recipe over 100 years old)

1 beef soupbone with meat
Salt to taste
2 tbsp. rice
1 med. potato, diced
1/4 c. corn
1/2 c. cut green beans
2 sm. carrots, diced
2 sm. kohlrabies, chopped
1 sm. onion, chopped
8 sm. pods of okra, sliced
2 sm. tomatoes, chopped
1/2 c. noodles

Place soupbone in pot; cover with water. Add salt; bring to a boil. Reduce heat; simmer until beef is partially done. Add rice, potato, corn, beans, carrots, kohlrabies, onion, okra and tomatoes; cook until vegetables are tender. Add noodles; cook until noodles are tender. May cook soupbone until beef is tender, then use only liquid to cook vegetables.

Magdalene Bauer
Fredericksburg Grange, No. 1650
Fredericksburg, Texas

BILL'S POTATO SOUP

2 or 3 med. potatoes, peeled
1/2 c. diced celery
1/4 c. chopped onion
1 c. boiling water
1 tsp. salt
2 1/2 c. milk
2 tbsp. butter
1 tbsp. fresh chopped parsley
Pepper to taste

Dice potatoes. Place potatoes, celery and onion in 1 or 1 1/2-quart saucepan. Add water and salt; cook for about 20 to 25 minutes or until vegetables are tender. Mash slightly with potato masher, if desired. Add milk, butter, parsley and pepper; heat thoroughly over low heat. Serve hot. One teaspoon dried parsley may be substituted for fresh parsley. Goes well with toasted cheese sandwiches for Saturday lunch. Yield: 4 servings.

Bill Steel, Natl. Youth Dir.
Potomac Grange, No. 1
Arlington, Virginia

★★★

QUICK MACARONI-CHICKEN SOUP

Salt
3 qt. rapidly boiling water
2 c. elbow macaroni
1/4 c. salad oil
2 c. chopped onions
2 c. coarsely chopped celery
    with tops
1 c. coarsely chopped green pepper
1 lg. garlic clove, crushed
3 qt. chicken stock or bouillon
2 c. cooked chicken or turkey chunks
1/2 tsp. crushed thyme leaves
1/8 tsp. pepper

Add 1 tablespoon salt to boiling water; add macaroni gradually so that water continues to boil. Cook, uncovered, stirring occasionally, until tender. Drain in colander; set aside. Heat oil in large saucepan. Add onions, celery, green pepper and garlic; saute over medium heat, stirring constantly, for about 7 minutes or until vegetables are tender. Add stock, chicken, thyme, pepper and 2 teaspoons salt; bring to boiling point. Add macaroni; cook until hot, stirring occasionally. Yield: Ten 1 1/2-cup servings.

Photograph for this recipe above.

BROWN FLOUR POTATO SOUP
(Recipe over 100 years old)

8 med. potatoes, peeled
1 med. onion, peeled
4 c. milk

1/4 c. flour
2 tbsp. butter or meat drippings
Salt and pepper to taste

Cube or slice potatoes and onion; cook in 4 cups boiling, salted water until tender. Add milk; simmer. Cook flour in butter over low heat until brown; add to soup. Blend carefully. Season with salt and pepper; bring to a boil. Serve at once. May be garnished with minced parsley or grated hard-boiled eggs. Yield: 6 servings.

Mrs. Gertrude Wymer
Kent Grange, No. 2371
Ravenna, Ohio

POTATO CHOWDER

2 strips bacon
1/3 c. chopped onion
2 c. diced potatoes
1/2 c. sliced fresh carrots
2 c. boiling water
1 1/4 tsp. salt
1/4 tsp. sage
1/8 tsp. pepper
1/4 tsp. paprika
2 tbsp. flour
2 c. milk

Cook bacon in large saucepan until crisp. Remove bacon; drain on absorbent paper. Add onion to saucepan; saute until tender. Add potatoes, carrots, boiling water and salt; cover. Reduce heat; simmer for about 10 minutes or until vegetables are tender. Add sage, pepper and paprika. Blend flour with 1/4 cup milk; stir into chowder. Add remaining milk; cook, stirring, until thickened. Crumble bacon over top; serve. Yield: 6 servings.

Joyce Bell
Sharon Grange, No. 1247
Shinglehouse, Pennsylvania

GAZPACHO ANDALUZ

1/4 lb. day-old Italian or French bread
1 med. green pepper
2 lb. fresh ripe tomatoes
1 1/2 c. pared and diced cucumber
1 or 2 cloves of garlic
2 tsp. salt
1/2 c. olive oil
1/4 c. wine vinegar

Place bread in shallow dish; add 1 inch of water. Let bread soak, turning once. Remove seeds from green pepper and tomatoes, then cut into cubes. Combine cucumber, green pepper, garlic, salt, oil and vinegar in electric blender container; blend until smooth. Add 1/2 of the bread; blend until smooth. Pour into bowl. Blend remaining bread and tomatoes; stir into mixture in bowl. Taste and season with more salt and vinegar, if desired. Chill thoroughly. Place 1 or 2 ice cubes in each bowl; add soup. Serve with accompaniments of sliced pimento-stuffed olives, diced cucumbers,

★ ★

chopped scallions or onion, diced tomatoes, chopped green peppers, croutons fried in olive oil, crisp crumbled bacon, sliced toasted almonds and chopped hard-cooked eggs. One quart hard rolls, cut into cubes, may be used instead of bread. Peel tomatoes, if desired. Color and flavor of soup are better if tomatoes are used unpeeled. Yield: About 7 cups.

Photograph for this recipe on page 35.

PUMPKIN SOUP

    3 onions, sliced
    1/4 c. butter
    3 to 4 c. shredded pumpkin
    3 c. water
    1 tsp. salt
    Pinch of pepper
    1 can chicken broth
    1 pt. sour cream

Saute onions in butter in saucepan until golden. Add pumpkin, water, salt, pepper and chicken broth; bring to a boil. Reduce heat; simmer for about 30 minutes or until pumpkin is tender. Remove from heat; stir in sour cream. Serve. Soup may be refrigerated for several days before sour cream is added. Add sour cream when ready to serve; heat until very hot, but do not boil. The longer the soup stands, the better it is. Yield: 8 servings.

Carolyn Scribner
Norfield Grange
Georgetown, Connecticut

RIVVEL SOUP
(Recipe at least 50 years old)

    2 c. unsifted flour
    1 egg, beaten
    1/2 tsp. salt
    8 c. chicken or beef broth
    1 sm. onion, chopped fine
    1/4 c. chopped celery
    2 c. corn (opt.)

Place flour, egg and salt in bowl; blend with fingers until crumbly. Pour broth into large saucepan; bring to a boil. Add flour mixture, onion, celery and corn; simmer for 12 minutes.
Rivvel is the Pennsylvania Dutch word for lump. This soup is full of little lumps resembling grains of rice. Originally, and frequently today, this soup was made by dropping the rivvels into salted and peppered hot milk.

Mrs. T. Gilpin Cooke
Eureka Grange, No. 1915
Dillsburg, Pennsylvania

EGGPLANT SUPPER SOUP

    1 lb. hamburger
    1 med. onion, chopped
    2 cans beef broth

    1 16-oz. can tomatoes
    1 c. water
    1 med. eggplant, peeled and diced
    1 lg. carrot, chopped
    1 celery stalk, sliced
    1 clove of garlic, crushed
    2 tsp. sugar
    1 1/2 tsp. salt
    1/2 tsp. pepper
    1 bay leaf
    1/4 tsp. nutmeg
    1/2 c. macaroni
    2 tbsp. chopped parsley

Crumble hamburger with fork in large saucepan or Dutch oven. Add onion; cook, stirring frequently, until hamburger is brown and onion is tender. Add beef broth, tomatoes, water, eggplant, carrot, celery, garlic, sugar, salt, pepper, bay leaf and nutmeg; cover. Simmer for 30 minutes; skim off all fat. Add macaroni and parsley; cook for 10 minutes or until macaroni is tender. Yield: 8 servings.

Marjorie H. Garland
Raymond Grange, No. 213
Raymond, New Hampshire

LENTIL SOUP

    1 c. lentils
    6 c. water
    1/2 c. diced carrots
    1/2 c. diced celery
    1/2 c. diced onions
    1 clove of garlic, minced
    1 to 2 c. tomatoes (opt.)
    1/2 tsp. salt
    1 tbsp. minced parsley

Cook lentils in water for about 1 hour or until lentils are soft. Add carrots, celery, onions, garlic, tomatoes and salt; continue cooking until vegetables are tender. Force half the vegetables through grinder; add to soup. Reheat; serve garnished with parsley. All of the vegetables may be ground, if desired. Yield: 4 to 6 servings.

Elnora M. Creswell
Ovid Grange, No. 155
Ovid, New York

SALMON SOUP

    1 qt. milk
    1/4 c. butter
    1/4 tsp. salt
    Pepper to taste
    1 sm. can salmon

Pour milk into large saucepan; bring just to boiling point. Add butter, salt and pepper. Flake salmon; add to milk mixture. Simmer, stirring, for 3 minutes. Serve. Yield: 3 to 6 servings.

F. E. Bringle
Sutherlin Comm. Grange, No. 714

★ ★

CONNECTICUT FISH CHOWDER

3 lb. codfish
2 qt. boiling water
1/2 lb. salt pork, diced
2 lg. onions, sliced
2 tbsp. flour
4 c. sliced potatoes
Salt and pepper to taste
6 crackers
1 pt. milk

Cook codfish in water for 15 minutes or until fish flakes easily; drain and reserve broth. Cool codfish; remove skin and bones and discard. Fry salt pork until fat is rendered. Add onions; cover. Cook over low heat for 5 minutes. Add flour; cook for 8 minutes longer, stirring frequently. Strain reserved broth; bring to a boil. Reduce heat; simmer for 5 minutes. Add salt pork mixture, potatoes and codfish; season with salt and pepper. Simmer for 15 minutes or until potatoes are tender. Soak crackers in milk for 3 minutes; add crackers and milk to chowder. Bring to a boil; serve. This recipe came from Center Congregational Church Cookbook, Torrington, Connecticut, published in 1907.

Mrs. Horton Gillette
Whigville Grange, No. 48
Bristol, Connecticut

NORWEGIAN FISH SOUP

2 lb. fresh fish, boned
6 med. potatoes, peeled and diced
1 tsp. salt
1/8 tsp. pepper
10 whole allspice
1/2 c. melted butter
Chopped parsley to taste

Cut fish into bite-sized pieces, including skin; place in large saucepan. Add potatoes and seasonings; add just enough water to cover all ingredients. Cook until potatoes are tender. Add butter; mix well. Sprinkle with parsley; serve immediately. Add 1 cup medium-thick cream sauce and 2 tablespoons finely chopped green onion and tops to make soup richer and tastier, if desired. Yield: 6 servings.

Mrs. Alma Irey
Rogue River Valley Grange, No. 469
Grants Pass, Oregon

PORTUGUESE BOATMAN'S STEW

3/4 tsp. salt
2 lb. boned fish
2 lg. onions, sliced
1/2 c. olive oil
1   1-lb. 4-oz. can tomatoes
1   8-oz. can tomato sauce
1 tsp. crushed sweet red pepper
Salt and pepper to taste
1/2 bunch parsley, chopped

1/2 c. white wine
1 1/2 c. water

Sprinkle salt over fish; let stand for several hours. Cook onions in olive oil until brown. Add tomatoes, tomato sauce, red pepper, salt, pepper, parsley, wine and water; simmer for 30 minutes. Add fish; simmer until fish is tender. Serve in bowls over French or Italian bread. Yield: 4 servings.

Sharon Marie Marsden
Harmony Grange
South Easton, Massachusetts

BICENTENNIAL FISH CHOWDER

1 lb. fresh of frozen codfish
2 or 3 med. potatoes, cubed
1 lg. onion, sliced
2 or 3 stalks celery, sliced
1 1/2 tsp. salt
1/8 tsp. pepper
2 to 3 tbsp. butter
3 c. water
3 c. milk
3 tbsp. flour

Thaw frozen codfish. Cut codfish into 2-inch slices; place in 4-quart kettle. Add remaining ingredients, except milk and flour; bring to a boil. Reduce heat; simmer until vegetables are tender. Add 2 cups milk. Mix flour with remaining 1 cup milk until smooth; add to chowder, stirring constantly to prevent sticking. Simmer until chowder is thick and creamy. Simmer over lowest heat for several minutes before serving. Yield: 6 to 8 servings.

Ethel Hanford
Norfield Grange, No. 146
Weston, Connecticut

CAPE COD FRIDAY CHOWDER
(Recipe about 150 years old)

1/2 lb. salt codfish
4 Bermuda or white onions, sliced
3 med. potatoes, cubed
1 1/2 tsp. butter
1 tbsp. chopped parsley
1/4 tsp. white pepper
Salt to taste
Milk

Soak codfish in cold water overnight; drain and flake. Place onions in large saucepan; add just enough boiling, salted water to cover. Simmer for about 15 minutes or until onions are partially done. Add potatoes; add enough boiling water to cover potatoes. Simmer for 40 minutes or until potatoes are tender. Add codfish; cook for 10 minutes. Add butter, parsley, pepper and salt; add enough milk for chowder consistency. Cook for 5 minutes longer. Serve with matzoth or

★ ★

large soda crackers, buttered, sprinkled with cheese and toasted in hot oven.

Margery R. White
Amesbury Grange, No. 127
Atkinson, New Hampshire

OYSTER STEW

2 c. milk
2 c. light cream
1 qt. oysters and liquor
2 tbsp. butter
Salt to taste
Pepper to taste
Celery salt to taste
Paprika (opt.)

This recipe is prepared quickly. Heat soup bowls before you start. Scald milk and cream together but do not boil. Drain oyster liquor into a saucepan; bring to a boil. Heat oysters in a separate saucepan with 2 tablespoons of oyster liquor and butter until oysters are plump and edges begin to curl. Remove from heat immediately. Combine milk mixture, hot oysters and hot oyster liquor. Season with salt, pepper and celery salt. Ladle into soup bowls; sprinkle with paprika. Serve with oyster crackers.

From a Grange Friend

NEW ENGLAND CLAM CHOWDER

1 qt. clams with liquor
3 c. water
2 slices salt pork, chopped
1 med. onion, sliced
3 med. potatoes, cut in sm. cubes
3 tbsp. butter
1 3/4 c. half and half
1 tbsp. salt
Dash of pepper

Combine clams, liquor and water in saucepan; bring to a boil. Drain clams, reserving liquid. Mince clam necks and coarse membranes; chop remaining clams. Fry salt pork until lightly browned. Stir in onion; cook until limp but not brown. Add reserved liquid and potatoes; cook until potatoes are tender. Stir in butter, half and half, salt, pepper and clams; heat through, but do not boil. Pour into large, warmed soup bowls immediately. Serve with crackers. Yield: 6 to 8 servings.

From a Grange Friend

RHODE ISLAND QUAHAUG CHOWDER
(Recipe 100 years old)

4 qt. large Rhode Island quahaugs
1 qt. milk
1   2 x 3 x 1-in. piece of lean salt
    pork, diced

2 c. finely chopped onions
4 c. diced potatoes
1/2 c. butter
Salt and pepper to taste

Open quahaugs; strain liquid through cheesecloth and reserve. Grind quahaugs through food chopper. Pour milk into pan; let heat until warm. Place salt pork and onions in 5-quart saucepan over medium heat; cook until salt pork is crisp and onions are tender. Add potatoes and reserved liquid; add just enough water to cover potatoes. Simmer until potatoes are tender; do not boil. Add quahaugs and 1/2 of the butter; cook for about 30 minutes. Do not boil. Add milk and remaining butter; simmer over very low heat for about 1 hour, stirring frequently. Season with salt and pepper. Serve piping hot with Pilot crackers and butter.

Jean M. Lynch
Central Grange, No. 34
West Warwick, Rhode Island

VENISON CHOWDER

5 slices bacon, cut in 1/2-in. pieces
1 c. sliced fresh mushrooms
1/2 c. chopped celery
1/4 c. sliced green onion
2 tbsp. all-purpose flour
3 1/2 c. Venison Brown Stock
2 c. 1/2-in. cubed venison
1 1/2 c. 1/2-in. pieces of peeled acorn
    squash
3/4 tsp. salt
1/8 tsp. white pepper
2 c. chopped fresh spinach
3 c. light cream or half and half

Cook bacon until lightly browned in 3-quart saucepan; pour off all but 2 tablespoons drippings. Add mushrooms, celery and onion; saute until tender. Stir in flour; blend in Venison Brown Stock gradually. Add venison, squash, salt and pepper. Simmer for 10 minutes. Add spinach; simmer for 5 minutes. Stir in cream; heat to serving temperature. Yield: About 10 cups.

VENISON BROWN STOCK

6 lb. venison bones with meat
2 1/2 qt. water
1/2 c. chopped celery
1 lg. bay leaf
8 whole peppercorns
2 tsp. salt

Place bones in large stockpot; add water. Cover; simmer for 3 hours. Remove bones; cut meat into 1/2-inch cubes. Refrigerate meat. Return bones to stock; add remaining ingredients. Simmer for 2 hours. Strain. Refrigerate overnight; remove fat layer. Extra meat and broth may be frozen for future use. Yield: 7 cups.

Photograph for this recipe on page 103.

★ ★

SQUIRREL SOUP

3 or 4 squirrels
1 tbsp. (scant) salt
Cut corn
Diced Irish potatoes
Diced tomatoes
Lima beans
Butter
Flour
Chopped celery leaves to taste
Chopped parsley leaves to taste
2 slices bread

Wash squirrels; cut into quarters. Place in large kettle; add salt and 1 gallon water. Bring to a boil; reduce heat. Cover; cook over very low heat until squirrels are nearly tender. Add desired amounts of vegetables; simmer until vegetables are tender. Pour through coarse colander into kettle; press squirrel meat and vegetables through colander, leaving bones. Simmer soup for several minutes. Coat desired amount of butter with generous amount of flour. Add to soup; add celery and parsley leaves. Simmer, stirring, until thickened and hot. Toast bread; cut into 1/2-inch cubes. Fry in butter until coated. Place toast squares in tureen; pour soup over toast. Serve.

Mrs. Leah Reekner, Master
Delphi Grange, No. 486
Manlius, New York

WIENER SOUP
(Recipe 40 years old)

4 med. potatoes, diced
1 onion, chopped
1 1/2 c. mushroom sauce
1 8-oz. can tomato sauce
1 1/2 lb. wieners

Combine potatoes and onion. Add enough water to cover; boil until almost done. Add sauces; bring to a boil. Cut wieners into 1-inch pieces; add to potato mixture. Heat through; serve immediately. Yield: 6 servings.

June Robinson
Dry Creek Grange, No. 646
Port Angeles, Washington

BASIC WHITE SAUCE

2 tbsp. butter
2 tbsp. flour
1 c. milk
1/2 tsp. salt

Melt the butter in saucepan; stir in flour. Cook until bubbly. Remove from heat; stir in milk slowly. Add salt. Return to heat; heat slowly, stirring constantly. Boil about 3 minutes, stirring to prevent burning. Yield: 1 cup sauce.

From a Grange Friend

HOLLANDAISE SAUCE

1/2 c. butter
3 egg yolks
2 tbsp. lemon juice
1/4 tsp. salt
Pinch of cayenne pepper

Place butter in small saucepan; heat to bubbling but not brown. Place egg yolks, lemon juice, salt and cayenne pepper in blender container. Process at low speed, pouring in hot butter in a slow steady stream until all is added.

Fran Eames
Meredith, New Hampshire

EDNA'S LEMON BUTTER

2 eggs, slightly beaten
Grated rind and juice of 1 lemon
1 c. sugar
2 tbsp. cornstarch
1 tbsp. butter

Mix eggs, lemon and sugar in saucepan. Stir in 1 cup boiling water slowly; bring to a boil. Mix cornstarch with 2 tablespoons cold water; stir into lemon mixture. Cook, stirring, until thickened. Add butter; cool. Mix well.

Edna Covington
Capital Grange, No. 18
Dover, Delaware

FAMILY LEMON BUTTER
(Recipe about 100 years old)

6 eggs, beaten
1/2 c. butter
2 c. sugar
Grated rind and juice of 3 lemons

Mix all ingredients in top of double boiler. Place over hot water; cook, stirring, until thick. Cool. May be spread on tarts or bread.

Mrs. Viola Miles
Millbrook Grange, No. 1864
Trivoli, Illinois

LUSCIOUS LEMON BUTTER SAUCE
(Recipe 60 years old)

2 eggs, well beaten
1 1/2 c. sugar
Juice and rind of 2 lemons
2 tbsp. butter

Combine eggs and sugar in small heavy saucepan; mix well. Stir in lemon juice and rind; add butter. Place over low heat; bring to a boil. Boil for 1 minute or until thickened, stirring constantly.

Mrs. Arthur C. Swartley
Chalfont Grange, No. 1545
Chalfont, Pennsylvania

Photo page 33 — Recipe on page 44.

Photo page 34 — Recipes on pages 41, 112, and 188.

★ ★

MILK GRAVY

2 tbsp. flour
Ham drippings
2 c. milk
Dash of pepper

Add flour to ham drippings in skillet after frying ham; mix well. Add milk slowly; cook, stirring constantly, until mixture comes to a boil. Stir in pepper. Add more milk if gravy is thicker than desired.
This was a favorite over hot biscuits, boiled potatoes or mashed potatoes. No salt was added, for country cured ham drippings were salty enough. Using today's hams, the gravy may require salt.

From a Grange Friend

CHICKEN PAN GRAVY

Drippings from fried or roasted chicken
4 c. milk
1/2 c. flour
1 1/2 tsp. salt
1/4 tsp. pepper
Finely chopped, cooked giblets (opt.)

Strain drippings from roasting or frying pan. Measure 1/2 cup and return to pan. Add browned bits left in strainer. Add milk; bring to a boil. Combine flour, salt, pepper and 1/2 cup water. Stir slowly into boiling milk. Scrape and stir thoroughly using a slotted pancake turner. Add giblets; taste and add more salt, if needed. Boil for 5 to 10 minutes or until flour is thoroughly cooked. Serve hot. Add 2 tablespoons cold water if fat separates. Stir, heat and serve at once.

From a Grange Friend

PENNSYLVANIA DUTCH MUSTARD
(Recipe over 100 years old)

5 tbsp. flour
1 tbsp. dry mustard
1 tsp. salt
1/2 tsp. pepper
2 tbsp. sugar
1/4 c. vinegar
1/4 c. water
Turmeric

Sift first 5 ingredients together into saucepan. Add vinegar and water and enough turmeric for coloring. Cook, stirring, to desired consistency; cool. Pour into jar; cover. May be refrigerated indefinitely.

Elsie L. Landgren
San Marcos Grange, No. 633
Encinitas, California

CREAMY MUSTARD SAUCE
(Recipe 30 years old)

3 eggs, beaten
2 tbsp. (heaping) dry mustard
3 tbsp. sugar
1/2 c. vinegar
Salt to taste
1/2 c. whipping cream, whipped

Mix first 5 ingredients in top of double boiler. Cook over boiling water, stirring, until thick. Remove from water; cool. Fold in whipped cream. Delicious served with baked ham.

Ann Westberg
Fairharbor Grange, No. 1189
Grapeview, Washington

TARTAR SAUCE EXTRAORDINAIRE

1 c. mayonnaise
1 tbsp. tarragon vinegar
3 tbsp. minced sweet pickles
1 tbsp. dillweed
1 tsp. dried minced parsley
1/8 tsp. salt
1/2 tsp. Worcestershire sauce
Dash of Tabasco sauce
1/4 tsp. dry mustard

Place all ingredients in bowl; mix well. Cover; refrigerate for 1 to 2 hours to blend flavors.

Mrs. Wayne George
North Bayside Grange, No. 691
Lakeside, Oregon

FRENCH MUSTARD
(Recipe 61 years old)

5 tbsp. dry mustard
2 tsp. cornstarch
2 tsp. sugar
2 eggs, beaten
1/2 c. dry white wine
1/2 tsp. salt
2 tbsp. vinegar
2 tbsp. salad oil

Mix mustard, cornstarch and sugar in saucepan. Add eggs; beat until smooth. Add wine, salt and vinegar gradually, stirring until smooth. Cook over low heat for 3 to 4 minutes, stirring constantly. Remove from heat; cool. Add oil gradually, stirring constantly. Store in covered jar in refrigerator; let mellow for 2 to 3 days before using. Keeps for 3 to 4 weeks. Yield: About 1 1/3 cups.
Recipe adapted from 1914 cookbook.

Karen Dorrah
Humptulips Grange, No. 730
Hoquiam, Washington

Photo page 35 — Recipe on page 28.
Photo page 36 — Recipes on pages 48 and 82.

Salads &
Salad Dressings

Salads, as we know them today, are relative newcomers to the American menu. In the pioneer days, salads, considered strictly company fare or a Sunday dinner treat, were man-sized meals in themselves. Big enough to satisfy the heartiest of appetites, they consisted of meat, fish, eggs, celery, lettuce and a homemade dressing. While the famous Chef's Salad and Caesar's Salad serve much the same purpose and are made with many of the same ingredients, the smaller salad is more commonly used as a complement to a meal. Because of the many necessary nutrients a salad provides, many Americans have made it their favorite light, diet-wise lunch.

Probably the most difficult task involved in preparing a delicious salad is choosing which taste-tempting ingredients to include. Thousands of farmers throughout this bountiful country take great pride in producing the very finest quality fruits and vegetables possible. This infinite variety of produce is available to the homemaker no matter what the season of the year. Learning to suit a salad to an entree by adding just the right color and texture can help make a meal as satisfying as it is nutritious. While a hearty meal of meat and potatoes calls for a fresh, green vegetable salad, a rich combination of meat and cheese can become the basis for a salad that is a meal in itself.

Several other types of salads, which originated many years ago, have become familiar sights on the American table. Gelatin salads were once quite a chore to prepare. However, since the farmer's wife no longer has to boil a calf's foot to obtain the ingredients she needs, congealed salads are cool, summer favorites across the nation. Two of our most popular salads, potato and coleslaw, came directly from our German forebearers. Easily prepared in large quantities, they are appealing flavor combinations that keep well over a short period of time.

Reaching their peak of popularity in this country, salads are as varied as the people who have made them famous. To be sure, they are a welcome addition to any meal.

★★★★★★★★★★★★★★★★★★★★★★★★★★★★★★★★★★★★★★

ASPARAGUS-FISH SALAD
(Recipe 40 years old)

1 c. shredded tuna or salmon
1/2 c. minced celery
1/2 tsp. salt
1/2 c. French dressing
1/2 c. sour cream
4 tsp. vinegar
1/2 tsp. sugar
1 1/2 tsp. minced onion
2 c. asparagus tips
Crisp lettuce leaves
1/4 tsp. paprika

Combine tuna, celery, 1/4 teaspoon salt and French dressing; let stand for 30 minutes. Combine sour cream, vinegar, sugar, remaining 1/4 teaspoon salt and onion, mixing well. Let chill. Arrange asparagus tips on lettuce leaves; top with mound of tuna mixture. Serve with sour cream salad dressing; sprinkle with paprika. Yield: 6 servings.

Mrs. Roger Koch
Powder River Grange, No. 68
Kaycee, Wyoming

CORNED BEEF SALAD

1 pkg. lemon gelatin
1 1/2 c. boiling water
1 c. salad dressing
1 pepper, chopped
1 onion, chopped
1/4 c. chopped olives
1 c. diced celery
2 tsp. vinegar
3 boiled eggs, diced
1 c. chopped corned beef

Dissolve gelatin in boiling water; let chill until partially congealed. Combine salad dressing and remaining ingredients; add to gelatin. Mix well. Chill until firm.

Mrs. Theresa Beason
Sonora Grange
Gilman, Iowa

TOSTADO SALAD

1 lb. ground beef
1 pkg. Lawry's taco seasoning
1/4 c. chopped onion
1 head lettuce, cut in pieces
2 tomatoes, cut in wedges
1/2 avocado, chopped
1 can kidney beans, drained
1 6-oz. package corn chips
Thousand Island dressing to taste

Brown beef with part of the taco seasoning and onion. Combine lettuce, tomatoes, avocado and beans; add beef mixture. Toss with remaining taco seasoning. Add corn chips and salad dressing; serve immediately. Yield: 6 servings.

Mrs. Robert Petersen, Master's Wife
C.W.A. Treas.
McFarland Grange, No. 543
McFarland, California

CURRIED CHICKEN SALAD

5 c. cooked chicken
2 c. pineapple chunks
1 c. diced celery
1/2 c. minced scallions or onion
1 c. sour cream
1 c. mayonnaise
4 tbsp. chutney or relish
1 tsp. curry powder
Chinese noodles
1/2 c. slivered almonds

Cut chicken into chunks. Mix chicken, pineapple, celery and scallions together. Combine sour cream, mayonnaise, chutney and curry powder; add to chicken and mix well. Arrange chicken salad on platter; spread noodles around edge of platter. Sprinkle almonds over top. Yield: 8-12 servings.

Frieda Bacon, Overseer, Past Master
Shrewsbury Grange, No. 101
Shrewsbury, Massachusetts

EASY CHICKEN SALAD

3 c. diced cooked chicken
1 c. minced celery
3 hard-cooked eggs, chopped fine
3 sweet pickles, chopped fine
1/8 tsp. pepper
1 tsp. (scant) salt
2/3 c. mayonnaise
3 tbsp. cream

Combine chicken, celery, eggs, pickles, pepper, salt, mayonnaise and cream. Toss carefully; serve. Yield: 10 servings.

Mrs. Margaret McGargle
Shavers Creek Grange, No. 353
Petersburg, Pennsylvania

COTTAGE CHEESE SALAD

1 1-lb. carton cottage cheese
3 hard-boiled eggs, chopped
3 tbsp. mayonnaise
1 sm. onion, minced
13 olives, minced

Combine all ingredients in salad bowl. Toss carefully to serve. Yield: 6 servings.

Mary L. Smith
Stillwater Grange, No. 2670
Covington, Ohio

★ ★

EGG-AVOCADO SALAD

8 hard-boiled eggs
2 lg. avocados
1 1/2 c. farmer-style cottage cheese
3 tbsp. mayonnaise
1/2 tsp. salt
Pepper to taste
Dash of paprika
1 tsp. Worcestershire sauce
1 sm. onion, grated
2 tbsp. chopped green chilies
Lettuce leaves

Mash hard-boiled eggs with fork; set aside. Mash avocados; mix into cottage cheese. Blend in mayonnaise, salt, pepper, paprika, Worcestershire and onion. Toss in chilies and eggs, mixing well. Mount on lettuce leaves to serve. Garnish with chopped sweet red peppers. Yield: 6 servings.

Ruth W. O'Neale
Rubidoux Grange, No. 611
Riverside, California

RED BEET EGGS

1 pt. home-canned beets with liquid
1 c. cider vinegar
1/3 c. sugar
3/4 tsp. salt
8 hard-cooked eggs, shelled

Pour beets and liquid into small saucepan. Add vinegar, sugar and salt; heat just until sugar dissolves. Cool to room temperature. Place eggs in medium-sized bowl; pour in beet mixture. Add water, if needed, to cover eggs with liquid. Cover; let marinate in refrigerator for 2 to 3 days before serving, stirring occasionally to color eggs evenly. Spoon beets, eggs and part of the liquid into bowl to serve. Eggs and beets may be arranged on lettuce leaves for individual servings, if desired. Good for picnics. Yield: 6-8 servings.
My grandmother brought this recipe to Illinois from the Pennsylvania Dutch area.

Betty J. Sites, Lecturer
Milledgeville Grange, No. 1883
Milledgeville, Illinois

PINEAPPLE AND CHEESE SALAD

1 8-oz. package cream cheese, softened
3 tbsp. confectioners' sugar
4 tbsp. salad dressing
1 c. drained crushed pineapple
9 maraschino cherries, minced
1 c. whipped cream

Stir cream cheese, sugar and salad dressing together until well mixed. Blend in pineapple and cherries. Fold in whipped cream. Chill in refrigerator until ready to serve. Yield: 6 servings.

Mrs. Frances McClure
Havana Grange, No. 1703
Caney, Kansas

FESTIVE RICE SALAD

2 pkg. strawberry gelatin
2 c. boiling water
3/4 c. cold water
1 c. cooked rice
1/2 c. cold milk
1 c. sweetened whipped cream
1 sm. can crushed pineapple with juice
1/2 c. chopped nuts

Dissolve gelatin in boiling water; stir in cold water. Chill until partially congealed. Fold in rice, milk, whipped cream, pineapple and nuts; chill until firm. Yield: 10 servings.

Shandon Towers
Hurricane Creek Grange
Joseph, Oregon

AVOCADO FRUIT SALAD

6 c. torn Boston lettuce and romaine
1 avocado, peeled, halved and sliced
2 c. seeded halved red grapes
4 tangerines, peeled and sectioned
1 c. sliced celery
Tangerine Dressing

Combine lettuce, avocado slices, grapes, tangerine sections and celery in large salad bowl. Toss lightly with Tangerine Dressing, if desired; mix well. Yield: 8 servings.

TANGERINE DRESSING

1/4 tsp. salt
1/8 tsp. pepper
1/4 tsp. dried leaf thyme
3 tbsp. fresh tangerine juice
1 tbsp. fresh lemon juice
1/4 c. salad oil
1/4 tsp. grated fresh onion

Mix salt, pepper and thyme together in small bowl. Add remaining ingredients; mix well.

Photograph for this recipe on page 34.

APPLE SALAD BOWL

2 c. diced unpared red apples
1 c. diced pineapple
1 c. diced American cheese
1/2 c. broken walnuts
1/3 c. mayonnaise
1/3 c. sour cream
1 tsp. lemon juice
1 tsp. sugar
1/4 tsp. salt

Combine all ingredients; toss to mix well. Serve on crisp salad greens.

Mrs. Laoma Edwards
Meander Grange
Youngstown, Ohio

★ ★

BLUEBERRY SALAD SUPREME

2 3-oz. packages blackberry gelatin
2 c. boiling water
1 15-oz. can blueberries
1 8 1/4-oz. can crushed pineapple
1 8-oz. package cream cheese, softened
1/2 c. sugar
1 c. sour cream
1/2 tsp. vanilla
1/2 c. chopped pecans

Dissolve gelatin in boiling water. Drain blueberries and pineapple; reserve juices. Add enough water to reserved juices to measure 1 cup liquid. Add liquid to gelatin mixture. Stir in blueberries and pineapple; pour into 2-quart shallow pan. Chill in refrigerator until firm. Blend softened cream cheese, sugar, sour cream and vanilla together; spread over congealed layer. Sprinkle with pecans; chill until ready to serve. Yield: 10-12 servings.

Mrs. Virgil W. Settle
Little Mountain Grange
Elkin, North Carolina

CHRISTMAS SALAD
(Recipe 60 years old)

1 pt. cranberries
3/4 c. boiling water
1 c. sugar
1 pkg. unflavored gelatin
1/4 c. cold water
1 c. diced pineapple
1 c. white grapes
1/2 c. chopped walnuts

Cook cranberries in boiling water until soft. Force through sieve. Combine cranberry juice and sugar in saucepan. Bring to a boil; boil until sugar is dissolved, stirring continuously. Soften gelatin in cold water. Add to cranberry juice; stir until dissolved. Stir in remaining ingredients. Chill in refrigerator until firm. May serve with mayonnaise mixed with whipped cream and topped with maraschino cherry, if desired.

Mary Merriman
Imnaha Grange, No. 677
Imnaha, Oregon

RED-WHITE AND BLUE SALAD
(Recipe 35 years old)

2 env. unflavored gelatin
1/3 c. sugar
Dash of salt
2 c. milk
1 1/4 c. cottage cheese
1 8-oz. can crushed unsweetened
     pineapple in juice
1 c. sliced strawberries
1/2 c. blueberries

Combine gelatin, sugar and salt in 1 1/2-quart saucepan; stir in 1/2 cup milk. Place over low heat, stirring constantly, until gelatin is dissolved. Add remaining

1 1/2 cups milk; stir in cottage cheese and pineapple. Arrange several of the strawberries and blueberries in 6-cup star-shaped mold. Pour 1 cup of the gelatin mixture over top; chill until set. Arrange more of the strawberries and blueberries in a design against the side of the mold. Fold remaining strawberries and blueberries into gelatin mixture; turn into mold. Chill until firm. Yield: 8-10 servings.

Mrs. Arthur Ebbert
Biglerville Grange, No. 2063
Biglerville, Pennsylvania

FROZEN STRAWBERRY SALAD

1 c. flour
1/2 c. butter
1/2 c. (packed) brown sugar
1/2 c. chopped nuts
1 pt. frozen strawberries
2 egg whites
1 c. (scant) sugar
1/2 pt. whipping cream, whipped

Combine flour, butter, brown sugar and nuts; mix well. Place in baking pan. Bake in preheated 350-degree oven for 20 minutes or until brown, stirring every 5 minutes. Place a layer of the nut mixture in 9 x 13-inch baking pan. Place strawberries, egg whites and sugar in bowl of electric mixer; beat for 20 minutes, stirring frequently. Fold in whipped cream. Spread over nut mixture in baking pan. Sprinkle remaining nut mixture over top. Freeze for 24 hours or until firm.

Mrs. Mabel Fair
Orange Grange
Ashland, Ohio

CRANBERRY WALDORF SALAD

2 c. fresh cranberries
3 c. miniature marshmallows
3/4 c. sugar
2 c. diced unpared tart apples
1/2 c. seedless green grapes
1/2 c. broken walnuts
1/4 tsp. salt
1 c. whipping cream, whipped

Grind cranberries; combine with marshmallows and sugar. Cover; chill overnight. Add apples, grapes, walnuts and salt. Fold in whipped cream; chill thoroughly. Serve in large bowl or individual lettuce cups. Garnish with clusters of green grapes and fresh cranberries, if desired. Yield: 8-10 servings.

Charlene Panter
Bandon Grange, No. 702
Bandon, Oregon

FROZEN CRANBERRY SALAD

1 lb. cranberries
3 lg. tart apples

★ ★

20 lg. marshmallows
1 c. sugar
1 pt. cream, whipped
1/2 c. finely cut pecans

Wash and stem cranberries; peel apples. Force cranberries and apples through food grinder alternately with marshmallows to have an even blend. Add sugar; mix thoroughly. Fold in whipped cream and pecans. Place in trays; freeze. May be served frozen or thawed.

Myrtle Moyer
Constantine Grange, No. 236
Constantine, Michigan

CHERRY CREAM SALAD

1   1-lb. can tart red cherries in syrup
2   3-oz. packages cherry gelatin
1   8 1/2-oz. can crushed pineapple
1   lg. ripe banana, diced
1 1/2 c. sour cream
1   tsp. grated lemon rind
Lettuce leaves

Drain cherries; reserve syrup. Add enough water to reserved syrup to make 2 cups liquid; pour into saucepan. Bring to boiling point. Add gelatin; stir until dissolved. Stir in undrained pineapple; chill until slightly thickened. Stir in cherries and banana. Pour 1/3 to 1/2 of the mixture into 7-cup heart-shaped mold; chill until set. Keep remaining gelatin at room temperature. Combine 1 cup sour cream and lemon rind; spread evenly over firm gelatin in mold. Pour remaining gelatin mixture over sour cream layer; chill until firm. Unmold onto lettuce-lined plate; pipe remaining 1/2 cup sour cream around outer top edge of heart. Yield: 8 servings.

Photograph for this recipe below.

STIFF CRANBERRIES
(Recipe 65 years old)

4 c. fresh cranberries
1 c. water
2 c. sugar

Cook cranberries and water for about 5 minutes; mash and strain. Add sugar; heat to dissolve sugar. Do not boil. Pour into mold; chill until firm. Will not fail to get stiff.

Mrs. Roy Glandt
Elkshorn Grange, No. 393
Omaha, Nebraska

★ ★

CRANBERRY-ORANGE RELISH
(Recipe over 50 years old)

    4 c. fresh cranberries
    2 oranges, quartered and seeded
    2 c. sugar

Force cranberries and oranges through food grinder, using coarse blade. Stir in sugar; chill. Keeps well for weeks stored in refrigerator. Yield: 2 pints.

Eva G. Barnaby, P.M., Sec., Master-elect
Kingston Grange, No. 323
Kingston, Massachusetts

SOUTH AFRICAN ROCK LOBSTER POTATO SALAD

    3 8-oz. packages frozen South African
       rock lobster tails
    3 lb. potatoes
    1/3 c. diced onion
    1 c. chopped celery
    1 1/2 tsp. salt
    1/2 tsp. white pepper
    2 c. mayonnaise
    1/2 c. sour cream
    1/2 c. heavy cream
    Lettuce leaves
    6 slices bacon, fried crisp and crumbled
    2 hard-cooked eggs, sieved

Drop frozen rock lobster tails into boiling salted water. Let water reboil; cook for 2 to 3 minutes. Drain immediately; drench with cold water. Cut away underside membrane with scissors; pull out lobster meat in one piece. Dice and chill. Peel potatoes; boil until tender. Drain; dice while still warm. Combine potatoes, onion, celery, salt, pepper, mayonnaise and creams; fold in lobster pieces carefully. Chill until ready to serve. Line bowl with lettuce leaves; spoon salad into bowl. Sprinkle top with crumbled bacon and sieved eggs. Yield: 8 servings.

Photograph for this recipe on page 33.

SHRIMP SALAD
(Recipe 40 to 50 years old)

    3/4 lg. head lettuce
    1/4 sm. head cabbage, minced
    2 stalks celery, diced
    4 green onions, diced
    Radishes to taste, diced
    2 hard-boiled eggs, chopped
    1 can shrimp
    Salt and pepper to taste
    Mayonnaise

Break lettuce into small pieces in salad bowl. Add remaining vegetables, eggs and shrimp; season with salt and pepper. Toss with enough mayonnaise to moisten. Yield: 6 servings.

Ora Nelson
Waller Road Grange, No. 1111
Puyallup, Washington

CHINESE TUNA SALAD

    Lettuce
    1 pkg. frozen green peas
    1 can tuna
    1 sm. can Chinese noodles
    Lemon juice to taste
    Mayonnaise

Break lettuce into pieces in salad bowl. Place frozen peas in colander; rinse with water to separate. Let drain. Mix lettuce, peas, tuna and noodles together; sprinkle with lemon juice. Toss with desired amount of mayonnaise. Yield: 4-6 servings.

Mrs. Robert Petersen, Master's Wife
C.W.A. Treas.
McFarland Grange, No. 543
McFarland, California

CRAB MEAT SALAD

    2 tbsp. unflavored gelatin
    1/2 c. cold water
    1/2 lb. cream cheese
    1 c. thick tomato soup
    1 c. mayonnaise
    2/3 c. diced celery
    1 green pepper, sliced
    1 onion, sliced
    1 6-oz. can crab meat

Soften gelatin in water; dissolve over low heat. Pour into blender container. Add cream cheese, soup, mayonnaise and vegetables; process until blended. Chill until thick. Stir in crab meat. Pour into oiled mold; chill until firm. Mince vegetables, then beat vegetable mixture until well blended if a blender is not available. Yield: 6 servings.

Deltah Dean
Trentwood Grange, No. 1056
Spokane, Washington

SALMON MOUSSE
(Recipe 35 years old)

    2 tbsp. gelatin
    2 c. red sockeye salmon
    Dash of cayenne pepper
    Dash of white or black pepper
    2 tbsp. cider vinegar
    2 tbsp. catsup
    1 c. salad dressing
    2 hard-cooked eggs, chopped
    18 to 24 stuffed olives, sliced
    2 tbsp. chopped gherkins
    1 c. cream, whipped

Soften gelatin in 1/2 cup cold water. Place over hot water; stir until dissolved. Remove bones and skin from salmon. Combine salmon, peppers, vinegar, catsup and salad dressing in mixing bowl. Add eggs, olives, gherkins and gelatin; mix carefully. Fold in whipped cream. Pour into large fish or ring mold; chill in refrigerator for 24 hours. Unmold onto serving

★ ★

plate; garnish with celery, hard-boiled egg halves, tomato wedges and sliced cucumbers. Yield: 10 servings.

Mrs. Earl Anderson, W.A.C.
Rinn Valley Grange, No. 466
Longmont, Colorado

DELICIOUS SALMON SALAD
(Recipe 65 years old)

1 can salmon
5 hard-boiled eggs, chopped
1 c. chopped English walnuts
1/2 c. chopped celery
2 tsp. mustard
2 tbsp. vinegar
3 tbsp. mayonnaise

Drain salmon; remove skin and bones, if desired. Combine all ingredients in salad bowl; toss carefully. Serve on lettuce leaves, if desired. Yield: 6 servings.

Bea Meader
Upper Klamath Grange
Klamath Falls, Oregon

ANTIPASTO SALAD

Romaine, leaf and iceberg lettuce
Cooked artichokes, quartered
Small shrimp, cooked
Swiss cheese, cut in strips
Salami, cut in strips
Onion, sliced thin
Hard-boiled eggs, chopped
Anchovies to taste
Capers to taste
Olives
Dressing

Combine romaine, leaf and iceberg lettuce, artichokes, shrimp, cheese, salami, onion, eggs, anchovies, capers and olives in large salad bowl. Pour Dressing over top; toss to mix well.

DRESSING

1 part wine vinegar
2 parts olive oil
Oregano to taste
Minced garlic to taste
Salt and pepper to taste
Dry mustard to taste
Dash of crushed red pepper

Combine all ingredients in jar with lid. Cover; shake thoroughly.

Judy Massabny
Potomac Grange, No. 1
Washington, D.C.

MIXED BEAN SALAD

1 can French-style green beans
1 can wax beans
1 can kidney beans
1/2 c. minced onion

1/2 c. diced green pepper
1/2 c. salad oil
1/2 c. vinegar
3/4 c. sugar
1 tsp. salt
1/2 tsp. pepper

Drain beans; rinse kidney beans. Combine beans, onion and green pepper in mixing bowl. Combine remaining ingredients; pour over bean mixture. Toss carefully. Let stand in refrigerator overnight to chill and marinate.

Camilie Twiss
Watatic Grange, No. 36
Amherst, New Hampshire

NAVY BEAN SALAD
(Recipe over 50 years old)

1 lb. dried navy beans
1 tsp. dry mint leaves, crushed fine
1 tsp. dry dill
2 lg. fresh tomatoes
1 lg. onion or 1 bunch green scallions
1 bunch parsley or 1 c. chopped parsley
Salad oil
Wine vinegar

Soak beans overnight; drain off water. Add fresh water; cook beans until tender. Drain beans well; place in salad bowl. Add mint leaves and dill; set aside. Cut tomatoes in pieces; chop onion fine. Chop parsley. Add vegetables to bean mixture; mix gently. Pour in salad oil and wine vinegar to taste; toss well. Chill for 1 hour or longer before serving. Yield: 8 servings.

Annni Nigohosian, Home Ec. Chm., Sec.
Salem Grange, No. 168
Lawrence, Massachusetts

FROZEN COLESLAW

1 tsp. salt
1 med. head cabbage, shredded
1 lg. carrot, grated
1 green pepper, chopped fine
1 pimento, chopped fine
1 sm. onion, chopped
1 c. vinegar
2 c. sugar
1 tsp. celery seed
1 tsp. mustard seed

Sprinkle salt over cabbage; let stand for 1 hour. Squeeze out liquid. Add carrot, green pepper, pimento and onion; mix well. Combine vinegar, 1/4 cup water, sugar, celery seed and mustard seed in saucepan; bring to a boil. Boil for 1 minute. Let stand until lukewarm. Pour over cabbage mixture; mix well. Place in containers; freeze. Can be refrozen several times. Yield: 6-8 servings.

Mrs. C. V. Roose
Hillsdale Grange, No. 77
Hillsdale, Michigan

★ ★

CABBAGE SALAD WITH CREAM DRESSING
(Recipe 65 years old)

1 med. head cabbage
3 tsp. sugar
1 tsp. (about) salt
Dash of pepper
3/4 c. thick cream
1/4 c. vinegar

Shave cabbage thin; chop crosswise once or twice, using sharp knife. Do not use a chopping bowl and chopping knife, as that bruises the cabbage and the juice will drain out. Combine sugar, salt and pepper in a cup. Add cream; stir until sugar and salt are dissolved. Stir in vinegar; pour over cabbage. Toss to mix well. This dressing will season about 1 quart cabbage. Yield: 8-10 servings.

Mrs. Iva Dell Stroud
Statesville Grange, No. 1236

NEW ENGLAND SLAW

6 c. shredded cabbage
1/3 c. chopped onion
1/2 c. thick sour cream
2 1/2 tbsp. vinegar
4 tsp. cream-style horseradish
1 tsp. salt
1/4 tsp. pepper

Combine all ingredients in salad bowl. Toss to mix well just before serving.

Freda Krebs, C.W.A. Chm.
Lake Creek Grange, No. 818
Harrisburg, Oregon

TWELVE-HOUR COLESLAW
(Recipe 40 to 50 years old)

1 lg. head cabbage, finely chopped
1 lg. onion, minced
1 c. chopped celery
1/4 green mango, chopped
1/2 c. vinegar
3/4 c. water
1 1/3 c. sugar
1/2 tsp. celery seed
3/4 tsp. salt
1/4 tsp. mustard seed

Combine all ingredients; mix well. Let stand for 12 hours before eating. The first 4 ingredients may be put through food grinder if fine slaw is desired.

Mrs. Jay Slates
Perry Township Grange, No. 1945
Carrollton, Ohio

PHOEBE'S CABBAGE SALAD

1 1/2 c. sugar
1 c. vinegar

1 tsp. salt
2 tsp. mustard seed
2 tsp. celery seed
1/4 tsp. turmeric
1 1/2 c. shredded cabbage
2 med. onions, chopped
1 red pepper, chopped
1 green pepper, chopped

Mix sugar, vinegar, salt, mustard seed, celery seed and turmeric together in saucepan. Bring to a boil. Combine remaining ingredients in mixing bowl; pour hot liquid over vegetables. Let cool. Seal in jars. Store in cool place for at least 24 hours before serving. This will keep for 3 to 4 weeks if kept cold.

Mrs. John W. Scott, Wife of Natl. Master
Unionville Grange, No. 1971
Mechanicsburg, Pennsylvania

CONGEALED CELERY-GREEN PEPPER SALAD

1 pkg. lemon gelatin
1 c. hot water
1 c. mayonnaise
1 c. cottage cheese
Pinch of salt
1 c. chopped celery
2 tbsp. minced onion
1/4 c. chopped green pepper
Chopped pimento to taste

Dissolve gelatin in hot water; let cool. Stir in mayonnaise, cottage cheese and salt; chill until partially congealed. Fold in celery, onion, green pepper and pimento; chill until set. Yield: 8 servings.

Blye Ellen Engel
Blanco Valley Grange, No. 1588
Blanco, Texas

SOUR CREAM-CUCUMBER SALAD
(Recipe over 150 years old)

1 1/4 lb. (about) med. cucumbers
2 tsp. salt
2 tbsp. vinegar
2 tbsp. water
1/4 tsp. pepper
1/2 tsp. sugar
1 c. thick sour cream
1/4 tsp. paprika

Wash and pare cucumbers; cut into thin slices. Place slices in bowl. Sprinkle with salt; mix lightly. Let stand for 1 hour. Squeeze cucumber slices, a few at a time, discarding liquid; place in serving bowl. Combine vinegar, water, pepper, sugar and sour cream. Pour over cucumbers; toss lightly. Sprinkle with paprika; chill in refrigerator for about 1 hour. Yield: 6-8 servings.

Betty Phillips
Progressive Grange, No. 1902
Liberal, Kansas

★ ★

DANISH CUCUMBERS
(Recipe 100 years old)

1 lg. firm cucumber
1 tsp. (about) salt
1/3 c. sugar
1/3 c. cider vinegar

Remove skin from cucumber, using potato peeler. Slice cucumber on large blade of grater. Place half the slices in bowl; sprinkle with salt. Place remaining slices in bowl. Place a tight-fitting plate over top; weight with heavy object. Let stand for 30 minutes. Pour off liquid; stir in sugar and vinegar. Cover; place bowl in refrigerator for at least 1 hour or until ready to use. Serve with the juice. May be served the following day, but is best if served fresh.

Astrid E. Campbell
Thermalito Grange, No. 729
Oroville, California

FRESH CUCUMBER SALAD

1 cucumber, sliced thin
1/6 green pepper, sliced thin
1 sm. onion, chopped
1 tsp. salt
Dash of pepper
1/4 c. sugar
3 tbsp. vinegar
1 tbsp. water
1/2 tsp. mustard seed
1/4 tsp. celery seed

Combine all ingredients; let stand in refrigerator overnight to blend flavors.

Mrs. Carl Heyman
North Fairfield Grange, No. 806
Norwalk, Ohio

GREEN PEA SALAD

2 med. cans green peas, drained
5 hard-boiled eggs, sliced
1 sm. jar red pimentos, diced
Mayonnaise to taste

Combine peas, sliced boiled eggs and pimentos in salad bowl. Toss with mayonnaise as for potato salad. Yield: 8-10 servings.

Helen Ludwig
Center Grange, No. 2428
Woodsfield, Ohio

KRAUT RELISH

2 c. sauerkraut, drained and chopped
1/2 c. chopped green pepper
1/4 c. canned pimento, cut in strips
1/2 c. mayonnaise
1 tbsp. prepared horseradish

1 tsp. Worcestershire sauce
1/2 tsp. salt
1/8 tsp. pepper

Combine all ingredients; mix well. Chill thoroughly. Serve with any chicken or meat dish. Relish will keep indefinitely. Flavor improves with age.

Florence Jeffrey, Master
Wide Awake Grange, No. 747
Phelps, New York

MARINATED CARROTS

2 lb. carrots
1 onion, sliced
1 green pepper, sliced
1/2 c. salad oil
3/4 c. vinegar
1 c. sugar
1 tsp. mustard
1 tsp. Worcestershire sauce
1/2 tsp. salt
1 tsp. pepper
1 1/4 c. homemade thick cream of tomato
    soup

Peel carrots; cook until tender. Let cool; cut into slices. Place half the carrots in bowl. Separate onion slices into rings; arrange onion rings and pepper slices over carrots. Place remaining carrots over onion rings. Combine remaining ingredients for dressing; mix well. Pour dressing over carrots. Let stand overnight before serving. Carrots will keep indefinitely if refrigerated. Yield: 12-15 servings.

Mrs. Velma Trumble
Papillion Grange, No. 401
Papillion, Nebraska

HOT GERMAN POTATO SALAD
(Recipe over 60 years old)

6 med. potatoes
2 hard-cooked eggs, sliced
4 slices bacon, cut up
1/4 c. minced onion
1 egg, beaten
4 tbsp. vinegar
3/4 tsp. salt
Lettuce

Boil potatoes in jackets until tender. Drain; peel and slice while still hot. Add eggs; toss carefully. Fry bacon and onion until golden brown. Strain to remove bacon and onion; reserve bacon fat. Add onion and bacon to potato mixture. Pour bacon fat slowly into beaten egg, beating constantly. Beat in vinegar and salt. Pour over potato mixture; mix well. Place in large double boiler; heat through. Serve hot on platter; garnish with lettuce.

Mrs. Norman Jahns
Riley Grange
Fremont, Ohio

★ ★

DUTCH POTATO SALAD
(Recipe 45 years old)

6 slices bacon
1/4 c. cider vinegar
2 tbsp. water
3 tbsp. sugar
1 tsp. salt
1 tsp. flour
2 tbsp. minced parsley
1 onion, cut fine
3 diced cooked potatoes

Cut bacon in small pieces; fry in large frypan until crisp. Blend in vinegar, water, sugar, salt and flour; bring to a boil. Add remaining ingredients; heat through. Serve warm. Yield: 4 servings.

Phyllis Peters
Constantine Grange, No. 236
Three Rivers, Michigan

POTATO SALAD FOR DINNER
(Recipe 75 to 100 years old)

4 qt. diced, cooked Irish potatoes
6 hard-boiled eggs, sliced
1/2 c. cider vinegar
2 eggs
1 c. sour cream
2 tbsp. sugar

Combine potatoes and sliced eggs in large bowl. Mix vinegar, eggs, sour cream and sugar together in saucepan; cook until thickened. Pour hot dressing over potatoes; toss carefully to mix. Let stand for about 1 hour before serving. May store in a cool place to let flavors blend, if desired. Yield: 6-8 servings.

Mrs. Lelah L. Mattock
Beecher Grange, No. 726
Pembine, Wisconsin

SPINACH WITH HOT BACON DRESSING

3 to 6 slices bacon
5 tbsp. sugar
1/2 tsp. salt
1 tbsp. flour
1 egg, slightly beaten
3 tbsp. vinegar
3 tbsp. water
1 lb. spinach

Dice bacon; fry in large frypan until crisp. Drain off excess fat. Combine sugar, salt and flour; blend in egg until smooth. Add vinegar; mix well. Add water; mix well. Add spinach to bacon; toss over low or medium heat. Add dressing; cook until dressing begins to thicken. Serve salad hot. Yield: 4-6 servings.

Mrs. Christina M. Landis
Dixie Grange, No. 2674
New Lebanon, Ohio

FRESH SPINACH SALAD

6 bunches spinach
2/3 c. salad oil
1/4 c. wine vinegar
2 tbsp. white dinner wine
2 tsp. soy sauce
1 tsp. sugar
1 tsp. dry mustard
1/4 tsp. curry powder
1/2 tsp. salt
1/2 tsp. garlic salt
1 tsp. pepper
3 or 4 strips bacon, fried crisp
2 to 4 hard-boiled eggs, chilled and
    quartered

Wash, drain and refrigerate spinach. Combine salad oil, vinegar, wine, soy sauce, sugar, mustard, curry powder, salt, garlic salt and pepper; mix well. Let chill thoroughly. Place spinach in large salad bowl; toss with chilled dressing. Crumble bacon over spinach; garnish with quartered eggs to serve.

Mildred Jones, Treas.
Riverside County Pomona Grange, No. 31
Riverside, California

BLUE CHEESE-SPINACH MOLD

1 10-oz. package frozen chopped spinach
1/2 c. cold water
2 env. unflavored gelatin
1 1/2 c. beef broth
1/2 c. bottled chunky blue cheese dressing
1 sm. onion, quartered
1/4 tsp. salt
2 tbsp. lemon juice
1 c. finely chopped seeded pared cucumber
1/2 c. chopped celery

Thaw spinach; drain. Pour water into electric blender container; sprinkle gelatin over water. Pour broth into small saucepan; bring to boiling point. Add to gelatin. Cover blender container; process at low speed until gelatin dissolves. Add blue cheese dressing and onion; cover. Process until smooth. Add salt, lemon juice and spinach; cover. Process just until smooth. Turn into bowl; chill, stirring occasionally, until mixture mounds slightly when dropped from spoon. Fold in cucumber and celery; turn into 4-cup mold. Chill until set. Unmold; garnish with tomatoes and parsley or small spinach leaves. Yield: 8 servings.

Photograph for this recipe on page 36.

HERBED TOMATOES
(Recipe over 100 years old)

6 ripe tomatoes
1 tsp. salt
1/4 tsp. pepper
1/2 tsp. thyme or marjoram
3 tsp. parsley

★ ★

1/4 c. chives or 1/4 c. chopped onion
2 c. salad oil
3 1/4 c. tarragon vinegar

Peel tomatoes; place in bowl. Sprinkle with seasonings and herbs. Combine oil and vinegar; pour over tomatoes. Cover; chill for several hours or overnight, spooning dressing over tomatoes occasionally. Lift tomatoes from dressing with slotted spoon when ready to serve. Dressing may be used several times.

Mrs. Arline Pitcher
Millerton Grange, No. 796
Millerton, New York

SEAFOOD-STUFFED TOMATOES

1   6-oz. package frozen crab meat
1 c. cooked shrimp
1 c. grated carrots
1 hard-cooked egg, chopped
2 tbsp. sliced green onions
1 c. sour cream
3 tbsp. chopped parsley
1 tsp. grated lemon rind
2 tbsp. lemon juice
1 tsp. prepared mustard
1 tsp. salt
1/8 tsp. pepper
6 lg. tomatoes

Thaw crab meat; drain well, then flake. Combine shrimp, crab meat, carrots, egg and onions in bowl; chill. Combine sour cream, parsley, lemon rind, lemon juice, mustard, salt and pepper in small bowl; chill.

Toss dressing with seafood mixture; chill. Remove slice from stem and blossom ends of tomatoes. Place each tomato on side; cut into thirds about two-thirds down. Place 1/4 cup seafood mixture into each sliced section, allowing 1/2 cup for each tomato. One 7-ounce package frozen shrimp, cooked, may be substituted for fresh shrimp. Yield: 6 servings.

Photograph for this recipe below.

TOMATO JELLY
(Recipe over 70 years old)

2 tsp. gelatin
1/2 c. cold water
2 c. tomatoes
4 peppercorns
2 cloves
1 slice onion
1 tsp. Worcestershire sauce
1/2 tsp. salt
1/2 tsp. paprika

Soften gelatin in cold water. Combine remaining ingredients in saucepan; cook for 15 minutes. Strain. Stir in gelatin until dissolved. Pour into individual molds or a ring mold. Chill until firm. Turn out of molds; serve with mayonnaise dressing, if desired. Yield: 4 servings.

Mrs. Robert Proctor
National Grange
Washington, D.C.

ZUCCHINI SALAD

4 sm. zucchini, sliced thin
2 juicy ripe tomatoes, chopped
1/2 green pepper, chopped fine
3 lg. green onions or 2 sm. dry onions,
    minced
1 tsp. salt
1/2 tsp. sugar
Dash of pepper

Combine all ingredients in salad bowl. Let stand at room temperature for 1 hour before serving. Yield: 10 servings.

Ruth Furro
Burston Grange, No. 892
Eatonville, Washington

DRESSING FOR COLESLAW

1/2 c. oil
1/2 c. vinegar
1 c. sugar
Salt and onion to taste

Combine all ingredients; mix well. Store in refrigerator; use as needed. May be used on garden lettuce salad, if desired.

Helen Thomas
Harvard Grange
Harvard, Illinois

★ ★

DRESSING FOR TOSSED SALAD
(Recipe 35 years old)

1 c. catsup
1 c. sugar
1 clove of garlic
1 c. salad oil
1 c. vinegar
1 sm. onion, chopped
1 1/2 tsp. paprika
1 tsp. salt

Combine all ingredients in blender container; blend for about 1 minute. Place all ingredients in quart container with lid; cover and shake well if blender is not available. Chill; serve over favorite tossed salad. Yield: 4 cups dressing.

Bethel Payne
Middlebury Grange, No. 192
Fredericktown, Ohio

CELERY SEED SALAD DRESSING

1 med. onion
1 tsp. salt
1 tsp. celery seed
1 tbsp. (heaping) prepared mustard
2/3 c. sugar
1/3 c. white or cider vinegar
1 c. vegetable oil

Process onion in blender; add salt, celery seed and mustard. Blend in sugar, vinegar and oil alternately until dressing is thick. Electric mixer may be used to mix dressing ingredients, if desired. Yield: 2 cups dressing.

Elodia Crooks
Blendon Grange, No. 708
Franklin, Ohio

EASY SALAD DRESSING
(Recipe more than 55 years old)

2 eggs, well beaten
1 c. water
3 tbsp. (or more) sugar
1 tbsp. (or more) butter
1/4 c. vinegar
1 tsp. dry mustard
1 tbsp. flour
Salt to taste
Minced onion (opt.)

Combine all ingredients in saucepan; mix well. Bring to boiling point; cook until thickened, stirring constantly. Yield: About 2 cups dressing.

Mrs. John V. Jacque
New London Grange, No. 2401
New London, Ohio

FRUIT SALAD DRESSING
(Recipe 80 years old)

4 eggs
1 c. sugar

1 1/2 tbsp. flour
1/2 c. lemon juice
2 c. pineapple juice
2 c. whipped cream

Beat eggs, sugar, flour and lemon juice together in saucepan until well blended. Add pineapple juice. Cook until mixture thickens, stirring constantly. Let cool. Fold in whipped cream just before using. Yield: 4 cups dressing.

Valerie Mueller
Whitethorn Grange, No. 792
Redway, California

MAYONNAISE
(Recipe 50 years old)

1 c. sugar
2 tbsp. cornstarch
2 tbsp. French mustard
1 tbsp. butter
1 tsp. salt
2 eggs, beaten
3/4 c. vinegar
1/4 c. water
1 c. milk

Mix all ingredients together in saucepan. Cook over slow heat until thick, stirring constantly. Chill; use as needed. Yield: 1 pint dressing.

Mrs. John Price, Youth Chm.
Perry Township Grange, No. 1945
No. Canton, Ohio

POTATO SALAD DRESSING
(Recipe over 50 years old)

3 tbsp. (heaping) flour
1 egg
2 tbsp. butter
1 tsp. salt
1 tbsp. (heaping) sugar
2 tbsp. mustard
Dash of pepper
1 c. milk
1/2 tsp. vinegar

Combine all ingredients except vinegar in small skillet or saucepan; cook over medium heat until thick, stirring constantly. Ingredients may be beaten with rotary beater before cooking, if desired. Remove from heat; stir in vinegar. Pour over warm, diced potatoes; sprinkle with paprika, if desired. Recipe can be doubled.

Mrs. J. Edwin Cook
Brandywine Grange, No. 60
West Chester, Pennsylvania

SALAD DRESSING WITHOUT OIL

2 eggs
1/2 tsp. mustard
1 tsp. salt
1 tbsp. sugar
2 tbsp. butter

★ ★

3 tbsp. vinegar
1 c. whipping cream

Beat eggs in top of double boiler. Add mustard, salt and sugar; beat until well mixed. Add butter and vinegar; cook until thick and smooth. Let cool. Stir in cream. Whip cream until almost stiff, and fold into cooled dressing if a fluffy dressing is desired. Yield: 1 1/2 pints dressing.
This recipe was taken from the 1905 Fisher Flour Recipe book.

Christina O'Neal
French Creek Grange, No. 396
Snohomish, Washington

SOUR CREAM SALAD DRESSING
(Recipe over 50 years old)

1 tsp. mustard
1 tsp. sugar
1/2 tsp. salt
Dash of pepper
1 tsp. flour
1 egg
1/2 c. milk
1/3 c. hot vinegar
1 1/2 tsp. butter
1/2 c. sour cream

Combine mustard, sugar, salt, pepper and flour in top of double boiler. Beat egg and milk together; stir into flour mixture gradually until smooth. Cook, stirring constantly, until mixture coats a spoon. Do not let water in bottom of double boiler boil. Add hot vinegar and butter; mix well. Remove from heat; let cool. Stir in sour cream. Excellent on potato salad.

Bryce Keene
Willows Grange, No. 672
Ione, Oregon

FRENCH DRESSING

1/2 c. sugar
1 tsp. salt
Dash of pepper
1/2 tsp. garlic salt
1/2 tsp. paprika
1/4 c. cooking oil
1/2 c. catsup
1/2 c. vinegar

Combine sugar, salt, pepper, garlic salt and paprika in bottle with lid. Add oil, catsup and vinegar. Cover; shake well to use. Store in same bottle in refrigerator; use as needed.

Mrs. Russell Fleming
Valley Grange, No. 1586
Cambridge, Ohio

MEXICAN TANGY DRESSING

1 c. mayonnaise
1/2 c. garlic vinegar
1/2 c. oil
1 tsp. celery seed

2 tsp. garlic powder
3 to 4 tsp. cumin

Blend all ingredients together until well mixed. Store in refrigerator; use as needed. Serve on green garden salad. Will keep for weeks.

Mrs. Alene Prunty
Guinda, California

TANGY HOMEMADE SALAD DRESSING
(Recipe 63 years old)

2 c. milk
2 tbsp. sugar
1/2 tsp. salt
1 tbsp. cornstarch
2 tsp. dry mustard
2 eggs, beaten
1 c. cider vinegar
1 1/2 to 2 tbsp. butter

Pour milk into double boiler; let scald. Combine sugar, salt, cornstarch and mustard. Add eggs; beat well. Stir slowly into milk. Cook until thick, stirring frequently. Heat vinegar to boiling point. Add butter; stir until melted. Pour vinegar mixture into milk mixture; beat until smooth.

Mrs. David H. Johnson
Ammonoosuc Grange, No. 55
Woodsville, New Hampshire

SWEET AND SOUR SALAD DRESSING

2 c. oil
2 1/2 c. catsup
1 c. vinegar
2 c. sugar
6 tbsp. onion flakes
4 tsp. paprika
4 tsp. salt
4 tsp. celery seed

Combine all ingredients in mixer bowl; beat until well blended. Store in refrigerator. Yield: 2 quarts dressing.

Mrs. Edward Sharp
Hocking Grange, No. 2029
Sugargrove, Ohio

TWA SALAD DRESSING

1/2 c. sugar
1 tsp. mustard
1 tsp. salt
2 tsp. celery seed or celery salt
2 tsp. grated onion
2 tsp. horseradish
1 c. salad oil
1/3 c. vinegar

Combine sugar, mustard, salt, celery seed, onion and horseradish in small bowl of electric mixer. Beat at high speed, slowly adding oil and vinegar. Mix well. Chill until ready to use.

Mrs. Clara Keller
Shavers Creek Grange, No. 353
Petersburg, Pennsylvania

Meats

Americans have always been famous meat eaters and, as a nation, are blessed with one of the most bounteous selections of meats and their various cuts to be found anywhere. Even in colonial times, visitors from Europe wrote of meals including beef, veal, venison, geese, turkey and wild fowl, all served in abundant proportions. Beef, the most frequently eaten meat in America today, began its rise to popularity in the middle of the 19th Century, when the first herd of Texas Longhorns arrived in New York City. The wearisome cattle drives made Longhorn meat rather tough and stringy by today's standards, but since that time, agriculture and technology have worked together to produce some of the meatiest and tastiest beef in the world.

During the days of the new Republic, lamb, mutton and pork were the most popular meats. Hogs were usually let loose to forage in the forest, then rounded up in the fall to be slaughtered for winter's meat. The quality of pork has vastly improved since then, and now, next to beef, pork is the most popular meat in America. A good reason for the popularity of pork, both then and now, is probably its versatility and variety. It appears as chops, roasts, ribs, bacon, sausage and ham. Can you think of another meat with such a variety of flavors and uses at so little cost? Today's popularity of wild game as an American food, although it can't be estimated, is known to be very great. The recipes for rabbit stew and squirrel pie, a regular part of the pioneer and settler diet, reflect the enduring tastiness of such meats.

For both hungry, growing children and hardworking parents, nothing can arouse and satisfy the appetite as fast as cooking and eating meat, whether on top of the stove, in the oven or over a charcoal grill. And, for the food value and versatility, there is hardly a better buy — an important consideration when you want to serve your family the best and be thrifty at the same time.

★ ★

BEEF-RICE PIE
(Recipe 50 years old)

1 onion, chopped
1 lg. potato, chopped
1 oz. fat salt pork, chopped
4 c. thinly sliced cooked beef or veal
2 tsp. salt
1/8 tsp. pepper
1 c. rice, cooked
1 c. stewed strained tomatoes
2 tbsp. butter
4 hard-boiled eggs

Mix onion, potato and salt pork in colander. Pour boiling water over onion mixture; drain. Cook in saucepan until light yellow. Add beef and seasonings; heat through, stirring carefully. Mix rice and tomatoes; add butter. Slice 2 eggs; stir into rice mixture gently. Turn beef mixture into buttered baking dish; place rice mixture over beef mixture carefully. Cut remaining 2 eggs into 4 slices each; press slices into rice mixture. Dot each slice with additional butter. Bake in preheated 350-degree oven for 30 minutes, adding beef stock or gravy, if needed. Yield: 4 servings.

Ivonette Coyne
Tunxis Grange, No. 13
Hartford, Connecticut

DRIED BEEF CASSEROLE

1 1/4 c. thick white sauce with chopped
    mushrooms
1 c. milk
1 c. shredded cheddar cheese
1 c. uncooked elbow macaroni
3 tbsp. finely chopped onion
1   3-oz. package dried beef, shredded
2 hard-boiled eggs, sliced

Mix sauce and milk until smooth. Add remaining ingredients except eggs; mix well. Fold in eggs; pour into buttered baking dish. Cover; store in refrigerator for at least 3 to 4 hours or overnight. Remove from refrigerator 30 minutes before baking. Bake in preheated 350-degree oven for 1 hour. Yield: 5 servings.

Mrs. Russell Lyford
Guilford Hope Grange, No. 6
Caledonia, Illinois

LIVER FRICASSEE
(Recipe over 50 years old)

1 lb. beef liver
Flour
3 tbsp. fat
Salt
Pepper to taste
1/2 c. catsup
2 c. diced potatoes
1 1/4 c. diced carrots
1 onion, chopped
4 stalks celery, chopped

Remove membrane from liver; cut liver into strips. Dredge with flour; cook in fat in skillet until brown. Season with salt to taste and pepper. Combine 3 cups water, catsup, and 2 teaspoons salt; add to liver. Bring to a boil. Add potatoes, carrots, onion and celery; cover. Cook for 30 minutes or until vegetables are tender. Yield: 4-5 servings.

Mrs. Oscar McNutt, C.W.A.
Pleasant Mt. Grange, No. 1112
Port Angeles, Washington

GLAZED CORNED BEEF AND VEGETABLE PLATTER

4 to 6 lb. corned beef brisket
1 tbsp. whole mixed pickling spices
1/3 c. orange marmalade
2 tbsp. brown sugar
2 tsp. prepared mustard
3 green pepper rings
8 sm. potatoes, pared
1   10-oz. package baby Brussels
    sprouts frozen in butter sauce
1   10-oz. package honey-glazed
    crinkle-cut carrots frozen in
    flavor-tight cooking pouch
1/4 c. sliced green onions including
    some green tops
Seasoned pepper

Place corned beef in Dutch oven; sprinkle with spices. Barely cover with water. Simmer for 3 to 4 hours or until beef is tender. Remove beef, reserving liquid in pan; place on rack in open roasting pan. Combine mar-

★ ★

malade, brown sugar and mustard in small saucepan; bring to a boil, stirring frequently. Brush mixture over corned beef. Bake in 350-degree oven for 20 minutes, brushing with glaze occasionally. Arrange green pepper rings on top of meat before applying final glaze. Add potatoes to cooking liquid; bring to a boil. Cook for 20 minutes or until tender, then drain. Cook Brussels sprouts and carrots according to package directions. Pour contents of pouches into bowl; stir in potatoes, green onions and seasoned pepper. Arrange vegetables around corned beef on serving platter.

Photograph for this recipe on page 54.

PIRATE HOUSE BEEF
(Recipe over 100 years old)

    3 lb. beef shanks
    1 tsp. salt
    Dash of pepper
    1 sm. bay leaf
    2 c. cooked rice
    2 c. stewed tomatoes
    1 sm. onion, minced
    1 green pepper, pureed

Place beef shanks in kettle; cover with boiling water. Add salt, pepper and bay leaf; reduce heat. Simmer until beef is fork tender. Remove from heat; remove beef shanks from liquid and cool. Remove beef from bones; cut into bite-sized pieces. Combine rice, tomatoes and onion in bowl; mix well. Line bottom and sides of casserole with rice mixture; fill center with beef. Dot rice mixture with green pepper pulp. Thicken beef broth as desired; pour over top of casserole to cover all ingredients. Bake in preheated 350-degree oven for 30 minutes or until gravy is absorbed by rice. Yield: 6 servings.

Iola Smith
Lawrence Grange, No. 117
Laconia, New Hampshire

HARVEST BEEF POT ROAST

    5 tbsp. flour
    2 tsp. salt
    1/4 tsp. pepper
    1   4 to 5-lb. beef blade pot roast
    1   16-oz. can whole tomatoes
    2 tsp. Worcestershire sauce
    2 tsp. basil
    1/2 tsp. cumin seed
    2 med. onions, cut in half
    3 sm. zucchini, cut in 1 to 2-in. pieces

Combine 2 tablespoons flour, salt and pepper; dredge meat with seasoned flour. Cook in 2 tablespoons fat in large frying pan or Dutch oven until brown; pour off drippings. Drain tomatoes, reserving liquid. Combine 1/2 cup reserved tomato liquid with Worcestershire sauce, basil and cumin seed; add to roast. Add onions; cover tightly. Bake in preheated 325-degree oven for 2 hours and 30 minutes or until roast is tender. Add

zucchini; cover. Bake for 15 minutes. Add tomatoes; cover. Bake for 5 minutes or until heated through. Remove roast, zucchini and tomatoes to warm platter. Add water, if necessary, to remaining reserved tomato liquid to make 1/3 cup liquid; combine with remaining flour. Stir into pan drippings; cook over low heat, stirring constantly, until thickened. Serve with roast.

Photograph for this recipe on page 102.

POT ROAST DELUXE
(Recipe 30 years old)

    1   3 to 4-lb. beef roast
    Salt and pepper to taste
    1/8 tsp. ginger
    2 cloves of garlic
    3 med. onions
    1/2 c. oil
    1 1/2 c. prunes
    1 can mushrooms
    1 c. pitted ripe olives

Sprinkle beef on all sides with salt, pepper and ginger. Chop garlic very fine; slice onions. Fry garlic and onions in hot oil in roasting pan until yellow. Add roast; sear on all sides. Add 1/2 cup water; cover tightly. Simmer for 1 hour and 30 minutes. Soak prunes in 1 1/2 cups water while beef is cooking. Add prunes, mushrooms and olives to beef; cook until beef is tender. Remove beef to platter; arrange prunes, mushrooms and olives around beef. Yield: 4-6 servings.

Mrs. Darrel Couch
Trout Lake Grange, No. 210
Trout Lake, Washington

SPICED POT ROAST
(Recipe about 100 years old)

    2 onions, chopped
    1/4 c. fat or salad oil
    1   4-lb. beef chuck, rump or bottom
         round roast
    1/4 c. flour
    1 tsp. salt
    2 1/2 c. cooked tomatoes
    1/4 tsp. pepper
    1 bay leaf
    1/4 tsp. whole cloves
    1/4 c. vinegar
    2 tbsp. brown sugar

Cook onions in fat in Dutch oven until tender. Dredge roast with flour; cook in Dutch oven with onions until brown on all sides. Place rack under roast. Combine salt, tomatoes, pepper, bay leaf, cloves, vinegar and brown sugar; pour over roast. Cover. Simmer for about 3 hours or until roast is tender. Yield: 8 servings.

Mrs. W. C. Harris, State Master's Wife
Elmira Grange, No. 523
Portland, Oregon

★ ★

JOAN'S ROAST BEEF

1   4 1/2-lb. beef roast
1 tbsp. vinegar
1 tbsp. brown sugar
1/4 tsp. allspice
1/4 tsp. pepper
1/2 tsp. dry mustard
1 tsp. paprika
2 tsp. salt

Place roast in roasting pan. Combine remaining ingredients; rub over roast, using all of the vinegar mixture. Do not add water to roasting pan. Bake in preheated 250-degree oven for 7 hours. Pan juices may be used for gravy.

Joan L. Mohler
Marlboro Grange
Hartville, Ohio

SAUERBRATEN
(Recipe 100 years old)

4 lb. bottom round beef
1 c. vinegar
2 c. water
1 tsp. mixed spices
2 bay leaves
2 tsp. salt
Pepper to taste
2 tbsp. flour
2 lg. onions, sliced
Browned flour

Place beef, vinegar, water, spices and bay leaves in an earthen crock; let stand in cool place for 2 to 3 days, basting frequently and turning beef once a day. Drain beef; reserve marinade. Sprinkle beef with salt, pepper and flour. Brown beef in hot fat in Dutch oven on all sides. Add marinade and onions; cover. Cook over low heat for 1 hour and 30 minutes or until tender. Remove beef from liquid. Strain liquid; thicken with browned flour mixed with water. Slice beef; add to gravy. Four pounds rabbit may be substituted for beef.

Fay O'Neill
Whitethorn Grange, No. 792
Whitethorn, California

CRABBY
(Recipe about 44 years old)

1 c. flour
Salt and pepper to taste
1   4 to 5-lb. round steak
Oil
2 onions, chopped
10 to 12 med. carrots, shredded
10 to 12 med. potatoes, shredded
1/2 pkg. corn flakes, crushed

Mix flour, salt and pepper. Cut steak into 10 to 12 pieces; dredge with seasoned flour. Cook in small amount of oil in skillet until brown. Place steak in 9 x 12-inch baking pan; pour pan juices from skillet over steak. Add 1/3 of the onions; sprinkle small amount of the remaining seasoned flour over onions. Add half the carrots; add half the remaining onions. Sprinkle with some of the seasoned flour; add remaining carrots. Sprinkle with seasoned flour. Add half the potatoes; add remaining onions. Sprinkle with seasoned flour; add remaining potatoes, then remaining seasoned flour. Add enough water to fill pan within 1/2 inch of top; sprinkle corn flake crumbs over top. Bake in preheated 300-degree oven for 3 hours or until water has evaporated. Yield: 8-10 servings.

Phyllis A. Hull, C.W.A.
Fertile Valley Grange, No. 1094
Elk, Washington

DANISH ONION-SMOTHERED STEAK

1/4 c. all-purpose flour
1 tsp. salt
1/4 tsp. pepper
1 1/2 lb. beef round steak, 3/4 in. thick
2 tbsp. cooking oil
3 med. onions, sliced
1 c. water
1 tbsp. vinegar
1 clove of garlic, minced
1 bay leaf
1/4 tsp. dried crushed thyme

Combine flour, salt and pepper; pound into steak. Cut steak into serving pieces; cook in hot oil in skillet until brown. Top with onion slices; add remaining ingredients. Bring to a boil; reduce heat. Cover. Simmer for 1 hour; remove bay leaf. Yield: 6 servings.

Mrs. Mary Babcock
Queen City Grange, No. 30
Winterport, Maine

DELICIOUS PEPPER STEAK

1   14-oz. can tomatoes
1   14-oz. can tomato sauce
1/4 c. soy sauce
2 green peppers, cut into strips
2 lb. round steak, cut into thin strips
Bacon fat (opt.)
1 tbsp. cornstarch

Mix tomatoes, tomato sauce, soy sauce and green peppers in saucepan; bring to a boil. Reduce heat; simmer while browning steak. Saute steak in small amount of bacon fat in skillet until light brown; drain. Add to tomato mixture; cook over low heat for 1 hour or until steak is tender. Thicken if sauce is too thin. Mix cornstarch with several tablespoons sauce; stir into remaining sauce. Simmer, stirring, until thickened. Serve over rice. May be frozen. Yield: 4 servings.

Mrs. Judy Massabny
Potomac Grange, No. 1
Washington, D.C.

★ ★

DUTCH DINNER CASSEROLE
(Recipe over 35 years old)

  1 1-lb. 4-oz. can tomatoes
  2 lb. round steak
  3 tbsp. shortening
  3 tbsp. flour
  1 tsp. salt
  1/4 tsp. pepper
  8 to 10 med. potatoes
  12 med. carrots
  6 sm. onions

Drain tomatoes; reserve juice. Pour reserved tomato juice back into can; add enough water to fill can. Cut steak into 7-inch squares; cook in hot shortening in skillet until brown. Remove steak to 3-quart greased casserole or baking pan. Add flour, salt and pepper to fat in skillet; stir until smooth. Add juice mixture slowly, stirring constantly; cook for 2 minutes. Place potatoes, carrots, onions and tomatoes on top of steak; pour gravy over vegetables. Cover tightly. Bake in preheated 350-degree oven for 2 hours. Yield: About 8 servings.

Nelson Lanchester
Crystal Grange, No. 1126
Bremerton, Washington

FAMILY RAGOUT
(Recipe over 50 years old)

  1/3 lb. sliced bacon
  1 lb. steak
  4 carrots, sliced
  Salt and pepper to taste
  4 onions, sliced
  4 potatoes, sliced

Cut bacon slices into 4 pieces; place in bottom of heavy skillet. Cut steak into strips; place on bacon. Add carrots; season with salt and pepper. Add onions; place potatoes on onions. Season with salt and pepper. Place skillet over heat; cook for 5 minutes. Add 1 cup water; cover tightly. Reduce heat; cook for 45 minutes. Yield: 4-6 servings.

Mrs. Carrol Ostrander
Masonville Grange, No. 1482
Sidney, New York

ROLLAMOPES
(Recipe 55 years old)

  1 1/2 lb. (about) round steak
  Prepared mustard
  Sm. onion slices
  1/2 x 2-in. bacon strips
  Seasoned flour

Cut steak into 2 x 3-inch pieces; pound both sides with steak hammer or thick saucer edge. Spread one side of each piece of steak with mustard; place 1 slice onion, then 1 strip bacon on each piece. Roll up, start-ing with narrow edge; secure each piece with tooth-pick. Roll in seasoned flour, cook in fat in cast-iron skillet until brown. Add 3/4 cup water; cover. Simmer for 1 hour and 30 minutes; thicken liquid to make gravy. Serve with rice. Yield: 4-6 servings.

Mrs. Tom Mills
Mt. Wheeler Grange, No. 696
Arlington, Washington

STUFFED ROUND STEAK
(Recipe 55 years old)

  2 c. toasted bread crumbs
  1 sm. onion, chopped
  1/2 green pepper, chopped
  1 tsp. sage
  2 tbsp. chopped parsley
  1/2 tsp. salt
  1 c. hot water
  1 1/2 lb. round steak
  Seasoned flour

Place crumbs, onion, green pepper, sage, parsley and salt in bowl; stir in water. Spread on steak; fold steak over. Tie or fasten with toothpicks. Spread melted fat on steak; dredge with seasoned flour. Cook steak in hot fat in skillet until brown. Cover tightly; reduce heat to very low. Cook until steak is tender.

Mrs. Clennen Reed
Watertown Grange, No. 1685
Vincent, Ohio

BEEF STEW WITH DUMPLINGS
(Recipe 100 years old)

  1 lb. beef flank, rump or plate
  2 1/4 c. flour
  1 tsp. salt
  1/4 tsp. pepper
  4 c. cubed potatoes
  1/2 sm. onion, sliced
  2 to 3 c. diced carrots and turnips
  4 tsp. baking powder
  1 c. (scant) milk

Wipe beef; cut into 1 1/2-inch cubes. Mix 1/4 cup flour, 1/2 teaspoon salt and pepper; dredge beef with seasoned flour. Cook beef in large kettle in small amount of fat until well browned. Cover with water; bring to a boil. Reduce heat; cover. Simmer for 2 hours and 30 minutes. Add vegetables; simmer for 30 minutes. Sift remaining 2 cups flour, remaining 1/2 teaspoon salt and baking powder into bowl; add enough milk to make soft dough, stirring constantly. Drop by spoonfuls into stew. Dip spoon into stew between spoonfuls to prevent dough from sticking to spoon. Cover tightly; cook for 15 minutes longer with-out removing cover. Yield: 4-6 servings.

Mrs. Harold Saultz, Ohio State Grange Sec.
Madison Grange
Lancaster, Ohio

★ ★

EASY BAKED STEW
(Recipe 50 years old)

1 1/2 lb. stew beef
4 carrots, sliced
3 to 4 stalks celery, chopped
1 c. tomatoes or tomato juice
1 green pepper, chopped
1 med. onion, chopped
1/3 c. tapioca
Salt and pepper to taste
1 tsp. sweet basil

Mix all ingredients in large casserole; cover. Bake in preheated 300-degree oven for 3 hours and 30 minutes to 4 hours. Yield: 6-8 servings.

Enez Birkett, W.A.C. Chm.
South Prairie Grange, No. 2077
West Liberty, Iowa

SWEET AND SOUR STEW

1/4 c. flour
2 tsp. MSG
Dash of pepper
2 lb. stew beef, cut in 1-in. cubes
1/4 c. cooking oil
2 c. water
1 c. catsup
1/2 c. (firmly packed) brown sugar
1/2 c. vinegar
2 tbsp. Worcestershire sauce
1 tsp. salt
1 onion, chopped
Diced potatoes, carrots and celery
   to taste

Combine flour, MSG and pepper. Coat beef with flour mixture; brown in oil in kettle. Combine water, catsup, brown sugar, vinegar, Worcestershire sauce and salt. Pour over beef; add onion. Cook over low heat for about 45 minutes. Add remaining vegetables; simmer for 1 hour and 30 minutes to 2 hours or until beef and vegetables are tender. Yield: 6 servings.

Dolly Dightman
Anderson Valley Grange, No. 669
Boonville, California

BEEF SHANK CROSSCUTS JARDINIERE

2 tbsp. flour
2 tsp. salt
1/4 tsp. pepper
3 lb. beef shank crosscuts
2 tbsp. lard or drippings
1 1/2 c. water

★ ★

3 carrots, cut in 1-in. pieces
4 stalks celery, cut in 3-in. pieces
1 10-oz. package frozen Brussels
   sprouts

Combine flour, salt and pepper. Dredge beef in seasoned flour. Cook in lard until brown; pour off drippings. Add 1 cup water. Cover tightly and cook over low heat for 2 hours. Add carrots, celery and remaining 1/2 cup water. Cook for 30 minutes longer. Add Brussels sprouts; cook for 30 minutes or until beef is done and vegetables are tender. Yield: 4 servings.

Photograph for this recipe on page 58.

SWEET-SOUR BEEF
(Recipe 100 years old)

2 lb. lean beef
4 med. onions, sliced
1 c. currants or seeded raisins
1/4 c. vinegar
4 whole cloves
1 bay leaf
1 tbsp. chopped orange rind

Cut beef into 2-inch cubes; cook in small amount of fat until brown. Add onions; cook until tender. Add about 1 cup water. Add remaining ingredients; simmer until beef is tender, adding water as needed. Thicken gravy; serve. Yield: 4 servings.

Vera Walker
Dorchester Grange
Rumney, New Hampshire

BEEFSAKA
(Recipe 50 years old)

6 link sausages
1 lb. hamburger
1 c. chopped onions
1/2 c. chopped celery
1 tsp. salt
1/2 tsp. pepper
6 c. thinly sliced potatoes
1 1-lb. can tomatoes

Cook sausages in heavy skillet until brown; remove from skillet. Cook hamburger, onions, celery, salt, pepper and potatoes in same skillet until hamburger and vegetables are lightly browned. Place alternate layers of hamburger mixture and tomatoes in 1 1/2-quart casserole, ending with potato mixture. Slice sausages thin; place on top of casserole. Cover. Bake in preheated 350-degree oven for 1 hour. Yield: 6 servings.

Ann York
Wethersfield Grange, No. 114
Wethersfield, Connecticut

CORNISH PASTIES
(Recipe 100 years old)

3 c. flour
Salt

1/4 c. lard
1 c. finely ground suet
6 to 7 tbsp. cold water
1 lb. finely diced flank or round steak
1/2 lb. finely diced pork
Finely chopped potatoes
Pepper
Sliced turnips
Chopped onions
6 tbsp. butter

Place flour, 1 teaspoon salt and lard in mixing bowl; work lard into flour with pastry blender. Add suet; work in thoroughly. Add enough water to make dough a little more moist than pastry. Divide dough into 4 parts; roll out each piece on floured surface into round shape the size of dinner plate. Mix steak and pork. Place 1/2-inch layer of potatoes on 1/2 of each piece of dough; season with salt and pepper to taste. Add thin layer of turnips, then thin layer of onions. Cover with 1/4 of the steak mixture; place 1 1/2 tablespoons butter on top of each. Fold dough over filled portion; seal edges with fork. Make a 1-inch slit on top of each pasty. Place pasties on cookie sheet or pie pan. Bake in preheated 400-degree oven for 1 hour or until done. Yield: 4 servings.

Beulah M. Sell
Guilford Grange, No. 934
Lisbon, Ohio

LASAGNA

1 lb. lasagna
2 tsp. olive oil
1/2 lb. mozzarella cheese
1 lb. hot bulk sausage
1 lb. hamburger
1 tsp. Italian seasoning
1 32-oz. jar spaghetti sauce
1 lb. ricotta cheese
1 egg
3 oz. grated Parmesan cheese
Parsley flakes to taste

Cook lasagna according to package directions, adding 1 teaspoon olive oil to water to prevent noodles from sticking. Cut 4 slices mozzarella cheese; reserve. Grate remaining mozzarella cheese. Heat remaining 1 teaspoon olive oil in deep skillet. Add sausage, hamburger and Italian seasoning; cook, stirring, until brown. Drain off excess grease. Stir in spaghetti sauce. Add small amount of water to jar to remove extra sauce; stir into hamburger mixture. Simmer for about 15 minutes. Place ricotta cheese, egg, 2 ounces Parmesan cheese, parsley flakes and grated mozzarella cheese in bowl; mix well. Place layers of hamburger mixture, lasagna and cheese mixture in large casserole until all ingredients are used, ending with layer of hamburger mixture. Place reserved mozzarella cheese slices on top; sprinkle with remaining 1 ounce Parmesan cheese. Bake in preheated 350-degree oven for 30 minutes or until cheese melts. Yield: 6-8 servings.

Mrs. Rexford R. Smith, State Master's Wife
West Springfield, Massachusetts

★ ★

BEVERLY'S BEEF-HAM LOAF
(Recipe 50 years old)

        3/4 lb. smoked ham
        3/4 lb. fresh pork
        1/2 lb. beef
        1 egg, slightly beaten
        1 tsp. pepper
        Corn flake crumbs
        1/2 c. tomato soup
        1/2 c. water

Grind all meats together. Add egg and pepper; mix well. Shape into loaf; roll in corn flake crumbs. Place in baking pan. Mix soup and water in small bowl. Bake loaf in preheated 325-degree oven for 1 hour and 30 minutes, basting with soup mixture occasionally. One-half cup raisins or 1 cup mushrooms may be added to baking pan and basted over loaf, if desired. Yield: 8 servings.

Beverly A. Gist
Centennial Grange, No. 2006

HARVEST MEAT LOAF
(Recipe 50 years old)

        1 1/2 lb. ground beef
        3/4 c. fine dry bread crumbs
        3/4 c. applesauce
        6 tbsp. catsup
        3/4 tsp. salt
        1/4 tsp. sage

Combine all ingredients in bowl; mix lightly with a fork. Shape into 6-inch square; place in baking pan. Bake in preheated 350-degree oven for 50 minutes or until done. May add chopped onions to beef mixture, if desired. Yield: 6 servings.

Wilma Martin
Willows Grange, No. 672

TAMALE PIE
(Recipe 75 years old)

        1/2 lb. diced pork shoulder
        1/2 lb. diced veal shoulder
        1/2 c. chopped celery
        2 tsp. salt
        1 slice bacon, diced
        2 tbsp. diced onion
        3/4 c. cornmeal
        1/2 tsp. chili powder
        1/2 c. cooked tomatoes
        1/2 c. canned corn
        1 egg

Place pork, veal, celery and salt in saucepan; add enough water to cover all ingredients. Bring to a boil; reduce heat. Cook for about 2 hours or until meats are tender. Drain; reserve broth. Cook bacon and onion in saucepan until brown. Cook cornmeal in 3 cups reserved broth, stirring constantly, until thick. Combine meat mixture, onion mixture, chili powder, cornmeal mixture, tomatoes and corn in bowl; beat in egg. Pour into 1-quart greased casserole. Bake in preheated 350-degree oven for 1 hour.

Shirley Engler
Mt. Allison Grange, No. 308
Ignacio, Colorado

SWEET AND SOUR MEAT LOAF

        2 tbsp. vinegar
        2 tbsp. brown sugar
        1 c. tomato sauce
        1 to 1 1/2 lb. ground beef
        1/2 lb. bulk pork sausage
        1 egg
        1/4 c. dry bread crumbs or cracker crumbs
        1/2 tsp. prepared mustard
        1 tsp. salt
        1/4 tsp. pepper
        1 tsp. Worcestershire sauce
        1/4 c. minced onion

Combine vinegar, brown sugar and tomato sauce in saucepan; cook, stirring, until sugar is dissolved. Place meats, egg, crumbs, mustard, salt, pepper, Worcestershire sauce and onion in large bowl; mix well. Stir in vinegar mixture; press into loaf pan. Bake in preheated 400-degree oven for 50 to 60 minutes.

Gladys Hager
West Wenatchee Grange, No. 1024
Wenatchee, Washington

POT OF BEEF AND VEGETABLES
(Recipe 50 years old)

        3 lb. beef brisket
        1 shinbone, marrow removed
        1 sm. chicken, disjointed
        2 onions, studded with several cloves
        6 sm. carrots
        3 sm. turnips
        5 leeks (opt.)
        4 qt. water
        1 1/2 tbsp. salt
        2 cloves of garlic
        1 bay leaf
        Pinch of thyme
        Several sprigs of parsley

Place all ingredients except parsley in kettle; bring to a boil. Boil hard for 5 minutes; skim off scum. Add parsley; cover. Reduce heat; simmer for 4 to 5 hours. Strain off broth; serve first. Serve meats and vegetables. May add potatoes, onions and carrots 1 hour before removing from heat. Any combination of meats and vegetables may be used.

Velma Yost
East Oakville Grange, No. 902
Oakville, Washington

★ ★

ROAST VENISON WITH SOUR CREAM GRAVY

3 c. dry wine
1/2 c. apple cider
3 bay leaves
4 whole peppercorns
1 6-lb. venison roast
Salt
1/4 c. butter
1 1/2 tbsp. all-purpose flour
1 c. sour cream

Combine 2 1/2 cups wine and apple cider in shallow dish; add bay leaves and peppercorns. Place venison in marinade; cover and refrigerate overnight, turning occasionally. Place venison on rack in roasting pan, fat side up; sprinkle with salt. Strain marinade and reserve. Insert meat thermometer in center of thickest part of roast not touching bone or resting in fat. Place in preheated 325-degree oven. Melt butter in 1-quart saucepan; add 1 cup reserved marinade. Brush roast occasionally with marinade mixture. Roast venison for 25 minutes per pound for medium-rare or to desired degree of doneness. Remove roast to warmed platter. Combine flour and salt in 1 1/2-quart saucepan. Add 3/4 cup drippings from roasting pan gradually, stirring until smooth. Add remaining 1/2 cup wine. Cook over medium heat, stirring constantly, until thickened. Reduce heat to low; stir in sour cream. Heat to serving temperature. Yield: 6-8 servings.

Photograph for this recipe on page 104.

RABBIT VEGETABLE STEW
(Recipe 71 years old)

1 2 1/2 to 3-lb. rabbit
6 sm. white onions
1 bay leaf
1 1/2 c. diced celery
4 1/2 tsp. salt
1/8 tsp. pepper
2 qt. boiling water
2 c. diced pared carrots
2 c. diced pared potatoes
1/2 lb. sliced fresh mushrooms
1/2 c. flour
3/4 c. cold water
1 tbsp. chopped parsley
Dash of Tabasco sauce

Cut rabbit into serving pieces; wash. Place in kettle; add onions, bay leaf, celery, salt, pepper and boiling water. Cover; bring to a boil. Reduce heat; simmer for 2 hours or until rabbit is nearly tender. Add carrots, potatoes and mushrooms; cover. Simmer for 30 minutes longer or until vegetables and rabbit are tender. Blend flour with cold water; stir into stew. Cook until thickened. Add parsley and Tabasco sauce; mix well. Serve. Yield: 6-8 servings.

Mrs. Eva Grochocki
Dorchester Grange, No. 280
Rumney, New Hampshire

STEWED RABBIT

1 rabbit
Vinegar
1/4 c. butter
1 onion, chopped
1 tbsp. flour
1 bay leaf
5 or 6 cloves
5 or 6 whole allspice

Wipe rabbit carefully with cloth soaked in vinegar; cut into serving pieces. Melt butter in skillet. Add rabbit; cook until brown on all sides. Remove to kettle. Cook onion in butter remaining in skillet until tender; spoon over rabbit. Stir flour into remaining butter in skillet; add 1 cup boiling water gradually, stirring constantly. Cook until smooth; add to kettle. Add remaining ingredients, 1 tablespoon vinegar and enough water to just cover rabbit; bring to a boil. Reduce heat; simmer until rabbit is tender, watching carefully as cooking time depends on age of rabbit. Remove rabbit to a serving dish; strain gravy over rabbit. Add flour and water mixture to thicken gravy, if thicker gravy is desired.

From a Grange Friend

SQUIRREL POTPIE

1 squirrel
Flour
1/4 lemon, sliced very thin
1 tsp. salt
1 sm. glass sherry
1 onion, minced
2 tbsp. butter
1 recipe biscuit dough

Cut squirrel into serving pieces; dredge with flour. Cook in small amount of fat in skillet until brown. Place rabbit in kettle; add 1 quart boiling water, lemon, salt and sherry. Cook onion in 1 tablespoon butter until brown; add to rabbit mixture. Bring to a boil; reduce heat. Cover tightly; simmer for 1 hour. Roll out biscuit dough on floured surface; cut with biscuit cutter. Place on squirrel mixture; cover tightly. Simmer for 15 minutes. Place squirrel in center of hot platter; arrange dumplings around squirrel. Melt remaining 1 tablespoon butter in skillet. Add 1 tablespoon flour; cook, stirring, until brown. Stir in rabbit broth; cook, stirring, until thickened. Pour over squirrel. The large gray and fox squirrels are the best for eating and are only fit to use when young. Their age may be known by their hairs and paws, which should be soft, the edges of the hairs smooth and the paws not worn. Squirrels are best in the fall and early winter. They should be drawn as soon as possible after killing, but should not be skinned until ready to use. Recipe from mother's turn-of-the-century cookbook.

Bee Warden, Sec.
Van Duzen River Grange, No. 517
Carlotta, California

★ ★

VEAL SHOULDER CASSEROLE

2 1/2 lb. veal shoulder
Salt and pepper to taste
Flour
4 slices bacon, diced
1 sm. onion, chopped
1 clove of garlic, chopped
1/2 lb. mushrooms, sliced
1 16-oz. can tomato sauce
1 1/2 c. water
1 tbsp. Angostura aromatic bitters

Cut veal into 1-inch cubes; sprinkle with salt and pepper. Roll cubes in flour. Fry bacon until crisp; remove from frypan and reserve. Cook veal until brown on all sides in bacon drippings. Add onion, garlic and mushrooms. Pour veal mixture into 2-quart casserole. Stir in tomato sauce, water and Angostura. Cover tightly. Bake in preheated 350-degree oven for 1 to 1 hour and 30 minutes or until veal is tender. Season with salt and pepper. Serve with hot cooked spaghetti and a green salad. Yield: 6 servings.

Photograph for this recipe above.

HOMEMADE RAVIOLI

3 c. flour
Salt
3 eggs

2 tbsp. butter or oil
1 c. (about) warm water
1 lb. hamburger
1 c. chopped cooked spinach
1/2 c. bread crumbs
1/3 c. grated Parmesan cheese
2 tbsp. chopped parsley
1/2 clove of garlic, chopped
1/8 tsp. rosemary
1/8 tsp. thyme
1/8 tsp. marjoram
1/2 tbsp. oregano
1 sm. onion, minced
Pepper to taste
Tomato sauce

Sift flour with 1/4 teaspoon salt. Place on board; place 1 egg in center. Add butter; mix well. Add enough water to make stiff dough; knead until smooth. Cover; let stand for about 10 minutes. Divide in half; roll out each half on lightly floured board until very thin. Place remaining 2 eggs in bowl; beat lightly. Blend remaining ingredients except tomato sauce in bowl; add salt to taste. Add enough beaten egg to hold ingredients together. Drop teaspoonfuls of hamburger mixture about 2 inches apart on 1 sheet of dough until all filling is used; cover with other sheet of dough. Press around each mound of filling with fingertips to form filled squares; cut squares apart with pastry cutter. Place 8 quarts of salted water in deep pot; bring to

★ ★ ★ ★ ★★★★★★★★★★★★★★★★★★★★★★★★★★★★★★★★★★★★★ ★ ★ ★ ★

a rapid boil. Cook filled squares in the boiling water for about 10 minutes or until dough is tender. Remove carefully with slotted spoon; place serving portions on individual heated plates. Top with tomato sauce; sprinkle with additional grated Parmesan cheese. Serve hot. Yield: 6 servings.

Mrs. Linda G. Sawyer
Berryessa Grange, No. 780
San Jose, California

OKLAHOMA CHILI

1 lg. bunch celery, chopped
1/2 lb. bacon, diced
2 lb. ground round steak
6 med. onions, chopped
2 cans kidney beans
2 lg. cans tomatoes
1/2 bottle catsup
1 can mushrooms
Chili powder to taste
1 tbsp. Worcestershire sauce
2 1/2 c. thick tomato soup
2 tbsp. (heaping) tapioca

Place celery in kettle; cover with boiling water. Simmer until tender. Fry bacon until crisp; place bacon in kettle. Cook steak and onions in bacon fat until light brown; add to kettle. Add celery and water; add remaining ingredients except tapioca. Bring to a boil; reduce heat. Simmer for several hours. Add tapioca just before serving; mix well.

Glorene Breckenridge
Lincoln Grange, No. 295
Pond Creek, Oklahoma

EASY MEAT LOAF
(Recipe about 50 years old)

2 lb. ground beef steak
1/2 lb. ground salt pork
1 c. cracker crumbs
1 c. milk
Salt and pepper to taste
Chopped onion to taste

Place all ingredients in bowl; mix well. Press firmly into loaf pan; cover with water. Bake in preheated 325-degree oven for 1 hour and 30 minutes.

Mrs. Clifford Cronk
Castile Grange, No. 1017
Fillmore, New York

JAPANESE SKILLET DINNER

2 tbsp. sugar
1 lb. ground beef
1 med. onion, diced
1 clove of garlic, minced
1 med. cabbage, shredded
1 1-lb. can tomatoes
1 8-oz. can tomato sauce
1/4 c. water

1 tsp. salt
1 to 2 tbsp. soy sauce

Place sugar in skillet; cook over low heat, stirring constantly, until melted. Stir in beef, onion and garlic; cover. Cook over low heat until lightly browned. Add cabbage and remaining ingredients; cook for about 20 minutes or until cabbage is tender. Serve with rice. Yield: 6 servings.

Mrs. Tom Fortune
Porterville Grange, No. 718
Porterville, California

1/2 cup water and 1/2 lemon before breakfast helps a torrid liver.

BEEF-ZUCCHINI SKILLET

3 lb. zucchini
1/3 c. vegetable oil
Pepper
3/4 lb. ground beef
1 1-lb. can tomatoes
Salt to taste

Wash and dry zucchini; cut in 1/8-inch slices. Heat oil in large skillet; add layer of zucchini. Sprinkle lightly with pepper; saute on both sides until lightly browned. Remove with slotted spoon. Repeat until all zucchini slices are cooked. Cook ground beef in same skillet until lightly browned; drain off excess fat. Add zucchini, tomatoes and salt to skillet; cover. Simmer for about 20 minutes. Yield: 4 servings.

Viola Blake, Home Ec Chm.
New Hampton Grange, No. 123
New Hampton, New Hampshire

MEXICAN CHILI
(Recipe over 100 years old)

2 lb. beef
1 lb. pork
3/4 c. fat
1 onion, chopped
2 cloves of garlic, chopped
1/2 tsp. cumin seed
3/4 c. chili pepper pulp
1 tsp. salt

Cut beef and pork into small cubes; do not grind. Heat fat in Dutch oven. Add meats, onion, garlic, cumin seed, pepper, pulp and salt; mix well. Cook, stirring, until meats are lightly browned. Cover with water; simmer for 3 hours, stirring occasionally. Use big red peppers to make pepper pulp. Split peppers; remove seeds. Steep in hot water for 20 minutes, then peel out pulp.

Leona Clayton
Rosedale Grange, No. 565
Kern County, California

✩ ☆ ★ ★ ★ ★ ★ ★ ★ ★ ★ ★ ★ ★ ★ ★ ★ ★ ★ ☆ ★ ★ ★ ★ ★ ★ ★ ★ ★ BARBECUE SAUCE ★ ★ ★ ☆ ★

ITALIAN DELIGHT

1 lb. hamburger
1 lg. onion, chopped fine
1 green pepper, chopped fine
2 c. spaghetti or macaroni, cooked
1/2 tsp. garlic salt
2 sm. cans tomato sauce
1 can whole-kernel corn
1 c. water
2 tsp. salt
1/2 tsp. pepper
2 tsp. chili powder
2 tsp. paprika
1/2 tsp. mace
Grated Cheddar cheese

Cook hamburger with onion and green pepper in skillet until brown. Add remaining ingredients except cheese; mix well. Place in casserole; cover with cheese. Bake in preheated 300-degree oven for 45 minutes.

Zella Chatburn
Albion Grange, No. 321
Albion, Idaho

GOURMET MEAT LOAF

1 c. fresh sliced mushrooms
1/2 c. chopped onion
2 tbsp. butter
1/3 c. sour cream
1 1/2 lb. ground beef
3/4 c. rolled oats
1 egg
2 tsp. salt
1/4 tsp. pepper
1 tbsp. Worcestershire sauce
2/3 c. milk

Cook mushrooms and onion in butter in saucepan until brown; remove from heat. Stir in sour cream. Combine remaining ingredients in bowl; mix thoroughly. Place half the beef mixture in shallow baking dish; shape to form an oval base. Make shallow well lengthwise down center for filling. Spoon mushroom mixture into well; shape remaining beef mixture over filling. Seal all around beef mixture. Bake in preheated 350-degree oven for 1 hour; let stand for 5 minutes before slicing. Yield: 6 servings.

Mrs. Roger Koch
Powder River Grange, No. 68
Kaycee, Wyoming

ZESTY MEAT LOAF

2 tbsp. prepared mustard
2 tbsp. molasses
2 tbsp. vinegar
1/2 c. tomato juice or catsup
2 eggs, beaten
1 c. rolled oats
1/2 c. finely chopped onion
2 tsp. salt
1/4 tsp. thyme
1/8 tsp. oregano
1/8 tsp. basil
1/8 tsp. celery seed
1/8 tsp. nutmeg
2 lb. lean ground beef

Combine mustard, molasses and vinegar in large bowl; reserve 1 tablespoon for glaze. Add remaining ingredients to remaining mustard mixture; mix well. Shape into loaf; place in foil-lined 9-inch square baking pan. Spread reserved glaze over top. Bake in preheated 350-degree oven for 1 hour, draining off excess fat, if needed. Two cups soft bread crumbs may be substituted for oats; Italian seasoning may be used instead of oregano and basil.

Grethel Capen, C.W.A. Sec.
American River Grange, No. 172
Rancho Cordova, California

CURRY BALLS
(Recipe 90 years old)

1 lb. hamburger
Salt
Pepper to taste
1/4 c. butter
1 sm. onion, finely chopped
Curry powder to taste
2 c. tomato puree
1/8 tsp. cayenne pepper
2 tbsp. flour

Combine hamburger, salt to taste and pepper; shape into balls size of walnuts. Melt 2 teaspoons butter in frying pan. Add onion; cook, stirring, until tender. Add curry powder; mix well. Add meatballs; cook for 10 minutes, shaking pan constantly. Mix tomato puree, remaining butter, teaspoon salt, cayenne pepper and flour in saucepan; cook until thickened. Pour over meatballs; cook until liquid is consistency of gravy.

Grace Hagen
Homestead Grange, No. 215
Roggen, Colorado

MEATBALLS IN BARBECUE SAUCE

2 lb. ground beef
1 1/2 c. soft bread crumbs
Chopped onion
1/2 c. chopped celery
Worcestershire sauce
2 eggs
1/4 tsp. pepper
2 1/4 tsp. garlic salt
1 tsp. butter
1/2 c. catsup
2 tsp. brown sugar
2 tbsp. prepared mustard

Combine ground beef, bread crumbs, 1/2 cup onion, celery, 1 tablespoon Worcestershire sauce, eggs, pepper and 2 teaspoons garlic salt in bowl; mix well. Shape into 24 balls; place in greased, shallow baking pan.

★ ★

Bake in preheated 375-degree oven for 20 minutes. Saute 1 teaspoon onion in butter in saucepan until transparent. Add catsup, brown sugar, mustard and remaining 1/4 teaspoon garlic salt; mix well. Simmer for 10 minutes. Pour over meatballs; bake for 30 minutes longer. Serve over rice. Yield: 8 servings.

Mrs. Mary E. Wisner
Champion Grange
Upper Sandusky, Ohio

OLD-TIME SPAGHETTI
(Recipe 70 years old)

1 1/2 lb. ground beef
2 tbsp. oregano
2 tbsp. grated cheese
2 cloves of garlic, minced
2 eggs
1/2 c. bread crumbs
2 cans tomato paste
1 qt. tomatoes
1 tbsp. salt
1 tsp. sugar
Mushrooms to taste
2 lb. spaghetti, cooked

Combine first 6 ingredients in bowl; mix well. Shape into balls. Cook in skillet until brown. Combine remaining ingredients except spaghetti in saucepan; bring to a boil. Add meatballs; simmer for 4 hours, stirring occasionally. Add spaghetti; mix well. Serve. Yield: 6 servings.

Sharon Taylor
Inavale Grange, No. 1248
Angelica, New York

HERBED MEATBALLS WITH SPAGHETTI
(Recipe 35 years old)

1 lb. ground beef
Salt and pepper to taste
1/4 tsp. marjoram
Shortening
2 med. onions, chopped
1 clove of garlic, pressed
1 c. chopped celery
2/3 c. chopped green pepper
3 1/2 c. chopped tomatoes
2 tsp. chili powder
1 c. mushrooms (opt.)
2 tbsp. Worcestershire sauce
1 c. spaghetti

Season beef with salt, pepper and marjoram; shape into 1-inch balls. Cook meatballs in small amount of shortening in skillet over medium-high heat until lightly browned. Add onions and garlic; cook until tender. Add celery, green pepper, tomatoes, chili powder, mushrooms and Worcestershire sauce; mix well. Break spaghetti into pieces; add to beef mixture. Push spaghetti down carefully so that tomatoes are over

spaghetti; cover. Bring to a boil over high heat; reduce heat to low. Simmer for 45 minutes. Garnish with chopped parsley. Serve with grated Parmesan cheese, if desired. May be cooled, packaged and frozen, then reheated. Yield: 8 servings.

Ethel M. Cooper
Mt. Wheeler Grange, No. 696
Arlington, Washington

SWEDISH MEATBALLS
(Recipe about 40 years old)

1 lb. ground beef
1 sm. onion, grated
1/4 c. chopped parsley
1 egg
1 slice bread, crumbled
3/4 tsp. salt
1/4 tsp. marjoram
Ground cloves
Pinch of thyme
1 1/4 c. brown gravy
1 tbsp. chopped onion
Dash of curry powder

Combine ground beef, grated onion, parsley, egg, bread, 1/2 teaspoon salt, marjoram, dash of cloves and thyme in large bowl; mix well. Shape into 48 balls. Combine dash of cloves, remaining 1/4 teaspoon salt, gravy, chopped onion and curry powder in large frying pan; bring to a boil. Add meatballs, one at a time; reduce heat. Simmer for about 15 minutes or until meatballs are just done. Yield: 6 servings.

Edna M. Kukkola
Webster Grange, No. 205
Marshfield, Massachusetts

MEAT ROLLS
(Recipe at least 40 years old)

Leftover beef gravy
Leftover pot roast, ground
2 c. sifted flour
3 tsp. baking powder
1/2 tsp. salt
1/4 c. shortening
2/3 to 3/4 c. milk

Heat beef gravy. Moisten roast well with some of the gravy; reserve remaining gravy. Mix flour, baking powder and salt in bowl; cut in shortening. Make well in center. Add milk all at once; stir with fork until mixed. Turn out onto floured board; knead for 30 seconds. Roll out until about 1/2 inch thick. Spread roast on dough; roll as for jelly roll. Cut into 1 to 1 1/2-inch thick slices. Place on greased cookie sheet. Bake in preheated 450-degree oven for 12 to 15 minutes. Serve topped with hot gravy. Yield: 4-5 servings.

June F. Hendrickson
Highline Grange, No. 1132
Seattle, Washington

★★★

MOCK RAVIOLI

2 med. onions, chopped
2 cloves of garlic, chopped
Salad oil
2 lb. ground beef
1   4-oz. can mushrooms
1 can tomato sauce
1 can tomato paste
1 1/2 c. water
1 1/2 tsp. mixed Italian herbs
1 1/2 c. finely chopped cooked spinach
1 c. soft bread crumbs
1/2 c. minced parsley
1 tsp. sage
1 tsp. salt
4 eggs, well beaten
1 lb. butterfly or seashell macaroni

Saute onions and 1 clove of garlic in 3 tablespoons oil in skillet until golden. Add ground beef; cook, stirring with a fork until brown. Add mushrooms, tomato sauce, tomato paste, water and Italian herbs; cover tightly. Cook over very low heat for 2 hours. Combine 1/2 cup oil, spinach, bread crumbs, remaining 1 clove of garlic, parsley, sage, salt and eggs in bowl; mix well. Cook macaroni in boiling water until tender; drain. Place layer of macaroni in large, greased baking dish or 2 smaller dishes. Add layer of spinach mixture, then layer of beef mixture. Repeat layers until all ingredients are used, ending with beef mixture. Bake in preheated 350-degree oven for 30 to 40 minutes. Use combination of thyme, sweet basil with small amount of rosemary and marjoram if Italian herbs are not available. Yield: 14-16 servings.

Betty Goeringer
Madera Grange, No. 783
Madera, California

HAMBURGER-CHEESE BAKE

1 lb. ground beef
1/2 c. chopped onion
2   8-oz. cans tomato sauce
1 tsp. sugar
3/4 tsp. salt
1/4 tsp. garlic salt
1/4 tsp. pepper
4 c. medium noodles
1 c. cream-style cottage cheese
1   8-oz. package cream cheese, softened
1/4 c. sour cream
1/3 c. sliced green onion
1/4 c. chopped green pepper
1/4 c. grated Parmesan cheese

Cook beef and onion in large skillet until beef is lightly browned and onion is tender. Stir in tomato sauce, sugar, salt, garlic salt and pepper; remove from heat. Cook noodles according to package directions; drain. Combine cottage cheese, cream cheese, sour cream, green onion and green pepper. Spread half the noodles in 11 x 7 x 1 1/2-inch baking pan; top with half the beef sauce. Cover with cheese mixture. Add

remaining noodles, then remaining beef sauce; sprinkle with Parmesan cheese. Bake in preheated 350-degree oven for 30 minutes. Yield: 8-10 servings.

Janice Peer
Rosedale Grange

GROUND BEEF-NOODLE DINNER

1/2 c. butter
1/2 c. flour
4 c. milk
1 1/2 c. grated cheese (opt.)
Salt and pepper to taste
1/2 lb. noodles, cooked
1 c. peas
Chopped onion to taste
1 1/2 lb. ground beef, ham or pork

Melt butter in saucepan. Add flour; stir until smooth. Add milk gradually; cook, stirring, until thickened. Add cheese; stir until melted. Season with salt and pepper. Arrange layers of noodles, peas, onion, beef and cheese sauce in greased casserole, ending with noodles. Bake in preheated 350-degree oven for 1 hour or until done.

Mrs. Jean Bagnick
Hope Grange
Waymart, Pennsylvania

JENNY'S LASAGNA

1/4 c. olive oil
1 lg. onion, finely chopped
2 lb. ground beef
4 cloves of garlic, pressed
1/2 c. parsley flakes
1/4 c. red wine
2   2-lb. cans Italian tomatoes
2   6-oz. cans tomato paste
1 stalk celery, finely chopped
1 carrot, finely chopped
1 1/2 tbsp. salt
1/2 tsp. freshly ground pepper
1 1/2 tsp. dried basil
1 1/2 tsp. oregano
Grated Romano or Parmesan cheese
2 eggs
1 lb. ricotta or cottage cheese
1 lb. lasagna, cooked
1 lb. mozzarella cheese, sliced

Heat olive oil in saucepan. Add onion and ground beef; saute until brown. Add garlic and 1/4 cup parsley flakes; cook over low heat for 10 minutes. Stir in wine; cover. Cook for 2 minutes. Add tomatoes, tomato paste, celery, carrot, salt, pepper, basil, oregano and 1/2 cup Romano cheese; mix well. Cover; cook over low heat for 1 hour, stirring occasionally. Beat eggs in bowl; stir in ricotta cheese and remaining 1/4 cup parsley flakes. Pour 1 cup beef sauce into 15 x 10 x 2-inch baking pan. Cover with 1/3 of the noodles, then layer of beef sauce. Add 1/3 of the moz-

★ ★

zarella cheese, 1/3 of the ricotta mixture and 2 table-spoons Romano cheese. Repeat layers twice, ending with beef sauce. Cover with Romano cheese. Bake in preheated 375-degree oven for 30 minutes or until bubbly; cut into squares. Recipe usually makes another small dish of lasagna; may be cooked at same time or frozen for later use. Yield: 10-12 servings.

Jenny Grobusky, Dir. of Women's Activities
National Grange
Washington, D.C.

BAKED HAMBURGER PATTIES

1 lb. ground beef
1 egg, beaten
1 c. crushed cereal
1 tsp. salt
1/4 tsp. pepper
1 tbsp. finely chopped onion
3 tbsp. (firmly packed) brown sugar
1/4 c. catsup
1/8 tsp. nutmeg
1 tsp. dry mustard

Combine ground beef, egg, 3/4 cup cereal, salt, pepper and onion. Combine sugar, catsup, nutmeg and dry mustard; mix well. Add half the sugar mixture to ground beef mixture; mix well. Shape into 6 balls; place in greased muffin tin. Pour remaining sauce in equal portions over ground beef balls. Sprinkle with remaining 1/4 cup cereal. Bake in preheated 400-degree oven for 30 minutes. Yield: 3 servings.

Mrs. Kenneth P. Thomas
Wife of Rhode Island State Master
North Kingstown, Rhode Island

RICE-BEEF CASSEROLE

1 lb. ground beef
1 lg. onion, chopped
1 c. rice
1 tbsp. salt
Pepper to taste
1/4 c. soy sauce
2 c. diagonally sliced celery
1 1/4 c. thick white sauce with chopped
    mushrooms
3 3/4 c. hot water
1/2 c. sliced carrots
1 sm. can pimento strips, drained
1/2 green pepper, chopped

Cook ground beef in small amount of fat in skillet until brown. Add onion, uncooked rice and remaining ingredients; mix well. Place in well-greased 9 x 13-inch baking pan; cover. Bake in preheated 350-degree oven for 1 hour; stir. Cover; bake for 1 hour longer. Yield: 12 servings.

Rose E. Laszlo
Sequim Prairie Grange
Sequim, Washington

GEORGE WASHINGTON'S STOVED POTATOES AND MUTTON CHOPS
(Recipe 200 years old)

10 med. potatoes
2 c. thick cream
3 lb. (about) thinly sliced mutton chips
Pepper
3 c. minced onions
Salt to taste
2 tbsp. butter

Peel and slice potatoes. Place 1/3 of the potatoes in greased Dutch oven or large casserole; pour half the cream over potatoes. Arrange 1/2 of the mutton chops over potatoes; sprinkle generously with pepper. Add 1/2 of the onions; sprinkle with salt. Repeat layers, ending with potatoes; dot with butter. Bake in preheated 300 to 325-degree oven for 1 hour and 30 minutes to 2 hours or until potatoes are tender. Yield: 8-10 servings.

This dish was supposed to have been served to George Washington for Christmas dinner in 1776.

Evelyn Ray
San Dimas Grange, No. 658
Glendora, California

ROAST LEG OF LAMB

1 6-lb. leg of lamb
1 1/2 tsp. salt
2 tsp. seasoned salt
1 tbsp. paprika
1/2 tsp. ground ginger
1/2 tsp. dry mustard
1 tsp. dried oregano
1 tsp. pepper
1/4 c. fresh lime juice
2 cloves of garlic, crushed
1/2 tsp. dried marjoram
3 or 4 dashes of Tabasco sauce
Stuffed olives

Trim excess fat from lamb. Mix 1 teaspoon salt with seasoned salt, paprika, ginger, mustard, oregano and pepper; rub over lamb thoroughly on all sides. Place lamb in baking pan. Combine lime juice, garlic, remaining 1/2 teaspoon salt, marjoram and Tabasco sauce; mix well. Gouge holes about 3/4 inch deep all over top of lamb by inserting sharp paring knife and scraping out meat. Pour lime mixture into each hole; insert a stuffed olive over lime mixture in each hole as for a stopper. Cover lamb; refrigerate overnight. Bake in preheated 350-degree oven for 3 hours or until lamb is tender, basting with remaining lime juice mixture and adding small amounts of hot water, if needed. Place lamb on platter. Skim off fat in baking pan; add enough boiling water to pan liquid to make rich gravy. Yield: 8-10 servings.

From a Grange Friend

★ ★

IRISH STEW

2 lb. shoulder of lamb
1/4 c. flour
1 tsp. salt
1/4 tsp. pepper
3 tbsp. bacon fat
1 tsp. minced parsley
1/2 tsp. oregano or marjoram
1/2 tsp. sweet basil
1 c. diced carrots
3 med. onions, sliced
2 c. diced potatoes
2 1/2 c. stewed tomatoes

Cut lamb into 1 1/2-inch cubes. Place flour, salt and pepper in paper bag. Add lamb; shake until coated. Heat fat in heavy skillet. Add lamb; cook, stirring frequently, until brown on all sides. Transfer to large pot; sprinkle parsley, oregano and basil over lamb. Add carrots, onions and potatoes to remaining fat in skillet; cook, stirring, for several minutes or until lightly browned. Add to lamb. Add tomatoes; stir to blend. Add 1 cup water to skillet; scrape up brown particles. Add to pot; simmer for 1 hour or until lamb is very tender and vegetables are well done. Mix small amount of flour with equal amount of water and stir into stew, if thicker liquid is desired. Let simmer for 5 minutes longer.

Mrs. Ralph W. Durkee
Saratoga Grange, No. 1209
Stillwater, New York

LAMB SOUFFLE

1 tbsp. butter
1 tbsp. flour
1 lg. tomato, pureed
1/4 c. soft bread crumbs
1/2 tsp. salt
1/4 tsp. pepper
1/2 tsp. onion juice
1 tsp. chopped parsley
2 eggs, separated
1 c. chopped lamb

Melt butter in saucepan; stir in flour. Add puree; bring to a boil, stirring constantly. Add crumbs, seasonings, lightly beaten egg yolks and lamb; mix thoroughly. Fold in stiffly beaten egg whites; turn into buttered 1 1/2-quart baking dish. Place in dish of boiling water. Bake in preheated 350-degree oven until firm. Serve with caper or tomato sauce. Yield: 2-3 servings. Recipe comes from Nyal Cookbook published in 1916.

Ruth Wiley, Lecturer
White Oak Grange, No. 182
Waldoboro, Maine

SCALLOPED VEGETABLES WITH LAMB
(Recipe 100 years old)

1 c. rice
1 lb. lean lamb
1 c. cooked peas
1 c. thickened stock
2 tsp. salt
2 tsp. grated onion
1/8 tsp. pepper

Pour 2 1/2 cups water into saucepan; bring to a boil. Add rice slowly so that water continues to boil; stir. Reduce heat; cover. Simmer until rice is tender. Cook lamb in simmering water until tender. Drain lamb; cut in thin slices. Place 1/3 of the rice in greased baking dish; add 1/2 of the lamb. Add 1/2 of the peas. Repeat layers, ending with rice. Mix stock, salt, onion and pepper; pour over rice. Bake in preheated 350 to 400-degree oven for 40 minutes. Yield: 4 servings.

Ruth C. Walters
Souhegan Grange
Milford, New Hampshire

BARBECUED PORK CHOPS

8 lean pork chops or pork steaks
1/2 c. catsup
1 tsp. salt
1 tsp. celery seed
1/2 tsp. nutmeg
1/2 c. vinegar
1 c. water
1 bay leaf

Cook pork chops in fat in skillet until brown, then arrange in baking pan. Combine remaining ingredients; pour over chops. Bake in preheated 325-degree oven for 1 hour and 30 minutes, turning chops once during baking.

Mrs. Philip Wheadon, Lecturer, C.W.A.
Adams Grange, No. 391
Adams, New York

BAKED PORK LOIN CHOPS WITH RICE
(Recipe over 50 years old)

Butter
6 pork loin chops, 1 in. thick
Salt and pepper to taste
6 slices onion, 1/4 in. thick
6 slices tomato, 1/4 in. thick
6 green pepper rings, 1/4 in. thick
Cooked rice
Paprika

Melt small amount of butter in large frying pan. Add pork chops; cook until brown on both sides. Season with salt and pepper; place in single layer in baking dish. Place 1 slice onion on each chop; add 1 slice tomato. Place 1 green pepper ring on each slice tomato; fill pepper ring with rice. Season with salt and pepper; sprinkle with paprika. Add about 1/4 cup water to frying pan; stir to remove brown particles from frying pan. Pour into baking dish; cover. Bake in preheated 350-degree oven for 1 hour or until done.

Mary T. Hironymous
American River Grange, No. 172
Sacramento, California

★ ★

BAKED PORK CHOPS WITH STUFFING

4 lean pork chops, cut 1 in. thick
1 tsp. prepared mustard
2 c. bread crumbs
1 tbsp. chopped onion
1/8 tsp. sage
1 tsp. salt

Trim bits of fat from chops; fry fat in heavy skillet until golden. Remove fat; set aside. Spread chops with mustard; cook until brown on one side. Turn chops. Combine crumbs, onion, sage, salt and just enough water to moisten; mix well. Pack stuffing on each chop, using all the stuffing; top each with bits of cooked fat. Cover. Bake in preheated 350-degree oven for 30 minutes. Uncover; bake for 20 minutes longer or until stuffing is brown. Yield: 4 servings.

From a Grange Friend

EASY PORK-POTATO CASSEROLE

4 thick pork chops
4 potatoes, quartered
2 med. onions, sliced
Salt and pepper to taste
1/2 c. butter
1/2 c. diced celery
1/2 c. diced onion
1 1/2 c. toasted bread cubes

Cook pork chops in small amount of fat in frying pan until brown on both sides. Remove chops from frying pan; set aside. Pour off grease from frying pan. Add 1/2 cup water to frying pan; scrape up brown particles from bottom to make gravy. Arrange potatoes in large casserole; spread onions over potatoes. Place pork chops over onions; pour gravy over chops. Season chops with salt and pepper. Mix remaining ingredients; spread over chops. Cover casserole with aluminum foil or lid. Bake in preheated 350-degree oven for 55 minutes. Remove cover; bake for 15 to 20 minutes longer. Yield: 4 servings.

Mrs. Palma Spera
Braintree Grange, No. 262
Braintree, Massachusetts

PORK CHOP AND POTATO SCALLOP

6 pork chops, cut 1/2 in. thick
4 tbsp. flour
2 tsp. salt
1 1/4 c. thick cheese sauce
1 1/4 c. milk
1/3 c. crumbled blue cheese (opt.)
6 med. baking potatoes
1 1/2 c. sliced onions
1 tsp. pepper

Trim excess fat from pork chops. Mix 2 tablespoons flour and 1 teaspoon salt; coat pork chops with flour mixture. Cook chops in small amount of fat in skillet until brown on both sides. Remove chops from skillet; set aside. Add cheese sauce to skillet; stir in milk gradually. Bring to a boil over medium heat. Remove from

heat; stir in cheese. Peel potatoes; slice thin. Arrange half the potatoes in greased 3-quart casserole; add half the onions. Combine remaining 2 tablespoons flour, remaining 1 teaspoon salt and pepper; sprinkle half the mixture over onions. Repeat layers; pour cheese sauce over top. Arrange pork chops on onion mixture; cover casserole with foil. Bake in preheated 350-degree oven for 1 hour to 1 hour and 15 minutes or until potatoes are tender.

Mrs. Jean Moffitt
Grafton Star Grange
Hanover, New Hampshire

BROILED PORK CHOPS WITH CRAB APPLES

6 to 8 pork chops, cut 1 in. thick
1   16-oz. jar crab apples
1/3 c. (firmly packed) brown sugar
1 tbsp. lemon juice

Place pork chops on rack in broiler pan. Insert pan so tops of chops are 5 inches from heat. Broil chops for 10 minutes; turn and broil for 15 minutes on second side. Prepare crab apple sauce while pork chops are broiling on first side. Drain crab apple liquid into saucepan; add brown sugar and lemon juice. Bring to a boil, stirring to dissolve sugar; cook over low heat for 5 to 8 minutes. Brush pork chops with crab apple sauce; broil, turning and brushing with sauce occasionally, for 15 minutes longer or until well done. Place crab apples on broiler rack for last 15 minutes of broiling time, brushing with sauce several times. Serve remaining sauce with chops. Yield: 6 to 8 servings.

Photograph for this recipe below.

★ ★ ★ ★ ★ ★ ★ ★ ★ ★ ★ ★ ★ ★ ★ ★ ★ ☆ ★ ★ ★ ★ ★ ★ ★ ★ ★ ★ ★ ★ ★ ★ ★ ★ ★ ★

PORK CHOP-TOMATO CASSEROLE
(Recipe 50 years old)

6 pork chops
8 lg. onions
1 1/2 c. long grain rice
1 1-lb. 13-oz. can stewed tomatoes
Salt and pepper to taste

Cook pork chops in skillet until brown on both sides; remove from skillet. Place in large casserole. Peel and slice onions; place over pork chops. Cover onions with rice; pour tomatoes over rice. Bake in preheated 350-degree oven for 1 hour or until chops are done. Sprinkle with salt and pepper to taste. Yield: 6 servings.

Mae E. Adams
Eclipse Grange, No. 311
Newton, New Hampshire

GLAZED HAM LOAF
(Recipe 50 years old)

1 1/2 lb. ground ham
1 lb. ground fresh pork
2 eggs
1 c. milk
1 c. cracker crumbs
1 tsp. salt
1/2 tsp. pepper
1/2 c. vinegar
1 c. (packed) brown sugar
1/2 c. water
1 tsp. dry mustard
Whole cloves

Place first 7 ingredients in bowl; mix well. Pack into 2 small bread pans. Place remaining ingredients except cloves in bowl; mix well. Pour over loaves. Stud each loaf with several cloves. Bake in preheated 325-degree oven for about 2 hours or until done. Yield: 10-12 servings.

Rose L. Albright
Mendon Grange, No. 855
Ruffsdale, Pennsylvania

HAM MOUNTAINS

2 eggs, slightly beaten
1 c. bread crumbs
1 c. tomato juice
1/2 c. chopped green pepper
1 tbsp. prepared mustard
2 lb. ground fresh pork
1 lb. ground smoked ham
8 to 12 pineapple slices
2 c. mashed sweet potatoes
8 to 12 marshmallows (opt.)

Combine eggs, crumbs, tomato juice, green pepper and mustard in bowl. Add pork and ham; mix well. Shape into patties the size of pineapple slices; place in greased, shallow baking pan. Place a pineapple slice on each patty; place heaping tablespoon sweet potatoes over each pineapple slice. Bake in preheated 350-degree oven for 50 minutes. Top each patty with a marshmallow; bake for 10 minutes longer or until marshmallows are melted and browned.

Genevieve Hughs
Hancock Grange, No. 1591
Eddy, New York

HAM-PINEAPPLE LOAF
(Recipe 80 years old)

2/3 c. crushed pineapple
2 c. bread crumbs
3 eggs, slightly beaten
1 lb. ground fresh pork
2 lb. ground smoked ham
1/2 sweet pepper, minced
Salt to taste
1/4 tsp. pepper

Reserve 2 tablespoons pineapple. Combine bread crumbs and remaining pineapple in bowl; let stand. Place eggs, meats, sweet pepper, salt and pepper in large bowl; mix well. Add pineapple mixture; mix until combined. Shape into loaf; place in baking pan. Spread reserved pineapple over top of loaf. Bake in preheated 350-degree oven for 1 hour and 30 minutes to 2 hours.

Frances Brackin
Petersburg Grange, No. 1819
Carrollton, Ohio

HAM POTPIE
(Recipe 95 years old)

3 lb. cured ham
1 lg. hambone
2 c. flour
1/2 tsp. salt
3 tsp. baking powder
1 c. milk

Pour 6 cups water into large pot. Add ham and hambone; bring to a boil. Reduce heat; cook for 1 hour or until ham is nearly tender. Sift flour, salt and baking powder together into bowl; stir in milk, mixing only until flour is moist. Drop by spoonfuls into boiling liquid. Cook, uncovered for 15 minutes. Cover pot; cook for 5 minutes longer without removing cover. Remove dumplings and ham to hot platter. Make gravy with liquid; pour some of the gravy over dumplings. Serve remaining gravy in sauceboat. Yield: 4-5 servings.

Mrs. Hubert Miller
Foxenkill Grange, No. 1579
East Berne, New York

DRIED APPLES AND DUMPLINGS

1 qt. dried apples
3 lb. (about) ham

★ ★

2 tbsp. brown sugar
2 c. sifted flour
1 tsp. salt
4 tsp. baking powder
1/4 tsp. pepper
3 tbsp. melted butter or shortening
1 egg, well beaten
2/3 c. (about) milk

Wash apples; place in bowl. Cover with water; soak overnight. Place ham in large kettle; cover with water. Cook for 3 hours. Add apples and water in which they were soaked; cook for 1 hour. Add brown sugar; mix well. Sift flour, salt, baking powder and pepper together into bowl. Add butter, egg and enough milk to make stiff batter; mix well. Drop by spoonfuls into hot liquid with apples and ham; cover kettle tightly. Cook for 18 minutes. Serve piping hot on large platter. Yield: 8 servings.

This is an old Pennsylvania Dutch recipe of the early eighteenth century before the Revolutionary War. It was used by my ancestors.

Mae W. Ross
Lake Worth Lucerne Grange, No. 167
West Palm Beach, Florida

SCRAMBLED HAM
(Recipe 90 to 100 years old)

2 c. minced ham
6 hard-boiled eggs, chopped
1/2 c. grated cheese
2 tbsp. butter
1 c. milk
Salt and pepper to taste
1/4 c. bread crumbs

Mix ham and eggs in bowl. Place half the ham mixture in baking dish; sprinkle half the grated cheese over ham mixture. Repeat layers; dot with butter. Add milk; sprinkle with bread crumbs. Bake in preheated 325-degree oven until heated through. Yield: 6 servings.

Mrs. Walter Cook
Harbor Springs Grange, No. 730
Harbor Springs, Michigan

ROAST PORK TENDERLOIN

1 lg. pork tenderloin
Bread crumbs
Salt
Minced onion
Milk

Cut tenderloin through center lengthwise, not cutting all the way through. Mix desired amounts of crumbs, salt, onion and milk for stuffing; place in center of tenderloin. Tie tenderloin into shape; cook in small amount of fat until well browned. Bake in preheated 350-degree oven, allowing 30 minutes per pound.

Mrs. Harold Saultz, State Sec.
Madison Grange
Lancaster, Ohio

SOUTHERN MARYLAND-STUFFED HAM
(Recipe 200 years old)

3 lb. watercress
2 lb. green cabbage
3 lb. kale
1 bunch celery
4 onions
6 tbsp. salt
2 tsp. red pepper
2 tsp. Tabasco sauce
2 tbsp. pepper
2 tbsp. celery seed
1 12-lb. boned corned or country ham

Wash first 5 ingredients thoroughly. Chop greens, celery and onions fine; place in large pan. Scald with boiling water; let ingredients remain submerged for about 5 minutes. Remove all ingredients; drain and reserve water. Cool mixture. Add seasonings; mix well. Stuff ham with greens mixture, filling boned area. Make gashes in top of the ham; fill. Place remaining stuffing on top and sides of ham; wrap ham tightly in muslin, discarded man's undershirt, or pillow case. Place ham in reserved water in large roasting pan; cover. Cook until ham is done, allowing 25 to 30 minutes per pound cooking time. Arrange greens mixture on large serving platter in mound; place slices of ham around greens mixture. Garnish with deviled eggs. Ham and greens may be served cold.

Danny Fluhart
Brandywine Grange, No. 348
East Waldorf, Maryland

JIFFY YAM AND SAUSAGE SKILLET

1 8-oz. package brown and serve sausage
  links
1 3-oz. package orange gelatin
1/2 c. water
1 c. (packed) brown sugar
2 tbsp. butter
1 tsp. minced onion
1/4 tsp. salt
1 tsp. grated lemon peel
Juice of 1 lemon
Dash of pepper
1 1/4 lb. cooked yams
1 1-lb. 4-oz. can sliced pineapple,
  drained

Brown sausage in large skillet according to package directions; remove sausage. Combine gelatin, water, sugar, butter, onion, salt, grated peel, lemon juice and pepper in same skillet; bring to a boil, stirring constantly. Add yams and pineapple; reduce heat. Simmer for 15 minutes, basting frequently. Add sausage; simmer, basting frequently, for 5 minutes longer. Garnish with parsley. Yield: 6 servings.

Mrs. Ann Guerrieri
Rubidoux Grange, No. 611
Riverside, California

★ ★

MOCK TURKEY
(Recipe 150 years old)

    1 loaf day-old bread, soaked in warm milk
    1 carrot, grated
    2 med. onions, finely chopped
    2 stalks celery, finely chopped
    1 lb. bulk pork sausage
    1 egg, beaten
    Salt and pepper to taste
    Poultry seasoning to taste

Place all ingredients in bowl; mix well. Place in buttered baking dish. Bake in preheated 350-degree oven for 1 hour or until done. May substitute 1/2 pound hamburger for 1/2 pound of the sausage. Yield: 6 servings.

Ethel Alford
Davis Lake Grange, No. 501
Newport, Washington

TOAD-IN-THE-HOLE
(Recipe 100 years old)

    8 pork sausages
    1 c. all-purpose flour
    1/4 tsp. salt
    1/4 tsp. pepper
    2 eggs
    1/2 c. milk

Melt small amount of fat in an ovenproof dish in preheated 400-degree oven. Add sausages; prick each sausage several times over top. Bake for 10 minutes or until lightly browned, turning once. Sift flour, salt and pepper into bowl. Make well in center; add eggs. Beat until smooth, adding enough milk to make thick batter. Pour over sausages; bake for 35 to 40 minutes or until brown. Serve at once. Yield: 4 servings.

Joan M. Ashworth
Westboro Grange, No. 716
Westboro, Massachusetts

FRESH CORN-SAUSAGE CUSTARD

    1/2 lb. bulk sausage
    8 ears of corn
    4 eggs
    1/2 tsp. salt
    1/8 tsp. pepper
    1 tsp. sugar

Break up sausage in skillet; cook until brown. Drain well on paper towels. Cut enough corn from cob to make 2 cups corn and liquid by running knife down center of each row of corn, then scrape corn and liquid from cob. Beat eggs in medium bowl, then add sausage, corn, salt, pepper and sugar. Mix well. Turn into individual custard cups or 1 1/2-quart baking dish. Place in pan of hot water. Bake in preheated 350-degree oven for 35 to 45 minutes for cups or 1 hour for baking dish or until tip of knife inserted in center comes out clean. Serve hot. Yield: 8 servings.

Photograph for this recipe on page 101.

ISLAND-STYLE SPARERIBS

    3 lb. spareribs
    Salt
    3 tbsp. brown sugar
    2 tbsp. cornstarch
    1/4 c. vinegar
    1/2 c. catsup
    1 sm. can crushed pineapple
    1 tbsp. soy sauce

Trim off all fat from spareribs; cut spareribs into serving pieces. Sprinkle each piece with salt. Combine sugar, cornstarch and 1/2 teaspoon salt in saucepan; stir in vinegar, catsup, pineapple and soy sauce. Cook for about 5 minutes or until slightly thickened, stirring constantly. Arrange half the spareribs in roasting pan; cover with half the sauce. Repeat with remaining spareribs and sauce. Cover pan tightly. Bake in preheated 350-degree oven for 1 hour and 30 minutes to 2 hours or until done. Yield: 5 servings.

Mrs. Alma Irey
Rogue River Valley Grange, No. 469
Grants Pass, Oregon

SWEET AND SOUR SPARERIBS

    2 lb. spareribs
    Salt to taste
    2 tbsp. soy sauce
    2 tbsp. Worcestershire sauce
    1/3 c. molasses
    1/2 c. (packed) brown sugar
    1/3 c. vinegar
    2 tsp. cornstarch

Cut through meat between each rib of spareribs; season spareribs with salt. Cook spareribs in small amount of fat in large frying pan until brown; drain off excess fat. Add soy sauce, Worcestershire sauce, molasses, 1/2 cup water, brown sugar and vinegar; simmer for 2 hours, adding more water, if needed. Mix cornstarch with 1/2 cup water until smooth; stir into sparerib mixture. Cook for 5 minutes longer. Yield: 4 servings.

Mattie M. Valline
Quincy Grange, No. 990
Quincy, Washington

FRANKFURTERS AND CABBAGE CASSEROLE
(Recipe 50 years old)

    3 tbsp. butter
    8 frankfurters
    2 c. shredded cabbage
    1 med. onion, sliced
    2 tsp. flour
    1/2 tsp. salt
    1/2 tsp. pepper
    2 c. stewed tomatoes
    2 tbsp. catsup

★ ★

Grease 1-quart baking dish with the butter. Cut frankfurters in halves lengthwise; arrange, cut side down, in baking dish. Cover with cabbage. Saute onion in small amount of fat for 3 minutes; blend in flour, salt and pepper. Add tomatoes; break up tomatoes with spoon. Simmer for 3 minutes, stirring constantly. Stir in catsup; pour over cabbage. Bake in preheated 350-degree oven for 25 minutes.

M. Miner
Ledyard Grange, No. 167
Gales Ferry, Connecticut

MACARONI-FRANKS CASSEROLE
(Recipe 35 years old)

1   8-oz. package elbow macaroni
3 tbsp. butter
3 tbsp. flour
2 tsp. salt
1 c. milk
2 eggs, well beaten
2 c. grated Cheddar cheese
1 tsp. dry mustard
10 frankfurters
Cheese strips

Cook macaroni according to package directions. Melt butter in saucepan. Add flour and salt; blend thoroughly. Add milk, stirring constantly; stir in eggs quickly. Cook, stirring, until thick; remove from heat. Add grated cheese and mustard; stir until cheese is melted. Add macaroni; mix well. Place half the macaroni mixture in greased baking dish; place 6 frankfurters on macaroni mixture. Add remaining macaroni mixture; top with remaining 4 frankfurters. Place strips of cheese on exposed frankfurters. Bake in preheated 375-degree oven for 30 minutes. Two teaspoons prepared mustard may be substituted for dry mustard. Yield: 6 servings.

Pamela Covington
West Suffield Grange, No. 199
Suffield, Connecticut

GROUND MEAT PASTIES

3 c. flour
1 tsp. salt
Butter
2   8-oz. cans mushrooms
1 tbsp. chopped onion
1 tbsp. minced celery
2 tbsp. catsup
1 lb. ground meat
1/2 c. milk
2 tsp. cornstarch

Place flour and 1/2 teaspoon salt in large bowl. Add 1 1/2 cups butter; cut into flour with pastry blender. Stir in just enough ice water to moisten ingredients; form into ball. Refrigerate for several hours or overnight. Drain mushrooms; reserve liquid and 1/4 of the mushrooms. Melt 2 tablespoons butter in saucepan. Add remaining mushrooms, onion and celery; cook, stirring, until onion is tender. Remove from heat; stir in catsup and ground meat. Divide pastry in half; roll out each half on floured surface into rectangle. Place half the meat mixture down center of each rectangle to within 1 inch of end. Fold pastry over meat mixture; seal edges. Fold ends over; seal. Place, seam side down, on cookie sheet. Bake in preheated 375-degree oven for 1 hour and 15 minutes. Pour reserved mushrooms and liquid into saucepan; stir in milk. Bring to a boil. Mix cornstarch with 1/4 cup water; stir into milk mixture. Cook, stirring, until thickened. Slice pasties; serve with sauce. Yield: 6 servings.

Mrs. Kenneth Lindsey
Madison Grange, No. 819
Madison, Ohio

POLISH SAUSAGE STEWED IN RED CABBAGE

1 head red cabbage, thinly sliced
Juice of 2 lemons
1 tbsp. butter
1 tbsp. flour
1/2 c. red wine
Salt and pepper to taste
1/2 tsp. Worcestershire sauce
Sugar to taste
1/2 lb. Polish sausage, diced

Scald cabbage with hot water; drain. Sprinkle with small amount of the lemon juice. Melt butter in saucepan; stir in flour, then stir in wine. Add cabbage, salt, pepper, Worcestershire sauce, sugar and remaining lemon juice. Cook over low heat for 15 minutes, stirring frequently; remove from heat. Add Polish sausage; cover. Cook for several minutes longer. Place cabbage mixture in serving dish; place sausage on top.

Mrs. Margaret Colson
Jefferson Grange, No. 2019
Sharpsville, Pennsylvania

VEAL WITH OYSTERS

2 lb. veal, cut in thin strips
Salt and pepper to taste
Flour
Lard
1 1/2 pt. small oysters
1 c. cream

Season veal with salt and pepper; dredge with flour. Fry in enough hot lard to prevent sticking until nearly done. Add oysters; cook until done. Add cream. Mix small amount of flour with water; stir into veal mixture. Cook, stirring, until thickened. Yield: 6 servings. This recipe came from Buckeye Cookery, published in 1891.

Mary Braynard
Chetco Grange, No. 765
Brookings, Oregon

Poultry

Chicken is one of the few foods which is less expensive today than it was years ago. In fact, that which is now everyday fare for us, was once considered to be strictly a company meal or a Sunday treat. Even on those occasions, the chicken was almost sure to be only a hen which had outlived her usefulness as an egg producer. Some of the most popular chicken recipes, such as chicken pie and chicken soup, were developed as ways to cook one of those older, tough hens, and when made with our more tender, plump chickens of today, these recipes are even tastier. In our great-grandmother's time, fried chicken was even more special because a young chicken was required for this dish — the family knew that she was planning a special dinner when great-grandmother killed a fryer.

The turkey can certainly be called the most American of birds; the Pilgrims feasted on them when they celebrated that first important Thanksgiving Day. The woods were full of these robust birds, which had helped to keep the Pilgrims fed during that difficult first year in New England. Turkey is still traditionally eaten on Thanksgiving Day to help us remember all that we have to be thankful for in this land of plenty. Soon, the settlers learned to make turkey even more delicious and filling with the addition of stuffings and gravies, and over the centuries, endless numbers of ingredients have made turkey dressing one of the most delicious and unique of American foods.

The smaller stout-bodied game birds such as partridges, squab and pigeons were also an early American favorite. A delicious roast duck is elegant and impressive on any occasion. Game birds, unless you have to purchase them, can always be depended upon to make pleasing and thrifty "family-type" dinners, whether served smothered in a warm gravy, baked in the oven, smoked or spitted on the grill.

★ ★

CHICKEN AND DRESSING SUPPER PIE

1 lg. hen
6 eggs, well beaten
1 c. flour
Milk
1 recipe bread dressing
Buttered bread crumbs

Cook chicken in salted water until tender. Lift out chicken to cool slightly; set broth aside to cool. Remove skin and bones from chicken; reserve skin. Dice chicken; grind reserved skin through food chopper. Mix chicken and skin together. Remove fat from cooled broth. Combine eggs and flour; mix until smooth. Add 1 cup chicken fat and enough milk to measure 8 cups mixture. Pour in double boiler; cook until sauce is thick, stirring frequently. Let cool. Prepare bread dressing, using chicken broth, giblets, sage and seasoning. Spread dressing in buttered large baking dish. Add layer of sauce; add diced chicken. Cover with remaining sauce; top with buttered crumbs. Bake in preheated 375-degree oven until dressing is done and top is browned.

Mrs. John Madison
Lower Naches Grange, No. 296
Yakima, Washington

CHICKEN AND DUMPLINGS
(Recipe 75 to 100 years old)

1 chicken
2 c. sifted flour
1/2 tsp. salt
1 tbsp. baking powder
1 tbsp. shortening
1 egg, well beaten
1 1/2 c. milk

Simmer chicken in large kettle filled with salted water until tender. Set aside. Sift flour, salt and baking powder together. Cut in shortening; mix in egg and milk. Add more flour if dough is too sticky. Roll out on floured board; cut into strips as desired for dumplings. Bring broth with chicken to a boil; drop dumplings into broth. Cook until done. Dumplings may be dropped into broth from a spoon, if desired.

Mrs. Lelah L. Matlock
Beecher Grange, No. 726
Pembine, Wisconsin

CHICKEN FRICASSEE
(Recipe over 50 years old)

4 to 5 lb. chicken
Salt and pepper to taste
Butter or pork fat
6 cloves
Sm. piece of bay leaf (opt.)
Parsley to taste
4 tbsp. flour
1 c. light cream
2 egg yolks

Cut chicken into serving pieces; season with salt and pepper. Saute in butter until golden brown. Cover with boiling water; add cloves, bay leaf and parsley. Simmer until tender. Remove chicken; reserve 2 1/2 broth. Melt 4 tablespoons butter in saucepan. Add flour; stir to make smooth paste. Stir in reserved broth; cook for 10 minutes, stirring constantly. Mix cream and egg yolks together; pour slowly into sauce, stirring constantly. Arrange chicken pieces on platter; pour sauce around pieces to serve. Brown butter, then stir in 5 tablespoons flour and brown well, if a brown sauce is preferred.

Robert G. Proctor, Natl. Sec.
National Grange
Washington, D.C.

CHICKEN MEDLEY

2 whole chicken breasts, split, skinned
and boned
1 tsp. salt
1/8 tsp. pepper
2 tbsp. butter
1   4 1/2-oz. jar mushrooms with liquid
1 1/4 c. thick cheese sauce
1 pkg. frozen broccoli spears
1/4 c. dry white wine

Season chicken breasts with salt and pepper; brown in butter, turning once. Combine mushrooms and cheese sauce; pour over chicken. Bake, covered, in preheated 300-degree oven for 45 minutes or until tender. Rinse broccoli under running water to remove ice crystals; separate spears carefully with fork. Split any large spears for even cooking; drain. Pour wine over chicken; top with broccoli spears. Cover; bake for 15 minutes longer or until broccoli is tender.

Alice Fetter
Progressive Grange
Marion, Ohio

CHICKEN-MUSHROOM CASSEROLE

1 tender roasting chicken
1/2 c. Crisco
Salt and pepper to taste
1 c. hot sweet cream
2 c. chopped mushrooms
1 tbsp. chopped parsley

Clean chicken; split down back. Place, breast side up, in casserole. Spread Crisco over breast; season with salt and pepper. Add a small amount of hot water; cover. Bake in preheated 400-degree oven for 1 hour. Pour cream over chicken; sprinkle with mushrooms and parsley. Cover; bake for 20 minutes longer or until chicken is tender. Serve hot in casserole. Oysters may be substituted for mushrooms, if desired.

Sarah Wautier
Manteca Dist. Grange, No. 507
Stockton, California

★ ★

CHICKEN POLENTA

1 fryer or rabbit
Flour
Oil
3 cans tomato paste
1   15-oz. can tomato puree
1 med. onion, chopped
3 cloves of garlic, minced
1 c. chopped celery
Salt and pepper to taste
Italian seasoning to taste
2 c. polenta or coarse cornmeal

Cut chicken into 1-inch pieces. Dredge with flour; brown in oil in large frypan. Add tomato paste, 3 tomato paste cans water and tomato puree; stir well. Add onion, garlic, celery, salt, pepper and Italian seasoning. Simmer for 2 hours, stirring frequently to prevent sticking. Bring 2 quarts salted water to a boil; add polenta meal slowly, stirring constantly. Cook until thickened. Spread polenta in large casserole; pour chicken mixture over all. Bake in preheated 350-degree oven for 30 to 45 minutes.

Elizabeth Cooper
Humboldt Grange, No. 501
Eureka, California

CHICKEN A LA REINE

4 c. chopped cooked broccoli, drained
4 c. chicken broth
2 tbsp. lemon juice
1 c. chopped mushrooms
2 c. cooked chicken
1 c. mayonnaise
1 pkg. bread dressing mixture with
    seasoning

Place broccoli in greased baking pan. Combine chicken broth, lemon juice, mushrooms, chicken and mayonnaise; pour over broccoli. Sprinkle bread dressing over chicken mixture; sprinkle seasoning over top of bread dressing. Bake in 350-degree oven for 30 to 45 minutes.

Ora R. Saalman
Sierra, Nevada Grange, No. 454
Weimar, California

CHICKEN ROLL-UPS

3 whole fryer chicken breasts, halved
1/4 c. chopped cooked shrimp
3/4 c. butter, softened
1/4 c. chopped green onions
1/2 tsp. salt
1/4 tsp. pepper
1/4 tsp. MSG
1 c. flour
1 1/4 tsp. baking powder
3/4 c. water
1 qt. cooking oil

Remove skin and bones from chicken breasts; pound to 1/4-inch thickness. Combine shrimp, butter, onions, 1/4 teaspoon salt, pepper and MSG in bowl; mix well. Divide into 6 portions. Spoon 1 portion into center of each chicken breast; spread to within 1/2 inch of edge. Roll up each breast as for jelly roll, starting at narrow end. Secure with toothpicks. Cover; refrigerate for at least 15 minutes. Combine flour, remaining 1/4 teaspoon salt and baking powder in bowl; stir in water to make a smooth batter. Dip roll-ups in batter. Fry, 2 rolls at a time, in cooking oil at 375 degrees for 10 minutes or until golden brown. Drain on paper toweling. Serve warm.

Mrs. Roger Koch
Powder River Grange, No. 68
Kaycee, Wyoming

CHICKEN ROLY-POLY
(Recipe is 100 years old)

1 tsp. soda
1 c. milk
4 c. flour
2 tsp. cream of tartar
1 tsp. salt
Cooked chicken, minced
Salt and pepper to taste

Dissolve soda in milk; combine flour, cream of tartar and salt. Stir milk into flour mixture to make a smooth dough. Roll out on floured board 1/2 inch thick. Remove any gristle from chicken; season with salt and pepper. Spread over dough; roll up as for jelly roll. Place on buttered plate; place plate in steamer. Steam chicken roll for 30 minutes. Slice and serve with gravy, if desired.

Brenda Cookson
Sebasticook Grange, No. 306
Veazie, Maine

CHICKEN STEW
(Recipe about 100 years old)

1   5-lb. chicken
1/4 c. fat or salad oil
1/2 c. flour
3/4 c. catsup
4 c. boiling water
3 tbsp. lemon juice
1 tsp. salt
1 tsp. Worcestershire sauce
1/2 tsp. pepper

Wash, dry and disjoint chicken. Heat fat in kettle; blend in flour. Stir in catsup, boiling water, lemon juice, salt, Worcestershire sauce and pepper. Add chicken; cover. Simmer for 3 hours or until chicken is tender. Serve with cornmeal mush or rice.

Mrs. W.C. Harris, State Master's Wife
Elmira Grange, No. 523
Portland, Oregon

★ ★

CHICKEN SOUFFLE

1 3-lb. chicken, cooked
6 slices bread, cut in 1-in. cubes
1/4 c. chopped green pepper
1 sm. onion, chopped
1/2 c. chopped celery
1/2 c. mayonnaise
Salt and pepper to taste
3 eggs
1 1/2 c. milk or chicken broth
2 slices buttered bread, cut in 1/2-in.
  cubes
1 1/4 c. thick white sauce with chopped
  mushrooms
Grated cheese (opt.)

Remove skin and bones from chicken; cut up as desired for salad. Arrange half the plain bread cubes in 2-quart rectangular Pyrex baking dish. Combine chicken, green pepper, onion, celery, mayonnaise, salt and pepper; mix well. Spread over bread cubes. Top with remaining plain bread cubes. Combine eggs and milk, mixing well; pour over bread cubes and chicken. Cover; let stand overnight in refrigerator. Sprinkle buttered bread cubes over top of casserole; spread sauce carefully over bread cubes. Bake in preheated 350-degree oven for 50 minutes. Sprinkle grated cheese over top; bake for 10 minutes longer or until done.

Mrs. Lloyd D. Wyant
Castile Grange, No. 1017
Castile, New York

CHICKEN STRATA

1/2 c. diced onion
1/2 c. diced celery
1/2 c. diced green pepper
2 to 3 c. diced chicken
1/2 c. mayonnaise
1 1/2 tsp. salt
1/2 tsp. pepper
8 slices bread, cubed
2 eggs, well beaten
1 1/2 to 2 c. chicken broth
1 1/4 c. thick white sauce with chopped
  mushrooms

Combine onion, celery, green pepper, chicken, mayonnaise, salt and pepper; toss carefully. Arrange bread cubes in baking dish; spread chicken mixture over top. Mix eggs and broth together; pour evenly over chicken. Chill overnight. Spread white sauce over chicken mixture. Bake in 350-degree oven for 1 hour or until heated through and bubbly. Freezes well. Yield: 6 servings.

Leone Thies
Trentwood Grange, No. 1056
Spokane, Washington

CHICKEN SPAGHETTI

1 4 to 5-lb. stewing chicken, disjointed
1/4 c. chicken fat or shortening

1 green pepper, chopped
1 onion, minced
1 veal knuckle, cracked (opt.)
1 1/2 tsp. salt
1 qt. boiling water
Dash of paprika
1/3 c. diced pimento
¶ lb. spaghetti
2/3 c. chopped pitted ripe or green olives
1/2 lb. grated American cheese

Brown chicken in hot fat. Add green pepper and onion; saute until golden brown. Place chicken mixture and veal knuckle in kettle. Add salt and boiling water; simmer for about 3 hours or until chicken is fork tender. Do not boil. Cool; remove chicken. Measure broth; add water to measure 2 cups liquid, if needed. Remove bones from chicken. Return chicken and 2 cups broth to kettle; add paprika and pimento. Cook spaghetti according to package directions; drain well. Add spaghetti, olives and half the cheese to chicken mixture; toss well. Cook over low heat for about 5 minutes or until cheese is melted. Top with remaining cheese; serve immediately. Freezes well. Chicken and veal can be cooked overnight in crock pot, if desired. Yield: 8-10 servings.

Mrs. Peter Meike
Powder River Grange, No. 68
Kaycee, Wyoming

GIBLET FILLING

1 lb. chicken gizzards
3 chicken livers
6 to 8 chicken hearts
1 c. chopped celery
3/4 c. chopped onions
1/2 loaf rye bread
3 eggs
1 tsp. salt
1/4 tsp. pepper
1 tsp. sage

Boil gizzards, livers and hearts until tender; let cool. Force gizzards, livers, hearts, celery and onions through food grinder. Soak rye bread in water. Squeeze out excess water; pull bread apart. Combine bread and ground mixture; add eggs and seasonings. Mix well. Spread in greased baking pan. Bake in preheated 350-degree oven for about 30 minutes or until done.

Mrs. Beatrice Waibel
Big Creek Grange, No. 1559
Lehighton, Pennsylvania

EASY CHICKEN CASSEROLE

2 1/2 c. chicken broth
2 eggs, slightly beaten
1/2 loaf bread, cubed
1 tsp. salt
1/2 c. diced celery, sauteed

★ ★ ★ ★ ★★★★★★★★★★★★★★★★★★★★★★★★★★★★★★★★★★★★★ ★ ★ ★ ★ ★

2 tbsp. minced onion (opt.)
2 c. cubed cooked chicken
Chicken gravy

Combine chicken broth, eggs and bread cubes; mix well. Add salt, celery and onion; fold in chicken. Pour into well-greased casserole. Bake in preheated 300-degree oven until done. Serve with chicken gravy.

Carrie Morse
Locke Grange
Moravia, New York

SAUTEED CHICKEN LIVERS AND MUSHROOMS

18 chicken livers
1/4 lb. sliced mushrooms
1 tbsp. minced green pepper
1 tbsp. minced parsley
1 tbsp. minced onion
1/4 c. butter
1 tbsp. flour
1/2 c. dry white wine
1/2 c. rich chicken broth
Pinch of thyme
Salt and pepper to taste

Saute chicken livers, mushrooms, green pepper, parsley and onion in butter over low heat for about 4 minutes, stirring frequently. Sprinkle flour over top; cook and stir until lightly browned. Add wine and chicken broth gradually, stirring constantly. Stir in thyme, salt and pepper. Cover; simmer for 10 to 15 minutes, stirring occasionally. Serve immediately with boiled rice or on triangles of hot buttered toast.

From a Grange Friend

gradually to rapidly boiling water so that water continues to boil. Cook, uncovered, until tender, stirring occasionally. Drain in colander. Return noodles to pan; stir in cheese, chopped parsley and remaining 2 tablespoons butter. Toss until well mixed. Place in serving bowl. Spoon sauce over noodles to serve. Garnish with parsley. Yield: 6 servings.

Photograph for this recipe above.

PARSLIED NOODLES WITH CHICKEN AND HAM SAUCE

4 tbsp. butter
1/2 c. chopped onion
1 sm. garlic clove, crushed
1 1/4 c. thick cream of celery soup
1 c. 1-in. chunks cooked chicken
3/4 c. 1-in. chunks cooked ham
3/4 c. milk
2 tsp. prepared mustard
1/4 tsp. rosemary, crushed
8 oz. fine egg noodles
1 tbsp. salt
3 qt. boiling water
1/2 c. shredded Cheddar cheese
1/4 c. chopped parsley
Parsley for garnish

Melt 2 tablespoons butter in medium saucepan. Add onion and garlic; saute over medium heat for about 5 minutes or until onion is tender, stirring constantly. Stir in soup, chicken, ham, milk, mustard and rosemary; cook over low heat until heated through, stirring constantly. Keep warm. Add noodles and salt

CHICKEN AND HOMEMADE NOODLES

2 c. flour
2 eggs
2 tbsp. milk or cream
Salt
1 stewing chicken
Pepper to taste

Sift flour in bowl; make well in center. Stir eggs, milk and 1/2 teaspoon salt together with fork until partially combined. Pour in well; stir with fork to make a stiff dough. Roll out thin on floured board; let dry for 1 to 2 hours. Cook chicken in boiling, salted water until tender. Lift from broth; remove skin and bones from chicken. Return chicken to broth. Cut noodle dough into 3-inch strips; stack and slice thin, using sharp knife. Drop noodles into boiling broth; season broth to taste. Add more water, if needed. Simmer, covered, for 15 minutes or until noodles are tender, stirring occasionally.

Mrs. Doris Fry
Pavillion Grange, No. 49
Riverton, Wyoming

★ ★

NOODLE-CHICKEN CASSEROLE

Salt
8 oz. medium egg noodles
1 4-oz. jar pimentos
1 14-oz. can artichoke hearts
1 c. chopped onions
2 tbsp. butter
1 med. green pepper, chopped
1 1/4 c. thick white sauce with chopped
    mushrooms
1 c. sour cream
1/4 tsp. pepper
2 c. cubed cooked chicken
2 c. cubed cooked ham
1 c. ripe or pimento-stuffed olives,
    halved
1/2 c. buttered bread crumbs
Grated Parmesan cheese

Add 1 tablespoon salt to 3 quarts rapidly boiling water; add noodles gradually so that water continues to boil. Cook, uncovered, stirring occasionally, until tender; drain in colander. Drain pimentos; dice. Drain artichoke hearts; cut each in half. Saute onions in butter until tender. Stir in green pepper; cook for 1 minute longer. Blend mushroom sauce, sour cream, 1 1/2 teaspoons salt and pepper in large bowl. Add noodles, onion mixture, chicken, ham, olives, pimentos and artichoke hearts; mix gently. Spoon into buttered 3-quart casserole; sprinkle buttered crumbs around edge. Bake in preheated 325-degree oven for about 1 hour; serve with Parmesan cheese.

Photograph for this recipe on page 270.

SHERRIED CHICKEN AND NOODLES
(Recipe over 40 years old)

5 chicken breasts
1 sm. onion, minced
2 carrots, chopped fine
3 stalks celery, chopped fine
1 lb. wide noodles
1/4 c. butter
2 tbsp. flour
1/2 c. heavy cream
2 c. cheddar cheese
1/4 c. sherry
Salt and pepper to taste
Bread crumbs

Place chicken breasts, onion, carrots and celery in large saucepan; cook until chicken is tender. Remove chicken breasts; reserve broth. Cook noodles in reserved broth until all broth has been absorbed. Melt butter in saucepan; stir in flour to make a smooth paste. Stir in cream, cheese, sherry and seasonings; cook until smooth and thick. Remove bones and slice chicken breasts. Place layer of noodles in casserole; top with layer of sliced chicken. Repeat layers until all ingredients are used. Pour cheese sauce over chicken; sprinkle crumbs over sauce. Bake in preheated 350-degree oven for 30 minutes or until heated through

and bubbly. Turkey may be substituted for chicken, if desired.

Doris S. White, P.M.
Chequesset Grange, No. 372
Wellfleet, Massachusetts

OVEN-FRIED HERB CHICKEN

2 c. Rice Chex, crushed
1/4 c. flour
1 tsp. salt
1/2 tsp. marjoram
1/4 tsp. pepper
1 chicken, disjointed

Combine crushed Rice Chex, flour, salt, marjoram and pepper; mix well. Place in paper bag. Add chicken pieces, one at a time; shake to coat well. Place chicken, skin side down, on cookie sheet. Bake in preheated 400-degree oven for 30 minutes. Turn; bake for 30 minutes longer.

Mrs. William Bivins
Manatee Grange, No. 179
Ellenton, Florida

CHICKEN-MUSHROOM CASSEROLE

1 c. broken wide noodles
2 c. diced cooked chicken
1 c. bread crumbs
1 c. grated cheese
1/4 c. chopped green pepper
2 tbsp. chopped pimento
1 sm. can mushroom pieces (opt.)
1 tsp. salt
1/4 c. melted butter
2 eggs, slightly beaten
1 1/2 c. milk
1 1/4 c. thick white sauce with chopped
    mushrooms

Combine all ingredients except sauce; toss carefully. Place in buttered baking dish. Bake in preheated 350-degree oven for 1 hour or until heated through and bubbly. Serve with hot mushroom sauce.

Ethel Smith
Forest City Grange, No. 288

CREAMY CHICKEN PIE
(Recipe over 100 years old)

1 lg. or 2 sm. chickens
3 tbsp. melted butter
3 tbsp. flour
Salt and pepper to taste
3 c. warm chicken stock
1 c. cream
Batter

Stew chicken until tender; remove bones. Place chicken in baking dish. Combine butter, flour, salt and

★ ★

pepper; mix well. Stir in stock to make a smooth mixture; stir in cream. Pour over chicken; spread Batter over top. Bake in preheated 400-degree oven until golden brown and bubbly.

BATTER

2 c. flour
1 tsp. salt
2 tsp. baking powder
2 tbsp. melted butter
1 egg, well beaten
1 c. milk

Sift flour, salt and baking powder together. Add remaining ingredients; mix until smooth.

Olive Ridenour
Quaker Grange, No. 1926
Vandalia, Ohio

VERMONT CHICKEN PIE
(Recipe over 100 years old)

1 chicken
2 tsp. salt
3 celery stalks with tops
1 med. onion
7 tbsp. flour
Biscuits

Place chicken in kettle; cover with water. Add salt, celery stalks and onion; bring to a boil. Simmer until chicken is tender. Lift out chicken; reserve broth. Remove bones from chicken; cut into rather large pieces. Place in casserole. Strain reserved broth. Mix a small amount of cold water with flour to make a smooth paste. Stir in 3 1/4 cups strained broth; pour over chicken. Cover top with Biscuits. Bake in preheated 400-degree oven for 30 minutes or until done.

BISCUITS

1 c. flour
1 1/2 tsp. baking powder
1/4 tsp. salt
5 tbsp. shortening
4 to 5 tbsp. milk

Sift flour, baking powder and salt together. Cut in shortening; mix in milk to make a soft dough. Pat out on floured board; cut into biscuits.

Mrs. William R. Thompson
Mt. Pleasant Grange, No. 1687
Mercer, Pennsylvania

CHICKEN-ALMOND CASSEROLE
(Recipe 65 years old)

1   5-lb. stewing chicken
2 stalks celery, chopped
2 med. carrots, chopped
1 med. onion, chopped
Salt and pepper to taste
2 c. cooked rice
1/4 c. chopped mushrooms
1/4 c. chopped red sweet pepper

1 c. slivered blanched almonds
2 tbsp. butter
2 tbsp. flour
1/4 tsp. marjoram
1/4 tsp. thyme
1/2 c. dried bread crumbs

Place chicken in kettle; add 8 cups water, celery, carrots, onion, salt and pepper. Bring to a boil; simmer until chicken is tender. Lift chicken from broth; reserve broth and vegetables. Remove skin and bones from chicken; chop chicken. Combine chicken, rice, reserved vegetables, mushrooms, red sweet pepper and 3/4 cup almonds. Stir 2 cups reserved broth gradually into flour in saucepan to make a smooth mixture. Cook until thick, stirring constantly. Stir in marjoram, thyme and more salt, if needed. Combine sauce with chicken mixture; place in heavy 11 x 7-inch baking pan. Sprinkle with bread crumbs and remaining 1/4 cup almonds. Bake in 375-degree oven for 1 hour or until heated through and bubbly.

Mrs. Elmer McCully
Winona Grange, No. 1038
Endicott, Washington

CHICKEN-VEGETABLE BAKE

1 fryer, disjointed
Butter
1/2 c. chopped onion
1/2 c. chopped carrots
1/2 c. chopped celery
1/2 c. rice
2 c. fine dry bread crumbs
2 c. boiling water

Fry chicken in butter until lightly browned; place in 3-quart casserole. Saute onion, carrots and celery in pan drippings until lightly browned; spoon over chicken. Sprinkle rice and bread crumbs over vegetables; pour water over top. Bake, covered, in 325-degree oven for 1 to 2 hours or until chicken is tender.

Dorothy E. Race
Grandview Grange, No. 151
Denver, Colorado

COMPANY CHICKEN SQUARES

9 slices bread, cubed
3 c. chicken broth
4 c. cooked chicken
2 c. cooked rice
2 tsp. salt
4 eggs, well beaten

Soak bread cubes in broth in mixing bowl. Add chicken, rice and salt; mix well. Stir in eggs. Place in greased 13 x 9 x 2-inch baking dish. Bake in 325-degree oven for 1 hour or until firm. Cut in squares; serve immediately. Serve with mushroom sauce, if desired.

Mrs. Lawrence Snyder
New London Grange, No. 2401
New London, Ohio

★ ★

DELICIOUS CHICKEN CASSEROLE

1 c. cooked rice
2 c. diced cooked chicken, turkey or ham
1 c. cream of chicken soup
1 c. diced celery
3/4 c. mayonnaise
3 hard-cooked eggs, chopped
1 tbsp. lemon juice
1 tbsp. grated onion
1/2 tsp. salt
1 c. buttered corn flakes

Combine all ingredients except corn flakes; place in 2-quart casserole. Sprinkle corn flakes over top. Bake in preheated 350-degree oven for 1 hour or until heated through. Serve immediately.

Mrs. Leon Wayand, Women's Activity Chm.
Louisville Grange, No. 1310
Morris, New York

EASY CURRIED CHICKEN
(Recipe 25 years old)

1 c. chopped celery
1/2 c. chopped onion
3 tbsp. butter
2 tbsp. flour
1 tsp. curry powder
1/2 tsp. salt
Dash of pepper
1 1/2 c. chicken broth
2 c. diced cooked chicken
Hot buttered rice

Saute celery and onion in butter until tender. Blend in flour, and seasonings. Add broth; cook, stirring constantly, until thick and smooth. Add chicken; cook until heated through. Serve over rice.

Susan Zimmerli
Hubbard Grange, No. 814
Park Rapids, Minnesota

ORANGE-GLAZED CHICKEN AND RICE

1 pkg. Uncle Ben's long grain and wild
   rice mix
1 1/2 c. hot water
1 broiler chicken, disjointed
1/3 c. orange juice concentrate
1/4 c. honey

Pour rice mixture into greased casserole; pour hot water over rice. Arrange chicken pieces on top of rice, skin side up. Combine orange juice concentrate and honey; pour 1/2 of the mixture over chicken. Bake, uncovered, in preheated 350-degree oven for 1 hour, basting with remaining orange juice mixture occasionally. Add water to chicken while baking, if needed.

Mrs. Gerald Hartmann
Ohio Grove Grange, No. 1842
Sycamore, Illinois

INDIAN CHICKEN CURRY

1/2 c. minced onion
5 tbsp. butter
6 tbsp. flour
2 1/2 tsp. curry powder
1 1/4 tsp. salt
1 1/4 tsp. sugar
1 chicken bouillon cube
1 c. boiling water
2 c. milk
4 c. cut-up chicken
1 tsp. lemon juice
6 c. cooked rice
Chopped salted peanuts

Saute onion in butter in top of double boiler over direct heat until tender. Stir in flour, curry powder, salt and sugar. Dissolve bouillon cube in boiling water and milk; stir into onion mixture. Cook over boiling water, stirring, until smooth and thick. Add chicken and lemon juice; heat through. Serve over rice; sprinkle peanuts over top.

Helan A. Higgins
Minerva Grange, No. 383
Levant, Maine

PARTY CHICKEN LOAF

5 c. diced chicken
2 c. cooked rice
4 c. bread crumbs
1/3 c. minced celery
1/4 c. pimento
1 tbsp. minced onion
3 eggs, beaten
2 tsp. salt
3 tbsp. poultry seasoning
2 1/2 c. chicken broth

Mix chicken, rice, bread crumbs, celery, pimento and onion together. Add remaining ingredients; mix well. Spread in baking pan. Bake in 350-degree oven for 55 minutes or until done. Pour mushroom sauce over each serving, if desired.

Mrs. Alvin Stoll
Platte Valley Grange, No. 455
Kersey, Colorado

ITALIAN-BARBECUED CHICKEN

1 8-oz. bottle Italian dressing
2 tbsp. chopped scallions or green onions
2 tbsp. Dijon mustard
1/4 c. dry white wine
2 fryers, quartered
1/2 tsp. salt

Mix Italian dressing, scallions, mustard and wine in large bowl. Add chicken quarters; turn to coat with dressing. Cover; refrigerate for at least 2 hours. Remove chicken from marinade; reserve marinade. Sprinkle chicken with salt; place, skin side up, on grill 3 to

★ ★

6 inches from heat. Cook over low coals for 1 hour to 1 hour and 15 minutes or until tender, turning and basting occasionally with reserved marinade. Leg should twist easily out of thigh joint and chicken should be fork tender when done. Yield: 8 servings.

Photograph for this recipe on page 36.

DIFFERENT SCALLOPED CHICKEN

    9 c. broth
    1/4 c. flour
    4 c. coarsely cubed chicken
    1 loaf bread, cubed
    1 sm. onion, chopped
    Salt and pepper to taste
    1/4 tsp. soda
    2 eggs

Pour 4 cups broth in large saucepan. Mix part of the broth with flour to make a smooth paste. Stir flour mixture into broth. Add chicken; bring to a boil, stirring constantly. Set aside. Combine bread cubes, onion, salt, pepper, soda and eggs in mixing bowl. Add 5 cups hot broth; mix well. Add more broth if dressing seems dry. Spread chicken mixture in shallow baking pan; cover with dressing. Bake in preheated 350-degree oven for 40 minutes or until bubbly and dressing is lightly browned.

Mrs. Esther Simmons
Sonora Grange
Malcom, Iowa

STUFFED DRUMSTICKS

    4 chicken legs and thighs
    1 c. chopped celery
    1/2 c. chopped onion
    1/4 tsp. poultry seasoning
    1 tsp. salt
    1/4 tsp. pepper
    1 egg, slightly beaten
    Fine bread crumbs

Remove bones from chicken legs and thighs, keeping meat in one piece. Saute celery and onion in 2 tablespoons hot fat in heavy skillet; add poultry seasoning. Rub inside of chicken pieces with salt and pepper; place 1 spoonful stuffing in each piece. Roll edges of chicken over stuffing; fasten with toothpicks. Dip in egg; dredge with bread crumbs. Saute in 1/4 inch hot fat in skillet until brown. Cover; cook slowly for 25 to 30 minutes or until chicken is tender.

From a Grange Friend

TARRAGON CHICKEN

    1 c. dry white wine
    1/4 c. lemon juice
    2 tbsp. red wine vinegar
    5 tbsp. salad oil
    2 lg. garlic cloves, crushed
    1 1/2 tsp. Spice Islands tarragon,
       crushed
    1 tsp. Spice Islands Beau Monde
       Seasoning
    1 1/4 tsp. salt
    1 3-lb. fryer, disjointed
    3 c. small whole frozen onions,
       thawed
    3 med. zucchini, cut into strips
    2 tbsp. butter
    1/8 tsp. white pepper
    2 med. tomatoes, cut into wedges

Combine wine, lemon juice, vinegar, 2 tablespoons salad oil, 1 garlic clove, tarragon, Beau Monde Seasoning and 1/2 teaspoon salt in a large bowl. Add chicken; turn to coat well. Cover; chill for at least 6 hours or overnight, turning chicken occasionally. Grill chicken about 4 to 5 inches from medium coals for about 45 to 60 minutes or until chicken is tender, turning with tongs occasionally and basting frequently with marinade. Heat remaining 3 tablespoons oil on grill in large ovenproof skillet. Add onions, zucchini and remaining garlic clove; saute for about 5 to 7 minutes or until zucchini is crisp-tender, stirring constantly. Stir in butter, remaining 3/4 teaspoon salt and white pepper. Add tomato wedges; cook just until tomatoes are heated through, stirring occasionally. Arrange chicken on large serving platter; arrange vegetables around chicken. Chicken may be placed on broiler pan rack and broiled 3 to 5 inches from source of heat for 45 minutes or until tender, turning occasionally and brushing frequently with marinade. Vegetables may be cooked on top of range over medium heat.

Photograph for this recipe below.

★ ★

AUNT MARGARET'S CHICKEN LOAF
(Recipe 75 years old)

1 lg. stewing hen
Chopped onion
Chopped celery
1 sm. loaf stale bread, cubed
1/2 tsp. sage
Salt
1/2 tsp. pepper
1/2 c. melted butter
3/4 c. flour
6 eggs, beaten

Place chicken in kettle; add 1 1/2 to 2 quarts water and chopped onion and chopped celery, as desired, for flavor. Cook until tender. Lift from broth; reserve broth. Remove bones from chicken; cut in pieces. Combine bread cubes, sage, 1/4 teaspoon salt, pepper, 2 tablespoons chopped onion and 2 tablespoons chopped celery in mixing bowl. Add as much reserved broth as needed for desired moistness. Spread in oiled 10 x 15-inch baking pan; cover with chicken. Combine butter and flour in large saucepan; stir until smooth. Stir in 4 cups hot reserved chicken broth; add 1 teaspoon salt. Cook over medium heat until custard is thick and smooth, stirring constantly. Stir part of the hot custard into beaten eggs; stir egg mixture into hot custard. Mix well. Pour over chicken. Bake in preheated 350-degree oven for 45 to 50 minutes or until heated through and custard is set. Cut in wedges to serve. Slice cold chicken loaf thin to serve, if desired.

Bee Bury
Whitethorn Grange, No. 792
Whitethorn, California

SWEET AND SOUR BAKED CHICKEN
(Recipe 25 years old)

1/2 c. chopped onion
1/2 c. coarsely chopped green pepper
1/2 c. coarsely chopped carrots
1/4 c. butter
3/4 c. catsup
1 c. pineapple juice
2 tbsp. vinegar
1/4 c. (firmly packed) brown sugar
2 tsp. soy sauce
1/2 tsp. garlic salt
1/4 tsp. salt
1/4 pepper
Dash of ginger
1 c. pineapple chunks
1 3-lb. fryer, cut up

Saute onion, green pepper and carrots in butter for about 5 minutes. Stir in catsup, pineapple juice, vinegar, brown sugar, soy sauce, garlic salt, salt, pepper and ginger; bring to a boil. Add pineapple chunks. Arrange chicken, skin side up, in baking pan. Pour pineapple mixture over top; cover. Bake in preheated

375-degree oven for 45 minutes. Uncover; bake for 30 minutes longer or until chicken tests done.

Florence Goff
Whitethorn Grange, No. 792
Whitethorn, California

PARTRIDGES WITH CABBAGE

2 partridges, dressed
Salt and pepper to taste
1 lg. apple, cored, peeled and diced
3 stalks celery, diced
Butter
2 slices bacon or salt pork
1 lg. onion quartered
1 head cabbage, quartered and cored
Flour

Rinse cavities of partridges with cold water; drain well. Season partridges, inside and out, with salt and pepper. Combine apple and celery for dressing. Fill cavities with dressing; secure openings. Rub partridges with butter; place in deep roasting pan. Arrange 1 bacon slice over breast of each partridge; place onion quarters in pan. Bake in preheated 350-degree oven for 45 minutes. Place cabbage in boiling water; cook until partially tender. Drain well. Place cabbage in pan around partridges; bake for 45 minutes longer or until tender. Remove partridges and cabbage to platter. Stir enough flour into pan drippings to make a smooth paste. Add water; cook and stir until gravy is thick.

Mrs. Helen A. Robbins
Saratoga Grange, No. 1209
Schuylerville, New York

ROAST PIGEONS
(Recipe over 80 years old)

Young pigeons, dressed
Butter
Cayenne pepper

Pat pigeons dry; truss wings. Dip 1 small pat of butter for each pigeon in cayenne pepper; place inside cavities. Secure openings. Bake in preheated 400-degree oven for 30 minutes or until tender. Serve with brown gravy and garnish with watercress or parsley, if desired. Bread dressing seasoned with nutmeg, apples or 3 oysters for each pigeon may be used as stuffing, if desired.

Mrs. F.R. Olin
Windsor Grange, No. 491
Windsor, Ohio

ROAST STUFFED DUCK

1 5 to 6-lb. dressed duck with giblets
1/2 lb. mushrooms, coarsely chopped
4 green apples, cored and sliced
1 1/2 c. halved and seeded sweet grapes

★ ★

2 c. chopped unblanched hazelnuts
1 tsp. salt
2 c. apple cider

Place giblets in saucepan; cover with water. Cook for 30 minutes. Drain, reserving 1/2 cup liquid; chop giblets. Combine mushrooms, apples, grapes, hazelnuts, salt, chopped giblets and reserved liquid; mix well. Stuff neck and body cavities of duck with mushroom mixture; secure openings. Prick skin on all sides of duck; place in baking pan, breast side up. Bake in preheated 400-degree oven for 1 hour, pricking skin and basting with cider every 20 minutes. Reduce oven temperature to 350 degrees; bake for 2 hours longer, pricking skin and basting with cider and pan drippings every 20 minutes.

Evelyn M. Delamarter
Georgetown Grange, No. 1540
Earlville, New York

STUFFED BRAISED YOUNG TURKEY GONDRECOURT

1 turkey liver, chopped
6 chicken livers, chopped
2 tbsp. minced parsley
2 tbsp. minced chives
2 tbsp. minced shallots
2 tbsp. chopped fresh mushrooms
2 tbsp. (heaping) turkey fat, melted
3 c. fresh bread crumbs
1/2 c. (scant) chopped onion
1/4 c. chopped green celery leaves
3 tbsp. brandy
Salt and pepper
1   8 to 10-lb. young turkey
Olive oil
2 c. dry white wine
1 sm. clove of garlic
5 or 6 slices onion
1 c. (scant) double-strength chicken
    consomme
6 whole mushrooms
12 black olives
1 c. hot chicken consomme
1 tbsp. (scant) flour
1 tbsp. (scant) butter
1 tsp. chopped orange rind, parboiled
2 tbsp. red currant jelly

Combine chopped livers, parsley, chives, shallots, chopped mushrooms, turkey fat, bread crumbs, chopped onion, celery leaves, brandy and salt and pepper to taste. Force stuffing mixture through food chopper at least 3 times or until smooth and fine. Pat turkey dry; rub with salt and pepper. Grease turkey with olive oil; stuff cavity with dressing. Secure opening. Sear turkey on all sides over medium heat until golden brown. Place in roaster; add 1 cup wine, garlic, onion slices and salt and pepper to taste. Pour in double-strength consomme; cover tightly. Bake in preheated 350-degree oven for 1 hour. Remove cover; add mushrooms, olives and remaining 1 cup wine quickly. Cover; bake for 1 hour longer or until turkey is done. Remove turkey, mushrooms and olives to platter; keep warm. Strain liquid from roaster into saucepan; remove all fat. Cook over high heat until sauce is reduced to smallest possible quantity. Add hot consomme; bring to a boil, stirring and scraping bottom of saucepan. Mix flour and butter together until well combined. Place in boiling sauce; simmer for 5 minutes or until thickened, stirring constantly. Drain orange rind well. Stir orange rind and jelly into sauce; serve immediately.

From a Grange Friend

STUFFED TURKEY LOAF

2 eggs, beaten
2/3 c. evaporated milk
1/3 c. chicken or turkey broth
1 1/2 c. soft bread crumbs
2/3 c. finely chopped celery
1/2 c. chopped onion
2 tbsp. chopped pimento
Dash of pepper
Dash of rosemary
4 c. coarsely ground turkey
Rice Stuffing
Mushroom Sauce

Combine eggs, milk, broth, bread crumbs, celery, onion, pimento and seasonings. Add turkey; mix well. Pat half the mixture in 8 x 8 x 2-inch pan. Spread Rice Stuffing over turkey mixture. Pat in remaining turkey mixture. Bake at 350 degrees for 45 minutes or until center of loaf is firm. Cut into squares; serve with Mushroom Sauce.

RICE STUFFING

1/2 c. brown rice
1 c. chicken broth
1/2 c. chopped onion
1/3 c. chopped celery
2 tbsp. butter
1 egg, beaten
1/2 tsp. salt
1/2 tsp. sage

Cook rice in broth in covered saucepan until rice is done. Saute onion and celery in butter until tender. Combine rice, onion, celery, egg and seasonings; mix well.

MUSHROOM SAUCE

1 c. sour cream
1 1/4 c. thick white sauce with chopped
    mushrooms
1/2 tsp. paprika

Combine sour cream and white sauce in saucepan. Add paprika; heat through.

Ruth W. O'Neale
Rubidoux Grange, No. 611
Riverside, California

Seafood

When the earliest settlers arrived in our country, the waters were teeming with fish of every variety, the shores were dotted with great oyster beds, the beaches contained vast amounts of clams, and the reefs yielded lobsters as large as 25 pounds. The abundance of good fish that awaited our forefathers was reason enough for devising simple ways to prepare them. It was then that people first realized how delicious fresh fish could be when taken straight from the water and cooked over a campfire.

Even though the current supply of seafood is not quite as great as it was in earlier times, everyday more Americans are discovering how much fun fishing as a sport can be. Seafood, one of the most popular foods served in this country, is one of the few kinds of wildlife that almost everyone enjoys eating. Besides being high in nutritional value, it is a fine food for even the most weight-conscious individuals.

Salmon has always been a favorite in this country. Nothing is more pleasing than freshly caught salmon which has been broiled in lemon juice and butter. The versatility of salmon is reflected in the number of mouthwatering recipes which our Grange members have contributed. By combining a single can of salmon with other ingredients, one can feed an entire family.

Shrimp and oysters are also most desirable on the American's table. Like salmon, there are a variety of ways to serve them including salads, creamed dishes and casseroles, as well as alone. While each region of the United States has its own characteristic seafood and own method of preparation, we are no longer limited only to the type of fish available close to home.

For a thrifty, yet elegant dish, make seafood an important part of your next meal.

★★★

CLAM-CORN CASSEROLE

1 7-oz. can clams
Milk
3 eggs, beaten
1 c. bread crumbs
1/2 c. cracker crumbs
1 c. cream-style corn
1 tbsp. melted butter
Dash of cayenne

Drain and reserve liquid from clams. Add enough milk to make 1 cup liquid. Combine with beaten eggs. Add clams, crumbs, corn, butter, cayenne and milk to cover; pour into greased casserole. Bake at 375 degrees for 45 minutes or until firm.

Luella M. Bain
Tuftonboro Grange, No. 142
Tuftonboro, New Hampshire

CLAM FRITTERS

1 pt. clams, shucked
2 tbsp. flour
1 tsp. baking powder
1 tsp. sugar
Salt and pepper to taste
1/2 c. rolled cracker crumbs
2 eggs, beaten

Drain clams, reserving juice. Remove and discard stomachs, then chop the remaining clam meat. Sift the flour, baking powder, sugar and seasonings over the cracker crumbs; mix well. Combine eggs and 1/2 cup reserved clam juice; mix well. Combine clams, egg mixture and crumb mixture; mix well. Let stand together for several minutes until crumbs are soaked. Add more clam juice, if needed. Drop by large spoonfuls into hot fat in frying pan. Flatten fritters if batter is thick. Cook until golden brown on both sides.

From a Grange Friend

PISMO CLAMS ON HALF SHELLS
(Recipe at least 65 years old)

12 Pismo clams
1 med. tomato, chopped
1 sm. onion, sauteed in oil
1 tbsp. chopped parsley
1 egg, beaten
Salt and pepper to taste
1/4 tsp. thyme
Dash of Worcestershire sauce
Dash of Tabasco sauce
Dry bread crumbs

Chop the clams fine; reserve juice. Combine clams, juice, tomato, onion, parsley, egg, seasonings and sauces; add enough crumbs to make sausage consistency. Fill half shells with clam mixture; dot with butter. Bake in 375-degree oven for 25 to 30 minutes.

Neola Kreiss
Pescadero Grange, No. 793
Pescadero, California

EASY CLAM CASSEROLE

1 egg, well beaten
1 can minced clams and juice
1/4 c. butter
1 c. cracker crumbs
1 c. warm milk
1/4 tsp. salt
Dash of pepper

Combine egg, clams and juice in medium bowl; mix well. Add remaining ingredients; mix well. Turn into casserole. Bake in 350-degree oven for about 40 minutes or until set. Yield: 3-4 servings.

Hester Gilpatric
West Minot Grange, No. 42
Auburn, Maine

FAMILY CLAM CASSEROLE

2 c. milk
2 c. crumbled saltines
2 7-oz. cans minced clams
4 eggs, well beaten
1/4 c. minced onion
1/4 tsp. pepper

Pour milk over saltines and let stand for several minutes. Add clams and juice, eggs, onion and pepper. Pour into greased casserole. Bake in 350-degree oven for about 1 hour or until firm. Yield: 4-6 servings.

Mrs. Alva D. Smith
Hollis Grange
Hollis Center, Maine

SCALLOPED CLAMS

1 can minced clams
1 egg, beaten
1 c. milk
1 c. cracker crumbs
1/4 c. melted butter

Combine clams, egg, milk, crumbs and butter; mix well. Turn into greased casserole. Bake in 350-degree oven for 50 minutes.

Mrs. Helen L. Chandler, Master
Quinnatissett Grange, No. 65
North Grosvenordale, Connecticut

BAKED CRAB MEAT AND SHRIMP

1 med. onion, chopped
1 med. green pepper, chopped
1 c. chopped celery
1 6 1/2-oz. can crab meat, flaked
1 6 1/2-oz. can shrimp, cleaned
1/2 tsp. salt
1/8 tsp. pepper
1 tsp. Worcestershire sauce
1 c. mayonnaise
1 c. buttered crumbs

★ ★

Combine all ingredients, except crumbs; place in individual seashells or in greased casserole. Sprinkle with buttered crumbs. Bake in 350-degree oven for 30 minutes. Yield: 6 servings.

Georgia M. Taylor
Potomac Grange, No. 1
Arlington, Virginia

DEVILED CRAB

2 c. finely chopped crab meat
1 c. cracker crumbs
1/2 c. light cream
3 tbsp. melted butter
1 tsp. Worcestershire sauce
2 eggs, beaten
1 tbsp. minced onion
1 tbsp. minced parsley
2 tbsp. mayonnaise
1 tsp. prepared mustard
Pepper to taste
1/2 tsp. salt

Combine crab meat, 1/2 cup cracker crumbs and remaining ingredients; mix well. Fill aluminum or natural crab shells with crab meat mixture; top with remaining cracker crumbs. Dot with butter. Bake in 350-degree oven until golden brown. Yield: 4 servings.

Lola Geil, Florida State Grange Lecturer
Indian Mound Grange, No. 177
Melbourne, Florida

MARYLAND CRAB CAKES

6 slices white bread
3/4 c. olive oil
3 eggs, separated
1/4 tsp. dry mustard
1/2 tsp. salt
2 tsp. Worcestershire sauce
1 1/2 lb. crab meat
Paprika
3 tbsp. butter

Trim crusts from bread; place slices on a shallow platter. Pour oil over bread; let stand until bread is thoroughly saturated. Break bread in small pieces with fork. Combine egg yolks with mustard, salt and Worcestershire sauce. Beat lightly. Stir in bread and crab meat; fold in stiffly beaten egg whites. Shape mixture into patties. Sprinkle with paprika; saute in heated butter until golden brown on both sides. Yield: 4-5 servings.

From a Grange Friend

TASTY CRAB MEAT CASSEROLE

1 sm. can evaporated milk
4 slices thin bread

1 can claw crab meat
1/2 c. butter, softened
1 c. Miracle Whip salad dressing
1 c. chopped celery
1 sm. bell pepper, chopped
Juice of 1 lemon
1 tbsp. minced onion
2 hard-boiled eggs, grated
1 tsp. Worcestershire sauce
Several drops of Tabasco sauce
Salt and pepper to taste

Pour milk over bread; let set until absorbed. Drain crab meat, discarding any shell. Combine bread, crab meat and remaining ingredients; mix thoroughly. Turn into buttered casserole. Bake in 350-degree oven for about 25 minutes. Toasted buttered crumbs may be sprinkled over casserole after baking for 20 minutes, then return to oven. Bake for 5 minutes longer. Sprinkle with paprika if desired. Serve hot.

Mrs. Daisy S. Moody
Pee Dee Grange, No. 679
Lake View, South Carolina

BEER DIP FOR FISH OR ONION RINGS

1 c. flour
1 c. pancake flour
1/2 c. yellow cornmeal
2 eggs, beaten
1 tsp. salt
Dash of pepper
1 can beer

Combine flours, cornmeal, eggs, salt and pepper; mix well. Add beer; stir to mix well. Dip fish or onion rings in beer batter; fry in hot deep fat until done.

Mrs. Clarence Scobee
Sonora Grange
Grinnell, Iowa

BROILED BROOK TROUT

6 3/4-lb. brook trout
1 tsp. salt
1/8 tsp. pepper
6 slices bacon
Lemon slices
Sliced cucumber
Parsley

Clean the trout. Wipe with damp cloth. Remove heads if desired, but leave tails on. Season well inside and out. Place a slightly undercooked slice of bacon inside the cavity of each trout. Lay trout in a shallow baking pan; pour a small amount of the bacon drippings over each fish. Broil for 3 to 4 minutes or until brown. Turn fish with a spatula; broil for 3 to 4 minutes on remaining side. Serve with lemon and cucumber slices. Garnish with parsley. Yield: 6 servings.

From a Grange Friend

★ ★

HALIBUT IN TARRAGON BUTTER SAUCE

    3/4 c. butter
    1/4 c. finely chopped onion
    1 lg. garlic clove, crushed
    2 tbsp. lemon juice
    1 tsp. Spice Islands Beau Monde
        Seasoning
    3/4 tsp. Spice Islands tarragon,
        crushed
    1/2 tsp. salt
    1/8 tsp. white pepper
    2 lb. halibut steaks, cut into
        4 serving pieces
    Parsley
    Cherry tomatoes
    Lemon wedges

Melt butter in medium saucepan. Add onion and garlic; saute over medium heat, stirring occasionally, for
about 2 minutes or until onion is tender. Stir in lemon
juice, Beau Monde Seasoning, tarragon, salt and white
pepper. Place each halibut piece on sheet of heavy-
duty aluminum foil; spoon butter mixture evenly over
each halibut piece. Wrap foil around halibut, sealing
edges well. Place foil packets about 4 inches over
medium-hot coals; grill for 30 to 40 minutes or until
fish flakes easily when tested with a fork. Remove
halibut to serving platter; garnish with parsley, tomatoes and lemon. Stir butter sauce; serve over halibut.
Two 16-ounce packages frozen fish steaks, thawed and
drained, may be substituted for halibut; grill for about
20 minutes. Yield: 4 servings.

Photograph for this recipe above.

FRESH ASPARAGUS AND FISH BAKE

    2 lb. fresh asparagus
    1/2 c. water
    3/4 tsp. salt
    4 fresh or frozen flounder fillets
    2 tbsp. butter
    1/4 c. chopped fresh onion
    2 tbsp. flour
    1 3/4 c. milk
    1/4 c. dry white wine
    2 tsp. fresh lemon juice
    1/4 tsp. dried dillweed
    1/8 tsp. pepper
    2 tbsp. chopped fresh parsley

Wash asparagus; break off each spear as far down as it
snaps easily. Place in large skillet; add water and 1/4
teaspoon salt. Bring to a boil, reduce heat. Simmer,
covered, just until tender, 2 minutes for thin asparagus
spears, 3 minutes for medium and 5 minutes for thick.
Drain. Divide into 4 portions, about 8 spears each.
Wrap 1 fillet around each bundle of asparagus; fasten
with wooden pick. Place in large baking dish. Melt
butter in medium saucepan. Add onion; cook over
medium heat until tender. Blend in flour. Remove
from heat; stir in milk. Return to heat; cook, stirring
constantly, until mixture thickens and comes to a boil.
Stir in wine, lemon juice, remaining 1/2 teaspoon salt,
dillweed, pepper and parsley. Spoon sauce over fillets;
cover. Bake in preheated 350-degree oven for 30 minutes or until fish flakes easily when tested with fork.
Yield: 4 servings.

Photograph for this recipe on page 101.

FISH BATTER

    1/2 c. oil
    1 c. flour
    1 1/2 c. milk
    1 egg
    2 tbsp. sugar

Combine oil, flour, milk, egg and sugar; mix well. Fish
fillets may be coated with flour, then dipped in batter
and fried in deep fat.

Willetta C. Eller
Nezperce Grange, No. 295
Nezperce, Idaho

FISH LOAF
(Recipe 75 years old)

    2 lb. fish, cooked
    2 eggs, separated
    1 1/4 c. milk
    1 3/4 c. bread crumbs
    1 sm. onion, chopped
    1/2 tsp. salt
    1/4 tsp. vinegar
    1 tsp. butter

Remove bones from fish. Beat egg yolks; add milk,
bread crumbs, onion, salt, vinegar and butter. Add

★ ★

fish; mix well. Beat egg whites until stiff peaks form; fold into fish mixture. Spread in greased 8 or 9-inch square pan. Place in a pan of water. Bake in 350-degree oven for 45 minutes.

Evelyn Payson, C.W.A. Chm.
White Oak Grange, No. 182
Thomaston, Maine

HADDOCK A LA RAREBIT

    4 lb. haddock fillets
    1/2 c. flour
    2 tsp. dry mustard
    1/2 tsp. salt
    2 c. milk
    2 c. shredded cheese
    1 tbsp. butter

Place fillets in well-buttered baking dish. Sift flour, mustard and salt together; add milk gradually, blending well. Cook, stirring constantly, until thickened. Add cheese and butter; stir until well blended. Pour cheese sauce over haddock. Bake in 350-degree oven for 30 minutes. Place carefully on a warm platter and surround with broiled or stuffed tomatoes.

From a Grange Friend

DILL-FLAVORED STUFFED FISH
(Recipe over 50 years old)

    Cleaned and boned fish
    Salt
    1 c. finely crushed potato chips
    1 c. day-old bread cubes
    2 tbsp. lemon juice
    1/3 c. chopped parsley
    1/3 c. chopped onion
    1/3 c. chopped dill pickles
    1/4 c. melted butter
    Capers (opt.)

Rub inside and outside of cleaned fish with salt. Combine potato chips, bread cubes, 1/4 teaspoon salt, lemon juice, parsley, onion, dill pickles and butter; mix well. Stuff fish with bread mixture. Close opening with toothpicks laced with cord. Cut 3 or 4 slashes in sides of fish to prevent skin from curling. Place in shallow baking pan. Bake in 550-degree oven for 15 minutes. Reduce oven temperature to 425 degrees; bake for 30 minutes longer. Serve hot; garnish with watercress or parsley garnish. Fish in this recipe may be haddock or rock fish. Yield: 4-6 servings.

Mrs. Robert G. Proctor
Natl. Secretary's Wife
National Grange
Washington, D.C.

ELEGANT BAKED STUFFED WHITEFISH

    1   3-lb. whitefish with head and tail
    2 tbsp. chopped onion

    1/4 c. sliced mushrooms
    1/2 c. butter
    2 1/2 c. soft bread crumbs
    1/4 c. chopped seeded peeled cucumber
    3 tsp. salt
    1/4 c. flour
    2 c. chicken broth
    1/4 c. lemon juice
    1/4 c. minced parsley

Clean fish thoroughly. Saute onion and mushrooms in 3 tablespoons butter in a large skillet. Add bread crumbs and cucumber. Season with 1/2 teaspoon salt; stir until ingredients are well mixed. Spoon stuffing into cavity of fish. Close sides of fish with toothpicks or skewers; sprinkle with 2 teaspoons salt. Dot with butter. Place in greased baking pan. Bake in 400-degree oven for about 25 minutes. Melt 1/4 cup butter in a saucepan; blend in the flour. Add the chicken broth. Cook, stirring constantly, until the sauce thickens. Add lemon juice and 1/2 teaspoon salt. Stir in parsley just before serving. Transfer fish to a hot platter; pour sauce over fish. Yield: 4-6 servings.

From a Grange Friend

FISH BALLS
(Recipe over 75 years old)

    1 lb. fresh salmon
    1 lb. fresh halibut
    1 med. onion, sliced
    1 carrot, quartered
    Salt and pepper
    3 eggs
    3 slices white bread
    Milk
    1/4 tsp. nutmeg
    1 tsp. lemon juice

Remove skin and bones from fish; place in large kettle. Cover with large amount of water; add 2 slices of onion and the carrot. Season to taste with salt and pepper. Cook for 45 minutes to 1 hour, then strain and set aside. Force fish and remaining onion through food chopper 3 times. Beat eggs; add 1/2 cup water. Stir until well mixed. Add to fish mixture. Dip bread into small amount of milk; squeeze lightly. Combine fish mixture, soaked bread, 1 1/2 teaspoon salt, 1/4 teaspoon pepper, nutmeg and lemon juice; mix well. Shape into 1-inch balls; let set on cookie sheet for 1 to 2 hours. Bring reserved broth to a boil; place several fish balls in broth. Bring to simmering point; cook for 3 to 7 minutes. Repeat until all fish balls are cooked. Prepare favorite recipe of white sauce using broth for part of the liquid. Pour over fish balls. Garnish with chopped chives or parsley and cooked diced carrots. May be served hot or cold. Yield: 12 servings.

Mrs. Hal Sundberg
Mt. Wheeler Grange, No. 696
Arlington, Washington

★ ★

FISH AND MACARONI PIE
(Recipe 50 years old)

1 1/2 c. macaroni
2 tbsp. butter
2 tbsp. flour
1/2 tsp. salt
2 1/2 c. milk
1/2 c. chopped onion
2 tbsp. parsley flakes
1 lb. cooked salmon
1 c. grated yellow cheese

Cook macaroni in boiling salted water according to package directions. Melt butter in saucepan; blend in flour and salt. Add milk gradually, stirring constantly. Cook and stir until thickened. Place a layer of macaroni in buttered 1 1/2-quart casserole; spoon over a small amount of white sauce, onion, parsley and cheese. Place a layer of salmon over white sauce; add more white sauce, onion, parsley and cheese. Continue layers, ending with white sauce and cheese on top. Bake in 350-degree oven for 30 minutes. One 1-pound can salmon may be used instead of fresh salmon. Yield: 6 servings.

Pearl L. Briggs, C.W.A. Chm.
Manteca Grange, No. 507
Manteca, California

BAKED SALMON SLICES
(Recipe over 45 years old)

1 c. milk
1 tbsp. salt
Salmon slices
Fine bread crumbs
Oil or melted butter

Combine milk and salt in shallow dish; stir until salt is dissolved. Dip salmon in milk mixture; coat with bread crumbs. Place on well-oiled baking sheet. Brush with oil. Bake in preheated 600-degree oven for 10 minutes. Bake for 11 minutes if oven only reaches 550 degrees. Remove to hot platter; serve immediately. Whitefish, trout, pike, haddock and fillets may be used instead of salmon.

Bee Warden, Sec.
Van Duzen River Grange, No. 517
Carlotta, California

PINK SALMON LOAF

1 can pink salmon
1 1/2 c. grated cheese
1 egg, beaten
3 tbsp. milk
1 tbsp. melted butter
Dash of pepper
1/2 tsp. salt
Bread crumbs

Remove bones and skin from salmon; flake salmon. Add cheese, egg, milk, melted butter, seasonings and enough crumbs to hold mixture together. Mix well and form in loaf. Cover with bread crumbs; sprinkle with cooking oil or melted butter. Bake in 375-degree oven until golden brown. Yield: 6-8 servings.

Mrs. Cora G. French, Past Flora
New Hampshire State Grange
Somersworth Grange, No. 264
Somersworth, New Hampshire

EASY SALMON LOAF

1 lb. cooked salmon
2 or 3 eggs, beaten
1/4 tsp. pepper
Dash of marjoram (opt.)
1 c. crushed soda crackers
1/2 c. cream or milk
1 tsp. salt

Remove bones and skin from salmon; flake with fork. Combine salmon, eggs, pepper, marjoram, crackers, cream and salt; mix well. Place in small loaf pan. Bake in 350-degree oven for 45 minutes. Yield: 6 servings.

Joan Lathrop
South Fork Grange, No. 605
Wallowa, Oregon

SALMON AND SPAGHETTI CASSEROLE
(Recipe over 40 years old)

1/2 pkg. spaghetti
2 c. chopped tomatoes
1 tsp. minced onion
1 tsp. salt
1 tsp. sugar
1/4 tsp. pepper
1 tbsp. flour
2 tbsp. butter
1 can salmon
1/2 c. buttered bread crumbs

Cook spaghetti in boiling salted water until tender. Drain and rinse with boiling water. Combine tomatoes, onion, salt, sugar, pepper, flour and butter in saucepan; simmer for 10 minutes. Arrange spaghetti, tomatoes and salmon in layers, ending with tomatoes. Sprinkle top with bread crumbs. Bake in 400-degree oven for 30 minutes.

Dorothy Graves
Bloomington Grange, No. 2057
Muscatine, Iowa

SALMON WITH PEAS
(Recipe 75 years old)

1 med. can red salmon
3 eggs
2 tbsp. (heaping) cracker crumbs
1 slice onion, chopped fine
Salt and pepper to taste
1 med. can small peas, drained

★ ★

2/3 c. milk
1 pat butter

Combine salmon and 1 slightly beaten egg; add cracker crumbs, onion, salt and pepper. Shape into a round loaf in center of casserole. Pour peas around salmon. Combine 2 remaining eggs, milk, salt and pepper; beat well. Pour over peas. Place butter on top of salmon. Bake in 300-degree oven for about 25 minutes or until set. Serve with a slice of lemon and parsley.

Mary E. Roe
Goldendale Grange, No. 49
Goldendale, Washington

TUNA PIE WITH CHEESE ROLL CRUST
(Recipe 25 years old)

3 tbsp. butter
1/2 c. sliced green peppers
2 slices onion
6 tbsp. flour
1/2 tsp. salt
3 c. milk
1 lg. can tuna, grated
1 tbsp. lemon juice

Melt butter in saucepan. Add green peppers and onion; cook until soft. Add flour and stir until well blended. Add salt; add milk slowly, stirring constantly until thick and smooth. Bring to a boil; cook for 2 minutes. Add remaining ingredients. Pour into large baking dish; cover with Cheese Rolls.

CHEESE ROLLS

1 1/2 c. flour
3 tsp. baking powder
1/2 tsp. salt
Dash of cayenne pepper
3 tbsp. shortening
1/2 c. milk
3/4 c. grated cheese
2 pimentos, chopped

Sift flour, baking powder, salt and cayenne pepper together in large bowl. Add shortening; mix thoroughly with fork. Add milk to make soft dough. Turn out on floured board; toss lightly until outside looks smooth. Roll out on 8 x 12-inch sheet. Sprinkle with cheese and pimentos. Roll up like jelly roll, starting at short side. Cut into 8 slices with sharp knife; flatten slightly. Place on top of creamed mixture in baking dish. Bake in 450-degree oven for about 30 minutes or until browned. Yield: 8 servings.

Mrs. James Donoghue
Garrison Hill Grange
Wiscasset, Maine

TUNA POTPIE
(Recipe about 45 years old)

1 c. chopped celery
1 1/2 c. diced carrots

1 1/2 c. diced potatoes
3 tbsp. chopped onion
1 No. 2 can peas
Milk
1/4 c. butter or margarine
1/4 c. flour
1 7-oz. can chunk white tuna
1/2 tsp. salt
1 recipe pie pastry

Cook celery, carrots, potatoes and onion in water to cover until just tender. Drain off liquid into a 2-cup measure. Add liquid from peas and enough milk to make 2 cups liquid. Melt butter; blend in flour. Add liquid slowly, stirring constantly, until thickened. Add 1 cup peas to vegetable mixture. Add tuna and salt. Mix gently; turn into a greased casserole. Cover with pie crust. Bake in 350-degree oven until crust is brown. Do not substitute fresh or frozen peas for canned peas; flavor will not be the same. Biscuit dough may be used for topping.

Myrna Thomas
French Camp-Lathrop Grange, No. 510
French Camp, California

TUNA CHOW MEIN

1 c. chopped onion
1 c. chopped celery
1 1/2 c. hot water
1/2 tsp. salt
Dash of pepper
1 can tuna, drained
1 can chow mein vegetables
1 can mushrooms
1/2 diced green pepper
1/2 jar pimento
1 jar water chestnuts
Soy sauce to taste

Cook onion in hot fat for 2 minutes or until golden. Add celery, water, salt and pepper. Cover and cook for 5 minutes. Add tuna, vegetables, mushrooms, green pepper, pimento and water chestnuts. Cover and cook for 5 minutes or longer. Add soy sauce. Serve on rice or noodles. Sprinkle with cashew nuts at serving time. Yield: 6 servings.

Mrs. Edwin Widell
Oak Leaf Grange, No. 569
Harris, Minnesota

BAKED TUNA AND DRESSING

1 can tuna
Partially cooked onions
Favorite dressing

Place tuna in the center of a greased baking dish; surround with onions. Fill in remaining space and over top with dressing. Bake in 350-degree oven until top is golden brown. Yield: 4-6 servings.

Frances Perkins, Chaplain
Fairview Grange, No. 273
Tillamook, Oregon

★ ★

green peppers under broiler until cheese is melted. Combine reserved cheese sauce and about 2 tablespoons milk; cook over low heat, stirring constantly, until hot. Place green peppers on serving platter; serve with cheese sauce. Yield: 6 servings.

Photograph for this recipe opposite.

FROGS' LEGS SAUTE

3 lb. frogs' legs
Flour (opt.)
1/4 c. butter
1 tsp. salt
1/4 tsp. pepper
Juice of 1/2 lemon
2 tbsp. minced parsley

Wash frogs' legs and pat dry. Dust with flour, if desired. Saute in butter until brown; turn and cook other side. Sprinkle with salt, pepper and lemon juice. Arrange on hot platter; pour the butter over frogs' legs. Sprinkle with parsley. Plan for 8 pairs of small frogs' legs or 3 pairs of large frogs' legs per person.

From a Grange Friend

MACARONI AND CHEESE GREEN PEPPERS

6 lg. green peppers
Salt
3 qt. rapidly boiling water
2 c. elbow macaroni
1/4 c. butter
1/4 c. all-purpose flour
Dash of cayenne pepper
Milk
2 1/2 c. shredded Cheddar cheese
1 6 1/2 or 7-oz. can tuna, drained
Cherry tomato halves

Slice off stem ends of green peppers; remove seeds and membranes. Add green peppers and 1 tablespoon salt to boiling water; cook for 5 minutes. Remove green peppers with slotted spoon; drain on paper towels. Reserve water. Add macaroni to reserved rapidly boiling water gradually so that water continues to boil. Cook, uncovered, stirring occasionally, until tender; drain in colander. Melt butter in large saucepan; stir in flour, 3/4 teaspoon salt and cayenne pepper until smooth. Cook over medium heat, stirring constantly, until mixture is bubbly. Reduce heat to low; stir in 2 cups milk gradually. Cook, stirring constantly, until mixture thickens and begins to boil; remove from heat. Add 2 cups cheese; stir until cheese is melted. Reserve 1 cup cheese sauce; cover and set aside. Stir tuna into remaining cheese sauce; stir in macaroni. Spoon macaroni mixture into green peppers; place in ungreased shallow baking pan. Cover with foil. Bake in preheated 375-degree oven for 30 minutes or until heated through. Remove pan from oven; discard foil. Garnish each stuffed pepper with a cherry tomato half. Sprinkle remaining 1/2 cup cheese over top of each green pepper. Increase temperature to broil; place

LOBSTER SHORTCAKE
(Recipe over 75 years old)

1/4 c. butter
4 c. lobster meat
2 c. cream
1 tbsp. flour
1/4 c. milk
Sugar to taste
Dash of paprika
Salt and pepper to taste

Melt butter in large skillet; add lobster meat. Fry until lobster turns pink. Add cream; bring to boiling point. Stir in flour; cook until slightly thickened. Stir in milk until smooth. Add seasonings. Serve over split and buttered biscuits.

Annie L. Fickett
Dexter Grange

LOBSTER A LA GRANGE

6 tbsp. butter
6 tbsp. flour
2 c. milk
3/4 tsp. salt
Pepper to taste
1 sm. can lobster
1/4 c. chopped pimento
1/4 c. sliced olives
Paprika to taste
3 hard-boiled eggs
2 egg yolks

★ ★

1/2 c. cream
Grated cheese

Melt butter in saucepan; stir in flour until smooth. Add milk, salt and pepper; cook, stirring constantly, until thickened. Add lobster, pimento, olives, paprika and 2 sliced eggs. Combine egg yolks and cream; beat until well blended. Add egg yolk mixture to lobster mixture; blend well. Pour into greased casserole. Garnish with remaining sliced hard-boiled egg and olives. Sprinkle cheese over all. Bake at 450 degrees for about 10 minutes. Yield: 8-10 servings.

Dorothy McCray
Slocum Grange, No. 36
Narragansett, Rhode Island

LOBSTER-SHRIMP PIE

1   14-oz. can lobster
1   10 1/2-oz. can shrimp
1 1/4 c. thick white sauce with
      mushrooms
2 pkg. or 1 box unsalted crackers
1 c. butter, softened
Grated cheese

Combine lobster, shrimp and mushroom sauce; mix well. Crush crackers with rolling pin. Combine crackers and butter; line a 2-quart casserole, reserving enough for topping. Pour in lobster mixture. Top with crackers and enough cheese to cover. Bake in 375-degree oven until hot and crackers and cheese on top are golden brown. Yield: 4 servings.

Ethel H. Cornforth
Danvers Grange, No. 263
Danvers, Massachusetts

OYSTERS ROCKEFELLER
(Recipe 75 years old)

6 tbsp. butter
6 tbsp. finely chopped fresh spinach
3 tbsp. finely chopped parsley
3 tbsp. finely chopped celery
3 tbsp. finely chopped onion
5 tbsp. fine bread crumbs
Several drops of Tabasco
1/2 tsp. salt
1/2 tsp. Pernod or anisette
Rock salt
36 oysters on the half shell

Melt butter in a saucepan; stir in all ingredients except rock salt and oysters. Cook over low heat, stirring constantly, for 15 minutes. Work through a sieve or food mill and set aside. Make a layer of rock salt in individual pie tins; place oysters on top. Place 1 teaspoonful of the vegetable mixture on each oyster. Broil under a preheated 400-degree broiler for 3 to 5 minutes or until topping begins to brown. Serve immediately in the pie tins. Yield: 6 servings.

From a Grange Friend

SCALLOPED OYSTERS
(Recipe over 50 years old)

1/2 lb. soda crackers, crushed
1 pt. fresh oysters
Salt and pepper to taste
1 c. sliced celery
1/4 c. butter
Milk
1/2 c. evaporated milk

Place layer of cracker crumbs in a well-buttered deep casserole. Add layer of oysters; sprinkle with salt and pepper. Add layer of celery; dot with butter. Repeat layers until all oysters are used, ending with crackers on top. Pour milk over ingredients until almost covered; top with evaporated milk. Bake in 350-degree oven for 1 hour. Large oysters may be sliced, if desired.

Mrs H. Love, Master
Selamona Grange

SHRIMP CASSEROLE

1/4 c. butter
1/4 c. flour
2 c. milk
1 c. grated cheese
2 egg yolks, beaten
2 slices bread, cubed
1 can shrimp
1/4 c. buttered crumbs

Melt butter; blend in flour. Add milk gradually, stirring constantly. Add cheese; cook and stir until thick. Pour small amount of cheese sauce over egg yolks, stirring constantly. Return egg yolk mixture to cheese sauce. Place bread cubes in greased 2-quart casserole. Arrange shrimp over bread. Cover with sauce. Top with buttered crumbs. Bake in 350-degree oven for 30 minutes. Yield: 6 servings.

Susie M. Weld, C.W.A.
Mt. Sugar Loaf Grange, No. 111

SHRIMP DE JONGHE
(Recipe 40 years old)

3 lb. fresh shrimp
Salt and pepper to taste
1/2 c. consomme
4 to 5 slivers garlic
1 c. butter
2 c. Pepperidge Farm herb stuffing
6 tbsp. minced parsley

Preheat oven to 400 degrees. Place 6 to 8 shrimp in individual baking dishes. Sprinkle with salt and pepper. Pour consomme over shrimp. Saute garlic in butter until butter browns, then remove garlic. Add stuffing and parsley to butter mixture. Sprinkle stuffing mixture over shrimp. Bake for 15 minutes. Do not overcook. Yield: 6-8 servings.

Dorothy Putnam, Master
Lucerne Grange, No. 167
Palm Beach Gardens, Florida

Vegetables

Two hundred years ago, life was simple and cooking was plain. Native vegetables such as corn and beans were staples in the American diet. When many of the seeds that the Pilgrims brought from their homelands would not grow, the Indians taught the settlers which foods were more suitable to their climate and how they could best be cultivated. The Pilgrims then devised ways to bring an extra touch to their simple dishes, such as using pure maple syrup to candy sweet potatoes and glaze carrots.

Farms of today bear little resemblance to those family plots tilled many years ago. Mechanization has resulted in the production of thousands of acres of the largest, highest grade and above all, tastiest vegetables ever known to man. However, there is still no comparison to the personal satisfaction derived from watching your own garden grow. A familiar sight behind most farmhouses is a small kitchen garden yielding every kind of vegetable from potatoes to peas.

Vegetables can be one of the most exciting courses of a meal. Besides adding color, vegetables lend a flavor variety which is unavailable in any other food. The importance of eating fresh vegetables for good nutrition cannot be overstressed. Because our sources of fresh vegetables are limitless, the smart and thrifty homemaker will use fresh fruits and vegetables as often as possible. Combine these luscious foods with the goodness of an old-fashioned recipe and a meal that is truly the best of the old and the new will result.

Inventive cooks, experimenting with new combinations of various vegetables, have come up with some original recipes that reflect the tastes of our ancestors. Why not use these recipes to discover a different way to fix an old family favorite or be adventurous and introduce your family to a vegetable they've never sampled!

★ ★

BOSTON-BAKED BEANS
(Recipe 100 years old)

    1 lb. small navy beans
    3/4 lb. salt pork, diced
    1 lg. onion, chopped
    1 tsp. salt
    2 tsp. dry mustard
    1/4 c. molasses
    1/4 c. (packed) dark brown sugar
    1 sm. can tomato sauce
    1/4 c. catsup

Place navy beans in large saucepan; cover with water. Bring to a boil; cook for 30 minutes. Drain beans; reserve liquid. Place beans in earthenware bean pot. Add pork, onion, salt, mustard, molasses, sugar and tomato sauce; mix well. Cover beans with reserved liquid; cover pot. Bake in preheated 200-degree oven for 12 hours; remove lid. Pour catsup over top; bake for 30 minutes longer. Yield: 12 servings.

Lena B. Martin
Chico Grange, No. 486
Chico, California

EASY BAKED BEANS
(Recipe 65 years old)

    2 lb. pea beans
    1 med. onion, chopped
    1 c. sugar
    4 tsp. salt
    2 tsp. dry mustard
    1/2 c. (scant) molasses
    1/2 lb. salt pork

Soak beans overnight in kettle. Add onion; bring to a boil. Reduce heat; simmer until beans are soft. Add remaining ingredients; mix well. Bake in preheated 250-degree oven for at least 8 hours. Yield: 15 servings.

Anna G. MacLaughlin
Central Grange, No. 34
Saunderstown, Rhode Island

NEW ENGLAND-BAKED BEANS
(Recipe 125 years old)

    2 lb. yellow-eye beans
    1/2 lb. salt pork
    3/4 c. sugar
    1/4 c. molasses
    1/2 c. Vermont maple syrup
    1/2 tsp. ginger
    1/2 tsp. dry mustard
    2 tsp. salt
    Dash of pepper

Sort and wash beans; place in kettle. Cover with water; soak overnight. Drain off most of the water; add enough cold water to cover beans. Bring to a boil over low heat. Simmer for 2 hours and 30 minutes, adding boiling water to keep beans well covered. Scrape rind of salt pork; cut through fat to rind in 1/2-inch cubes. Scald pork with boiling water; drain. Place in center of beans. Pour 2 cups water into saucepan. Add remaining ingredients; mix well. Bring to a boil; stir into beans. Add enough boiling water to cover 1 inch over beans. Bake in preheated 325-degree oven for 2 hours and 30 minutes. Yield: 12 servings.

Zelda Sweeney
Banner Grange, No. 356
St. Albans, Vermont

DILLED GREEN BEANS

    2 lb. fresh green beans
    3 tbsp. butter
    2 tsp. dillseed, crushed

Break beans into 1-inch pieces; cook, uncovered, in rapidly boiling, salted water for 20 to 30 minutes or until tender. Drain; set aside. Melt butter in large skillet. Add dillseed; cook, stirring, for 3 minutes. Add beans; stir to coat thoroughly. Cook until beans are heated thoroughly. Yield: 8 servings.

From a Grange Friend

LIMA BEAN AND SAUSAGE BAKE

    1 c. dried baby lima beans
    3/4 tsp. salt
    1/2 lb. bulk sausage
    1/4 tsp. poultry seasoning
    Dash of pepper
    2 tbsp. minced onion
    2 tbsp. minced green pepper
    1 c. undiluted evaporated milk

Place lima beans in saucepan; add just enough water to cover. Soak overnight. Bring to a boil over moderate heat. Reduce heat; add salt. Cover. Simmer for about 1 hour or until beans are just tender; drain. Cook sausage in skillet until lightly browned, breaking apart with fork. Drain off fat; add sausage to beans. Add poultry seasoning and pepper; stir in onion and green pepper. Turn into buttered casserole; add milk. Cover. Bake in preheated 325-degree oven for about 45 minutes or until beans are tender. Yield: 4 servings.

Bertha Sweet, Sec.
Gardner Grange, No. 130
Gardner, Massachusetts

HARVARD BEETS

    6 med. beets
    1/2 c. sugar
    1/2 tbsp. cornstarch
    1/2 c. vinegar
    2 tbsp. butter

Cook beets in small amount of boiling salted water until tender, then slice. Combine sugar and cornstarch in saucepan; stir in vinegar. Boil for 5 minutes, stirring

★ ★

constantly. Add butter; stir until melted. Pour sauce over beets. Yield: 4 servings.

Mrs. Perley Sweetland
Manchester Grange, No. 172
Manchester, Maine

BROCCOLI-CORN BAKE

1 10-oz. package frozen chopped
   broccoli, thawed
1 1-lb. can creamed corn
Cracker crumbs
1 egg, beaten
3 tbsp. melted butter
1/2 tsp. salt
1 tbsp. minced onion
Dash of pepper

Combine broccoli, corn, 1/4 cup cracker crumbs, egg, 1 tablespoon melted butter, salt, onion and pepper; mix well. Turn into greased 1 1/2-quart casserole. Combine 2 tablespoons melted butter and 1/4 cup cracker crumbs; sprinkle over broccoli. Bake in 350-degree oven for 45 minutes.

Frieda Palm
North Fairfield Grange, No. 806
North Fairfield, Ohio

BRUSSELS SPROUTS IN ONION CREAM

1 1/2 lb. Brussels sprouts
1/2 c. chopped onion
1 pt. sour cream
2 tbsp. butter

Cook Brussels sprouts in steamer for 15 minutes or until tender. Saute onion in butter until rich brown. Stir in sour cream and heat, stirring constantly. Add Brussels sprouts and mix well. Yield: 6 servings.

From a Grange Friend

DUTCH RED CABBAGE
(Recipe over 70 years old)

1 2-lb. head red cabbage
4 lg. cooking apples, sliced
3/4 c. raisins
2 tbsp. cider vinegar
1 to 2 tbsp. butter
1/2 tsp. salt
Sugar to taste

Cut red cabbage coarsely. Combine cabbage, apples, raisins, vinegar, butter, salt and water to almost cover in saucepan; sprinkle sugar over top. Cook until cabbage is tender, stirring occasionally. Add more water as needed. Add small amount of vinegar at a time to increase sour flavor, if desired. Liquid should be almost evaporated when done. Yield: 6 servings.

Mrs. C. Ida Herman
Denmark Grange, No. 1544
Jefferson, Ohio

HUNGARIAN CASSEROLE

2 lb. bacon
1 head cabbage
1 8-oz. package kluski noodles

Dice bacon; cook in skillet until brown. Remove from skillet; drain on paper towels. Shred cabbage; add to bacon drippings. Cook and stir until browned. Cook noodles according to package directions. Stir noodles and bacon into cabbage in skillet.

Mrs. Margaret Colson
Jefferson Grange, No. 2019
Sharpsville, Pennsylvania

RED CABBAGE WITH APPLES

1 head red cabbage, chopped
4 or 5 tart apples, chopped
Pinch of salt
2 tsp. sugar
1 tsp. butter
1/2 c. vinegar

Combine cabbage, apples, salt and small amount of water in saucepan; boil until tender. Add sugar, butter and vinegar just before servings. Yield: 8 servings.

Mattie Vriezelaar
Sugar Grove Grange, No. 2044

STUFFED CABBAGE ROLLS

20 lg. cabbage leaves
2/3 c. rice
1 lb. ground beef
1 lb. ground pork
1 tsp. salt
1/2 tsp. thyme
Dash of pepper
1 lg. onion, chopped
2 eggs
2 c. tomato juice
2 c. water
1 onion, chopped
5 bouillon cubes
4 tbsp. parsley
Salt to taste

Boil cabbage leaves for 5 minutes or just long enough to wilt. Cook rice until tender; drain. Combine rice, beef, pork, salt, thyme, pepper, onion and beaten eggs; mix well. Shape into small rolls. Wrap each roll in cabbage leaf; place in skillet. Mix tomato juice, water, onion, bouillon cubes, parsley and salt; pour over rolls in skillet. Cover; simmer for about 1 hour and 30 minutes to 2 hours. Turn rolls occasionally. Thicken sauce slightly with paste made with flour and water if desired.

Miss Dorothy Collett
Empire Grange, No. 1228
Wheelersburg, Ohio

★★

CABBAGE ROLLS WITH SAUERKRAUT
(Recipe 85 years old)

1 1/2 lb. hamburger
1 sm. onion, cut fine
1 1/4 c. cooked rice
1 egg, beaten
Salt and pepper to taste
1 head cabbage
1 sm. can sauerkraut
1 med. can tomatoes
1 sm. can tomato puree

Combine hamburger, onion, rice, egg, salt and pepper. Steam cabbage leaves in pan of boiling water for 5 minutes. Form hamburger mixture into balls; wrap each ball in a cabbage leaf. Place layer of rolls in Dutch oven; cover with sauerkraut. Add half the tomatoes and puree. Make another layer of rolls; add remaining tomatoes and puree. Cover and cook for 45 minutes to 1 hour. Yield: 6 servings.

Mrs. George Baxter
Central Grange, No. 61
Middletown, Delaware

HONEY CARROTS

10 to 12 sm. carrots
3 tbsp. butter
1 tbsp. brown sugar
2 tbsp. honey

Cook carrots in small amount of boiling, salted water until tender; drain. Melt butter in saucepan; add sugar, honey and carrots. Cook over low heat for 5 to 6 minutes or until carrots are well glazed, turning frequently. Yield: 4 servings.

Mrs. Alma Irey
Rogue River Valley Grange, No. 469
Grants Pass, Oregon

POTATO-CARROT CAKES

1 1/2 c. shredded pared potatoes
1 1/2 c. shredded pared carrots
1 tbsp. grated fresh onion
2 tbsp. flour
2 tbsp. wheat germ
3 tbsp. chopped fresh parsley
1 tsp. salt
1/8 tsp. pepper
1/4 tsp. dried leaf tarragon
4 eggs, slightly beaten
2 tbsp. butter

Use coarse grater to shred potatoes and carrots. Combine potatoes, carrots and onion in large bowl. Sprinkle with flour; toss to mix well. Stir in remaining ingredients except butter. Melt 1 tablespoon butter in large skillet; spoon 1/4 cup mixture for each pancake onto skillet and flatten. Cook for 5 minutes; turn and cook for 5 minutes longer or until golden brown. Repeat with remaining mixture, adding remaining butter as needed. Yield: 12 pancakes.

CREAMED FRESH BEANS AND CELERY

1 lb. fresh green beans
1 c. diagonally sliced celery
1/4 c. water
1/2 tsp. salt
2 tbsp. butter
1/4 c. chopped fresh onion
2 tbsp. chopped fresh celery leaves
2 tbsp. flour
1 3/4 c. milk
4 tsp. fresh lemon juice
1/8 tsp. pepper

Cut off tips of green beans; cut beans into 1-inch pieces. Combine with celery, water and 1/4 teaspoon salt in saucepan. Cover; simmer for 15 to 20 minutes or until beans are crisp-tender. Drain. Melt butter in medium saucepan; add onion and celery leaves. Cook until onion is tender. Blend in flour. Remove from heat; stir in milk. Return to heat; cook, stirring constantly, until mixture thickens and comes to a boil. Stir in lemon juice, remaining 1/4 teaspoon salt, pepper, cooked beans and celery. Serve over Potato-Carrot Cakes.

Photograph for this recipe on page 101.

GINGER CARROTS

3 to 4 c. sliced carrots
1 c. orange juice
1/2 c. chicken broth
3 whole cloves
3/4 tsp. ground ginger
1 1/2 tsp. grated lemon rind
3 tbsp. sugar

Place all ingredients except sugar in saucepan; mix well. Bring to a boil. Stir in sugar; cover. Reduce heat; simmer for about 30 minutes or until carrots are tender. Do not omit lemon rind. Yield: 6 servings.

From a Grange Friend

FAMILY CARROT CASSEROLE

8 carrots, sliced
1 onion, chopped
1 bell pepper, diced
4 stalks celery, sliced
1 1/4 c. thick tomato soup
Salt and pepper to taste

Parboil carrots; drain. Saute onion, bell pepper and celery in small amount of oil in saucepan until tender. Add to carrots; stir in tomato soup and seasonings. Place in 9 x 6-inch baking pan. Bake in preheated 350-degree oven until bubbly. Yield: 8 servings.

Fern E. Konkel
Central Grange, No. 626
Fresno, California

Photo page 101 —
Recipes on pages 72, 90, and 100.
Photo page 102 — Recipe on page 55.

★ ★

SURPRISE CARROT LOAF
(Recipe 50 years old)

1 c. ground carrots
1 c. ground peanuts
1 c. fine bread crumbs
1 c. chopped tomatoes
1 tbsp. butter
4 eggs

Mix carrots, peanuts and bread crumbs in bowl. Add tomatoes and butter; mix well. Beat eggs until foamy; stir into carrot mixture. Place in greased bread pan. Bake in preheated 350-degree oven for about 1 hour. Yield: 6 servings.

Dorothy M. Cordes
Eclipse Grange, No. 311
Plaistow, New Hampshire

SCALLOPED CORN WITH OYSTERS

1 8-oz. can oysters
1/4 tsp. salt
1/8 tsp. pepper
1/4 c. melted butter
2 c. cracker crumbs
1 can corn
1/2 c. coffee cream

Place sieve over saucepan; empty oysters into sieve to drain. Lift oysters from sieve, one by one; remove bits of shell. Reserve liquid. Mix salt, pepper, butter and cracker crumbs. Spread 1/3 of the crumbs mixture over bottom of shallow baking dish; cover with half the oysters, then half the corn. Add half the remaining crumbs mixture. Repeat layers of oysters and corn; top with remaining crumbs mixture. Mix reserved oyster liquid and cream; pour over crumbs mixture. Bake in preheated 425-degree oven for 20 minutes. Yield: 4 servings.

Mrs. David Schock
Banner Grange
Holton, Kansas

CORN FRITTERS
(Recipe 70 years old)

1 egg
1 c. fresh corn
1 c. flour
2 tsp. salt
Dash of cayenne pepper
1/2 c. milk
1 tbsp. olive oil
Powdered sugar (opt.)

Beat egg in bowl. Add remaining ingredients except sugar; mix well. Drop by spoonfuls into deep hot fat; fry for 6 to 8 minutes or until done. Drain; sprinkle with powdered sugar. Serve hot. Canned corn may be used instead of fresh corn. Yield: 4 to 6 servings.

Mrs. Robert Proctor
National Grange
Washington, D.C.

Photo page 103 — Recipe on page 31.

Photo page 104 — Recipe on page 61.

CORN SOUFFLE
(Recipe about 100 years old)

1 tbsp. melted butter
4 egg yolks, well beaten
2 c. cream-style corn
1 tbsp. sugar
3 tbsp. flour
1 tsp. salt
1/8 tsp. pepper
1 1/2 c. light cream

Mix butter and egg yolks in bowl. Add corn; mix well. Mix sugar, flour, salt and pepper in bowl. Add cream; beat until smooth. Stir in corn mixture; place in greased casserole. Place in pan of hot water. Bake in preheated 325-degree oven for 1 hour to 1 hour and 30 minutes or until firm. Yield: 6 servings.

Valerie Mueller
Whitethorn Grange, No. 792
Redway, California

CHEESE WOODCHUCK

1 sm. onion, minced
2 tbsp. butter
1/2 tsp. salt
1/2 tsp. savory or poultry seasoning
2/3 c. milk
1 1/2 c. corn, scraped from cob
1/2 lb. cheese, diced
2 eggs, well beaten
6 slices toast

Saute onion in butter in saucepan until tender. Add seasonings, milk and corn; cook over low heat, stirring, for 10 minutes. Stir in cheese; cook until melted. Add eggs; cook for 2 to 3 minutes, stirring constantly. Serve on toast slices. Canned corn may be used instead of fresh corn. Yield: 6 servings.

This recipe came from Yankee Magazine, which dates it about 1710, from Peaks Island, Casco Bay, Maine. After a shipwreck, the people had so much salvaged cheese that they had to think up many ways to use it. This was one of them.

Ruth McCall
North Haven Grange, No. 35
North Haven, Connecticut

CREAM-STYLE CORN

Fresh white or yellow ears of sweet corn
1 c. water
1 tsp. salt
2 tbsp. sugar

Remove husks and silks from corn. Cut corn off cob halfway through kernels; scrape cobs. Measure 4 cups corn; place in large saucepan. Stir in water, salt and sugar; bring to a boil. Reduce heat; simmer, stirring constantly, for 10 minutes. May be canned or frozen, if desired. Yield: 6 servings.

Mrs. Floyd Grommet
Turkey Hill Grange, No. 1370
Belleville, Illinois

★ ★

CORN CUSTARD

1 can corn
1 1/2 c. milk
2 tsp. cornstarch
1 tbsp. sugar
3 eggs, well beaten
1/2 c. melted butter
1 1/2 tsp. salt

Mix all ingredients in bowl; place in greased baking dish. Bake in preheated 300-degree oven for 35 minutes or until firm. One pint frozen corn, thawed, may be substituted for canned corn. Yield: 6 servings.

Mrs. John F. Hull
Wayne Township Grange, No. 1951
Lisbon, Ohio

CHEESE AND CORN CASSEROLE

1 c. milk
1 1/2 c. bread crumbs
1 c. corn
1 c. grated cheese
1 tbsp. butter
1 tsp. salt
3 eggs, separated

Combine milk, bread crumbs, corn, cheese, butter, salt and beaten egg yolks in bowl; mix well. Beat egg whites until stiff; fold into corn mixture. Bake in preheated 350-degree oven for 30 minutes or until firm.

Mrs. Amos E. Stuart
Sterling Grange, No. 53
Sterling, Massachusetts

DELICIOUS CORN OYSTERS
(Recipe 50 years old)

1 egg
1 c. corn
1/4 c. flour
Salt and pepper to taste
Crisco

Beat egg in bowl until foamy; stir in corn. Add flour, salt and pepper; beat well. Drop by spoonfuls into deep, hot Crisco; cook until golden brown. Fritters should be size of large oysters. Yield: 2 dozen corn oysters.

Mrs. Alma Rolla
Ware Grange, No. 164
Ware, Massachusetts

GLAZED VEGETABLES

1 lb. parsnips
3/4 c. water
1/2 tsp. salt
3 tbsp. Smucker's Caramel Flavor
    Topping
2 tbsp. butter
1 tbsp. lemon juice

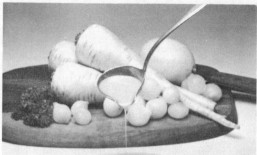

Peel parsnips; cut into 2 x 3/8-inch strips. Combine parsnips, water and salt in medium saucepan; bring to a boil. Cover; simmer for 8 minutes or until tender. Drain thoroughly. Heat caramel flavor topping, butter and lemon juice together in small saucepan. Pour over drained parsnips; toss gently until evenly coated. Two cups frozen small onions or 1 pound carrots may be substituted for parsnips. Cook onions according to package directions. Cut carrots into strips; cook in boiling salted water for 12 minutes or until tender. Yield: 4 servings.

Photograph for this recipe above.

CUCUMBER AU GRATIN

3 med. cucumbers, peeled and sliced
2 tbsp. butter
2 tbsp. flour
1 1/4 c. milk
1 bouillon cube
1/4 tsp. onion juice or grated onion
Salt and pepper to taste
1 c. grated mild cheese
1/3 c. buttered bread crumbs

Cook cucumbers in just enough salted boiling water to cover for 5 minutes; drain well. Melt butter in saucepan; add flour, stirring until blended. Add milk gradually; cook and stir until smooth. Add bouillon cube and onion juice; stir until dissolved. Season with salt and pepper. Add cheese; simmer, stirring constantly, until melted. Add cucumbers; pour into greased small casserole. Top with bread crumbs. Bake in 350-degree oven for about 20 minutes or until browned. Yield: 6 servings.

Mrs. Ralph W. Durkee
Saratoga Grange, No. 1209
Stillwater, New York

★ ★

GRANDMOTHER'S CREAMED CUCUMBERS
(Recipe over 100 years old)

    4 med. cucumbers
    2 med. onions, diced
    3 tbsp. salt
    1 c. heavy cream
    3 tbsp. vinegar
    3 tbsp. sugar

Peel and thinly slice cucumbers. Place cucumbers and onions in large bowl; add salt, stirring to coat. Cover with dish and weight. Let set for 12 to 18 hours, draining periodically. Cucumbers will be limp, but crunchy. Drain cucumber mixture. Add cream, vinegar and sugar; chill. Serve over boiled new potatoes. Yield: 6 servings.

Mrs. Alyene A. Rollins
Hamilton-Wenham Grange, No. 297
South Hamilton, Massachusetts

CORN AND ZUCCHINI CASSEROLE

    4 c. cooked sliced zucchini
    1 c. shredded yellow cheese
    3 eggs, well beaten
    Salt and pepper to taste
    1 sm. onion, chopped
    1/3 c. rich milk
    2 tbsp. flour
    1 can cream-style corn

Combine all ingredients in a greased baking dish. Bake in 325-degree oven for about 1 hour or until set. For variation, 2 cloves of garlic, chopped and 1 pound ground beef, cooked until brown, may be added and additional cheese sprinkled on top. One cup bread crumbs may be added to serve a larger group. Yield: 7-8 servings.

Myrna Thomas
French Camp-Lathrop Grange, No. 510
French Camp, California

DANDELION FRITTERS

    1 1/2 qt. (about) dandelion blossoms
    1 c. flour
    1 tsp. baking powder
    1/2 tsp. salt
    1/8 tsp. pepper
    2 eggs, beaten
    2/3 c. milk
    2 tbsp. melted butter

Wash and drain dandelion blossoms. Sift flour, baking powder, salt and pepper in large bowl. Combine eggs, milk and butter; mix well. Add egg mixture and dandelion blossoms; stir until blended. Drop by spoonfuls in hot butter; fry until brown on both sides.

Aletha E. Hemenway
Ripley Grange, No. 462
Dexter, Maine

HOT DANDELION GREENS
(Recipe at least 60 years old)

    2 qt. dandelion greens
    1 c. water
    1 tsp. salt
    3 strips bacon
    1/2 c. sugar
    1 tbsp. flour
    1/2 c. vinegar
    1 c. sour cream
    1 hard-boiled egg, sliced

Cook greens in boiling salted water for 5 minutes; drain. Fry bacon until crisp; drain, reserving 2 tablespoons drippings. Combine sugar, flour, vinegar, sour cream and bacon drippings. Add bacon and greens; bring to a boil, stirring gently. Remove from heat. Garnish with egg.

Elma Burgard, W.A.C. Chm.
Flemingville Grange, No. 1333
Owego, New York

BAKED EGGPLANT WITH CHEESE

    2 med. eggplant
    1 c. grated sharp cheese
    1 c. cracker crumbs
    1 c. rich milk
    1 bell pepper, chopped fine
    1 med. onion, chopped fine
    4 eggs, well beaten
    2 tbsp. oil
    Salt and pepper to taste

Peel and dice eggplant; cook in boiling water until tender. Drain; mash. Combine remaining ingredients in bowl; stir in eggplant. Place in well-greased baking pan. Bake in preheated 375-degree oven for 35 to 40 minutes or until done.

Mrs. Tom Fortune
Porterville Grange, No. 718
Porterville, California

EGGPLANT SICILIANA

    3 tbsp. cooking oil
    1 med. onion, chopped
    1 lg. eggplant
    1 green pepper, diced
    1 15-oz. can tomato sauce
    1 tsp. Italian seasoning
    Salt and pepper to taste

Heat oil in saucepan. Add onion; saute until transparent. Peel eggplant; cut into 1/2-inch cubes. Add eggplant and green pepper to onion; cook, stirring, until eggplant is coated with oil. Add tomato sauce; mix well. Bring to a boil; reduce heat. Simmer for 30 minutes. Stir in Italian seasoning, salt and pepper; simmer for 15 minutes longer. May be cooled and refrigerated, then heated next day. Flavor is improved if reheated. Yield: 5 to 6 servings.

John Ortolani
Pioneer Grange, No. 737
Annandale, Virginia

★ ★

BAKED EGGPLANT WITH TOMATO
(Recipe over 125 years old)

    1 med. eggplant
    1 egg, beaten
    1 tomato, chopped
    1 onion, chopped
    1 c. bread crumbs
    Salt and pepper to taste
    Butter

Cut eggplant in half; scoop out pulp, leaving about 1/4-inch shell. Chop or grind pulp medium-fine; soak in salt water for about 1 hour. Squeeze out water; place pulp in bowl. Add egg, tomato, onion, bread crumbs, salt and pepper; mix well. Pack in eggplant shells; dot with butter. Place shells in baking pan; add small amount of water. Bake in preheated 375-degree oven for 40 to 50 minutes or until done.

Mrs. Virginia S. Cummings
Essex Grange, No. 381
Essex, Massachusetts

EGGPLANT PIE

    2 med. eggplant
    1/2 c. flour
    Salt
    Pepper
    1/2 c. vegetable oil
    1/2 c. finely chopped onion
    1/2 c. chopped green pepper
    2 tbsp. chopped parsley
    2 8-oz. cans tomato sauce
    1/4 lb. sliced mozzarella cheese
    2 eggs, slightly beaten
    3 tbsp. grated Parmesan cheese

Peel eggplant; cut into 1/2-inch slices. Mix flour with salt and pepper to taste. Dip eggplant slices in seasoned flour; cook in oil until lightly browned. Drain slices on paper towels. Saute onion and green pepper in remaining oil for 5 minutes or until tender. Add parsley, 1/2 teaspoon salt, dash of pepper and tomato sauce; simmer for 5 minutes. Spoon half the sauce into large, shallow casserole; arrange half the eggplant slices on sauce. Add mozzarella cheese slices. Add remaining sauce, then add remaining eggplant slices. Combine eggs and Parmesan cheese; pour over eggplant. Bake in preheated 325-degree oven for 35 to 40 minutes. Yield: 6 servings.

Dorothy Krause
Guiding Star Grange, No. 1
Greenfield, Massachusetts

BAKED CREAMED MUSHROOMS

    1 lb. mushrooms, coarsely chopped
    2 sm. onions, chopped
    3 tbsp. butter
    2 eggs, beaten
    2/3 c. fine bread crumbs
    3/4 c. milk
    3/4 c. light cream

    2 tsp. salt
    1/4 tsp. pepper

Saute mushrooms and onions in butter until golden. Combine eggs, crumbs, milk, cream, salt and pepper in 1 1/2-quart casserole; mix well. Blend in mushrooms and onions. Bake, uncovered, in 350-degree oven for about 1 hour or until golden and set. Serve with chicken or fish.

Mrs. Laoma Edwards
Meander Grange
Youngstown, Ohio

BAKED STUFFED MUSHROOMS

    1 lb. fresh med. mushrooms
    1 c. chopped pecans
    3 tbsp. chopped parsley
    1/4 c. soft butter
    1 clove of garlic, crushed
    1/4 tsp. thyme
    1/2 tsp. salt
    Dash of pepper
    1/2 c. cream

Wipe mushrooms with a damp cloth; remove caps. Arrange in shallow baking dish with hollow side up. Chop the stems; mix with pecans, parsley, butter, garlic, thyme, salt and pepper. Mix well; heap into mushroom caps. Press down firmly. Pour cream over mushrooms; cover. Bake at 350 degrees for 30 to 45 minutes or until tender. Baste once or twice with the cream. Add more cream, if necessary.

From a Grange Friend

ONION SHORTCAKE

    8 to 10 med. onions
    Salt
    3 tbsp. butter, melted
    1 c. flour
    1 1/2 tsp. baking powder
    2 tbsp. shortening
    1/3 c. milk
    1 egg, beaten
    3/4 c. thick cream

Peel onions; slice thin. Season with 1/2 teaspoon salt. Place onions in butter in frypan; cover. Simmer, stirring occasionally, until onions are tender but not browned; let cool. Sift flour, 1/2 teaspoon salt and baking powder together; add shortening, mixing well. Combine milk and half the egg; add to flour mixture. Stir until well mixed. Spread in greased pie pan; arrange onions over pie shell. Combine remaining part of egg and cream; pour over onions. Bake in 425-degree oven for 25 minutes or until done. Serve hot. Yield: 6 servings.

Edith Atwell
Manitou Park Grange, No. 430
Woodland Park, Colorado

CAJUN CHUCK ROAST

7 lb. charcoal briquets
Starter
1 stick hickory wood
3 sm. zucchini
3 sm. summer squash
2 16-oz. cans stewed tomatoes
1 20-oz. package frozen sm. whole
 onions
2 1/2 tsp. salt
12 new potatoes
1 4-lb. beef chuck cross rib pot roast
1 tsp. lemon pepper
1 tsp. garlic powder

Allow at least 1 pound charcoal briquets for each hour of cooking time. Place charcoal in bottom pan of charcoal water smoker; use a good starter. Try electric or chimney type, or choose a liquid, jelly or solid fibrous cubes. Place hickory wood on top of hot coals, or use other flavor-producing woods like bourbon barrel, applewood chips, pecan or mesquite. Place second pan into smoker; fill with water according to manufacturer's instructions. Place rack above water. Cut zucchini and squash into 1/2-inch thick slices. Drain tomatoes; chop coarsely. Place squash in 3-quart casserole. Add onions, tomatoes and 1 teaspoon salt; stir to blend well. Place uncovered casserole on rack; surround casserole with potatoes. Add second rack. If charcoal water smoker is a single rack unit, a step-up attachment can be used to hold a second rack; may improvise by placing a baking rack over single rack. The meal may be cooked on a single rack, but be sure that the roast does not touch casserole. Mix lemon pepper, garlic powder and remaining 1 1/2 teaspoons salt; rub over roast. Place on rack above casserole; cover with lid. Cook according to manufacturer's instructions, removing lid only to check water level and adding water according to manufacturer's instructions. Cook for 6 hours. Yield: 6-8 servings.

Photograph for this recipe above.

CREAMED ONIONS

12 med. onions
2 c. milk
2 tbsp. butter
2 tbsp. flour
Salt and pepper to taste
Buttered crumbs

Cook the onions in boiling salted water until tender, but firm; drain. Scald 1 1/2 cups milk with the butter. Stir flour into remaining 1/2 cup milk; add salt and pepper. Add the paste to scalded milk mixture; stir until smooth and creamy. Place onions in buttered baking dish; pour the sauce over them. Sprinkle top with crumbs. Bake in 375-degree oven for about 30 minutes.

From a Grange Friend

★ ★

ONION-CHEESE PIE

6 tbsp. butter
1 1/2 c. cracker crumbs
3 c. thinly sliced onions
2 eggs, beaten
1 c. milk
1 tsp. salt
1/4 tsp. pepper
1/2 c. Cheddar cheese, shredded

Melt 4 tablespoons butter in saucepan; add cracker crumbs, mixing well. Press on side and bottom of pie pan, reserving 1/2 cup for top. Saute onions in 2 tablespoons butter until tender. Place onions in crust. Beat eggs with milk; add salt, pepper and cheese. Place over low heat, stirring until cheese melts. Pour sauce over onions. Sprinkle reserved crumbs on top. Bake in 325-degree oven for 30 minutes. Yield: 6 servings.

Carrie Morse
Locke Grange
Moravia, New York

ONION CHOWDER DISH
(Recipe at least 40 years old)

2 c. chopped onions
2 tbsp. butter
2 c. diced potatoes
Salt
3 c. milk
Dash of pepper

Simmer onions in butter until transparent, adding just enough water to prevent burning. Add potatoes, 1/4 teaspoon salt and small amount of water; cook over low heat until potatoes are done. Add milk, pepper and salt. Cook over low heat for 10 minutes before serving. Serve with hot biscuits. Yield: 4 servings.

Mrs. Nella H. Ashley
Dorchester Subordinate Grange, No. 280
Dorchester, New Hampshire

PARSNIPS AU GRATIN

2 lb. parsnips
4 tbsp. butter
2 tbsp. flour
1 1/2 c. milk
1/2 tsp. salt
Dash of pepper
1/2 c. dried bread crumbs
1/2 c. grated Cheddar or Parmesan cheese

Scrape or pare parsnips; cut in fourths lengthwise. Trim out woody core, Cut in large chunks. Cook in boiling salted water until tender; drain well. Melt 2 tablespoons butter in a saucepan; stir in flour until smooth. Add milk gradually. Cook over low heat, stirring constantly, until mixture bubbles. Season with salt and pepper. Combine parsnips and white sauce in greased casserole. Melt remaining butter in skillet; add

crumbs. Cook, turning constantly, until brown. Combine buttered crumbs and cheese; sprinkle over parsnips. Bake in 350-degree oven for 15 to 20 minutes.

Carrie Morse
Locke Grange
Moravia, New York

BEEF-STUFFED GREEN PEPPERS

3 green peppers
1 1/2 lb. ground beef
2 c. bread crumbs
2 eggs
1 tsp. salt
1/4 tsp. pepper
2 tbsp. chopped onion
3 tbsp. melted butter
Tomato sauce

Remove stem ends and seeds from green peppers; cut green peppers in half lengthwise. Combine beef, bread crumbs, eggs, salt, pepper, onion and butter. Fill green pepper shells with beef mixture; place in shallow baking pan. Bake in preheated 350-degree oven for 45 minutes; serve with tomato sauce.

Mrs. Richard H. Will
Easton Grange
Easton, Pennsylvania

HAM-STUFFED PEPPERS

2 c. cooked tomatoes
1 1/2 lb. ground ham
1/2 tsp. salt
Dash of pepper
1 tbsp. butter
1/2 to 3/4 c. bread crumbs
1 clove of garlic, diced
6 green peppers
1 can tomato sauce
Grated Parmesan cheese

Heat tomatoes in saucepan; stir in ham, salt, pepper, butter, bread crumbs and garlic. Slice tops from green peppers; remove seeds. Cook green peppers in boiling water for 10 minutes; drain. Stuff green peppers with ham mixture; place in shallow casserole. Add tomato sauce. Bake in preheated 350-degree oven for 35 minutes. Cover with Parmesan cheese; bake for 10 minutes longer.

Marge Holl
Fair Harbor Grange, No. 1129
Allyn, Washington

PEPPERS STUFFED WITH TUNA

1 7 1/2-oz. can tuna
1 c. stale bread crumbs
1 c. tomato pulp
1 tsp. salt

★ ★

1/4 tsp. pepper
1 tsp. onion juice
6 med. green peppers
Buttered bread crumbs
Sliced or grated Cheddar or American
   cheese
Tomato sauce

Drain tuna; flake. Place in bowl. Add stale bread crumbs, tomato pulp, salt, pepper and onion juice; mix well. Remove tops from green peppers, then remove seeds and membranes. Parboil for 3 minutes; drain and cool. Place in muffin cups; stuff with tuna mixture. Cover with buttered bread crumbs; top with Cheddar cheese. Bake in preheated 350-degree oven for 20 minutes. Serve with tomato sauce.

Viola K. Swishu
Grange No. 361
Greencastle, Pennsylvania

REICHERT POTATOES

4 Idaho potatoes, pared
2 tbsp. salad oil
2 onions, thinly sliced
1/2 c. chopped green pepper
1/2 tsp. dried dillweed
1 1/2 tsp. salt
1/4 tsp. pepper

Slice potatoes on coarse wide opening on 4-sided grater. Heat oil in very large skillet; add potatoes, onions and green pepper. Sprinkle with dillweed, salt and pepper. Cook over medium-high heat, stirring frequently, for about 15 minutes or until lightly browned and potatoes are tender. Yield: 4 to 6 servings.

Photograph for this recipe on page 272.

GERMAN POTATO PANCAKES
(Recipe 80 years old)

4 c. grated potatoes
1 med. onion
1/4 c. flour
2 tsp. salt
Dash of pepper (opt.)
3 lg. eggs, well beaten

Pare and grate potatoes and onion together. Grating may be done with a blender, but taste is different if done by hand on a regular metal grater. Add flour, salt, pepper and eggs; mix well. Drop batter by tablespoonfuls onto well-greased medium-hot griddle, spreading batter thin. Bake on each side until light brown and slightly crisp. Stir batter in bowl to keep well mixed. Pancakes may be placed on baking sheet and kept warm in oven. Serve with butter and brown sugar or syrup. May be served as side dish with bacon or ham and applesauce.

Bertha Norman
Courtland Grange, No. 563
Rockford, Michigan

POTATOES A LA JACK

6 c. prepared Idaho mashed potatoes
1/2 c. butter, softened
2 3-oz. packages cream cheese, softened
1/2 c. grated Parmesan cheese
1/2 c. shredded Cheddar cheese
1/4 tsp. saffron
1/4 c. chopped scallions
1/3 c. chopped green pepper
1 2-oz. can pimento, drained and diced

Prepare mashed potatoes without butter. Turn into large bowl; add butter and cheeses. Beat until well blended. Add saffron, scallions, green pepper and pimento; mix well. Turn into 2-quart casserole; refrigerate for several hours for flavors to blend. Bake in preheated 350-degree oven for 1 hour or until thoroughly heated. Garnish with parsley. Yield: 8 to 12 servings.

Photograph for this recipe on page 272.

FRIED MASHED POTATO CAKES
(Recipe over 40 years old)

1 c. mashed potatoes
1 tsp. (heaping) butter, melted
1 1/2 c. sugar
1 c. milk
2 eggs, well beaten
Pinch of salt
Nutmeg to taste
3 tsp. baking powder
4 to 5 c. flour

Combine mashed potatoes, butter and sugar; stir until well blended. Add milk, eggs, salt, nutmeg, baking powder and enough flour to make a soft dough, blending well. Let stand in refrigerator overnight. Fry in preheated 375-degree deep fat until browned.

Leta Shader
Wheeler Grange, No. 1416
Bath, New York

EASY SCALLOPED POTATOES

6 med. potatoes
2 tbsp. flour
1 1/2 tsp. salt
1/8 tsp. pepper
2 tbsp. butter
2 c. hot milk

Peel and slice the potatoes. Place a layer of potatoes in a greased baking dish. Sprinkle with part of the flour, salt and pepper. Dot with butter. Repeat until all the potatoes are used. Pour milk over all. Bake in 350-degree oven for 1 hour or until potatoes are tender and browned on top. Bread crumbs may be sprinkled on top of potatoes before baking, if desired. Yield: 6 servings.

Mildred Henzler
Barberton Grange, No. 571
Vancouver, Washington

★ ★

POTATOES SUPREME

1 8-oz. carton sour cream
2 c. cottage cheese
2 tsp. salt
1 tbsp. onion powder
1/4 tsp. garlic powder
5 c. diced cooked potatoes
1/2 c. grated American cheese
Dash of paprika

Combine sour cream, cottage cheese, salt, onion and garlic. Fold in diced potatoes; pour into a buttered 1 1/2-quart casserole. Top with cheese and sprinkle lightly with paprika. Bake at 350 degrees for 40 to 45 minutes or until thoroughly heated and lightly browned on top. Yield: 6 servings.

Agnes Ingwersen
Dir. of Jr. Grange Activities
National Grange
Le Roy, Kansas

POTATO CAKES

1 c. leftover mashed potatoes
1 egg
1/2 tsp. baking powder
4 tbsp. (rounded) flour
1 tsp. salt
1/4 c. milk

Mix all ingredients together; fry in melted shortening in skillet until brown and edges are well set. Turn and cook other side until brown. Yield: 4 servings.

Hazel L. Cooper
Hillstown Grange, No. 87
East Hartford, Connecticut

CHEESE-SCALLOPED POTATOES
(Recipe over 85 years old)

9 to 10 c. sliced potatoes
6 tbsp. butter
6 tbsp. flour
1 tsp. salt
1/4 tsp. pepper
3 c. milk
1 1/2 c. grated sharp cheese
1 sm. onion, grated

Cook potatoes in small amount of water until just glossy. Melt butter in saucepan; blend in flour, salt and pepper. Add milk gradually, stirring constantly. Cook and stir until thick and smooth. Remove from heat; add cheese, stirring until melted. Spoon potatoes in baking dish; arrange onion over potatoes. Pour cheese sauce over all. Bake in 350-degree oven for about 1 hour and 30 minutes. Yield: 10-12 servings.

Zella Chatburn
Albion Grange, No. 321
Albion, Idaho

OLD-STYLE SCALLOPED POTATOES

6 med. potatoes, sliced thin
2 onions, sliced thin
3 stalks celery, sliced
2 tbsp. chopped green parsley
2 tbsp. flour
1 tsp. salt
1/2 tsp. pepper
7 tbsp. butter
2 1/4 c. hot milk

Make layers of potatoes, onions and celery in buttered baking dish. Sprinkle with parsley. Sprinkle with flour, salt and pepper; dot with butter. Continue until all vegetables are used. Pour hot milk over all. Cover. Bake in 325-degree oven for 1 hour, or until potatoes are tender. Add milk if mixture becomes dry. Yield: 4 servings.

Ellen F. Storb
Chester Valley Grange, No. 1496
West Chester, Pennsylvania

SPINACH-TOMATO AND CHEESE LOAF

2 c. drained cooked spinach
2 1/4 c. canned tomatoes
1/4 c. chili sauce
1/2 lb. grated cheese
1 c. cracker crumbs
Juice of 1/2 onion
1/4 tsp. salt
1/4 tsp. pepper

Toss all ingredients together until blended. Place in a greased loaf pan. Bake in preheated 350-degree oven for about 1 hour. Serve garnished with crisp bacon. Yield: 8 servings.

Mrs. Jane Brace
Ferrisburg Grange, No. 539
Ferrisburg, Vermont

CREAMED SPINACH AND CAULIFLOWER

1 cauliflower, cut in flowerets
1 1/4 tsp. salt
3 tbsp. butter
8 c. chopped fresh spinach
2 tbsp. flour
1 c. milk
1/2 c. light cream
1/2 c. shredded Swiss cheese
1/8 tsp. pepper
1/16 tsp. nutmeg

Cook cauliflowerets in 1 inch boiling water with 1/2 teaspoon salt in large skillet for 10 minutes or until cauliflower is crisp-tender. Drain; set aside. Melt butter in skillet. Add spinach; cook over low heat for 5 minutes. Sprinkle with flour; mix well. Stir in milk and cream; cook over low heat, stirring constantly, until

★ ★

sauce thickens and comes to a boil. Stir in Swiss cheese, remaining 3/4 teaspoon salt, pepper and nutmeg. Add cooked cauliflowerets; heat through and serve immediately. Yield: 8 servings.

Photograph for this recipe on page 34.

GRANDMOTHER'S DELICIOUS BAKED SQUASH
(Recipe 40 years old)

2 sm. acorn squash
1/2 c. cream
2 tbsp. butter
3 tbsp. sugar
Salt to taste
1/2 c. (packed) brown sugar
1/2 c. chopped pecans

Cut squash in half; remove seeds. Place squash, cut side down, in baking dish. Bake in preheated 350-degree oven until tender. Remove pulp from squash; mash in bowl. Add cream, butter, sugar and salt; mix well. Fill squash halves with butter mixture. Sprinkle tops with brown sugar, then pecans; place on cookie sheet. Broil until brown. Yield: 4 servings.

Antoinette K. Barschaw
Sammamish Valley Grange, No. 286
Seattle, Washington

MOTHER'S OLD-TIME SQUASH PATTIES
(Recipe about 75 years old)

3 c. cooked mashed yellow, summer or
    zucchini squash
3 eggs, beaten
1/2 tsp. salt
Pepper to taste
1 tbsp. melted butter
1 1/2 to 2 c. flour

Mix all ingredients in bowl; drop by spoonfuls onto hot, greased griddle. Cook until brown on both sides. May add diced leftover ham or other meats and serve with gravy.

Myrna Thomas
French Camp-Lathrop Grange, No. 510
French Camp, California

SQUASH CASSEROLE

4 med. summer or zucchini squash
4 strips bacon
1 onion, chopped
1/2 green pepper, chopped
1 1/2 c. crushed saltine crackers
2 eggs, beaten well
Salt and pepper to taste
Butter
Paprika

Cook squash in boiling, salted water until tender; drain and chop. Fry bacon until crisp; drain and crumble. Saute onion and green pepper in bacon drippings until tender. Add bacon, onion mixture, 1 cup crushed crackers, eggs, salt and pepper to squash; mix well. Place in greased casserole; top with remaining 1/2 cup cracker crumbs. Dot with butter; sprinkle with paprika. Bake in preheated 350-degree oven for 30 minutes or until done. Yield: 6 to 8 servings.

Doris Wilson
Tamarack Grange, No. 1388
Renovo, Pennsylvania

CHEESED ZUCCHINI CASSEROLE

1 c. crumbled crackers
6 med. zucchini, sliced
3 tomatoes, sliced
1 onion, sliced
3/4 tsp. salt
1/4 tsp. garlic salt
1/4 tsp. oregano
Dash of pepper
6 slices sharp American process cheese
3 strips bacon, halved

Sprinkle crackers into 13 x 9-inch baking dish. Layer zucchini, tomatoes and onion over crackers; add seasonings. Top with cheese, then bacon. Bake in preheated 350-degree oven for 45 minutes or until done. Yield: 8 servings.

Mildred Arnett
Unity Grange
Pemberton, Ohio

ZUCCHINI-CHEESE BAKE

1 lg. zucchini
1 sm. can evaporated milk
2 tbsp. butter
2 tbsp. flour
1/2 c. grated American cheese
3 tbsp. slivered blanched almonds
2 tbsp. melted butter
1 c. soft bread crumbs

Slice zucchini or cut into cubes; cook in small amount of boiling, salted water for 5 minutes. Drain; reserve liquid. Place zucchini in greased casserole. Add enough evaporated milk to reserved liquid to make 1 cup liquid. Melt butter in small saucepan; stir in flour. Add milk gradually; cook, stirring constantly, until thickened. Add cheese; cook over low heat until melted. Add almonds; pour over zucchini. Mix melted butter with bread crumbs; sprinkle over zucchini mixture. Bake in preheated 350-degree oven for 30 to 35 minutes or until crumbs are golden brown; garnish with parsley. Cucumbers may be substituted for zucchini.

Mrs. Raymond J. Meehan
Northumberland Grange, No. 218
Lewisburg, Pennsylvania

★ ★

CHARLEY'S SWEET POTATOES
(Recipe over 60 years old)

    4 med. sweet potatoes
    1 c. brown sugar
    1/4 c. butter
    Vinegar

Boil sweet potatoes in water to cover until almost done. Let cool, then peel. Cut in slices about 1/2 inch thick. Arrange slices in oiled shallow pan. Cream butter and sugar together; spread over sweet potatoes. Drop several drops of vinegar on each slice from tip of spoon. Bake in 350-degree oven for 30 to 40 minutes. Yield: 6 servings.

Christina O'Neal
French Creek Grange, No. 396
Snohomish, Washington

CRUSTED SWEET POTATO CASSEROLE

    3 c. cooked mashed sweet potatoes
    1 c. sugar
    Butter
    2 eggs, beaten
    1 tsp. vanilla
    1 c. brown sugar
    1/3 c. flour
    1 c. chopped nuts

Combine sweet potatoes, sugar, 1/2 cup melted butter, eggs and vanilla; stir until well mixed. Turn into greased casserole. Combine brown sugar and flour; blend well. Stir in 1/3 cup melted butter and the nuts; pour evenly over sweet potato mixture. Bake in 375-degree oven for about 30 minutes or until brown. Yield: 8 servings.

Juanita Gentry, Home Ec. Chm.
Little Mountain Grange
Roaring River, North Carolina

YAM-PECAN CASSEROLE

    2 16 or 17-oz. cans Louisiana yams
    1/2 c. orange juice
    1 tbsp. lemon juice
    1/3 c. chopped pecans
    Marshmallows
    Whole pecans for garnish
    Parsley for garnish

Drain yams, reserving 1/2 cup yam syrup; slice yams. Combine yams, reserved yam syrup, orange juice and lemon juice in large mixer bowl; beat at low speed until yams are mashed. Increase speed to medium; beat until mixture is light and fluffy. Stir in chopped pecans. Spoon yam mixture into ungreased 6-cup souffle dish or casserole; cover with foil. Bake in preheated 375-degree oven for 20 minutes. Remove from oven; top with marshmallows. Return to oven; bake, uncovered, for 5 minutes longer or until marshmallows are slightly melted. Garnish with whole pecans and parsley. Yield: 4 servings.

Photograph for this recipe above.

GINGER SWEET POTATOES

    5 lb. sweet potatoes
    1/4 c. butter
    1/2 tsp. salt
    3/8 c. cream
    1/2 lb. gingersnaps, crushed

Wash, peel and slice sweet potatoes; cook in boiling salted water until tender. Drain, then mash. Add butter, salt and cream. Place potatoes in shallow baking pan. Sprinkle gingersnaps on top. Dot with additional butter. Bake in 350-degree oven until brown. Yield: 15 servings.

Mrs. Mary Jane Kent
Harveys Grange, No. 1444
West Finley, Pennsylvania

SWEET POTATO BALLS

    3 c. cooked mashed sweet potatoes
    1/4 c. butter
    3/4 c. brown sugar
    2 tbsp. milk
    1/4 tsp. salt
    1/2 tsp. grated lemon rind
    Miniature marshmallows
    1/2 c. crushed corn flakes

Combine sweet potatoes, butter, sugar, milk, salt and lemon rind; mix well. Combine 6 marshmallows and as much sweet potato mixture as desired; shape in balls. Roll balls in corn flakes. Place in buttered baking dish. Bake in 350-degree oven for 45 minutes. Each ball may be placed in a piece of aluminum foil shaped like a cup, then set in baking dish for ease in handling. Yield: 8 servings.

Mrs. Frederick A. Holbert
Indian Orchard Grange, No. 1020
Honesdale, Pennsylvania

★ ★

OUR FAVORITE YAM CASSEROLE

2 c. cooked and strained yams
1/3 c. sugar
2 eggs, beaten
1/2 tsp. salt
1/2 tsp. cinnamon
1/4 tsp. nutmeg
1 tbsp. lemon juice
1/4 c. rich milk or cream
3 tbsp. melted butter
1/4 c. raisins
1/4 c. chopped pecans
Large marshmallows

Combine all ingredients except raisins, nuts and marsh-mallows; beat until well mixed. Stir in raisins and nuts. Pour into 1-quart casserole. Bake in 350-degree oven for 30 minutes. Cover top with marshmallows; return to oven. Bake until marshmallows are brown. Yield: 6 servings.

Margaret H. Woodward
Orlando Park Grange, No. 172
Casselberry, Florida

BAKED STUFFED TOMATOES

2 c. soft bread crumbs
1 tsp. salt
1/8 tsp. pepper
2 tbsp. sugar
2 tbsp. melted butter
6 tomatoes
1 tbsp. butter

Mix bread crumbs with salt, pepper, 1 tablespoon sugar and melted butter. Cut thin slices from stem end of tomatoes; remove centers, leaving thick shells. Sprinkle centers with additional salt and pepper to taste and remaining 1 tablespoon sugar. Fill with stuffing; dot with butter. Place in baking pan. Bake in preheated 350-degree oven for 1 hour.

Anna Heikens
Eastside Grange, No. 109
Bigfork, Montana

MEDITERRANEAN TOMATOES

1/2 c. butter
8 lg. ripe tomatoes, peeled
2 tsp. brown sugar
6 tbsp. minced chives
1/2 c. minced celery
1/4 c. minced parsley
1 tsp. crushed oregano
Salt and pepper to taste

Melt butter in small skillet. Place whole tomatoes, stem side down in saucepan; add sugar. Cover; cook over low heat for about 10 minutes. Remove cover. Turn tomatoes carefully; add remaining ingredients. Spoon butter over tomatoes; cover. Cook over low heat for about 10 minutes. Place tomatoes on heated platter; spoon pan juices over tomatoes. Serve immediately. Yield: 8 servings.

From a Grange Friend

FRIED TOMATOES

1/2 c. cornmeal
1/2 c. flour
2 tbsp. sugar
1 tsp. salt
1/4 tsp. pepper
Firm ripe tomatoes, sliced

Mix all ingredients together except tomatoes. Coat both sides of tomato slices with cornmeal mixture. Fry in hot shortening until browned on both sides. Serve hot. Green or partially ripe tomatoes may be used. Store leftover cornmeal mixture in plastic container for future use.

Cora Wolfe
Brandywine Grange, No. 348
Brandywine, Maryland

TASTY TURNIPS
(Recipe 40 years old)

4 strips bacon
2 c. diced white turnips
1 c. diced potatoes
3/4 tsp. salt
1/8 tsp. pepper
1/2 tsp. sugar
1/4 c. cream

Fry bacon until crisp; chop and set aside. Combine vegetables, 1 tablespoon bacon drippings, seasonings and sugar; add water just to cover. Cook until tender, then drain. Add cream; mash. Add chopped bacon; mix well. Serve immediately. Yield: 6 servings.

Mrs. Walter Sager
Orchard Park Grange, No. 1335
Orchard Park, New York

VEGETABLES EN CASSEROLE
(Recipe over 50 years old)

1/2 tbsp. corn syrup
2 tbsp. vegetable oil
1 c. diced onion
1 c. diced celery
1 c. diced string beans
2 c. thinly sliced potatoes
1/2 tsp. salt
Dash of pepper
1 tbsp. cornstarch
1 pt. canned tomatoes
1/2 c. fine dry bread crumbs
1/4 c. grated American cheese

Combine syrup and oil in frypan. Add onion; cook until yellowed. Add celery, string beans and potatoes. Stir in salt, pepper and cornstarch. Arrange the onion mixture in layer in baking dish; add tomatoes. Add enough water to barely cover vegetables. Combine crumbs and cheese; sprinkle over casserole. Place cover on casserole. Bake in 350-degree oven for 1 hour. Uncover, bake for 30 minutes longer.

Mrs. Trula Baird
Muncey Grange, No. 1204

Side Dishes

Side dishes are the "other foods" that go on the dinner plate with meats and vegetables. They include a number of delicious dishes from the simple baked potato with butter to the most enjoyable combinations of cheeses, spices, fruits, eggs and rice or pasta. Cornmeal mush, homemade noodles and dumplings served to feed the larger families of yesterday — and stretched the food supply while adding nourishment when meat and fresh vegetables were in short supply.

Macaroni and cheese, rice and gravy and baked or mashed potatoes have all been longtime favorite side dishes for American families. They are easy to prepare, filling and always good. But, how long has it been since you have cooked up a hearty pot of chicken and dumplings to surprise your hungry family? Hominey and grits, like potatoes, rice and noodles, are simple foods to which you can add a variety of ingredients to make them taste exactly as you wish.

Fruit is also important as a side dish, whether fresh, canned, cooked with the meal, or as a garnish. A baked ham decked with pineapple slices and cherries, baked chicken surrounded by golden peach slices or most any cut of pork accompanied by applesauce or apple slices all make appetite and eye-pleasing dishes. Cranberry sauces or spiced pears, peaches and crabapples, not only pretty at Christmas, all make delicious complements for all fowl and poultry dishes. For an elegant touch, serve frosted grapes or strawberries with the entree.

Side dishes can be simple or elegant, but because they are usually cereals, pastas or fruits (often with the addition of cheese and eggs), they are always nutritious. They may sometimes take a little extra time to prepare, but the difference in interest and taste appeal of a dinner is well worth the extra effort.

★ ★

BOILED POTPIE
(Recipe 100 years old)

1/4 tsp. salt
1 1/2 c. flour
2 tbsp. shortening
1/4 to 1/2 c. water
3 or 4 potatoes
4 c. beef stock

Combine salt and flour; cut in shortening until mixture resembles cornmeal. Mix in just enough water to hold ingredients together. Roll out as for pie dough on well-floured board or between 2 sheets of waxed paper. Cut into 2-inch squares; let stand for several minutes. Peel and quarter potatoes; heat stock. Cook potatoes in stock for about 5 minutes. Drop potpies into boiling stock, stirring to keep separated. Boil for 20 to 30 minutes, stirring occasionally to keep from sticking together. Add more water, if needed. Serve with sliced, boiled beef, if desired.

Mrs. J. Herbert Snyder, Past Delegate
Natl. Grange
Glade Valley Grange
Walkersville, Maryland

CHEESE CASSEROLE

10 slices stale bread, cut in 1/2-in. pieces
3/4 lb. sharp cheese, grated
1/4 lb. butter
2 c. milk
2 eggs, beaten
1/2 tsp. Worcestershire sauce
Salt and pepper to taste

Place layer of bread in buttered 8 x 12 x 2-inch baking dish. Add layer of cheese. Continue adding layers of bread and cheese, ending with cheese. Melt butter; add milk, eggs, Worcestershire sauce, salt and pepper. Pour over bread and cheese. Cover; let stand in refrigerator overnight. Let stand at room temperature for 2 hours. Place in pan of water. Bake in preheated 350-degree oven for 1 hour. Cut in squares; serve with desired sauce.

Mrs. Lloyd Fillmore
Plymouth Grange, No. 389
Plymouth, Michigan

HOMEMADE CHEESE

3 gal. clabbered milk
1/2 tsp. soda
1/2 c. butter, melted
1 1/2 c. sour cream
1 tbsp. salt
1 tsp. butter coloring

Scald milk; remove from heat. Let stand for 30 minutes. Place in cloth sack; let drip for several hours to remove all whey. Add soda and butter; let stand for 2 hours. Mix with 1 cup sour cream; cook in double boiler, stirring until smooth. Add remaining sour cream, salt and coloring. Place in well-buttered glass pan; let stand in cool place for at least 5 days.
This is a very old recipe given to me by mother in 1925.

Mrs. Lois Keyser
Millbrook Grange, No. 1864
Elmwood, Illinois

QUICHE LORRAINE

1 1/2 c. soda cracker crumbs
1/4 c. melted butter
1 1/2 c. milk
3 eggs
1 tsp. Worcestershire sauce
1/2 tsp. salt
1/2 lb. Swiss cheese, cubed
1/4 c. grated Parmesan cheese
1/2 lb. bacon
1/2 c. chopped onion

Mix crumbs and butter together; press into 10-inch pie plate. Bake in preheated 350-degree oven for 10 minutes. Remove from oven. Reduce oven temperature to 325 degrees. Combine milk, eggs, Worcestershire sauce, salt and cheeses; mix well. Cut up bacon; fry bacon and onion until brown. Drain; spread in baked crust. Pour in egg mixture. Bake for 45 to 55 minutes or until quiche is set in center. Let cool for 5 minutes; cut into pie-shaped wedges to serve.

Mrs. Ruth S. Duffield
Community Grange, No. 1994
New Alexandria, Pennsylvania

WELSH RAREBIT

1 lb. soft rich cheese, diced
1 8-oz. glass ale or milk
1 tsp. dry mustard
1/2 tsp. paprika or dash of cayenne pepper
1/2 c. cream or 1/4 c. butter

Place cheese in chafing dish; add ale gradually, stirring until cheese is melted. Add mustard, paprika and cream; heat thoroughly. Serve immediately over toast or crackers. May add dash of Worcestershire sauce if milk is used.
This recipe is from the 1897 Hood's Practical Cook's Book.

Mrs. Herma Jane Huseby
Lexington Grange, No. 94
Bonner Springs, Kansas

GRANDMOTHER'S CORNMEAL MUSH
(Recipe 100 years old)

5 c. water
2 tbsp. salt
2 c. cornmeal
1/2 c. flour

★ ★

Combine water and salt in heavy kettle; bring to a rolling boil. Add cornmeal slowly, beating constantly to prevent lumping. Mix flour and a small amount of water to make a smooth paste; stir flour slowly into cornmeal mixture. Simmer for at least 1 hour and 30 minutes, stirring frequently. Serve with pork, if desired. Pour leftover cornmeal mush into casserole to mold. Slice and fry in butter until browned and heated through; serve for breakfast.

Mrs. Edward F. Holter
Middletown Valley Grange, No. 331
Frederick, Maryland

OLD-FASHIONED CORNMEAL MUSH

8 c. cornmeal
4 c. cold water
2 tbsp. salt
4 qt. boiling water

Combine cornmeal and cold water; mix well. Add salt to boiling water; add cornmeal mixture gradually to keep water boiling, stirring constantly. Let boil for at least 2 hours, stirring frequently. Serve hot with milk, cream and sugar or butter and syrup. May be chilled and sliced for frying. Oiling mush on top prevents formation of a crust.
Cornmeal mush is sometimes called Hasty Pudding from the custom of making it as wanted and serving it after 15 minutes cooking. The cornmeal was not thoroughly cooked and therefore was said to disagree with many persons.

Trudy Rendon
San Dimas Grange, No. 658
Azusa, California

CORN BREAD STUFFING

1/2 c. (scant) butter
4 c. crumbled corn bread
4 c. soft bread crumbs
1/2 c. (scant) bacon fat
2/3 c. diced celery
2 med. onions, diced
1/2 c. chopped green pepper
1 1/3 tsp. salt
1/4 tsp. pepper
1 1/3 tsp. monosodium glutamate
2 tsp. poultry seasoning
2 eggs, beaten
1 c. water

Cut butter into small pieces. Combine butter, corn bread and bread crumbs. Melt bacon fat. Add celery and onions; cook for 5 minutes. Stir into crumb mixture. Add remaining ingredients, using just enough water to make a moist stuffing; mix well. Yield: Stuffing for one 8-pound turkey.

Gail Turcotte
Centennial Grange, No. 185
Barrington, New Hampshire

GRANDMOTHER'S DRESSING
(Recipe 100 years old)

1 loaf bread
Butter
Salt and pepper to taste
Nutmeg to taste
2 eggs
1 c. milk

Cut bread into small cubes. Fry 1 cup of bread cubes at a time in small amount of butter over low heat until lightly browned. Season bread cubes with salt, pepper and nutmeg. Beat eggs and milk until well blended; add to bread cubes. Toss until well coated. Stuff into fowl or place in baking dish to bake. Yield: 8 servings.

Mrs. Patricia Carncross
Wife of Michigan State Master

DANISH DUMPLING
(Recipe 120 years old)

1/2 c. milk
2 tbsp. butter
1/4 tsp. salt
1/2 c. flour
2 eggs
Vegetable or beef soup

Bring milk, butter and salt to a boil in saucepan. Stir in flour; mix well. Mixture will be very thick. Remove from heat; add eggs, one at a time, beating vigorously after each addition. Dip teaspoon into simmering soup so dough will not stick. Drop dough from teaspoon into soup; dumplings are done when they rise to top of soup.
This recipe was used by my great grandmother who was a native of Denmark.

Anne Johnson
Meridian Grange, No. 265
Kent, Washington

EGG DUMPLINGS

2 c. flour
3/4 tsp. salt
2 1/2 tsp. baking powder
2 eggs
2/3 c. cream
2 tbsp. melted shortening
4 to 6 c. beef or chicken broth
   or stock

Sift flour, salt and baking powder together. Beat eggs; add cream and shortening. Stir egg mixture into dry ingredients; mix well. Drop by spoonfuls into simmering broth. Cook, covered, for 10 minutes. Uncover; cook for 10 minutes longer.

Kathryn Karnes
Rainboro Grange, No. 2653
Greenfield, Ohio

★ ★

ONION DUMPLINGS
(Recipe about 300 years old)

4 or 5 med. onions, chopped
Butter
2 c. flour
2 tsp. baking powder
1/2 tsp. salt
2 eggs
Milk
1/2 c. cream

Saute onions in butter until browned and tender; set aside. Sift flour, baking powder and salt together; stir in eggs and enough milk to make a soft dough. Drop by spoonfuls into boiling salted water; cook until done. Combine sauteed onions and cream in saucepan; bring to a boil. Place dumplings in serving dish; pour onion sauce over dumplings.
This recipe has been in my family for 5 generations.

Marie Coe
Plains Grange, No. 101
Plains, Montana

QUICK DROP DUMPLINGS
(Recipe 50 to 60 years old)

2/3 c. flour
1/4 tsp. salt
1 tsp. baking powder
1 egg
3 tbsp. milk
Broth

Sift flour, salt and baking powder together. Beat egg until light. Add milk; beat well. Fold in dry ingredients quickly, stirring only until moistened. Drop by spoonfuls into rapidly boiling broth. Boil, covered, for 15 minutes. Do not lift cover. Serve immediately.

From a Grange Friend

PROSCIUTTO SOUFFLE
(Recipe 60 years old)

1/4 lb. prosciutto
4 eggs, separated
1/8 tsp. salt
1/8 tsp. white pepper
2 tbsp. grated Parmesan cheese
1/2 c. melted butter

Cut prosciutto into thin strips. Mix egg yolks, salt, pepper, cheese and prosciutto together lightly with wooden spoon. Fold in stiffly beaten egg whites and melted butter; pour into greased large casserole. Mixture must not fill more than 1/3 of the casserole. Bake in preheated 350-degree oven for 20 minutes. Serve immediately.

Mrs. Genevieve Granito
Fall River Grange, No. 392
Fall River, Massachusetts

BAKED EGGS WITH MASHED POTATOES

Hot mashed potatoes
Melted butter
Eggs

Fill buttered casserole or baking dish with mashed potatoes. Make depressions in potatoes large enough to hold an egg, using a tablespoon. Brush potatoes with melted butter. Break 1 egg carefully into each depression. Bake in preheated 375-degree oven until eggs are set and potatoes are lightly browned.

Mary T. Hironymous
American River Grange, No. 172
Sacramento, California

EGGS BENEDICT

1/2 English muffin
1 slice ham, sauteed lightly
1 egg, poached
1 1/2 tbsp. Hollandaise Sauce

Toast muffin lightly. Place ham on cut side of muffin; top with poached egg. Cover with Hollandaise Sauce. Yield: 1 serving.

HOLLANDAISE SAUCE

4 egg yolks
2 tbsp. lemon juice
1/2 lb. butter, melted
1/4 tsp. salt
White pepper to taste

Beat egg yolks in top of double boiler; stir in lemon juice. Cook over low heat, never allowing water in bottom pan to come to a boil. Add butter, a small amount at a time, stirring constantly with a wooden spoon. Add salt and pepper; cook slowly until thickened. Yield: 1 cup sauce.
This dish is said to have been created in the Vatican kitchen around 1760 for Pope Benedict XIII.

From a Grange Friend

CREAMED EGGS ON TOAST
(Recipe about 30 years old)

2 tbsp. (heaping) butter
Flour
2 c. milk
Salt and pepper to taste
6 hard-boiled eggs, chopped
Toast

Melt butter in saucepan; stir in enough flour to make a smooth paste. Add milk, a small amount at a time, stirring constantly; cook until smooth and thick. Season with salt and pepper. Stir in eggs; heat through. Serve over toast.

Clella Reitmyer
Jordan Grange, No. 758
Coolport, Pennsylvania

★ ★ ★ ★ ★★★

SALT PORK OMELET
(Recipe over 100 years old)

    6 1/4-in. thick slices salt pork
    6 eggs, separated
    1/2 c. milk
    1/4 c. flour
    1 tsp. baking powder
    Salt and pepper to taste

Cut pork slices into 1/2-inch squares; fry in cast-iron frypan over medium heat until lightly browned. Drain off all but 2 tablespoons fat. Spread out pork squares evenly in frypan; set aside. Beat egg whites until stiff. Beat yolks until creamy; add milk, flour, baking powder and seasonings, beating until smooth. Fold in egg whites. Heat frypan; pour egg mixture over pork squares. Cook over medium heat until eggs are set and bottom starts to brown. Bake in preheated 350-degree oven until cooked through. Cut into 6 wedges to serve. Bacon or canned sandwich meat may be substituted for salt pork slices, if desired.

Mildred Chalifoux
Hudson Grange, No. 11
Hudson, New Hampshire

SCALLOPED EGGS

    Bread crumbs
    12 hard-boiled eggs, sliced crosswise
    Butter
    Salt and pepper to taste
    1 c. cream or milk

Sprinkle a layer of bread crumbs in well-buttered large baking dish. Add layer of egg slices; dot with butter. Season with salt and pepper. Repeat layers until all eggs are used, ending with crumbs. Pour cream over top. Bake in preheated 350-degree oven until heated through and browned.

Georgia Schultz
Apple Valley Grange
Apple Valley, California

FRIED APPLES
(Recipe 100 years old)

    6 apples
    2 tbsp. butter
    2 tbsp. sugar
    2 tbsp. molasses
    1 tbsp. water

Cut apples into eighths; peel 1 strip of skin from each piece. Melt butter in frypan; add sugar, molasses and water. Mix well. Add apples; cover and cook until tender. Remove cover; cook until juice is boiled away and apples are brown. Good served with pork or sausage. Yield: 6-8 servings.

Mrs. Elsie M. Gould
Somersworth Grange, No. 264
Exeter, New Hampshire

DRIED APPLE SAUCE

    1 qt. dried apples
    1 lemon, sliced and seeded
    Sugar to taste

Combine apples with water to cover; let stand for 2 hours. Pour off water. Place apples in saucepan; cover with water. Boil slowly until almost done, adding hot water as needed. Add lemon and sugar; cook until done. Yield: 4 servings.

Gertrude A. Pratt
Nemasket Grange
Bridgewater, Massachusetts

SPICED APPLES

    4 apples
    2 c. sugar
    1 c. water
    1 1/2 c. vinegar
    Whole cloves to taste
    Stick cinnamon to taste

Peel, core and quarter apples. Combine sugar, water and vinegar. Tie cloves and cinnamon in a bag; add to sugar mixture. Cook, stirring, until sugar is dissolved. Add apples; cook until transparent but not broken. Chill before serving.

Mary T. Hironymous
American River Grange, No. 172
Sacramento, California

PINEAPPLE CASSEROLE

    6 slices white bread, diced
    1/2 c. butter
    2 tbsp. flour
    3/4 c. sugar
    1 No. 2 1/2 can crushed pineapple
    3 eggs, well beaten

Saute bread cubes in butter; set aside. Mix flour with sugar; add pineapple. Mix well. Stir in eggs. Pour into shallow 9-inch square pan or casserole; top with sauteed bread cubes. Bake in preheated 350-degree oven for 45 minutes.

Evalyn Leithe
Home Economist, Washington Wheat Commission
Spokane, Washington

STEAMED RHUBARB

    4 c. 1-in. pieces of unpeeled rhubarb
    1/2 to 3/4 c. sugar

Place rhubarb in top of double boiler over boiling water. Cover tightly; steam for 20 to 30 minutes or until almost tender. Do not stir at any time. Dissolve sugar in 1/2 cup hot water. Pour over rhubarb; steam for 2 minutes longer.

Dorothy McCray
Slocum Grange
Narragansett, Rhode Island

★ ★

SCALLOPED PINEAPPLE

4 c. bread cubes
1/2 c. butter, melted
1 1/2 c. sugar
3 eggs, beaten
1/2 c. evaporated milk
1 No. 2 can crushed pineapple

Place bread cubes in mixing bowl; pour butter over top. Toss until coated. Add sugar, eggs, milk and pineapple; mix thoroughly. Pour into well-greased 1 1/2-quart casserole. Bake in preheated 350-degree oven for 40 minutes to 1 hour or until firm and browned. Serve with baked ham or ham loaf.

Mrs. Charles B. Forney
Star Grange, No. 993
Nazareth, Pennsylvania

CURE FOR NEURITIS OR ARTHRITIS

1 1/2 lb. figs
1 box seeded raisins
1 1/2 oz. olive oil
1/2 oz. glycerine
1/2 oz. slippery elm
1 1/2 oz. powdered senna
1 oz. charcoal

Grind figs and raisins — then put the drug store ingredients in. Mix thoroughly with hands. Shape into balls the size of small walnuts. Take one morning and evening for a week, then one a day for 6 months. The balls are to be chewed. Keep in refrigerator.

Josie Davis
Lyndell Grange, No. 1179
Downingtown, Pennsylvania

HOMINY GRITS

2 c. grits
1/2 c. butter
1 lb. sharp cheese, diced
1 lb. Velveeta cheese, diced
1 med. onion, minced
3/4 c. milk
6 eggs, beaten

Cook grits according to package directions; stir in butter. Add remaining ingredients in order listed; spread in baking dish. Bake for about 40 minutes in preheated 350-degree oven. Cut into squares to serve, if desired.

Sylvia Bomer, Home Ec. Chm.
Hurricane Creek Grange
Joseph, Oregon

MACARONI AND CHEESE FOR SIXTEEN

1   1-lb. package elbow macaroni
6 tbsp. butter
6 tbsp. flour
6 c. milk
1 tsp. salt
1 lb. extra sharp cheese, grated

Cook macaroni according to package directions. Melt butter in large saucepan; blend in flour. Add milk slowly, stirring constantly, until mixture is smooth; cook for about 10 minutes or until sauce thickens. Add salt and 2/3 of the cheese. Combine sauce and cooked macaroni; pour into two 8 x 11 x 2-inch baking dishes. Sprinkle remaining cheese on top; dot with additional butter. Bake at 375 degrees for 15 to 20 minutes. Freezes well.
Recipe has been in our family for 3 generations.

Mrs. William W. Campbell, Lady Asst. Steward
Middletown Grange, No. 684
Langhorne, Pennsylvania

JIFFY MACARONI AND CHEESE
(Recipe 25 years old)

1/2 c. mayonnaise
1/4 tsp. salt
1/8 tsp. pepper
1 tsp. minced parsley
1/2 c. milk
1 c. grated American cheese
3 c. hot cooked macaroni
6 frankfurters, sliced

Combine mayonnaise, salt, pepper and parsley in top of double boiler; add milk gradually, stirring constantly until smooth. Add cheese, macaroni and four frankfurters; cook over boiling water for about 15 minutes. Place in casserole; garnish with remaining 2 frankfurters. Bake in preheated 400-degree oven until browned.

Edith Cooper
Liberty Grange, No. 152
Meridian, Idaho

SUPER MACARONI AND CHEESE

1 1/2 c. macaroni
2 c. milk, heated
6 oz. Cheddar cheese, grated
1/4 c. butter, melted
1 can mushrooms
1 sm. jar pimento, chopped
3 eggs, beaten slightly

Cook macaroni in salted water until tender; drain well. Combine all ingredients; mix carefully. Place in buttered casserole; place casserole in pan of water. Bake in preheated 350-degree oven for 50 minutes.

Winifred Clark
Quartz Hill Grange, No. 697
Lancaster, California

BAKED MACARONI AND CHEESE SPECIAL

Salt
3 qt. rapidly boiling water
2 c. elbow macaroni
1 c. grated Muenster cheese
1 c. grated Cheddar cheese
1 c. grated Swiss cheese
8 tbsp. butter
1 c. soft fresh fine bread crumbs
1/3 c. all-purpose flour
Dash of cayenne pepper
3 c. milk
1 lg. tomato, cut into wedges

Add 1 tablespoon salt to boiling water; add macaroni gradually so that water continues to boil. Cook, uncovered, stirring occasionally, until tender; drain in colander. Combine Muenster, Cheddar and Swiss cheeses; set aside. Melt 2 tablespoons butter in small saucepan; remove from heat. Stir in bread crumbs and 1/2 cup cheese mixture; set aside. Melt remaining 6 tablespoons butter in large saucepan; stir in flour, 3/4 teaspoon salt and cayenne pepper until smooth. Cook over medium heat, stirring constantly, until mixture is bubbly; reduce heat to low. Stir in milk gradually; cook, stirring constantly, until mixture thickens and begins to boil. Remove from heat. Add remaining cheese mixture; stir until cheeses are melted. Add macaroni; stir well to combine. Pour into an ungreased 3-quart casserole; sprinkle crumb mixture around edges. Cover with foil. Bake in preheated 375-degree oven for 25 minutes or until bubbly; remove from oven. Increase temperature to broil. Remove foil from

casserole; place tomato wedges over macaroni mixture. Place under broiler; broil until crumbs are lightly browned. Yield: 4-6 servings.

Photograph for this recipe opposite.

RING OF PLENTY
(Recipe 85 years old)

1 1/2 c. cooked macaroni
1 c. diced cheese
1 c. soft bread crumbs
1 tbsp. minced parsley
3 tbsp. minced pimento or red sweet pepper
3 tbsp. melted butter
1 tbsp. minced onion
1 c. scalded milk
1 egg, well beaten
1 tsp. salt
1/8 tsp. pepper

Cut macaroni in small pieces. Combine all ingredients in order listed; place in well-greased ring mold. Place mold in pan of hot water. Bake in preheated 375-degree oven for about 35 minutes or until firm. Unmold; serve hot. Can be filled with leftover creamed meat or fish. Grease outside of a jelly glass with shortening, then place glass upside down in center of deep baking dish, if a ring mold is not available.

Ruth Halladay
Suffield Grange, No. 27
Suffield, Connecticut

MANICOTTI

1 lb. ricotta
5 eggs
1/4 tsp. salt
1/4 tsp. cinnamon
1/4 c. grated cheese
1 tbsp. chopped parsley
1 c. flour
Spaghetti sauce
Grated cheese

Combine ricotta, 1 egg, salt, cinnamon, cheese and parsley; mix well. Refrigerate filling until ready to use. Beat remaining 4 eggs in small deep bowl, adding 1 cup water slowly. Add flour gradually, beating until smooth. Drop by spoonfuls onto medium-hot griddle; spread thin to form 4-inch circles. Cook until easy to turn but not brown; turn and cook other side. Fill center of each circle with row of filling; fold each side of circle over filling to form a roll. Place in greased baking dish; cover with spaghetti sauce. Sprinkle with grated cheese. Bake in preheated 300-degree oven for 20 to 30 minutes or until heated through.

Mrs. Mary Cottone
Delaware Valley Grange, No. 1565
Grand Gorge, New York

★★★★★★★★★★★★★★★★★★★★★★★★★★★★★★★★★★★★★★★

SPANISH MACARONI CASSEROLE

1/2 lb. macaroni
1/4 lb. cheese, diced or grated
1/2 c. diced celery
2 med. onions, chopped
1 can whole tomatoes, cut up
2 tbsp. chopped green pepper
3 tbsp. melted butter
Salt and pepper to taste
2 c. medium white sauce

Cook macaroni in boiling salted water until tender; drain well. Combine macaroni, cheese, celery, onions, tomatoes, green pepper and butter; mix well. Pour into buttered 2-quart casserole; season with salt and pepper. Pour white sauce over top. Bake in preheated 350-degree oven for 1 hour and 15 minutes or until done. Yield: 6-8 servings.

Mrs. Charles Wertman
Jackson Grange, No. 2650
West Salem, Ohio

EGG NOODLES WITH POPPY SEED

1 lb. egg noodles
1/2 c. milk
1/2 c. poppy seed
2 tbsp. sugar
3 tbsp. honey
3 tbsp. butter
1/2 c. raisins (opt.)

Cook noodles in salted water until tender; drain. Combine milk, poppy seed, sugar, honey, butter and raisins in saucepan; cook over low heat for 3 minutes. Pour poppy seed mixture over noodles; toss carefully. Serve immediately.

Mrs. Margaret Colson
Jefferson Grange, No. 2019
Sharpsville, Pennsylvania

HOMEMADE GERMAN NOODLES
(Recipe about 100 years old)

4 lg. eggs
3 c. sifted flour

Mix eggs and flour together to make a very stiff dough. Knead with hands until dough starts to blister and bubbles form. Divide dough into 5 parts; roll out each part until paper thin on lightly floured board. Place on towel to dry until layers will not stick together, turning several times. Roll each layer into tight roll; slice very thin. Loosen noodles; spread out on towel to dry before using or storing.

Betty Goeringer
Madera Grange, No. 783
Madera, California

OLD-FASHIONED HOMEMADE NOODLES
(Recipe 4 generations old)

4 egg yolks
1 whole egg
4 tbsp. water

1 tsp. salt
2 1/4 c. unbleached flour

Mix egg yolks and egg together. Add water and salt; beat until well blended. Mix in flour with spoon until dough becomes very stiff, then knead dough with the heels of the hands. Divide dough into 2 equal parts; roll out each part on floured board until paper thin. Place on table to partially dry. Roll up tight; cut into thin strips. Shake out strips; let dry thoroughly before storing. Yield: 7 cups dry noodles.

Oneita McMurchy
Rickreall Grange, No. 671
Dallas, Oregon

PILAF EXTRAORDINAIRE

1/2 c. butter
2 c. long grain rice
1 tsp. salt
1/4 tsp. saffron
Freshly ground pepper to taste
4 c. consomme
2 med. onions
1 c. dark seedless raisins

Melt 1/4 cup butter in heavy skillet. Add rice; cook over moderately low heat, stirring occasionally, until golden brown. Add seasonings and consomme; cover. Bake in preheated 325-degree oven for 1 hour and 30 minutes. Peel onions; slice paper thin. Cook in remaining 1/4 cup butter over very low heat until soft and yellow. Stir raisins into rice; let stand for 5 minutes before serving. Mound rice mixture on serving platter; garnish with onion rings. Yield: 6 servings.

Photograph for this recipe below.

★ ★

EASY HOMEMADE NOODLES

1 c. flour
1 tsp. salt
3 eggs, beaten
1 to 1 1/2 qt. meat stock

Beat flour, salt and eggs together to make a smooth mixture. Press through a finely tipped cookie press or cake decorator tube into boiling stock to form long narrow noodles. Let cook for at least 10 minutes or until done. Yield: 3 cups noodles.

Evelyn Doerge
Black Diamond Grange, No. 1128
Port Angeles, Washington

TILLAMOOK LOAF

1 c. rice, cooked
1/4 c. Wesson oil
1 egg
Salt and pepper to taste
1 c. grated Tillamook cheese
1/2 c. chopped parsley
3 green onions, chopped

Combine all ingredients; mix well. Place in well-oiled ring mold or loaf pan. Let stand for 30 minutes. Bake in preheated 325-degree oven for 35 minutes.

CREAM SAUCE

1 tbsp. flour
1 1/2 c. milk
Tuna, crab or shrimp to taste

Combine flour and milk in saucepan; add tuna. Simmer for 3 minutes. Serve over Tillamook Loaf.

Bertha Tomko
Loomis Grange, No. 638
Loomis, California

RICE A LA KEITH

4 unsalted chicken bouillon cubes
2 tsp. curry powder
1 tbsp. parsley flakes
2 tbsp. Worcestershire sauce
2 tbsp. minced onion
3 c. water
1 c. rice
1 tbsp. safflower oil or butter

Combine all ingredients except rice and oil in saucepan; bring to a boil. Add rice and oil; cover. Reduce heat; simmer for about 25 to 30 minutes or until rice is done. Serve with chicken sauce and grated Parmesan cheese.

Florence M. Keith
Fairfax Grange, No. 570
Bakersfield, California

RICE MILANESE
(Recipe over 80 years old)

1 sm. onion, chopped
Butter
1 chicken gizzard, chopped
2 c. rice
1 glass Marsala or red wine
6 to 8 c. chicken broth
2 tsp. salt
Dash of pepper
1/4 tsp. saffron
2 c. grated Parmesan cheese

Saute onion in 1/2 cup butter until browned. Add chicken gizzard and uncooked rice; cook over low heat until browned, stirring constantly. Stir in Marsala; cook for 1 minute. Add chicken broth, a small amount at a time, stirring constantly; cook over low heat for 15 minutes. Add salt, pepper and saffron; cook for 15 minutes longer or until done, stirring frequently. Blend in Parmesan cheese and additional butter just before serving. Yield: 6-8 servings.

Mrs. Kenneth Fairbanks
Lompoc Grange, No. 646
Lompoc, California

GREEN RICE

4 tbsp. butter
4 or 5 green onions with tops,
    finely chopped
1/2 green pepper, finely chopped
1/3 c. minced parsley
3 c. chicken broth
1 1/2 c. long grain rice
1/4 tsp. salt
1/8 tsp. pepper

Heat butter in saucepan; add onions and green pepper. Saute slowly for 5 to 10 minutes or until tender. Stir in remaining ingredients; bring to a boil. Reduce heat; check seasonings. Cover; simmer for about 20 minutes or until rice is done. Rice may be served immediately or may be turned into casserole with tight-fitting cover and placed in warm oven until serving time. Yield: 6 servings.

From a Grange Friend

YORKSHIRE PUDDING

2 lg. eggs
1 c. milk
1 c. flour
Salt to taste
6 tbsp. butter or pan drippings

Beat eggs slightly. Add 1/3 cup milk, flour and salt; beat gently until smooth. Add remaining 2/3 cup milk gradually; beat until smooth. Heat butter in baking pan; pour in batter. Bake in preheated 275-degree oven for 40 minutes. Serve immediately. May bake with meat loaf, if desired. Move meat loaf to side of large baking pan; add hot butter to meat loaf drippings, if needed. Pour batter next to meat loaf to bake.

Gladys Arnold, Flora
Lucerne Grange, No. 167
West Palm Beach, Florida

Breads

Remember those cold, winter mornings when you woke up to the wonderful aroma of Grandma's homemade bread baking in the oven? It was so hard to wait for that first warm slice, covered with soft, creamy butter, that almost melted in your mouth. While baking day was one of the busiest times of the week, it was also one of the most rewarding, a time when grandma could stand back and be proud of the results of her labors.

Grandma wasn't the only proud one. Farmers spent hours plowing, planting and cultivating to produce the beautiful, golden wheat fields that stretched for miles. Overflowing harvests often resulted, keeping the mills busy grinding grain. Milling was an honorable profession and, even today, there are still a few quaint mills remaining to remind us of days gone by.

Although times have changed and many kinds of breads are available commercially, families still come running when the smell of freshly baked bread fills the air. It's true — home baking is no longer a necessity. Instead, it's a pleasure that can be enjoyed by people of all ages. Getting away from the fast-paced world in which we live today is often difficult, but it can be done right in your own kitchen. Whether you live in the bustling city or the quiet countryside, baking a loaf of bread can be one of the most entertaining things you've experienced in months.

Loaf breads are just one of the types of breads you can make. Doughnuts, crullers and rich apple strudel, all sweet breads, and quick breads such as mouthwatering biscuits, hearty bran muffins and popovers will satisfy the need to create and yield the unmistakable flavor and aroma of home baked goodness.

By bringing back the flavor and goodness of the breads of the past, we can add fresh enjoyment to almost every meal we serve.

★ ★

MOTHER'S BREAD

12 c. flour
1/3 cake household yeast or
   1 cake commercial yeast
3 1/2 c. warm water
2 tbsp. (rounded) sugar
1 tbsp. (heaping) salt
1 tbsp. lard or shortening

Place flour in large pan; make nest in center. Dissolve yeast in 1/2 cup warm water. Mix sugar, salt and shortening with remaining warm water; pour into center of flour. Add yeast; mix with spoon or use hands to squeeze flour and liquid until much of the flour has been worked in. Continue mixing by drawing dough toward center and punching the flour into dough; knead for 8 to 10 minutes or until all flour is kneaded into dough and the dough is elastic. Amount of flour may vary slightly with different brands. Remove dough from pan. Grease pan; replace dough, turning so top is greased. Cover with cloth; set into warm place away from drafts. Let rise until doubled in bulk, then punch down. Cover; let rise until doubled in bulk. Form into 3 loaves, kneading and shaping in greased hands to remove any large bubbles. Place in greased loaf pans; let rise until doubled in bulk. Bake in preheated 350 to 375-degree oven for 45 minutes to 1 hour or until bread tests done. Grease tops of loaves; cover. Let cool.

Mrs. John W. Scott
Wife of National Master
Mechanicsburg, Pennsylvania

EASY-TO-MAKE BREAD

Vegetable shortening
6 to 7 c. flour
1/4 c. sugar
1 tbsp. salt
2 pkg. dry yeast
2 1/4 c. milk
1/4 c. cooking oil
1 egg

Grease two 9 x 5 or 8 x 4-inch loaf pans generously with shortening. Combine 2 cups flour, sugar, salt and yeast in large mixing bowl. Pour milk and oil into saucepan; heat until very warm. Add to flour mixture. Add egg; beat with mixer at low speed for 30 seconds. Beat at medium speed for 3 minutes; stir in enough remaining flour to make soft dough. Knead on floured surface for about 1 minute or until smooth and elastic. Place in greased bowl; turn to grease all sides. Cover dough; let rise in warm place for 45 to 60 minutes or until doubled in bulk. Punch down; shape into 2 loaves. Place in greased loaf pans. Cover; let rise in warm place for 30 to 45 minutes or until doubled in bulk. Bake in preheated 350-degree oven for 40 to 45 minutes or until loaf sounds hollow when lightly

tapped. Remove from pans immediately; cool on rack. Brush top of loaves with melted butter, if desired.

Betty Huckins
New Hampton Grange, No. 123
New Hampton, New Hampshire

BLUE RIBBON WHITE BREAD
(Recipe over 75 years old)

2 pkg. dry yeast
4 c. warm water
1/2 c. sugar
2 tbsp. (or less) salt
1/3 c. lard
11 to 12 c. all-purpose flour

Soak yeast in 1/2 cup warm water in large bowl for 5 minutes; stir until dissolved. Add sugar, salt, lard, 3 1/2 cups warm water and 4 cups flour; beat with electric mixer for 2 minutes or until well blended. Mix in enough remaining flour with large spoon until dough is easy to handle, stirring until blended. Knead on floured surface until smooth and satiny. Place in bowl; let rise until doubled in bulk. Punch down; divide into 4 equal parts. Roll each part out on floured surface to 9 x 7 x 1-inch rectangle. Roll as for jelly roll; tuck in ends. Place in greased 9 x 5 x 3-inch bread pans. Let rise till doubled in bulk. Place in preheated 425-degree oven; reduce temperature to 375 degrees. Bake for 45 minutes to 1 hour or until well browned; cool on rack. Loaves may be frozen.
This bread won blue ribbons frequently at County Fair. Several years ago this loaf won first place in this State Grange contest.

Mrs. J. Merle Rife
Batavia Grange, No. 2450
Amelia, Ohio

ANADAMA BREAD

1/2 c. water-ground cornmeal
2 c. boiling water
1/4 c. butter
1/2 c. molasses
3 tsp. salt
2 pkg. or cakes yeast
1/2 c. lukewarm water
7 to 8 c. sifted flour
Melted butter

Add cornmeal to boiling water gradually, stirring constantly. Add butter, molasses and salt; mix well. Cool to lukewarm. Dissolve yeast in lukewarm water; stir into cornmeal mixture. Add enough flour to make stiff dough. Place on floured board; knead well. Place in buttered bowl; turn to grease top. Cover with waxed paper, then towel. Let rise in warm place until doubled in bulk. Place on floured board; knead well, adding more flour, if necessary. Shape into 3 medium loaves; place in greased loaf pans. Cover; let rise until doubled in bulk. Bake in preheated 425-degree oven

★ ★

for 10 minutes. Reduce temperature to 350 degrees; bake for about 30 minutes. Remove from oven; brush with melted butter.

Mrs. Lewis W. Pyle
Chester Valley Grange, No. 1496
Chester Springs, Pennsylvania

DELICIOUS POP-UP BREAD

    3 to 3 1/4 c. flour
    1 pkg. dry yeast
    1/2 c. milk
    1/2 c. water
    1/2 c. oil
    1/4 c. sugar
    1 tsp. salt
    2 eggs
    1 c. grated Cheddar cheese (opt.)

Mix 1 1/2 cups flour and yeast in large bowl. Mix milk, water, oil, sugar and salt in saucepan; place over low heat until lukewarm, stirring occasionally. Add to yeast mixture; beat with electric mixer at medium speed for 2 minutes or 300 strokes by hand. Blend in eggs and cheese; stir in enough remaining flour to make stiff dough. Beat until smooth and elastic. Divide into 2 parts; place in 2 well-greased 1-pound coffee cans. Cover with plastic lids; let rise for about 1 hour or until dough is 1/4 to 1/2 inch below lids. Remove lids. Bake in preheated 375-degree oven for 30 to 35 minutes or until done. Cool for 15 minutes; remove from cans.

Velva Jackson
Scholls Grange, No. 338
Hillsboro, Oregon

BRAID BREAD

    4 to 4 1/2 c. flour
    2 pkg. dry yeast
    2 c. warm water
    1/4 c. melted butter or oil
    2 tbsp. sugar
    1 tbsp. salt

Combine 2 cups flour and yeast in large mixing bowl; add warm water, butter, sugar and salt. Beat with electric mixer at low speed for 30 seconds, scraping side of bowl constantly. Beat for 3 minutes at high speed. Stir in enough remaining flour to make easily handled dough; knead on lightly floured board for 10 minutes. Shape into ball; place in greased bowl, turning once to grease surface. Cover; let rise for 1 hour and 30 minutes. Punch down; divide in half. Divide each half into thirds; shape into 6 balls. Cover for 10 minutes. Roll each ball into 16-inch rope; place 3 ropes 1 inch apart on greased baking sheet. Braid loosely; pinch ends and tuck under. Repeat with remaining 3 ropes. Cover; let rise in warm place for 40 minutes. Bake in preheated 375-degree oven for 30 minutes or until lightly browned. Brush top with additional butter while warm.

This recipe won a blue ribbon at Washington State Baking Contest.

Mrs. David G. Miles
Sequim Prairie Grange
Sequim, Washington

COLONIAL BREAD

    1 c. cornmeal
    2/3 c. (packed) dark brown sugar
    2 tbsp. salt
    4 c. boiling water
    1/2 c. corn oil
    4 pkg. yeast
    1 c. warm water
    1 c. rye flour
    1 1/2 c. whole wheat flour
    9 c. (about) flour

Combine cornmeal, sugar, salt, boiling water and oil in large bowl; let stand until lukewarm. Dissolve yeast in warm water; let stand for 10 minutes. Add yeast to cornmeal mixture; add rye flour and whole wheat flour. Beat with electric beater until mixed. Stir in flour. Turn out onto board; knead for about 10 minutes. Let rise for about 1 hour and 30 minutes. Punch down; divide into 4 parts. Let rest for 10 minutes. Shape into loaves; place in greased 8 1/2 x 4 1/2 x 3-inch pans. Let rise until doubled in bulk. Bake in preheated 350-degree oven for 30 minutes.

Mrs. Howard Preslan
New London Grange, No. 2401

ESTELLE'S WHITE YEAST BREAD
(Recipe over 100 years old)

    3 c. lukewarm water
    1/2 c. sugar
    2 pkg. yeast
    14 c. sifted all-purpose flour
    2 c. milk
    2 tbsp. salt
    6 tbsp. shortening

Pour water into large bowl. Add 1/4 cup sugar; stir until dissolved. Sprinkle yeast over top; let stand for about 5 minutes. Stir until dissolved. Add 4 cups flour; beat until smooth. Cover with cloth; let rise in warm place for about 1 hour. Scald milk in saucepan. Add salt, remaining 1/4 cup sugar and shortening; mix well. Cool to lukewarm. Stir yeast mixture to break bubbles; add milk mixture. Add remaining 10 cups flour to make workable dough; mix well. Turn onto floured board; knead. Place in greased bowl; let rise until doubled in bulk. Punch down; divide into 4 equal portions. Place in greased 7 1/2 x 3 1/2 x 2 1/2-inch loaf pans; let rise until doubled in bulk. Bake in preheated 400-degree oven for 50 minutes.

Mrs. William B. Worthington, Sr.
Wacohu Grange, No. 415
Hagerstown, Maryland

★ ★

FLORENCE'S PRIZEWINNING RYE BREAD

2 1/2 c. unsifted rye flour
2 1/2 c. unsifted flour
1 tbsp. sugar
1 tbsp. salt
1 tbsp. caraway seed (opt.)
1 pkg. dry yeast
1 c. milk
1 tbsp. honey
1 tbsp. butter
1/4 c. cornmeal
1 egg white

Combine flours in large bowl. Mix 1 2/3 cups flour mixture, sugar, salt, caraway seed and yeast in bowl. Combine milk, 3/4 cup water, honey and butter in saucepan; place over low heat until lukewarm. Add to yeast mixture; beat with electric mixer at medium speed for 2 minutes, scraping bowl occasionally. Add 1 cup flour mixture or enough to make thick batter; beat at high speed for 2 minutes. Stir in enough flour mixture to make soft dough. Add more flour to make desired dough, if necessary. Turn out onto lightly floured board; knead for 8 to 10 minutes or until smooth and elastic. Place in greased bowl, turning to grease top; cover. Let rise in warm place until doubled in bulk. Punch down; turn out onto floured board. Divide in half; form into smooth balls. Cover; let rest for 10 minutes. Roll lightly on board to form loaves with tapered ends. Sprinkle baking sheet with cornmeal; place loaves on sheet. Combine egg white and 2 tablespoons water; brush on loaves. Let rise, uncovered, in warm place for 35 minutes. Bake in preheated 400-degree oven for 25 minutes or until done. Remove from baking sheet; cool on wire racks. This recipe won 1st place in yeast breads at 1975 Washington State Grange.

Florence Seiffert
Cape Horn Grange, No. 70
North Bonneville, Washington

NORWEGIAN RYE BREAD
(Recipe 100 years old)

2 pkg. dry yeast
2 c. warm milk
1 c. (packed) brown sugar
1 c. dark unsulphured molasses
2 tbsp. salt
5 c. rye flour
1/2 c. soft butter
Flour
Butter

Dissolve yeast in 1/4 cup warm water. Mix milk, 3 cups warm water, sugar, molasses, salt, rye flour, yeast and soft butter in bowl. Stir in about 2 cups flour; beat vigorously. Cover; let rise in warm place until bubbly. Stir in enough flour to make stiff dough; place

on floured surface. Knead until smooth and elastic. Return to well-buttered bowl; butter top of dough. Cover; let rise until doubled in bulk. Punch down; let rise until doubled in bulk. Shape into 5 loaves; place on greased cookie sheet. Let rise until very light. Bake in preheated 350-degree oven for 45 minutes. Two teaspoons caraway seed or 3 tablespoons chopped candied orange peel may be added to dough, if desired.

Olga M. Day
Randle Grange, No. 865
Randle, Washington

BOHEMIAN BREAD

5 to 5 1/2 c. Bohemian-style rye and wheat flour
2 pkg. active dry yeast
2 c. milk
1/4 c. butter
3 tbsp. sugar
4 tsp. salt
1/3 c. dark molasses

Combine 2 cups flour and yeast in large mixing bowl. Combine milk, butter, sugar and salt in 1-quart saucepan; heat until warm. Stir in molasses. Add to flour mixture. Beat for 30 seconds at low speed, scraping bowl constantly, then for 3 more minutes at high speed. Add 1 cup flour and beat for 1 minute longer. Stir in enough remaining flour to make a soft dough. Turn onto lightly floured surface; knead for 5 to 10 minutes or until smooth and satiny. Place in buttered bowl, turning once to butter top. Cover bowl. Let rise on a rack over hot water for about 1 hour or until doubled in bulk. Punch down; divide in half. Roll each half into 9 x 12-inch rectangle on lightly floured surface. Roll dough tightly beginning with 9-inch edge; seal final seam well with thumbs. Seal ends of loaf and fold under loaf. Place, seam side down, in 2 buttered 9 x 5 x 3-inch pans. Cover; allow to stand in warm place for about 1 hour or until doubled in bulk. Bake in preheated 375-degree oven for 30 to 35 minutes or until loaf sounds hollow when tapped. Turn out of pans onto wire rack to cool. Yield: 2 loaves.

Photograph for this recipe on back cover.

OLD-ENGLISH WHOLE WHEAT BREAD

2 c. milk
1 tbsp. butter
2 tsp. salt
1/2 c. sugar
1 pkg. yeast
1/2 c. lukewarm potato water
2 c. sifted flour
2 c. unsifted whole wheat flour
Lard

Scald milk in saucepan; stir in butter, salt and sugar. Cool to lukewarm; pour into bowl. Dissolve yeast in

★ ★

potato water; stir into milk mixture. Add flour; beat until very smooth. Let rise until bubbly. Add whole wheat flour, small amount at a time, beating vigorously after each addition. Place in 2 well-greased small bread pans; grease tops with lard. Let rise until doubled in bulk. Bake in preheated 375-degree oven for 40 minutes.

Mrs. Robert C. Earl, Sr.
Fitchville Grange, No. 2356
North Fairfield, Ohio

PIZZA-STYLE FRENCH BREAD

1 pkg. dry yeast
1 1/2 c. warm water
1   8-oz. can spaghetti sauce
1 tbsp. sugar
1 tbsp. grated Parmesan cheese
1 1/2 tsp. garlic salt
1/2 tsp. sweet basil
1/2 tsp. leaf oregano
3 tbsp. olive or cooking oil
6 3/4 to 7 c. all-purpose flour

Dissolve yeast in warm water in large mixing bowl. Stir in remaining ingredients, adding enough flour gradually to form stiff dough. Knead on floured board for 3 to 5 minutes or until smooth. Place in greased bowl; cover. Let rise in warm place for about 1 hour or until doubled in bulk. Divide dough into 3 parts; shape each part into 12-inch long loaf. Place on greased cookie sheets; cover. Let rise in warm place for about 45 minutes or until doubled in bulk. Bake in preheated 375-degree oven for 30 to 35 minutes or until golden brown. Remove from cookie sheet; cool. Brush crust with melted butter, if desired.

Mrs. Paul E. Syphrit
Brady Grange, No. 1218
Punxsutawney, Pennsylvania

GRANDMOTHER'S FRENCH BREAD
(Recipe 75 years old)

2/3 c. sugar
2 tbsp. salt
2/3 c. lard
1 cake yeast
12 c. (about) flour

Place sugar, salt and lard in large bowl. Add 4 cups warm water; stir until sugar and lard are melted. Combine yeast and 1/4 cup warm water in measuring cup. Sprinkle with dash of additional sugar; let stand for 5 to 10 minutes. Add 1/3 of the flour to sugar mixture; stir well. Add yeast mixture; mix well. Add remaining flour, small amount at a time, stirring well after each addition. Dough will be sticky. Let dough rise in bowl until doubled in bulk. Punch down; stir in enough flour to make dough easy to handle. Turn onto floured board; knead well. Shape into 5 or 6 loaves; place on baking sheets. Let rise until doubled in bulk.

Bake in preheated 325-degree oven for about 45 minutes or until done.

Mrs. Pauline Applin
Pleasant Valley Grange, No. 136
Bethel, Maine

CRUSTY FRENCH BREAD

1 pkg. dry yeast
1 1/2 c. warm water
1 tbsp. sugar
1 1/2 tbsp. salt
1 tbsp. soft shortening
4 c. flour
Cornmeal

Sprinkle yeast into 1/2 cup warm water; stir until dissolved. Place sugar, salt and shortening in large bowl. Add remaining 1 cup warm water; stir until dissolved. Add yeast mixture; mix well. Add flour; stir until smooth. Let stand for 1 hour, stirring 5 times. Turn out onto floured board; cut in half. Shape into balls; let rest for 10 minutes. Roll each half out into 10 x 8-inch rectangle; roll as for jelly roll. Place on cookie sheet sprinkled with cornmeal; slash 6 times diagonally. Let rise for 1 hour and 30 minutes. Bake in preheated 400-degree oven for 30 to 35 minutes or until done.

Lila Gannett
Hollis Grange, No. 132

DILLY BREAD

1 pkg. dry yeast
1/4 c. lukewarm water
1 c. creamed cottage cheese
2 tbsp. sugar
1 tbsp. instant minced onion
1 tsp. butter
2 tsp. dillseed
1 tsp. salt
1/4 tsp. soda
1 egg
2 1/4 to 2 1/2 c. flour
Garlic salt

Sprinkle yeast over water; let stand. Heat cottage cheese to lukewarm; place in mixing bowl. Stir in sugar, onion, butter, dillseed, salt, soda, egg and yeast mixture. Stir in enough flour to make stiff dough; knead on floured surface for 10 to 15 minutes. Place in bowl; cover. Let rise until doubled in bulk; form into loaf. Place in well-greased loaf pan; let rise until doubled in bulk. Bake in 350-degree oven for 40 to 45 minutes or until done. Brush with additional butter; sprinkle with garlic salt. May be made into 2 small loaves; baking time will be shorter.

Mrs. Grace Riedel
Eden Grange, No. 2550
Tiffin, Ohio

★ ★

SOURDOUGH BREAD

1 1/2 c. warm water
1 pkg. or cake yeast
1 c. Sourdough Starter
6 c. unsifted all-purpose flour
2 tsp. salt
2 tsp. sugar
1/2 tsp. soda

Pour water into large mixing bowl. Sprinkle yeast over water; stir until dissolved. Add Sourdough Starter, 4 cups flour, salt and sugar; stir vigorously for 3 minutes. Place in large, greased bowl; cover with towel. Let rise in warm place for about 2 hours or until doubled in bulk. Mix soda with 1 cup flour; stir into dough. Turn out onto floured board; knead in remaining 1 cup flour. More flour may be added, if necessary. Knead until dough is smooth and not sticky. Shape it into large, round loaf or 2 oblong loaves; place on lightly greased cookie sheet. Cover; let rise in warm place until nearly doubled in bulk. Brush surface with water; score or slash top diagonally with sharp knife. Place shallow pan of hot water in bottom of oven. Bake bread in preheated 400-degree oven for 45 to 50 minutes or until done.

SOURDOUGH STARTER

1 c. flour
1 c. water
1 tbsp. sugar

Mix flour, water and sugar in bowl; cover. Let stand in warm place for 2 to 3 days or until fermented. Starter may also be purchased.

Sourdough may be the oldest of all breads, dating as far back as 4,000 B.C. According to one theory, it was unknown in America until Columbus landed with a Sourdough Starter in the hold of his ship. Sourdough Starter is simply a selfperpetuating yeast mixture made by combining flour, sugar and water. The bread became identified with America because of the Alaskan sourdoughs made by prospectors who carried Sourdough Starter pots strapped to their packs. They could make a batch of bread whenever they felt the need without walking fifty miles to the nearest town for a bit of yeast.

Evangeline Stoskopf
Dover Grange, No. 1939
Sharon Springs, Kansas

SALLY LUNN

1 c. milk
1/2 c. shortening
4 c. flour
1/3 c. sugar
2 tsp. salt
2 pkg. dry yeast
3 eggs

Grease 10-inch tube or bundt pan. Mix milk, shortening and 1/4 cup water in saucepan; heat until lukewarm. Blend 1 1/3 cups flour, sugar, salt and yeast in large mixing bowl; blend in milk mixture. Beat well for about 2 minutes. Add 2/3 cup remaining flour gradually. Add eggs; beat for 2 minutes. Add remaining flour; mix well. Batter will be thick, but not stiff. Cover; let rise in warm place for about 1 hour and 15 minutes. Beat down; place in greased pan. Cover; let rise for about 30 minutes. Bake in preheated 350-degree oven for 40 to 50 minutes. Turn out of pan onto plate to cool.

Ardys Holmes, Musician
Buffalo Valley Grange
Strykersville, New York

OATMEAL BATTER BREAD

1 c. rolled oats
2 c. scalded milk
1 pkg. dry yeast
1/2 c. warm water
1/2 c. molasses
2 tsp. (or less) salt
1 tbsp. melted butter
4 1/2 c. flour

Place oats in mixing bowl. Pour milk over oats; let stand until lukewarm. Dissolve yeast in warm water; add to oats mixture. Add molasses, salt and butter; mix well. Add half the flour; beat well. Add remaining flour; mix thoroughly. Cover; let rise until doubled in bulk. Place in 2 greased 9 x 5 x 2-inch loaf pans; let rise until doubled in bulk. Bake in preheated 425-degree oven for 15 minutes. Reduce temperature to 350 degrees; bake for 35 minutes or until done. Remove from pans at once; cool on wire rack, if possible.

Mrs. Marian Agard
Ulysses Grange, No. 419
Trumansburg, New York

OLD-FASHIONED OATMEAL BREAD
(Recipe 100 years old)

1 c. rolled oats
3 1/2 tbsp. shortening
1 tbsp. salt
1/3 c. cold molasses
2 yeast cakes
Flour

Mix 2 cups boiling water with first three ingredients in bowl; cool to lukewarm. Mix 1/4 cup boiling water and molasses in bowl; cool to lukewarm. Dissolve yeast in molasses mixture. Add oats mixture and enough flour to make soft dough; mix well. Let rise until doubled in bulk. Stir in enough flour to make dough just stiff enough to handle. Shape into loaves; place in 2 greased loaf pans. Bake in preheated 400-degree oven for 10 minutes. Reduce oven temperature to 325 degrees; bake for 40 minutes longer. Milk may be substituted for water.

Barbara Annear
Montague Grange, No. 141
Montague, Massachusetts

★ ★

EASY OATMEAL BREAD

1 1/4 pkg. yeast
1/2 c. warm water
2 c. boiling water
1 c. quick-cooking rolled oats
1/2 c. molasses
1 tbsp. butter
2 tsp. salt
6 c. flour

Dissolve yeast in warm water. Mix boiling water and oats in bowl; cool to lukewarm. Add molasses, butter, salt and yeast; mix well. Add flour gradually; mix well to form stiff dough. Let rise for 3 hours and 30 minutes. Knead well on floured surface. Shape into 2 loaves; place in greased loaf pans. Let rise for 1 hour and 30 minutes. Bake in preheated 350-degree oven for 50 minutes.

Mrs. W. Walter Rodgers
Plain Grove Grange, No. 1431
Slippery Rock, Pennsylvania

HOMEMADE YEAST
(Recipe 60 years old)

1 qt. buttermilk
Cornmeal
3 cakes yeast

Pour buttermilk into saucepan; bring to a boil. Stir in enough cornmeal to make thick mush; boil for several minutes. Remove from heat; let set until lukewarm. Dissolve yeast in 1 cup warm water in large bowl; stir in mush. Sprinkle small amount of cornmeal over top. Cover; let rise in warm place until light. Stir in enough cornmeal until mixture is stiff enough to form into cakes. Shape into cakes 1/2 inch thick. Place on flat surface, turning and moving every 6 hours until dry. Store in paper sack; use as for commercial yeast.

Mrs. Wayne Clinesmith
Centerville Grange, No. 1468
Centerville, Kansas

MA'S YEAST
(Recipe about 100 years old)

2 handfuls hops
6 lg. potatoes
1/2 c. sugar
3/4 c. flour
1/4 c. salt

Cook hops in 2 quarts boiling water until done. Strain hops; reserve liquid. Boil potatoes in reserved liquid until tender. Strain potatoes; reserve liquid. Mix hops, potatoes, sugar, flour and salt in saucepan; stir in reserved liquid. Bring to a boil; remove from heat. Cool.

Mrs. Nyle Katz
Fredonia Grange, No. 1713
Marshall, Michigan

PERPETUAL YEAST
(Recipe 60 years old)

1 cake yeast
Sugar
Potato water

Break up yeast; add 1 cup sugar. Place in 1-quart jar; fill jar with potato water to within 2 inches of top. Cover; let stand until yeast is dissolved. Stir well; let stand for 24 hours. Yeast is ready to use. Stir well when ready to bake; pour out all except 1 cup, which must be left in jar for next use. Mix sponge with liquid from jar. To renew, fill jar with potato water day before baking. Add 1/2 cup sugar; stir well. Yeast is ready for use. Keep in a cool place in summer; do not freeze in winter.

Mrs. Wayne Clinesmith
Centerville Grange, No. 1468
Centerville, Kansas

EASY GRAHAM BREAD

2/3 c. sugar
1/2 c. molasses
2 c. buttermilk
1 tsp. soda
1/2 tsp. salt
2 1/2 c. graham flour
1 1/2 c. whole wheat flour
1 tsp. baking powder

Mix all ingredients in bowl; pour into 2 greased loaf pans. Bake in preheated 350-degree oven for 50 minutes or until bread tests done. Add 1 tablespoon vinegar to 1 cup milk if no buttermilk is available.

Mrs. Elwyn G. Wrisley
Fassett Grange, No. 1567
Gillett, Pennsylvania

OLD-FASHIONED GRAHAM BREAD
(Recipe 70 years old)

1/2 c. sugar
1/2 c. molasses
1 egg
1/4 tsp. salt
1 tsp. soda
2 c. sour milk
1 c. all-purpose flour
2 c. graham flour

Combine sugar and molasses in bowl. Add egg and salt; beat well. Dissolve soda in sour milk; add to sugar mixture. Mix well. Add all-purpose flour and graham flour; blend well. Batter will be thin. Pour into 2 greased loaf pans. Bake in preheated 350-degree oven for about 1 hour or until bread tests done.

Mrs. Edith M. Tucker
East Clay Grange
Clay, New York

★ ★

RANCH LOAF

2 c. warm water
1 pkg. or cake Fleischmann's yeast
2 tbsp. sugar
2 tsp. salt
2 1/2 c. unsifted all-purpose flour
1/2 c. instant nonfat dry milk
1/2 c. water
1/2 c. (firmly packed) dark brown sugar
3 tbsp. Fleischmann's margarine
1 tbsp. dark molasses
5 3/4 c. (about) unsifted whole wheat
    flour

Measure warm water into large warm bowl; sprinkle or crumble in yeast. Stir until dissolved. Stir in sugar, salt and all-purpose flour; beat until smooth. Cover; let rise in warm place, free from draft, for about 30 minutes or until light and spongy. Dissolve dry milk solids in water; bring to a boil. Stir in brown sugar, margarine and molasses. Cool to lukewarm. Stir yeast sponge down; stir in lukewarm brown sugar mixture and half the whole wheat flour. Beat until thoroughly blended. Stir in enough additional whole wheat flour to make a soft dough. Turn out onto lightly floured board. Cover; let rest for 10 minutes. Knead for about 10 minutes or until smooth and elastic. Place in greased bowl, turning to grease top. Cover; let rise in warm place, free from draft, for about 1 hour or until doubled in bulk. Punch dough down; turn out onto lightly floured board. Divide dough in half; shape into loaves. Place each loaf in greased 9 x 5 x 3-inch loaf pan. Cover; let rise in warm place, free from draft, for about 1 hour or until doubled in bulk. Bake in preheated 350-degree oven for about 50 minutes or until bread tests done.

Photograph for this recipe above.

ANGEL BISCUITS

2 cakes yeast
2 tbsp. water
5 c. flour
1 tsp. soda
3 tsp. baking powder
4 tbsp. sugar
1 tsp. salt
1 c. shortening
2 c. buttermilk
Butter

Soften yeast in water. Sift flour, soda, baking powder, sugar and salt together; cut in shortening. Add yeast and buttermilk. Knead until dough holds together; roll to 1/4-inch thickness. Spread with butter; fold over. Cut in desired shapes. Bake at 400 degrees for 20 minutes. Yield: 5 to 6 dozen.

Audrey Shaffer
Sunshine Grange, No. 1823
Minford, Ohio

★ ★

MASTER BISCUIT MIX

9 c. flour, sifted
.1/3 c. baking powder
1 tbsp. salt
2 tsp. cream of tartar
1/4 c. sugar
2 c. Crisco

Sift flour, baking powder, salt, cream of tartar and sugar together 3 times. Cut shortening into flour mixture until mixture is consistency of cornmeal. Store in a covered container; mixture does not need to be refrigerated. To make 1 recipe biscuits, measure 3 cups Master Biscuit Mix lightly into bowl; add 2/3 cup milk, mixing well. Cut or shape in rounds; place on baking sheet. Bake in 425-degree oven for 12 to 15 minutes or until browned.

Etta Drake
Lake Shore Grange, No. 128
Wolfeboro, New Hampshire

POTATO BISCUITS
(Recipe over 100 years old)

2 c. mashed potatoes
1 c. sugar
1/2 lg. yeast cake
1 c. lukewarm potato water
1 c. lard
2 eggs
3 tsp. (about) salt
7 to 8 c. flour
Melted butter

Cool potatoes to lukewarm; add sugar. Soak yeast in potato water, then add to potato mixture. Let rise until doubled in bulk. Add lard; mix well. Add eggs, salt and flour, a small amount at a time, until soft dough is formed. Knead until smooth. Let rise until doubled in bulk. Turn out on floured board; roll out to 1/2-inch thickness. Cut in rounds; place on baking pan. Let rise until doubled in bulk. Brush tops with melted butter; sprinkle with additional sugar. Bake in 350-degree oven for about 20 minutes.

Roxanna J. Hively
Eagle Grange, No. 1
Montgomery, Pennsylvania

BLUEBERRY CURRY BISCUITS

3 c. homemade biscuit mix
1 1/2 tsp. curry powder
1/3 c. soft butter
1/3 c. grated sharp Cheddar cheese
1 c. milk
1 15-oz. can blueberries, drained

Combine biscuit mix and curry. Cut in butter until particles are very fine. Stir in cheese and milk until dough cleans the bowl. Knead on a lightly floured board several times until dough is smooth. Roll out to 1/4-inch thickness; cut into thirty-six 2 1/2-inch rounds. Place half the rounds on greased cookie sheet; top each round with spoon of drained blueberries. Top with second round. Brush top with additional milk.

Bake in preheated 400-degree oven for 10 to 12 minutes or until lightly browned. Serve biscuits hot with assorted cheese wedges and slices. Yield: 18 biscuits.

Photograph for this recipe on page 271.

RANCH BISCUITS
(Recipe 100 years old)

2 c. flour
1 tbsp. baking powder
2 tbsp. sugar
1/2 tsp. salt
1/2 c. shortening
3/4 c. milk

Sift flour, baking powder, sugar and salt into bowl; make a well in center. Melt shortening in baking pan; add with the milk to dry ingredients, stirring well. Turn onto floured board; knead several times. Cut; turn in shortening left in pan to coat top. Bake in a 400-degree oven for 15 to 20 minutes. Yield: 16 biscuits.

Virginia Lee
Priest Lake Grange, No. 447
Priest River, Idaho

BUTTERMILK BISCUITS

2 c. flour
1/2 tsp. salt
2 tsp. baking powder
1/2 tsp. soda
5 tbsp. shortening
1 c. buttermilk

Sift flour, salt, baking powder and soda together. Cut in shortening. Add buttermilk all at once. Knead 20 times. Roll 3/8 inch thick. Cut out; place on baking sheet. Bake in 450-degree oven for 15 minutes.

Mrs. Mildred Henzler
Barberton Grange, No. 571
Vancouver, Washington

DEPRESSION BISCUITS
(Recipe over 40 years old)

2 c. flour
1/2 tsp. salt
4 tsp. baking powder
2 tbsp. fat
3/4 c. milk

Measure flour into mixing bowl; stir in salt and baking powder. Flour may be measured into a sifter, then salt and baking powder added and sifted together. Work in fat with pastry blender or fork. Add milk; stir until dough comes together in ball. Do not handle dough more than necessary. Roll on floured board; cut in rounds. Place on greased baking sheet. Bake in 425-degree oven until brown. Bacon fat and rendered chicken fat produce same results as lard or commercial shortenings.

Mrs. Paul W. Morton
Freeport Grange, No. 2337
Freeport, Ohio

★ ★

CRACKLIN' BREAD

2 c. cornmeal
1/4 tsp. salt
1/2 tsp. soda
1 c. buttermilk
1 c. cracklings

Sift first 3 ingredients together; place in bowl. Add milk; stir in cracklings. Form into oblong cakes; place on baking dish. Bake in preheated 450-degree oven for 20 to 30 minutes or until brown. Yield: 6 servings.

Bettie M. Edwards
Gold Sand Grange
Louisburg, North Carolina

INDIAN HOECAKES
(Recipe over 200 years old)

1 c. water-ground white cornmeal
1/2 tsp. salt
1 tbsp. melted lard or shortening

Combine cornmeal with salt. Add lard and enough boiling water to make dough that will hold shape. Form into 2 thin, oblong cakes; place in hot, well-greased heavy pan. Bake in preheated 375-degree oven for about 25 minutes; serve hot. Yield: About 4 servings.
Washington was an early riser, usually up by five or six A.M. He would occupy himself with a ride or a book until breakfast was served, usually between seven and eight o'clock. A favorite breakfast, Samuel Stearns noted, was three small Indian hoecakes, and as many dishes of tea. George Washington Parke Custis confirmed this: Indian cakes, honey and tea formed this temperate repast. Washington was also inordinately fond of honey.
Hoecakes, a favorite in the South during Colonial times, were originally baked right on a hoe in the open hearth. They were commonly served as accompaniments to vegetable soup. Soup was a typical breakfast dish of the time, as was meat.

Trudy Rendon
San Dimas Grange, No. 658
Azusa, California

JALAPENO CORN BREAD

1/2 lb. sliced bacon
1/2 c. sifted flour
3 tsp. baking powder
1 tsp. salt
2 tsp. sugar
1 1/2 c. cornmeal
1 egg, beaten
3 tbsp. melted butter
3/4 c. buttermilk
1 c. Mexicorn, drained
1/3 c. diced canned green chilies

Fry bacon in skillet until crisp; drain. Reserve drippings; crumble bacon. Sift flour, baking powder, salt and sugar together into bowl; stir in cornmeal. Combine egg, butter and buttermilk in bowl; mix well. Add to flour mixture. Add Mexicorn, chilies and bacon; mix until just blended. Batter will be stiff. Heat 3 tablespoons bacon drippings in 10-inch iron skillet; pour batter into skillet. Bake in preheated 400-degree oven for 20 minutes or until brown.

Ruth W. O'Neale
Rubidoux Grange, No. 611
Riverside, California

CORN BREADSTICKS

1 c. all-purpose flour
1 c. yellow cornmeal
3 tbsp. sugar
1 tbsp. baking powder
1 tsp. salt
1 egg
1 c. milk
1/4 c. butter, melted

Combine flour, cornmeal, sugar, baking powder and salt in bowl. Beat egg and milk together; stir in butter. Add to dry ingredients, stirring just until moistened. Turn into buttered cornstick pans, filling each about 2/3 full. Bake in preheated 425-degree oven for 15 to 18 minutes or until golden brown. Yield: 18.

Photograph for this recipe on back cover.

CRISPY CORN STICKS

1/2 c. finely chopped onion
2 tbsp. butter or margarine, melted

★ ★

1 14-oz. package corn muffin mix
1 12-oz. can vacuum-pack golden whole
   kernel corn, drained
Corn syrup

Saute onion in butter until tender. Prepare muffin mix according to package directions, stirring in onion and corn with dry ingredients. Do not overmix. Brush corn stick pans liberally with oil. Fill pans with corn mixture until batter is level with top. Keep remaining batter refrigerated until baked. Bake at 400 degrees for about 20 minutes. Remove corn sticks from pan; brush tops with corn syrup. Yield: 21 corn sticks.

Photograph for this recipe on page 136.

OLD-FASHIONED CORN BREAD MUFFINS
(Recipe 200 years old)

1 c. yellow cornmeal
1 c. flour, sifted
1/2 tsp. salt
2 tsp. baking powder
1 egg, well beaten
1/4 c. shortening
1/4 c. sugar
1 c. milk

Mix first 4 ingredients in bowl; add egg. Mix shortening and sugar well; add to cornmeal mixture. Add milk; mix well. Place in greased muffin pans. Bake in preheated 375-degree oven for 25 minutes or until done. Batter may be placed in small, square pan and baked for 25 to 30 minutes.

Mrs. Charles Mull
Whitewater Valley Grange
Richmond, Indiana

EASY CORNMEAL MUFFINS

1/4 c. butter
1/2 c. sugar
2 c. flour
1 c. cornmeal
4 tsp. baking powder
3/4 tsp. salt
2 eggs
1 c. milk

Cream butter and sugar in bowl. Sift flour, cornmeal, baking powder and salt together. Beat eggs until lemon colored and thick; stir in milk. Add to creamed mixture alternately with cornmeal mixture; beat thoroughly. Place in muffin tins lined with baking cups. Bake in preheated 400-degree oven for 20 minutes or until done. Yield: 12 muffins.

Mrs. Paul Henzler
Barberton Grange, No. 571
Vancouver, Washington

CORN CAKES
(Recipe over 50 years old)

1 egg, well beaten
1/3 c. sugar
2/3 c. cornmeal
1 1/3 c. flour
1/2 tsp. salt
1 tsp. soda
2 tsp. cream of tartar
1 c. milk

Mix egg and sugar in bowl. Sift cornmeal, flour, salt, soda and cream of tartar together; add to egg mixture. Add milk; stir until just mixed. Do not overbeat. Place in greased muffin cups. Bake in preheated 350-degree oven for about 25 minutes or until done. May be placed in baking pan and baked as for corn bread. Three teaspoons baking powder may be used instead of cream of tartar.

Alice E. Gray
Enterprise Grange, No. 173
Orrington, Maine

CORNMEAL YEAST BREAD

5 1/2 to 6 c. all-purpose flour
1 c. yellow cornmeal
2 pkg. dry yeast
2 c. milk
3/4 c. butter
1/2 c. sugar
1 1/2 tsp. salt
2 eggs
Melted butter
Sesame seed

Combine 2 cups flour, cornmeal and yeast in mixing bowl. Combine milk, butter, sugar and salt in 1-quart saucepan; heat until warm or to 120 to 130 degrees. Add to flour mixture. Add eggs. Beat for 30 seconds at low speed, scraping bowl constantly, then 3 minutes longer at high speed. Add 1 cup flour; beat for 1 minute longer. Stir in enough remaining flour to make a soft dough. Turn onto lightly floured surface; knead for 5 to 10 minutes or until smooth and satiny. Place in buttered bowl, turning once to butter top. Cover bowl. Let rise on a rack over hot water for about 1 hour or until doubled in bulk. Punch down; divide in half. Roll each half on lightly floured surface into 9 x 12-inch rectangle. Roll dough tightly, beginning with 9-inch edge; pinch seam together to seal. Seal ends of loaf; fold under loaf. Place, seam side down, in two 9 x 5 x 3-inch buttered loaf pans. Brush with melted butter; sprinkle tops with sesame seed. Cover; let stand in warm place for about 1 hour or until doubled in bulk. Bake in preheated 375-degree oven for 35 to 40 minutes or until loaf sounds hollow when tapped. Turn out of pans onto wire rack to cool.

Photograph for this recipe on back cover.

★ ★

BLUEBERRY CORN BREAD

    1 c. fresh blueberries
    1 1/2 c. flour
    1 c. yellow cornmeal
    1/4 c. sugar
    1/2 tsp. salt
    4 tsp. baking powder
    2 eggs, beaten
    2 c. milk
    1/4 c. shortening, melted

Wash blueberries; drain well in a colander or on paper towels. Sift flour, cornmeal, sugar, salt and baking powder into a bowl. Mix eggs, milk and shortening. Add to dry ingredients; beat until smooth. Fold in drained blueberries. Preheat electric skillet to 250 degrees and grease. Pour batter into skillet; bake, covered, with vent open from 25 to 30 minutes. Serve hot from skillet at breakfast table. May be baked in well-greased pan in preheated 425-degree oven for 30 minutes.

Photograph for this recipe above.

OLD-FASHIONED CORN PONE
(Recipe 100 years old)

    1/2 c. butter
    1/2 c. sugar

    3 eggs, separated
    1 c. cornmeal
    2 c. flour
    Pinch of salt
    3 tsp. baking powder
    1 c. milk

Cream butter and sugar in bowl; stir in beaten egg yolks. Sift cornmeal, flour and salt together several times. Add baking powder; sift again. Stir into creamed mixture alternately with milk; fold in beaten egg whites. Place in greased bread pans. Bake in preheated 350-degree oven for about 1 hour or until done.

Rose Albright
Mendon Grange, No. 855
Ruffsdale, Pennsylvania

SPOON BREAD
(Recipe 150 years old)

    1 c. white cornmeal
    3 c. milk
    1 tsp. salt
    1 tsp. baking powder
    2 tbsp. melted butter
    1 tbsp. sugar
    3 eggs, separated

★ ★

Cook cornmeal and 2 cups milk in double boiler until consistency of mush. Remove from heat; stir in salt, baking powder, butter, sugar and remaining 1 cup milk. Stir in well-beaten egg yolks; fold in stiffly beaten egg whites. Place in greased 2-quart iron skillet. Bake in preheated 325-degree oven for about 1 hour or until done. Spoon into warm dishes; top with additional butter. Yield: 6 servings.

Edna C. Mashl
Quonochontaug Grange, No. 48
Bradford, Rhode Island

PERFECT CORN BREAD

    1 c. sifted all-purpose flour
    1/4 c. sugar
    4 tsp. baking powder
    3/4 tsp. salt
    1 c. yellow cornmeal
    2 eggs
    1 c. milk
    1/4 c. shortening

Sift flour with sugar, baking powder and salt into bowl; stir in cornmeal. Add eggs, milk and shortening; beat with rotary or electric beater until just mixed. Do not overbeat. Pour into greased 9 x 9 x 2-inch pan. Bake in preheated 425-degree oven for 20 to 25 minutes. Batter may be spooned into greased corn stick pans, filling 2/3 full, and baked in 425-degree oven for 12 to 15 minutes.

Carolyn Jadriano
Quonochontaug Grange, No. 48
Pawcatuck, Connecticut

MUFFIN MIX THAT KEEPS IN REFRIGERATOR

    2 c. boiling water
    2 c. All-Bran
    1 1/4 c. butter
    2 1/2 c. sugar
    4 eggs
    1 qt. buttermilk
    4 c. Bran Buds
    6 c. flour
    5 tsp. soda

Pour boiling water over All-Bran; set aside. Cream butter and sugar together. Add eggs, one at a time, beating well after each addition. Combine buttermilk, Bran Buds, flour and soda in large bowl. Blend in All-Bran mixture. Store in gallon jar or plastic bowls. Do not fill too full as mixture expands slightly. Keep covered lightly. Batter will keep in refrigerator for several weeks. Bake only as many muffins as needed. Fill muffin tins 1/2 full of batter. Bake in preheated 400-degree oven for 10 to 15 minutes or until done.

Mrs. Loren Pendell
Windsor Grange, No. 980
Spokane, Washington

SOURDOUGH ENGLISH MUFFINS

    1 c. Starter
    2 tbsp. honey
    2 c. warm milk
    Flour
    1 tsp. soda
    2 tsp. salt
    Cornmeal

Combine Starter, honey, milk and 4 cups flour in glass or plastic bowl. Let rise in warm place overnight. Stir down; mix in soda and salt. Sprinkle kneading board with 1 cup flour; turn out sourdough mixture onto board. Knead for about 5 minutes, working in as much flour as needed to make a smooth dough. Flour board lightly; roll out dough to 1/2-inch thickness. Cut into 3-inch rounds. Sprinkle waxed paper with cornmeal. Place muffins on waxed paper; sprinkle tops lightly with cornmeal. Cover; let rise in warm place for about 30 minutes. Heat griddle over low heat for 5 minutes. Cook each muffin for 4 to 5 minutes on each side, turning once. Press top gently with pancake turner after turning muffin to even shape, if necessary. A tuna can with both ends removed may be used to cut muffins, if desired. Yield: 18-20 muffins.

STARTER

    1/2 pkg. yeast
    2 c. flour
    2 tbsp. sugar
    2 1/2 c. water

Combine all ingredients in glass or crockery bowl; beat well. Cover with towel; let stand in warm place for 2 days. Store starter in glass jar in refrigerator.

Karen Dorrah
Humptulips Grange, No. 730
Hoquiam, Washington

RYE MUFFINS
(Recipe 100 years old)

    1 c. rye flour
    1/2 c. all-purpose flour
    1/2 tsp. salt
    1 tsp. soda
    1 egg
    1/4 c. molasses
    1 c. sour milk
    2 tbsp. melted butter or oil

Sift rye flour, all-purpose flour, salt and soda together. Beat egg in mixing bowl. Add molasses and milk; mix well. Add sifted dry ingredients; stir in butter. Pour batter in greased muffin pans. Bake in preheated 400-degree oven for 20 to 25 minutes or until done. Sweet milk combined with 1 tablespoon vinegar may be substituted for sour milk, if desired.

Priscilla S. Roberts
Raymond, New Hampshire

★ ★

BLUEBERRY ENGLISH MUFFINS

1 recipe prepared yeast dough for
    12 rolls
1 15-oz. can blueberries, drained

Let dough rise until doubled in bulk. Roll out dough to 1/4-inch thickness on a lightly floured board. Cut out twenty-four 3-inch rounds. Place half the rounds on cornmeal-sprinkled cookie sheet. Top with blueberries. Cover blueberries with second round of dough. Sprinkle top with cornmeal. Let rise in warm place until doubled in bulk. Bake rounds on ungreased hot griddle over low heat for 7 to 8 minutes. Turn and brown on the other side. Serve, split and toasted, with butter and blueberry preserves. Yield: 12 muffins.

Photograph for this recipe on page 271.

OATMEAL ROLLS
(Recipe 60 years old)

2 c. oatmeal
2 c. flour
2 c. sour milk
1 tsp. salt
1 tsp. soda
3 tbsp. sugar
1 egg

Mix oatmeal, flour and sour milk together; let stand for several minutes. Add salt, soda, sugar and egg; stir well. Drop by spoonfuls into greased muffin tins. Bake in preheated 400-degree oven for 20 minutes or until done.

Mrs. Bertha Perkins, C.W.A. Chm.
Queen City Grange, No. 30
Orono, Maine

BUTTERMILK ROLLS

1 pkg. yeast
1/4 c. lukewarm water
2 c. buttermilk
1/4 c. sugar
2 tsp. salt
1/4 c. melted shortening
1/2 tsp. soda
2 c. all-purpose flour
2 1/2 c. whole wheat flour
Melted butter

Dissolve yeast in lukewarm water. Scald buttermilk; stir in sugar, salt, shortening and soda. Cool to lukewarm. Add to yeast mixture; mix well. Add all of the flour; mix thoroughly. Knead on floured surface until smooth and elastic. Shape into rolls; place in greased pans. Brush with melted butter. Cover; let rise until doubled in bulk. Bake in preheated 425-degree oven for 20 minutes or until brown.

Mrs. Howard Miller
Hall of Fame Grange, No. 2003
Bonner Springs, Kansas

YEAST PAN ROLLS

4 1/2 to 5 c. all-purpose flour
2 pkg. dry yeast
1 1/2 c. milk
Butter
1/4 c. sugar
1 tsp. salt
2 eggs, slightly beaten

Combine 1 cup flour and yeast in mixing bowl. Combine milk, 1/4 cup butter, sugar and salt in 1-quart saucepan; heat until warm. Add to flour mixture; add eggs. Beat for 30 seconds with electric mixer at low speed, scraping bowl constantly; beat for 3 minutes at high speed. Add 1 cup flour; beat for 1 minute longer. Stir in enough remaining flour to make soft dough. Turn out onto lightly floured surface; knead for 5 to 10 minutes or until smooth and satiny. Place in buttered bowl, turning once to butter top; cover bowl. Let rise on rack over hot water for about 1 hour or until doubled in bulk; punch down. Divide dough into 3 equal pieces. Form each piece into 9-inch roll; cut each roll into 8 equal pieces. Form into smooth balls; place in buttered 15 x 10 1/2 x 1-inch jelly roll pan. Cover; let rise in warm place for 30 to 40 minutes or until doubled in bulk. Bake in preheated 375-degree oven for 15 to 20 minutes; brush with butter. Yield: 24 rolls.

Photograph for this recipe on back cover.

POPOVERS

1 egg, well beaten
1/8 tsp. salt
1/4 c. water
1/2 c. flour
1/4 c. milk
Oil

Mix egg and salt in bowl; blend in water. Add flour; beat until smooth. Stir in milk. Fill hot, well-oiled muffin cups 2/3 full. Bake in preheated 450-degree oven for 30 to 40 minutes or until done.

From a Grange Friend

CLOVERLEAF ROLLS
(Recipe 65 years old)

1 cake yeast
2 eggs, lightly beaten
2 tbsp. butter
1 tsp. salt
3/4 c. sugar
6 c. flour
Melted butter

Dissolve yeast in 1 cup lukewarm water. Combine eggs, butter, salt, sugar and 1 cup boiling water in bowl; mix well. Cool. Add yeast and flour; mix thoroughly. Place in cool place overnight. Shape dough

★ ★

into small balls; dip in melted butter. Place 3 balls in each greased muffin cup; let rise for 4 hours or until very light. Bake in preheated 350-degree oven for 15 to 20 minutes. Yield: 3 1/2 dozen.

Margaret Medlar
South Deer Creek Grange, No. 440
Roseburg, Oregon

COCKTAIL BUNS

    1 pkg. dry yeast
    1/4 c. warm water
    3/4 c. lukewarm milk
    1/4 c. sugar
    1 tsp. salt
    1 egg
    1/4 c. soft butter
    3 1/2 to 4 c. flour

Dissolve yeast in lukewarm water in large bowl. Stir in remaining ingredients except half the flour; mix until smooth. Add enough of the remaining flour to make dough easy to handle, mixing by hand. Turn onto lightly floured board; knead for about 5 minutes or until smooth and elastic. Place in greased bowl, turning to grease top. Cover with damp cloth; let rise in warm place for 1 hour and 30 minutes or until doubled in bulk. Punch down; let rise for about 30 minutes or until almost doubled in bulk. Shape balls of dough 3/4 to 1 inch in diameter. Place 1 inch apart on greased baking sheet; flatten slightly. Let rise for about 20 minutes or until doubled in bulk. Bake in preheated 400-degree oven for 10 minutes or until lightly browned. Yield: About 7 dozen.

Mrs. Kenneth E. Wilkin
Newark Grange, No. 1004
Heath, Ohio

CRESCENT DINNER ROLLS

    3/4 c. warm water
    2 pkg. dry yeast
    1/2 c. sugar
    1 tsp. salt
    2 eggs
    1/4 c. soft shortening
    1/4 c. butter
    4 c. sifted flour
    Soft butter
    Melted butter

Pour warm water into mixing bowl. Add yeast; stir until dissolved. Stir in sugar, salt, eggs, shortening, butter and 2 cups flour. Add remaining flour; mix until smooth. Scrape dough from sides of bowl; cover bowl with damp cloth. Let dough rise for about 1 hour and 30 minutes or until doubled in bulk. Punch down; knead on floured surface 10 times. Roll half the dough into 12-inch circle 1/4 inch thick; spread with soft butter. Cut into 16 wedges. Roll each wedge as for jelly roll, beginning at wide edge. Place on baking sheet, point side down; curve ends to form crescent. Brush with melted butter. Repeat with remaining dough. Let rise for about 1 hour or until doubled in

bulk. Bake in preheated 400-degree oven for 12 to 15 minutes or until done. Rolls may be baked and frozen. Yield: 32 rolls.

Betty Hall, Past Delegate, National Grange
Silverton Grange, No. 506
Ravenswood, West Virginia

COTTAGE CHEESE ROLLS

    2 pkg. dry yeast
    1/2 c. lukewarm water
    2 c. cottage cheese
    1/2 c. sugar
    2 tsp. salt
    1/2 tsp. soda
    2 eggs, slightly beaten
    4 1/4 c. flour

Dissolve yeast in lukewarm water. Heat cottage cheese in saucepan until lukewarm; place in bowl. Stir in sugar, salt, soda, eggs and yeast mixture. Add enough flour gradually to make soft dough; place in greased bowl. Let rise for 1 hour and 30 minutes or until doubled in bulk. Punch down; turn out onto floured surface. Divide into 24 pieces; shape each piece into a ball. Grease two 9-inch square pans; place 12 rolls in each pan. Bake in preheated 350-degree oven for 20 minutes or until golden brown.

Mrs. John Carman
Broadbent Grange, No. 729
Gaylord, Oregon

FEATHERBEDS
(Recipe 100 years old)

    1 med. potato
    1 env. yeast
    1/3 c. sugar
    1 tsp. salt
    1/4 c. butter
    1 egg, beaten
    4 1/2 c. sifted flour
    Melted butter

Peel potato; place in small saucepan. Cover with water; cook until done. Drain potato; reserve 3/4 cup potato water. Mash potato. Dissolve yeast in 1/4 cup warm water. Mix sugar, salt and butter in bowl; stir in reserved potato water. Cool to lukewarm. Add yeast mixture, mashed potato, egg and 2 cups flour; stir or beat with electric mixer until smooth. Add remaining flour; mix well. Knead on floured surface until smooth and satiny. Place in greased bowl; turn to grease top. Cover; let rise in warm place until doubled in bulk. May preheat oven to warm for 2 to 3 minutes, then turn off oven. Place dough in oven to rise, if desired. Punch dough down; shape into 24 small balls. Place 12 balls each in 9-inch layer pans. Brush with melted butter; let rise in warm place until doubled in bulk. Bake in preheated 375-degree oven for 20 minutes or until done. Yield: 24 rolls.

Ruby E. Stoops
Highland Grange, No. 1771
Norwich, Ohio

★ ★

DOLLY MADISON TEA ROLLS
(Recipe 75 to 100 years old)

1 pt. milk
1/2 c. butter or lard
1 cake yeast
6 to 7 c. flour
2 lg. eggs
1 tsp. salt
1/2 c. sugar

Heat milk and butter in saucepan until butter is melted; cool to lukewarm. Dissolve yeast in 1/2 cup warm water. Pour milk mixture into large mixing bowl; add 2 cups flour, eggs and yeast. Mix well. Add salt, sugar and enough remaining flour to make stiff dough; mix well. Cover; let rise in warm place until doubled in bulk. Shape into desired rolls; place on greased baking pan. Let rise until doubled in bulk. Bake in preheated 350-degree oven for 15 to 20 minutes.

Mrs. Allen R. McClelland
Pataskala Grange, No. 1884
Pataskala, Ohio

FAMILY REFRIGERATED YEAST ROLLS
(Recipe 75 years old)

1/2 c. sugar
1 pkg. dry yeast
2 c. warm water
5 c. sifted flour
1 tsp. salt
1/2 c. shortening

Mix sugar, yeast and water in bowl; let stand for 15 minutes. Place flour in bowl. Add salt and shortening; mix with pastry blender or fork. Pour yeast into flour mixture; stir until mixed. Cover; refrigerate overnight. Roll out 1/3 of the dough on floured board, rolling in only 1 direction. Cut with biscuit cutter; place in muffin cups. Let rise for about 1 hour. Bake in preheated 350-degree oven until golden brown. Remaining dough will keep in refrigerator for several days. Yield: 2-2 1/2 dozen.

Beatrice Sturtevant, Sec.
Maine State Grange
Auburn, Maine

KANSAS BUTTERHORN ROLLS

1 c. milk
1/2 c. sugar
1/2 c. butter
1 pkg. dry yeast
1/4 c. warm water
3 eggs, beaten
1/2 tsp. salt
5 c. flour
Melted butter

Mix milk, sugar and butter in saucepan; heat until scalded. Cool to lukewarm. Dissolve yeast in water. Pour milk mixture into bowl; stir in yeast. Add eggs and salt; mix well. Add flour; mix thoroughly. Knead on floured surface until smooth; place in bowl. Let rise until doubled in bulk. Punch down; let rise until doubled in bulk. Divide into 3 parts; roll out each part on floured surface into circle size of pie pan. Brush with melted butter. Cut each circle into 16 wedges; roll each wedge as for jelly roll, starting with wide end. Place on greased baking sheet, point side down; let rise until light. Bake in preheated 375-degree oven for 12 to 15 minutes. Yield: 48 rolls.

Margeret Jones
Cloverleaf Grange, No. 1923
Hugoton, Kansas

PARKER HOUSE ROLLS
(Recipe 100 years old)

Sugar
1 cake yeast
1 c. lukewarm water
2 tsp. salt
1 c. scalded milk
1 egg, beaten
6 tbsp. melted shortening
6 c. sifted flour
Melted butter

Add 1 teaspoon sugar and yeast to lukewarm water in bowl; let stand for 5 minutes. Dissolve salt and 1/4 cup sugar in milk; cool to lukewarm. Stir in yeast, egg and shortening. Add flour; mix well. Let rise in warm place until doubled in bulk. Knead on floured board; roll out about 1/4 inch thick. Cut with cookie cutter; spread melted butter over each round. Fold each round in half; place on greased cookie sheet. Let rise until doubled in bulk. Bake in preheated 350-degree oven for 25 minutes. Yield: 3 dozen.

Ruth Williams
Charlotte Grange, No. 398
Charlotte, Vermont

RUSKS

1 c. scalded milk
1 pkg. dry yeast
1/4 c. warm water
1/2 c. shortening
3 1/2 c. (about) flour
3/4 tsp. salt
2 tbsp. sugar
1 egg

Cool milk to lukewarm. Dissolve yeast in warm water; add to milk. Stir in shortening. Sift flour, salt and sugar together; add half the mixture to yeast mixture. Stir in egg. Add remaining flour mixture; mix well. Turn out onto floured board; knead lightly. Place in bowl; let rise in warm place until doubled in bulk. Roll out on floured board; cut with large cookie or biscuit cutter. Place on greased cookie sheet; let rise for about 30 minutes. Bake in preheated 400-degree oven for 15 to 20 minutes. Yield: 12 buns.

Mrs. Mary Shumaker
Kent Grange, No. 2371
Kent, Ohio

★ ★

RICH REFRIGERATOR ROLLS

1 cake yeast
3 eggs, beaten
1/2 c. melted butter
1 tsp. salt
1 c. lukewarm milk
1/2 c. sugar
5 c. unsifted flour

Dissolve yeast in 1/2 cup warm water in bowl. Add eggs, butter, salt, milk and sugar; mix well. Add flour; mix thoroughly. Cover; let rise until doubled in bulk. Punch down. Place dough in greased bowl; cover. Place in refrigerator. Roll or pat dough on lightly floured surface 3 hours before baking. Shape into desired rolls. Place in greased pan; grease top of rolls with additional butter. Let rise for 3 hours. Bake in preheated 350 to 375-degree oven for 15 to 20 minutes.

Katie M. Renkert
Lower Naches Grange, No. 296
Yakima, Washington

SWEDISH BULLER
(Recipe 65 years old)

1/2 c. butter or shortening
2 c. scalded milk
1 pkg. or cake yeast
1/2 c. warm water
1 1/2 tsp. cardamom seed
2 eggs
1 1/2 tsp. salt
1/2 c. sugar
7 1/2 c. unsifted all-purpose flour
1/4 c. melted butter

Stir butter into milk until melted; cool to lukewarm. Stir yeast into warm water; let stand for about 5 minutes. Crush cardamom in mortar with pestle, blender, or with bottom of flat-surfaced jar. Blend milk mixture, yeast mixture, cardamom, eggs, salt and sugar in large bowl. Add flour, one cup at a time, blending in as much flour as possible. Turn out onto board with remaining flour; knead until smooth, adding more flour, if needed. Wash mixing bowl in warm water; dry. Rub bowl with additional butter or shortening. Place dough in bowl, turning to grease top. Cover; let rise in warm place for about 1 hour or until about doubled in bulk. Punch down; place on floured board. Knead until smooth. Divide dough in half. Pour melted butter equally into two 9-inch square baking pans. Divide each half dough into 20 pieces of equal size. Shape each piece, drawing edges under to make smooth-topped ball. Turn balls in butter in baking pan as shaped; arrange 20 pieces, smooth side up, in each pan. Cover without touching dough; let rise in warm place for about 30 minutes or until doubled in bulk. Brush tops of rolls with additional milk. Bake in preheated 375-degree oven for about 25 minutes or until well browned. Yield: 40 rolls.

Evelyn H. Nielsen
Eastlake Grange, No. 727
Glenhaven, California

THERESA'S BUTTERHORNS

1 c. scalded milk
1/2 c. sugar
2 tsp. salt
1/4 c. shortening
5 c. flour
2 pkg. yeast
1/4 c. warm water
2 eggs
Melted butter

Pour milk into bowl. Add sugar, salt and shortening; mix well. Add 2 cups flour; stir until mixed. Dissolve yeast in warm water in measuring cup; pour over sugar mixture. Beat eggs in cup in which yeast was dissolved; pour over sugar mixture. Mix well. Add remaining 3 cups flour gradually; mix well. Knead on floured surface until smooth and elastic, adding more flour, if needed. Place in large, greased bowl; let rise until doubled in bulk. Punch down; divide into 5 balls. Roll out each ball on floured surface into circle size of pie pan; spread melted butter over top. Cut each circle into 8 wedges with pizza cutter. Roll each wedge as for jelly roll, starting with wide end. Place on cookie sheet, point side down; let rise until doubled in bulk. Bake in preheated 400 to 425-degree oven for 15 minutes. Yield: 40 rolls.

Mrs. Theresa Beason
Sonora Grange
Gilman, Iowa

WHOLE WHEAT ROLLS

1 c. milk
1 c. water
6 tbsp. shortening
1/4 c. sugar
1/2 tbsp. salt
2 c. Wheat Chex
2 pkg. or cakes yeast
2/3 c. warm water
1 egg
5 c. (about) flour
Melted shortening or butter

Mix milk, water, shortening, sugar and salt in saucepan; heat until scalded. Pour over Wheat Chex in large bowl; cool to lukewarm. Dissolve yeast in warm water; add to milk mixture. Add egg; beat until mixed. Add flour, one cup at a time, mixing thoroughly after each addition. Place on well-floured board; knead well. Place in bowl; grease top of dough. Cover with waxed paper, then towel moistened with warm water. Let rise in warm place, free from draft, for about 1 hour. Turn onto floured board; knead well. Shape into rolls; place on baking sheets. Let rise for about 45 minutes. Bake in preheated 375-degree oven for 15 minutes. Remove from oven; brush with melted shortening. Return to oven. Bake until brown; brush with melted shortening again.

Mrs. Lucy E. Newton
Sunapee Mt. Grange, No. 144
Newport, New Hampshire

★ ★

BLUEBERRY BUCKLE

3/4 c. sugar
1/4 c. butter
1 egg
1/2 c. milk
2 c. flour
2 tsp. baking powder
1/2 tsp. salt
2 c. blueberries
Topping

Combine sugar, butter, egg and milk; mix well. Blend in flour, baking powder and salt well. Stir in blueberries. Pour into buttered 9 x 9-inch pan. Sprinkle Topping over batter. Bake in preheated 375-degree oven 30 to 35 minutes. Serve as coffee cake or warm with whipped cream.

TOPPING

1/2 c. sugar
1/2 tsp. cinnamon
1/4 c. butter

Combine all ingredients; mix until crumbly.
This recipe was used in the White House in George Washington's time.

Mrs. Gene Henning
Kenova Grange
Malden, Washington

CRUMB KUCHEN

2 1/4 c. all-purpose flour
1 c. sugar
1/2 tsp. salt
1/2 c. shortening
1 tsp. baking powder
1 c. sour milk
1 tsp. soda
1 egg, beaten
1 tsp. cinnamon

Sift flour, sugar and salt together into large bowl; add shortening. Mix with pastry blender or knives until mixture is crumbly. Remove 1 cup flour mixture; reserve for topping. Combine remaining flour mixture with baking powder. Combine sour milk and soda, stirring until soda is dissolved; Add milk mixture and egg to flour mixture; mix well. Pour into tube pan. Add cinnamon to reserved flour mixture; sprinkle over batter in tube pan. Bake in preheated 350-degree oven for 35 to 40 minutes. Yield: 8-10 servings.

Gladys Lyday, Sec.
Honeoye Falls Grange, No. 6
Honeoye Falls, New York

CINNAMON COFFEE CAKE

2 pkg. yeast
1 1/2 c. water
Flour
Cinnamon

Vegetable shortening
1 1/2 tsp. salt
Sugar
1 egg
1/3 c. dry milk powder
1 c. raisins

Soften yeast in warm water. Sift 3 cups flour and 1 teaspoon cinnamon together. Combine yeast mixture, 1/3 cup shortening, salt, 1/2 cup sugar, egg, dry milk powder and flour mixture; beat well. Stir in raisins and enough flour to make a soft dough. Turn out on floured board; knead until dough is smooth and elastic. Place in greased bowl. Cover; let rise in warm place for about 1 hour and 30 minutes or until doubled in bulk. Divide in 2 parts; shape each to fit 8 x 8-inch greased pan. Cover; let rise for about 1 hour or until light. Spread tops generously with 2 tablespoons melted shortening. Combine 1/3 cup sugar and 1/2 teaspoon cinnamon; sprinkle over tops. Bake in preheated 375-degree oven for 40 minutes or until done.

Florence Proctor
Delavan Lake Grange, No. 681
Elkhorn, Wisconsin

OLD TIMEY COFFEE CAKE
(Recipe over 100 years old)

1 c. sugar
1/2 c. butter or shortening
2 eggs, beaten
1 c. molasses
1 tsp. soda
1 c. cold coffee
3 c. flour
1 tsp. baking powder
1/4 tsp. cinnamon
1/4 tsp. allspice
1/4 tsp. nutmeg
1/4 tsp. cloves
1/4 tsp. salt
1 c. raisins
1/2 c. currants

Cream sugar and butter; add eggs and molasses. Dissolve soda in coffee. Sift dry ingredients together. Add coffee mixture and flour mixture alternately to butter mixture, mixing well after each addition. Dredge fruits with small amount additional flour. Add to batter. Place in greased loaf pan. Bake in preheated 350-degree oven for 40 minutes or until toothpick inserted in center comes out clean.

Ellen B. Engelmann
Kalama Grange, No. 197
Kalama, Washington

QUICK DATE COFFEE CAKE

1 1/2 c. dates
1 c. hot water

★ ★

2 eggs, beaten
2 c. sugar
1/4 tsp. salt
1 c. chopped walnuts
3 c. flour
2 tsp. soda
2 tsp. baking powder
1/2 c. soft butter
1 3/4 c. hot coffee
1 tsp. vanilla
Topping

Place dates in large bowl; cover with hot water. Let soak for several minutes. Add eggs, sugar and salt; mix well. Mix walnuts with flour until coated; add to date mixture. Combine soda, baking powder and soft butter; add to date mixture. Stir in hot coffee and vanilla. Pour into greased 9 x 13-inch pan. Bake in 350-degree oven for 40 minutes to 1 hour. Remove from oven; sprinkle with Topping.

TOPPING

2/3 c. (firmly packed) brown sugar
1/4 c. butter

Mix brown sugar and butter until mixture is crumbly.

Mrs. Helen Campbell, W. A. C.
Junction Grange, No. 239
Quenemo, Kansas

TEA RING

(Recipe 50 years old)

2 c. lukewarm milk
1 1/2 c. sugar
2 tsp. salt
2 cakes yeast or 2 pkg. dry yeast
2 eggs
Soft butter
7 to 7 1/2 c. sifted flour
4 tsp. cinnamon
1 c. (or more) raisins
Powdered sugar icing

Mix milk with 1/2 cup sugar and salt. Crumble in yeast; stir until dissolved. Stir in eggs and 1/2 cup butter. Stir in enough flour to make soft dough, then add flour to make stiff dough. Knead well. Place in greased bowl; let rise until doubled in bulk. Punch down. Let rise again. Divide dough in 2 parts. Shape into 2 balls; cover. Let rest for 15 minutes. Roll dough into two 9 x 18-inch shapes. Spread each rectangle with 2 tablespoons soft butter; sprinkle each with 1/2 cup sugar and 2 teaspoons cinnamon, then sprinkle with raisins. Roll up like a jelly roll, then shape into rings. Pinch edges together. Cut 3/4 way through with scissors, about 1 inch apart. Turn cut pieces on sides. Let rise for about 30 minutes. Bake in preheated 350-degree oven for 25 to 30 minutes. Drizzle powdered sugar icing on top while still warm.

Mrs. Roy Hardman
Lexington Grange
Alliance, Ohio

SOUR CREAM COFFEE CAKE

1/2 c. butter
1 c. sugar
2 eggs
1 c. thick sour cream
2 c. flour
1 tsp. baking powder
1/2 tsp. soda
1/2 tsp. salt
1 tsp. vanilla
Streusel Topping

Cream butter and sugar until light; add eggs. Beat until smooth; stir in sour cream. Add flour, baking powder, soda, salt and vanilla; mix until thoroughly blended. Place half the batter in greased tube pan; sprinkle with half the Streusel Topping. Add remaining batter; sprinkle remaining Streusel Topping evenly over top. Bake at 350 degrees for about 45 minutes.

STREUSEL TOPPING

1/2 c. (firmly packed) brown sugar
2 tbsp. flour
2 tsp. cinnamon
1/2 c. chopped nuts
2 tbsp. melted butter

Combine all ingredients in small bowl; stir until well blended.

Catherine L. Kyle
Patuccoway Grange
West Nottingham, New Hampshire

YUM-YUM COFFEE CAKE

1/2 c. butter
1 c. sugar
2 eggs
2 c. sifted flour
1 tsp. soda
1 tsp. baking powder
1/2 tsp. salt
1 c. sour cream
1 tsp. vanilla extract
Topping

Cream butter until soft; add sugar. Mix well. Beat until light and fluffy. Add eggs, one at a time, beating well after each addition. Sift flour, soda, baking powder and salt together. Add dry ingredients to creamed mixture alternately with sour cream, beginning and ending with flour mixture. Stir in vanilla. Place in greased 8 or 9-inch square pan; sprinkle on Topping. Bake in preheated 325-degree oven for 40 minutes.

TOPPING

1/3 c. (firmly packed) brown sugar
1/4 c. sugar
1 tsp. cinnamon
1 c. finely chopped pecans

Combine all ingredients, mixing well.

Mrs. Viola McConkey
Millbrook Grange, No. 1864
Morton, Illinois

★ ★

AFTERNOON TEA DOUGHNUTS
(Recipe 50 years old)

2 eggs
6 tbsp. sugar
3/4 tsp. salt
1/4 tsp. nutmeg (opt.)
2 tbsp. melted shortening
6 tbsp. milk
2 c. flour
3 tsp. baking powder
Powdered sugar
Cinnamon sugar

Beat eggs until very light; add sugar, salt, nutmeg and shortening. Mix well. Add milk, flour and baking powder; beat well. Drop by teaspoonfuls into deep hot fat; fry until brown. Drain well on paper toweling. Sprinkle with powdered sugar, then roll in cinnamon sugar.

Mrs. Charles H. Gray
Central Grange, No. 396
St. Maries, Idaho

CAKE DOUGHNUTS
(Recipe 45 years old)

2 eggs, beaten
1 c. sugar
1 c. milk
4 tsp. baking powder
4 c. flour
1/2 tsp. salt
1 tsp. vanilla extract
1 1/2 c. shortening

Combine eggs, sugar and milk; beat until sugar is dissolved. Combine baking powder, flour and salt; stir into egg mixture. Add vanilla extract. Cover; chill thoroughly. Roll out on floured board; cut with doughnut cutter. Fry in 370-degree shortening until golden on both sides. Yield: 3 dozen.

Mrs. Clarence Grewell
Cloverleaf Grange, No. 1923
Hooker, Oklahoma

CHOCOLATE DOUGHNUTS

4 tbsp. vegetable shortening
1 1/4 c. sugar
2 eggs, slightly beaten
2 tbsp. melted chocolate
1 c. mashed potatoes
4 c. flour
1 tsp. soda
2 tsp. baking powder
1 tsp. cinnamon
1 tsp. salt
1 c. sour milk
1/4 tsp. vanilla extract

Cream shortening and sugar together until light and fluffy. Add eggs, melted chocolate and mashed potatoes, stirring well after each addition. Sift flour, soda,

baking powder, cinnamon and salt together. Add dry ingredients alternately with sour milk to creamed mixture, stirring well after each addition. Stir in vanilla extract. Roll dough out on floured board; cut with doughnut cutter. Drop into hot 390-degree fat; fry until golden brown, then flip over. Drain on unglazed paper. May roll in powdered or granulated sugar, if desired. Yield: 3 to 4 dozen.

Mrs. E. H. Amidon
Goldendale Grange, No. 49
Goldendale, Washington

CRULLERS
(Recipe 100 years old)

1 c. sugar
1 tbsp. butter
2 eggs, beaten
1 c. milk
4 c. flour
2 tsp. cream of tartar
1 tsp. soda
1 tsp. salt
1 tsp. nutmeg

Cream sugar and butter together; beat in eggs and milk. Sift flour, cream of tartar, soda, salt and nutmeg together; stir into milk mixture. Add more flour if needed to make a soft dough. Roll dough out 1/2 inch thick. Cut with doughnut cutter. Fry in deep fat until golden brown on both sides. May use homemade lard for butter.

Mrs. Floyd E. Conklin
Lawsville Grange, No. 1455
Montrose, Pennsylvania

RAISED POTATO DOUGHNUTS
(Recipe about 150 years old)

2 med. potatoes, boiled and mashed
2 c. scalded milk
1 tsp. salt
3/4 c. sugar
2 cakes yeast
1/4 c. warm water
2 eggs, well beaten
1/2 c. melted butter
Flour
Lard

Stir potatoes into scalded milk; add salt and sugar. Set aside to cool. Dissolve yeast in warm water. Add eggs and yeast to milk mixture. Let rise until light. Add butter; stir well. Add enough flour to make stiff dough. Let rise in a warm place for about 4 hours. Roll out; cut with doughnut cutter. Let rise until doubled in bulk. Fry in hot lard. These are delicious with maple syrup.

Irene Chase
Mt. Cube Grange, No. 236
Orford, New Hampshire

★ ★

EASY-DO DOUGHNUTS

Sugar
1/2 c. milk
1 egg
Melted shortening
1 1/2 c. all-purpose flour
2 tsp. baking powder
1/2 tsp. salt
1/2 c. seedless raisins
1/2 tsp. nutmeg or cinnamon

Blend 1/3 cup sugar, milk, egg and 2 tablespoons melted shortening together. Sift flour, baking powder and salt together; add to liquid mixture, stirring lightly. Mix in raisins. Drop heaping teaspoonfuls into melted 365-degree shortening. Fry for 2 to 3 minutes or until golden brown. Drain on paper towels. Mix 1/4 cup sugar and nutmeg into bag; shake warm doughnuts in sugar. May coat in confectioners' sugar, if desired.

Mrs. Harry Brazeau
Bolton Grange, No. 142
Bolton, Massachusetts

RAISED SPICY DOUGHNUTS
(Recipe 25 years old)

1 1/4 c. m   scalded
1/4 c. sho   ling
1/2 tsp. salt
1 cake yeast
5 c. (about) sifted flour
3 eggs
3/4 c. sugar
1 1/2 tsp. cinnamon
1/4 tsp. nutmeg
1/8 tsp. mace

Combine milk, shortening and salt; cool to lukewarm. Crumble in yeast; let stand for 5 minutes. Add 2 1/2 cups sifted flour; beat until smooth. Cover; let rise until bubbly. Add eggs, sugar and spices; mix well. Add enough remaining flour to make a dough that can be easily handled. Knead until smooth. Cover; let rise until doubled in bulk. Roll out 1/2 inch thick. Cut or shape doughnuts; let rise on board until doubled in bulk. Fry, a few at a time, in deep fat at 375 degrees for 3 minutes or until lightly browned, turning once. Drain on absorbent paper. Yield: About 3 dozen doughnuts.

Signa M. Allen, C.W.A. Chm.
Lucerne Grange, No. 167
Loxahatchee, Florida

OLD-FASHIONED JELLY DOUGHNUTS

1/2 c. milk
1/2 c. butter
1/3 c. sugar
1 tsp. salt
1/2 c. warm water
2 pkg. active dry yeast
2 eggs, slightly beaten
1 tbsp. grated lemon peel
4 1/2 to 5 c. unsifted all-purpose flour
1 c. (about) Smucker's Red Raspberry Jelly
Confectioners' sugar

Heat milk in small saucepan until small bubbles appear at edge; stir in butter, sugar and salt. Cool to lukewarm. Measure water into large warm bowl. Sprinkle in yeast; stir until dissolved. Add lukewarm milk mixture, eggs, lemon peel and 2 1/2 cups flour; mix until moistened. Beat until well blended. Stir in enough additional flour, 2 to 2 1/2 cups, to make a stiff dough. Turn out onto lightly floured board; knead for 8 to 10 minutes or until smooth and elastic. Place in greased bowl; turn over to grease top. Cover with waxed paper and towel; let rise in warm place, free from draft, for about 1 hour or until doubled in bulk. Punch dough down; knead on floured board for 2 to 3 minutes. Roll out half the dough at a time to 1/2-inch thickness with lightly floured rolling pin; cut into rounds with 3-inch cookie cutter. Place doughnuts on ungreased baking sheets. Knead trimmings, then roll and cut. Cover. Let rise in warm place, free from draft, for about 30 minutes or until doubled in bulk. Pour oil 3 to 4 inches deep in deep fat fryer or kettle; preheat to 375 degrees. Drop doughnuts, 3 or 4 at a time, into hot oil; fry for 2 to 3 minutes or until golden brown, turning once. Drain on absorbent paper. Cut a slit in side of each doughnut before serving. Fill center of each with about 2 teaspoons jelly, using small spoon or pastry tube. Sprinkle with confectioners' sugar. Yield: About 2 dozen.

Photograph for this recipe below.

★ ★

SOUR DOUGH DOUGHNUTS
(Recipe 60 years old)

1 c. sour dough
1/2 c. milk
2 eggs, beaten
Sugar
3 tbsp. shortening, softened
1 tsp. soda
1/2 tsp. salt
1/4 tsp. nutmeg
2 c. flour

Combine sour dough, milk, eggs, 1/2 cup sugar and shortening; mix well. Add soda, salt and nutmeg; mix well. Stir in enough flour to make a soft dough. Roll out on floured surface; cut with doughnut cutter. Place on floured board to rise for at least 1 hour or until light. Fry in hot Crisco until golden brown. Sprinkle with sugar; serve hot.

Sophia A. Friel
Thompson Falls Grange, No. 123
Thompson Falls, Montana

SPICY DOUGHNUTS
(Recipe over 60 years old)

1 c. sugar
1/2 tsp. ginger
1/2 tsp. nutmeg
1 tsp. salt
2 tbsp. melted butter or shortening
2 eggs
1 c. milk
4 c. flour
4 tsp. baking powder

Mix sugar, ginger, nutmeg and salt together; add butter and eggs. Beat well. Add milk, flour and baking powder; mix well. Roll on floured board to 1/3 inch thick. Cut out with doughnut cutter. Fry slowly in deep hot fat until golden on both sides. Yield: 2 1/2 dozen.

Mrs. Anna Niles
Masonville Grange, No. 1482
Masonville, New York

SQUAW BREAD

1 c. flour
1/4 c. sugar
2 tsp. baking powder
1/2 tsp. salt
Powdered sugar

Combine flour, sugar, baking powder and salt; add enough water to make soupy paste. Drop small amounts into hot fat over medium heat; fry until brown. This will make a variety of shapes. Roll in powdered sugar.

Dr. Sam Lacina
Chester Royal Grange, No. 2181
Grinnell, Iowa

HUNGARIAN CSOROGE

1 c. sour cream
4 egg yolks, lightly beaten
2 c. sifted flour
Powdered sugar

Combine sour cream and egg yolks; add all or enough flour to make soft dough. Knead until smooth. Roll out very thin; cut into diamond shapes. Make slit in center of each diamond; pull one end through slit. Fry in deep hot fat until very light brown. Dust generously with powdered sugar.

Mrs. Margaret Colson
Jefferson Grange, No. 2019
Sharpsville, Pennsylvania

KREBLE
(Recipe over 100 years old)

2 eggs
1 c. cream
2 to 3 c. flour
2 tsp. baking powder
1/8 tsp. soda
2 tbsp. sugar
1 tsp. salt

Beat eggs; add cream. Combine 2 cups flour with baking powder, soda, sugar and salt; mix into cream mixture. Add enough flour to make workable dough. Roll out dough; cut into 3 x 5-inch strips. Cut slit lengthwise to within about 1 inch from each end. Fry in deep hot fat until golden on each side. Drain on paper toweling. Sprinkle with additional sugar.

Mrs. Adalia M. Gillett
Homestead Grange, No. 215
Kersey, Colorado

GREAT GRANDMOTHER'S GINGERBREAD
(Recipe over 100 years old)

1/2 c. sugar
1/4 c. lard
1/4 c. butter
1 egg, beaten
1 c. Brer Rabbit or sorghum molasses
2 1/2 c. sifted flour
1 1/2 tsp. soda
1 tsp. cinnamon
1 tsp. ginger
1/2 tsp. cloves
1/2 tsp. salt
1 c. hot water

Cream sugar, lard and butter together until light and smooth; add egg and molasses. Beat until fluffy. Sift flour, soda, cinnamon, ginger, cloves and salt together. Add dry ingredients to molasses mixture; add hot water, beating until smooth. Batter will be soft. Pour into greased shallow pan. Bake in 350-degree oven for

★ ★

40 to 45 minutes or until gingerbread tests done. Yield: 15 servings.

Alice Slater
Laurel Grange, No. 1678
Beverly, Ohio

BLUEBERRY GINGERBREAD
(Recipe 100 years old)

1 c. shortening
Sugar
1 egg
2 c. all-purpose flour
1 tsp. soda
1/2 tsp. salt
1 tsp. cinnamon
1/2 tsp. ginger
1 c. sour milk or buttermilk
3 tbsp. molasses
1 c. Maine blueberries

Combine shortening and 1 cup sugar in large bowl; cream until light. Add egg; beat until fluffy. Sift flour, soda, salt and spices together. Add to creamed mixture alternately with sour milk, mixing well after each addition. Stir in molasses and blueberries. Pour into greased and floured 9 x 9-inch pan. Sprinkle 3 tablespoons sugar over batter. Bake at 350 degrees for 50 minutes to 1 hour. Yield: 12 servings.

Fay W. Corbett
Farmington Grange, No. 12

MARY BALL WASHINGTON'S GINGERBREAD
(Recipe about 200 years old)

1/2 c. butter
1/2 c. (firmly packed) dark brown sugar
1/2 c. light molasses
1/2 c. honey
1/4 c. sherry
1/2 c. warm milk
3 c. sifted flour
2 tbsp. ginger
1 1/2 tsp. cinnamon
1 1/2 tsp. mace
1 1/2 tsp. nutmeg
1 tsp. cream of tartar
3 eggs, well beaten
1 tsp. soda
2 tbsp. warm water
2 tbsp. grated orange rind
1/4 c. orange juice
1 c. raisins

Preheat oven to 350 degrees. Grease 13 x 9 x 2-inch pan; line with waxed paper. Cream butter until light. Add brown sugar; beat well. Add molasses, honey, sherry and milk; beat well. Sift flour, spices and cream of tartar together; add to sugar mixture alternately with eggs. Dissolve soda in warm water. Add orange rind, orange juice, raisins and soda water to sugar mixture. Pour in prepared pan. Bake for 45 to 50 minutes

or until gingerbread is firm in center.
This was a favorite of George Washington's mother.

Jenny E. Mathison
Fawn Grove Grange, No. 1736
Fawn Grove, Pennsylvania

APPLE-NUT LOAF
(Recipe about 75 years old)

1/2 c. shortening
1 c. sugar
1 egg, well beaten
1 c. (packed) chopped peeled apples
1/4 c. chopped dates
1/4 c. chopped nuts
2 c. all-purpose flour
1/2 tsp. salt
1 tsp. soda
1/2 tsp. cinnamon
1/2 c. sour milk

Cream shortening and sugar together. Add egg; beat well. Mix in apples, dates and nuts. Sift flour, salt, soda and cinnamon together; add flour mixture to apple mixture alternately with milk. Pour into loaf pan. Let stand in pan for 10 minutes before baking. Bake in preheated 350-degree oven for 55 minutes or until loaf tests done.

Dorothy Carlson
Shirley Grange, No. 254
Shirley, Massachusetts

APPLESAUCE BREAD

1 1/4 c. applesauce
1 c. sugar
1/2 c. cooking oil
2 eggs
3 tbsp. milk
2 c. sifted all-purpose flour
1 tsp. soda
1/2 tsp. baking powder
1 tsp. cinnamon
1/4 tsp. salt
1/4 tsp. nutmeg
1/4 tsp. allspice
3/4 c. chopped pecans
1/4 c. (packed) brown sugar

Combine applesauce, sugar, oil, eggs and milk in mixer bowl; mix well. Sift flour, soda, baking powder, 1/2 teaspoon cinnamon, salt, nutmeg and allspice together. Stir into applesauce mixture; beat well. Fold in 1/2 cup pecans; turn into well-greased 9 x 5 x 3-inch loaf pan. Combine remaining 1/4 cup pecans, brown sugar and remaining 1/2 teaspoon cinnamon; sprinkle over batter. Bake in preheated 350-degree oven for 1 hour or until bread tests done. Remove from pan; cool on rack.

Elsie Howard
Albion Center Grange, No. 270
Pulaski, New York

★ ★

CINNAMON-APPLE BREAD
(Recipe over 50 years old)

   1/2 c. shortening
   1 c. sugar
   2 eggs
   1 tsp. vanilla extract
   2 tbsp. lemon juice
   2 c. flour
   1/2 tsp. cinnamon
   1/4 tsp. salt
   1 tsp. soda
   1 tsp. grated lemon rind
   1 1/2 c. coarsely grated apples

Cream shortening and sugar together. Beat in eggs; add vanilla extract and lemon juice. Sift flour, cinnamon, salt and soda together; stir into sugar mixture. Add lemon rind and apples; pour into greased loaf pan. Bake in preheated 350-degree oven for 50 to 60 minutes or until bread tests done. Add 2 tablespoons water to batter if apples are dry and mealy. Freezes well.

Mrs. Edward Holler, State Sec.
Harmony Grange, No. 12
Wilmington, Delaware

OLD-FASHIONED APPLE BREAD
(Recipe over 100 years old)

   1 c. sugar
   1/2 c. shortening
   2 eggs
   1 1/2 tbsp. sour milk
   2 c. flour
   1 tsp. soda
   1/2 tsp. salt
   1 tsp. baking powder
   1/2 tsp. vanilla extract
   1 c. ground unpeeled apples
   1/2 c. chopped nuts

Cream sugar and shortening together. Add eggs and sour milk; mix well. Sift flour, soda, salt and baking powder together; stir into shortening mixture. Add vanilla extract, apples and nuts; pour into 2 loaf pans. Bake in preheated 325-degree oven for about 50 minutes or until loaves test done.

Leota M. Ford
Marion Grange, No. 207
Wildwood, Florida

BANANA NUT BREAD

   1/3 c. shortening
   1/2 c. sugar
   2 eggs
   1 3/4 c. sifted all-purpose flour
   1 tsp. baking powder
   1/2 tsp. soda
   1/2 tsp. salt
   1 c. mashed ripe bananas
   1/2 c. chopped walnuts

Cream shortening and sugar together. Add eggs, one at a time, beating well after each addition. Sift flour, baking powder, soda and salt together. Add to creamed mixture alternately with bananas, blending well after each addition. Stir in walnuts. Pour into well-greased 9 x 5 x 3-inch loaf pan. Bake in preheated 350-degree oven for 45 to 50 minutes or until done. Remove from pan; cool on rack. Wrap; store overnight.

Carolyn J. Adriano
Quonochontaug Grange, No. 48
Pawcatuck, Connecticut

FAMILY FAVORITE BANANA BREAD
(Recipe 35 years old)

   1 c. sugar
   2 tbsp. butter
   1 egg, beaten
   2 bananas, mashed
   2 tbsp. sour cream or milk
   2 c. flour
   1 tsp. soda
   1/2 tsp. baking powder
   1/2 tsp. salt

Cream sugar and butter together. Add egg, bananas and sour cream; mix well. Sift flour, soda, baking powder and salt together; stir into banana mixture. Pour in loaf pan. Bake in preheated 375-degree oven for 50 minutes or until done.

Mrs. Henry G. Sager
Deputy Jr. Matron, Lecturer, Treas.
Logan Grange, No. 2041
Buckland, Ohio

YULETIDE BANANA BREAD

   1 c. Crisco
   2 c. sugar
   4 eggs
   Flour
   1/2 tsp. salt
   2 tsp. soda
   1 tsp. cinnamon
   6 ripe bananas, mashed
   1/2 c. maraschino cherries, finely
      chopped
   1 c. chopped pecans
   1/2 c. flaked coconut

Beat Crisco for 2 minutes; add sugar gradually, beating constantly. Add eggs, one at a time, beating well after each addition. Sift 2 1/2 cups flour, salt, soda and cinnamon together; add to egg mixture alternately with bananas. Toss cherries and pecans with 1 tablespoon flour; fold into banana mixture with coconut. Turn into greased and floured 9 x 5 x 3-inch loaf pan. Bake at 350 degrees for 1 hour or until bread tests done. Decorate with candied pineapple and cherries, if desired.

Ruth W. O'Neale
Rubidoux Grange, No. 611
Riverside, California

★ ★

GRANDMA'S BANANA BREAD
(Recipe over 100 years old)

    1/4 c. butter
    1 c. (scant) sugar
    1 egg
    2 c. all-purpose flour
    1 tsp. soda
    Salt to taste
    3 bananas, beaten

Cream butter and sugar together. Add egg; beat well. Sift flour, soda and salt together. Add to sugar mixture alternately with bananas; mix well. Pour into loaf pan. Bake in preheated 350-degree oven for 1 hour or until bread tests done.

Mrs. Edward Abbott
Windsor, Vermont

BRAN BROWN BREAD

    2 c. All-Bran
    1 1/4 c. milk
    1/2 c. molasses
    1 egg, beaten
    1 c. flour
    1/2 tsp. salt
    1 tsp. soda
    1/2 c. currants or raisins

Combine bran, milk and molasses; let stand until liquid is absorbed. Add egg and remaining ingredients; mix well. Pour batter into greased loaf pan. Bake in preheated 350-degree oven for 45 minutes or until bread tests done.

Virginia Huckins
New Hampton Grange, No. 123
New Hampton, New Hampshire

BAKED WALNUT BROWN BREAD

    1 1/4 c. sifted all-purpose flour
    2 tsp. baking powder
    3/4 tsp. soda
    1 1/4 tsp. salt
    1 1/4 c. graham flour
    1 c. chopped California walnuts
    1 egg
    1/3 c. (packed) brown sugar
    1/2 c. light molasses
    3/4 c. buttermilk
    3 tbsp. melted shortening

Resift all-purpose flour with baking powder, soda and salt. Stir in graham flour and walnuts. Beat egg lightly; beat in brown sugar, molasses, buttermilk and shortening. Stir into dry mixture just until all of flour is moistened. Spoon into 3 greased 1-pound size cans. Bake in preheated 350-degree oven for 45 minutes or until bread tests done. Let stand for 10 minutes, then turn out onto wire rack. Serve warm or cold. May spoon batter into a 9 x 5 x 3-inch loaf pan and bake for 50 to 55 minutes, if desired.

Photograph for this recipe below.

★ ★

BOSTON BROWN BREAD WITH WALNUTS
(Recipe over 100 years old)

2 c. graham flour
1 c. all-purpose flour
1 egg
1/2 c. sugar
1/2 c. molasses
2 c. buttermilk
2 tsp. soda
Pinch of salt
1/2 c. raisins
1/2 c. chopped walnuts

Mix graham flour and all-purpose flour together. Stir in remaining ingredients; mix well. Pour batter into well-greased bread pans; let rise for 2 hours. Bake in preheated 300-degree oven for 1 hour or until bread tests done.

Mrs. Dan Robinson, State Lecturer
Westmond Grange, No. 302
Sagle, Idaho

DELICIOUS BROWN BREAD
(Recipe 60 years old)

1 c. sugar
1 c. molasses
Graham flour
1 c. raisins
2 eggs
2 c. buttermilk
1 tsp. salt
1 tsp. soda
1/4 c. hot water

Combine sugar, molasses, 4 cups flour, raisins, eggs, buttermilk and salt in large mixing bowl. Dissolve soda in hot water; add to flour mixture. Mix well. Grease Number 303 size cans; dust with graham flour. Pour in batter to fill cans 1/2 full. Bake at 400 degrees for 45 minutes. Reduce oven temperature to 350 degrees; turn cans on side. Bake for 15 minutes longer. Let cool. Slice thin; spread with butter or cream cheese to serve. Bread freezes well.

Leagh E. Ritchey
Ozone Grange, No. 845
Salus, Arkansas

OLD BOSTON BROWN BREAD
(Recipe over 75 years old)

2 c. milk
3/4 c. molasses
2 c. cornmeal
2 c. all-purpose flour
1/2 tsp. salt
1 tsp. soda

Combine milk and molasses in large mixing bowl. Stir in cornmeal, flour and salt. Combine soda and about 1 teaspoon boiling water in molasses measuring cup; stir into milk mixture. Place in greased deep 2-quart pan; place pan over boiling water. Cover; steam for 3 hours.

Dissolved soda may be added before flour and cornmeal, if desired.

Mrs. L. A. Meeker
Hawleyton Grange, No. 575
Binghamton, New York

HOLIDAY FRUIT BREAD

2 pkg. yeast
1/4 c. warm water
1/2 c. sugar
1 tsp. salt
1/3 c. shortening
1 c. scalded milk
2 eggs
5 c. flour
1/2 c. raisins
3/4 c. candied fruit
1/2 c. chopped nuts (opt.)
1 1/2 tsp. grated lemon rind
3 tsp. grated orange rind

Soften yeast in warm water. Add sugar, salt and shortening to scalded milk; let cool to lukewarm. Add yeast mixture; beat in eggs and 2 cups flour until smooth. Add remaining flour to make a soft dough; knead until smooth and elastic. Place in oiled bowl; let rise until doubled in bulk. Combine remaining ingredients; knead into dough. Shape into 2 balls; place on oiled baking sheet. Let rise until doubled in bulk. Bake in preheated 375-degree oven for about 35 minutes or until loaves test done.

Mrs. Frank Prelli
Wife of State Master
Winsted, Connecticut

LEBKUCHEN
(Recipe 4 generations old)

2 c. milk, scalded
1 pkg. yeast
Sugar
Flour
3 eggs, beaten
1 tsp. salt
1 c. soft shortening
2 1/2 c. raisins
1/4 c. citron
1/4 c. orange rind
1/4 c. lemon rind
1/2 c. blanched almonds
Grated rind and juice of 1 lemon
1/4 tsp. cinnamon
1/4 tsp nutmeg

Cool scalded milk to lukewarm. Dissolve yeast and 1 teaspoon sugar in 1/4 cup warm water; let stand for 5 minutes. Add milk and 1 1/2 cups flour; let stand in warm place till bubbly. Blend in eggs, 1 cup sugar, salt and shortening. Chop raisins, citron, orange rind, 1/4 cup lemon rind and almonds; dredge with 1/4 cup flour. Add grated lemon rind and lemon juice to egg mixture. Sift 5 3/4 cups flour, cinnamon and nutmeg together; add to egg mixture to make a stiff dough.

★ ★

Work in raisin mixture; let rise until doubled in bulk. Braid in wreath; place on cookie sheet. Bake in preheated 375-degree oven for 30 minutes or until done. Frost with powdered sugar icing; decorate with candies, nuts or cherries.

Agnes Mae Lampert
Worley Grange, No. 348
Worley, Idaho

JULEKAKE
(Recipe over 75 years old)

1 yeast cake
1/4 c. lukewarm water
1/4 c. butter
1 1/2 c. milk, scalded
6 tbsp. sugar
1 tsp. salt
6 c. flour
1 egg, beaten
1/4 c. currants
1/4 c. chopped citron
6 tbsp. raisins
1/4 c. chopped candied cherries

Dissolve yeast in lukewarm water. Add butter to scalded milk; let cool to lukewarm. Combine milk mixture, yeast mixture, sugar and salt; mix well. Stir in 1 1/2 cups flour, egg, currants, citron, raisins and cherries. Add remaining flour gradually to make a soft dough; knead until smooth. Place in greased bowl; cover. Let rise until doubled in bulk. Punch down; let rise again until doubled in bulk. Shape into 2 loaves; place in greased 5 x 9-inch loaf pans. Let rise until doubled in bulk. Bake in preheated 350-degree oven for 35 to 40 minutes or until loaves test done. Frost as desired.

Otis Maynard Master
Buffalo Valley Grange
Arcade, New York

CHERRY-WALNUT BREAD

3/4 c. (packed) brown sugar
1/3 c. oil
1 egg, beaten
1/2 c. mixed milk and cherry juice
1/2 tsp. almond extract
1 1/4 c. flour
1/2 tsp. salt
1/2 tsp. soda
1/4 tsp. cinnamon
3/4 to 1 c. sour cherries, diced
1/4 to 1/3 c. chopped walnuts

Combine brown sugar and oil; add egg, milk and almond extract. Mix well. Beat in dry ingredients; stir in cherries and walnuts. Place in greased loaf pan. Bake in preheated 325-degree oven for 40 minutes or until done. May use glass pan and bake at 350 degrees for 60 to 65 minutes. Fresh or drained canned cherries may be used.

Grethel Capen, C.W.A. Sec.
American River Grange, No. 172
Rancho Cordova, California

CRANBERRY-NUT BREAD
(Recipe 45 years old)

2 c. flour
1 tsp. baking powder
1 tsp. salt
3/4 c. sugar
1 egg, slightly beaten
2/3 c. milk
1/4 c. melted butter
1 c. whole cranberry sauce
1 c. chopped nuts

Sift dry ingredients into large bowl; add remaining ingredients. Mix just to moisten. Turn into greased loaf pan. Bake in preheated 350-degree oven for about 1 hour.

Bertha Perkins, C.W.A. Chm.
Queen City Grange, No. 30
Orono, Maine

CRANBERRY-ORANGE BREAD
(Recipe about 40 years old)

8 c. sifted flour
4 c. sugar
2 tbsp. baking powder
2 tsp. soda
4 tsp. salt
Juice and grated rind of 4 med. oranges
1/2 c. (scant) melted shortening
4 med. eggs, well beaten
2 c. chopped nuts
1 1/2 lb. cranberries, coarsely chopped

Sift flour, sugar, baking powder, soda and salt together. Pour orange juice into 4-cup measuring cup; add orange rind and shortening. Add enough boiling water to make 3 cups liquid. Make a well in center of dry ingredients; pour in liquid and eggs. Stir just until dry ingredients are dampened. Fold in nuts and cranberries. Divide into 4 greased and paper-lined loaf pans, pushing batter into corners. Bake in preheated 350-degree oven for 1 hour. Remove from pans; cool. Wrap and store for several days in refrigerator for easy slicing.

Lucille J. Scanlon
Quonochontaug Grange, No. 48
Bradford, Rhode Island

GRAPE NUTS BREAD

1 c. Grape Nuts
2 c. sour milk
1 tsp. soda
1/2 c. sugar
3 1/2 c. flour
4 tsp. baking powder

Mix Grape Nuts and milk together; let stand for 15 minutes. Add soda. Combine sugar, flour and baking powder; stir into milk mixture. Place in greased loaf pan. Bake in preheated 350-degree oven until bread tests done.

Mrs. Clifton Oakley
Windy Ridge Grange, No. 1573
Grand Gorge, New York

★ ★

DATE AND CHEESE BREAD

3/4 c. boiling water
1/2 lb. dates, cut fine
1 3/4 c. flour
1/4 tsp. salt
1 tsp. soda
1/2 c. sugar
1 egg, beaten
1 c. grated Cheddar cheese

Pour boiling water over dates; let stand for 5 minutes. Mix and sift flour, salt, soda and sugar. Add date mixture, egg and cheese. Mix well. Place in greased loaf pan. Bake in preheated 350-degree oven for 50 minutes.

Mrs. Thelma Plummer, Overseer
Fairview Grange, No. 273
Tillamook, Oregon

DATE NUT BREAD

1 1/2 c. boiling water
2 c. chopped dates or·raisins
2 tbsp. butter
2 eggs, well beaten
2 c. (scant) sugar or 1 1/2 c. (packed)
    brown sugar
5 c. flour
2 tsp. soda
1/2 tsp. salt
1 tbsp. vanilla extract
1 c. chopped walnuts

Pour boiling water over dates; add butter. Let stand for 15 minutes. Add eggs to date mixture. Add dry ingredients, vanilla extract and walnuts; mix well. Turn into greased loaf pans. Bake in preheated 350-degree oven for 45 minutes. Slice thin and serve.

Celesta Nice
Wolf Creek Grange, No. 596
North Powder, Oregon

FRESH BLUEBERRY-LEMON BREAD

Flour
4 tsp. baking powder
1 1/2 tsp. salt
2 eggs
1 c. sugar
1 c. milk
3 tbsp. melted shortening
1 tsp. vanilla
1 tsp. grated lemon rind
1 c. fresh blueberries
1/2 c. chopped walnuts

Sift 3 cups sifted flour, baking powder and salt together. Beat eggs well; beat in sugar gradually. Combine milk and shortening; add to egg mixture. Add vanilla and lemon rind; mix well. Add sifted dry ingredients; stir to blend well. Combine blueberries, walnuts and 1 tablespoon flour; fold carefully into batter. Pour into greased 9 x 5 x 3-inch loaf pan. Bake in preheated 350-degree oven for 1 hour or until bread tests

done. Cool in pan on rack for 10 minutes. Remove from pan; cool on rack. One 10-ounce package frozen blueberries, thawed and drained, may be substituted for fresh blueberries.

Rose M. Robinson, C.W.A. Dir.
New Jersey Grange

EASY HOBO BREAD

2 c. raisins
2 c. boiling water
4 tbsp. oil
1 1/2 c. sugar
1 c. (packed) brown sugar
2 eggs, beaten
4 c. whole wheat flour
2 tsp. soda
1 tsp. salt
2 tsp. vanilla
1 c. chopped nuts

Combine raisins and boiling water; set aside. Mix remaining ingredients together in order listed. Pour in raisin mixture; mix well. Fill three 1-pound coffee cans half full. Bake in preheated 350-degree oven for 1 hour or until the loaves test done. Loaves may be frozen. One and one-half cups honey may be substituted for sugars, if desired.

Mildred Jones, Treas.
Pomona Grange, No. 31
Riverside, California

GINGER YEAST BREAD

1/2 c. milk
2 tbsp. shortening
1 1/2 tsp. grated orange peel
2 tsp. salt
1/4 c. dark molasses
3 1/2 c. sifted all-purpose flour
3/4 tsp. cinnamon
1/2 tsp. ginger
1/8 tsp. cloves
1 pkg. dry yeast
3/4 c. warm water
1 egg

Heat milk in heavy saucepan; add shortening, orange peel, salt and molasses. Stir until shortening melts. Cool to lukewarm. Sift flour, cinnamon, ginger and cloves together. Dissolve yeast in warm water in warm bowl. Add milk mixture, egg and 2 cups flour mixture. Blend at low speed of electric mixer; beat at medium speed for 2 minutes. Add remaining flour; beat for 1 minute. Cover; let rise in warm place for about 45 minutes or until doubled in bulk. Stir down. Pour batter into well-greased 9 x 5-inch loaf pan. Cover; let rise for about 40 minutes or until doubled in bulk. Bake in preheated 375-degree oven for 45 minutes. Serve with cream cheese.

This recipe dates back to colonial days.

Cecilia S. Lamb
Wheatland Grange, No. 273
Hillsdale, Michigan

★ ★

IRISH BREAD

2 c. flour
1/2 c. sugar
1 1/2 tsp. baking powder
1/2 tsp. soda
1/4 tsp. salt
1 egg
1/2 c. raisins or currants
1 tbsp. caraway seed
1 c. buttermilk

Sift flour, sugar, baking powder, soda and salt together into bowl. Add egg, raisins, caraway seed and buttermilk; mix well. Place in greased loaf pan. Bake in preheated 350-degree oven for 50 to 60 minutes.

Betty C. Purdy
Norfield Grange
Georgetown, Connecticut

NAPFKUCHEN

(Recipe over 100 years old)

1 cake yeast
1/4 c. warm milk
1/2 c. butter
1/2 c. sugar
2 eggs, well beaten
1 c. milk, scalded and cooled
3 c. flour
1 c. raisins
Grated rind of 1/2 lemon
Chopped almonds

Dissolve yeast in warm milk. Cream butter and sugar together. Add eggs and cooled milk; mix well. Stir in yeast mixture. Add flour, raisins and lemon rind; mix thoroughly. Sprinkle buttered loaf pan with chopped almonds; fill half full of dough. Let rise until doubled in bulk. Bake in preheated 300-degree oven for 45 minutes or until done. Turn out of pan; sprinkle with additional sugar.

Leona Clayton
Rosedale Grange, No. 565
Bakersfield, California

LEMON-WALNUT BREAD

1/2 c. butter
1 1/2 c. all-purpose flour
1 1/4 c. sugar
1 tsp. baking powder
1/4 tsp. salt
2 eggs, beaten
1/2 c. milk
Juice and grated rind of 1 lemon
1/2 c. chopped walnuts

Cream butter until light. Sift flour, 1 cup sugar, baking powder and salt together. Combine eggs and milk. Add flour mixture and milk mixture alternately to butter mixture, mixing well after each addition. Stir in grated rind and walnuts. Turn into greased bread pan. Bake in preheated 350-degree oven for 1 hour. Combine lemon juice and remaining 1/4 cup sugar. Remove loaf from oven; spread sugar mixture over loaf. Let cool before removing from pan.

May E. Marcy
Seekonk Grange, No. 341
Seekonk, Massachusetts

OATMEAL HEALTH BREAD

2 c. rolled oats
1/2 c. wheat germ
1 c. raisins
3/4 c. molasses
1 tbsp. shortening
1 tbsp. salt
1 pkg. yeast
10 c. all-purpose flour

Combine oats, wheat germ, raisins and 4 cups water; cook for about 10 minutes. Stir in molasses, shortening and salt. Let cool. Soften yeast in 1/2 cup lukewarm water; add to cooled oats mixture. Add 9 cups flour; turn out on floured board. Knead in remaining flour. Place in greased bowl; let rise for about 1 hour and 30 minutes. Punch down; let rise again for about 1 hour and 30 minutes. Punch down; turn out on board. Let rest for 10 minutes. Cut into 3 parts; roll out each part to break bubbles. Form into loaves; place in bread pans. Let rise for about 1 hour and 30 minutes. Bake in preheated 375-degree oven for 20 minutes. Cover with aluminum foil. Reduce temperature to 350 degrees; bake for 15 to 20 minutes longer or until bread tests done.

Shirley R. Gaspar
Beverly Grange, No. 306
Wenham, Massachusetts

PUMPKIN BREAD

1/3 c. shortening
1 1/3 c. sugar
2 eggs
1 1/2 c. flour
1/4 tsp. baking powder
1 tsp. soda
1/2 tsp. salt
1/2 tsp. cinnamon
1/4 tsp. cloves
1 c. strained pumpkin
3/4 c. water
1/3 c. white raisins
1/3 c. chopped nuts

Cream shortening, sugar and eggs together. Sift dry ingredients together; mix pumpkin and water. Add pumpkin mixture alternately with sifted dry ingredients to egg mixture. Stir in raisins and nuts. Place in greased 4 x 10-inch loaf pan. Bake in 350-degree oven for 1 hour or until done.

Mrs. Mary Cottone
Delaware Valley Grange, No. 1565
Grand Gorge, New York

★ ★

PEAR BREAD

2 c. flour
1 tsp. baking powder
1/2 tsp. soda
1/2 tsp. salt
1 c. sugar
1/3 c. oil or shortening
1 egg
1/3 c. orange juice
1 tbsp. orange peel
1 c. chopped unpeeled pears
1 c. bran flakes
1 c. chopped nuts
Topping

Place first 5 ingredients in bowl; add oil, egg, juice and peel. Mix well. Add pears, bran flakes and nuts; stir until well combined. Pour into greased loaf pan. Sprinkle Topping over batter. Bake in preheated 350-degree oven for 50 minutes.

TOPPING

1 tbsp. butter
3 tbsp. brown sugar
1/4 tsp. mace
1 tbsp. flour

Combine all ingredients; mix well.

Pauline M. Fisher
Morning Star Grange, No. 311
Halsey, Oregon

PECAN LOAF
(Recipe 75 years old)

1 c. butter
2 c. sugar
6 eggs, beaten
1 lg. wine glass whiskey
1/2 c. raisins
2 tsp. nutmeg
4 c. flour
4 c. chopped pecans

Cream butter and sugar together. Add eggs, whiskey, raisins and nutmeg; mix well. Add flour slowly, mixing until smooth after each addition. Stir in pecans. Pour in well-greased loaf pan. Bake in preheated 350-degree oven until a toothpick inserted in center comes out clean.

Mrs. Olive Elliott
Morgan Hill Grange, No. 408
Morgan Hill, California

RAISIN RYE BREAD

4 c. (about) all-purpose flour
2 pkg. active dry yeast
2 c. milk
1/4 c. light molasses
2 tbsp. butter
1 tbsp. sugar

2 tsp. salt
1 c. seedless raisins
1 tsp. grated lemon peel
2 c. Bohemian-style rye and whole wheat
   flour

Combine 2 cups all-purpose flour and yeast in a large mixing bowl. Combine milk, molasses, butter, sugar and salt in 1-quart saucepan; heat until warm. Add milk mixture to flour. Beat for 30 seconds at low speed, scraping bowl constantly, then 3 minutes longer at high speed. Add 1 cup all-purpose flour and beat for 1 minute longer. Add raisins and lemon peel. Stir in rye and whole wheat flour and enough remaining all-purpose flour to make a soft dough. Turn onto lightly floured surface; knead for 5 to 10 minutes or until smooth and satiny. Place in buttered bowl, turning once to butter top. Cover bowl. Let rise on a rack over hot water for about 1 hour or until doubled in bulk. Punch down; divide in half. Shape each into a round loaf; flatten slightly. Place on buttered baking sheet. Cover; let stand in warm place for about 1 hour or until doubled in bulk. Bake in preheated 375-degree oven for 25 to 30 minutes or until loaf sounds hollow when tapped. Remove to wire rack to cool. Yield: 2 loaves.

Photograph for this recipe on back cover.

EASY RAISIN BREAD

1 1/2 tsp. salt
1/4 c. sugar
1/4 c. shortening
2/3 c. hot water
2 pkg. yeast
1/2 c. warm water
1 egg, beaten
1 c. seedless raisins
3 c. sifted flour
1/4 tsp. cinnamon

Stir salt, sugar and shortening into hot water; cool to lukewarm. Sprinkle yeast in warm water; stir until dissolved. Stir into lukewarm water mixture. Add remaining ingredients; stir until well blended. Let rise for about 50 minutes or until more than doubled in bulk. Stir down; beat vigorously for about 30 seconds. Turn into greased 1 1/2-quart casserole or large bread pan. Bake, uncovered, in preheated 400-degree oven for 45 minutes or until done. Do not let dough rise before putting in oven; dough will rise while baking.

Helen Placy
Mohawk Grange, No. 217
Colebrook, New Hampshire

GRANNY'S RAISIN BREAD
(Recipe over 125 years old)

1 1/2 c. milk
1 c. sugar
1/2 c. shortening
1 tsp. salt
2 cakes yeast

★ ★

1/2 c. warm water
1 lb. raisins
4 eggs, beaten
Flour

Scald milk; stir in sugar, shortening and salt. Let cool to lukewarm. Dissolve yeast in water. Combine yeast, milk mixture, raisins and eggs; add enough flour to make stiff dough. Turn out onto floured board; knead well. Place dough in large greased bowl; let rise until doubled in bulk. Punch down. Let rise again until doubled in bulk. Divide dough in 3 parts; shape into loaves. Place in well-greased loaf pans. Let rise until doubled in bulk. Bake in preheated 350-degree oven for 45 to 60 minutes. Cinnamon-raisin bread may be made by flattening dough for each loaf and sprinkling with cinnamon and sugar to taste. Shape into loaves. Two finely chopped apples may be added to dough, if desired.

Eva Jeanne Steffey, State Youth Dir.
Pleasant View Grange, No. 1459
Lawrence, Kansas

RHUBARB BREAD

1 1/2 c. (firmly packed) brown sugar
Melted butter
1 egg
1 c. sour milk or buttermilk
1 tsp. vanilla
1 tsp. soda
2 1/2 c. flour
1 1/2 c. diced rhubarb
1/2 c. chopped nuts
1/2 c. sugar
1/2 tsp. cinnamon

Combine brown sugar and 2/3 cup butter. Stir in egg, sour milk and vanilla; mix well. Sift soda and flour together; stir into butter mixture. Stir in rhubarb and nuts. Pour into 2 well-greased loaf pans. Combine remaining ingredients with 1 tablespoon melted butter; sprinkle over top. Bake in preheated 325-degree oven for about 40 minutes or until done. Do not overbake. Let stand for 2 to 3 minutes. Remove from pan; cool on rack.

Marie Presler
Glendale Grange, No. 135
Wheat Ridge, Colorado

MOLASSES DUMPLINGS
(Recipe 200 years old)

2 c. flour
1 tsp. salt
1 tsp. soda
2 tsp. cream of tartar
2 tsp. melted fat
3/4 c. milk
1 pt. molasses

Sift flour, salt, soda and cream of tartar together. Add melted fat and milk; mix well. Roll out on floured board. Cut out with small round cutter. Drop dump-

lings, several at a time, into deep hot fat. Fry until browned. Bring molasses to a boil; drop dumplings into molasses to coat. Remove; drain on racks. Yield: 4 servings.

Shirley R. Gaspar
Beverly Grange, No. 306
Wenham, Massachusetts

STRAWBERRY MUFFIN SHORTCAKE

2 pt. California strawberries
Honey
Grated lemon peel
1 c. sour cream
1 1/2 c. unsifted all-purpose flour
1/2 c. sugar
1 tbsp. poppy seed
2 tsp. baking powder
1/2 tsp. salt
1/4 c. shortening
1 egg
3/4 c. milk

Slice strawberries; sweeten with about 1/4 cup honey or to taste. Add 1 teaspoon grated lemon peel; stir gently and chill for 30 minutes. Combine sour cream, 1/4 cup honey and 1 teaspoon grated lemon peel in a medium-sized bowl; stir just until ingredients are combined. Do not overstir. Chill. Combine flour, sugar, poppy seed, baking powder and salt in medium-sized bowl. Cut in shortening with pastry blender or 2 knives until mixture resembles coarse crumbs. Beat egg; stir in milk. Add egg mixture to flour mixture. Stir quickly with fork just until dry ingredients are moistened. Batter will be lumpy. Divide mixture evenly among twelve 2 1/2 x 1 1/4-inch greased muffin cups. Bake in preheated 400-degree oven for 20 minutes or until toothpick inserted in center of muffins comes out clean. Remove muffins from pans. Split warm muffins; top with strawberry mixture, then top each serving with sour cream mixture. Yield: 12 muffins.

Photograph for this recipe below.

★ ★

GINGER BUNS

3 c. flour
2 tsp. salt
2 tsp. soda
1 tsp. cinnamon
1 tsp. cloves
1 tsp. ginger
1 egg
3/4 c. shortening, melted
1 c. molasses
1/2 c. sugar
1 c. boiling water

Sift flour, salt, soda and spices together; add egg, shortening, molasses and sugar. Mix thoroughly; add boiling water. Spoon in greased muffin tins. Bake at 350 degrees for 20 to 25 minutes. Cupcake paper liners may be used in muffin tins, if desired. Yield: 18 large or 25 medium buns.

Mrs. Perley Sweetland
Manchester Grange, No. 172
Manchester, Maine

MARMALADE DROPS

1 pkg. dry yeast
1/4 c. warm water
1 c. milk
1/4 c. sugar
1 tsp. salt
1/2 c. melted shortening
2 eggs, beaten
3 1/4 c. sifted flour
1/2 tsp. vanilla
Marmalade

Soften yeast in warm water. Scald milk; add sugar, salt and shortening. Cool to lukewarm. Add eggs; beat until blended. Add 1 cup flour; beat well. Add yeast mixture; mix well. Add more flour, stirring until batter is stiff. Stir in vanilla. Cover; let rise for about 1 hour or until bubbly. Place 1 teaspoon marmalade in each greased cup of muffin pan. Stir dough thoroughly; drop by spoonfuls into muffin pan. Let rise until doubled in bulk. Bake in 375-degree oven for 20 to 30 minutes. Yield: 12-18 muffins.

Edith Atwell
Manitou Park Grange, No. 430
Woodland Park, Colorado

NEALIE'S APPLE MUFFINS
(Recipe about 100 years old)

2 1/4 c. flour
3 1/2 tsp. baking powder
1/2 tsp. cinnamon
1/2 tsp. nutmeg
1/4 c. shortening or lard
Sugar
1 egg

1 c. milk
1 c. finely chopped apples

Sift flour, baking powder, 1/4 teaspoon cinnamon and 1/4 teaspoon nutmeg together on waxed paper or in bowl. Cream shortening and 1/2 cup sugar until smooth. Add egg; beat until fluffy. Add flour mixture alternately with milk, mixing well after each addition. Fold in apples. Pour in well-greased muffin tins. Combine 2 tablespoons sugar, 1/4 teaspoon cinnamon and 1/4 teaspoon nutmeg; stir to mix well. Sprinkle over batter in muffin tins. Bake in 400-degree oven for 20 minutes or until golden brown. Yield: 12 muffins.

Jean Stubblefield, Lady Asst. Steward
Imnaha Grange, No. 677
Imnaha, Oregon

ORANGE-FILLED ROLLS
(Recipe about 50 years old)

2 c. milk
1 pkg. yeast
Sugar
1/4 c. melted shortening
6 c. sifted flour
2 tsp. salt
3 tbsp. cornstarch
Grated rind and juice of 1 orange
Grated rind and juice of 1/2 lemon

Scald milk; let cool to lukewarm. Sprinkle yeast and 2 tablespoons sugar over milk; let soak until dissolved. Add shortening and half the flour; beat until smooth. Add salt and remaining flour; knead until smooth. Place in greased bowl; cover. Let rise until doubled in bulk. Roll out on floured board to 1/4-inch thickness. Combine cornstarch and 3/4 cup sugar in saucepan; blend. Stir in 1/2 cup water; add rinds and juices. Bring to a boil; cook and stir until thick. Set aside to cool. Spread filling over dough; roll up as for jelly roll. Cut into 1-inch slices. Place in greased muffin tins; let rise for about 45 minutes or until light. Bake in 375-degree oven for 20 to 25 minutes or until golden.

Lois M. Mecklenburg
Bluestem Grange, No. 776
Davenport, Washington

CINNAMON ROLLS

2 to 2 1/4 c. all-purpose flour
1 pkg. dry yeast
3/4 c. milk
1/4 c. butter
Sugar
3/4 tsp. salt
1 egg
Melted butter
1 tsp. cinnamon
1/4 c. seedless raisins (opt.)

Combine 1 cup flour and yeast in small mixing bowl. Combine milk, butter, 1/4 cup sugar and salt in 1-quart saucepan; heat until warm. Add to flour mixture; add egg. Beat for 30 seconds with electric mixer

★ ★

at low speed, scraping bowl constantly; beat for 3 minutes at high speed. Add 1/2 cup flour; beat for 1 minute longer. Stir in enough remaining flour to make soft dough. Turn onto lightly floured surface; knead for 5 to 10 minutes or until smooth and satiny. Place in buttered bowl, turning once to butter top; cover bowl. Let rise on rack over hot water for about 1 hour or until doubled in bulk; punch down. Roll out dough on lightly floured surface to measure 8 x 15 inches; brush to within 1/2 inch of edge with melted butter. Mix 3 tablespoons sugar and cinnamon in small bowl; spread over dough. Sprinkle with raisins; roll lengthwise as for jelly roll. Cut into 1 1/4-inch slices; place, cut side up, in buttered 9-inch square pan. Cover; let rise in warm place for 30 to 40 minutes or until doubled in bulk. Bake in preheated 375-degree oven for 25 to 30 minutes; remove to wire rack to cool. Brush with melted butter; sprinkle with sugar. Yield: 12 rolls.

Photograph for this recipe on back cover.

BLUEBERRY CRUMPETS

1 pkg. yeast
1/2 c. lukewarm water
2 eggs
1 1/2 c. lukewarm milk
2 tbsp. melted butter
1/2 tsp. salt
2 tsp. sugar
Grated rind of 1 orange
3 1/2 c. all-purpose flour
1 c. dry-pack frozen blueberries, thawed
   or 1   15-oz. can blueberries,
   drained

Dissolve yeast in lukewarm water. Combine eggs, milk, butter, salt, sugar and grated rind; mix well. Stir in dissolved yeast. Stir in flour gradually; beat until smooth. Let stand for 15 minutes. Stir in blueberries; spoon batter into well-greased muffin pans, filling cups 2/3 full. Bake in a preheated 400-degree oven for 15 minutes or until lightly browned. Serve immediately with butter and blueberry preserves. Yield: 24 crumpets.

Photograph for this recipe on page 271.

A PHILADELPHIA SPECIALTY TRADITIONAL STICKY BUNS

1/2 c. pecan halves
6 tbsp. butter
1/4 c. light corn syrup
3/4 c. (packed) light brown sugar
1 lb. white bread dough
3/4 tsp. ground cinnamon

Place pecans into twelve 3 x 1 1/2-inch well-greased muffin pan cups. Melt 4 tablespoons butter in small saucepan; stir in corn syrup and 1/2 cup brown sugar. Cook until sugar dissolves, stirring occasionally. Divide mixture evenly between muffin pan cups; set aside. Roll out dough into a 12 x 10-inch rectangle on lightly floured surface. Spread with remaining 2 tablespoons butter; sprinkle on cinnamon and remaining 1/4 cup brown sugar. Roll dough jelly-roll fashion starting at 12-inch side. Pinch seam to seal edge. Cut into twelve 1-inch slices. Place, cut side up, in prepared pans. Cover; let rise in a warm place, free from draft, for about 30 minutes or until doubled in bulk. Bake in preheated 350-degree oven for 25 minutes or until golden. Invert rolls onto plate lined with waxed paper to cool. Serve with tea flavored with cinnamon stick.

Photograph for this recipe on page 201.

DANISH AEBLESKIVER
(Recipe 50 years old)

3 eggs, separated
1 1/2 c. buttermilk
1 tsp. soda
1 3/4 c. flour
2 tsp. baking powder
1/2 tsp. salt
1/2 c. shortening, melted

Beat egg yolks well; beat in buttermilk and soda. Sift flour, baking powder and salt together; add with shortening to buttermilk mixture. Fold in stiffly beaten egg whites. Place 1/2 teaspoon additional shortening in each cup of hot aebleskiver pan. Fill each cup 3/4 full with batter. Bake both sides to a golden brown, turning with sharp fork. Serve hot with syrup, powdered sugar or jelly. May also be baked in waffle iron.

Marie Christians
Homestead Grange, No. 215
Denver, Colorado

NORWEGIAN KRINGLE
(Recipe at least 75 years old)

2 c. warm milk
2 pkg. yeast
Sugar
1 tbsp. salt
2 eggs, beaten
6 1/2 c. flour
1 tsp. crushed cardamom seed
Cream
1 egg yolk

Combine milk, yeast, 1 cup sugar, salt and eggs; mix well. Add half the flour and cardamom seed; mix well. Add remaining flour; mix until smooth. Let rise until doubled in bulk. Pinch off pieces of dough; roll in narrow strips about 8 inches long. Form into figure 8. Place on greased cookie sheet; let rise over pan of steam until doubled in bulk. Add enough cream to egg yolk to make brushing consistency; stir in sugar to taste. Brush cream mixture on rolls. Bake in 375-degree oven for 20 to 25 minutes or until browned.

Mrs. O. A. Reitzel
Oak Leaf Grange, No. 569
Harris, Minnesota

★ ★

CINNAMON ROLLS

1 yeast cake, crumbled
Sugar
1 c. lukewarm milk
1/2 c. soft butter
3 eggs, well beaten
1 tsp. salt
4 2/3 c. flour
2 tbsp. melted butter
Cinnamon sugar

Stir yeast cake with 1 tablespoon sugar. Add milk, soft butter, eggs, salt and flour; mix until soft dough forms. Cover; let dough rise from 2 hours to overnight. Cut dough in half. Roll out into 1/4-inch thick rectangle. Spread each rectangle with 1 tablespoon melted butter, then with cinnamon sugar. Roll up as for jelly roll; cut into 1-inch thick pieces. Place in greased muffin tins. Cover; let rise for 2 hours. Bake in preheated 375-degree oven for 12 to 15 minutes. Let set in pans for about 5 minutes. May frost with powdered sugar icing. Yield: 2 dozen rolls.

Sharon Pearse
Guilford Hope Grange, No. 6

CINNAMON KNOTS

1 c. milk
1/3 c. butter
1 c. hot mashed potatoes
2 tsp. salt
Sugar
1 tbsp. yeast
1/2 c. warm water
2 eggs, beaten
5 to 6 c. flour
2 tbsp. (or more) cinnamon
1/2 c. melted butter

Scald milk; pour over butter in large bowl. Add potatoes, salt and 1/3 cup sugar; let cool. Dissolve yeast in warm water; add yeast, eggs and 2 cups flour to potato mixture. Cover; let rise until bubbly. Add enough flour to make dough manageable; knead until smooth. Place in buttered bowl; cover. Let rise until doubled in bulk. Divide in 3 portions. Form into balls, one portion at a time; roll out to 1/2-inch thickness on a floured board. Cut dough in 1 x 5-inch strips. Combine 1 1/2 cups sugar and the cinnamon in shallow dish. Dip each strip of dough in melted butter, then roll in cinnamon-sugar mixture. Tie in a knot; place on greased cookie sheet, tucking ends under. Cover with waxed paper; let rise until doubled in bulk. Bake in 375-degree oven for 20 minutes or until lightly browned.

Eloise Potts, C.W.A.
Lamont Grange, No. 889
Lamont, Washington

BASIC SWEET DOUGH

2 pkg. dry yeast
1/2 c. warm water
4 c. flour
1/2 c. sugar
1 tsp. salt
3/4 c. butter
1/2 c. milk, scalded and cooled
2 eggs, slightly beaten
Butter, melted

Sprinkle yeast over water; stir until dissolved. Combine flour, sugar and salt in large mixing bowl. Cut in butter until mixture resembles coarse crumbs. Combine milk, eggs and yeast; add to dry ingredients. Mix well; brush with butter. Cover; chill overnight.

PECAN ROLLS

Basic Sweet Dough
1/4 c. butter
1 c. (firmly packed) brown sugar
1/4 c. light corn syrup
Pecan halves
Butter, melted
1 tsp. cinnamon

Bring dough to room temperature. Combine butter, 1/2 cup sugar and syrup in saucepan; bring to a boil. Spoon 1 1/2 teaspoons sugar mixture into buttered muffin cups; top with 2 or 3 pecan halves. Divide dough in half. Roll each half in a 18 x 12-inch rectangle on a lightly floured surface. Brush with butter. Combine remaining 1/2 cup brown sugar and the cinnamon. Sprinkle over buttered dough rectangle. Roll up; cut in 1-inch slices. Place in muffin cups. Brush with butter. Cover; let dough rise in warm place until doubled in bulk. Bake in preheated 375-degree oven for 15 to 20 minutes or until golden brown. Invert immediately. Yield: 36 rolls.

Photograph for this recipe below.

★ ★

CAPE COD BUTTER BUNS

1 yeast cake
1/4 c. water
1 c. scalded milk
3 1/2 c. all-purpose flour
1/4 c. sugar
1/4 c. melted butter
2 egg yolks
1/2 tsp. salt
Grated rind of 1 lemon
Softened butter
Brown sugar

Make a sponge by combining yeast cake, water, milk and 1 1/2 cups flour. Let stand in warm place until light, then add sugar, melted butter, egg yolks, salt, lemon rind and remaining flour. Knead until smooth and elastic. Cover tightly; let set until doubled in bulk. Turn upside down on floured board; roll into a rectangle. Spread with softened butter; sprinkle with brown sugar. Roll as for jelly roll. Cut into 1-inch slices; place on well-buttered pan. Sprinkle top with brown sugar. Let rise for 15 minutes. Bake at 400 degrees for about 20 minutes. Yield: 8 servings.

Mrs. Della L. Macomber, Sec.
Eastham Grange, No. 308
Eastham, Massachusetts

SHORTBREAD
(Recipe 150 years old)

1 c. butter
1/2 c. sugar
1/4 tsp. salt
1 egg yolk
2 c. (about) flour

Soften butter in bowl; stir in sugar, salt and egg yolk with wooden spoon. Add flour, small amount at a time, until mixture is too stiff to stir. Turn onto floured board; knead lightly. Divide in half; pat onto 2 ungreased plates. Pinch edges; prick all over with fork. Place on cookie sheet. Bake in preheated 325-degree oven until lightly browned.

Mrs. Daryl Lowry
Wife of State Master
Vergennes, Vermont

MOM NOH'S APPLE STRUDEL
(Recipe over 100 years old)

1 egg
2 c. flour
Pinch of salt
Butter
8 to 9 apples
2 1/2 c. bread crumbs
1 1/2 c. raisins
1 c. chopped walnuts
1 1/2 c. sugar
1 tbsp. cinnamon
Confectioner's sugar

Beat egg well; pour in 1-cup measuring cup. Fill with lukewarm water. Combine flour and salt in large bowl; add egg mixture and 1 tablespoon melted buttter. Mix until moistened, then knead and pound until dough blisters. Cover; let set in warm place for about 1 hour. Peel and core apples; cut in thin slices. Measure slices to fill 7 cups. Spread kitchen table with large pastry cloth or any clean cloth; sprinkle with generous coating of flour. Place ball of dough in center; roll out in circle as evenly as possible. Using hands in gentle hand over hand motion, work from center and stretch toward outer edge of table. Keep moving around table, stretching dough with backs of hands until dough is paper thin. Trim off uneven or thick edges. Brush with 1/4 cup melted butter; sprinkle with half the bread crumbs. Combine apples, raisins and walnuts; spread over bread crumbs. Combine sugar and cinnamon. Sprinkle over apple mixture. Sprinkle remaining bread crumbs evenly over sugar; drizzle with 1/4 cup melted butter. Roll strudel up, using hands under cloth to guide rolling dough. Work into horseshoe shape. Brush edges with water; seal. Lift into baking pan. Brush top with melted butter. Bake in preheated 400-degree oven for 10 minutes. Reduce oven temperature to 350 degrees; bake for about 30 minutes or until brown. Sprinkle with confectioners' sugar; cool.

Mrs. Chester Noh
Fairview Grange, No. 178
Buhl, Idaho

OLD VIENNA APPLE STRUDEL
(Recipe over 80 years old)

1 1/2 c. flour
1/4 tsp. salt
1 egg
1 tbsp. (heaping) lard
4 lb. apples
1/4 c. butter
1 c. bread crumbs
Sugar to taste
1/2 c. (or more) raisins
Grated rind of 1 lemon
Cinnamon to taste
Powdered sugar

Combine flour, salt, egg and lard in large bowl; add 1/3 to 1/2 cup water or enough to make soft dough. Beat until dough blisters. Cover with warm bowl; let set in warm place for about 30 minutes. Peel, core and slice apples as for pie. Melt butter in pan; add bread crumbs, tossing until coated and lightly browned. Place tablecloth on table; sprinkle lightly with flour. Roll dough to about 1/2-inch thickness with rolling pin. Put hand under dough in center; pull and stretch gently, being careful not to make holes, until dough is paper thin. Spread bread crumbs over dough. Place a thin layer of apples over crumbs, then sprinkle with sugar. Dot with additional butter; add raisins and lemon rind. Sprinkle with cinnamon. Holding one end of tablecloth, roll up dough. Form into horseshoe with hand still under tablecloth. Flip into greased 8 x 12-inch pan. Bake in preheated 350-degree oven for 45 to 60 minutes. Cut in slices; sprinkle with powdered sugar.

Aurelia Bryant
Priest Lake Grange, No. 447
Coolin, Idaho

★ ★

FINNISH PANCAKES
(Recipe over 100 years old)

> 3 eggs
> 2 c. milk
> 1/4 c. sugar or honey
> 3/4 c. flour
> 1/2 tsp. salt
> 4 tbsp. butter

Combine eggs and milk; beat until blended. Add sugar, flour and salt. Melt butter in hot iron skillet. Drop batter in 4 equal portions into skillet. Bake in 450-degree oven for 20 to 30 minutes. Serve with jam or berry syrup or strawberries and cream.

Ellen Johnson Austin
Washington Grange, No. 82
Vancouver, Washington

BUCKWHEAT GRIDDLE CAKES
(Recipe over 100 years old)

> 4 c. warm water or milk
> 1 tsp. salt
> 1/2 cake compressed yeast
> 4 c. buckwheat flour
> 1 c. flour
> 1 tsp. soda

Pour warm water into small earthen jar; add salt and yeast. Stir in buckwheat flour and flour; beat well. Thin batter, if too thick, with warm water. Beat again; cover with plate. Place folded cloth over plate. Set in warm place; let rise overnight. Dissolve soda in 1 teaspoon water. Add to batter to remove any sourness and improve lightness. Let stand for 20 to 25 minutes. Pour batter in desired amounts on griddle; bake on both sides until light brown. Save enough of batter to start next new batter. May be used several times, especially in cold weather, until batter becomes sour.

Mrs. Thelma Hylton
Price's Fork Grange, No. 786
Blacksburg, Virginia

HUCKLEBERRY GRIDDLE CAKES

> 3 c. flour
> 1 tbsp. brown sugar
> 1 tsp. salt
> 2 tsp. baking powder
> 2 eggs, beaten
> 2 c. milk
> 1 c. huckleberries

Sift flour, sugar, salt and baking powder together in large bowl. Add eggs, milk and huckleberries; mix well. Batter should be thin. Pour batter in desired amount onto greased hot griddle. Turn quickly to form crust on both sides to keep juice from escaping. Turn again on both sides; cook until browned. Yield: About 20 griddle cakes.

Mrs. Dora Wilson
Laurel Valley Grange, No. 2708
Rockbridge, Ohio

NORWEGIAN PANCAKES
(Recipe over 100 years old)

> 6 eggs
> 1/2 tsp. salt
> 2 tbsp. sugar
> 2/3 c. flour
> Milk

Beat eggs until lemon colored. Add salt, sugar and flour; beat until well mixed. Add enough milk to make a thin batter. Pour just enough batter to barely cover the bottom of heavy greased skillet. Cook until lightly browned on both sides. Roll as for jelly roll; place on warm platter. May be buttered and sprinkled with sugar before rolling. Yield: 16 pancakes.

Marcia Hunt
Columbia Grange, No. 87
Vancouver, Washington

RAISED GRIDDLE CAKES

> 2 c. flour
> 1 tbsp. sugar
> 1 tsp. salt
> 1 c. milk
> 1 1/2 c. water
> 1/2 cake fresh yeast
> 1 egg, well beaten

Sift and measure flour; sift with sugar and salt. Heat milk until bubbles form around edge. Add water; cool to lukewarm. Add crumbled yeast; stir until dissolved. Add dry ingredients all at once and mix. Cover with damp cloth; let rise in warm place overnight. Add egg to yeast batter; let stand for 10 minutes before baking. Drop by tablespoonfuls onto lightly greased hot griddle or frying pan. Turn cakes when bubbles break. Yield: 3 dozen.

Helen Herbst
Platte Valley Grange, No. 455
Kersey, Colorado

BOHEMIAN PANCAKES
(Recipe more than 50 years old)

> 1 c. scalded milk
> 1 cake or 1 pkg. dry yeast
> 2 eggs, well beaten
> 1/2 tsp. salt
> 1 tbsp. sugar
> 1 1/2 c. flour

Cool milk to lukewarm; add yeast. Let soak until softened; add eggs, salt and sugar. Add flour; beat until smooth. Cover; let rise for about 30 minutes or until light. Do not stir again, but lift carefully with tablespoon and drop on greased hot griddle. Cook until brown on both sides. Serve hot with fruit jam and whipped cream for dessert or with honey or jam for breakfast. Pancakes may be mixed and left to rise at room temperature overnight to cook for breakfast.

Mrs. Fred Stuth
Colon Grange
Colon, Michigan

★ ★

CORNMEAL BATTER CAKES

1 c. white cornmeal
1/2 c. flour
1/2 tsp. salt
2 eggs
2 c. buttermilk
1 tsp. soda
3 tbsp. melted butter

Sift cornmeal, flour and salt together. Beat eggs well; add 1 1/2 cups buttermilk. Pour buttermilk mixture into dry ingredients; mix until smooth. Dissolve soda in remaining buttermilk; stir into batter. Stir in melted butter. Drop by spoonfuls onto greased hot griddle. Be sure griddle is not smoking hot, but very hot. Turn with pancake turner when top surface is covered with little holes. Serve with melted or creamed butter with cream and cinnamon mixed with powdered sugar.

Evelyn Jones
Nezperce Grange, No. 295
Stites, Idaho

UNUSUAL PANCAKES

1 tbsp. cooking oil
1 egg
1 c. buttermilk
1 tsp. soda
1/8 c. yellow cornmeal
1/4 c. quick-cooking oats
1/2 c. flour
1/2 tsp. salt
1 tsp. baking powder

Combine oil, egg, buttermilk and soda; beat until well mixed. Add cornmeal and oats; stir until mixed. Sift flour, salt and baking powder together; add to oats mixture. Add more buttermilk if batter is too thick. Drop from tablespoon into electric frypan at 380 degrees or in hot frypan on top of stove. Cook until browned on both sides.

Bernardine Huffmaster
Golden State Grange, No. 429
Glenn, California

SCOTCH PANCAKES (BANNOCKS)

1 c. quick-cooking oatmeal
1 c. cornmeal
1/3 c. toasted diced almonds
1/2 tsp. salt
1/2 tsp. ground ginger
1 tbsp. brown sugar
2 c. buttermilk
1 tbsp. molasses
1 tsp. grated lemon peel
2 eggs
2 tbsp. melted butter

Combine oatmeal, cornmeal, almonds, salt, ginger and brown sugar in large bowl. Combine buttermilk, molasses and lemon peel in medium bowl; add eggs and butter, beating until thoroughly mixed. Add buttermilk mixture to oatmeal mixture; mix well. Spoon batter about 1/4 inch thick on hot well-greased heavy frypan or griddle. Fry for about 10 minutes, then turn. Fry for 5 minutes longer or until done. Cut or fold in half; spread with butter and jelly. May be served with creamed chipped beef, shredded ham or slivered chicken.

Elsie Seaton
Whitethorn Grange, No. 792
Whitethorn, California

BASIC WAFFLES

1 1/2 c. flour
2 tsp. baking powder
2 tbsp. sugar
1/2 tsp. salt
1 c. milk
2 eggs, separated
1/4 c. melted butter

Sift flour, baking powder, sugar and salt together into large bowl. Combine milk, beaten egg yolks and butter; mix well. Add to flour mixture; beat until blended. Beat egg whites until stiff but not dry; fold into batter. Bake in hot waffle iron until steam ceases to appear.

Mrs. Russell Rountree
Cherry Creek Grange, No. 58
Denver, Colorado

VIRGINIA WAFFLES
(Recipe about 75 years old)

1/2 c. white cornmeal
2 c. flour
3 tbsp. sugar
2 tsp. baking powder
1 1/2 tsp. salt
1 1/2 c. milk
2 eggs, separated
2 tbsp. melted butter

Bring 1 1/2 cups water to a boil; stir in cornmeal. Sift flour, sugar, baking powder and salt together. Add milk, flour mixture, beaten egg yolks and butter to cornmeal mixture; mix well. Fold in stiffly beaten egg whites. Cook in waffle iron according to manufacturer's instructions. Yield: 4-6 waffles.

Mrs. Leonard Holtzclaw
Crescent Grange, No. 136
Broomfield, Colorado

To make your pie crust look rich and flaky: When two-crust pies are ready for the oven, spread top with soft lard and sprinkle lightly with flour. Hold pie slightly slanted over sink and pour cold water from a dipper over it until flour is washed off.

Desserts
& Beverages

In 1896 Charles Joseph Latrobe wrote, "No where is the stomach of the traveler or visitor put in such constant peril as among the cake-inventive housewives and daughters of New England . . . I greatly suspect that some of the Pilgrim fathers must have come over to the country with the Cookery book under one arm and the Bible under the other." It is no wonder that American cooks have invented such simple and delicious desserts as Apple Pie, Strawberry Shortcake, Chocolate Chip Cookies and Angel Food Cake for the delight of family and friends. They have taken the abundance of dairy products and eggs from the farms, high-quality wheat from the fields, and fruits, berries and nuts growing all around them to come up with a delicious and nourishing variety of desserts to serve to their families.

Even with the modern ease and availability of one-step cake mixes, premixed refrigerator cookie dough, instant puddings and frozen pies and sweets, the typical American homemaker still prefers to serve her family sweets and desserts that she has made "from scratch" as often as possible. Many American homemakers today feel that there isn't enough time to bake homemade desserts for their families. But, as many of the recipes in this section show, pies, puddings and cakes are really very simple. Families can always tell the difference between cakes and other desserts made "from scratch" and the "box variety" because home baked flavors are fuller and more distinct — and experts agree that the foods made with fresh ingredients are more nutritious and more economical than prepackaged foods.

Plan a tasty, homemade dessert for your next meal and make it a special occasion. If you need an occasion, make a cherry pie for the Bicentennial! Your family will appreciate the little extra effort and better flavor of the treat, because no matter how satisfying the meal, a well-prepared, homemade dessert is always the perfect complement.

★ ★

FLORIDA WEDDING PUNCH

3 12-oz. cans Florida frozen orange
   juice concentrate, reconstituted
3 fifths champagne
Florida orange slices

Chill orange juice and champagne well. Combine
orange juice and champagne in punch bowl just before
serving. Add 2 quarts ice cubes; garnish with orange
slices. Four and one-half quarts Florida orange juice
may be substituted for reconstituted frozen juice.
Yield: About sixty 1/2-cup servings.

Photograph for this recipe on page 202.

NEW ENGLAND MAPLE MILK

4 c. milk
3/4 c. pure maple syrup
Butter pecan ice cream

Blend milk and maple syrup together in a large bowl;
stir until combined. Top each serving with scoop of
butter pecan ice cream.

Cynthia L. Mason
Holden Grange, No. 78
Holden, Massachusetts

FRUIT PUNCH

1 1/2 c. sugar
6 c. cold medium-strong tea
3 c. grape juice
2 cans frozen orange juice
2 cans frozen lemon juice
1 can pineapple juice
1/2 bottle Zarex raspberry syrup
2 (or more) bottles ginger ale

Stir enough hot water into sugar to dissolve. Stir in
tea, fruit juices and raspberry syrup, mixing well. Let
stand for at least 8 hours. Pour into punch bowl; pour
in ginger ale carefully. Garnish with orange and lemon
slices. Serve immediately.

Evelyn Hamilton
Narragansett Grange, No. 1
Wakefield, Rhode Island

MULLED CIDER PUNCH
(Recipe 200 years old)

4 qt. cider
2 2/3 c. (packed) brown sugar
4 c. white sugar
1 tsp. salt
24 whole cloves
24 whole allspice
16 cinnamon sticks
8 qt. orange juice
8 qt. lemon juice

Combine cider, sugars, salt and spices in kettle; place
over low heat. Bring to boiling point; simmer for 5

minutes. Strain. Add orange juice and lemon juice;
mix well. Serve in heated bowl; garnish with orange
and lemon slices. Yield: 4 gallons.

Neil C. Hansen, Master
Wilbraham Grange, No. 153
Wilbraham, Massachusetts

RHUBARB-LEMONADE PUNCH

2 12-oz. packages frozen rhubarb,
   partially thawed
1/4 to 1/2 c. sugar
1 6-oz. can frozen lemonade concentrate
3 c. water
2 7-oz. bottles lemon-lime carbonated
   beverage, chilled

Place rhubarb in blender container; blend until
smooth. Pour into saucepan. Cook for 5 minutes; let
cool. Strain pulp, if desired. Combine rhubarb, sugar,
lemonade concentrate and water; mix well. Pour rhubarb mixture over ice cubes or garnished ice ring in
punch bowl. Pour lemon-lime carbonated beverage
carefully into bowl; serve immediately.

Frances A. Hoffman
Northumberland Grange, No. 218
Northumberland, Pennsylvania

REFRESHING SUMMER DRINK

2 c. tea
2 cans cranberry or other juice
1 bottle ginger ale

Combine all ingredients; mix carefully. Serve over ice
cubes or crushed ice.

V. K. Swisher
Grange No. 361
Greencastle, Pennsylvania

SWITCHEL

2 qt. water
3/4 c. sugar
4 tbsp. vinegar
1 tsp. ginger

Mix all ingredients together; stir until sugar is dissolved. Chill or serve over ice.

Shirley R. Gaspar
Beverly Grange, No. 306
Wenham, Massachusetts

RHUBARB NECTAR
(Recipe 100 years old)

8 qt. finely chopped rhubarb
Juice of 4 lemons
4 lb. sugar
8 qt. hot water
1 yeast cake

★ ★

Combine rhubarb, lemon juice and sugar; mix thoroughly. Let stand overnight. Add hot water; let stand until lukewarm. Strain through flannel bag. Dissolve yeast cake in 1/2 cup lukewarm water; stir into rhubarb mixture. Let stand for 6 hours. Strain through flannel bag; store in refrigerator or other cool place.

Priscilla Savage
Sebasticook Grange, No. 306
Pittsfield, Maine

WHEY LEMONADE
(Recipe over 80 years old)

1 qt. whey
6 tbsp. sugar
Juice of 2 lemons
Lemon slices

Combine whey, sugar and lemon juice; mix well. Chill until ready to serve. Garnish with lemon slices. Grated or diced lemon rind, nutmeg or cinnamon may be substituted for lemon slices, if desired. Whey is made by straining sour milk which has been cooked until curd separates.

Mrs. Diane Godin
Seymour Grange, No. 91
Shelton, Connecticut

AUNT JESSIE'S POPCORN BALLS
(Recipe 40 years old)

3/4 c. vinegar
1/4 c. water
2 c. sugar
1/2 c. butter
5 to 6 qt. popped popcorn

Combine vinegar, water, sugar and butter in saucepan; bring to a boil. Cook until mixture forms a hard ball when dropped in cold water. Pour over popcorn; shape into balls, being careful not to burn fingers.

Edith Deering
Delavan Lake Grange, No. 681
Elkhorn, Wisconsin

BUTTERY ALMOND BRITTLE

2 c. sugar
1 c. light corn syrup
1/2 c. water
1 c. butter
2 c. almonds
1 tsp. soda

Combine sugar, syrup and water in 3-quart saucepan; cook, stirring, until sugar dissolves. Bring to a boil; blend in butter. Cook to 230 degrees on candy thermometer, without stirring. Cook to 280 degrees, stirring frequently. Add almonds; cook to 305 degrees or hard-crack stage, stirring constantly. Remove from heat; stir in soda quickly, mixing well. Pour into 2 well-greased cookie pans. Stretch thin by lifting and pulling from edges with fork. Cool. Loosen from pan; break into pieces.

Bettie M. Edwards
Gold Sand Grange, No. 6
Louisburg, North Carolina

DIVINITY

3 c. sugar
1/2 c. light corn syrup
1/4 tsp. salt
1/2 c. hot water
2 egg whites, stiffly beaten
1 tsp. vanilla extract
3/4 c. chopped nuts or coconut (opt.)

Combine sugar, syrup, salt and hot water. Cook, stirring constantly, until sugar is dissolved. Cook, without stirring, to 248 degrees on candy thermometer or to firm-ball stage. Remove from heat; pour slowly over egg whites, beating constantly with an electric mixer or wire whip. Add vanilla; continue beating until mixture will hold shape when dropped from spoon. Add nuts; drop onto waxed paper. Yield: About 80 pieces.

Donna R. Cole
Bunker Hill Grange, No. 676
Longview, Washington

GRANDMA'S MARSHMALLOWS

3 c. sugar
2 env. unflavored gelatin
1 tsp. vanilla extract
Powdered sugar

Cook sugar with 6 tablespoons water until thread spins. Place gelatin in enough cold water to soften. Pour sugar syrup slowly into gelatin, beating constantly. Add vanilla; beat for 25 minutes longer. Sprinkle powdered sugar generously in 9 x 13-inch pan. Pour candy into pan. Cover top with powdered sugar. Let stand until cold. Marshmallows may be cut in desired size with shears, dipping in water when shears become sticky. Marshmallows may then be rolled in powdered sugar.

Mrs. Ray Miles
Millbrook Grange, No. 1864
Elmwood, Illinois

MASHED POTATO CANDY

2 med. potatoes, quartered
2 lb. (about) powdered sugar
Peanut butter

Cook potatoes in water until done; drain, then mash. Beat in enough powdered sugar to make thick enough to roll like pie dough. Sprinkle board with powdered sugar; roll out. Spread with peanut butter; roll up and slice.

Karen L. Texter
Donegal Grange
Karns City, Pennsylvania

★ ★

HICKORY NUT PRALINES
(Recipe over 50 years old)

2 c. white sugar
1/2 c. (packed) brown sugar
1 c. cream or top milk
1 tsp. butter
Pinch of salt
1 tsp. vanilla
1/2 to 1 c. hickory nuts or chopped
walnuts

Combine white sugar, brown sugar and cream in sauce-pan; bring to a rolling boil. Add butter; reduce heat and add salt. Cook to 230 to 235 degrees on candy thermometer or soft-ball stage. Cool in pan of cold water until lukewarm. Add vanilla; beat until light. Stir in hickory nuts; drop from teaspoon onto waxed paper.

Mrs. Judy Groeper
Millbrook Grange, No. 1864
Elmwood, Illinois

MOLASSES TAFFY

1 c. light molasses
1/2 c. sugar
2 tsp. vinegar
1 tbsp. butter
3 drops of oil of peppermint (opt.)

Combine first 4 ingredients in saucepan. Cook slowly to 260 degrees on candy thermometer or to brittle stage, stirring constantly last part of cooking time. Pour into greased pans. Add peppermint when cool enough to handle. Grease hands; pull taffy until light in color and hard. Twist and cut into bite-sized pieces.

From a Grange Friend

NEW DEAL FUDGE
(Recipe over 150 years old)

2 c. sugar
2/3 c. milk
5 tsp. cocoa
1 tsp. vinegar
1 egg, beaten
2 tbsp. butter
1 tsp. vanilla extract

Combine all ingredients except vanilla; cook to soft-ball stage. Add vanilla; beat until candy loses gloss. Spread in buttered square pan. Let cool.

Martha J. West, Lecturer
Sterling Grange, No. 53
Clinton, Massachusetts

MOLDED MINTS

1/3 c. shortening
1/3 c. white syrup
1 egg white

1 3/4 lb. confectioners' sugar
1 tsp. flavoring
Food coloring
Sugar

Combine shortening, syrup, egg white, 1 pound confectioners' sugar, flavoring and food coloring in mixer bowl; beat well. Beat in as much remaining confectioners' sugar as needed to make a stiff consistency. Shape into balls; roll in sugar. Press into candy mold; let dry for 1 day. May be frozen. Mint mixture can be divided for different flavoring and coloring.

Mrs. John Rorabaugh
Sugar Grove Grange, No. 2044
Colfax, Iowa

NUT CARAMELS

2 c. sugar
2 c. light corn syrup
Dash of salt
1/2 c. butter
2 c. evaporated milk
1 tsp. vanilla
3/4 c. chopped nuts

Combine sugar, corn syrup and salt in large heavy saucepan; boil, stirring occasionally, to 310 degrees on candy thermometer. Add butter; pour in milk slowly, stirring constantly. Cook rapidly to 246 degrees on candy thermometer or firm-ball stage. Remove from heat; add vanilla. Beat for 1 to 2 minutes if mixture curdles. Add nuts; pour into buttered 8 x 8 x 2-inch pan. Let stand until cold. Cut into 1-inch squares; wrap individually in waxed paper. Keeps well for 3 months.

Mrs. Robert Zimmerman
New London Grange, No. 2401
New London, Ohio

PEANUT BRITTLE

2 c. sugar
1 c. white corn syrup
1/2 c. water
2 c. peanuts
1 tsp. butter
1 tsp. vanilla extract
1 tsp. soda

Combine sugar, syrup and water in saucepan; cook until hard ball forms in cold water. Add peanuts and butter; cook until syrup turns brown. Add vanilla; remove from heat. Add soda, mixing well. Pour into buttered pans, spreading thin. Cool. Break into pieces. Yield: About 2 pounds.

Mrs. Lydia Schultz
Bluestem Grange, No. 776
Harrington, Washington

POPCORN CAKE

2 c. sugar
2 c. syrup

★ ★ ★ ★ ★ ★★ ★ ★ ★ ★ ★

2 c. medium cream
4 qt. popped popcorn
10 lg. marshmallows, quartered or 40
    miniature marshmallows
1 c. coconut
1 c. (or more) nuts

Combine sugar, syrup and cream in saucepan; cook to soft-ball stage. Add popcorn, marshmallows, coconut and nuts; mix well. Mold in well-buttered pan or shape into balls. Unmold in about 1 hour or before cake cools completely.

Mrs. Earl Claycomb, W.A.C.
Bedford Grange, No. 619
Bedford, Pennsylvania

SEAFOAM CANDY

5 c. sugar
1 c. dark Karo syrup
1 c. water
3 egg whites
Pinch of salt
1 c. chopped nutmeats

Combine sugar, syrup and water; cook to soft-ball stage. Beat egg whites until stiff peaks form; add salt. Remove 1 cup syrup; add to beaten egg whites slowly, stirring constantly. Continue to boil remaining syrup until drop will crack when dropped in cold water. Pour slowly over egg white mixture, beating constantly. Add nutmeats; continue stirring until the shine begins to crack. Pour at once into buttered pan.

Dan Robinson
National Grange Gatekeeper
Sagle, Idaho

PENUCHE CANDIED WALNUTS

1 c. (packed) brown sugar
1 c. white sugar
1/2 c. thick cream or evaporated milk
1 tbsp. butter
1 tsp. vanilla extract
2 1/2 to 3 c. walnut halves

Combine sugars, cream and butter in saucepan; cook to 240 degrees on candy thermometer or to soft-ball stage. Add vanilla; remove from heat. Stir in the walnuts until all are coated. Drop on waxed paper; separate. May drop by spoonfuls and leave in clusters, if desired.

Myrna Thomas
French Camp-Lathrop Grange, No. 510
French Camp, California

VINEGAR CANDY

2 tbsp. butter
2 c. sugar
1/2 c. vinegar

Melt butter in large saucepan; add sugar and vinegar. Stir until sugar is dissolved. Cook to brittle stage, stir-ring occasionally. Turn onto buttered platter to cool. Pull and cut as for molasses candy.

Mrs. Lendon Layr
Knox Pomona Grange, No. 3
Rockland, Maine

NEVER-FAIL PENUCHE

1 c. (packed) brown sugar
2 c. sugar
1 1/2 c. milk
2 tbsp. butter
1/8 tsp. soda
1 tsp. vanilla
1 c. chopped nuts

Combine sugars, milk, butter and soda in heavy saucepan; bring to boiling point, stirring frequently. Cook over low heat, without stirring, to 236 degrees on candy thermometer or until a small amount forms a soft ball when dropped into cold water. Remove from heat; cool to room temperature without stirring. Add vanilla and nuts; beat until candy holds shape. Pour into buttered pan; cut when cool.

Mrs. Sammie Ceaser
Sonora Grange
Grinnell, Iowa

COCONUT CAKE FROSTING

3 egg whites
1 tbsp. sugar
1 tsp. vanilla extract
1 lg. bag flaked coconut

Beat egg whites until soft peaks form; add sugar and vanilla. Beat until stiff peaks form. Spread on layer cake, 1 layer at a time. Cover meringue with coconut. Place in cake saver or under a large bowl; let stand for 24 hours before serving. Egg white mixture will soak into cake leaving coconut on top of layers.

Beatrice Walton
Hessel Grange, No. 750
Sebastopol, California

LEMON CAKE FILLING
(Recipe 46 years old)

2 eggs
1 c. sugar
Juice of 1 1/2 lemons
Grated rind of 1 lemon
1/2 pt. whipping cream, whipped

Beat eggs well; add sugar. Beat until thick. Stir in lemon juice and rind. Pour in top of double boiler; cook over hot water, stirring constantly, until thick. Let cool. Fold in whipped cream.

Evelyn Harm
Vale Grange, No. 696

★ ★

NEVER-FAIL FLUFFY WHITE FROSTING

2 egg whites
3/4 c. sugar
1/3 c. light corn syrup
2 tbsp. water
1/4 tsp. salt
1/4 tsp. cream of tartar
1 tsp. vanilla extract

Combine all ingredients except vanilla in top of double boiler. Cook over rapidly boiling water, beating with rotary beaters or electric mixer until mixture stands in peaks. Remove from heat. Add vanilla; continue beating until thick enough to spread.

Louise Dunbar
Deahaga Grange, No. 1951
Athens, Pennsylvania

MAPLE FROSTING
(Recipe 50 years old)

1 c. maple syrup
1/2 c. sugar
1 egg white

Place syrup, sugar and egg white in top of double boiler over hot water. Beat until mixture stands in peaks. Remove from heat and beat until cool.

Ella Wrisley
Charlotte Grange, No. 398
Charlotte, Vermont

QUICK CARAMEL FROSTING

1/2 c. butter
1 c. (packed) brown sugar
1/4 c. milk
1 3/4 to 2 c. confectioners' sugar

Melt butter in 8-inch skillet; add brown sugar. Cook over low heat, stirring constantly, for 2 minutes. Add milk; stir until mixture comes to a boil. Remove from heat; cool. Add confectioners' sugar slowly, beating well with spoon until thick enough to spread. Yield: Frosting for two 8-inch layers.

Mrs. Doris Price
Painter Creek Grange, No. 1923
Kenton, Ohio

STRAWBERRY FLUFF
(Recipe over 100 years old)

1 egg white
3/4 c. sugar
3/4 c. crushed strawberries, raspberries or blackberries

Beat egg white until stiff. Add sugar and strawberries alternately, about 2 tablespoons at a time, beating well after each addition. Beat until mixture is very stiff. Serve immediately over cake. Leftover fluff may be whipped again.

Karen F. Wilcox
Almond Grange, No. 1102
Almond, New York

BEER AND SAUERKRAUT FUDGE CAKE

2/3 c. butter
1 1/2 c. sugar
3 eggs
1 tsp. vanilla extract
1/2 c. cocoa
2 1/4 c. sifted flour
1 tsp. baking powder
1 tsp. soda
1/4 tsp. salt
1 c. beer
2/3 c. sauerkraut

Cream butter and sugar until light. Add eggs, one at a time, beating well after each addition. Add vanilla extract; mix well. Sift cocoa, flour, baking powder, soda and salt together; add to creamed mixture alternately with beer, beginning and ending with dry ingredients. Stir in sauerkraut. Turn into 2 greased and floured layer cake tins. Bake in preheated 350-degree oven for 35 minutes. Cool and frost as desired.

Connie Pipes
Narragansett Grange, No. 1
Narragansett, Rhode Island

MINCEMEAT CAKE

1 box raisins
1 pkg. dry mincemeat
3 c. water
2 tsp. soda
1/2 c. butter
1 1/3 c. sugar
2 eggs
3 c. flour
1 tsp. cinnamon
1 tsp. cloves
1 tsp. salt
1 c. chopped nuts

Combine raisins, mincemeat and water in saucepan; bring to a boil. Let cool; add soda. Cream butter and sugar; add eggs. Combine mincemeat mixture and butter mixture. Sift flour, spices and salt together; add to mincemeat mixture. Fold in nuts. Place in greased tube pan. Bake in preheated 300-degree oven for 1 hour and 30 minutes to 2 hours or until cake tests done.

Nancy Wolfe
Brandywine Grange, No. 348
Brandywine, Maryland

★ ★

HICKORY NUT CAKE
(Recipe 50 years old)

1 1/2 c. sugar
3/4 c. butter or shortening
3 c. sifted flour
3/4 tsp. salt
1 tsp. baking powder
1 1/2 c. milk
1 c. chopped hickory nuts
3 egg whites, stiffly beaten
1 tsp. vanilla extract
1 recipe Seven-Minute Icing

Cream sugar and butter. Sift flour, salt and baking powder together; add alternately with milk to butter mixture. Stir in hickory nuts. Fold in egg whites and vanilla. Pour into 3 greased and floured 8-inch round cake pans. Bake in preheated 375-degree oven for 20 to 25 minutes. Remove from oven; cool on cake racks. Frost between layers, on top and around side with Seven-Minute Icing.

Mable G. Benn
Wheatland Grange
North Adams, Michigan

FOOD FOR THE GODS CARROT CAKE

3/4 c. salad oil
2 eggs, beaten
1 tsp. soda
1/4 tsp. salt
1 c. sugar
1 c. flour
1 tsp. cinnamon
1 1/2 c. grated carrots
1/2 c. raisins
1/2 c. chopped nuts

Combine all ingredients except carrots, raisins and nuts; beat for about 5 minutes. Add remaining ingredients; mix well. Pour into a greased and floured 9 x 9-inch baking pan or bundt pan. Bake in preheated 350-degree oven for about 35 minutes or until just done when tested with toothpick. Do not overbake or cake will be dry. Allow to cool in pan for several minutes. Turn out on cake plate; cool completely. May dust with confectioners' sugar, if desired.

Ann Pike
Tuftonboro Grange, No. 142
Wolfeboro, New Hampshire

CONGRESS CAKE
(Recipe over 100 years old)

2 c. diced green apples
1 c. molasses
1 c. sugar
1 egg, lightly beaten
3/4 c. shortening
1 tsp. cinnamon
1 c. sour milk

1 1/2 tsp. soda
2 1/2 c. all-purpose flour

Cook apples in molasses until thick; cool. Add remaining ingredients; mix well. Spread in 9-inch square pan. Bake in preheated 350-degree oven for 30 to 35 minutes or until cake tests done.

Lela Wilsie
Potter Hollow Grange, No. 1555
Preston Hollow, New York

OLD-TIME BUTTER SPONGE CAKE
(Recipe over 85 years old)

2 1/4 c. sifted flour
2 tsp. baking powder
1 tsp. salt
11 egg yolks
2 c. sugar
1 c. scalded milk
1 tsp. vanilla extract
1/2 tsp. lemon extract
1/2 c. melted butter

Sift dry ingredients together. Beat egg yolks until thick and lemon colored; add sugar gradually, beating thoroughly after each addition. Add milk, vanilla and lemon extracts; beat until well blended. Fold in sifted dry ingredients gradually, blending thoroughly. Add butter; mix well. Pour into ungreased 10-inch tube pan. Cut through batter with spatula to break large air pockets. Bake in preheated 350-degree oven for 50 to 60 minutes. Cool in inverted pan for about 1 hour.

June Fredrickson, Lady Asst. Steward
Freshwater Grange, No. 499
Eureka, California

SWEET WATERMELON RIND PICKLE CAKE

1 c. sugar
1 c. water
1/2 c. butter
1 10-oz. jar sweet watermelon rind
    pickles, chopped
2 c. flour
1 tsp. cinnamon
1/2 tsp. cloves
1 tsp. salt
1 tsp. soda
1 c. chopped nuts

Combine sugar, water, butter and watermelon rind in saucepan; bring to a boil. Simmer until butter melts; cool for 5 minutes. Add remaining ingredients; mix well. Spread in greased 9 x 13-inch pan. Bake in preheated 350-degree oven for 25 to 30 minutes or until cake tests done. May frost with caramel frosting.

Mrs. Ruth Stoll
Platte Valley Grange, No. 455
Kersey, Colorado

★ ★

LANE CAKE

1 c. butter
2 c. sugar
1 tsp. vanilla extract
3 1/4 c. sifted all-purpose flour
3 1/2 tsp. baking powder
3/4 tsp. salt
1 c. milk
8 egg whites, stiffly beaten

Cream butter and sugar until fluffy; add vanilla. Combine flour, baking powder and salt; add to sugar mixture alternately with milk. Mix well after each addition. Fold in egg whites. Grease and flour bottoms of four 9-inch round cake pans. Divide batter in pans. Bake in preheated 325-degree oven until cake tests done. Cool.

FROSTING

8 egg yolks
1/2 c. butter
1 1/4 c. sugar
1 c. chopped seeded raisins
1 c. chopped pecans
1 c. shredded coconut
1 c. chopped candied cherries
1/4 tsp. salt
1/3 c. whiskey

Combine all ingredients except whiskey in top of double boiler over hot water. Cook, stirring constantly, until thick. Remove from heat; stir in whiskey. Spread between layers, on top and around side.

Mrs. Doris Holtz
Wilkins Run Grange, No. 1979
Newark, Ohio

MILKLESS-EGGLESS-BUTTERLESS SPICE CAKE

1 c. (firmly packed) dark brown sugar
1 c. water
1/3 c. vegetable shortening
1 c. seedless raisins
1 tbsp. Angostura aromatic bitters
2 c. unsifted all-purpose flour
1/2 tsp. baking powder
1/2 tsp. soda
1/2 tsp. salt
1 c. coarsely broken walnuts

Combine sugar, water, shortening, raisins and Angostura bitters. Bring to a boil; boil for 1 minute. Cool to lukewarm. Stir in remaining ingredients until well blended. Pour into greased and floured 9-inch square baking pan. Bake in preheated 350-degree oven for 35 minutes or until firm in center. Cut into squares. Serve warm or cold, dusted with confectioners' sugar. May also be served topped with vanilla ice cream or sweetened whipped cream.

Photograph for this recipe below.

★ ★

PINK ANGEL FOOD CAKE

1 1/2 c. sugar
1 1/4 c. sifted flour
11 egg whites
1 tsp. cream of tartar
1 tsp. vanilla extract
1/4 tsp. red food coloring

Combine sugar and flour; sift 5 times. Beat egg whites until frothy; add cream of tartar. Beat until stiff peaks form. Fold in vanilla extract and red food coloring. Sift flour mixture onto egg whites gradually, folding gently until all flour is mixed in. Turn into ungreased angel cake pan. Bake in preheated 350-degree oven for 40 minutes.

Charlotte Cordon
North Fairfield Grange, No. 806
North Fairfield, Ohio

PRIZEWINNING ANGEL FOOD CAKE

1 1/2 c. egg whites
Pinch of salt
1 1/4 tsp. cream of tartar
1 1/2 c. sugar
1 c. plus 1 tbsp. sifted cake flour
1 tsp. vanilla

Beat egg whites and salt with a wire beater until egg whites are frothy. Add cream of tartar; continue beating until soft peaks form. Sift sugar 6 times; fold into egg whites, one tablespoon at a time. Sift flour 6 times. Fold into egg white mixture, one tablespoon at a time. Fold in vanilla last. Turn into angel food cake pan. Place in a cold oven; turn temperature to 150 degrees. Bake 10 minutes. Increase temperature to 200 degrees for another 10 minutes, then increase temperature 25 degrees every 10 minutes until 300 degrees is reached. Bake for 10 minutes longer. Increase temperature to 350 degrees and bake for 10 minutes longer. Full time for baking is 1 hour and 10 minutes. Place on rack upside down; let cool for 2 hours.
This cake won first prize at the Clearfield County Fair in 1957.

Helen Baughman
Bradford Grange
Clearfield County

SPECIAL YELLOW ANGEL CAKE
(Recipe about 50 years old)

6 eggs, separated
1/2 c. cold water
1 1/2 c. sugar
1/2 tsp. vanilla extract
1/2 tsp. orange or lemon extract
1/4 tsp. almond extract
1 1/2 c. cake flour
1/4 tsp. salt
3/4 tsp. cream of tartar

Beat egg yolks until thick and lemon colored; add cold water and continue beating until thick. Add sugar gradually, beating constantly; add extracts. Sift flour and salt together; fold into egg yolk mixture, a small amount at a time. Beat egg whites until foamy; add cream of tartar. Beat until peaks form. Fold egg whites into egg yolk mixture. Place in ungreased tube pan. Bake in a preheated 325-degree oven for 1 hour. Invert to cool. Frost with butter frosting or boiled frosting, if desired.

Anna G. MacLaughlin
Central Grange, No. 34
Saunderstown, Rhode Island

CHOCOLATE ANGEL FOOD CAKE
(Recipe over 50 years old)

1/4 c. cocoa
1 1/2 c. sugar
3/4 c. flour
1/4 tsp. salt
1 1/2 c. egg whites
1 tsp. cream of tartar
1 tsp. vanilla extract

Sift cocoa with 1 cup sugar. Sift flour with remaining 1/2 cup sugar. Add salt to egg whites; beat until foamy. Add cream of tartar. Beat until stiff peaks form. Fold in cocoa mixture. Add vanilla. Fold in flour and sugar mixture. Pour in ungreased tube pan. Bake in preheated 325-degree oven for 50 to 55 minutes. Invert pan until cool, then remove. May be frosted or served plain.

Mrs. Fred Proctor
Delavan Lake Grange, No. 681
Elkhorn, Wisconsin

FRESH APPLE CAKE

2 c. flour
2 tsp. soda
2 tsp. cinnamon
1 tsp. salt
2 eggs, well beaten
2 c. sugar
1/2 c. salad oil
2 tsp. vanilla extract
4 c. unpeeled diced apples
1 c. chopped nuts (opt.)

Sift flour, soda, cinnamon and salt together. Beat eggs with sugar with an electric mixer until creamy; add oil gradually. Add vanilla and apples. Fold in flour mixture and nuts. Spread in greased 9 x 12 x 2-inch pan. Bake in preheated 350-degree oven for about 45 minutes or at 325 degrees for 1 hour or until toothpick inserted in center comes out clean.

Evelyn Doerge
Black Diamond Grange, No. 1128
Port Angeles, Washington

BOTTOMS-UP APPLE CAKE

2 tbsp. butter
1/2 c. (firmly packed) light brown sugar
1/2 tsp. cinnamon
2 c. peeled thinly sliced cooking apples
2 c. sifted all-purpose flour
1 c. sugar
2 1/2 tsp. baking powder
1/2 tsp. salt
1/2 c. softened butter
3/4 c. milk
1 egg, beaten
Rum Sauce

Melt butter in 9-inch square baking pan. Mix brown sugar and cinnamon; sprinkle over butter. Arrange apple slices in rows in bottom of pan. Sift flour, sugar, baking powder and salt together into large mixing bowl. Add softened butter and 1/2 cup milk; beat with electric mixer at medium speed for 2 minutes. Add remaining 1/4 cup milk and egg; beat at medium speed for 2 minutes. Spread batter over apples in pan. Bake in preheated 375-degree oven for 30 to 40 minutes or until done; cool in pan on wire rack for 10 minutes. Invert onto serving plate. Cut into squares; serve warm with Rum Sauce.

RUM SAUCE

1/2 c. sugar
2 tbsp. cornstarch
1 c. water
1/4 c. butter
1 tbsp. rum extract
1/8 tsp. salt

Combine sugar and cornstarch in 1-quart saucepan; stir in water. Cook over medium heat, stirring constantly, until thickened; cook for 2 minutes longer. Remove from heat; stir in butter, rum extract and salt.

Photograph for this recipe above.

AUNT KATE'S ONE-EGG CAKE
(Recipe over 100 years old)

1 2/3 c. flour
1 c. sugar
2 tsp. cream of tartar
1 tsp. soda
Pinch of salt
1 egg yolk
3 tbsp. butter
2/3 c. milk
1 tsp. vanilla extract

Combine flour, sugar, cream of tartar, soda and salt; sift 3 times. Combine egg yolk and butter; beat until creamy. Add milk, blending well. Add flour mixture; beat until smooth. Blend in vanilla. Spread in greased cake pan. Bake in preheated 350-degree oven until

★ ★

cake tests done. Ice with favorite egg white frosting, if desired.

Caroline Cutts
West River Grange, No. 511
Townshend, Vermont

AUNT IOLA'S EGG YOLK CAKE

11 egg yolks
1 3/4 c. sugar
1 c. boiling milk
2 c. flour
1 3/4 tsp. baking powder
1/4 tsp. salt
6 tbsp. melted butter
1 tsp. vanilla extract

Beat egg yolks until light. Add sugar gradually, mixing until well blended. Add milk; mix well. Sift flour, baking powder and salt together. Add to egg mixture; mix until smooth. Fold in melted butter and vanilla. Pour into 2 layer pans or 1 oblong baking pan. Bake in preheated 350-degree oven for 25 to 30 minutes for layers and 40 minutes for oblong pan. This is a great cake to use egg yolks from making an angel food cake.

Mrs. Kenneth Koch
Wife of State Master
Kaycee, Wyoming

BICENTENNIAL CAKE
(Recipe over 65 years old)

RED LAYER

1 c. sugar
1/2 c. butter
1/2 c. milk
4 egg whites, stiffly beaten
2 c. flour
1 tsp. cream of tartar
1/2 tsp. soda
Red food coloring

Cream sugar and butter until light. Blend in milk. Fold in egg whites. Sift flour, cream of tartar and soda together. Add to egg mixture gradually, mixing well after each addition. Blend in enough food coloring to color red. Grease and flour bottom of 9-inch cake pan. Spread batter in pan.

WHITE LAYER

1 c. sugar
1/2 c. butter
1/2 c. milk
4 egg whites, beaten
1/2 c. cornstarch
1 c. flour
1 tsp. cream of tartar
1/2 tsp. soda
Lemon extract to taste

Cream sugar and butter until light. Blend in milk. Fold in egg whites. Combine cornstarch, flour, cream of tartar and soda; sift. Add to egg white mixture, mixing until well blended. Stir in lemon extract. Grease and flour bottom of 9-inch cake pan. Spread batter in pan.

BLUE LAYER

Repeat ingredients and method for Red Layer, substituting blue food coloring for red. Bake all layers in preheated 350-degree oven until cake tests done. Frost between layers, top and sides with favorite white icing. Decorate as desired. This may be baked in sheet pans or bundt pans, in stripes, layers or marbleized.
This recipe was in a 1909 cookbook and was called The National Cake.

Mrs. Fred V. Herrian
Wife of State Master
Covington, Oklahoma

BLACK WALNUT CAKE

3 c. cake flour
3 tsp. baking powder
3/4 c. butter
1 1/2 c. sugar
1 c. milk
1/2 c. chopped black walnuts
1 tsp. vanilla extract
6 egg whites, stiffly beaten

Sift flour once; measure. Add baking powder; sift 3 times. Cream butter thoroughly; add sugar gradually, beating until light and fluffy. Add flour alternately with milk, a small amount at a time, beating well after each addition. Add walnuts and vanilla; fold in stiffly beaten egg whites. Place in 3 greased layer pans. Bake in preheated 350-degree oven for 20 minutes or until cake tests done.

Camilla Erickson
Issaquah Valley Grange, No. 581
Issaquah, Washington

BROWN MERINGUE CAKE
(Recipe over 50 years old)

1/2 c. butter or shortening
2/3 c. white sugar
2 eggs, separated
1 1/2 c. sifted flour
2 tsp. baking powder
1/2 tsp. salt
1/2 c. milk
1 tsp. vanilla extract
1 1/2 c. (packed) brown sugar

Cream butter and white sugar; stir in egg yolks. Beat until light and fluffy. Combine flour, baking powder and salt; add to creamed mixture alternately with milk. Stir in vanilla. Pour into greased and floured 9 x 13-inch pan. Beat egg whites until stiff peaks form but not until dry. Beat in brown sugar gradually. Spread over batter. Bake in preheated 350-degree oven for 45 minutes.

Mable L. Bagley, Sec.
Beverly Grange, No. 306
Beverly, Massachusetts

★ ★

BRAZIL NUT SENSATION

3/4 c. sifted all-purpose flour
3/4 c. sugar
1/2 tsp. baking powder
1/2 tsp. salt
3 c. shelled Brazil nuts, finely chopped
1 lb. pitted dates, chopped
1 c. well-drained maraschino cherries,
    chopped
3 eggs
1 tsp. vanilla extract

Line a greased 9 x 5 x 3-inch loaf pan with waxed paper. Place first 4 ingredients in sifter. Place nuts, dates and cherries in large bowl; sift flour mixture over top. Mix with hands until nuts and fruits are well coated. Beat eggs until foamy; add vanilla. Stir into nut mixture until well mixed. Spread evenly in prepared pan. Bake in preheated 300-degree oven for about 1 hour and 30 minutes or until done. Cool in pan on wire rack for 15 minutes. Remove from pan; peel off paper. Cool on rack. Wrap in aluminum foil; store in refrigerator. May be kept in freezer for several months.

Mrs. Marshall Moore
Volunteer Grange, No. 1250
Knoxville, Tennessee

CARROT AND PINEAPPLE CAKE

1   8-oz. can crushed pineapple, well
    drained
2 c. grated carrots
1 c. flaked coconut
1 c. all-purpose flour
1 c. whole wheat flour
1 1/2 c. sugar
1 tsp. soda
2 tsp. cinnamon
1/2 tsp. nutmeg
1/2 tsp. salt
3 eggs
1/2 c. salad oil
3/4 c. buttermilk
2 tsp. vanilla extract
Buttermilk Glaze

Combine pineapple, carrots and coconut. Mix flours, sugar, soda, spices and salt in plastic bag. Beat eggs with oil, buttermilk and vanilla in large mixing bowl; add flour mixture. Mix well. Add carrot mixture; mix just until combined. Pour into greased and floured 13 x 9 x 2-inch cake pan. Bake in preheated 350-degree oven for about 45 minutes or until pick inserted in center comes out dry. Prepare Buttermilk Glaze. Prick hot baked cake with fork at about 1/2-inch intervals. Pour Buttermilk Glaze slowly over cake.

BUTTERMILK GLAZE

2/3 c. sugar
1/4 tsp. soda
1/3 c. buttermilk
1/3 c. butter
1/2 tsp. vanilla extract

Combine all ingredients in saucepan; bring to a boil. Boil slowly for 5 minutes.

Mary E. Gosney
Goldendale Grange, No. 49
Goldendale, Washington

EASY SOUR CREAM CHOCOLATE CAKE

2 sq. chocolate
1/2 c. boiling water
2 eggs
1 c. sugar
1 tsp. vanilla extract
1 1/2 c. flour
1/4 tsp. salt
1 tsp. soda
1 c. homemade sour cream or half and half

Melt chocolate; add boiling water. Beat eggs; add sugar slowly, beating constantly. Stir in vanilla extract. Combine flour with salt and soda. Add chocolate mixture to egg mixture. Add flour mixture alternately with sour cream. Place in oblong greased pan. Bake in preheated 350-degree oven for 35 minutes.

CHOCOLATE FROSTING

1 c. sugar
1 sq. chocolate
1/2 c. half and half
1 tbsp. butter
1 1/2 tsp. vanilla extract

Combine first 3 ingredients in saucepan; boil for 5 minutes or until soft ball forms when dropped in cold water. Add butter and vanilla extract. Do not stir. Let cool. Beat until of spreading consistency.

Maude Mathis
Fair Harbor Grange, No. 1129
Grapeview, Washington

RED VELVET CAKE

1/2 c. shortening or butter
1 1/2 c. sugar
2 eggs
1/4 c. red food coloring
2 tbsp. cocoa
1 tsp. vanilla extract
1 c. buttermilk
1 tsp. salt
2 1/4 c. sifted cake flour
1 tbsp. vinegar
1 tsp. soda

Mix shortening, sugar and eggs until fluffy. Combine food coloring and cocoa; add to cake mixture. Combine vanilla extract and buttermilk. Combine salt and flour. Add milk mixture and flour mixture alternately to sugar mixture, mixing well after each addition. Add vinegar and soda; mix well. Place in two 9-inch cake pans. Bake in preheated 350-degree oven for 25 to 30 minutes. Cool.

★ ★

FROSTING

1 c. milk
5 tbsp. flour
1/2 c. butter, softened
1 c. sifted powdered sugar
1 tsp. vanilla extract

Combine milk and flour in saucepan; cook, stirring, until thick. Cool. Combine butter, powdered sugar and vanilla extract until smooth. Blend in milk mixture, small amount at a time, until well blended and smooth.

Ann White
Sequim Prairie Grange, No. 1108
Sequim, Washington

MARAMOR FUDGE CAKE

(Recipe 50 years old)

1/4 c. butter
2 c. sugar
2 eggs, separated
1 1/2 c. milk
2 c. Swans Down cake flour
2 tsp. baking powder
1/2 tsp. salt
2 tsp. vanilla extract
4 sq. Baker's bitter chocolate, melted
1 c. chopped nuts

Cream butter and sugar until smooth; add egg yolks, half the milk, flour, baking powder and salt. Add remaining milk, vanilla extract, melted chocolate, nuts and stiffly beaten egg whites. Pour into 2 layer pans. Bake in preheated 350-degree oven for 30 minutes.

MARAMOR FROSTING

1 box confectioners' sugar
1/4 lb. butter
1 unbeaten egg white
1 sq. chocolate, melted
1 tsp. lemon juice
1 tsp. vanilla
1 c. chopped nuts

Combine sugar and butter; blend until smooth. Add egg white, melted chocolate, lemon juice, vanilla and nuts; mix well. Hot water may be added, if necessary, for spreading consistency. Spread over cake layers.

Patricia A. Sterling
Lawrence Valley Grange
Kenton, Ohio

SUNDAY CHOCOLATE CANDY CAKE

3 tsp. baking powder
1 tsp. salt
2 1/8 c. cake flour
2 c. sugar
1/2 c. shortening
1 1/3 c. milk
3 eggs

3 sq. melted chocolate
1 tsp. red food coloring

Sift baking powder, salt, flour and sugar into bowl; add shortening and half the milk. Beat for 2 minutes. Add eggs and remaining milk; blend well. Add chocolate and food coloring. Beat for 2 minutes on medium speed. Pour into two 9-inch layer cake pans. Bake in preheated 350-degree oven for 35 minutes.

ANGEL'S CHOCOLATE FROSTING

4 1/2 1-oz. squares unsweetened
    chocolate
5 1/2 c. sifted powdered sugar
6 3/4 tbsp. hot water
1 lg. egg
3/4 c. soft butter
2 tsp. vanilla

Melt chocolate in mixing bowl over hot water; remove from heat. Blend in sugar and water with electric mixer. Beat in egg, butter and vanilla. Place bowl in ice water; beat until of spreading consistency. Frosts between layers, top and sides of two 9-inch layers.
This cake has won 1st place prizes in county and state fairs, also "Champion Cake" twice in Washington State Grange baking contests.

Violet Eshelman
Centerville Grange, No. 81
Centerville, Washington

COCONUT CRUST CAKE

(Recipe about 35 years old)

2 eggs
1 c. sugar
1 c. flour
1 1/2 tsp. baking powder
3/4 tsp. salt
1/2 c. milk
2 tbsp. butter
1 tsp. vanilla extract

Beat eggs; add sugar gradually, beating until fluffy. Sift flour; measure. Add baking powder and salt; sift again. Add to egg mixture; beat thoroughly. Heat milk and butter to boiling point; add with vanilla to batter. Mix quickly; place in greased 8 or 9-inch square pan. Bake in preheated 350-degree oven for 30 minutes. Cool slightly.

TOPPING

6 tbsp. brown sugar
2 tsp. cream
2 tsp. butter
1/2 c. coconut
1/2 c. chopped nutmeats

Combine all ingredients; mix until well blended. Spread over slightly cooled cake. Return to oven; bake until topping is browned.

June F. Hendrickson
Highline Grange, No. 1132
Seattle, Washington

★ ★

CRANBERRY CLOUD CAKE

2 1/2 c. flour
1 tsp. soda
1 tsp. salt
1 c. sugar
1/2 c. (firmly packed) brown sugar
1/2 c. shortening
2 eggs
1 egg yolk
1 tbsp. grated lemon rind
1 c. milk
2 tbsp. lemon juice
1 c. whole cranberry sauce

Sift flour, soda and salt together; set aside. Cream sugar, brown sugar and shortening until fluffy. Add eggs and egg yolk, one at a time, beating well after each addition. Blend in lemon rind. Combine milk and lemon juice; add to creamed mixture alternately with flour mixture, beating after each addition on low speed of mixer. Stir in cranberry sauce. Turn into well-greased and floured 13 x 9 x 2-inch pan. Bake in preheated 375-degree oven for 30 to 35 minutes or until cake tests done. Cool.

FROSTING

1/2 c. (packed) brown sugar
1 tbsp. cornstarch
1/2 c. whole cranberry sauce
2 tbsp. butter

Combine all ingredients in saucepan; bring to a boil. Simmer for 3 minutes. Spread on cake.
This cake recipe won 1st Prize at the County Fair.

Christina O'Neal
French Creek Grange, No. 396
Snohomish, Washington

ADD-A-LAYER STRAWBERRY SHORTCAKE

Unsifted all-purpose flour
Sugar
1 tbsp. baking powder
1 tsp. salt
1/3 c. shortening
3/4 c. milk
Melted butter
2 pt. California strawberries, halved
1 c. heavy cream

Measure 1 3/4 cups flour by spooning lightly into measuring cup; do not pack flour or tap cup. Level off with spatula. Combine flour, 2 tablespoons sugar, baking powder and salt in bowl. Cut in shortening with pastry blender or 2 knives until mixture resembles coarse crumbs. Make well in center of flour mixture; pour in milk. Mix quickly and lightly with fork until dough is moist enough to leave side of bowl. Pat into greased 8-inch or 9-inch round cake pan. Brush top lightly with melted butter; sprinkle lightly with sugar. Bake in preheated 450-degree oven for about 25 minutes for 8-inch pan or 15 minutes for 9-inch pan or

until golden brown. Sweeten strawberries with sugar to taste while shortcake is baking. Whip cream until stiff, adding sugar to taste. Remove shortcake from pan; place on serving plate. Top with strawberries and whipped cream. Double biscuit recipe only for 2-layer shortcake; bake in 2 cake pans. Top each baked layer with strawberries and whipped cream; stack layers. Triple biscuit recipe for 3-layer shortcake; bake in 3 cake pans. Increase strawberries to 3 pints and heavy cream to 1 1/2 cups. Top each baked biscuit layer with strawberries and whipped cream; stack layers.

Photograph for this recipe on page 203.

HOLIDAY FRUITCAKE
(Recipe over 30 years old)

1 c. butter or shortening
2 1/2 c. (packed) brown sugar
4 eggs
3 3/4 c. flour
3 tsp. baking powder
1/2 tsp. soda
1 tsp. salt
1/2 tsp. cloves
2 tsp. cinnamon
1 tsp. nutmeg
2 c. halved cranberries
1 1/2 c. seedless raisins
1 1/2 c. currants
1 c. chopped dates
1/2 c. chopped mixed candied fruit peels
1 c. slivered almonds
Grated rind of 1 lemon
1 1/4 c. cranberry, orange or pineapple
   juice

Cream butter and brown sugar together until light and creamy. Add eggs, one at a time, beating well after each addition. Sift flour, baking powder, soda, salt, cloves, cinnamon and nutmeg together; stir in cranberries, raisins, currants, dates, candied peels, almonds and lemon rind. Stir flour mixture and cranberry juice alternately into butter mixture; mix well. Pour batter into greased and floured tube pan. Decorate top with whole cranberries, slivered almonds or other fruits and nuts, if desired. Bake in preheated 275-degree oven for 3 hours or until cake tests done.

Mrs. Frances Thompson, Sec.-Treas.
Thurmond Grange
State Road, North Carolina

MARTHA WASHINGTON FRUITCAKE

1 lb. fresh currants
1 lb. chopped raisins
1/2 lb. sliced citron
7 c. flour
2 c. butter or shortening
3 c. sugar
6 eggs, separated

★ ★

1 tsp. soda
1/4 tsp. salt
1 nutmeg, grated
1/4 tsp. mace
2 c. sour cream
Juice and grated rind of 1 lemon

Wash currants; remove stems. Rub vigorously in coarse towel; shake in colander. Combine raisins, citron and currants; dredge with part of the flour. Line bottoms of 2 large loaf pans with 2 thicknesses of brown paper. Cream butter and sugar until light and fluffy; add well-beaten egg yolks gradually, beating constantly. Sift remaining flour, soda, salt, nutmeg and mace together; add to creamed mixture alternately with sour cream. Stir in fruits, lemon juice and rind; fold in stiffly beaten egg whites. Turn into loaf pans; cover with greased paper. Bake in preheated 325-degree oven for 2 hours and 30 minutes or until cake tests done. This recipe was published in 1929 in New Delineator Cookbook.

Mrs. Vernon R. Maw
Mansfield Grange, No. 883
Mansfield, Washington

WHITE FRUITCAKE

1 c. butter
2 c. sugar
1/2 tsp. soda
2 tbsp. hot water
1 tbsp. ground mace
1/2 c. brandy or whiskey
1 lb. citron, julienned
1 c. maraschino cherries, halved
1 1/4 lb. flour
1 tsp. cream of tartar
1/2 lb. almonds, blanched, chopped
12 egg whites
1 fresh coconut, grated

Cream butter and sugar. Dissolve soda in water; add mace and brandy. Dredge citron and cherries in part of the flour. Add flour and cream of tartar to creamed mixture alternately with liquids, then add fruits and almonds. Fold in stiffly beaten egg whites, then coconut. Pour into tube pan. Bake in preheated 275-degree oven for 1 hour and 30 minutes to 2 hours or until cake tests done. This recipe is believed to be from the family of Patrick Henry.

Mrs. Margaret Sullivan, D.W.A.
Virginia State Grange
Blacksburg, Virginia

HONEY CAKE
(Recipe over 50 years old)

1/2 c. shortening
1 c. honey
1/4 c. milk
1/3 tsp. lemon extract
2 eggs, separated

1 1/2 c. sifted flour
1 1/2 tsp. baking powder
1/2 tsp. salt

Cream shortening; add honey. Beat well. Add milk and lemon extract; beat until well blended. Add slightly beaten egg yolks; mix well. Sift dry ingredients together; add gradually, stirring just until mixed. Fold in stiffly beaten egg whites. Pour in waxed paper-lined 9 x 9-inch pan. Bake in preheated 350-degree oven for about 30 minutes or until cake tests done by pressing lightly with finger.

Mrs. Betty Lord
Garland Grange, No. 1568
Garland, Kansas

HUNDRED-YEAR OLD PORK CAKE
(Recipe over 125 years old)

1 lb. all-fat salt pork
1 pt. boiling water
4 c. sugar
1 tsp. nutmeg
1 tsp. cloves
1 tsp. cinnamon
1 tsp. soda
1 egg, well beaten
1/2 c. molasses
6 c. flour
1 lb. raisins

Put pork through food grinder; pour boiling water over pork. Let stand until lukewarm. Stir in sugar, spices, soda, egg and molasses. Sift flour before measuring. Add flour and raisins to pork mixture, stirring until well blended. Pour into well-greased loaf pans. Bake in preheated 300-degree oven for 2 hours or until done. This cake may be eaten as soon as baked and cooled and is especially good for outdoor meals and picnics.

Sandra K. Hunt
Springwater Grange, No. 263
Estacada, Oregon

EASTERN CAKE

1 1/2 c. sugar
1/2 c. cold water
6 eggs, separated
1/2 tsp. salt
1 tsp. vanilla extract
1 c. cake flour
1/2 tsp. cream of tartar

Cook sugar and water until thread spins. Beat egg whites and salt until stiff peaks form. Pour syrup slowly into egg whites, beating constantly until cold. Fold in well-beaten egg yolks and vanilla. Sift flour 5 times before measuring, then add cream of tartar. Fold into egg mixture. Place in ungreased tube pan. Bake in preheated 350-degree oven for 50 minutes. Turn upside down; let cool before cake loosens from pan.

Mrs. Henry G. Sager, Deputy Jr. Matron
Lecturer, Treas.
Logan Grange, No. 2041
Buckland, Ohio

★ ★

LADY BALTIMORE CAKE

> 3 1/2 c. sifted cake flour
> 3 1/2 tsp. baking powder
> 1 c. butter
> 3 c. sugar
> 4 eggs
> 1 c. milk
> 1/2 c. water
> 2 tsp. vanilla extract
> 2 tsp. almond extract

Sift flour and baking powder together. Cream butter until soft. Beat in 2 cups sugar gradually until mixture is light and fluffy. Add eggs, one at a time, beating thoroughly after each addition. Add flour mixture alternately with milk, blending until smooth after each addition. Pour into 2 greased and floured 9-inch layer pans. Bake in preheated 350-degree oven for 30 to 35 minutes. Combine remaining 1 cup sugar and water; cook until a thick syrup is formed. Stir in extracts. Remove cakes from pans; spread tops with syrup. Cool.

LADY BALTIMORE FROSTING

> 2 c. sugar
> 2/3 c. water
> 2 tsp. corn syrup
> 2 egg whites
> 2 c. seeded raisins, chopped
> 12 figs, chopped
> 2 c. chopped pecans
> Almond and vanilla extracts to taste

Combine sugar, water and corn syrup. Stir over low heat until sugar is dissolved. Boil gently to 244 degrees on candy thermometer or until a small amount of syrup forms a firm ball in cold water. Beat egg whites until stiff. Pour syrup in a fine stream over egg whites, beating constantly. Continue to beat unil frosting is cool and is of spreading consistency. Blend in raisins, figs and pecans. Add extracts. Spread frosting between layers and on top and side of cake. Raisins and figs may be soaked overnight in a small amount of sherry or brandy, if desired.

> *Mrs. Ira Shea*
> *Wife, Deputy National Master*
> *Mesa, Arizona*

LEMON CHEESE CAKE AND FILLING

> 2 c. sugar
> 1/2 c. shortening
> 4 egg whites, stiffly beaten
> 2 1/2 c. flour
> 2 tsp. baking powder
> 1/4 tsp. salt
> 1 c. milk

Cream sugar and shortening until light. Fold in egg whites. Combine flour, baking powder and salt. Add to creamed mixture alternately with milk, mixing after each addition. Remove 2 tablespoons batter; reserve for filling. Pour remaining batter into 3 greased and floured cake pans. Bake in preheated 350-degree oven for 25 minutes. Remove from pans; cool.

FILLING

> Juice and grated rind of 2 lemons
> 1 c. sugar
> 4 egg yolks
> 1/2 c. milk
> 2 tbsp. reserved cake batter

Combine all ingredients in saucepan; mix well. Cook over low heat, stirring constantly, until thick. Spread between layers and over top of cake. May sprinkle with coconut, if desired.

> *Bettie M. Edwards*
> *Gold Sand Grange*
> *Louisburg, North Carolina*

MAINE BLUEBERRY CAKE

> 3 c. sifted flour
> 3 tsp. baking powder
> 1 tsp. salt
> 1 c. butter or shortening
> 1 1/2 c. sugar
> 2 eggs
> 1 c. milk
> 2 1/2 c. fresh blueberries

Sift flour once, then measure; add baking powder and salt. Sift again. Cream butter thoroughly; add sugar gradually, beating constantly until sugar is dissolved. Add eggs; beat well. Add flour alternately with milk, a small amount at a time, beating well after each addition until smooth. This makes a stiff batter. Fold in blueberries. Turn into a greased 13 x 9 x 2-inch pan, spreading batter evenly. Sprinkle with sugar, if desired. Bake in preheated 350-degree oven for 1 hour. Serve warm or cold.

> *Mrs. Russell G. Jones, Sec.*
> *Shrewsbury Grange, No. 101*
> *Shrewsbury, Massachusetts*

OLD-FASHIONED STACK CAKE
(Recipe 60 years old)

> 1 c. butter
> 1 c. sugar
> 2 eggs
> 1 tsp. vanilla
> 4 c. sifted flour
> 2 tsp. baking powder
> 1/2 tsp. salt
> 1/4 c. milk

Cream butter; add sugar slowly, mixing until creamy. Beat eggs slightly; add with vanilla to creamed mixture. Sift flour, baking powder and salt together; add alternately with milk. Chill dough thoroughly in refrigerator. Divide dough into 7 equal parts. Roll each part into a circle. Turn cake pan upside down; place circle of dough on ungreased pan. Trim to fit pan. Bake in

★ ★

preheated 350-degree oven for 20 minutes or until edges are golden brown. Cool on wire racks. Layers will be thin and crisp.

FILLING

2 lb. dried apricots, cooked
1/2 c. liquid from cooked apricots
1 c. sugar
1 tsp. lemon extract
1/4 tsp. salt

Mash apricots; add liquid, sugar, lemon extract and salt. Cool. Should be thick. Spread between layers, but do not spread on top layer. Let cake set overnight for flavors to blend.

Mrs. Charles Patterson
Deemston Grange, No. 1372
Brownsville, Pennsylvania

ORANGE DREAM CAKE

2 c. sifted cake flour
1 1/3 c. sugar
2 tsp. baking powder
1/4 tsp. soda
1 tsp. salt
2/3 c. shortening
1 tsp. grated orange rind
1/4 tsp. grated lemon rind
1/3 c. orange juice
1/3 c. water
2 eggs
2 tbsp. lemon juice

Sift flour, sugar, baking powder, soda and salt into a mixing bowl; add shortening. Beat until creamy. Add rinds, orange juice, water and eggs. Beat for 200 strokes or for 2 minutes with mixer. Blend in lemon juice. Place in 2 greased and floured square or round pans. Bake in preheated 375-degree oven for 25 to 30 minutes. Ice as desired.

Mrs. Willie Lewis
Fredericksburg Grange, No. 1650
Fredericksburg, Texas

ORANGE WEDDING CAKE

1 c. soft butter
1 1/2 c. sugar
4 eggs
1/2 c. chopped nuts
1/3 c. chopped candied pineapple
2 c. unsifted cake flour
1 tsp. baking powder
1/2 tsp. salt
1/2 c. Florida orange juice
1 tsp. grated orange rind

Cream butter and sugar in large bowl until light and fluffy; beat in eggs, one at a time. Place nuts and pineapple in small bowl; sprinkle 1/4 cup flour over nut mixture. Mix remaining flour, baking powder and salt together; blend into creamed mixture alternately with orange juice. Add grated rind; fold in nut mixture. Turn into greased 8-inch springform pan. Bake in

preheated 350-degree oven for about 1 hour and 40 minutes or until cake tester inserted in center comes out clean. Cool for 10 minutes; remove from pan. Cool completely on rack. Prepare double recipe of batter for 8-inch cake; pour into a greased 6-inch spring-form pan and a greased 10-inch springform pan. Bake 6-inch cake for about 1 hour and 30 minutes and 10-inch cake for 1 hour and 50 minutes or until cakes test done. Cool for 10 minutes; remove from pans. Cool completely on racks.

MERINGUE

12 egg whites, at room temperature
1 1/2 tsp. cream of tartar
1/4 tsp. salt
3 3/4 c. sugar
Orange Peel Roses
Mint sprigs

Beat egg whites, cream of tartar and salt in large bowl until frothy. Beat in sugar, two tablespoons at a time; continue beating for 15 to 20 minutes or until very stiff. Frost top of each cake layer; assemble layers on large, heatproof platter or tray. Cover sides of layers with Meringue. Place remaining Meringue in pastry bag with large star tip. Pipe small rosettes along top edge of each layer and around base of bottom layer. Bake in preheated 250-degree oven for 30 minutes or until Meringue is dry, but not brown. Garnish with Orange Peel Roses and mint sprigs. Cake may be frosted and baked on foil-covered baking sheet if heatproof platter is not available, then transferred to platter. Meringue will probably crack slightly during transfer. Yield: 50-60 servings.

ORANGE PEEL ROSES

Cut thin peel from oranges in long spirals with very sharp knife. Peel needs to be thinly cut with as little of the white pith as possible in order to roll well without breaking. Roll up a strip of peel, orange side out for each rose; fasten with small pin or food pick. Place roses in water or wrap in plastic wrap to keep from drying out; place on cake just before guests arrive.

Photograph for this recipe on page 202.

CORNSTARCH CAKE

2 c. sugar
1 c. butter
1 c. milk
1/2 tsp. soda
1 c. cornstarch
2 c. flour
1 tsp. cream of tartar
5 egg whites

Cream sugar and butter; add milk and soda. Mix well. Sift cornstarch, flour and cream of tartar together. Beat egg whites until stiff peaks form. Blend flour mixture and egg whites into sugar mixture. Place in 2 layer pans or 1 loaf pan. Bake in preheated 350-degree oven until cake tests done.

Vivian Headrick
Oak Hill Grange, No. 809
Rogers, Arkansas

★ ★

PATRIOTIC CAKE
(Recipe 199 years old)

1 lb. bread dough
2 c. (packed) brown sugar
1 c. butter
3 eggs
2 tbsp. cream
1 tsp. cloves
1 tsp. nutmeg
1 tsp. soda
1 tbsp. water
1/2 lb. dried currants, washed and drained
1/2 lb. seeded raisins, washed and drained

Let dough rise; add brown sugar, butter, eggs, cream, cloves and nutmeg. Mix well. Dissolve soda in water; mix into dough. Add currants and raisins; mix well. Turn into greased pan. Let rise for 20 minutes. Bake in preheated 325-degree oven for 1 hour or until cake tests done. Cool. Ice as desired and garnish with candied cherries.
This is a 1776 recipe.

Ada H. Mason
San Marcos Grange, No. 633
Escondido, California

PEANUT ROLLS
(Recipe over 50 years old)

3 eggs, separated
1 c. sugar
1 c. flour
1 tsp. baking powder
1 tsp. salt
6 tbsp. boiling water
2 c. confectioners' sugar
3/4 c. butter
Finely chopped or ground peanuts

Beat egg yolks. Add sugar; beat until creamy. Add dry ingredients; beat until well blended. Stir in water. Fold in stiffly beaten egg whites. Spread on paper-lined cookie sheet with sides or shallow baking pan. Bake in preheated 350-degree oven for about 25 minutes. Cut into 2 x 3/4-inch strips. Combine confectioners' sugar and butter; mix until smooth. Ice each strip on all sides; roll in peanuts until well covered.

Mrs. James A. Kegel
Valley Grange, No. 1360
Lewisberry, Pennsylvania

DELICIOUS PINEAPPLE CAKE

1/2 c. butter
1 1/2 c. sugar
1 tsp. vanilla extract
3 eggs, separated
1 c. crushed pineapple with juice
2 1/2 c. sifted flour
2 1/2 tsp. baking powder
1/8 tsp. salt
1/4 c. water

Cream butter until light; add sugar and vanilla. Cream until fluffy. Add egg yolks and pineapple; mix well. Sift dry ingredients together, then add to creamed mixture. Blend in water. Beat egg whites until stiff peaks form; fold into batter. Turn into sheet cake pan or layer pans. Bake in preheated 350-degree oven for 35 to 40 minutes or until cake tests done. Frost as desired.

Alberta Horst
Beech Grove Grange
Seelyville, Pennsylvania

PINEAPPLE UPSIDE-DOWN CAKE

1/2 c. butter
1 c. (packed) brown sugar
6 slices pineapple
Maraschino cherries
3 eggs, separated
1 c. sugar
5 tbsp. pineapple juice
1 c. flour
1 tsp. baking powder

Melt butter in a round, deep pan; add brown sugar, spreading evenly over bottom of pan. Place slice of pineapple in center, then arrange half slices around edge. Place cherries in holes. Beat egg yolks; add sugar and pineapple juice. Sift flour and baking powder together; add to egg mixture. Fold in stiffly beaten egg whites. Pour over fruit. Bake in preheated 350-degree oven for 45 minutes to 1 hour.

Catherine L. Marolf
Beaver Falls Grange, No. 554
Castorland, New York

SAVARIN

Butter
All-purpose flour
1 pkg. dry yeast
1/4 c. warm water
1/4 c. milk
2 tbsp. sugar
1/2 tsp. salt
4 eggs
Syrup
Sweetened whipped cream

Butter 6 1/2-cup ring mold generously; dust with flour. Sprinkle yeast over warm water. Scald milk in small saucepan. Add 3/4 cup butter, sugar and salt; stir until butter is dissolved. Cool to lukewarm. Beat eggs in large mixing bowl; stir in yeast and butter mixture. Beat in 2 cups sifted flour gradually; mix until smooth. Cover; let rise in warm place for about 1 hour or until doubled in bulk. Stir down; turn into prepared mold. Let rise in warm place until almost doubled in bulk. Bake in preheated 350-degree oven for 20 to 25 minutes; cool on wire rack for 5 minutes. Loosen around edges, if necessary; remove from mold. Prick top of cake with fork immediately; drizzle Syrup over cake until cake is thoroughly soaked. Serve with whipped cream. Yield: 12 servings.

SYRUP

1 c. sugar
1 tbsp. grated orange rind
1/2 c. orange juice
1/2 tsp. rum extract

Combine sugar, orange rind and orange juice in small saucepan; bring to a boil. Boil for 1 minute. Stir in rum extract; cool to lukewarm.

Photograph for this recipe above.

EIGHTEEN EIGHTY-FOUR POUND CAKE

1 lb. sugar
3/4 lb. butter
8 eggs
2 tsp. lemon extract
2 tsp. vanilla extract
1 lb. flour, sifted

Cream sugar and butter in mixer until smooth; add eggs, one at a time, with lemon and vanilla extracts. Beat until sugar is dissolved. Add flour; beat until smooth. Pour into tube pan. Bake on middle rack in 350-degree oven for 1 hour and 20 minutes.

Mrs. Emmet L. Gaston
Muncy Grange, No. 1204
Lebanon, Tennessee

OLD-FASHIONED POUND CAKE
(Recipe 150 years old)

9 lg. eggs, separated
2 c. sugar
2 c. butter
4 c. flour, sifted

1 tsp. baking powder
1/2 tsp. salt
1 tsp. lemon extract

Beat egg yolks until fluffy; add sugar gradually, beating until pale yellow color. Place butter in another bowl; cream until light. Add flour, baking powder and salt; cream well. Add egg mixture to creamed mixture; beat well. Add lemon extract and unbeaten egg whites; beat until well mixed. Pour into well-greased tube pan. Bake in 300-degree oven for 1 hour and 45 minutes or until done.

Ada H. Mason
San Marcos Grange, No. 633
Escondido, California

RAISIN AND ORANGE CAKE
(Recipe about 100 years old)

1 c. sugar
1/2 c. lard
2 eggs, beaten
1 orange, ground
1 c. raisins
1 tsp. soda
1 c. sour milk
2 c. flour
1/4 tsp. salt
Chopped nuts to taste (opt.)
Juice of 1 orange
1 c. confectioners' sugar

Mix sugar and lard; beat until creamy. Add eggs, ground orange and raisins. Mix soda in sour milk; sift flour and salt. Add milk and flour alternately to sugar mixture, beating well after each addition. Stir in nuts. Place in loaf pan. Bake in preheated 350-degree oven until cake tests done. Combine orange juice and confectioners' sugar. Pour over slightly warm cake.

Dee Meanes
Imnaha Grange, No. 677
Imnaha, Oregon

RHUBARB CAKE

1/2 c. shortening
Sugar
1 egg
1 tsp. soda
1 tsp. vanilla extract
1 c. sour milk
2 c. flour
1/2 tsp. salt
1 1/2 c. chopped rhubarb
1/3 c. chopped nuts
1 tsp. cinnamon

Cream shortening and 1 1/2 cups sugar. Add egg; beat thoroughly. Combine soda, vanilla and milk. Combine flour and salt; add alternately with milk mixture to creamed mixture. Stir in rhubarb. Pour into greased cake pan. Combine 1/3 cup sugar, nuts and cinnamon; sprinkle over top. Bake in preheated 350-degree oven for 30 minutes.

Mrs. Sophie Fisol
West Warren, Massachusetts

★ ★

QUICK RAISED CAKE
(Recipe 150 years old)

1 yeast cake
1 c. butter
2 c. sugar
1 egg, well beaten
1 c. milk
4 c. flour
2 tsp. (heaping) baking powder
1/2 tsp. nutmeg
1 tsp. salt
1/2 c. chopped citron
1 c. seeded raisins
1 c. chopped walnuts

Dissolve yeast cake in 1 cup lukewarm water; cover. Let stand while preparing other ingredients. Cream butter and sugar; add egg. Mix well. Blend in milk and yeast. Combine dry ingredients; sift. Add to yeast mixture, blending well. Add fruits and walnuts. Place in greased tube pan. Bake in preheated 350-degree oven for 1 hour and 20 minutes.
This recipe used in family for 5 generations.

Mrs. Doris T. Shaw, State C.W.A. Director
Tunxis Grange, No. 13
Hartford, Connecticut

CHOCOLATE ROLL
(Recipe 57 years old)

6 eggs, separated
1 c. sugar, sifted
3 tbsp. cocoa
2 tbsp. flour
1/2 tsp. baking powder
1/2 tsp. vanilla extract
Sweetened whipped cream

Mix egg yolks with sugar. Sift cocoa, flour and baking powder. Add to egg mixture; blend well. Fold in stiffly beaten egg whites and vanilla. Pour batter into 10 x 13-inch shallow pan. Bake in preheated 300-degree oven for 15 minutes. Turn onto dampened tea towel; roll up. Cool. Unroll; spread with sweetened whipped cream. Roll again.

ICING

1 tbsp. butter
2 tbsp. hot water
2 c. confectioners' sugar
4 tbsp. cocoa
1 tsp. vanilla extract

Melt butter in hot water. Mix sugar and cocoa; add slowly to butter mixture. Stir in vanilla. Spread over roll.

Alice V. McComb
Wife of Past State Master
Maryville, Tennessee

PRIZE JELLY ROLL

3 eggs
1 c. sugar

1/3 c. water
1 tsp. vanilla extract
1 c. cake flour
1 tsp. baking powder
1/4 tsp. salt
Powdered sugar
1 10-oz. jar jelly

Beat eggs until thick; add sugar gradually, beating constantly. Beat in water and vanilla. Sift flour, baking powder and salt together; fold into batter, mixing carefully until smooth. Pour into brown paper-lined and greased jelly roll pan. Bake in preheated 350-degree oven for 15 minutes. Invert quickly on towel dusted with powdered sugar. Remove brown paper; trim crusty edges. Cool. Spread with jelly. Roll carefully.

Mrs. Robert Beecher
Livonia Grange, No. 1180
Livonia, New York

GRANDMOTHER SMITH'S JELLY ROLL
(Recipe over 100 years old)

1 c. sugar
3 eggs
1/2 tsp. soda
4 tsp. warm water
1 c. flour
1 tsp. cream of tartar
Jelly

Cream sugar and eggs together until foamy. Dissolve soda in warm water; add to creamed mixture. Add flour and cream of tartar; mix well. Spread in jelly roll pan. Bake in preheated 350-degree oven for 15 to 20 minutes or until cake tests done. Turn out on cloth. Spread with jelly; roll up.

Mrs. Olive Chandler
Laurel Grange
Dexter City, Ohio

SOUR CREAM-CHERRY-NUT CAKE

1 1/2 c. sugar
3 eggs
1 c. thick sour cream
2 c. flour, sifted
1 tsp. soda
1/2 tsp. nutmeg
1/2 tsp. cinnamon
1/2 tsp. salt
1/2 c. chopped nuts
1 c. drained and chopped cherries

Beat sugar and eggs together until smooth. Add cream; beat until smooth. Sift dry ingredients together; add to sugar mixture. Blend well. Stir in nuts and cherries. Place in greased layer pan. Bake in preheated 350-degree oven for 30 minutes.

ICING

1 c. sugar
1/2 c. milk

★ ★ ★ ★ ★★★ ★

1 tbsp. butter
1 tsp. burnt sugar
Vanilla to taste

Combine first 4 ingredients in saucepan; cook until soft ball forms in cold water. Add vanilla and additional 1 tablespoon milk. Beat for 4 minutes or until thick. Frost cake with Icing.

Mrs. Cecil Lynch
Cloverleaf Grange, No. 1923
Hugoton, Kansas

POPPY SEED TEA CAKE

1/3 c. poppy seed
1 c. buttermilk
1 c. butter
1 1/2 c. sugar
4 eggs
2 1/2 c. sifted all-purpose flour
2 tsp. baking powder
1 tsp. soda
1/2 tsp. salt
1 tsp. orange extract
Cinnamon Sugar

Combine poppy seed and buttermilk; refrigerate overnight for full flavor. Cream butter with sugar until light and fluffy. Add eggs, one at a time, beating after each addition. Sift flour, baking powder, soda and salt together. Add orange extract to creamed mixture; blend in sifted ingredients alternately with seed mixture, beginning and ending with dry ingredients. Turn half the batter into a greased and floured 10-inch tube pan or bundt pan. Sprinkle Cinnamon Sugar on top. Add remaining batter. Bake in 350-degree oven for 1

hour or until cake tests done. Cool for 10 minutes, then remove from pan to finish cooling. Cinnamon Sugar may be made by mixing 2 tablespoons sugar with 1 teaspoon cinnamon.

Photograph for this recipe below.

WASHINGTON CAKE

1/2 lb. butter
1 lb. sugar
4 eggs, separated
1 c. milk
1/2 nutmeg, grated
1 lb. flour
1 lb. raisins
1 tsp. soda

Cream butter and sugar together. Beat egg yolks until creamy; add to butter mixture. Beat well. Add milk and nutmeg. Stir in part of the flour; add stiffly beaten egg whites. Sprinkle about 2 tablespoons of the remaining flour over raisins; mix well. Add remaining flour to egg mixture; mix well. Dissolve soda in 1 tablespoon water; stir into mixture. Stir in raisins. Line 2 loaf pans with buttered paper; fill 2/3 full. Bake in preheated 350-degree oven until cake tests done.

Mrs. Margaret Sullivan, D.W.A.
Virginia State Grange
Blacksburg, Virginia

PRUNE CAKE
(Recipe 65 years old)

1 1/2 c. sugar
2/3 c. shortening
4 eggs
1 tsp. cloves
1 tsp. cinnamon
1 tsp. nutmeg
1/4 tsp. salt
1 tsp. soda
1/2 c. sour milk
1 1/2 c. flour, sifted
1 c. cooked dried seeded prunes, chopped

Cream sugar, shortening and eggs together; mix in spices and salt. Dissolve soda in milk. Add flour and milk mixture alternately to creamed mixture, mixing well. Add prunes; mix well. Pour into greased and floured 9-inch layer pans. Bake in preheated 350-degree oven for 30 to 35 minutes or until cake tests done.

PRUNE CAKE ICING

2 c. sugar
1 c. thick cream

Combine sugar and cream in saucepan; boil to soft-ball stage. Beat until cool enough to spread on cake.

Carmen Dawson
South Fork Grange, No. 605
Lostine, Oregon

★ ★

TEMPTATION SPICE CAKE
(Recipe over 40 years old)

2 c. sifted flour
1 tsp. salt
3 1/2 tsp. baking powder
1 1/3 c. sugar
1 tsp. cinnamon
1/2 tsp. nutmeg
1/4 tsp. cloves
1/2 c. shortening
1 c. milk
1 tsp. vanilla extract
2 lg. eggs

Sift first 7 ingredients into mixer bowl. Add shortening, milk and vanilla. Beat for 2 minutes. Add eggs; beat for 2 minutes longer. Turn into 2 greased and floured 9-inch cake pans. Bake in preheated 350-degree oven for 35 to 40 minutes. Cool for 10 minutes; remove from pans.

CREAMY NUT FILLING AND FROSTING

1/2 c. milk
2 1/2 tbsp. flour
1/2 c. butter
1/2 c. sugar
1/4 tsp. salt
1/2 tsp. vanilla extract
1/2 c. coarsely chopped nuts
1 c. sifted confectioners' sugar

Blend milk gradually into flour; cook, stirring constantly, for about 10 minutes or to a very thick paste. Cool to lukewarm. Combine butter, sugar and salt; cream until light. Add lukewarm paste; beat with rotary beater until fluffy. Fold in vanilla and nuts. Spread about 1/3 of the mixture between 2 cake layers. Blend confectioners' sugar in remaining nut mixture. Spread over top and side of cake.

Mrs. Clinton Walton
Upper Rogue Grange, No. 825
Central Point, Oregon

TWO-EGG CHIFFON CAKE

2 eggs, separated
1 1/2 c. sugar
2 1/4 c. cake flour
1 tsp. salt
3 tsp. baking powder
1/3 c. cooking oil or butter
1 c. milk
1 1/2 tsp. vanilla extract

Grease generously and dust with flour two 8 or 9-inch layer pans. Beat egg whites until frothy; beat in 1/2 cup sugar gradually. Continue beating until very stiff and glossy. Sift remaining sugar, flour, salt and baking powder into bowl; add oil, 3/4 cup milk and vanilla extract. Beat for 1 minute at medium speed, scraping side and bottom of bowl. Add remaining milk and egg yolks; beat for 1 minute longer, scraping side to mix thoroughly. Fold in egg whites. Pour into prepared

pans. Bake in preheated 350-degree oven for 25 to 30 minutes. Frost with favorite frosting; spread lemon filling between layers, if desired.

Mae Blatt
Camas Valley Grange, No. 842
Springdale, Washington

WINTERGREEN CANDY CAKE

1/2 lb. wintergreen candy
1 1/4 c. milk
1/2 c. shortening
1/2 c. sugar
1 tsp. vanilla extract
3 c. flour
3 tsp. (heaping) baking powder
1/4 tsp. salt
4 egg whites, stiffly beaten

Soak wintergreen candy in milk overnight. Cream shortening; add sugar, then vanilla. Mix well. Sift flour, baking powder and salt together. Add to shortening mixture alternately with candy mixture. Fold in egg whites. Place in tube pan. Bake in preheated 350-degree oven until cake tests done.

Lois Dietterick
Lightstreet Grange
Bloomsburg, Pennsylvania

POPPY SEED LEMON-ORANGE TORTE

1 c. milk
1/3 c. poppy seed
1/2 c. butter
1 1/4 c. sugar
1 1/2 tsp. vanilla
2 c. sifted cake flour
1 tbsp. baking powder
1/4 tsp. salt
4 egg whites
Lemon-Orange Cream Filling
Sifted confectioners' sugar

Heat milk; pour over poppy seed. Cool, then place in refrigerator for about 2 hours. Line two 9-inch round cake pans with waxed paper. Cream butter in mixing bowl. Add 1 cup sugar gradually; beat until light and fluffy. Beat in vanilla. Sift flour, baking powder and salt together; add to creamed mixture alternately with poppy seed mixture, beginning and ending with dry ingredients. Beat egg whites in small mixing bowl until frothy. Add remaining 1/4 cup sugar gradually; beat until stiff peaks form. Fold into batter; pour into the prepared pans. Bake in preheated 350-degree oven for 25 to 30 minutes or until cake tests done. Cool in pans on wire racks for 5 minutes. Turn onto racks; cool completely. Split cake layers horizontally; fill with Lemon-Orange Cream Filling. Place a doily on top of cake; sift confectioners' sugar over doily to make a design. Remove doily.

LEMON-ORANGE CREAM FILLING

3/4 c. sugar
1/2 c. all-purpose flour

1/4 tsp. salt
1 1/2 c. milk
4 egg yolks, beaten
1 tbsp. grated orange rind
1 tbsp. grated lemon rind
1/4 c. orange juice
1/4 c. lemon juice

Combine sugar, flour and salt in saucepan; stir in milk gradually. Cook over medium heat, stirring constantly, until thickened. Cook for 2 minutes longer. Stir small amount of hot mixture into egg yolks; stir back into hot mixture. Cook for 1 minute longer; do not boil. Cool slightly; stir in orange and lemon rinds and juices.

Photograph for this recipe above.

ALMOND CHEESECAKE

1/2 c. butter
2 c. graham cracker crumbs
2 tsp. cinnamon
1/2 c. chopped walnuts
2 8-oz. packages cream cheese
3 eggs
1 c. sugar
2 tsp. vanilla extract
1/2 tsp. almond extract
1/4 tsp. salt
3 c. sour cream

Beat butter until creamy; blend in crumbs and cinnamon. Stir in walnuts. Reserve small amount of crumb mixture for topping. Press remaining crumb mixture in bottom and around side of springform pan. Beat cream cheese until smooth; add eggs, one at a time, beating well after each addition. Beat in sugar, vanilla, almond extract and salt. Fold in sour cream until well blended. Pour into prepared pan. Sprinkle with reserved crumbs. Bake in preheated 375-degree oven for about 1 hour or until crack appears on top. Cool on rack. Chill thoroughly in refrigerator.

Marie G. Scheiblauer
Greece Grange, No. 311
Rochester, New York

CHERRY CHEESECAKE

1/2 c. butter
1 1/4 c. fine graham cracker crumbs
Sugar
1 tsp. cinnamon
1 lg. package cream cheese, softened
2 eggs
1 tsp. vanilla
1 tsp. almond extract
2 c. sour cream
1 can sweet cherries
3 tbsp. cornstarch
1 tsp. lemon juice

Melt butter; mix in graham cracker crumbs, 2 teaspoons sugar and cinnamon. Press in 8 x 8 x 2-inch pan. Combine cream cheese and 1 cup sugar. Add eggs, vanilla, almond extract and sour cream; mix well. Pour over crust. Bake in preheated 350-degree oven for 40 minutes or until knife inserted in center comes out clean. Let cool. Combine cherries, cornstarch and lemon juice in saucepan; cook until thick and clear. Let cool; spread on cheesecake.

Gladys Arnold, Flora
Lucerne Grange, No. 167
West Palm Beach, Florida

FAVORITE CHEESECAKE

5 graham crackers, crushed fine
1 1/2 lb. cream cheese
1 1/4 c. sugar
1 tsp. salt
1/4 c. flour
5 eggs, separated
2 1/2 tbsp. lemon juice
1/4 tsp. nutmeg
1 tsp. vanilla
1/2 tsp. almond extract
1 c. sour cream

Spread graham cracker crumbs in well-buttered tube pan. Combine cheese, 1 cup sugar and salt; blend well. Add flour and egg yolks; beat well. Mix in lemon juice, nutmeg, vanilla, almond extract and sour cream. Beat egg whites with remaining 1/4 cup sugar until stiff but not dry. Fold into cheese mixture. Pour into pan. Bake in preheated 325-degree oven for 1 hour and 15 minutes. Turn off oven heat; cool in oven for 1 hour. Remove from oven; cool completely on rack. Refrigerate until thoroughly chilled. Remove from pan.

Oleta Frye, Master's Wife
Bartonsville Grange, No. 481
Bartonsville, Vermont

★ ★

ORANGE-CRANBERRY CHEESECAKE

1 c. all-purpose flour
1/4 c. sugar
1 tbsp. grated fresh orange rind
6 tbsp. butter
1 egg yolk
1/2 tsp. vanilla extract
Cheesecake Filling
Orange sections
Cranberry Topping

Combine flour, sugar and grated orange rind in bowl. Add butter, egg yolk and vanilla extract; cut in with pastry blender and then knead with fingers until smooth. Pat 1/3 of the dough over bottom of 9-inch springform pan. Bake in preheated 400-degree oven for 5 minutes or until golden brown. Let cool. Pat remaining dough evenly around side to 1/2 inch from top. Pour Cheesecake Filling into prepared pan. Bake in preheated 400-degree oven for 8 minutes. Reduce oven temperature to 225 degrees; bake for 1 hour and 20 minutes longer. Let cool slowly; refrigerate until ready to serve. Arrange orange sections on top of cheesecake. Spoon Cranberry Topping in center of cheesecake; serve immediately. Yield: 12-18 servings.

CHEESECAKE FILLING

5 8-oz. packages cream cheese,
    softened
1 3/4 c. sugar
3 tbsp. flour
1/4 tsp. salt
1 tsp. grated fresh lemon rind
1 tbsp. fresh lemon juice
1 tbsp. grated fresh orange rind
1/4 tsp. vanilla extract
5 eggs
2 egg yolks
1/4 c. fresh orange juice

Combine cheese, sugar, flour, salt, lemon rind, lemon juice, orange rind and vanilla extract in large bowl of electric mixer; beat at low speed until smooth. Add eggs and egg yolks, one at a time, beating well after each addition. Stir in orange juice.

CRANBERRY TOPPING

1 c. sugar
1 c. water
4 strips fresh orange rind
2 whole cloves
2 c. fresh cranberries

Combine sugar, water, orange rind and cloves in medium saucepan; stir over low heat until sugar dissolves. Add cranberries; cook over medium heat until cranberries begin to pop. Remove from heat; chill until needed.

Photograph for this recipe on page 34.

WILLIAM PENN'S CHEESECAKE
(Recipe about 200 years old)

1 1/2 c. all-purpose flour
1 c. butter

4 lg. eggs
1 tbsp. cold water
3 8-oz. packages cream cheese, softened
3/4 c. sugar
1 tsp. ground nutmeg
1 tsp. rose extract or 2 tbsp. rose water
1/2 c. dried currants

Place flour in bowl; cut in 1/2 cup butter. Combine 1 egg and cold water; sprinkle over flour mixture. Stir gently with fork until pastry clings together. Roll out into 12-inch circle; lift onto foil-lined 10-inch quiche dish. Press to fit dish; trim off pastry overhang. Fit piece of waxed paper into pastry shell; fill with beans, rice or broken bread crusts. Bake in preheated 400-degree oven for 15 minutes. Set aside to cool slightly. Reduce oven temperature to 350 degrees. Beat cheese and remaining 1/2 cup softened butter until fluffy; beat in sugar and 3 remaining eggs gradually. Stir in nutmeg, rose extract and currants. Remove beans and paper; turn cheese mixture into pastry shell. Bake for 30 minutes. Turn off oven heat; let cheesecake stand in oven for 15 minutes. Remove; let cool to room temperature. Chill. Lift from dish with foil; place on serving plate. Vanilla extract may be substituted for rose extract. Place cheesecake under broiler to brown top, if desired.

This cheesecake was created by Gulielma Penn, wife of Pennsylvania's founder, who never set foot in the colony. Her son brought a handwritten manuscript of her recipes to Penn's estate in the 1700's.

Donna Wagner
Homestead Grange, No. 215
Roggen, Colorado

BANANA BROWNIES

2/3 c. shortening
1 1-lb box brown sugar
2 eggs, slightly beaten
2 lg. ripe bananas, mashed
3 1/2 c. flour
1 tbsp. baking powder
1 tsp. salt
1 tsp. vanilla extract
1 c. chopped nuts
1 6-oz. package butterscotch bits
Glaze

Cream shortening and sugar in bowl; blend in eggs and bananas. Stir in flour, baking powder and salt, then vanilla, nuts and butterscotch bits. Spoon into greased 10 x 15-inch baking pan. Bake in preheated 350-degree oven for 40 minutes. Remove from oven; spread with Glaze. Cut into squares while warm.

GLAZE

2 tbsp. mashed banana
1 1/2 tsp. lemon juice
2 1/4 to 2 1/2 c. powdered sugar

Mix all ingredients.

Denise Smith
Sonora Grange
Grinnell, Iowa

★ ★

DELICIOUS BROWNIES

1/2 c. shortening
4 eggs
1 lb. confectioners' sugar
4 sq. chocolate, melted
1 3/4 c. flour, sifted
1/4 tsp. salt
1 tsp. vanilla
1 c. chopped nuts

Cream shortening, eggs and sugar together. Stir in re-maining ingredients in order listed. Pour into greased 9 x 13-inch pan. Bake in preheated 360-degree oven for 25 to 30 minutes or until done.

Mrs. Priscilla Puckey
Garrison Hill Grange, No. 497
Newcastle, Maine

FROSTED BROWNIES

2 c. flour
2 c. sugar
1/2 tsp. salt
1 c. butter
1/4 c. cocoa
1 c. water
1/2 c. buttermilk
2 eggs, beaten
1 tsp. soda
1 tsp. vanilla extract
Frosting

Mix flour and sugar together. Combine salt, butter, cocoa and water in saucepan; bring to a boil. Pour over flour mixture; mix well. Add milk, eggs, soda and va-nilla; mix well. Pour into greased jelly roll pan. Bake in preheated 400-degree oven for 20 minutes or until done. Spread Frosting over hot brownies. Cut into squares to serve.

FROSTING

1/2 c. butter
1/4 c. cocoa
6 tbsp. milk
1 lb. powdered sugar
1 tsp. vanilla extract
1 c. chopped nuts

Combine butter, cocoa and milk in saucepan; bring to a boil. Remove from heat; stir in sugar, vanilla extract and nuts. Mix well.

Mrs. William Hatfield
Kinney Grange, No. 754
Nunica, Michigan

CHEWY PEANUT BUTTER STRIPS

1/3 c. shortening
1/2 c. peanut butter
1 c. sugar
1/4 tsp. salt
2 eggs
1 tsp. vanilla extract
1 c. sifted flour

1 tsp. baking powder
1 c. shredded coconut
Confectioners' sugar

Blend shortening, peanut butter, sugar, salt, eggs and vanilla in bowl. Sift flour with baking powder; stir into shortening mixture. Stir in coconut; spread in greased 8 x 12-inch baking pan. Bake in preheated 350-degree oven for 25 to 30 minutes. Cut into strips; roll in confectioners' sugar. Yield: 2 1/2 dozen.

Isabelle S. Covington
West Suffield Grange, No. 199
West Suffield, Connecticut

LUSCIOUS LEMON SQUARES

1 c. soft butter
1/2 c. powdered sugar
2 1/4 c. flour
Dash of salt
2 c. sugar
4 eggs, beaten
6 tbsp. lemon juice

Combine butter, powdered sugar, 2 cups flour and salt in bowl; mix well. Press mixture into 9 x 13-inch pan. Bake in preheated 350-degree oven for 15 minutes or until well browned; cool slightly. Combine remaining flour and sugar in bowl; mix in eggs and lemon juice. Pour onto crust. Bake for 25 minutes longer or until set. Cool; sprinkle with additional powdered sugar. Cut into 1 1/2-inch squares.

Mrs. Gordon Krupke
Spring Creek Grange, No. 951
Reardan, Washington

CHERRY DROP COOKIES

1 c. lard
2 c. sugar
2 eggs, beaten
1 tsp. soda
1 c. sour milk
1 c. tart red cherries
1/2 c. chopped nuts
1 c. raisins
Flour
1 tsp. baking powder
1/2 tsp. cinnamon
1/2 tsp. nutmeg

Cream lard and sugar in bowl. Add eggs; mix well. Dissolve soda in sour milk; stir into sugar mixture. Add cherries, nuts and raisins; mix well. Sift 1 cup flour with baking powder and spices; stir into sugar mixture. Add enough flour to make stiff dough; mix thoroughly. Drop by spoonfuls onto greased baking sheet. Bake in preheated 350-degree oven for about 15 minutes or until brown.

Christne Kearne
Yucaipa Grange, No. 582
Yucaipa, California

★ ★

RASPBERRY JAM SQUARES

1/2 c. butter
3/4 c. sugar
2 eggs
1/2 tsp. salt
1 1/2 c. flour
1 tsp. baking powder
Raspberry jam
3/4 c. (packed) brown sugar
1/2 c. chopped walnuts or coconut

Cream butter and sugar in bowl. Beat 1 egg with 1 egg yolk; stir into creamed mixture. Stir in salt, flour and baking powder. Spread in 9 x 13-inch baking pan; spread layer of jam over flour mixture. Beat remaining egg white until stiff; beat in brown sugar. Fold in walnuts; spread over jam. Bake in preheated 350-degree oven for 20 minutes; cut into squares.

Norma O'Neal
Garrison Hill Grange, No. 497
Sheepscott, Maine

AMISH COOKIES

2 c. (packed) brown sugar
1 1/2 c. butter
2 eggs
5 1/2 c. flour
1 tsp. salt
1 tsp. soda
3 tsp. baking powder
1 tsp. vanilla extract
1/2 tsp. maple flavoring
1 1/2 c. milk

Cream sugar and butter in bowl. Add eggs; mix well. Sift flour, salt, soda and baking powder together. Mix flavorings with milk; add to creamed mixture alternately with flour mixture. Beat well. Drop by spoonfuls onto greased cookie sheet. Bake in preheated 350-degree oven for 12 to 15 minutes; cool. Frost with desired powdered sugar icing flavored with maple flavoring. Yield: 5-6 dozen.

Maxine Patterson
Keene Hill Grange, No. 1602
Millersburg, Ohio

CARROT COOKIES

2 c. sifted flour
1/4 tsp. salt
2 tsp. baking powder
1 c. shortening
3/4 c. sugar
1 c. grated carrots
1/2 tsp. orange extract
1 egg

Sift flour with salt and baking powder. Cream shortening and sugar in bowl thoroughly. Add carrots, orange extract and egg; beat well. Stir in flour mix-

ture; mix well. Drop by spoonfuls on cookie sheet. Bake in preheated 400-degree oven for 10 to 12 minutes or until done. One tablespoon grated orange rind may be substituted for orange extract. Yield: 3 dozen.

Rose M. Lewis
Rosedale Grange
Bakersfield, California

BOILED MOLASSES COOKIES

(Recipe over 150 years old)

1 c. molasses
2 tsp. soda
2 tsp. salt
1 c. butter
2/3 c. sugar
2 eggs
1 tsp. ginger
1 tsp. cinnamon
1 tsp. nutmeg
1 tsp. vanilla extract
5 c. flour

Pour molasses into saucepan; bring to a boil. Add soda and salt; let foam. Pour into bowl. Add butter, sugar, eggs, spices and vanilla; mix well. Add flour; stir until mixed. Drop by spoonfuls onto greased cookie sheet. Bake in preheated 350-degree oven for 10 minutes.

Mrs. Martha J. West, Lecturer
Sterling Grange, No. 53
Clinton, Massachusett

COCONUT DROPS

(Recipe 60 to 75 years old)

1/2 c. butter
1 c. sugar
2 eggs
2 c. flour
1/4 tsp. salt
2 tsp. baking powder
2/3 c. milk
1 c. coconut
1 tsp. vanilla extract

Cream butter, sugar and eggs in bowl. Sift flour, salt and baking powder together; add to creamed mixture alternately with milk. Add coconut and vanilla; mix well. Drop from teaspoon onto greased baking sheet. Bake in preheated 375-degree oven for 15 minutes or until done. Yield: 3 dozen.

Edna C. Mashl
Quonochontaug Grange, No. 48
Bradford, Rhode Island

CHRISTMAS ROCKS

1 lb. shelled walnuts
1/2 lb. blanched almonds
1/2 lb. Brazil nuts

★ ★

2 lb. dates
1 1/2 lb. candied cherries
24 slices candied pineapple
2 1/2 c. sifted flour
1 c. butter
1 1/2 c. (packed) brown sugar
2 eggs, beaten
1 tsp. cinnamon
1 tsp. soda
1 1/2 tsp. vanilla extract

Chop nuts and fruits medium fine; mix. Stir in 1/2 cup flour. Cream butter and sugar in bowl; stir in eggs. Add remaining flour, cinnamon, soda and vanilla; stir until mixed. Add fruit mixture; mix well. Drop by small spoonfuls on greased baking sheet. Bake in preheated 350-degree oven until light brown. Store in airtight container. Yield: Over 200 cookies.

Mrs. Roy Plaster
Spring Creek Grange, No. 951
Reardan, Washington

DATE AND NUT KISSES

4 egg whites
1 1/4 c. sugar
2 c. chopped dates
1 c. chopped English walnuts

Beat egg whites in bowl until soft peaks form; beat until stiff, adding sugar gradually. Fold in dates and walnuts; drop by spoonfuls onto greased cookie sheet. Bake in preheated 300-degree oven for 25 to 30 minutes or until lightly browned.

Mrs. Roland J. Byers
Wayne Trail Grange
Arcanum, Ohio

DROP COOKIES OF GRANDMA SLACK
(Recipe 125 years old)

1 c. sugar
1/2 c. shortening
1/4 c. molasses
1 egg
1 tsp. (scant) soda
3/4 c. milk
1/2 c. chopped nuts (opt.)
1/2 c. raisins
1/2 tsp. cinnamon
1/2 tsp. cloves
2 1/2 c. flour

Cream sugar and shortening in bowl. Add molasses and egg; mix well. Dissolve soda in milk; stir into sugar mixture. Add remaining ingredients; stir until well mixed. Drop by spoonfuls onto greased cookie sheet. Bake in preheated 350-degree oven for about 15 minutes or until brown.

Madelin D. Andrews
Wife of State Master
Sarasota, Florida

GINGER PUFFS
(Recipe 75 years old)

1 c. shortening
1 c. sugar
3 eggs
1 c. molasses
1 c. warm coffee
4 c. flour
1 tsp. ginger
1 tsp. cinnamon
1 tsp. salt
2 tsp. soda
1 c. raisins
1 c. chopped nutmeats

Cream shortening and sugar in bowl; beat in eggs. Add molasses and coffee; mix well. Sift flour with spices, salt and soda; stir into molasses mixture. Add raisins and nuts; mix well. Drop from teaspoon onto greased baking sheet. Bake in preheated 375-degree oven for 10 to 12 minutes. Yield: 4 dozen.

Victoria Maxwell, W.A.C. Chm.
Lawrence Grange, No. 937
Lindley, New York

MINCEMEAT COOKIES

1 c. shortening
1 1/2 c. sugar
1 egg, beaten
1 1/2 tsp. hot water
1 tsp. salt
1 tsp. soda
1 c. (heaping) mincemeat
3 c. flour

Cream shortening and sugar in bowl; stir in egg. Mix hot water, salt and soda; stir into egg mixture. Add mincemeat and flour; mix well. Drop by spoonfuls onto greased cookie sheet. Bake in preheated 400-degree oven for 10 to 12 minutes.

Helen Verney
Garrison Hill Grange, No. 497
Wiscasset, Maine

SUGARLESS COOKIES

1 c. orange marmalade
1 egg
1/2 c. soft shortening
2 c. sifted flour
1 tsp. soda
1/4 tsp. salt
1 tsp. vanilla extract
1/2 c. raisins
1/2 c. chopped nuts (opt.)

Mix all ingredients in order listed. Drop by small spoonfuls on greased baking sheet. Bake in preheated 350-degree oven for about 12 minutes or until done. Yield: 35-40 cookies.

Mrs. Margueritte E. Freethy
Somersworth Grange, No. 264
Somersworth, New Hampshire

★ ★

MRS. FOX'S OATMEAL COOKIES
(Recipe over 80 years old)

1 c. lard or butter
2 c. (packed) brown sugar
2 or 3 eggs, beaten
3 c. flour
2 c. rolled oats
1 tsp. soda
1 tsp. cinnamon
3/4 c. sour milk
1 c. raisins
1 c. chopped nuts
1 tbsp. vanilla extract

Cream lard and sugar in bowl. Add eggs; mix well. Mix flour, oats, soda and cinnamon; add to sugar mixture alternately with sour milk. Add raisins, nuts and vanilla; mix well. Drop by spoonfuls onto greased cookie sheet. Bake in preheated 350-degree oven for about 15 minutes or until brown. Yield: 5 dozen.

Mrs. Lowell Green
Rushcreek Grange, No. 1687
Rushsylvania, Ohio

SOFT ORANGE COOKIES

1 c. sugar
1/2 c. shortening
1 egg
1/4 c. orange juice
1/2 c. milk
2 1/2 c. flour
1/2 tsp. baking powder
1/2 tsp. soda
1/8 tsp. salt

Cream sugar and shortening in bowl. Add egg; beat well. Stir in orange juice and milk. Add remaining ingredients; mix well. Drop by spoonfuls onto greased cookie sheet. Bake in preheated 350-degree oven for 10 to 12 minutes or until lightly browned. Ice while warm with powdered sugar mixed with orange juice, if desired.

Mrs. James Bender
Fredericksburg Grange, No. 1650
Fredericksburg, Texas

PERSIMMON COOKIES

1/2 c. butter
1 c. sugar
1 c. chopped nuts
1 to 2 c. raisins
1 egg (opt.)
1 c. persimmon pulp
2 c. flour
1 tsp. soda
1/4 to 1/2 tsp. cinnamon
1/4 to 1/2 tsp. nutmeg
1/4 to 1/2 tsp. cloves

Cream butter and sugar in bowl. Add nuts and raisins; mix well. Beat egg; stir in persimmon pulp. Add to butter mixture; stir until mixed. Add remaining ingredients; mix well. Drop from teaspoon onto greased baking sheet. Bake in preheated 350-degree oven for 10 to 15 minutes. Yield: 3 dozen.

Jo Nachreiner
Centerville Grange, No. 797
Redding, California

SUNFLOWER SEED COOKIES
(Recipe 40 years old)

1 c. shortening
1 c. (packed) brown sugar
1 c. white sugar
2 eggs
1 1/2 c. flour
1 1/2 c. unsalted sunflower seed
1/2 tsp. salt
1 tsp. soda
3 c. rolled oats
1/2 c. chopped walnuts

Cream shortening and sugars in bowl; stir in eggs. Add remaining ingredients; mix well. Drop by spoonfuls onto greased cookie sheet; press down with fork. Bake in preheated 350-degree oven for 10 to 12 minutes or until done.

Orpha Geise
Waller Road Grange, No. 1111
Tacoma, Washington

ANGEL FOOD COOKIES
(Recipe 50 years old)

1 c. shortening
1/2 c. (packed) brown sugar
1/2 c. white sugar
1 egg, beaten
1/4 tsp. salt
2 c. flour
1 tsp. soda
1 tsp. cream of tartar
1 c. coconut
1 tsp. banana flavoring

Cream shortening, brown sugar and white sugar in bowl; stir in egg. Sift salt, flour, soda and cream of tartar together. Add to creamed mixture; mix well. Stir in coconut and flavoring. Roll dough into small balls. Dip top into water, then into additional sugar. Place on greased cookie sheet, sugared side up. Bake in preheated 350-degree oven for 15 minutes or until done. Yield: 4 dozen.

Willie Mai Griffin
Statesville Grange, No. 1236
Watertown, Tennessee

ALMOND SPICE COOKIES
(Recipe 100 years old)

1 1/2 c. strained honey
3/4 c. shortening

★ ★

2 c. sugar
1/4 c. fruit juice
Grated rind of 1 orange
Grated rind of 1 lemon
2 c. chopped unblanched almonds
10 c. cake flour
1 tsp. salt
1 tsp. cinnamon
2 tsp. nutmeg
1 tsp. cloves
4 tsp. baking powder
Icing

Mix honey and shortening in top of double boiler; place over hot water until shortening is melted. Add sugar and juice; stir until sugar is dissolved. Pour into large bowl; stir in grated rinds and almonds. Sift remaining ingredients together except Icing; stir into honey mixture. Place in refrigerator until chilled. Roll out on floured surface 1/8 inch thick; cut into strips or fancy shapes. Place on greased cookie sheet. Bake in preheated 350-degree oven for about 20 minutes or until done. Frost with Icing while warm. Dough may be refrigerated for several days before baking. Yield: 15 dozen.

ICING

2 c. confectioners' sugar
1 tbsp. melted butter
3 to 4 tbsp. cream
1 tsp. vanilla extract

Combine all ingredients in bowl; mix well.

Mrs. Doris Spencer, W.A.C. Chm.
Mosherville Grange, No. 1351
Jonesville, Michigan

FARMHOUSE COOKIES
(Recipe 125 years old)

1 c. butter
2 c. sugar
2 eggs
1 c. sour cream
Vanilla extract to taste
1/2 tsp. soda
4 tsp. baking powder
4 to 4 1/2 c. flour
Pinch of salt
3/4 c. chopped nuts

Cream butter and sugar in bowl. Add eggs; beat well. Add sour cream and vanilla; stir until mixed. Add remaining ingredients; mix well. Roll out on floured board 1/4 inch thick; cut with large, round cutter or glass. Place on cookie sheet. May be decorated or sprinkled with sugar and cinnamon, if desired. Bake in preheated 350 to 375-degree oven for 15 minutes or until light brown. Yield: 5 dozen.

Ann J. Schroeder
Melrose Grange, No. 434
Roseburg, Oregon

GRAMMY LOWD'S SOUR CREAM COOKIES

2 eggs
2 c. sugar
1/2 tsp. salt
1 c. melted butter
1 c. sour cream
1 tsp. soda
3 3/4 c. (about) flour

Mix eggs, sugar and salt in bowl; stir in butter. Mix sour cream with soda; stir into sugar mixture. Stir in flour. Roll out on floured surface; cut with desired cutter. Place on greased cookie sheet. Bake in preheated 375 to 400-degree oven for 8 to 10 minutes or until golden brown. May be frozen. Yield: 5-6 dozen.

Theda Pease
Mt. Cube Grange, No. 236
Orford, New Hampshire

ICEBOX GINGER COOKIES
(Recipe 85 years old)

1 c. Crisco
1 c. sugar
2 eggs
1 c. molasses
4 c. flour
1 tsp. soda
2 tsp. ginger
1 tsp. salt

Cream Crisco and sugar in bowl. Add eggs; mix well. Add molasses; stir until mixed. Stir in remaining ingredients. Shape into 3 or 4 rolls according to size desired; wrap in waxed paper. Refrigerate overnight. Slice dough; place on greased cookie sheet. Bake in preheated 375-degree oven for 8 to 12 minutes.

Mrs. Marian Blass
Central Grange, No. 1216
Coudersport, Pennsylvania

GREEN MOUNTAIN GINGERSNAPS

3/4 c. shortening
1 c. sugar
1/4 c. molasses
1 egg
2 c. flour
2 tsp. soda
1 tsp. salt
1 tsp. cinnamon
1 tsp. cloves
1 tsp. ginger

Cream shortening in bowl. Add sugar, molasses and egg; mix thoroughly. Sift remaining ingredients together; stir into creamed mixture. Roll into small balls; dip in additional sugar. Place 2 inches apart on greased cookie sheet. Bake in preheated 375-degree oven for about 10 minutes or until done. Yield: About 5 dozen.

Florence S. Wyeth
Blackwater Grange
Andover, New Hampshire

★ ★

COUNTRY RAISIN GINGERSNAPS

2 c. raisins or currants
2 tbsp. brandy
1 1/2 c. shortening
1 1/2 c. sugar
2 eggs
1 tbsp. vanilla extract
1/2 c. molasses
4 c. flour
4 tsp. soda
2 tsp. salt
2 tsp. ginger
1/2 tsp. cloves
1 tsp. cinnamon
1/2 c. wheat germ
1 c. chopped walnuts

Soak raisins in brandy for at least 2 hours. Cream shortening and sugar in bowl; stir in eggs, vanilla and molasses. Sift flour, soda, salt and spices together; stir into shortening mixture. Stir in wheat germ, walnuts and undrained raisins; cover. Chill for 1 to 2 hours. Roll into 1-inch balls; roll in additional sugar. Place on greased cookie sheets. Bake in preheated 350-degree oven for 9 to 10 minutes or until done. Mixture of raisins and currants may be used instead of raisins or currants. Brown sugar, packed, may be substituted for sugar. Yield: 9-10 dozen.

Karen Dorrah
Humptulips Grange, No. 730
Hoquiam, Washington

CURRANT COOKIES

1 c. butter
3 c. rolled oats
1 c. sugar
3/4 c. sifted flour
1 tsp. soda
1/2 tsp. ground cloves
1/2 tsp. cinnamon
1/2 c. dried currants
1/4 c. milk

Soften butter in large mixing bowl; blend in oats and sugar. Add flour, soda, cloves and cinnamon; mix well. Stir in currants and milk. Shape into balls about 1 inch in diameter. Place 3 inches apart on greased baking sheets. Bake in preheated 350-degree oven for 12 to 15 minutes or until golden brown. Remove from baking sheets; cool. Yield: About 3 dozen.

Mildred Rice, Ceres
West Randolph Grange
Randolph, Vermont

GRIDDLE COOKIES

3 1/2 c. flour
1 1/2 tsp. baking powder
1 c. sugar
1 tsp. salt
1/2 tsp. soda
1 c. butter
1 egg, beaten
3/4 c. milk
1 tsp. vanilla extract
1 c. raisins or chopped nuts (opt.)
Salad oil

Sift first 5 ingredients together into bowl. Add butter; mix with pastry blender or cut in with 2 knives until consistency of meal. Add egg, milk, vanilla and raisins; stir until mixed. Roll out on floured board 1/4 inch thick; cut with cookie cutter. Heat griddle until drop of water will dance on surface; oil griddle lightly. Place cookies on griddle; cook until golden brown. Turn; cook until brown. Yield: 4 dozen.

Lucille Kellett
Atascadero Grange, No. 563
Atascadero, California

JOE FROGGERS

7 c. flour
1 tbsp. salt
1 tbsp. ginger
1 tsp. nutmeg
1 tsp. cloves
1/2 tsp. allspice
1 c. shortening
2 c. sugar
3/4 c. hot water
1/4 c. rum
2 tsp. soda
2 c. dark molasses

Sift flour, salt, ginger, nutmeg, cloves and allspice together. Cream shortening and sugar in bowl; stir in sifted ingredients. Mix hot water and rum; stir into sugar mixture. Mix soda and molasses; add to sugar mixture. Mix well; chill. Roll out dough on floured surface, one-fourth at a time; cut into large circles, using large can with both ends cut out. Lift cookies carefully with spatula onto cookie sheet. Bake in preheated 375-degree oven for 10 minutes or until done.

Shirley R. Gaspar
Beverly Grange, No. 306
Wenham, Massachusetts

LEMON CRACKERS
(Recipe 150 years old)

1 oz. baking ammonia
2 c. milk
1 c. lard
2 c. sugar
1/2 tsp. salt
1 tsp. oil of lemon
3 eggs, well beaten
Flour

Add ammonia to milk; stir until dissolved. Set aside. Cream lard and sugar in bowl. Add salt, oil of lemon and eggs; mix well. Add 1 cup flour and ammonia mixture; stir until mixed. Add enough flour to make dough that is not sticky. Roll out on floured board

★ ★

about 1/8 inch thick; cut in 2-inch squares. Prick with fork; place on a very lightly greased baking pan. Bake in preheated 400-degree oven about 9 minutes or until very lightly browned; cookies will blister on top like crackers. Remove from baking sheet; cool. Store in an airtight container. Ammonia and oil of lemon may be purchased at drug store; do not use household ammonia in recipe.

Mrs. Archie B. Roberts
Pinola Grange
LaPorte, Indiana

NURNBERG LEBKUCHEN

1 c. honey
3/4 c. (packed) brown sugar
1 egg, beaten
1 tbsp. lemon juice
1 tsp. grated lemon rind
2 1/2 c. sifted flour
1/2 tsp. soda
1 tsp. cinnamon
1/4 tsp. cloves
1/2 tsp. allspice
1/2 tsp. nutmeg
1/2 c. chopped citron
1/3 c. chopped almonds
Almond halves
Citron pieces
Glaze

Pour honey into saucepan; bring to a boil. Cool thoroughly. Pour into bowl. Add brown sugar, egg, lemon juice and rind; mix well. Sift flour, soda, cinnamon, cloves, allspice and nutmeg together; stir into honey mixture. Add chopped citron and almonds; mix well. Chill overnight. Roll out on floured surface to about 1/2-inch thickness; cut into rectangles 2 1/2 to 3 1/2 inches long. Decorate with almond halves and citron pieces; place on greased cookie sheet. Bake in preheated 350-degree oven for 10 minutes or until done. Brush with Glaze immediately upon removing from oven.

GLAZE

1 c. sugar
1/2 c. water
1/4 c. powdered sugar

Mix sugar and water in saucepan; bring to a boil. Cook to 230 degrees on candy thermometer or until mixture spins thread when dropped from spoon. Remove from heat; stir in powdered sugar. Add 2 drops more water and reheat if glaze gets stiff before all cookies are glazed.

Mrs. Bernhardt Seibert
Shiloh Valley Grange
Belleville, Illinois

OLD-FASHIONED MOLASSES COOKIES
(Recipe 65 years old)

2 c. lard
2 c. sugar
4 c. molasses
10 to 12 c. flour
1 tbsp. ginger
1 tbsp. cinnamon
1 tsp. cloves
1 tsp. allspice
2 c. sour milk
4 tsp. soda
1 c. chopped nuts

Cream lard and sugar in bowl. Add molasses; mix well. Sift flour with spices. Mix sour milk with soda; add to creamed mixture alternately with flour mixture. Stir in nuts. Chill for 2 to 3 hours. Roll out on floured surface; cut with 3-inch cookie cutter. Place on greased cookie sheet. Bake in preheated 350-degree oven for about 15 minutes. Yield: 5 dozen.

Theresa Siegel
Emerald Mound Grange, No. 1813
Mascoutah, Illinois

OLD-FASHIONED ROLLED SUGAR COOKIES

4 c. flour
1 tsp. salt
2 tsp. baking powder
1 tsp. soda
1 c. buttermilk or sour milk
1 c. shortening
2 c. sifted sugar
2 eggs
1 tsp. vanilla extract or orange flavoring

Sift flour with salt and baking powder. Dissolve soda in buttermilk. Cream shortening in bowl. Add sugar; mix well. Add eggs; beat thoroughly. Add buttermilk mixture alternately with flour mixture; mix well. Stir in vanilla; chill thoroughly. Roll out on floured surface; cut with cookie cutter. Place on greased cookie sheet. Bake in preheated 350 to 400-degree oven for 8 to 10 minutes or until done. May add 1 cup cut-up dates or steamed raisins to dough, if desired.

These cookies took first prize at Ulysses Grange contest and at Tompkins County Pomona Grange in 1975.

Sarah Nivison
Ulysses Grange, No. 419
Ithaca, New York

FRUIT ICE CREAM

Juice of 3 lemons
3 oranges, peeled and cut into bite-sized pieces
3 bananas, quartered and sliced
3 c. sugar
2 cans evaporated milk
1 No. 2 can crushed pineapple
3 c. milk
Pinch of salt

Combine all ingredients in freezer container; mix well. Freeze according to directions.

Mrs. Doris Price
Painter Creek Grange, No. 1923
Kenton, Ohio

PINEAPPLE A LA MODE WITH STRAWBERRY-ALMOND TOPPING

1 fresh pineapple
2 pt. strawberry ice cream
Strawberry-Almond Topping

Slice pineapple. Remove rind and core; cut into pieces. Chill. Divide into 8 serving dishes; add scoop of ice cream. Top with Strawberry-Almond Topping.

STRAWBERRY-ALMOND TOPPING

1/3 c. slivered almonds
1 pt. strawberries, sliced
1/3 c. sugar

Spread almonds in shallow pan. Bake in preheated 400-degree oven for 5 to 6 minutes or until toasted. Place strawberries, sugar and almonds in bowl; toss until mixed. Chill.

Photograph for this recipe above.

CANTALOUPE A LA MODE WITH BLUEBERRY SAUCE

1 lg. cantaloupe
2 pt. vanilla ice cream
Blueberry Sauce

Slice cantaloupe into 8 rings; peel and remove seeds. Place slices on chilled plates; place scoop of ice cream in center. Top with Blueberry Sauce.

BLUEBERRY SAUCE

2 c. fresh blueberries
1/3 c. water
1/2 c. sugar
1 tbsp. cornstarch
1 tbsp. lemon juice

Combine blueberries, water, sugar and cornstarch in 1-quart saucepan. Cook over medium heat, stirring constantly, until thickened; cook for 2 minutes longer. Stir in lemon juice; chill.

Photograph for this recipe opposite.

PEACH A LA MODE WITH CARAMEL BUTTER SAUCE

8 or 16 canned or fresh peach halves, chilled
2 pt. maple nut ice cream
Caramel Butter Sauce

Place 1 or 2 peach halves in each serving dish; place a scoop of ice cream in center. Top with Caramel Butter Sauce.

CARAMEL BUTTER SAUCE

3/4 c. sugar
Dash of salt
1/2 c. light corn syrup
1/4 c. butter
1 c. light cream or half and half
1/2 tsp. vanilla extract

Combine sugar, salt, corn syrup, butter and 1/2 cup cream in 1 1/2-quart saucepan. Cook over low heat, stirring frequently, to 250 degrees on candy thermometer or until small amount dropped into cold water forms hard ball. Stir in remaining 1/2 cup cream gradually; cook to 216 degrees or until small amount forms thread when dropped from spoon. Remove from heat; stir in vanilla. Serve warm.

Photograph for this recipe opposite.

FRENCH VANILLA ICE CREAM
(Recipe over 100 years old)

3 qt. milk
6 eggs, lightly beaten
1 1/2 c. sugar
1/2 c. cornstarch
1 tsp. salt
3 tbsp. vanilla extract
2 c. cream

Pour 1 quart milk in heavy saucepan. Combine eggs, sugar, cornstarch and salt. Mix just until well combined. Stir into milk. Cook over low heat until thick, stirring constantly. Remove from heat; cool. Add vanilla. Pour into freezing container; add cream and remaining milk, mixing well. Freeze according to freezer directions, using 3 parts ice to 1 part salt.

Mrs. Beatrice Bredbenner
Mahoning Grange, No. 2039
Lehighton, Pennsylvania

OLD-FASHIONED VANILLA ICE CREAM

Milk
6 eggs
3 c. sugar

★ ★

6 tbsp. (heaping) flour
Dash of salt
2 tbsp. vanilla extract

Pour 3 quarts milk in top of double boiler; place over direct heat. Bring to boiling point. Beat eggs thoroughly; stir in 1 1/2 cups sugar. Mix well. Pour slowly into hot milk, stirring constantly. Mix flour with a small amount of cold milk to make a smooth thin paste. Add to milk mixture, stirring constantly; add salt. Cook over hot water until mixture starts to thicken; cook for 20 minutes longer, stirring constantly. Add remaining 1 1/2 cups sugar; mix well. Remove from heat; let mixture cool. Add vanilla extract; refrigerate for at least 2 hours. Pour into ice cream freezer container; add crushed ice and rock salt to bucket. Freeze according to freezer directions. Maple extract may be substituted for vanilla extract, adding about 1 cup chopped walnuts to custard before completely frozen for maple walnut ice cream.

Mrs. Earl Crego
Baldwinsville Grange, No. 1251
Baldwinsville, New York

MAPLE SYRUP ICE CREAM

1 c. Vermont maple syrup
4 eggs, separated
1 pt. whipping cream, whipped

Combine syrup and egg yolks in saucepan; bring slowly to boiling point, stirring constantly. Strain and cool. Add whipped cream to custard, folding in carefully; fold in stiffly beaten egg whites until just combined. Pour into ice cream freezer container; freeze according to freezer instructions.
This recipe was first printed in Westford Ladies Aid Cookbook published in the early 1900's.

Irene E. Allen, Home Ec. Chm.
Brown's River Grange, No. 556
Westford, Vermont

NEAPOLITAN SHERBET
(Recipe 40 years old)

1/2 c. orange juice
1/2 c. lemon juice
2 c. sugar
3 c. cold milk
1/2 c. mashed bananas
1 c. crushed apricots

Combine lemon and orange juices with sugar; add milk. Beat well. Add bananas and apricots. Pour into freezer container. Freeze according to freezer instructions. Yield: 2 quarts.

Mrs. Fred Goeglein
Rocksprings Grange, No. 2565
Rocksprings, Texas

RHUBARB SHERBET
(Recipe 30 years old)

3 c. sliced tender young rhubarb
2 c. water

1 1/2 c. sugar
1/2 tsp. unflavored gelatin
1 c. pineapple juice

Combine rhubarb and water; cook until tender. Press through sieve; add sugar to juice. Heat, stirring, until sugar is melted. Soften gelatin in 1 tablespoon pineapple juice; stir into mixture. Add remaining pineapple juice; pour into freezer tray. Freeze until partially frozen. Place in bowl; beat with rotary beater until smooth. Return to tray; freeze until firm.

Mrs. Elvin V. Huckins, C.W.A. Chm.
Santa Cruz Live Oak Grange, No. 503
Santa Cruz, California

APPLE PAN DOWDY

1 c. sugar
1/4 tsp. salt
1/2 tsp. cinnamon or nutmeg
6 to 8 sour apples
Grated rind of 1/2 lemon
2 tsp. lemon juice
1 tbsp. hot water
2 tsp. butter
1 recipe rich 1-crust pie pastry

Combine sugar, salt and cinnamon. Pare, core and cut apples into eighths; place in deep baking dish. Add sugar mixture, lemon rind, lemon juice and water; dot with butter. Cover with pie crust. Bake in preheated 350-degree oven for 1 hour or until apples are tender. Slow baking gives the apples rich color. May serve with cream, ice cream or hard sauce.

Dorothy Eller
Trentwood Grange, No. 1056
Spokane, Washington

BROWN BETTY
(Recipe over 50 years old)

2 c. crumbs from 3-day old bread
3 tbsp. melted butter
3 or 4 med. apples
1 tbsp. lemon juice
1/2 tsp. grated lemon peel
1/2 c. (packed) brown or white sugar
1/3 c. hot water

Combine bread crumbs and butter in skillet; cook over low heat until lightly browned, stirring constantly. Place 1/3 of the crumbs in greased baking dish. Pare, core and slice apples; arrange half the apples in layer over crumbs. Sprinkle with half the lemon juice, lemon peel and brown sugar. Add half the remaining crumbs; cover with remaining apples, lemon juice, lemon peel and sugar. Top with remaining crumbs. Pour water over crumbs. Bake in preheated 375-degree oven for 30 to 40 minutes or until apples are tender. May serve warm with second cream or lemon sauce.

Barbara Staples
Whitethorn Grange, No. 792
Whitethorn, California

★ ★

YANKEE APPLE JOHN
(Recipe 100 years old)

    6 tart apples, sliced thin
    1/3 c. sugar
    3/4 tsp. cinnamon
    1/2 tsp. nutmeg
    2 c. sifted flour
    3 tsp. baking powder
    1/2 tsp. salt
    1/2 c. shortening
    2/3 c. milk
    Nutmeg Sauce

Fill greased, shallow baking dish with sliced apples. Combine sugar and spices; sprinkle over apples. Sift flour, baking powder and salt together. Cut in shortening. Add milk; mix to form a soft dough. Roll out; fit over apple mixture. Brush with additional milk. Bake in preheated 425-degree oven for 25 minutes. Serve with Nutmeg Sauce.

NUTMEG SAUCE

    1 c. sugar
    1/4 tsp. nutmeg
    2 tbsp. flour
    1/8 tsp. salt
    2 c. boiling water
    1 tbsp. butter
    1 tbsp. vinegar

Mix sugar, nutmeg, flour and salt together in saucepan. Add boiling water; stir constantly until blended. Add butter; bring to a boil for 5 minutes. Stir in vinegar. Serve hot.

Mary Crahan
Marble Valley Grange, No. 567
Pittsford, Vermont

OLD-FASHIONED APPLE DUMPLINGS
(Recipe 103 years old)

    6 med. baking apples
    2 c. flour
    2 1/2 tsp. baking powder
    1/2 tsp. salt
    2/3 c. shortening
    1/2 c. milk
    Cinnamon sugar to taste
    2 c. (packed) brown sugar
    2 c. water
    1/4 tsp. cinnamon
    1/4 c. butter

Pare and core apples. Sift flour, baking powder and salt together. Cut in shortening until size of small peas. Sprinkle milk over mixture; press together lightly, working dough only enough to hold together. Roll out dough; cut into 6 squares. Place apple on each square. Fill cavity with cinnamon sugar. Pat dough around apple to cover, pinching edges together securely. Place 1 inch apart in greased baking pan. Combine brown sugar, water and cinnamon; cook for 5 minutes. Remove from heat; add butter. Pour over apples. Bake in

preheated 375-degree oven for 35 to 40 minutes, basting occasionally during baking. Serve hot with rich milk.

Mrs. Areva Haldeman
Williamsport Grange, No. 1815
Mt. Gilead, Ohio

DELICIOUS APRICOT COBBLER
(Recipe 75 years old)

    2 c. flour
    1 tsp. salt
    4 tsp. baking powder
    6 tbsp. shortening
    2/3 c. milk
    1 1/2 qt. stewed apricots
    1 3/4 c. sugar
    3 tbsp. cornstarch
    1/2 tsp. nutmeg
    1 tbsp. butter

Combine first 3 ingredients in bowl; cut in shortening. Add milk; stir until mixed. Drain apricots; reserve liquid. Place apricots in 9 x 13-inch baking dish. Heat reserved juice in saucepan. Add sugar; thicken with cornstarch. Pour over apricots. Sprinkle with nutmeg; dot with butter. Drop dough by spoonfuls over apricot mixture. Bake in preheated 400-degree oven for 20 to 25 minutes or until brown; serve warm. Cream may be poured over cobbler, if desired. Peaches may be used instead of apricots; cinnamon may be substituted for nutmeg. Yield: 8 servings.

Mrs. Leonard Leth
Fairview Grange, No. 178
Buhl, Idaho

BLACKBERRY DUMPLINGS
(Recipe 60 years old)

    1 qt. blackberries
    Sugar
    3/4 tsp. salt
    1/2 tsp. lemon extract
    1 1/2 c. flour
    1 1/2 tsp. baking powder
    1/4 tsp. nutmeg
    2/3 c. milk

Mix blackberries, 1 cup sugar, 1/4 teaspoon salt and lemon extract in square baking pan; bring to a boil. Reduce heat; simmer while preparing dumplings. Sift flour, remaining 1/2 teaspoon salt, baking powder, 1 tablespoon sugar and nutmeg into bowl. Add milk; stir until ingredients are just mixed. Drop from teaspoon onto blackberry mixture; cover tightly. Cook for 15 minutes without removing cover. Place in serving dishes; serve with additional milk and sugar. Yield: 4 servings.

Mrs. Charles Patterson
Deemston Grange, No. 1372
Brownsville, Pennsylvania

★ ★

BLUEBERRY ROLYPOLY
(Recipe 50 years old)

1/2 tsp. salt
2 1/2 tsp. baking powder
2 c. sifted flour
1/4 c. butter
2/3 c. milk
Melted butter
Blueberries
6 tbsp. sugar

Sift salt, baking powder and flour together into bowl; cut in butter. Add milk all at once; stir until flour is dampened and pastry forms ball. Turn out on floured board; knead for 30 seconds. Roll out 1/4 inch thick; brush with melted butter. Cover with blueberries; sprinkle with sugar. Roll as for jelly roll; place in buttered pan, seam side down. Brush with melted butter. Bake in preheated 400 to 450-degree oven for 20 to 30 minutes; serve hot. Yield: 6 servings.

SAUCE

1 c. blueberries
1 c. water
1 tbsp. flour
1/2 c. sugar
1/4 tsp. salt
Dash of cloves
2 tsp. butter
2 tbsp. lemon juice

Place blueberries in saucepan; add water. Bring to a boil; cook for 3 minutes. Stir in flour, sugar, salt and cloves; cook until thick. Add butter and lemon juice. Serve with blueberry roll. Yield: 1 1/2 cups.

Octavia J. Stearns
Wilmot Grange, No. 309
Danbury, New Hampshire

CREME BLEU

1 c. heavy cream
1/2 c. milk
1/2 c. sugar
Dash of salt
1 env. unflavored gelatin
1/4 c. cold water
1 c. sour cream
1/2 tsp. almond flavoring
1 1/2 c. fresh blueberries

Combine heavy cream, milk, sugar and salt in saucepan; cook, stirring, over low heat until sugar is dissolved. Remove from heat. Soften gelatin in cold water; stir into cream mixture until dissolved. Add sour cream; beat with a rotary beater until thoroughly blended and smooth. Add flavoring; stir in blueberries gently, being careful not to crush them. Pour mixture into wet individual molds. Chill until firm. Loosen from molds with hot spatula and by rubbing bottom of molds with hot towel. Unmold. Yield: 6 to 9 individual servings, depending on size of molds.

Photograph for this recipe below.

★ ★

BANANA FRITTERS

1 c. flour
1 1/2 tsp. baking powder
1/4 tsp. salt
3 tbsp. confectioners' sugar
1/3 c. milk
1 egg
2 c. sliced bananas

Sift flour, baking powder, salt and sugar together into bowl; stir in milk gradually. Beat until smooth. Add egg; beat well. Dip bananas in batter. Fry in shallow fat or oil at 375 degrees until lightly browned; drain on absorbent paper. Sprinkle with additional confectioners' sugar; serve hot with sauce or whipped cream. Apples, peaches or pineapple may be substituted for bananas. Yield: 4 servings.

Pearl Estabrook, Overseer
Bolton Grange, No. 142
Bolton, Massachusetts

RASPBERRY SHORTCAKE

Sugar
1 1/2 tsp. baking powder
1/4 tsp. soda
1 1/2 c. sifted flour
1/2 tsp. salt
1/3 c. butter
1/2 to 2/3 c. milk
3 c. fresh or frozen raspberries
1 c. sour or heavy cream

Sift 2 tablespoons sugar with next 4 ingredients into bowl; blend in butter. Add enough milk to make soft dough. Press into well-buttered 8 x 12-inch baking dish. Spread raspberries evenly over dough. Sprinkle with 1 cup sugar; pour cream over top. Bake in preheated 375-degree oven for 40 to 45 minutes or until done; serve warm.

Grace Palm
Dalbo Grange, No. 670
Dalbo, Minnesota

RASPBERRY-WALNUT TORTE

1 1/4 c. flour
1/3 c. powdered sugar
1/2 c. soft butter
1   10-oz. package frozen red raspberries, thawed
3/4 c. chopped walnuts
2 eggs
1 c. sugar
1/2 tsp. salt
1/2 tsp. baking powder
1 tsp. vanilla extract
Raspberry Sauce

Combine 1 cup flour, powdered sugar and butter in bowl; blend well. Press mixture into bottom of 13 x 9-inch pan. Bake in preheated 350-degree oven for 15 minutes; cool. Drain raspberries; reserve liquid.

Spoon raspberries over crust; sprinkle with walnuts. Beat eggs with sugar in small mixing bowl until light and fluffy. Add salt, remaining 1/4 cup flour, baking powder and vanilla; blend well. Pour over walnuts. Bake in preheated 350-degree oven for 30 to 35 minutes or until golden brown; cool. Cut into squares; serve with whipped cream and Raspberry Sauce.

RASPBERRY SAUCE

1/2 c. water
1/2 c. sugar
2 tbsp. cornstarch
1 tbsp. lemon juice

Combine water, reserved raspberry liquid, sugar and cornstarch in saucepan. Cook, stirring constantly, until thickened and clear. Stir in lemon juice; cool.

Mrs. Dennis Fiess
Spring Creek Grange, No. 951
Edwall, Washington

GRANDMOTHER'S PEACH COBBLER

Sliced peaches
2 c. flour
1/2 tsp. salt
4 tsp. baking powder
1/2 c. shortening
2 eggs, beaten
2/3 c. peach juice

Cover bottom of square baking pan with peaches. Place in preheated 350-degree oven while preparing batter. Mix remaining ingredients in bowl; drop by spoonfuls over peaches. Bake for about 30 minutes or until brown. Yield: 6 servings.

Jane Woodbury
Hooksett Grange, No. 148
Manchester, New Hampshire

QUICK CHERRY COBBLER

1 1/2 c. pitted cherries
1 1/2 c. sugar
1 c. flour
Pinch of salt
1 tsp. baking powder
1/2 c. milk
2 tbsp. soft butter

Cook cherries and 3/4 cup sugar in saucepan until cherries are tender. Sift flour, remaining 3/4 cup sugar, salt and baking powder together into bowl. Add milk and butter; beat well. Pour boiling cherry mixture into square baking pan; pour batter over cherries. Bake in preheated 350-degree oven for 30 minutes. Any fruit may be substituted for cherries.

Mrs. J. A. Kennedy
Oregon Trail Grange, No. 84
Casper, Wyoming

Photo page 201 — Recipe on page 159.

Photo page 202 — Recipes on pages 166 and 181.

★ ★

FRESH RHUBARB ROLL

2 c. sugar
1 1/2 c. water
3 c. flour
3 tsp. baking powder
1/2 tsp. salt
1/3 c. shortening
1 c. milk
3 tbsp. melted butter
3 c. cut rhubarb
Sauce

Combine 1 1/2 cups sugar and water in saucepan; cook for 5 minutes. Pour into greased oblong baking pan. Sift flour, baking powder, salt and remaining sugar together into bowl; cut in shortening. Add milk; stir lightly. Knead on floured board; roll out into 12-inch square. Brush with melted butter. Spread rhubarb over dough; roll as for jelly roll. Cut into 1 1/2-inch slices; place in syrup in pan. Bake in preheated 400-degree oven for 40 minutes, basting with Sauce occasionally. Yield: 8 servings.

SAUCE

1 c. cut rhubarb
1/2 c. sugar
2/3 c. water
Drop of red food coloring

Mix all ingredients in saucepan; cook until rhubarb is tender.

Mrs. Max Bailey
Wife of State Master
Delia, Kansas

All fruits for jelly making should be gathered just before they are fully ripe and on a dry day.

SHIRLEY'S BAKED RHUBARB

4 c. cut rhubarb
3/4 c. flour
1 1/2 to 2 c. sugar
1 tsp. cinnamon
1/2 c. butter

Place rhubarb in greased 8-inch square baking pan. Mix flour, sugar, cinnamon and butter; spoon over rhubarb. Bake in preheated 350-degree oven for 45 minutes; top with whipped cream, if desired.

Shirley King
Mountain Home Grange, No. 285
Princeton, Idaho

Photo page 203 — Recipe on page 178.

Photo page 204 — Recipe on page 214.

CREAM PUFFS
(Recipe about 70 years old)

1 c. water
1/2 c. butter
1 c. flour
4 eggs
Whipped cream
Powdered sugar

Heat water and butter in saucepan until water boils and butter melts. Add flour all at one time; stir vigorously until dough forms a ball in center of pan. Remove from heat; let stand for 5 minutes. Add eggs, one at a time, beating well after each addition. Drop by heaping tablespoonfuls onto buttered baking sheet 2 inches apart. Bake in preheated 350-degree oven for 30 minutes or until done. Cut a slit in each puff; fill with whipped cream. Sift powdered sugar over tops. Yield: 18 servings.

Ellen Adams
Crescent Grange, No. 136
Broomfield, Colorado

OLD-FASHIONED PIE CRUST
(Recipe 50 years old)

3 c. flour
1 tsp. salt
1 c. (heaping) shortening
1 egg
3 tbsp. water
2 tsp. vinegar

Sift flour and salt together; cut in shortening until mixture resembles coarse crumbs. Beat egg slightly. Add water and vinegar; mix well. Add to flour mixture; mix well. Form into 2 balls on lightly floured board. Roll out to make 2 pie crusts.

Mrs. Forrest Clymer
Sugar Grove Grange, No. 2044
Newton, Iowa

EGG YOLK PASTRY

5 c. sifted flour
4 tsp. sugar
1/2 tsp. salt
1/2 tsp. baking powder
1 1/2 c. lard
2 egg yolks

Combine dry ingredients; cut in lard until mixture resembles coarse crumbs. Place egg yolks in measuring cup; mix with fork until smooth. Blend in enough cold water to make a scant cupful. Sprinkle gradually over dry ingredients; toss with fork to make a soft dough. Roll out on floured board. Dough may be frozen and used as needed. Yield: Pastry for three 9-inch 2-crust pies.

Mrs. Gordon Tate
Mica Flats Grange, No. 436
Coeur d'Alene, Idaho

★ ★

OLD-FASHIONED APPLE PIE
(Recipe 103 years old)

6 c. sliced peeled apples
2 tbsp. cornstarch
1 c. sugar
Pastry for one 9-inch 2-crust pie
1 tsp. nutmeg or cinnamon

Combine apples, 1 tablespoon cornstarch and sugar; mix well. Cover; refrigerate overnight. Drain apples; reserve juice. Line 9-inch pie pan with pastry; arrange apples in pastry. Cover with top crust; seal pastry edges together. Make 3 slits in top crust. Bake in preheated 425-degree oven for 50 minutes or until apples are done. Add enough water to reserved juice to measure 1 cup liquid. Combine liquid, nutmeg and remaining 1 tablespoon cornstarch in saucepan; bring to a boil. Boil for several minutes to thicken. Remove pie from oven; pour hot juice into slits in crust. Let cool.

Mrs. George Hein
Spring Creek Grange, No. 951
Reardan, Washington

PRIZEWINNING APPLE PIE
(Recipe over 50 years old)

2 c. flour
Salt
2/3 c. plus 2 tbsp. shortening
1/4 c. cold water
5 or 6 apples, pared and sliced
1 tsp. lemon juice
Sugar
1/4 tsp. nutmeg
1 tsp. butter
Milk

Mix flour and 1 teaspoon salt together; cut in shortening until mixture resembles coarse crumbs. Mix in water until pastry clings together. Divide in half. Roll out half the pastry on floured board; place in pie pan. Roll out remaining half for top crust. Place apple slices in pie crust; sprinkle with lemon juice. Sprinkle 2/3 cup sugar, nutmeg and a dash of salt over top; dot with butter. Cover with top crust; press edges together. Brush top crust with milk; sprinkle with sugar. Bake in preheated 400-degree oven for 10 minutes. Reduce oven temperature to 350 degrees; bake for 45 minutes longer or until done.
This pie won first prize at the Washington County Pomona Fair in August 1974 and at the Narragansett Grange Number 1 Fair in June 1975.

Ethel Rosenbalm, W.A.C.
Narragansett Grange, No. 1
Wakefield, Rhode Island

BACK TO NATURE PIE

2 tbsp. butter
1/2 c. (packed) brown sugar

2 eggs
2 tbsp. flour
1 c. dark corn syrup
1/4 tsp. salt
1 tsp. vanilla
1 unbaked pie crust
1 c. hickory nuts

Cream butter and brown sugar together. Add eggs, flour, syrup, salt and vanilla; beat well, using electric mixer. Pour into pie crust; sprinkle hickory nuts over top. Bake in preheated 450-degree oven for 10 minutes. Reduce oven temperature to 350 degrees; bake for 20 to 25 minutes longer or until done.

Mrs. William B. Brown
Whetstone Grange, No. 2628
Bucyrus, Ohio

BLUEBERRY-APRICOT PIE

2 c. blueberries
2 c. halved pitted fresh apricots
1 1/4 c. sugar
3 tbsp. quick-cooking tapioca
1/2 tsp. cinnamon
1/4 tsp. salt
Pastry for one 2-crust pie
2 tbsp. butter

Combine blueberries, apricots, sugar, tapioca, cinnamon and salt in large bowl; toss lightly to mix. Line pie pan with pastry; pour in fruit mixture. Dot with butter. Cover with top crust; seal pastry edges together. Bake in preheated 425-degree oven for 40 minutes or until done. One 1-pound 14-ounce can apricot halves, drained, may be substituted for fresh apricots; reduce sugar measurement to 1 cup.

Rita P. Armstrong
Nute Ridge Grange, No. 316
Farmington, New Hampshire

BLUEBERRY-BANANA PIE

1 can blueberries
2 1/2 tbsp. cornstarch
1/2 c. sugar
2 tbsp. butter
2 tbsp. lemon juice
1 baked 9-in. pie shell
2 bananas, sliced crosswise
1 c. heavy cream, whipped

Drain blueberries; reserve juice. Mix cornstarch and sugar together in saucepan; stir in reserved juice. Cook until thick, stirring constantly. Remove from heat; add butter and lemon juice. Stir in blueberries carefully; let cool. Line pie shell with sliced bananas; pour blueberry mixture over bananas. Refrigerate until thoroughly chilled. Spread whipped cream over top before serving.

Mrs. Anthony W. Salerno
Centre Grange, No. 11
Wilmington, Delaware

★ ★

SCHNITZ PIE
(Recipe over 100 years old)

1 lb. schnitz (dried sour apples)
1 qt. cold water
2 tsp. cinnamon
2 c. sugar
Juice and grated rind of 1 orange
Pastry for two 8-inch 2-crust pies

Combine schnitz and water in saucepan; cook to a soft pulp. Add cinnamon, sugar, orange juice and grated rind; mix well. Let stand until cool. Line two 8-inch pie pans with pastry; fill with schnitz mixture. Place top crusts over schnitz mixture; seal and flute edges. Cut several slits in center of each top crust. Bake in preheated 425-degree oven for 10 minutes. Reduce oven temperature to 350 degrees; bake for 30 minutes longer or until done.

Mrs. James E. Werner
Gouglersville Grange, No. 1743
Wernersville, Pennsylvania

APPLE-MINCEMEAT PIE

All-purpose flour
1/4 tsp. salt

3 tbsp. butter
2 tbsp. lard
3 to 4 tbsp. milk
4 c. peeled sliced cooking apples
2 c. prepared mincemeat
1 c. sour cream
2 tbsp. confectioners' sugar
1 tbsp. grated orange rind

Combine 1 cup flour and salt in bowl; cut in butter and lard until mixture resembles small peas. Sprinkle milk over flour mixture, 1 tablespoon at a time, mixing lightly with fork after each addition. Gather up dough with fingers; shape into ball. Place on lightly floured surface; flatten slightly. Roll out 1/8 inch thick into circle 1 inch larger than diameter of 9-inch pie plate. Fold circle in half over rolling pin; lift onto pie plate. Fold extra dough over; build up on rim of pie plate. Flute edge. Combine apples and 2 tablespoons flour in bowl; turn into crust. Top with mincemeat. Bake in preheated 400-degree oven for 35 to 40 minutes; remove from oven. Blend sour cream with confectioners' sugar and orange rind in small bowl. Place dollops of sour cream mixture around edge of pie; return to oven for 3 to 4 minutes to set topping.

Photograph for this recipe below.

★ ★

Combine 1/2 cup sugar, flour, salt and mace in 2-quart saucepan; stir in milk gradually. Cook over medium heat, stirring constantly, until thickened; cook for 2 minutes longer. Blend small amount of hot mixture into slightly beaten egg yolks; stir back into hot mixture. Cook for 1 minute; stir in vanilla. Cover; cool thoroughly. Beat egg whites in small mixing bowl until soft peaks form; beat in 2 tablespoons sugar. Fold into milk mixture; fold in whipped cream. Chill. Parfaits may be made by spooning about 1/3 cup Foamy Custard into each of 6 parfait glasses; top with strawberries. Repeat with custard and strawberries.

Photograph for this recipe opposite.

STRAWBERRY SHORTCAKE

2 c. flour
1/2 tsp. salt
2 tbsp. sugar
4 tsp. baking powder
3 tbsp. shortening
3/4 c. milk
Butter
4 c. sweetened crushed strawberries

Sift first 4 ingredients together into bowl; cut in shortening. Add milk; mix well. Press into greased, deep layer pan. Bake in preheated 400 to 450-degree oven for 25 to 30 minutes or until done. Cut in half crosswise; spread with butter. Spread strawberries between and on top of layers. Yield: 4-6 servings.

Mrs. Ruth A. Nixon
Vincentown Grange, No. 67
Vincentown, New Jersey

FOAMY CUSTARD STRAWBERRY SHORTCAKE

2 c. sifted all-purpose flour
1/4 c. sugar
1 tbsp. baking powder
1/2 tsp. salt
1/2 c. butter
3/4 c. milk
Foamy Custard
Sweetened sliced strawberries

Sift flour, sugar, baking powder and salt together into bowl. Cut in butter until mixture resembles coarse meal. Add milk all at once; stir until dough holds together. Turn out onto lightly floured surface; knead gently for about 10 times. Pat or roll dough about 1/2 inch thick; cut out 8 biscuits from dough with floured 2 3/4-inch round cutter. Place on baking sheet; brush tops with additional milk. Bake in preheated 450-degree oven for 10 to 15 minutes. Split shortcakes; place bottom halves in serving dishes. Spoon about 1/4 cup Foamy Custard and sweetened sliced strawberries over each bottom half. Replace shortcake tops; place 1/4 cup Foamy Custard and strawberries over each top.

FOAMY CUSTARD

Sugar
2 tbsp. all-purpose flour
1/4 tsp. salt
1/4 tsp. mace
1 1/2 c. milk
2 eggs, separated
1 tsp. vanilla extract
1/2 c. whipping cream, whipped

APRICREAM PIE
(Recipe 25 years old)

1 tbsp. gelatin
1/4 c. cold water
3 eggs, separated
1 c. (packed) brown sugar
1/2 tsp. salt
1 1/2 c. apricot pulp
1 tbsp. lemon juice
2 tbsp. sugar
1/2 c. heavy cream, whipped
1 baked pie shell

Soften gelatin in water. Combine egg yolks, brown sugar, salt, apricot pulp and lemon juice in saucepan; cook over low heat until thick, stirring constantly. Add gelatin; chill until firm. Beat egg whites with sugar until stiff. Fold egg whites and whipped cream into apricot mixture. Pour into pie shell. Chill until ready to use. Top with additional whipped cream, if desired.

Lois Lettow
Whitethorn Grange, No. 792
Whitethorn, California

★ ★

BRANT PIE
(Recipe 119 years old)

    Pastry for two 2-crust pies
    2 c. chopped cranberries
    2 c. sugar
    1 c. chopped raisins
    1 c. cold water
    Salt to taste (opt.)
    Butter (opt.)

Line 2 pie pans with pastry. Roll out remaining pastry for top crusts; cut into strips for latticing. Combine cranberries, sugar, raisins, cold water and salt; mix well. Spoon filling into 2 pie pans. Dot with butter. Arrange lattice strips over top; seal pastry edges together. Bake in preheated 350-degree oven until done.

Cecelia Kihl
Stafford Grange, No. 1
Stafford Springs, Connecticut

GRANDMOTHER'S BUTTERMILK PIE
(Recipe 100 years old)

    1 c. sugar
    1 tsp. flour
    1/2 tsp. salt
    2 eggs
    1/2 tsp. lemon extract
    2 c. buttermilk
    1 unbaked pie shell

Combine sugar, flour and salt. Add eggs, lemon extract and buttermilk; mix well. Pour into pie shell. Bake in preheated 400-degree oven for about 30 minutes or until filling is set.

Priscilla Savage
Sebasticook Grange, No. 306
Pittsfield, Maine

LEMONY BUTTERMILK PIE
(Recipe over 50 years old)

    Sugar
    1 tbsp. flour
    1/2 tbsp. butter
    1 c. buttermilk
    1 tsp. lemon flavoring
    1/8 tsp. salt
    1 tbsp. lemon juice
    2 eggs, separated
    1 unbaked 9-in. pastry shell

Combine 2/3 cup sugar, flour and butter. Add buttermilk, lemon flavoring, salt, lemon juice and slightly beaten egg yolks; mix thoroughly. Pour into pastry shell. Bake in preheated 425-degree oven until knife inserted in center comes out clean. Beat egg whites and 2 tablespoons sugar together until stiff peaks form; spread over top of pie to edge. Bake at 350 degrees for 20 minutes or until meringue is golden.

Wanda Lakey
Eagle Valley Grange, No. 656
Richland, Oregon

DELICIOUS BUTTERSCOTCH PIE FILLING
(Recipe over 40 years old)

    3 tbsp. butter
    1 1/2 c. (packed) brown sugar
    3/4 c. boiling water
    3 egg yolks
    1 1/2 c. milk
    6 tbsp. flour
    3/8 tsp. salt
    1 baked pastry shell
    1 recipe meringue

Melt butter in skillet. Stir in sugar; cook until sugar is dissolved and caramelized, stirring constantly. Stir in water gradually. Beat egg yolks. Stir a small amount of milk into flour until smooth; stir in remaining milk. Stir in egg yolks. Add salt; pour slowly into sugar mixture, stirring constantly. Cook until thick. Let cool. Pour into pastry shell. Spread meringue over top, sealing to crust. Bake in preheated 400-degree oven until browned.

Jeannette Lewis, W.A. Dir.
Ohio State Grange
Lebanon, Ohio

CALVIN COOLIDGE'S CUSTARD PIE

    2 lg. eggs
    3/4 c. sugar
    1 tbsp. (rounded) flour
    1/2 tsp. salt
    3 c. boiling milk
    Nutmeg to taste
    1 unbaked pie shell

Beat eggs. Add sugar, flour and salt; mix well. Stir in boiling milk; sprinkle with nutmeg. Pour into pie shell. Bake in preheated 400-degree oven for 15 minutes. Reduce oven temperature to 325 degrees; bake for 15 minutes longer or until knife inserted in center comes out clean.

Hazel Washburn
Tally-Ho Grange
St. Petersburg, Florida

COTTAGE CHEESE PIE
(Recipe 50 years old)

    2 c. cottage cheese
    4 tbsp. flour
    1 c. sugar
    2 eggs, separated
    2 c. milk
    1 tsp. vanilla
    1 unbaked 9-in. pie shell

Mix cheese, flour, sugar and egg yolks together. Add milk and vanilla; mix well. Fold in stiffly beaten egg whites. Pour into pie shell. Bake in preheated 400-degree oven for 10 minutes. Reduce oven temperature to 350 degrees; bake for 30 minutes longer or until firm.

Mrs. Merrill Fellman
Chalfont Grange, No. 1545
Chalfont, Pennsylvania

★ ★

BUTTERSCOTCH MERINGUE PIE
(Recipe over 50 years old)

3 eggs, separated
1 1/2 c. (packed) brown sugar
5 tbsp. flour
Salt
2 c. milk
Vanilla extract
2 tbsp. butter
1 baked pie shell
1/8 tsp. cream of tartar
6 tbsp. sugar

Beat egg yolks, brown sugar, flour, 1/2 teaspoon salt and milk together until smooth. Pour in saucepan; cook until thick, stirring constantly. Add 2 teaspoons vanilla extract and butter; mix well. Pour in pie shell. Beat egg whites until stiff; beat in cream of tartar, sugar, 1/2 teaspoon vanilla and several grains of salt. Spread over pie filling. Bake in preheated 400-degree oven until browned.

Mrs. Walter Canode
East Union Grange, No. 2397
Apple Creek, Ohio

CHESS PIES
(Recipe 75 years old)

3 c. flour
1 tsp. salt
1 1/2 c. shortening
3 eggs
3 tbsp. vinegar
3 tbsp. cold water
1/2 c. butter
1 c. sugar
Juice and grated rind of 1 lemon
1 c. dried currants
1 c. coarsely chopped walnuts

Combine flour and salt in mixing bowl; cut in shortening until mixture resembles coarse crumbs. Beat 1 egg, vinegar and cold water together; mix lightly into flour mixture until pastry forms a ball. Roll out as for pie crust. Cut into circles; fit into 36 small tart pans or muffin tins. Wrap remaining pastry securely for future use. Cream butter and sugar together. Add remaining 2 eggs; beat well. Stir in lemon juice, lemon rind, currants and walnuts; mix well. Place 1 rounded teaspoon filling in each tart shell. Bake in preheated 350-degree oven for 25 minutes or until light brown and bubbly.

Ella Nichols
Skagit Valley Grange, No. 620
Woolley, Washington

GERMAN CHOCOLATE PIE

1 1/2 c. sugar
2 tbsp. flour
3 tbsp. cocoa
2 eggs, beaten
1/2 c. butter, melted
1 1/4 c. evaporated milk
1/4 c. water

3/4 c. chopped pecans
1/2 c. coconut
1 unbaked pie shell

Combine sugar, flour and cocoa; stir in eggs and butter. Add milk, water, pecans and coconut; mix well. Pour into pie shell. Bake in preheated 350-degree oven for 30 minutes or until set.

Pency H. Eades
Iron Bridge Grange
Blackstone, Virginia

BLACK BOTTOM PIE

1 tbsp. unflavored gelatin
3/4 c. sugar
4 tsp. cornstarch
2 c. rich milk, scalded
4 egg yolks, beaten
1 1/2 oz. chocolate, melted
1/2 tsp. vanilla extract
1 baked 9-in. deep crumb crust or pastry crust
3 egg whites
1/4 tsp. salt
1/4 tsp. cream of tartar
1 tbsp. rum
1 c. whipping cream
2 tbsp. confectioners' sugar
1/2 oz. shaved chocolate

Soften gelatin in 1/4 cup cold water. Combine 1/2 cup sugar and cornstarch; stir into milk until dissolved. Stir a small amount of hot milk into egg yolks, mixing well; stir egg yolks into hot milk. Cook over hot water for 20 minutes or until custard is thick, stirring occasionally. Remove 1 cup custard; blend in melted chocolate. Let cool. Stir in vanilla; spread in pie shell. Stir softened gelatin into remaining hot custard until dissolved; let cool. Do not let custard set. Beat egg whites until soft peaks form. Add salt, cream of tartar and 1/4 cup sugar slowly, beating constantly; beat until stiff peaks form. Fold egg whites carefully into custard; stir in rum. Pour over chocolate custard in pie shell; chill until set. Whip cream until almost stiff. Add confectioners' sugar; whip until stiff. Spread whipped cream over top of pie; sprinkle with shaved chocolate.

Hazel Fox
Sterling Grange, No. 53
Clinton, Massachusetts

CHOCOLATE FUDGE PIE

1 env. unflavored gelatin
2 tbsp. sugar
1/4 tsp. salt
2 eggs, separated
1 c. milk
1 c. Smucker's chocolate fudge topping
1/2 tsp. vanilla extract
1 c. whipping cream, whipped
1 baked 9-in. pie shell

Mix gelatin, 1 tablespoon sugar and salt in medium saucepan. Beat egg yolks with milk and chocolate fudge topping; stir into gelatin mixture. Cook over low heat, stirring constantly, for 6 to 8 minutes or until gelatin dissolves. Remove from heat; stir in vanilla. Chill, stirring occasionally, until mixture mounds slightly when dropped from spoon. Beat egg whites until stiff but not dry. Add remaining 1 tablespoon sugar; beat until very stiff. Fold 1/4 the egg whites into chocolate mixture, then fold in whipped cream and remaining egg whites gently. Pour into pie shell; chill until firm. Garnish with additional whipped cream and chocolate fudge topping.

Photograph for this recipe above.

lemon juice. Cook over low heat until thick and clear, stirring constantly. Add cherries; cook for 3 minutes longer. Let cool; stir in almond extract. Pour into pie shell. Bake in preheated 450-degree oven for 10 minutes. Reduce oven temperature to 400 degrees; bake for 10 to 15 minutes longer or until done. Cool on rack. Pie filling will thicken as it cools. Spread whipped cream over top before serving. A pastry lattice top crust may be used, if desired. Three and one-half tablespoons cornstarch or 1/3 cup flour may be substituted for tapioca.

Grethel Capen, C.W.A. Sec.
American River Grange, No. 172
Rancho Cordova, California

DELICIOUS CHERRY PIE

    2 No. 2 cans tart cherries
    1 c. sugar
    2 tbsp. tapioca
    1 tbsp. cornstarch
    1/4 tsp. salt
    1/8 tsp. cloves
    1/4 tsp. cinnamon
    1/4 tsp. red food coloring (opt.)
    1 tsp. lemon juice
    1/2 tsp. almond extract
    1 unbaked 9-in. pie shell
    Whipped cream

Drain cherries; reserve 1 cup juice. Combine sugar, tapioca, cornstarch, salt, cloves and cinnamon in saucepan; stir in reserved juice. Add food coloring and

IMPOSSIBLE PIE

    1/2 c. flour
    1 1/2 c. sugar
    1/4 c. melted butter
    4 eggs, well beaten
    2 c. milk
    1 tsp. vanilla
    1 7-oz. package coconut

Combine flour and sugar. Add butter, eggs, milk and vanilla; mix well. Stir in coconut; pour into greased 10-inch pie pan. Bake in preheated 350-degree oven for 45 minutes or until filling is firm. Cool thoroughly before serving. This pie makes its own crust.

Connie Pipes
Narragansett Grange, No. 1
Narragansett, Rhode Island

★ ★

COCONUT MACAROON PIE
(Recipe over 65 years old)

2 eggs
1 1/2 c. sugar
1/2 tsp. salt
1/2 c. soft butter
1/4 c. flour
1/2 c. milk
1 1/2 c. shredded coconut
1 unbaked 9-in. pie shell

Beat eggs, sugar and salt until lemon colored. Add butter and flour; blend well. Stir in milk. Fold in 1 cup coconut; pour into pie shell. Top with remaining 1/2 cup coconut. Bake in preheated 325-degree oven for about 1 hour or until done.

Ethel M. Bennett
Louisville Grange
Milford, New York
Mrs. Kenneth E. Wilkin
Newark Grange, No. 1004
Heath, Ohio

DEEP OATMEAL PIE
(Recipe 150 years old)

3/4 c. white sugar
3/4 c. (packed) brown sugar
1/4 tsp. salt
3 eggs, beaten
3/4 c. milk
3/4 c. oatmeal
3/4 c. coconut
1 tsp. vanilla
1 unbaked deep 9-in. pie shell

Combine white sugar, brown sugar and salt. Stir in eggs and milk; mix well. Add oatmeal, coconut and vanilla; pour into pie shell. Bake in preheated 350-degree oven for 35 to 40 minutes or until done.

Mrs. Eleanore Gorman
Washington Grange, No. 82
Vancouver, Washington

GREEN TOMATO PIE
(Recipe over 50 years old)

1 c. sugar
2 tbsp. flour
1 tsp. salt
1/2 tsp. cinnamon
1/2 tsp. nutmeg
3 c. thinly sliced green tomatoes
3 tbsp. lemon juice
Pastry for one 8-in. 2-crust pie
1 tbsp. butter

Combine sugar, flour, salt, cinnamon and nutmeg. Add tomatoes; toss lightly. Stir in lemon juice. Line 8-inch pie pan with pastry; spoon tomato mixture into pie pan. Dot with butter. Cover with top crust; flute edges. Cut slits in top. Bake in preheated 350-degree oven until done.
This pie won 1st prize at County Fair.

Mrs. Arthur N. Winnesterfer
Tri Community Grange, No. 1008
Otis Orchards, Washington

FRESH STRAWBERRY PIE

1/2 c. sugar
3 tbsp. cornstarch
1/4 c. cold water
1 tsp. red food coloring
1 tsp. lemon juice
1/4 c. grenadine syrup
1/2 c. boiling water
4 1/2 c. fresh strawberries
1 baked pie shell
Whipped cream

Combine sugar, cornstarch and cold water in heavy cooking pan. Add food coloring, lemon juice, grenadine syrup and boiling water; cook until thick, stirring constantly. Stir in strawberries; remove from heat. Let cool. Pour into pie shell; top with whipped cream. Chill until ready to serve.

Henry M. Rumsey
Deerpark Grange, No. 1518
Port Jervis, New York

LEMON CHESS PIE

2 c. sugar
2 tbsp. flour
2 tbsp. cornmeal
4 eggs
1/4 c. melted butter
1/4 c. lemon juice
1/4 c. milk
1 unbaked pie shell

Combine sugar, flour and cornmeal. Add eggs, one at a time, beating well after each addition. Add butter, lemon juice and milk gradually; mix well. Pour into pie shell. Bake in preheated 350-degree oven for 35 minutes or until firm.

Mrs. J. L. Lucy
Iron Bridge Grange
Blackstone, Virginia

LEMON SPONGE PIE
(Recipe 60 years old)

1 c. sugar
2 eggs, separated
1/4 c. butter, softened
2 tsp. (heaping) flour
Dash of salt
Juice and grated rind of 1 lemon
1 c. milk
1 baked pie shell

★ ★

Combine sugar, egg yolks, butter, flour, salt, lemon juice, lemon rind and milk; mix well. Beat egg whites until stiff; fold into lemon mixture. Pour into pie shell. Bake in preheated 350-degree oven until browned and filling is firm.

Franklin C. Nixon
Vincentown Grange, No. 67
Vincentown, New Jersey

LEMON TRIFLE

2 tsp. grated lemon peel
1/3 c. fresh lemon juice
1 1/2 c. sugar
1/2 c. butter
3 eggs, slightly beaten
1 c. sour cream
1 pt. strawberries
1 to 2 tbsp. sherry
1   11 1/4-oz. pound cake
2 tbsp. toasted sliced almonds

Combine lemon peel, lemon juice, sugar and butter in saucepan; cook over low heat until butter is melted and sugar is dissolved. Remove from heat. Blend small amount of sugar mixture into eggs; stir back into sugar mixture. Cook over medium heat, stirring constantly, until mixture is slightly thickened; do not boil. Cool; stir in sour cream. Reserve 8 strawberries for garnish. Slice remaining strawberries; toss with sherry. Cut cake into 18 slices 1/4 inch thick. Place 6 slices cake in 1 1/2-quart oblong casserole, cutting slices to cover bottom of casserole. Top with half the sliced strawberries; add 1 cup lemon sauce. Repeat layers. Arrange remaining 6 slices cake over lemon sauce; spoon remaining lemon sauce over cake. Sprinkle with al-monds. Slice reserved strawberries to make fans; garnish top. Chill for several hours or overnight. Yield: 8 servings.

Photograph for this recipe below.

TANGY LEMON PIE

1 c. sugar
Pinch of salt
1 2/3 c. water
5 tbsp. cornstarch
1/2 c. lemon juice
2 tsp. grated lemon rind
3 egg yolks, slightly beaten
2 tbsp. butter
1 baked pie shell
Several drops of lemon extract
1 recipe meringue

Bring sugar, salt and water to a boil in saucepan. Mix cornstarch, lemon juice and 1 teaspoon lemon rind together; pour into boiling mixture, stirring constantly. Boil over moderate heat for 1 minute or until mixture thickens. Stir half the hot mixture slowly into egg yolks; pour egg mixture into saucepan, stirring constantly. Cook for 1 minute. Remove from heat. Add butter; beat until smooth. Pour into pie shell. Fold remaining teaspoon grated lemon rind and lemon extract into meringue; spread meringue over top of pie. Bake in preheated 350-degree oven for about 15 minutes or until golden.

Betty Conroy
Mission Grange, No. 767
Riverside, California

★ ★

OLD-FASHIONED CREAM PIE
(Recipe 65 years old)

3 tbsp. (heaping) sugar
2 tbsp. flour
Pinch of salt
3 tbsp. sour cream
1 c. whipping cream
1 c. rich milk or half and half
2 egg whites, stiffly beaten
1 unbaked 9-in. pie shell
Nutmeg to taste

Combine sugar, flour, salt and sour cream. Stir in whipping cream and milk; fold in stiffly beaten egg whites. Pour into pie shell; sprinkle with nutmeg. Bake in preheated 400-degree oven until top begins to brown. Reduce oven temperature to 350 degrees; bake until firm.

Mrs. Vernie E. Stahr
Laurel Valley Grange
Rockbridge, Ohio

ORANGE PIE

1 c. chopped pecans
1 c. shredded coconut
3/4 c. sugar
1/2 c. melted butter
1 3/4 c. orange juice
3 tbsp. cornstarch
2/3 c. orange marmalade
1 tbsp. vanilla extract
6 oranges
Whipped cream (opt.)

Combine pecans, coconut, 1/4 cup sugar and butter; mix well. Reserve 1/2 cup coconut mixture; press remaining mixture in pie pan to form crust. Bake in preheated 375-degree oven for 10 minutes or until browned. Combine orange juice, cornstarch, remaining 1/2 cup sugar, orange marmalade and vanilla extract in saucepan; cook over medium heat until thickened and clear, stirring constantly. Remove from heat; let cool. Peel oranges and remove membrane from slices. Line pie crust with orange slices; sprinkle reserved coconut mixture over slices. Spread filling over slices; top with whipped cream.

Leona Clayton
Rosedale Grange, No. 565
Bakersfield, California

FRESH PEACH PIE

1 c. ripe peaches, mashed
1 c. sugar
1/4 c. water
1 tbsp. lemon juice
3 tbsp. cornstarch
1/2 tsp. almond extract
1 baked pie shell
Thinly sliced fresh peaches
Whipped cream

Combine mashed peaches, sugar, water, lemon juice, cornstarch and almond extract in saucepan; cook until thick. Let cool. Cover bottom of pie shell with sliced peaches. Pour cooked mixture over peach slices; refrigerate until ready to use. Top with whipped cream; serve immediately.

Mrs. Grace P. Little
Bear Creek Grange
Mt. Pleasant, North Carolina

CREAMY PEACH PIE

4 c. miniature marshmallows
1 tbsp. lemon juice
2 tbsp. orange juice
1 c. cream, whipped
1 c. (or more) diced peaches
1 vanilla wafer crumb crust

Melt marshmallows over hot water. Stir in lemon juice and orange juice; let cool. Mix in whipped cream and peaches; pour into crust. Chill until ready to serve.

Mrs. John Brommer
Spring Creek Grange, No. 951
Reardan, Washington

CHERRY-BERRY-PEACH PIE

3 c. sliced peeled fresh peaches
1 c. fresh blueberries
1 c. pitted halved fresh sweet cherries
1 tbsp. fresh lemon juice
1/4 c. (packed) light brown sugar
Sugar
3 tbsp. flour
1/8 tsp. salt
1/4 tsp. cinnamon
Pastry for 2-crust 9-in. pie
Milk

Mix peaches, blueberries and cherries in large bowl; sprinkle with lemon juice. Stir in brown sugar, 1/2 cup sugar, flour, salt and cinnamon gently. Line 9-inch pie plate with half the pastry; trim overhang to 1 inch. Turn fruit mixture into pastry. Roll out remaining pastry on floured surface; cut into 3/4-inch strips. Arrange strips over fruit mixture in lattice fashion. Fold strips under edge of pastry; make rim and flute edge. Brush with milk; sprinkle with sugar. Bake in preheated 450-degree oven for 10 minutes. Reduce temperature to 350 degrees; bake for 45 to 50 minutes longer or until pastry is brown and fruits are tender. Serve warm or cool. Yield: 6-8 servings.

Photograph for this recipe on page 204.

PEAR CRUMBLE PIE

Sugar
Flour
1/2 tsp. salt
1 egg, beaten

★ ★

1 c. thick freshly soured cream
2 c. finely chopped pears
1/2 tsp. vanilla
1 unbaked pie shell
Nutmeg to taste
1/4 c. butter

Combine 1/2 cup sugar, 2 tablespoons flour and salt. Add egg and sour cream; mix well. Stir in pears and vanilla; pour into pie shell. Sprinkle nutmeg over top. Bake in preheated 425-degree oven for 15 minutes. Reduce oven temperature to 325 degrees; bake for 20 minutes longer or until firm. Combine 1/3 cup sugar, 2/3 cup flour and butter to make a crumbly mixture; sprinkle over top of pie. Bake for 10 minutes longer or until golden brown. Chill before serving.

Mary Brezden
Kittltas Grange, No. 1059
Ellensburg, Washington

PECAN PIE
(Recipe 75 years old)

1 tbsp. butter
1 c. (packed) brown sugar
1 c. light corn syrup
3 eggs, well beaten
Dash of salt
1 tsp. vanilla
1 c. pecan halves
1 unbaked pie shell

Cream butter and sugar together. Add syrup, eggs, salt and vanilla; mix well. Stir in pecan halves; turn into pie shell. Bake in preheated 350-degree oven until filling is firm.

Beverly A. Gist
Centennial Grange, No. 2006
Lawrence, Kansas

MAPLE PUMPKIN PIE

5 c. flour
Salt
1 lb. lard
3 eggs
2 tbsp. vinegar
1 c. cooked pumpkin
1 tbsp. cornstarch
1/3 c. sugar
1/2 tsp. cinnamon
1/4 tsp. nutmeg
1 tbsp. melted butter
1/2 c. milk
1 1/2 c. maple syrup

Combine flour and a pinch of salt in mixing bowl; cut in lard until mixture resembles coarse crumbs. Beat 1 egg in 1 cup measure; beat in vinegar. Add enough water to measure 1 cup liquid; mix well. Stir egg mixture into flour mixture until ingredients are moistened and pastry clings together. Roll out enough pastry for one 8-inch pie shell; place in pie pan. Flute edge. Wrap remaining pastry securely; store for future use. Beat pumpkin until smooth. Sift cornstarch, sugar, 1/4 teaspoon salt, cinnamon and nutmeg together; mix with pumpkin. Add butter, milk and maple syrup; mix well. Beat remaining 2 eggs; stir into pumpkin mixture. Pour into pie shell. Bake in preheated 450-degree oven for 15 minutes. Reduce oven temperature to 325 degrees; bake for 40 minutes longer or until filling is set.

Lillie M. Mason
Winthrop Grange, No. 538
Winthrop, New York

AMERICAN PUMPKIN PIE

2 c. cooked mashed pumpkin
3/4 c. (firmly packed) light brown sugar
2 tsp. cinnamon
3/4 tsp. salt
3/4 tsp. ginger
1/2 tsp. nutmeg
1/4 tsp. mace
1/8 tsp. ground cloves
4 eggs, slightly beaten
1 1/2 c. light cream or half and half
1 unbaked 9-in. pie shell
Sweetened whipped cream

Combine pumpkin and brown sugar in large bowl; blend in cinnamon, salt, ginger, nutmeg, mace and cloves. Add eggs; stir in cream gradually. Pour into pie shell. Bake in preheated 400-degree oven for 40 to 45 minutes or until knife inserted in center comes out clean; cool on wire rack. Top with whipped cream.

Photograph for this recipe below.

★ ★

PUMPKIN-RAISIN PIE

1 1/2 c. mashed pumpkin
3/4 c. (packed) brown sugar
2 eggs, slightly beaten
1 3/4 c. light cream, scalded
1 c. raisins, chopped
1/4 c. brandy
1 tsp. cinnamon
1/2 tsp. allspice
1/2 tsp. cloves
1/2 tsp. salt
1 unbaked pie shell
Shredded coconut

Combine pumpkin, brown sugar, eggs, cream, raisins, brandy, cinnamon, allspice, cloves and salt; mix well. Pour into pie shell. Bake in preheated 400-degree oven until filling is firm. Reduce oven temperature if filling begins to bubble. Remove from oven; sprinkle coconut over top of pie. Return to oven; bake until coconut is browned.

Mrs. Lorene M. Walker
Contoocook Grange, No. 216
Bow, New Hampshire

RAISIN CRUMB PIE

1 lb. seeded raisins
1 1/2 c. cold water
3 c. sugar
2 c. flour
1/4 c. shortening
2 eggs, well beaten
1 c. milk
2 tsp. baking powder
Pastry for two 1-crust pies

Wash and drain raisins. Combine raisins, water and 1/2 of the sugar in saucepan; cook until raisins are plump. Set aside to cool. Combine flour, remaining sugar and shortening; crumble and mix together with fingertips. Set aside 1 cup crumbs. Add eggs and milk to remaining crumbs; mix well. Stir in baking powder. Line 2 pie pans with pastry; fill with raisin mixture. Pour batter over raisins; sprinkle top with reserved crumbs. Bake in preheated 440-degree oven for 10 minutes. Reduce oven temperature to 350 degrees; bake for 35 minutes longer or until done.

Mrs. Helen Updike
Aurora Grange, No. 874
Wellsboro, Pennsylvania

SOUR CREAM-RAISIN PIE
(Recipe 100 years old)

1 c. cooked raisins
Sugar
1 tsp. cinnamon
1 tsp. cloves
1 1/2 tbsp. flour
1 c. sour cream

2 eggs, separated
1 c. (scant) milk
1 baked 9-in. pie shell

Combine raisins, 1 cup sugar, cinnamon, cloves, flour, sour cream, egg yolks and milk in large heavy kettle. Place over medium heat; bring to a boil, stirring constantly. Boil until thickened to pie filling consistency. Remove from heat; cool slightly. Pour into pie shell. Beat egg whites until soft peaks form. Add 4 tablespoons sugar gradually; beat until stiff peaks form. Spread over raisin filling to edge of shell. Bake in preheated 425-degree oven until browned.

Dorlene Laird
Unity Grange, No. 416
Weiser, Idaho

FRESH RHUBARB PIE

4 c. 1-in. pieces of rhubarb
Pastry for one 9-in. 2-crust pie
1 1/3 to 2 c. sugar
1/3 c. tapioca
1 1/2 tbsp. butter

Wash rhubarb; let drain. Line 9-inch pie pan with pastry. Mix sugar and tapioca toegether; mix with rhubarb. Pour into pastry-lined pie pan; dot with butter. Cover with top crust. Seal pastry edges together; cut slits in top crust. Sprinkle with sugar. Bake in preheated 425-degree oven for 40 to 50 minutes or until crust is browned and juice bubbles through slits. Serve slightly warm.

Carole L. Stafford
Rowe Grange, No. 167
Charlemont, Massachusetts

MOTHER'S FAVORITE RHUBARB CUSTARD MERINGUE PIE
(Recipe 75 years old)

3 eggs, separated
1 c. milk
3 tbsp. flour
Sugar
1/4 tsp. salt
3 c. chopped rhubarb
1 unbaked 9-in. pie shell
1/4 tsp. cream of tartar

Beat egg yolks and milk together. Add flour, 1 cup sugar and salt; beat slowly until smooth. Place rhubarb in pie shell; pour egg mixture over rhubarb. Bake in preheated 350-degree oven for about 35 minutes or until firm. Beat egg whites until frothy. Add cream of tartar and 2 tablespoons sugar; beat until soft peaks form. Add 4 tablespoons sugar gradually; beat until stiff peaks form. Spread on hot pie. Bake in 325-degree oven for 15 minutes or until lightly browned.

Mrs. Margarete Leathers
Oak Lawn Grange, No. 42
Cranston, Rhode Island

★ ★

SPRING FRUIT PIE

Pastry for one 2-crust pie
2 c. sliced strawberries
2 c. 1-in. pieces of rhubarb
1/2 c. drained crushed pineapple
2 tbsp. lemon juice
1 c. sugar
1/4 c. cornstarch
Dash of salt

Line pie pan with pastry. Combine strawberries, rhubarb, pineapple, lemon juice, sugar, cornstarch and salt; pour into pie pan. Cover with top crust; seal pastry edges together. Cut slits in top crust. Bake in preheated 425-degree oven for 40 to 45 minutes or until done.

Carol Crawford
Paris Grange
Sauquoit, New York

SWEET POTATO PIE

1 1/2 to 2 c. hot cooked sweet potatoes
1/4 c. butter
3/4 c. miniature marshmallows
3/4 c. sugar
1/8 tsp. cinnamon
1/8 tsp. nutmeg
Vanilla and rum flavorings to taste
2 eggs
Chopped nuts (opt.)
1 unbaked pie shell

Combine sweet potatoes, butter and marshmallows; stir until butter and marshmallows are melted. Add sugar, spices and flavorings. Add eggs; beat well, using electric mixer. May add about 1/4 cup milk if mixture is too stiff. Sprinkle nuts in pie shell; pour in filling. Bake in preheated 350-degree oven for 50 to 60 minutes or until filling is set.

Pearl Thompson, Sec.
North Carolina State Grange
Salisbury, North Carolina

VINEGAR PIE

1 c. sugar
3 tbsp. butter
2 eggs
3 tbsp. vinegar
1 tsp. lemon extract
1 unbaked pie shell

Cream sugar and butter together; beat in eggs. Stir in vinegar and lemon extract. Pour into pie shell. Bake in preheated 350-degree oven until filling is firm.

Mrs. F. M. Buchanan
McLeansville Grange, No. 999
McLeansville, North Carolina

SURPRISE PIE

12 saltines, rolled fine
12 dates, chopped
1/2 c. chopped walnuts
1 c. sugar
1/2 tsp. baking powder
1 tbsp. water
1 tsp. almond flavoring
3 egg whites, beaten stiff
Whipped cream or vanilla ice cream

Combine saltine crumbs, dates, walnuts, sugar, baking powder, water and almond flavoring; mix well. Fold carefully into egg whites. Pour into buttered pie pan. Bake in preheated 350-degree oven for 30 minutes or until done. Top with whipped cream to serve.

Jessie E. Ordway, Pomona
New Hampton Grange, No. 123
New Hampton, New Hampshire

WALNUT PIE

2 eggs, beaten
1 c. dark corn syrup
1 c. sugar
2 tbsp. melted butter
1/2 tsp. salt
1 tsp. vanilla flavoring
3/4 c. chopped black walnuts
1 unbaked pastry shell

Mix eggs and syrup together. Stir in sugar, butter, salt and vanilla; mix well. Stir in walnuts; pour into pastry shell. Bake in preheated 400-degree oven for 15 minutes. Reduce oven temperature to 350 degrees; bake for 30 to 35 minutes longer or until toothpick inserted in center of pie comes out clean.

Susie Qualls
Statesville Grange, No. 1236
Lebanon, Tennessee

CHOCOLATE BREAD PUDDING
(Recipe 95 years old)

1 tbsp. butter
1 sq. unsweetened chocolate
2 c. scalded milk
1 c. bread crumbs
2 eggs, separated
1/2 c. sugar

Melt butter and chocolate in scalded milk; pour over bread crumbs in bowl. Beat egg yolks; blend in sugar. Stir into milk mixture; fold in stiffly beaten egg whites. Pour into buttered casserole. Bake in preheated 350-degree oven for about 1 hour or until firm.

Fay O'Neill
Whitethorn Grange, No. 792
Whitethorn, California

★ ★

BASIC PUDDING MIX

1 1/2 c. sugar
2 1/2 c. powdered nonfat dry milk
1 1/4 c. flour
1 tsp. salt

Combine sugar, dry milk, flour and salt in bowl; stir until well mixed. Store in tightly covered container in cool place.

VANILLA PUDDING MADE FROM MIX

1 1/4 c. Basic Pudding Mix
2 1/2 c. warm water
1 tbsp. butter
1 egg, beaten
3/4 tsp. vanilla extract

Combine mix with water in saucepan; cook over low heat until thick, stirring constantly. Stir in butter, egg and vanilla extract; cool, then chill. Yield: 6 servings.

Loretta Lauderback
Gresham Grange, No. 270
Gresham, Oregon

BATTER-TOPPED APPLE PUDDING

8 med. apples
3/4 c. maple syrup
2 tbsp. butter
1 tbsp. cinnamon
1/4 c. shortening
3/4 c. sugar
1 egg
2 c. flour
2 tsp. cream of tartar
1 tsp. soda
1/2 tsp. salt
1 c. milk
Dash of vanilla extract

Slice apples into large baking pan; pour syrup over apples. Dot with butter; sprinkle with cinnamon. Combine shortening, sugar, egg, flour, cream of tartar, soda, salt, milk and vanilla in bowl; mix well. Pour over apples. Bake in preheated 350-degree oven for 50 to 60 minutes or until done. Yield: 12 servings.

Barbara Bierly
Charity Grange, No. 103
Eugene, Oregon

MASTER'S APPLE PUDDING
(Recipe 70 years old)

Sliced apples
Sugar
Cinnamon
Butter
1 tbsp. shortening
2 c. flour
1/4 tsp. salt
2 tsp. baking powder
Milk

Line bottom of 4-quart baking dish with apples. Season with sugar and cinnamon to taste; dot with butter. Cream 1/2 cup sugar and shortening in bowl. Sift flour, salt and baking powder together; add to creamed mixture. Stir in enough milk to make medium-thick batter; pour over apples. Bake in preheated 375-degree oven for about 1 hour or until done.

D. Vincent Andrews
Master of Florida State Grange
Sarasota, Florida

RAISIN-APPLE BREAD PUDDING

3 apples, peeled
4 c. diced oatmeal or wheat germ bread
1/2 c. raisins
1 qt. milk
3 eggs, beaten
1/2 c. sugar
1 tsp. vanilla extract
1/2 tsp. cinnamon
1/2 tsp. nutmeg

Core and dice apples. Mix bread, raisins and apples in greased 2 1/2-quart casserole. Combine remaining ingredients in bowl; beat until well blended. Pour over bread mixture. Bake in preheated 350-degree oven for 1 hour or until firm in center. Serve with topping or ice cream. Yield: 6-8 servings.

Mrs. George Smullen
Rock District Grange, No. 780
Cobleskill, New York

RAISIN BREAD PUDDING
(Recipe 90 years old)

2 c. bread crumbs
1 qt. milk
4 eggs, separated
1 c. sugar
Grated rind of 1 lemon
Raisins to taste
1/2 c. powdered sugar

Place bread crumbs in bowl; pour milk over crumbs. Soak for 30 minutes. Beat egg yolks with sugar until well mixed; stir in grated rind. Add to milk mixture. Add raisins; mix well. Place in greased casserole. Bake in preheated 350-degree oven for about 30 minutes or until done. Beat egg whites until stiff peaks form, adding powdered sugar gradually. Spread over pudding, sealing to edge of casserole. Return to oven; bake until lightly browned.

Mary Balis
Colville Valley Grange, No. 249
Colville, Washington

CHERRY PUDDING WITH SAUCE

1 c. sifted flour
1 1/2 c. sugar

★ ★ ★ ☆ ★

1 tsp. baking powder
1/8 tsp. salt
2 tsp. melted butter
1/2 c. milk
1 c. canned tart pitted cherries
1/2 c. cherry juice

Sift flour, 1/2 cup sugar, baking powder and salt together into bowl. Add 1 teaspoon butter and milk; mix until blended. Pour into greased 9 x 4 1/2 x 3-inch loaf pan. Mix remaining 1 teaspoon butter, cherries, cherry juice and remaining 1 cup sugar; pour over flour mixture. Bake in preheated 325-degree oven for 45 minutes or until done. Yield: 6-8 servings.

Mrs. Lula Rappole
Philadelphia Grange, No. 114
Philadelphia, New York

BOILED CUSTARD
(Recipe 65 years old)

3 c. milk
2/3 c. sugar
2 tbsp. flour
2 eggs, beaten
1 tsp. vanilla extract

Pour milk into saucepan; stir in sugar. Place flour in bowl; stir in small amount of milk mixture. Add eggs; beat well. Scald milk mixture; add egg mixture slowly, stirring constantly. Bring to a boil over low heat, stirring constantly; remove from heat. Stir in vanilla; cool, then chill. Serve in dessert dishes. Yield: 6 servings.

Mona Johnston
Garland Grange, No. 1568
Garland, Kansas

CHARLOTTE
(Recipe over 50 years old)

5 c. milk
Sugar
2 tbsp. flour
3 eggs, separated
1 tsp. vanilla extract
2 tbsp. unflavored gelatin
1 pt. cream
1/2 c. wine

Heat 4 cups milk in saucepan until warm. Mix 1 cup sugar, flour and egg yolks; stir in small amount of the milk until smooth. Stir back into milk; cook over low heat, stirring constantly, until custard just coats spoon. Remove from heat; stir in vanilla. Soften gelatin in remaining 1 cup milk for 5 minutes. Add to hot custard; stir until dissolved. Chill until custard begins to thicken. Fold in beaten egg whites. Whip cream until stiff; beat in about 2 tablespoons sugar. Stir in wine; fold into gelatin mixture. Place in mold. Chill until firm.

Alice V. McComb
Maryville, Tennessee

MAPLE CUSTARD

1/4 c. maple syrup
2 c. scalded milk
4 eggs, well beaten
1/2 tsp. salt
Butter

Combine maple syrup and milk in bowl; beat well. Add eggs slowly, stirring constantly; stir in salt. Pour into 8 custard cups; dot each with butter. Place cups in pan of water. Bake in preheated 350-degree oven for 30 to 35 minutes or until set. One tablespoon maple syrup may be placed in each cup before adding custard mixture for more distinct maple flavor, if desired.

Avis Shannon
Protective Grange, No. 22
Brattleboro, Vermont

CARAMELIZED PUDDING
(Recipe over 100 years old)

2 1/2 c. sugar
2 1/2 c. hot water
3 tbsp. butter
2 tsp. vanilla extract
1/2 tsp. salt
1/2 c. milk
1 tsp. baking powder
1 c. flour

Place 1/2 cup sugar in heavy skillet; cook over low heat, stirring constantly, until melted and golden brown. Add 1 1/2 cups sugar and hot water; mix well. Bring to a boil; reduce heat. Cook for 15 minutes. Add 2 tablespoons butter, 1 teaspoon vanilla and 1/4 teaspoon salt; mix well. Reduce heat to very low; let simmer. Cream remaining 1/2 cup sugar with remaining 1 tablespoon butter; stir in milk. Add remaining 1/4 teaspoon salt, remaining 1 teaspoon vanilla, baking powder and flour; mix well. Bring caramel sauce to a boil; drop batter from teaspoon onto sauce. Bake in preheated 350-degree oven for 20 minutes or until brown. Serve with cream. Yield: 12 servings.

Mrs. Robert Lord
Garland Grange, No. 1568
Garland, Kansas

OLD-FASHIONED BAKED RICE PUDDING
(Recipe 75 to 100 years old)

1/2 c. rice
2 qt. milk
1 c. sugar
1/2 tsp. salt
1/4 tsp. cinnamon
1 c. raisins

Mix all ingredients; place in baking pan. Bake in preheated 325-degree oven for 2 hours, stirring about 3 times.

Sylvia L. Wheeler
Shelburne Grange, No. 68
Shelburne Falls, Massachusetts

★ ★

OLD-FASHIONED BAKED CUSTARD
(Recipe 100 years old)

5 eggs
1 c. sugar
1 tsp. vanilla extract
1 qt. milk
Nutmeg

Place eggs in bowl; beat thoroughly. Add sugar; beat well. Stir in vanilla and milk; pour into casserole. Sprinkle with nutmeg; place casserole in pan of warm water. Bake in preheated 225-degree oven until knife inserted in center comes out clean. Do not overbake. Recipe calls for long, slow baking, but custard will never curdle if baked this way. Yield: 8 servings.

Mrs. Edwin Horton
Lawtons Grange, No. 1176
Eden, New York

HUCKLEBERRY PUDDING
(Recipe 75 years old)

2 c. sugar
3/4 c. butter or shortening
2 eggs
3 1/2 c. flour
2 tsp. (heaping) baking powder
1/4 tsp. salt
1 c. milk
1 qt. huckleberries or blueberries

Cream sugar and butter in bowl; stir in eggs. Sift flour, baking powder and salt together; add to creamed mixture alternately with milk. Stir in huckleberries; place in well-greased pudding pan. Bake in preheated 350-degree oven for 45 minutes or until done. Yield: 10 servings.

Mrs. Ray Kanouff
Blue Ball Grange, No. 1331
West Decatur, Pennsylvania

INDIAN PUDDING
(Recipe 324 years old)

3 1/2 c. milk
5 tbsp. yellow cornmeal
1/2 tsp. salt
1/2 c. currants
1/2 c. sorghum syrup
2 eggs, beaten
1/3 c. sugar
Nutmeg to taste

Scald 2 cups milk in top of double boiler. Stir in cornmeal; cook over boiling water until done. Remove from heat; add remaining milk, salt, currants and syrup. Mix well; cool. Mix eggs, sugar and nutmeg. Stir into cornmeal mixture; turn into well-greased baking dish. Bake in preheated 350-degree oven for several minutes. Stir so that the currants will not sink to bottom; bake for about 1 hour or until mixture looks watery, not milky.

Gladys True, D.W.A.
California State Grange
Middletown, California

ORANGE MARMALADE PUDDING

2 c. bread crumbs
1/2 c. finely chopped suet
1/4 c. orange juice
1 tsp. soda
1 c. orange marmalade
1 egg, beaten

Place bread crumbs in bowl; add suet and orange juice. Add soda to marmalade; stir just until mixed. Combine with suet mixture; stir in egg. Pour into buttered top of double boiler; cover. Place over boiling water; steam for 3 hours. Serve with Lemon Hard Sauce or whipped cream. Yield: 6 servings.

LEMON HARD SAUCE

1/2 c. butter
1 1/2 c. powdered sugar
1 egg, separated
2 tbsp. lemon juice
1 tsp. grated orange peel

Cream butter, powdered sugar and egg yolk in bowl. Stir in lemon juice and grated peel; fold in stiffly beaten egg white.

Grace E. Adams
Mount Gardner Grange, No. 325
Woodsville, New Hampshire

PEACH-TOPPED PUDDING
(Recipe about 90 years old)

1 c. sugar
2 tbsp. butter
1 egg
1 c. milk
1 tsp. vanilla extract
2 c. flour
2 tsp. baking powder
Peach halves
Whipped cream

Cream sugar and butter in bowl. Add egg; mix well. Stir in milk and vanilla. Add flour and baking powder; mix well. Pour into greased square baking pan. Bake in preheated 350-degree oven for about 1 hour or until done. Cool; cut into squares. Place on serving plates. Place peach halves on each square; serve with whipped cream. Yield: 9 servings.

Mrs. George Selbher
Sugar Grove Grange

PERSIMMON PUDDING
(Recipe 100 years old)

2 c. persimmon pulp
2 c. sugar
1 1/2 c. flour
1 tsp. soda
1 1/2 c. buttermilk
1 tsp. baking powder
1/8 tsp. salt
2 eggs
1/2 tsp. cinnamon

★ ★

1 tsp. vanilla extract
1/4 c. cream
1/4 c. butter

Mix all ingredients except butter in large bowl in order listed. Melt butter in large loaf pan; pour batter into loaf pan. Bake in preheated 300-degree oven for 1 hour and 30 minutes or until done. Yield: 12-15 servings.

Dorothy B. Marshall
Windom Grange
Mitchell, Indiana

CHRISTMAS PLUM PUDDING
(Recipe 100 years old)

4 eggs, separated
1 c. sugar
1 c. finely chopped suet
1 tsp. salt
1 c. molasses
1/2 c. milk
1/2 c. brandy
2 tsp. grated nutmeg
2 tsp. cinnamon
1/2 tsp. ground cloves
Juice and grated rind of 1 lemon
2 c. fine stale bread crumbs
2 c. flour
1 tsp. soda
1 c. seeded raisins
1/2 c. thinly sliced citron

Place egg yolks in large bowl; beat until very light. Add sugar; beat well. Add suet, salt, molasses, milk, brandy, spices, lemon rind and juice and bread crumbs; mix well. Sift in 1 cup flour. Dissolve soda in 1 teaspoon cold water; add to suet mixture. Stir thoroughly. Beat egg whites until stiff peaks form; fold into suet mixture. Mix some of the remaining flour with raisins and citron. Stir remaining flour into suet mixture; stir in raisin mixture. Spoon into buttered pudding mold with tube in center, filling 2/3 full; cover closely. Place in kettle of boiling water reaching nearly to top of mold. Cover kettle closely; reduce heat. Simmer for 5 to 6 hours, adding water as needed. Pour an additional 1/3 glass brandy over pudding just before serving. Place small branch of holly in top of pudding; light match to brandy just as carried to table. Serve with wine sauce or brandy sauce.

Mrs. Thelma Hylton
Price's Fork Grange, No. 786
Blacksburg, Virginia

GRANDMA WILSON'S OLD ENGLISH PLUM PUDDING
(Recipe about 175 years old)

4 eggs
1 tsp. soda
1 1/2 c. ground or chopped suet
1/2 c. (packed) brown sugar
1/2 c. white sugar

1 c. molasses
1 tsp. salt
1/4 tsp. allspice
1/4 tsp. nutmeg
1/4 tsp. cloves
1/2 tsp. cinnamon
3 tbsp. milk
5 c. flour
1 lb. raisins, floured
Hard Sauce

Beat eggs in large bowl; mix soda with 1 tablespoon hot water. Add suet, brown sugar, white sugar, molasses, salt, spices, soda, milk and flour to eggs; mix well. Fold in floured raisins. Place in wet, floured heavy cloth; tie. Place in large kettle of boiling water; simmer for 3 to 4 hours or until done, adding water as needed. Loosen bag and tie knot about 2 inches higher if pudding gets too tight. Serve warm topped with Hard Sauce. Yield: 20-24 servings.

HARD SAUCE

1 c. sugar
3 tbsp. (or more) flour
2 tbsp. butter
Vanilla extract to taste
Brandy to taste

Pour 2 cups water into saucepan; bring to a boil. Mix sugar with enough flour for desired thickness; stir into water. Cook, stirring, until thickened. Remove from heat; stir in butter, vanilla and brandy.

Raymond G. Wilson, Past Master
Riverview Grange, No. 392
Blair, Nebraska

SNOW PUDDING WITH CUSTARD SAUCE

1/2 c. cold water
1 env. unflavored gelatin
Sugar
1/4 tsp. salt
1 c. boiling water
1/4 c. lemon juice
4 eggs, separated
2 c. milk
1 tsp. vanilla extract

Pour cold water into large bowl; sprinkle gelatin over cold water to soften. Add 1/3 cup sugar, 1/8 teaspoon salt and boiling water; stir until thoroughly dissolved. Add lemon juice; stir. Chill until nearly firm. Beat egg whites until stiff peaks form; fold into gelatin mixture. Chill until firm. Scald milk in top of double boiler; cool slightly. Combine beaten egg yolks, remaining 1/8 teaspoon salt and 1/4 cup sugar; stir in milk gradually. Cook over hot, not boiling, water until mixture coats metal spoon, stirring constantly. Remove from heat; cool at once by placing pan in bowl of cold water and stirring for several minutes. Stir in vanilla; chill. Spoon pudding into serving dishes; top with sauce.

Mrs. William Buffington, Lecturer
Pennsylvania State Grange
Chadds Ford, Pennsylvania

Quantity Recipes

Eating together, like working together, has long been a part of the American way of life. Large groups of people gathered for fun, fellowship and food were as much a common sight in pioneer days as they are now. Rather than cooking for just one family, the women combined their culinary skills, preparing large kettles full of food that would feed hundreds. Those were the times when cooperative harvesting was done by day and barn raisings were enjoyed by night.

While rural America has changed considerably, its people seem to have changed very little. They are still down-to-earth country folks who treat everyone in their community as a respected member of the family. Quite important are the traditional community outings such as Sunday picnics by the pond and Fourth of July barbecues when hearty dishes of all kinds completely cover the table. Preparing meals in large quantities that are as delicious as they are inviting does not have to be difficult.

Included in this section are quantity recipes that, having been personally tested, were found to be supremely suitable for large gatherings. They transport well, are generally liked by people of all ages and do not require an excess amount of preparation. Many are flexible enough to be stretched if a larger crowd than expected arrives for dinner and many can be made ahead of time, frozen or refrigerated, and then reheated. None require exotic, expensive ingredients, so they are well suited to a food committee's budget.

A variety of recipes for main dishes, vegetables, salads, breads, desserts and even punches can be found here. And for the men, the pioneers of American barbecue, there are sauce and meat recipes that are sure to please. All of these are the product of good times and good friends gathering at Grange tables.

★ ★

QUANTITIES TO SERVE ONE-HUNDRED PEOPLE

Baked beans	.5 gallons	Loaf sugar	3 pounds
Beef	40 pounds	Meat loaf	24 pounds
Beets	30 pounds	Milk	.6 gallons
Bread	10 loaves	Nuts	3 pounds
Butter	3 pounds	Olives	1 3/4 pounds
Cabbage for slaw	20 pounds	Oysters	18 quarts
Cakes	.8	Pickles	2 quarts
Carrots	33 pounds	Pies	.18
Cauliflower	18 pounds	Potatoes	35 pounds
Cheese	3 pounds	Potato salad	12 quarts
Chicken for chicken pie	40 pounds	Roast pork	40 pounds
Coffee	3 pounds	Rolls	.200
Cream	3 quarts	Salad dressing	3 quarts
Fruit cocktail	1 gallon	Scalloped potatoes	.5 gallons
Fruit juice	4 No. 10 cans	Soup	.5 gallons
Fruit salad	20 quarts	Tomato juice	4 No. 10 cans
Ham	40 pounds	Vegetables	4 No. 10 cans
Hamburger	30 to 36 pounds	Vegetable salad	20 quarts
Ice Cream	.4 gallons	Whipping cream	4 pints
Lettuce	.20 heads	Wieners	25 pounds

BARBECUE SAUCE

1 qt. vinegar or apple cider
1 pt. corn oil
1/8 jar onion salt
1/2 c. sugar
1/4 c. salt
Pepper to taste
1/4 c. catsup
1/4 c. mustard
6 tbsp. Worcestershire sauce

Place all ingredients in blender container; process until blended. Yield: Enough sauce for 40 to 50 chicken halves.

Mrs. Jenny Grobusky, D.W.A.
National Grange
Walhalla, South Carolina

CREAM OF TOMATO SOUP
(Recipe 75 years old)

1 peck ripe tomatoes
1 bunch celery, chopped
6 onions, chopped
Pinch of soda
3 sweet green peppers
3 sweet red peppers
1 c. sugar
Salt and pepper to taste
1 c. flour
Cream
Butter to taste

Peel and chop tomatoes. Cook tomatoes, celery, onions, soda and green and red peppers in kettle until tender; press through colander. Add sugar, salt and pepper; mix well. Bring to a boil; cook for 15 minutes. Mix flour with 1 cup water until smooth; stir into tomato mixture. Cook until thickened. Add desired amount of cream and butter just before serving; heat through. Serve with toasted breadsticks. Yield: 20 servings.

Dorothy B. Marshall
Windom Grange
Mitchell, Indiana

MABEL'S SALAD DRESSING

4 eggs, beaten
3 c. sugar
4 tbsp. (heaping) flour
2 tsp. salt
4 tsp. prepared mustard
1 c. vinegar
3 c. hot water or milk
4 chunks butter
1/2 c. salad dressing

Mix all ingredients except salad dressing in saucepan; bring to a boil. Remove from heat. Add salad dressing; mix well. Yield: Enough dressing for 10 pounds potato salad.

Mrs. James R. Kilgore
Harmony Grange, No. 1692
Nazareth, Pennsylvania

★ ☆ ★

WEDDING CAKE POTATO SALAD

    10 lb. potatoes
    1 8-oz. bottle Hellmann's or Best
         Foods Italian dressing
    8 c. chopped celery
    2. chopped onions
    2 tbsp. salt
    1 tsp. white pepper
    Hellmann's or Best Foods real mayonnaise
    Tomato Roses
    Celery leaves
    Filled Cucumber Cups
    Cucumber half slices
    Tomato points

Cook potatoes until just tender; peel, dice and toss with Italian dressing while still warm. Let marinate in refrigerator for about 2 hours. Combine potatoes, celery, onions, salt and pepper. Add 4 cups mayonnaise; toss until well mixed. Line bottom and sides of 3 tier pans, 10 x 2 inches, 8 x 2 inches and 6 x 2 inches, with waxed paper. Pack firmly with potato salad. Cover; chill for several hours. Uncover 10-inch layer; invert serving plate over pan and turn upright, holding pan firmly against center of plate. Place on flat surface; remove pan and waxed paper. Turn out 8-inch layer on center of 10-inch layer; remove pan and waxed paper. Turn out 6-inch layer on top of 8-inch layer; remove pan and waxed paper. Garnish base of salad with Tomato Roses on celery leaves. Circle base of middle layer with Filled Cucumber Cups. Stand cucumber half slices and place tomato points around base of top layer. Decorate top with tomato rose and celery leaves. Yield: Forty-two 3/4-cup servings.

TOMATO ROSES

Peel tomatoes with vegetable peeler, starting at top and peeling around and around to bottom of tomato. Roll peeling around itself into rose shape.

FILLED CUCUMBER CUPS

Make a cut from center through outer edge of tissue thin cucumber slices; overlap edges, forming cup. Place on salad, overlapped edges down. Force mayonnaise through pastry tube into cups.

Photograph for this recipe opposite.

DELICIOUS POTATO SALAD

    1 tbsp. salt
    1 tbsp. paprika
    2 tbsp. onion juice
    1 c. French dressing
    5 qt. cooked cubed potatoes
    6 hard-cooked eggs, quartered
    5 c. thinly sliced celery
    1/2 c. chopped pimentos
    1/2 c. chopped green peppers
    1/2 c. chopped parsley
    1 c. mayonnaise
    1 c. cooked dressing

Combine salt, paprika, onion juice and French dressing in bowl. Add potatoes; mix well. Let stand for 15 minutes. Add eggs and vegetables; mix lightly. Combine mayonnaise and cooked dressing. Add to salad; mix lightly. Yield: 5 1/2 quarts.

From a Grange Friend

GREEN BEAN SALAD

    1 qt. green beans
    8 stalks celery, diced
    2 green peppers, diced
    1 pt. peas
    2 sm. onions, chopped
    1 pimento, chopped
    1 tsp. salt
    1/2 c. salad oil
    1 c. vinegar
    1 tbsp. water
    1 1/2 c. sugar

Mix beans, celery, green peppers, peas, onions and pimento in bowl. Mix remaining ingredients; stir into bean mixture. Place in refrigerator for 24 hours before serving. Yield: 20 servings.

Mrs. Mendal Jordan
Columbia Grange, No. 2435
Albany, Ohio

CREAMY CABBAGE SLAW

    1 1/2 c. cream or sour cream
    1/2 c. vinegar
    3/4 c. sugar
    2 tbsp. salt
    1/2 tsp. pepper
    8 qt. shredded cabbage, chilled

Mix cream, vinegar, sugar, salt and pepper in bowl. Add cabbage; mix well. Serve immediately. Yield: 50 servings.

From a Grange Friend

★ ★

MARINATED CARROT SALAD

2 lb. carrots
1 med. onion, sliced thin
1 green pepper, diced
1 1/4 c. thick homemade tomato soup
1/2 c. Wesson oil
1 c. sugar
3/4 c. cider vinegar
1 tbsp. prepared mustard
1 tbsp. Worcestershire sauce
1 tsp. salt
Dash of pepper

Wash, peel and slice carrots. Cook in boiling water until crisp tender; drain. Combine remaining ingredients in bowl; stir in carrots. Cover tightly; place in refrigerator for at least 12 hours before serving. May be refrigerated for at least 3 weeks. Yield: 20 servings.

Mrs. Vetrie Jones
Woodpecker Community Grange
Chester, Virginia

MARINATED COLESLAW

3/4 c. (packed) brown sugar
2 c. vinegar
1 c. water
3 to 4 tbsp. celery seed
3 tbsp. salt
1/2 tsp. pepper
8 qt. shredded cabbage

Mix brown sugar, vinegar, water, celery seed, salt and pepper in bowl. Add cabbage; mix well. Chill for at least 30 minutes before serving. Yield: 50 servings.

From a Grange Friend

DELICIOUS MACARONI AND CHEESE

3 1/2 lb. macaroni
3/4 c. salt
1 c. butter
2 c. flour
1 gal. milk
1 tsp. paprika
1/2 tsp. pepper
2 1/2 lb. cheese, chopped
1 7-oz. can pimento strips, drained (opt.)

Cook macaroni in 3 1/2 gallons boiling water with 1/2 cup salt until tender. Drain in colander; rinse with water. Melt butter in kettle; stir in flour until smooth. Add milk; cook, stirring constantly, until thickened. Add remaining 1/4 cup salt, paprika, pepper and cheese; cook, stirring, until cheese melts. Stir in macaroni; pour into greased baking pans. Garnish with pimento strips. Bake in preheated 375-degree oven for 30 minutes or until brown. Yield: 50-55 servings.

From a Grange Friend

MACARONI AND CHEESE FOR FIFTY

5 lb. macaroni
1/4 c. salt
2 lb. cheese, cut in pieces
6 qt. thin white sauce
1 qt. soft bread crumbs
1/2 c. melted butter

Cook macaroni in 2 gallons boiling water with salt until tender; drain. Add cheese to white sauce; heat, stirring constantly, until cheese is melted. Stir in macaroni; place in greased baking pans. Mix bread crumbs with butter; sprinkle over macaroni mixture. Bake in preheated 375-degree oven until bubbly and brown. Yield: 50 servings.

From a Grange Friend

BEEF BARBECUE

1 8 to 9-lb. boneless lean chuck roast
1/2 c. vinegar
3 c. water
1/2 c. sugar
8 tsp. mustard
1/2 tsp. pepper
1/2 tsp. red pepper
4 1/4-in. slices lemon
4 med. slices onion
1 c. butter
2 c. catsup or chili sauce
1/4 c. Worcestershire sauce

Bake roast as desired until well done. Combine vinegar, water, sugar, mustard, pepper, red pepper, lemon and onion in saucepan; simmer for 30 minutes. Add butter, catsup and Worcestershire sauce; remove from heat. Remove roast from oven; let stand until cool. Cut into 1/4 to 1/2-inch thick slices; arrange in deep platter. Pour sauce over roast; refrigerate for at least 24 hours. Reheat before serving. Yield: 24-32 servings.

Mrs. Blanche Newsom
Wife of Past National Master
Washington, D.C.

BEEF AND NOODLES

5 lb. ground or chopped beef
1/3 c. chopped onion
Beef drippings or butter
3 1/2 qt. meat stock
1 c. flour
Salt
Pepper to taste
1/2 c. chili sauce
2 1/2 lb. noodles

Brown beef and onion in 1/4 cup drippings in kettle, stirring frequently. Add stock; simmer for 30 minutes or until beef is tender. Melt 1/2 cup drippings; stir in flour to make a smooth paste. Stir hot stock into flour mixture; stir back into hot stock. Cook until thickened, stirring constantly. Add salt and pepper to taste;

stir in chili sauce. Stir 1/2 cup salt into 2 1/2 gallons boiling water. Add noodles slowly; cook until tender. Drain in colander, rinsing well with water. Combine noodles and ground beef sauce to serve. Ground beef sauce may be served over noodles, if desired. Add more seasoning, if needed. Yield: 50-55 servings.

From a Grange Friend

NEVER-FAIL MEAT LOAF

3 loaves bread
24 lb. ground beef
1 1/2 gal. milk
16 eggs, beaten
1 lb. butter, melted
1/3 c. Lawry's seasoning salt
1/3 c. onion salt

Toast bread slices until browned; crush or blend into crumbs. Combine all ingredients; mix thoroughly. Line 16 loaf pans with aluminum foil. Pieces may be large enough to fold over loaves and wrap for freezing, if desired. Divide beef mixture equally in loaf pans. Bake in preheated 350-degree oven for 1 hour. Eight loaf pans may be used, if more convenient. Lift loaves from pans after baking; seal tightly. Prepare and fill pans; bake remaining loaves. Three strips bacon may be placed over each loaf before baking, if desired. Yield: 100-120 servings.

Michael T. Curran, W.A.C. Asst. Dir.
Massachusetts

CALICO HAM CASSEROLE

3 c. bread cubes
1/4 c. melted butter
1 c. butter
1 c. flour
1 tsp. salt
1/4 tsp. pepper
2 tsp. dry mustard
2 tsp. Worcestershire sauce
6 c. milk
2 1/2 c. grated cheese
1 med. onion, grated
4   10-oz. packages frozen mixed
    vegetables, cooked
2 lb. ham, cut into cubes
Minced celery to taste (opt.)

Combine bread cubes and melted butter; set aside. Place 1 cup butter in large saucepan; heat until melted. Add flour, salt, pepper and mustard; stir until smooth. Stir in Worcestershire sauce and milk; cook over medium heat, stirring constantly, until thickened. Add cheese; stir until melted. Remove from heat. Add remaining ingredients; mix well. Pour into 2 greased 18 x 8 x 2-inch baking pans. Bake in preheated 350-degree oven for about 40 minutes or until brown. Yield: 25 servings.

Mrs. Edward Andersen
Wife of State Master
Waterloo, Nebraska

LITTLE HAM LOAVES

1 loaf bread
2 doz. eggs, beaten
Milk
20 lb. ground ham
10 lb. ground beef
1 c. catsup
Brown sugar to taste

Break bread into fine pieces. Stir in eggs and enough milk to make a batter. Add ground ham and ground beef; mix well. Shape into small loaves, using a custard cup or ice cream scoop; place in baking pans. Bake in preheated 350-degree oven for 45 minutes. Combine catsup and brown sugar; brush over tops of loaves. Bake for 15 minutes longer. A topping made with crushed pineapple may be used, if desired. Yield: 100-105 servings.

Mrs. J. William Steel
Big Knob Grange, No. 2008
Freedom, Pennsylvania

CHICKEN TAMALES
(Recipe over 90 years old)

1   4 to 5-lb. chicken
2 c. yellow cornmeal
1 lg. onion, diced
1 tsp. red pepper
1 c. catsup
1 1/2 tsp. chili powder
2 1/2 c. thick tomato soup
1 1/2 c. butter
1/4 c. Worcestershire sauce
1 tsp. mace
1/2 tsp. cloves
1/2 tsp. allspice
Salt to taste
2 or 3 doz. large dried cornhusks
Olives

Cook chicken in water to cover until tender; remove chicken from broth. Reserve 2 quarts broth. Cut chicken into small chunks. Bring reserved broth to a boil; stir in cornmeal. Cook until thick. Add onion, red pepper, catsup, chili powder, tomato soup, butter, Worcestershire sauce, mace, cloves, allspice and salt. Cook until thick, adding more cornmeal, if needed. Wash cornhusks; pour boiling water over husks. Let stand for 15 minutes. Overlap 2 or 3 husks in one hand; spread 1/4-inch thick layer of cornmeal mixture over husks. Add layer of chicken; place olive in center. Spread with another layer cornmeal mixture. Place 1 or 2 husks over top; roll up. Tie ends securely with string or strips of husks. Continue until all ingredients are used. Refrigerate for 1 to 2 days for flavors to blend. Place in steamer; steam until heated through. May be frozen for future use. These tamales are easier if 2 people work together to fill and tie. Yield: 20 servings.

Zella Chatburn
Albion Grange, No. 321
Albion, Idaho

★ ★

VENISON STEW
(Recipe 50 years old)

2 c. salad oil
1 lb. bacon, diced
12 lb. venison, cubed
5 lb. onions, chopped
6 or 7 cloves of garlic, minced (opt.)
3 No. 2 cans solid-pack tomatoes or 6 c.
   fresh tomatoes, chopped
5 lb. carrots, diced
25 lb. potatoes, cut
3 or 4 glasses claret or Burgundy

Heat salad oil in 25-gallon kettle. Add bacon; saute until browned. Add venison, a small amount at a time; saute until browned. Remove part of the venison and keep hot until all is browned, if necessary. Add onions and garlic to venison; stir in tomatoes, carrots, potatoes and wine. Cover; cook slowly until venison is tender, stirring frequently. Do not add water. Other vegetables may be added to stew. Wine vinegar may be substituted for claret, if desired. Yield: 50 servings.

Elsie Craig
Calaveras Grange, No. 715
San Andreas, California

CHICKEN A LA KING

1 lb. mushrooms, sliced thin
3 tbsp. butter
6 qt. cubed cooked chicken
3 qt. medium white sauce
1 sm. can pimento, chopped
4 tbsp. chopped parsley
2 tbsp. salt
2 tsp. pepper

Saute mushrooms in butter until browned. Stir chicken into white sauce. Add mushrooms and remaining ingredients; mix together carefully. Cook slowly, stirring frequently, until heated through. May serve over toast, patty shells or biscuits. Yield: 50 servings.

From a Grange Friend

SCALLOPED CHICKEN FOR A CROWD

1   5-lb. fat hen with giblets
1 carrot
1 onion
5 tsp. salt
1 1/2 loaves 2 day-old bread
Butter
6 sprigs of parsley, chopped
1 med. onion, chopped
2 lg. stalks celery with tops, chopped
Dash of pepper
1 tsp. poultry seasoning
1 c. sifted flour
1 c. milk
4 eggs, slightly beaten
1 c. bread crumbs

Place hen in large kettle; add carrot, onion, 2 teaspoons salt and 2 quarts boiling water. Cover; simmer for 2 hours and 30 minutes or until chicken is tender. Cool chicken in broth. Remove chicken from broth; grind skin. Cut chicken into bite-sized pieces. Cook giblets in boiling water until tender; drain broth into kettle containing broth. Strain broth; chill. Grind giblets. Remove crusts from bread; grind crusts for later use. Crumble bread into large bowl. Melt 1/2 cup butter in heavy pan. Add parsley, chopped onion and celery; cook, stirring, for 5 minutes. Add to bread crumbs; mix lightly with fork. Add giblets, 1 teaspoon salt, pepper and poultry seasoning. Skim fat from chicken stock; reserve. Heat chicken broth; do not boil. Add 6 tablespoons chicken broth to bread mixture; mix lightly. Set aside. Add enough butter to reserved chicken fat to make 1 cup, if needed. Melt fat mixture in large saucepan; stir in flour until smooth. Add 4 cups chicken broth and milk gradually; stir in remaining 2 teaspoons salt. Cook, stirring constantly, until thick. Stir small amount of sauce into eggs; stir back into sauce. Cook over low heat for 3 to 4 minutes, stirring constantly; stir in ground skin. Place bread mixture in large, greased casserole; pour half the sauce over bread mixture. Add chicken; add remaining sauce. Melt 1/4 cup butter; mix with bread crumbs. Sprinkle over casserole. Bake in preheated 375-degree oven for 20 minutes or until heated through and golden brown. May be frozen. Yield: 20 servings.

Glorene Breckenridge
Lincoln Grange, No. 295
Pond Creek, Oklahoma

SCALLOPED CHICKEN WITH GIBLET DRESSING

2   5 to 6-lb. hens
2 c. flour
8 eggs, beaten
3 qt. milk
3 qt. giblet dressing
4 c. cracker crumbs

Cook chickens in boiling salted water until tender. Lift chickens from broth; set broth aside to cool. Remove skin and bones from chickens; grind skin through food chopper. Dice chickens; set aside. Remove 2 cups fat from chicken broth; pour fat in top of large double boiler. Stir in flour to make a smooth paste. Add eggs, stirring constantly; mix in milk. Cook until thick and smooth, stirring constantly. Stir in ground chicken skin. Spread giblet dressing in 2 large baking pans. Pour a layer of sauce over dressing, using half the sauce. Arrange diced chicken over sauce; top with remaining sauce. Cover with cracker crumbs. Bake in preheated 350-degree oven for 30 minutes or until heated through and bubbly. Sprinkle milk over crumbs, if top seems dry. Chicken stock may be used as liquid in giblet dressing, if desired. Yield: 50 servings.

Mrs. Bruce T. Metzger
Union Center Grange, No. 784
Canton, Pennsylvania

★ ★

TURKEY PIE

    1   25-lb. turkey, roasted and boned
    8 c. flour
    2 gal. turkey broth
    2 1/2 c. thick celery soup
    4 No. 303 cans sm. onions
    4 pkg. frozen peas
    1 c. ground fresh celery
    1/2 c. grated onions
    1 c. butter
    12 c. bread crumbs
    Salt and pepper to taste
    Poultry seasoning to taste

Break turkey into small pieces; place in large baking pan. Place flour in large kettle; stir in broth until smooth. Add soup and onions. Cook, stirring, until thick. Stir in peas just before removing from heat. Pour over turkey. Saute celery and onions in butter until golden. Add to bread crumbs; add seasonings. Toss until well blended. Spread on cookie sheets. Bake in preheated 350-degree oven until browned. Sprinkle over sauce in baking pan. Bake until heated through. Yield: 50 servings.

Margaret Thomson
El Camino Grange, No. 462
Gerber, California

GRANDMA WELLES' RAISED BISCUITS
(Recipe 75 to 100 years old)

    3 c. milk
    1 cake yeast
    1 c. lard
    1 c. sugar
    1/2 tsp. (about) salt
    Flour

Mix all ingredients, using enough flour to make soft dough; let rise until doubled in bulk. Knead on floured surface, adding more flour, if needed. Roll out; cut with biscuit cutter. Place in greased pans; let rise until doubled in bulk. Bake in preheated 350-degree oven for 15 minutes. Reduce temperature to 325 degrees; bake until done. Yield: 50 biscuits.

Ora Mae Gaylord
Tunxis Grange, No. 13
Bloomfield, Connecticut

JITNEY SUPPER SPECIAL BISCUITS

    10 lb. flour
    10 oz. baking powder
    3 oz. salt
    3 lb. fat
    4 qt. milk

Sift dry ingredients together in bowl. Add fat; mix with pastry blender. Add milk; mix well. Dough should be soft and light. Roll out on floured board; cut with biscuit cutter. Place on greased baking sheets.

Bake in preheated 375-degree oven for 12 to 15 minutes. Yield: 150 biscuits.

Arline Marsh
Trout Lake Grange, No. 210
Trout Lake, Washington

COFFEE FOR ONE HUNDRED

    8 c. coffee
    4 1/2 gal. water

Tie 2 cups coffee loosely into each of 4 pieces of double thickness cheesecloth, allowing room for coffee to swell. Bring water to a boil in large kettle. Drop in bags of coffee; reduce heat. Cover. Simmer for 10 to 13 minutes or to desired strength; do not boil. Remove bags; serve at once.

From a Grange Friend

BEVERLY'S FRUIT PUNCH
(Recipe 75 years old)

    4 c. sugar
    8 c. water
    1 box strawberries
    1 pineapple, shredded
    4 bananas, sliced
    1 c. fruit juice
    Juice of 6 oranges
    Juice of 3 lemons
    2 qt. Apollinaris

Mix sugar and water in saucepan; boil for 5 minutes. Chill. Hull strawberries; cut into small pieces. Mix sugar syrup, strawberries, pineapple, bananas, juices and Apollinaris; add ice. Stir in enough water to make punch desired strength. One cup maraschino cherries may be added, if desired. Yield: 25 servings.

Mrs. Beverly L. Martin
Bloomingburg Grange, No. 1197
Bloomingburg, New York

PINK WEDDING PUNCH

    4   3-oz. packages pink lemonade
        powder mix
    4 qt. iced water
    2   46-oz. cans pineapple juice
    2   46-oz. cans Hawaiian punch
    2   1-qt. bottles Seven-Up or ginger ale
    1 qt. pineapple sherbet

Combine lemonade mix and iced water. Add pineapple juice and Hawaiian punch; stir thoroughly. Add Seven-Up. Scoop sherbet into punch bowl; pour punch over sherbet slowly. Punch will be frothy. Yield: One hundred 4-ounce servings.

Mrs. Glen Garber
Spring Creek Grange, No. 951
Reardan, Washington

well. Chill. Add ginger ale and sherbet just before serving. Yield: 30 servings.

Mrs. William B. Brown
Whetstone Grange, No. 2628
Bucyrus, Ohio

DELICIOUS WEDDING PUNCH

    2 c. sugar
    2 c. water
    1 c. strained fresh lemon juice, chilled
    2 c. strained fresh orange juice, chilled
    1 46-oz. can apricot juice, chilled
    2 46-oz. cans pineapple juice, chilled
    2 qt. ginger ale, chilled

Mix sugar and water in saucepan; heat until sugar is dissolved. Chill. Stir in juices; refrigerate until ready to serve. Add ginger ale; serve. Yield: 50 servings.

Bessie Wischmeyer
Sodom Grange
Bryan, Ohio

TEAHOUSE PINEAPPLE PUNCH

    1 qt. water
    1/2 c. tea
    3 qt. cold water
    2 bunches fresh mint
    1/4 c. sugar
    2 1-pt. 2-oz. cans pineapple juice
    2 c. orange juice
    2 c. lemon juice
    2 c. grapefruit juice
    2 sm. jars maraschino cherries
    1 qt. ginger ale
    1 qt. club soda

Bring 1 quart water to a full rolling boil. Remove from heat and immediately add tea; let stand for 4 minutes. Stir; strain into container holding 3 quarts cold water. Crush mint leaves and stems in sugar in large mixing bowl, using a wooden spoon. Stir in fruit juices and cherries. Add tea; mix well. Pour over ice ring in punch bowl when ready to serve. Add ginger ale and club soda carefully; add more sugar, if desired. Yield: About 70 punch-cup servings.

Photograph for this recipe above.

PARTY PUNCH

    6 tbsp. lemon juice
    1 1/2 c. sugar
    1 1/2 c. water
    1 1-qt. 14-oz. can orange juice
    1 1-qt. 14-oz. can pineapple juice
    1 1/2 qt. ginger ale
    1 1/2 qt. pineapple sherbet

Combine lemon juice, sugar and water; stir until sugar is dissolved. Add orange juice and pineapple juice; mix

BROWNIE BARS

    8 1-oz. squares chocolate
    1 1/3 c. butter
    4 c. sugar
    1 1/2 c. eggs
    2 c. all-purpose flour
    1 tbsp. salt
    1 tbsp. vanilla extract
    4 c. coarsely chopped nuts

Melt chocolate and butter over hot water. Add sugar; mix well. Beat in eggs. Add flour, salt, vanilla and nuts; mix thoroughly. Spread evenly in greased and floured 17 x 11-inch baking pan to about 3/4-inch thickness. Bake in preheated 325-degree oven for 25 to 40 minutes. Remove pans from oven when mixture is still slightly sticky but not doughy; cool slightly. Cut into 1 x 2-inch bars.

From a Grange Friend

DIFFERENT SAND TARTS
(Recipe about 175 years old)

    2 lb. flour
    2 lb. sugar
    1 1/4 lb. butter
    3 eggs
    Finely chopped blanched almonds
    Cinnamon sugar

Place flour and sugar in bowl; cut in butter. Add eggs; mix thoroughly. Roll out thin, using additional sugar instead of flour. Sprinkle with desired amount of almonds; press lightly into dough. Sprinkle with cinnamon sugar. Cut into desired shapes with sharp knife; place on greased cookie sheet. Bake in preheated

★ ★

400-degree oven until golden brown. Yield: About 200 cookies.

Edith Rogers
Floris Grange, No. 749
Herndon, Virginia

DROP CAKES
(Recipe about 175 years old)

2 c. sugar
4 c. flour
1 c. butter
5 eggs, slightly beaten
1 tsp. soda
1 c. sour cream
Grated rind and juice of 2 lemons
1 lb. raisins
1/2 lb. currants
1/2 lb. citron, chopped

Place sugar and flour in bowl; cut in butter. Add eggs; mix well. Dissolve soda in sour cream; stir into sugar mixture. Add lemon rind and juice. Add fruits; mix thoroughly. Drop by teaspoonfuls on greased cookie sheet. Bake in preheated 375-degree oven until golden brown. Yield: About 100 cookies.

Edith Rogers
Floris Grange, No. 749
Herndon, Virginia

LIBBY'S COOKIES
(Recipe 125 years old)

2 c. shortening
2 c. sugar
2 c. molasses
2 eggs
2 tbsp. ginger
1/2 tsp. salt
1 c. milk
2 tbsp. vinegar
2 tbsp. soda
Flour

Cream shortening and sugar in large bowl; stir in molasses, then eggs. Add ginger, salt and milk; mix well. Combine vinegar and soda; stir into molasses mixture. Stir in enough flour to make stiff dough. Roll out on floured board, rolling thin for crisp cookies or thick for soft cookies. Cut with large cookie cutter; place on greased cookie sheets. Bake in preheated 350-degree oven for about 15 minutes or until done. Remove from cookie sheet; cool. Yield: 6 dozen.

Violet M. Chase
Cape Horn Grange
Bonneville, Washington

PARTY SUGAR COOKIES
(Recipe about 75 years old)

1 c. lard
2 c. sugar

2 eggs, well beaten
1 tsp. soda
1 c. sour milk
Pinch of salt
Flavoring to taste
Flour

Cream lard and sugar in bowl; stir in eggs. Mix soda and sour milk; stir into creamed mixture. Add salt and flavoring; mix. Add enough flour to make stiff dough; mix well. Roll out on floured surface; cut with cookie cutter. Place on greased cookie sheets. Bake in preheated 425 to 450-degree oven for about 10 minutes or until done. Remove from cookie sheet; cool. Yield: 5 dozen.

Mrs. Robert George
Willard Grange, No. 1440
New Castle, Pennsylvania

SPECIAL GINGER COOKIES
(Recipe about 85 years old)

2 c. molasses
1 c. sugar
1 c. lard or butter
1 c. sour milk
2 eggs
2 tsp. soda
1 tsp. ginger
Flour

Mix all ingredients in order listed, adding enough flour to make soft dough. The softer the dough the better the cookie. Roll out on floured surface; cut with cookie cutter. Place on greased cookie sheets. Bake in preheated 425 to 450-degree oven for about 10 minutes or until done. Remove from cookie sheet; cool. Yield: 6 dozen.

Mrs. Wendell Dean
Willard Grange, No. 1440
New Castle, Pennsylvania

OLD-FASHIONED LEMON PIES
(Recipe 65 to 70 years old)

8 c. water
Juice of 3 lemons
4 c. sugar
1/4 c. cornstarch
4 egg yolks, beaten
Dash of salt
Butter
4 baked pie shells, cooled
Whipped cream or meringue

Mix water, lemon juice, sugar and cornstarch in saucepan; cook until clear. Add small amount of the hot mixture to egg yolks, stirring constantly; stir back into hot mixture. Add salt and small amount of butter; mix well. Pour into pie shells; cool. Cover pies with whipped cream. Yield: 24 servings.

Hazel Bills Butterfield
Loch Lomond Grange, No. 76
Golden, Colorado

Special Diabetic Recipes

This section of special diabetic and dietetic recipes is the result of requests from our Grange members for suggestions on how to prepare special dishes for diabetic family members and friends. Many weight-conscious Grange members have also asked for help with low-calorie dishes suitable for dieting. We feel that these recipes will be a great help in planning special diets for family members so that meals will be more interesting and varied. If under the care of a doctor, show him the recipes and see if they meet his approval. In most cases, we are sure that they will.

Sticking to a low-sugar or a low-calorie diet is difficult for anyone, but it is especially hard for children. They see their friends eating cookies, cakes and other delicious desserts and sweets. For your diabetic child's next birthday, use the recipe for *Chocolate Cake* and top it with *Fluffy Frosting* — then watch his eyes light up when you tell him that he can eat this cake because it was made just for him and is on his diet! On other occasions, fix *Applesauce Cookies* or *Chocolate-Walnut Brownies* for a delicious surprise.

Americans are becoming more and more weight conscious. Pilgrims, pioneers and settlers may have missed the ready availability of sweets, but now, sweets are almost too available for our own good. But, with recipes in this section such as *Refrigerator Cheesecake* and *Coconut Custard Pie*, you can enjoy desserts and still stay on your diet. When dieting friends come to supper, they won't have to turn down scrumptious *Cherry Tarts* in *Dieter's Pie Crust* topped with *Mock Whipped Cream*. Everyone will want to know your recipes for preparing such rich foods without exceeding your diet allowance.

Suggestions for using these recipes successfully include being sure to measure carefully, oiling pans with spray-on nonstick coatings and noticing when a recipe calls for a liquid or a granulated diet sweetener. If a recipe does not have the calorie count listed, you can be sure the amount is nominal.

★ ★

LOW-CALORIE CREAMY FRENCH DRESSING

1/2 sm. onion, chopped
1 sm. can diet tomato juice
1 tbsp. Worcestershire sauce
2 tsp. salt
1 tsp. dry mustard
1/2 tsp. pepper
1/2 tsp. paprika
1/8 tsp. garlic powder
2 tsp. Sugar Twin
1 pkg. MCP pectin (opt.)
1 1/2 c. salad oil

Place onion and 1/2 cup tomato juice in blender container; process until onion is pureed. Add remaining tomato juice, Worcestershire sauce and remaining ingredients except oil; process until blended. Add oil, 1/2 cup at a time, blending well after each addition. Place in container; cover. Refrigerate; dressing will not separate.

Mrs. Jenny Grobusky, D.W.A.
National Grange
Walhalla, South Carolina

The following recipes were submitted by Mrs. Mattie M. Valline, Quincy Grange, No. 990, Quincy, Washington.

APRICOT-OATMEAL BREAD

2 c. biscuit mix
1 c. oatmeal
1/4 tsp. salt
1 tsp. baking powder
1/2 c. dried apricots, chopped
1/3 c. coarsely chopped walnuts
4 1/2 tsp. Sucaryl
1 egg, beaten
1 1/4 c. milk

Combine biscuit mix, oatmeal, salt, baking powder, apricots and walnuts. Combine Sucaryl, egg and milk; blend well. Add to dry mixture; mix well. Turn into a greased 9 x 5-inch loaf pan or 2 small loaf pans. Bake in preheated 350-degree oven for 1 hour. Yield: 20 servings, 94 calories each.

APPLE CUSTARD PIE WITH LO-CAL SHELL

1/3 c. flour
1/8 tsp. salt
2 tbsp. shortening
1/2 c. dry cottage cheese
3 c. apple slices
3 eggs, beaten
1 tbsp. Sucaryl
1 1/2 c. skim milk
1/2 tsp. vanilla extract
Nutmeg to taste

Combine flour and salt; cut in shortening. Force cheese thru a sieve; add to flour mixture. Mix until dough forms a ball. Roll out on lightly floured board. Turn into 9-inch pie plate. Fill crust with apple slices. Combine eggs with Sucaryl, milk and vanilla; mix well. Pour over apples. Sprinkle with nutmeg. Bake in preheated 350-degree oven for 40 to 50 minutes or until knife inserted in center comes out clean. 178 calories each serving.

APPLESAUCE-PUMPKIN PIE

1 c. pumpkin
1 c. unsweetened applesauce
1 tbsp. Sucaryl
1/2 c. non-dairy Pream
1 1/2 tsp. cinnamon
1 1/2 tsp. nutmeg
1/2 tsp. salt
4 eggs, well beaten
1 c. boiling water
1 9-in. unbaked pie shell

Combine pumpkin, applesauce, Sucaryl, Pream, spices and salt; beat well. Add eggs and boiling water; mix well. Pour into pie shell. Bake in preheated 425-degree oven for 10 minutes. Reduce temperature to 350 degrees; bake until knife inserted in center comes out clean.

BAKED VANILLA PUFF

5 tsp. dietetic margarine
3 tbsp. flour
1/4 tsp. salt
3/4 c. skim milk
1 1/2 tsp. vanilla extract
Granulated or liquid no-calorie sweetener
    to equal 4 tbsp. sugar
3 eggs, separated

Melt margarine in medium-sized saucepan; blend in flour and salt. Stir in milk, vanilla and half the sweetener. Cook, stirring constantly, over low heat until sauce thickens and boils for 1 minute. Cool. Beat egg whites until foamy and doubled in volume; sprinkle in remaining sweetener. Beat until meringue stands in firm peaks. Beat egg yolks well; stir in cooled sauce. Fold in meringue. Pour into ungreased souffle dish. Cut deep circle in mixture with knife. Set dish in baking pan; pour boiling water into pan to depth of 1 inch. Bake in preheated 350-degree oven for 45 minutes or until firm and golden. Serve at once. Yield: 6 servings, 109 calories each.

★ ★

The following recipes were submitted by Mrs. Melvin Stepon, Quincy Grange, No. 990, Quincy, Washington.

Helpful Hints for These Recipes: Measure carefully. Always soften gelatin in at least 1 tablespoon cold water. Always check with Doctor when using any sweetener. Sugar Twin has both white and brown sugar substitutes. Sweet Ten, S & W and MCP have recipes for canning fruits and you may write for them. Where recipes call for lightly oiled or greased dishes, you may use Cooking Ease as directed on can as this has no calorie count.

COOKED DRESSING

1 egg
2 tsp. liquid sweetener
1 tsp. dry mustard
1/8 tsp. paprika
1/4 c. lemon juice
1 1/2 tsp. salt
3/4 c. salad oil
4 tbsp. cornstarch
1 c. water
1/4 c. cider vinegar

Place egg, sweetener, mustard, paprika, lemon juice, salt and salad oil in mixing bowl; do not mix. Mix cornstarch and 1/2 cup water to a smooth paste in top of double boiler over hot water. Cook over low heat, stirring constantly and adding remaining water and vinegar gradually. Cook until clear. Add to ingredients in bowl, beating constantly on medium speed of electric mixer until smooth. Cool. May add 1/8 teaspoon curry powder for Indian Dressing or substitute 1/2 cup unsweetened pineapple juice for 1/2 cup water for Fruit Dressing.

FRUIT SALAD DRESSING

1 tbsp. unflavored gelatin
1 tbsp. cold water
1/4 c. boiling water
1/4 tsp. salt
1 tbsp. liquid sweetener
1/4 c. lemon juice
1/8 tsp. dry mustard
1/2 tsp. paprika

Soften gelatin in cold water; dissolve in boiling water. Combine remaining ingredients; mix with dissolved gelatin. Store in refrigerator. Dressing will become firm; may soften by reheating, if desired. Yield: 1/2 cup, 6 calories.

APPLE CIDER SALAD

1 1/2 tbsp. unflavored gelatin
1/3 c. cold water
2 tsp. liquid sweetener
2 c. apple cider or juice
2 tbsp. lemon juice
1/2 tsp. salt
2 med. apples, finely chopped
1/2 c. finely chopped celery

Soften gelatin in cold water. Combine sweetener, cider, lemon juice and salt; heat. Add to the softened gelatin, stirring until gelatin dissolves. Cool until mixture begins to thicken. Fold in apples and celery. Place in 4-cup mold. Chill until set. Yield: 8 servings, 57 calories.

CRANBERRY JELLY

2 c. fresh cranberries
1/2 c. water
1 1/2 tbsp. liquid sweetener
2 tbsp. lemon juice
1 tbsp. unflavored gelatin

Cook cranberries in water until skins pop. Cool slightly; force through strainer. Add sweetener and lemon juice and cook for about 1 minute longer. Remove from heat. Soften gelatin in 1/4 cup water; add to hot cranberry mixture. Stir until dissolved. Turn into mold; chill until set. Yield: 6 servings, 25 calories each.

CRANBERRY-ORANGE RELISH

2 c. cranberries
1 orange
3 tsp. liquid sweetener

Wash and sort cranberries; remove orange seeds. Grind cranberries and orange with peel through food grinder, using finest blade. Stir in sweetener; chill before serving.

JELLIED SPRING VEGETABLE SALAD

1 tbsp. unflavored gelatin
1/4 c. cold water
2 c. boiling water
1/2 tsp. salt
1/4 c. lime juice
2 tbsp. liquid sweetener
Green food coloring
1 c. diced peeled cucumber
1 c. sliced radishes
1/4 c. sliced scallions

Soften gelatin in cold water; dissolve in boiling water. Add salt, lime juice, sweetener and enough food coloring to tint desired color. Chill until mix begins to thicken. Fold in remaining ingredients. Place in 5-cup mold; chill until set. Yield: 8 servings, 17 calories each.

★ ★

MOLDED SALAD

    2 env. unflavored gelatin
    1 pkg. lime-flavored unsweetened Kool-Aid
    3 1/2 c. boiling water
    1/2 pt. cottage cheese
    1 tbsp. liquid sweetener
    1 8-oz. can unsweetened crushed
        pineapple

Combine gelatin and Kool-Aid in bowl; add boiling water. Stir until dissolved. Chill until thickened. Stir in cottage cheese, sweetener and pineapple. Chill until set. May substitute flavored dietetic gelatin for Kool-Aid, sweetener and unflavored gelatin. Use pineapple canned in its own juice.

NO-SUGAR FRUIT SALAD

    1 can pineapple chunks canned in own juice
    1 tbsp. cornstarch
    1 tsp. sweetener
    1 tsp. vanilla extract
    Banana slices

Drain juice from pineapple into saucepan. Stir a small amount of juice into cornstarch; return to saucepan. Cook until thickened, stirring constantly. Stir in sweetener and vanilla. Dice pineapple chunks. Combine pineapple and equal amount of banana slices. Pour thickened juice over fruits; toss until well coated. Refrigerate until well chilled.

CHOCOLATE SAUCE

    1 tbsp. butter or diet margarine
    2 tbsp. cocoa
    1 tbsp. cornstarch
    Dash of salt
    1 c. skim milk
    2 tsp. liquid sweetener
    1/2 tsp. vanilla extract

Melt butter in saucepan. Combine cocoa, cornstarch and salt; blend with melted butter until smooth. Add milk and sweetener; cook over moderate heat, stirring constantly, until slightly thickened. Stir in vanilla. Place saucepan in ice water; stir for about 5 minutes or until cold. Yield: 1 cup, 16 calories.

LEMON SAUCE

    1 tbsp. cornstarch
    1/8 tsp. salt
    2 tsp. liquid sweetener
    1 c. water
    1 tbsp. grated lemon rind
    3 tbsp. lemon juice
    2 tbsp. butter or diet margarine
    Drop of yellow food coloring

Combine cornstarch and salt in saucepan. Blend in sweetener and water gradually; cook over medium heat, stirring constantly, until thickened. Remove from heat; blend in lemon rind, lemon juice, butter and coloring. Cool. Grated orange rind and orange juice may be substituted for lemon rind and juice for orange sauce; add 1/8 teaspoon cinnamon. Yield: Five 1/4-cup servings, 48 calories each.

MOCK MAPLE SYRUP

    1 tsp. maple flavoring
    1 tsp. liquid sweetener
    1/8 tsp. salt
    1 c. hot water
    1 tbsp. cornstarch
    1/4 c. cold water

Add flavoring, sweetener and salt to hot water in top of double boiler. Blend cornstarch with cold water; add to hot mixture. Cook over boiling water, stirring constantly, until thickened. Yield: 1/2 pint, 3 1/2 calories per tablespoon.

TANGY SEAFOOD COCKTAIL SAUCE

    1/2 c. tomato juice
    1/4 tsp. liquid sweetener
    1 tsp. prepared horseradish
    1 tsp. lemon juice
    1/2 tsp. Worcestershire sauce
    1/2 tsp. salt
    1 tsp. finely chopped parsley

Combine all ingredients; chill to blend flavors. Spoon over seafood cocktails. Yield: 1/2 cup, 3 1/2 calories per tablespoon.

DIETER'S ANTIPASTO

    1/2 lb. mushrooms, sliced
    Low-Calorie Dill Dressing
    1 tsp. salad oil
    3 dill pickles, sliced
    Salt to taste
    1 lb. cooked shrimp
    6 ribs celery
    3 hard-cooked eggs, halved
    1 6 1/2-oz. can tuna, drained
    3 med. tomatoes, cut in wedges
    2 dill pickles, cut in strips
    Lettuce

Combine mushrooms, 1/2 cup dill dressing, oil, half the sliced pickles and salt; chill. Combine remaining sliced pickles, shrimp and 1/4 cup dill dressing; chill. Arrange celery, eggs, tuna, tomatoes and dill pickle strips on lettuce-lined platter. Serve with remaining dressing and marinated mushrooms and shrimp.

★ ★

LOW-CALORIE DILL DRESSING

  1 c. vegetable juice cocktail
  3/4 c. dill pickle liquid
  1 tbsp. chopped onion
  1 clove of garlic, crushed
  1/2 tsp. basil leaves
  Dash of pepper

Combine all ingredients in jar; cover. Chill thoroughly. Shake well before using.

Photograph for this recipe on page 269.

APPLE MUFFINS

  1 2/3 c. all-purpose flour
  2 1/2 tsp. baking powder
  1/2 tsp. salt
  1/4 tsp. nutmeg
  1 tsp. cinnamon
  1 egg, slightly beaten
  2/3 c. skim milk
  1/4 c. oil or melted shortening
  2 tsp. liquid sweetener
  1 c. minced apples

Sift flour, baking powder, salt, nutmeg and cinnamon together. Combine egg, milk, oil and sweetener; blend into flour mixture. Do not overmix; batter will be lumpy. Fold in apples; pour into cupcake liners, filling 2/3 full. Bake in preheated 400-degree oven for 20 to 25 minutes or until done. Yield: 12-14 muffins.

BREAKFAST COFFEE CAKE

  1/4 c. skim milk
  1/3 c. butter or diet margarine
  1 tsp. salt
  1 1/2 tsp. liquid sweetener
  2 pkg. yeast
  1/2 c. lukewarm water
  2 eggs, beaten
  3 c. sifted flour
  1/3 c. chopped walnuts
  Powdered sweetener to taste
  Cinnamon to taste

Scald milk. Add butter, salt and liquid sweetener; stir until butter is melted. Cool to lukewarm. Dissolve yeast in warm water; add to milk mixture. Add eggs and sifted flour; mix well. Spoon into greased 9-inch square cake pan. Let rise, covered, in warm place until doubled in bulk. Sprinkle walnuts, powdered sweetener and cinnamon over top. Bake in preheated 400-degree oven for 20 minutes or until done. Yield: 9 servings, 246 calories each.

APRICOT-DATE BREAD

  1 c. all-purpose flour
  2 tsp. baking powder
  1/4 tsp. soda
  1/2 tsp. salt
  3/4 c. skim milk
  1 egg, beaten
  1/2 c. granular sweetener
  1 tbsp. grated orange rind
  1 tbsp. melted shortening
  1/2 c. whole wheat flour
  1/2 c. finely cut or ground pitted dates
  1/2 c. finely cut or ground dried apricots

Sift all-purpose flour, baking powder, soda and salt together. Combine milk, egg, sweetener, orange rind and shortening. Stir in flour mixture; mix well. Mix whole wheat flour, dates and apricots together; stir into milk mixture until combined. Do not overmix. Pour in oiled loaf pan. Bake in preheated 350-degree oven for 50 minutes or until bread tests done. Turn out on rack to cool.

BANANA-NUT BREAD

  1 tbsp. liquid sweetener
  1 lb. ripe bananas
  2 eggs, well beaten
  1 3/4 c. cake flour
  3 tsp. baking powder
  1/4 tsp. salt
  1/4 c. chopped walnuts

Sprinkle sugar substitute over bananas; blend well. Blend in eggs. Sift flour, baking powder and salt together; blend into banana mixture thoroughly but do not overmix. Stir in walnuts. Pour batter into well-greased 4 x 7-inch pan. Bake in preheated 350-degree oven for 25 minutes. Reduce oven temperature to 300 degrees; bake for 35 to 40 minutes longer or until done.

CRANBERRY-NUT LOAF

  2 c. sifted flour
  1 c. granular sweetener
  1 1/2 tsp. baking powder
  1/2 tsp. soda
  1 tsp. salt
  1/4 c. shortening
  3/4 c. orange juice
  1 tbsp. grated orange rind
  1 egg, well beaten
  1/2 c. chopped nuts
  1 c. fresh cranberries, coarsely chopped

Sift flour, sweetener, baking powder, soda and salt together. Cut in shortening until mixture resembles coarse cornmeal. Combine orange juice, orange rind and egg. Pour into flour mixture; mix just enough to dampen. Fold in nuts and cranberries carefully; spoon into greased loaf pan. Spread corners slightly higher than center. Bake in preheated 350-degree oven for about 1 hour or until crust is golden brown and toothpick inserted in center comes out clean. Cool; store overnight for easy slicing.

★ ★

DATE BREAD

1 c. chopped fine or ground dates
1 tsp. soda
1 c. boiling water
2 c. all-purpose flour
1 tsp. salt
1/4 tsp. nutmeg
1 tbsp. butter or diet margarine
1 c. brown granular sweetener
1 egg
1/2 c. chopped nuts
1/2 tsp. vanilla

Combine dates, soda and water; let cool. Sift flour, salt and nutmeg together. Cream butter and sweetener together; add egg. Add flour mixture and date mixture alternately, blending well. Stir in nuts and vanilla; do not overmix. Pour into lightly oiled loaf pan. Bake in preheated 350-degree oven for 40 to 50 minutes or until done. Turn out on rack to cool.

OATMEAL-PRUNE BREAD

1/2 c. shortening
6 tbsp. brown granular sweetener
1 egg, beaten
2 c. flour, sifted
2 tsp. baking powder
1 c. rolled quick oats
1 1/4 c. buttermilk
1/2 c. chopped walnuts
3/4 c. pitted cooked prunes, chopped fine

Cream shortening; beat in sweetener gradually. Beat in egg. Sift flour and baking powder together; stir in oatmeal. Add to shortening alternately with buttermilk; mix well. Spoon layer of batter into greased loaf pan; sprinkle with walnuts and prunes. Repeat layers until all ingredients are used, ending with a layer of batter. Bake in preheated 350-degree oven for 1 hour and 15 minutes or until bread tests done. Turn out on rack to cool.

ORANGE MARMALADE NUT BREAD

2 c. sifted flour
1 1/2 tsp. baking powder
1/2 tsp. salt
1/3 c. skim milk
1 egg
2 tbsp. butter or diet margarine
1 tbsp. liquid sweetener
1/2 c. dietetic orange marmalade
1/4 c. chopped walnuts

Sift flour, baking powder and salt together into mixing bowl. Combine milk, egg, butter and sweetener. Add to flour mixture; stir only until flour is dampened. Fold in marmalade and walnuts, mixing as little as possible. Spoon batter into lightly greased 9 x 5 x 3-inch pan. Bake in preheated 350-degree oven for 1 hour and 40 minutes or until done. Cool before slicing. Yield: 12 servings, 110 calories each.

PUMPKIN NUT BREAD

1 c. brown granular sweetener
1/2 c. shortening
2 eggs
1 c. canned pumpkin
1/4 c. skim milk
2 c. sifted flour
2 tsp. baking powder
1/2 tsp. salt
1/4 tsp. soda
1/2 tsp. ginger
1/4 tsp. cloves
1/2 c. chopped walnuts

Cream sweetener and shortening together until light and fluffy. Add eggs, one at a time, beating well after each addition; stir in pumpkin and milk. Sift flour, baking powder, salt, soda, ginger and cloves together; stir into pumpkin mixture. Beat for 1 minute with electric mixer. Stir in walnuts. Turn into greased 9 1/2 x 5 x 3-inch loaf pan. Bake in preheated 350-degree oven for about 55 minutes or until done. Let cool.

BASIC ROLL DOUGH

1 pkg. dry yeast
1/4 c. warm water
1 c. low-fat milk, scalded
1 tsp. granular sweetener
1 tsp. salt
1/4 c. shortening
3 1/2 c. sifted flour
1 egg, beaten

Soften yeast in warm water. Combine milk, sweetener, salt and shortening in bowl; cool to lukewarm. Add 1 1/2 cups flour; beat well. Stir in yeast and egg. Add remaining flour gradually to form soft dough; beat well. Place in greased bowl; turn once to grease surface. Cover; let rise for 1 hour and 30 minutes to 2 hours or until doubled in bulk. Turn out on lightly floured pastry cloth; form into desired shapes. Place on greased baking sheet or in muffin cups; let rise until doubled in bulk. Bake in preheated 400-degree oven for 12 to 15 minutes. Yield: 2 dozen cloverleaf, butter fan or bowknot rolls or 3 dozen Parker House rolls.

RAISIN-CINNAMON ROLLS

1/2 recipe Basic Roll Dough
1/4 c. granular sweetener
2 tbsp. melted butter or diet margarine
1 tsp. cinnamon
1/4 c. raisins

Roll out dough on lightly floured pastry cloth into 16 x 8-inch rectangle. Combine sweetener, butter and cinnamon; spread over dough. Sprinkle with raisins. Roll as for jelly roll; seal edge. Cut in 1-inch slices; place in greased 9 x 9 x 2-inch pan, cut side down. Cover; let rise for about 30 to 40 minutes or until

★ ★

doubled in bulk. Bake in preheated 375-degree oven for 20 to 25 minutes or until golden brown; remove from pan. May ice with 1/2 cup granular sweetener, if desired. May substitute 2 teaspoons grated orange peel for cinnamon, omit raisins and add 2 tablespoons chopped walnuts for Orange Rolls.

PINEAPPLE STICKY BUNS

1/2 recipe Basic Roll Dough
Melted diet margarine or butter
1 8-oz. can diet crushed pineapple
1 tbsp. liquid sweetener
1/2 tsp. (about) cornstarch
1/4 c. walnut halves
8 maraschino cherries, halved

Roll out dough on lightly floured pastry cloth as thin as possible. Cut with cookie or biscuit cutter to make 144 rounds. Spread melted margarine on each; stack 6 rounds together, making 24 stacks. Drain pineapple; reserve juice. Mix sweetener with reserved juice; pour into saucepan. Add cornstarch; mix well. Cook, stirring, until thickened. Remove from heat; stir in pineapple and 1/4 cup melted margarine. Arrange walnut halves and cherry halves in bottom of 2-quart tube pan or bundt pan; spoon pineapple mixture over walnuts and cherries. Place roll stacks on edge around pan over pineapple mixture; let rise for 25 minutes. Bake in preheated 375-degree oven for 20 to 25 minutes or until done. Turn out on large plate to cool. One-half cup brown granular sweetener may be substituted for liquid sweetener and cornstarch.

SWEET ROLLS

Butter or diet margarine
1/2 tsp. salt
1/2 c. skim milk, scalded
1 pkg. dry yeast
1 tsp. liquid sweetener
Flour
Dietetic fruit conserve or peach preserves
40 raisins

Add 1 teaspoon butter and salt to milk; let cool to lukewarm. Sprinkle in yeast; stir until dissolved. Stir in sweetener and 1 cup flour; mix well. Sprinkle 3 to 4 tablespoons flour onto pastry cloth; turn out dough on cloth. Knead well. Grease small mixing bowl with 1/8 teaspoon butter; turn dough into bowl. Let rise until doubled in bulk. Place dough on pastry cloth; divide into 8 equal portions. Flatten each portion to 3 inches in diameter; make an indentation in center of each. Place 1 teaspoon fruit conserve and 5 raisins in each indentation; place rolls on lightly greased cookie sheet. Let rise until doubled in bulk. Melt 1/2 teaspoon butter; brush lightly over rolls. Bake in preheated 375-degree oven for 25 minutes or until done. Conserve and raisins may be placed inside rolls and the rolls folded for turnovers, if desired.

CRANBERRY PUNCH

2 qt. low-calorie cranberry cocktail
2 12-oz. cans unsweetened pineapple
   juice
2 tsp. liquid sweetener
1 qt. low-calorie ginger ale, chilled

Combine cranberry cocktail, pineapple juice and sweetener; chill. Stir in ginger ale and ice cubes just before serving. Yield: 3 3/4 quarts, 20 calories per 1/2-cup serving.

BASIC LEMONADE

1 c. lemon juice
8 c. cold water
2 1/2 to 3 tsp. liquid sweetener

Combine all ingredients. Add ice cubes just before serving. Yield: Nine 1-cup servings, 7 calories each.

PINK LEMONADE

1 c. lemon juice
1 c. low-calorie cranberry cocktail
6 c. cold water
4 tsp. liquid sweetener

Combine all ingredients. Add ice cubes just before serving. Yield: 8 cups, 10 calories per cup.

MOCK SPARKLING BURGUNDY

2 c. unsweetened grape juice
2 tsp. liquid sweetener
1 qt. low-calorie lemon-lime carbonated
   beverage, chilled
1 qt. low-calorie ginger ale, chilled

Combine grape juice and sweetener; chill. Stir in carbonated beverage, ginger ale and ice cubes just before serving. Yield: 2 1/2 quarts, 20 calories per 1/2-cup serving.

PARTY PUNCH

1 pkg. unsweetened grape beverage
   powder
2 c. unsweetened pineapple juice
2 tbsp. liquid sweetener
1 qt. sparkling water, chilled

Dissolve grape powder in pineapple juice. Add sweetener; mix well. Chill. Add sparkling water just before serving. Yield: 1 1/2 quarts, 20 calories per 4-ounce serving.

★ ★

DRIED FRUIT CANDY

1/2 c. dried apricots
1 c. raisins
1/2 c. nuts
1/2 tsp. liquid sweetener
Grated coconut

Grind apricots, raisins and nuts. Add sweetener; mix thoroughly. Roll into small balls. Roll balls in coconut and additional ground nuts. Wrap each ball in foil. Store in refrigerator. 30 calories each.

FRUIT AND NUT CANDY

1 tbsp. unflavored gelatin
2 tbsp. cold water
1/2 c. boiling water
2 tbsp. liquid sweetener
2 tsp. unsweetened orange beverage powder
1/2 c. raisins, finely chopped
17 roasted peanuts, finely chopped
1 tbsp. cornstarch
1/4 tsp. powdered sweetener

Soak gelatin in cold water for 5 minutes. Add to boiling water; stir until dissolved. Add liquid sweetener and orange beverage powder. Refrigerate until partially congealed. Add raisins and peanuts; stir until blended. Turn into cold water rinsed 3 x 7-inch shallow pan. Refrigerate until firm. Cut into 1-inch squares. Combine cornstarch and powdered sweetener; sift over squares. 20 calories per piece.

CREAMY FROSTING

1/2 c. cottage cheese, sieved
1 tbsp. liquid sweetener
1/8 tsp. salt
1 tbsp. melted butter

Combine all ingredients, beating until smooth. Flavor as desired; spread on cakes or cookies.

LOW-CALORIE TOPPING

1/2 c. instant nonfat dry milk
1/2 c. ice water
1 tsp. liquid sweetener
1/2 tsp. vanilla extract

Combine milk, ice water and sweetener in mixing bowl. Beat with mixer at high speed until consistency of whipped cream. Add vanilla. May be spread on pie and garnished with grated lemon rind. Yield: 8 servings, 102 calories.

MOCK WHIPPED CREAM

1/2 c. instant nonfat dry milk
1/2 c. cold water

2 tbsp. lemon juice
2 tsp. liquid sweetener

Combine all ingredients in small mixing bowl. Beat with mixer at high speed until stiff peaks form. Yield: 1 quart or sixteen 12-calorie servings.

CHOCOLATE CAKE

3/4 c. sifted flour
1 tsp. baking powder
1/4 tsp. soda
1/4 tsp. salt
3 tbsp. cocoa
1/4 c. cold coffee
1 egg
1 tbsp. liquid sweetener
1/4 c. water
1 tbsp. salad oil
1 tsp. vanilla extract
1 tsp. butter or diet margarine
Fluffy Frosting

Sift flour, baking powder, soda and salt together. Blend cocoa and coffee. Beat egg; stir in sweetener, water, salad oil and vanilla. Stir into flour mixture, mixing only until smooth. Stir in cocoa mixture. Line 8-inch round layer pan with white paper; grease with butter. Pour batter into pan; cover pan with foil. Place in shallow pan of water. Bake in preheated 350-degree oven for 25 minutes. Remove onto cake rack; cool. Cut layer in half; ice with Fluffy Frosting. Yield: 8 slices, 71 calories each.

FLUFFY FROSTING

1/2 tsp. unflavored gelatin
2 tbsp. water
2 tbsp. instant nonfat dry milk
1/2 tsp. liquid sweetener
1 1/2 tsp. lemon juice
1 tsp. vanilla extract

Soften gelatin in water for 5 minutes; dissolve over hot water. Combine remaining ingredients in small bowl; beat with mixer at high speed for about 15 minutes. Add gelatin very gradually; continue beating until frosting stands in peaks. Total calories, 64.

CHOCOLATE SPONGE ROLL

5 eggs
5 tsp. liquid sweetener
1 tbsp. lemon juice
2 tsp. vanilla extract
1/4 tsp. red food coloring
3/4 c. sifted cake flour
1/4 c. sifted cocoa
1/4 tsp. salt
1 tbsp. cornstarch
1/4 c. granular sweetener
Cream Filling

★ ★

Have eggs at room temperature. Beat eggs in large mixing bowl with mixer at high speed for about 5 minutes or until light. Add liquid sweetener, lemon juice, vanilla and food coloring; continue beating at high speed until stiff peaks form. Sift dry ingredients together 3 times. Blend into egg mixture gradually at low speed; beat for 2 minutes. Line bottom of 15 1/2 x 10 1/2 x 1-inch jelly roll pan with well-oiled waxed paper. Pour in batter; smooth top. Bake in preheated 300-degree oven for 20 minutes or until top springs back when lightly touched. Sift cornstarch with granular sweetener onto sheet of waxed paper. Turn out cake onto waxed paper. Peel waxed paper from bottom of cake; trim off crisp edges. Roll up cake with waxed paper; cool. Unwrap; spread cake with Cream Filling. Rewrap; place in refrigerator for at least 2 hours before serving.

CREAM FILLING

1/4 tsp. salt
2 tbsp. cornstarch
1 c. water
1 tbsp. cream
1 1/2 tsp. liquid sweetener
1 egg yolk, slightly beaten
1/4 tsp. vanilla extract

Place salt and cornstarch in saucepan. Add water; stir until smooth. Add cream and sweetener; cook over medium heat until mixture comes to a boil and is medium thick. Mix small amount of the sauce with egg yolk; return to saucepan. Cook for about 3 minutes longer or until well thickened, stirring constantly. Stir in vanilla; cool.

SPONGE CAKE

7 eggs, separated
1/2 c. cold water
3 tbsp. liquid sweetener
1/2 tsp. vanilla extract
2 tbsp. lemon juice
3/4 tsp. cream of tartar
1 1/2 c. sifted cake flour
1/4 tsp. salt

Have eggs at room temperature. Beat egg yolks in bowl for about 5 minutes or until thick and lemon colored. Combine water, sweetener, vanilla and lemon juice. Add to egg yolks; beat for 10 minutes or until thick and fluffy. Beat egg whites in bowl until foamy. Add cream of tartar; beat until stiff peaks form. Fold into egg yolk mixture carefully. Combine flour and salt in sifter; sift, small amount at a time, over egg mixture, folding in gently. Place in ungreased 9 or 10-inch tube pan. Bake in preheated 325-degree oven for 1 hour and 15 minutes. Yield: 12 servings, 91 calories each.

ORANGE CUPCAKES

1 c. sifted flour
1/2 tsp. salt
3 tsp. baking powder
1 tsp. vanilla extract

Liquid sweetener
1 c. water
2 egg whites
2 1/2 tsp. grated orange rind
1/4 c. Wheaties or other prepared cereal
1/4 tsp. cinnamon
1 tsp. melted butter or diet margarine

Sift flour, salt and baking powder together into bowl. Mix vanilla, 1 tablespoon sweetener and water. Add to flour mixture; stir just until moistened. Beat egg whites until stiff, but not dry; fold into flour mixture, using spatula. Fold in 1 1/2 teaspoons orange rind; pour into muffin pan lined with fluted baking cups. Mix Wheaties, cinnamon, remaining 1 teaspoon orange rind, butter and 1/2 teaspoon sweetener; sprinkle over batter in cups. Bake in preheated 375-degree oven for 30 minutes or until done. Remove from pan immediately; cool on cake rack. Yield: 12 muffins, 42 calories each.

SUNSHINE MARMALADE CAKE

2 c. sifted cake flour
3 tsp. baking powder
1/4 tsp. salt
1/3 c. soft butter or diet margarine
3/4 c. skim milk
4 tsp. liquid sweetener
4 drops of yellow food coloring
1/3 c. egg whites
1 8-oz. jar dietetic orange marmalade

Sift dry ingredients into mixing bowl. Add butter; beat with mixer at low speed for 3 to 5 minutes. Combine milk, sweetener and coloring. Add all except 1/4 cup milk mixture to flour mixture; beat with mixer at medium speed for 30 seconds. Add remaining milk mixture; beat for 1 minute. Add unbeaten egg whites; beat for 1 minute. Mixture will have a curdled appearance. Pour into 8-inch round cake pan lined with greased waxed paper. Bake in preheated 375-degree oven for 20 minutes. Cool in pan for 10 minutes, then remove from pan. Cut cake in half, making 2 semicircles. Place together in layers, using marmalade as filling and topping. Yield: 12 servings, 118 calories each.

PRUNE WHIP

1/2 lb. dried prunes
1 tsp. unflavored gelatin
4 egg whites
2 tsp. lemon juice
2 tbsp. liquid sweetener

Simmer prunes in 1 cup water until soft. Remove pits; force prunes with liquid through food mill. Soften gelatin in 1 tablespoon water; dissolve over hot water. Beat egg whites until foamy; beat in dissolved gelatin, lemon juice and sweetener gradually. Fold into prune pulp; place in mold. Chill until firm. Yield: 6 servings, 98 calories each.

★ ★

APRICOT DESSERT JELLY

3 8-oz. cans dietetic apricots
1 env. unflavored gelatin
6 whole cloves
1 c. boiling water
4 tsp. liquid sweetener
1/8 tsp. salt
2 tsp. lemon juice

Drain apricots; reserve liquid. Press apricots through sieve or food mill. Mix 3/4 cup reserved apricot liquid with gelatin; set aside. Add cloves to boiling water; reduce heat. Cover; simmer for 5 minutes. Remove from heat; remove cloves. Add gelatin to water; stir until dissolved. Add sweetener, salt, lemon juice and apricots; mix well. Pour into 3-cup mold or 6 individual molds; chill until firm.

FOUNDATION RECIPE FOR GELATIN DESSERTS

1 env. unflavored gelatin
1/2 c. cold water
2 tsp. liquid sweetener
1/8 tsp. salt
1 c. boiling water
1/4 c. lemon juice

Sprinkle gelatin over cold water to soften. Add sweetener, salt and boiling water; stir until thoroughly dissolved. Add lemon juice; mix well. Pour into mold; chill until firm. To make orange juice, grape juice, apple cider, pineapple juice or grapefruit juice gelatins in above recipe, use 1/4 cup cold water, 1 cup boiling water and 1/4 cup pure juice or 1 1/2 cups boiling juice, 1 tablespoon lemon juice and 1 to 2 teaspoons liquid sweetener.

GELATIN DESSERT

10 graham crackers, crushed
1 env. unflavored gelatin
1/2 env. unsweetened flavored Kool-Aid
1 1/2 c. boiling water
1 tbsp. liquid sweetener
1/2 c. evaporated milk, chilled
1 sq. unsweetened baking chocolate, shaved
Flaked coconut

Place graham cracker crumbs in 9-inch pie plate; spread crumbs over bottom and up side of plate to rim. Mix gelatin and Kool-Aid in bowl. Add boiling water; stir until dissolved. Stir in liquid sweetener; chill until partially set. Whip evaporated milk until thick. Add gelatin mixture; beat until mixture forms stiff peaks. Pour into crust; sprinkle with chocolate, then small amount of coconut. Cover with an inverted pie plate; refrigerate until served. Instant nonfat dry milk mixed with ice water may be substituted for evaporated milk. Low-calorie flavored gelatin may be used instead of unflavored gelatin and Kool-Aid. Yield: 6 servings.

CHOCOLATE BAVARIAN

1 env. unflavored gelatin
1/4 c. cocoa
1 c. skim milk
2 tsp. liquid sweetener
1/2 tsp. vanilla extract
1 c. instant nonfat dry milk
1 c. ice water

Soften gelatin in 2 tablespoons water. Mix cocoa and skim milk in top of double boiler until smooth; place over boiling water. Add softened gelatin and sweetener; stir until gelatin is dissolved. Remove from heat; add vanilla. Chill until thickened. Combine dry milk and ice water; beat with mixer at high speed until consistency of whipped cream. Beat gelatin mixture until smooth; add to whipped milk gradually. Spoon into lightly oiled 6-cup mold; chill for about 3 hours or until firm. Yield: 10 servings, 64 calories each.

REFRIGERATOR CHEESECAKE

10 crushed graham crackers
1 1/4 tbsp. melted butter or diet
    margarine
1 tbsp. unflavored gelatin
3/4 c. cold water
2 eggs, separated
1/4 tsp. salt
1/2 c. skim milk
1 12-oz. carton cottage cheese, drained
3 tsp. liquid sweetener
1 tbsp. grated lemon rind
4 tbsp. lemon juice
1/2 tsp. vanilla extract
1/2 c. instant nonfat dry milk

Combine cracker crumbs and melted butter; reserve 1/4 cup crumb mixture. Press remaining crumb mixture over bottom of 9-inch square cake pan; chill. Soften gelatin in 1/4 cup cold water. Beat egg yolks in top of double boiler. Add salt and skim milk; cook over boiling water until slightly thickened, stirring constantly. Add gelatin; stir until dissolved. Cool. Rub cottage cheese through a sieve; add to custard. Add 2 teaspoons sweetener, lemon rind, 3 tablespoons lemon juice and vanilla. Combine dry milk and remaining cold water, lemon juice and sweetener; beat for about 10 minutes or until very thick. Beat egg whites until stiff, but not dry; fold in whipped milk. Pour into custard mixture. Pour into cake pan crumb mixture; sprinkle with reserved crumb mixture. Chill for about 4 hours. Yield: 12 servings, 101 calories each.

STRAWBERRY SPONGE

1 env. unflavored gelatin
1/2 c. cold water
1 tbsp. liquid sweetener
1 1/2 tbsp. lemon juice

★ ★

1 pt. strawberries, crushed
2 egg whites

Soften gelatin in water in top of double boiler. Add sweetener and lemon juice; place over boiling water. Heat, stirring, until gelatin dissolves. Remove from heat; stir in strawberries. Chill until mixture begins to thicken, then beat until light and fluffy. Beat egg whites until stiff; fold into gelatin mixture. Spoon into lightly oiled 3-cup mold or 6 individual molds; chill until firm. Yield: 6 servings, 94 calories each.

APPLESAUCE COOKIES

1 3/4 c. flour
1/2 tsp. salt
1 tsp. cinnamon
1/2 tsp. cloves
1/2 tsp. nutmeg
1 tsp. soda
1/2 c. butter or diet margarine
1 tsp. liquid sweetener
1 egg
1 c. unsweetened applesauce
1/3 c. raisins
1 c. All-Bran or quick-cooking rolled oats

Sift dry ingredients together. Cream butter, sweetener and egg until light and fluffy. Add flour mixture alternately with applesauce, mixing well after each addition; fold in raisins and All-Bran. Drop by spoonfuls about 1 inch apart onto oiled cookie sheet. Bake in preheated 350-degree oven for about 20 minutes or until brown. Chopped nuts or ground dates may be substituted for raisins. May add more applesauce, making a thinner batter, and bake in pan. Cut into squares when done. Yield: 4 dozen cookies, 39 calories each.

LEMON COOKIES

1/2 c. shortening
1 tbsp. liquid sweetener
1 egg
1 tbsp. lemon juice
1 tbsp. water
1 tbsp. grated lemon peel
1 tsp. vanilla extract
1/2 c. shredded coconut
2 c. sifted flour
1 tsp. baking powder
1/2 tsp. salt

Cream shortening in small mixing bowl with mixer at high speed. Add sweetener, egg, lemon juice, water, lemon peel and vanilla; beat until thoroughly blended. Mix in coconut. Sift dry ingredients together; add to creamed mixture, mixing thoroughly. Form into roll 2 inches in diameter; wrap in waxed paper. Chill until firm. Cut in thin slices; place on ungreased cookie sheet. Bake in preheated 400-degree oven for 10 to 15 minutes. Yield: 4 1/2 dozen cookies, 35 calories each.

CHOCOLATE-WALNUT BROWNIES

1 sq. unsweetened chocolate
1/3 c. butter or diet margarine
2 tbsp. liquid sweetener
2 tsp. vanilla extract
2 eggs, beaten
1 c. sifted cake flour
1/2 tsp. salt
1/2 tsp. soda
3/4 c. chopped walnuts

Melt chocolate and butter in saucepan over low heat; remove from heat. Add sweetener, vanilla and eggs; stir until well blended. Add cake flour, salt and soda; mix until well blended. Stir in walnuts; pour into greased 8-inch square baking pan. Level batter in pan. Bake in preheated 325-degree oven for 20 minutes; cool. Cut into bars. Yield: 32 brownies, 55 calories each.

CINNAMON COOKIES

5 tbsp. butter or diet margarine
1 c. sifted flour
1/2 tsp. baking powder
1 tsp. liquid sweetener
1 tsp. vanilla extract
1 tbsp. milk, fruit juice or coffee
1 tsp. cinnamon

Cream butter until light and fluffy; blend in flour and baking powder. Combine liquid ingredients. Stir into flour mixture; mix thoroughly. Sprinkle cinnamon over dough; knead on floured surface until dough has streaked appearance. Shape into balls about 1/2 inch in diameter; arrange on cookie sheet. Flatten balls with fork dipped in cold water. Bake in preheated 375-degree oven for 15 minutes or until edges are well browned. Yield: 30 cookies, 30 calories each.

ORANGE REFRIGERATOR COOKIES

1 c. sifted flour
1/4 tsp. baking powder
1/4 tsp. salt
1/4 c. butter or diet margarine
1 3/4 tsp. liquid sweetener
1 tsp. vanilla extract
1/4 c. orange juice
1 tbsp. grated orange rind
1 tsp. grated lemon rind

Sift flour, baking powder and salt together. Cream butter in bowl. Combine remaining ingredients; add to butter alternately with flour mixture. Shape into roll; wrap in waxed paper. Chill until firm. Cut in 1/8-inch slices; place on ungreased cookie sheet. Bake in preheated 400-degree oven for 12 minutes. Yield: 30 cookies, 28 calories each.

★ ★

PEANUT DROP COOKIES

3/4 c. sifted flour
1/2 tsp. salt
1 1/2 tsp. baking powder
1/2 tsp. cinnamon
3/4 c. bran flakes
2 tbsp. chopped peanuts
1/4 c. finely chopped raisins
1 egg
1 tbsp. liquid sweetener
1/4 c. water
1 tbsp. salad oil
1/2 tsp. vanilla extract

Sift dry ingredients together; add bran flakes, peanuts and raisins. Beat egg in bowl; add remaining ingredients. Stir into flour mixture; do not overmix. Drop from teaspoon onto lightly greased cookie sheet. Bake in preheated 350-degree oven for 10 minutes. Yield: 30 cookies, 27 calories each.

SESAME WAFERS

1/3 c. sifted flour
1/4 tsp. salt
1 1/4 tbsp. granular sweetener
2 tbsp. butter or diet margarine
1/2 c. drained cottage cheese
1 tbsp. toasted sesame seed

Combine flour, salt and sweetener in bowl; cut in butter until mixture resembles cornmeal. Place cottage cheese in cheesecloth; squeeze until as much moisture as possible is removed. Press cottage cheese through sieve; add to flour mixture. Stir in sesame seed. Roll out on floured surface until very thin; cut with 1 1/4-inch cookie cutter. Prick each cookie several times with fork; place on greased cookie sheet. Bake in preheated 400-degree oven for 8 minutes or until lightly browned. Yield: 30 cookies, 15 calories each.

LOW-CALORIE ICE CREAM

1 1/2 tsp. unflavored gelatin
2 c. skim milk
1 egg, separated
1 tsp. liquid sweetener
1/8 tsp. salt
1 tsp. vanilla extract

Soften gelatin in 1/4 cup milk. Blend egg yolk with sweetener, salt and remaining milk in saucepan. Cook over low heat, stirring constantly, until mixture coats spoon; remove from heat. Add gelatin mixture; stir until dissolved. Cool. Add vanilla; pour into refrigerator tray. Freeze until firm. Remove to chilled bowl; beat until light. Fold in stiffly beaten, but not dry, egg white; return to freezer tray. Freeze until firm. Yield: 6 servings, 45 calories per 1/2-cup serving.

SMACKEROONS

3 egg whites
1/4 tsp. cream of tartar
1/4 tsp. almond extract
2 tsp. liquid sweetener
3 c. Rice Krispies
1/4 c. flaked coconut

Beat egg whites until foamy. Add cream of tartar; beat until stiff, but not dry. Add almond extract and sweetener; beat until blended. Fold in Rice Krispies and coconut. Drop from teaspoon 1 inch apart on lightly greased cookie sheet. Bake in preheated 350-degree oven for 12 to 15 minutes or until lightly browned. Yield: 2 dozen cookies, 15 calories each.

ORANGE-PINEAPPLE SHERBET

1 6-oz. can frozen unsweetened orange juice concentrate
1 6-oz. can frozen unsweetened pineapple juice concentrate
3 1/2 c. cold water
2 tbsp. liquid sweetener
1 c. instant nonfat dry milk

Set refrigerator control at coldest setting. Mix all ingredients in 2-quart mixing bowl in order listed; beat just enough to blend. Pour into ice cube trays; freeze for 1 to 2 hours or until partially frozen. Remove to large chilled mixing bowl; beat with electric mixer at low speed until softened. Beat at high speed for 3 to 5 minutes or until creamy but not liquid. Pour into freezer containers or ice cube trays; freeze until firm. Yield: Twenty 1/2-cup servings, 58 calories each.

VANILLA FROZEN DESSERT

1 1/4 c. skim milk
1/2 c. evaporated milk
2 tbsp. unflavored gelatin
1/2 c. cold water
1 tbsp. liquid sweetener
2 tsp. vanilla extract
1/2 c. instant nonfat dry milk
1/2 c. ice water

Combine skim milk and evaporated milk in saucepan; heat until scalded. Soften gelatin in cold water. Add sweetener and vanilla; blend into milk. Pour into freezer tray; cool to room temperature. Place in freezer until frozen around edges and thick in center. Remove to chilled bowl; beat until smooth. Combine dry milk and ice water; beat until consistency of whipped cream. Fold into gelatin mixture; pour into 2 freezer trays. Freeze until firm. Yield: Eight 65-calorie servings.

★ ★

DIETER'S PIE CRUST

1/2 c. cottage cheese
1/3 c. sifted all-purpose flour
1/8 tsp. salt
2 tbsp. shortening

Squeeze cottage cheese in cloth until very dry; discard liquid. Press cheese through sieve. Combine flour and salt; cut in shortening. Add cottage cheese. Mix lightly with fork until ball of dough is formed. Turn out on lightly floured pastry cloth; roll to fit 9-inch pie plate. Bake in preheated 400-degree oven for about 20 minutes. One crust is 461 calories.

APPLE PIE

1   6-oz. can apple juice
2 tbsp. cornstarch
1 tbsp. butter or diet margarine
1 tsp. cinnamon
Pinch of salt
5 lg. apples, peeled and sliced
Pastry for 2-crust pie

Combine apple juice and cornstarch; cook until thickened. Add butter, cinnamon and salt. Pour over apples; mix well. Turn into pastry-lined pie pan. Cover with top crust; cut 5 or 6 air vents in top. Bake in preheated 350-degree oven for 45 minutes.

APRICOT GLACE PIE

1 1/4 tsp. unflavored gelatin
2 tbsp. cold water
1 c. dietetic apricot preserves
1/4 c. sherry
1 tsp. liquid sweetener
Pinch of salt
2   1-lb. cans dietetic apricots
1   8-in. baked pie shell

Soften gelatin in cold water. Combine preserves, sherry, sweetener and salt. Bring to a boil. Remove from heat; stir in gelatin until dissolved. Cool until mixture begins to set. Drain apricots; place rounded side up in pie shell. Cover with gelatin mixture; let stand until set. Yield: 6 servings, 187 calories each.

BANANA CREAM PIE

1/4 c. flour
1 1/2 c. cold skim milk
1 tsp. liquid sweetener
1/2 tsp. vanilla
1/8 tsp. salt
1 tsp. lemon juice
1 egg
1 banana
1 baked pie shell

Blend flour with 1/2 cup cold milk. Scald remaining 1 cup milk; add all ingredients except banana and pie shell. Place in top of double boiler; cook, stirring constantly, until thick. Slice banana into pie shell; spread filling over top. Cool. May top with Fluffy Frosting or Mock Whipped Cream, if desired. Yield: 6 servings, 154 calories each.

CHERRY TARTS

1 1/4 c. sifted flour
1/2 tsp. salt
1/3 c. shortening
3 tbsp. (about) ice water
2 c. sour cherries
4 1/2 tsp. cornstarch
1 tbsp. liquid sweetener
1/4 tsp. almond extract

Combine flour and salt in small mixing bowl; cut in shortening. Add water gradually, blending until dough holds together. Roll on lightly floured pastry cloth. Cut circles 4 inches in diameter; place in tart pans. Bake in preheated 450-degree oven for 10 to 15 minutes or until golden. Cool. Drain cherries, reserving juice. Place cornstarch in small saucepan. Blend in reserved cherry juice and sweetener gradually. Cook over low heat, stirring until thickened. Add almond extract; cool. Place cherries in cooled tart shells. Pour cooled cherry juice mixture over cherries. Yield: 8 tarts, 166 calories each.

LIGHT LEMON CHIFFON PIE

1 env. unflavored gelatin
1/4 c. lemon juice
2 tsp. grated lemon rind
4 egg whites
2 egg yolks
1/4 c. water
1/4 tsp. salt
5 tbsp. liquid sweetener
1/4 c. cake flour
3/4 c. boiling water
1/2 c. nonfat dry milk
1/2 c. ice water
1/8 tsp. yellow food coloring
Oil
1/4 c. fine toasted bread crumbs

Combine gelatin, lemon juice and rind; set aside to soften. Beat egg whites until soft peaks form. Beat egg yolks; add water, salt and sweetener. Mix until well combined. Add flour; mix until blended. Stir in boiling water. Place in saucepan over high heat; bring to a boil. Cook, stirring vigorously, for about 1 minute or until thickened. Remove from heat; stir in softened gelatin until well blended. Fold in egg whites. Combine milk, ice water and food coloring; beat until soft peaks form. Fold into filling mixture. Brush 9-inch pie plate with oil; sprinkle crumbs over bottom and around side. Pour filling in pan; chill until firm.

COCONUT CUSTARD PIE

2 2/3 c. skim milk
5 eggs
1 tbsp. liquid sweetener
1/4 tsp. salt
1 tsp. vanilla extract
Nutmeg to taste
3/4 c. toasted unsweetened coconut

Scald milk. Combine eggs, sweetener, salt and vanilla in large mixer bowl; blend well. Add scalded milk slowly, beating lightly. Pour into 8-inch pie plate. Sprinkle with nutmeg. Bake in preheated 450-degree oven for 5 minutes. Reduce temperature to 350 degrees; bake for 15 minutes or until knife inserted in center comes out clean. Cool; garnish with toasted co-conut. May use fresh coconut, if desired. Yield: 6 servings, 146 calories each.

TANGY LEMON CHIFFON PIE

2 tbsp. diet margarine
2 tbsp. cold water
1 1/4 tsp. liquid sweetener
1 1/4 c. graham cracker crumbs

Melt margarine in small saucepan. Remove from heat. Add water and sweetener. Stir in graham cracker crumbs until thoroughly combined. Press onto bottom and side of 9-inch pie pan. Bake in preheated 400-degree oven for 8 to 10 minutes or until deep golden brown. Cool.

★ ★

FILLING

1 env. unflavored gelatin
1/2 c. cold water
2 eggs, separated
1/2 tsp. grated lemon peel
Lemon juice
1 tbsp. liquid sweetener
1/4 tsp. salt
2 or 3 drops of yellow food coloring (opt.)
1/3 c. instant nonfat dry milk
1/3 c. ice water

Soften gelatin in cold water in medium saucepan. Stir in egg yolks, lemon peel, 1/4 cup lemon juice, sweetener, salt and food coloring; blend well. Cook over low heat, stirring constantly, until mixture comes to a boil. Remove from heat; cool. Beat egg whites, nonfat dry milk, ice water and 1 tablespoon lemon juice together at high speed until stiff peaks form. Fold into gelatin mixture. Turn into pie shell; chill until firm. Yield: 8 servings, 110 calories per serving.

PUMPKIN PIE

3/4 c. granulated sugar substitute
1 tsp. cinnamon
1/4 tsp. ginger
2 eggs, beaten
1 1/2 c. pumpkin
1 1/2 c. rich milk or evaporated milk
Few drops of maple flavoring (opt.)
1   9-in. pastry shell

Combine all ingredients except pastry shell; mix well. Pour into pastry shell. Bake in preheated 425-degree oven for 20 minutes. Reduce temperature to 300 degrees; bake until custard is set. May substitute 1 1/4 teaspoons pumpkin pie spice for cinnamon and ginger.

DIABETIC APPLE PIE

1 c. soy-carob flour
1/2 c. shortening
1/4 tsp. salt
2 or 3 tsp. cold water

Mix flour, shortening and salt until crumbly. Add water; mix until dough holds together. Roll 1/2 the dough to fit 9-inch pie plate. Place in plate.

FILLING

4 apples, peeled, cored and sliced
1/3 c. granulated sugar substitute
2 tbsp. flour
1/4 tsp. cinnamon
1/2 tsp. nutmeg
1 tbsp. butter

Combine Filling ingredients except butter; toss until apples are coated. Place in pie shell. Sprinkle with additional tablespoon sugar substitute; dot with butter. Roll out remaining dough; place over pie. Cut air vents in crust. Bake in preheated 400-degree oven for 40 minutes.

DIABETIC JELLY

1 env. MCP low-sugar pectin
1 c. hot water
1 c. fruit juice
1 tbsp. lemon juice
1 tbsp. MCP sweetener

Dissolve pectin thoroughly in hot water. Strain any fruit juice used through a cloth. Pour fruit juice into 2-quart kettle; stir in lemon juice and sweetener. Place over heat; bring to a simmering boil. Stir in pectin mixture; bring to a simmering boil, stirring constantly. Remove from heat. Pour into 2 sterilized 8-ounce jelly glasses; seal tightly. Invert glasses for several minutes, then turn upright. Two and one-half calories per teaspoon.

SUGARLESS JAM

1   1-lb. can water-pack or artificially
     sweetened fruit
MCP liquid sweetener
1 c. MCP low-sugar liquid pectin

Place fruit in small kettle. Crush tree fruits, but not berries. Add 3 teaspoons liquid sweetener if using water-pack fruit; add 2 1/2 teaspoons liquid sweetener if using artificially sweetened fruit. Add liquid pectin; stir well. Mixture will thicken quickly. Place in containers; cover. Store in refrigerator. May place kettle over high heat and bring to a full boil, stirring constantly. Pour into clean, hot 1/2-pint jars; seal. May increase recipe several times, if desired. Two and one-half calories per teaspoon.

TOMATO CATSUP

18 med. tomatoes
1 c. chopped onion
1 1/2 tsp. celery seed
1/2 tsp. mustard seed
1/4 tsp. allspice
1/2 stick cinnamon
1 tbsp. salt
2 tbsp. liquid sweetener
3/4 c. vinegar
1 1/2 tsp. paprika

Wash and drain tomatoes; peel and remove cores. Chop tomatoes; place in kettle. Add onion; cook until soft. Press tomato mixture through sieve; return to kettle. Cook over high heat until reduced to half. Tie celery seed, mustard seed, allspice and cinnamon in bag; add to tomato mixture. Add salt and sweetener; cook until thick. Stir in vinegar and paprika; boil for 5 minutes or to desired thickness. Remove spice bag. Pour catsup into clean hot pint jar; seal at once. Yield: 1 pint, 18 calories per tablespoon.

Food Preservation

Ever since that first New England winter when many Pilgrims starved, families have been devising ways to preserve their harvests for the times when food would be scarce. They learned to preserve in brine the cod and fish they could catch as well as the meat from the livestock on their farms. The Indians taught them to dry strips of venison to make jerky, which lasts for an indefinite period of time and carries easily on long journeys. Today, food preservation is not as much a necessity as it was then. We have refrigerators and freezers and most vegetables and fruits are available in the store, fresh, all the year through. The canning and preserving of foods is more and more being considered an art and a boost to the budget than a necessity.

With ever-spiraling food costs, Americans are renewing their interest in both home gardening and food preservation. Unprecedented numbers of people are learning the age-old, time-tested methods of canning, curing and salting, as well as the newer ways of preserving and freezing. Thanks to the hard-working farmer and his thrifty, busy wife, these arts are still alive for all to learn, enjoy and benefit from.

In canning, there are two methods which the USDA approves as safe for use at home. These are the water bath and steam pressure canning methods. Water bath is safe to use with high-acid foods such as tomatoes, fruits, rhubarb, relishes, and pickles as well as preserves, fruit butters and marmalades. You *MUST NOT* use anything but a steam pressure canner with low-acid foods such as peas, beans, carrots, corn, asparagus, okra, squash, beef, pork, chicken, turkey and fish. Low-acid foods require a higher temperature than 212 degrees in order to kill dangerous bacteria. If you live at an altitude of 1,000 feet or more above sea level, add 1 minute to the processing time per thousand feet if the processing time is 20 minutes or less. For more than 20 minutes, add 2 minutes to the processing time per thousand feet.

★ ★

Some recipes have been altered slightly to conform to USDA canning standards. USDA recommends all foods be processed either by water bath method or pressure canner.

1891 APPLE BUTTER

1 gal. apple cider
3 lb. apples

Boil cider until volume is reduced by half. Peel and core apples; add to cider. Cook slowly, stirring frequently, for 8 to 10 hours or until mixture will adhere to an inverted plate. Pack into hot sterilized jars; seal. Process pints and quarts in simmering water bath for 10 minutes.
In 1891 apple butter was stored in stone jars covered with writing paper cut to fit the jars and thick brown paper tied securely over tops.

Florence D. Andrews
Melrose Grange, No. 434
Roseburg, Oregon

SPICED APPLE BUTTER

3 c. cider or apple juice
4 qt. unpeeled cored chopped apples
3 c. sugar
1 tsp. cinnamon
1 tsp. allspice
1/2 tsp. (heaping) cloves

Pour cider over chopped apples in kettle; simmer until tender. Cool. Sieve or rice apples to remove skins. Add sugar and spices to pulp. Cook, stirring, until butter mounds when dropped onto saucer and there is no liquid around edge of mound. Place in hot sterilized jars; seal. Process in boiling water bath for 10 minutes. May add 1 or 2 tablespoons lemon or orange juice if tartness is needed. Sugar measurement should be no more than 1/2 cup to each cup apple puree.

Grethel Capen, C.W.A. Sec.
American River Grange, No. 172
Rancho Cordova, California

SWEET APPLE BUTTER

1 peck sweet apples
1 gal. cider
6 c. sugar
1 tbsp. cinnamon
1/2 tsp. cloves

Wash and slice apples; place in kettle. Add cider; cook until apples are soft. Press through sieve or food mill. Boil pulp until thick enough to round up in a spoon. Add sugar and spices; cook, stirring frequently, until thick and no liquid runs off when placed on a cold plate. Pour into hot sterilized jars; seal. Process pints and quarts in simmering water bath for 10 minutes.

Mrs. Merle Lewis
Green Grove Grange, No. 1955
Dalton, Pennsylvania

CHIPPED PEARS

2 qt. pears
6 c. sugar
Grated rind and juice of 2 lemons
1 c. chopped crystallized ginger

Peel pears; cut in thin slivers. Place pears and sugar in preserving kettle; let stand for at least 10 hours or overnight. Add lemon rind, lemon juice and ginger; bring to a boil. Reduce heat; simmer for about 2 hours or until pears are clear and mixture is thick. Pack in sterilized jars; seal. Process in boiling water bath for 10 minutes. May be placed in plastic containers and covered tightly, then frozen. One tablespoon ground ginger may be used instead of crystallized ginger. Yield: Eight 8-ounce jars.
Recipe of A. V. Armstrong, taken from an Oak Lawn Grange Cookbook published in 1914.

Oak Lawn Grange, No. 42
Cranston, Rhode Island

LOUISIANA YAM BUTTER

2 c. cooked and sieved Louisiana yams
2 c. apple juice
3 tbsp. lemon juice
Dash of cloves
1/4 to 1/2 tsp. (scant) cinnamon
1/4 to 1/2 tsp. (scant) allspice
1 1/2 to 2 tsp. honey or sugar

Combine all ingredients in large heavy pot or Dutch oven. Cook, stirring frequently, over medium heat for about 10 minutes. Reduce heat to low; continue cook-

★ ★

ing to obtain consistency of apple butter or soft jelly, stirring frequently. Remove from heat; add honey to taste. Serve warm or cold. Refrigerate yam butter in covered container for up to 1 week. Yam butter may be frozen in airtight container for up to 4 to 6 months.

Photograph for this recipe opposite.

CANTALOUPE CONSERVE

6 cantaloupes, peeled
6 oranges, unpeeled
3 lemons, unpeeled
Sugar

Cut cantaloupes in large chunks; cut oranges and lemons in quarters. Put through food chopper, using coarse blade; measure. Add one scant cup sugar for each cup of pulp. Cook to desired thickness, stirring occasionally. Ladle into hot sterilized jars; place caps on jars. Process in simmering water bath for 10 minutes. Yield: 5 half-pints.

Robin Hayes
Davis Lake Grange, No. 501
Spokane, Washington

DELUXE GRAPE CONSERVE
(Recipe 60 years old)

2 1/2 lb. grapes
2 oranges
2 1/2 lb. sugar
1/2 c. chopped walnuts

Wash grapes; do not let stand in water. Drain well. Separate skins from pulp. Place half the skins in saucepan; simmer for 5 minutes. Discard remaining grape skins. Cook pulp until soft; force through colander. Peel oranges; put peelings and grape skins through meat grinder. Chop oranges. Mix pulp, grape skin mixture and oranges together in saucepan. Stir in sugar; boil for 5 minutes. Stir in walnuts. Pack into hot sterilized jars; seal. Process in boiling water bath for 10 minutes.

Mrs. Norman Jahns
Riley Grange
Fremont, Ohio

PEACH NUT CONSERVE

4 c. peeled diced peaches
1/4 c. lemon juice
1 pkg. powdered pectin
Grated rind of 1 lemon
6 c. sugar
1/4 c. chopped maraschino cherries
1/2 c. chopped nuts

Combine peaches, lemon juice, pectin and lemon rind. Place in heavy saucepan; bring to a hard boil. Add sugar; bring to a full rolling boil. Boil for exactly 4 minutes. Add cherries and nuts. Remove from heat;

skim and stir for 5 minutes. Pour into hot sterilized jars; seal immediately. Process in boiling water bath for 10 minutes to complete seal.

Mrs. Alma Irey
Rogue River Valley Grange, No. 469
Grants Pass, Oregon

PEACH CONSERVE

1 lg. tart seedless orange
Peaches
5 1/2 c. sugar
1 c. fresh or canned sm. pineapple chunks
1/2 tsp. salt
1/4 tsp. ground ginger
1/4 tsp. ground nutmeg
1/4 tsp. ground mace

Use sharp knife to remove thin, yellow part of orange peel. Cut remaining orange in paper-thin slices; cut slices in 1/8 to 1/4-inch wedges. Place in saucepan; add just enough water to cover orange. Cook over low heat until peel is soft. Freestone peaches may be scalded 30 seconds to 1 minute in boiling water to loosen skins. Clingstone peaches require peeling with knife. Discard peach pits; cut peaches in 1/2-inch chunks. Measure 7 cups, shaking cup to settle peaches. Place all ingredients, including water used for cooking orange, in kettle or saucepot. Boil rapidly, stirring frequently, until fruits are translucent and very little syrup is left. Do not overcook; conserve will thicken more after canning. Remove foam; quickly pour boiling hot conserve to 1/8 inch of top of jars. Wipe off anything spilled on top or threads of jars. Place dome lids on jars; screw bands tight. One-half cup coarsely chopped almonds, filberts or pecans or 2 to 3 tablespoons apricot cordial or kirsch may be added 5 minutes before conserve is removed from heat. Yield: 7-8 half-pint jelly jars.

Photograph for this recipe opposite.

YAM-APRICOT CONSERVE

1/2 c. diced dried California apricots
3/4 c. sugar
2/3 c. water
2 c. cooked, peeled and diced fresh
    Louisiana yams
1 c. dark raisins
1 c. apple juice
1 tbsp. lemon juice
1/4 c. toasted slivered almonds

Combine apricots with sugar and water in large pot; bring to a boil. Reduce heat; simmer, uncovered, stirring occasionally, for about 10 minutes or until liquid is absorbed and apricots are tender. Add remaining ingredients except almonds; bring to a boil. Stir gently over medium heat for about 5 minutes or until most of liquid has evaporated. Stir in almonds. Serve conserve hot or cold. Conserve may be stored, covered, in refrigerator for up to 1 week. Yield: About 2 cups.

Photograph for this recipe opposite.

★ ★

PRUNE CONSERVE
(Recipe over 60 years old)

10 lb. prunes
2 lb. raisins
3 oranges
13 c. sugar
1 lb. walnuts, shelled and chopped

Put prunes, raisins and oranges through food chopper. Place in kettle. Add remaining ingredients; mix well. Cook, stirring constantly, for 20 minutes. Ladle into hot sterilized jars; seal. Process in simmering water bath for 10 to 15 minutes. Yield: 12 pints.

Mary E. Gosney
Goldendale Grange, No. 49
Goldendale, Washington

RHUBARB CONSERVE
(Recipe 60 years old)

3 qt. chopped rhubarb
12 c. sugar
1 lg. orange
1 lb. raisins
1/4 lb. chopped walnuts

Place rhubarb in kettle; cover with sugar. Let stand overnight. Mix well. Bring to a boil; cook for 30 minutes. Cut unpeeled orange into quarters; remove seeds. Grind orange; add to rhubarb mixture. Add raisins; cook for 15 minutes longer. Add walnuts; remove from heat. Place in sterilized pint jars; seal. Process in boiling water bath for 10 minutes.

Mrs. Roy Burgy
Rome Grange, No. 226
Bellingham, Washington

GRAPE FUDGE

4 qt. Concord grapes
2 oranges
2 lemons
Sugar
1 c. chopped nuts
1/2 tsp. salt

Wash grapes; remove stems. Separate pulp from skins of grapes. Cook the pulp until soft; force through sieve to remove seeds. Place the sieved pulp and skins in kettle. Extract juice from oranges and lemons, then put rinds through food chopper. Add juices and rinds to grapes. Cook for 1 hour. Measure, then add equal amount of sugar. Add nuts and salt. Cook until thick, stirring frequently. Place in hot sterilized jars; seal. Process in boiling water bath for 10 minutes.

Martha Isaacs
Sunny Valley Grange, No. 870
Outlook, Washington

CLOVER HONEY

10 lb. sugar
4 c. water

80 white clover blossoms
40 red clover blossoms
20 roses
Small piece of alum

Boil sugar and water together for 10 minutes. Add clover blossoms, roses and alum; remove from heat. Let stand for 30 minutes. Strain; pour liquid into hot sterilized jars. Process in simmering water bath for 10 to 15 minutes.

Eloise Bean
Mt. Cube Grange, No. 236
Orford, New Hampshire

QUINCE HONEY
(Recipe 50 years old)

3 lb. sugar
1 pt. water
3 quince
1 apple

Combine sugar and water in saucepan; cook for 15 minutes. Grate quince and apple finely; add to syrup. Boil for 10 minutes longer. Pour into jelly glasses; cover with 1/8-inch melted paraffin.

Mrs. Russell Metzger
Master, State W.A.C. Mem.
Central Grange, No. 1650
Germansville, Pennsylvania

TOMATO HONEY

1 lb. ripe tomatoes
Grated rind of 1 lemon
Sugar
Juice of fresh lemons

Cut tomatoes into small pieces; add lemon rind. Cook until thick. Press through sieve and measure. Add 2 cups sugar and juice of 1 1/2 lemons for each pint. Cook, stirring frequently, until consistency of honey. Pour into jars; place caps on jars. Process in simmering water bath for 10 minutes.

Eloise Bean
Mt. Cube Grange, No. 236
Orford, New Hampshire

CITRON JAM

1 lg. citron, peeled
5 oranges
4 lemons
Sugar
Mace (opt.)

Cut citron, oranges and lemons in chunks; force through food chopper. Measure fruit mixture into saucepan; add 1 cup sugar per 1 cup fruit mixture. Add mace, if desired. Cook over low heat for about 2 hours or until thick and clear, stirring frequently to prevent sticking. Pack in hot sterilized jars; place caps on jars. Process in simmering water bath for 10 min-

★ ★

utes. Yield: 5-6 pints. Our grange is promoting citron this year, so we save the seed from citron used to make jam.

Mrs. Harold Fahy, C.W.A.
Indian Orchard Grange, No. 1020
Lake Ariel, Pennsylvania

PEACH JAM

    4 c. coarsely chopped peaches or
      nectarines
    3 c. sugar
    1/4 c. water or orange juice
    2 tbsp. lemon juice
    2 or 3 pits

Shake cup to settle peaches when measuring. Place peaches, sugar and water into kettle. Add lemon juice and pits. Cook over moderate heat until sugar dissolves, then boil rapidly, stirring frequently until jam thickens. Discard pits. Skim off foam quickly; pour hot jam to 1/8 inch of top of jar. Wipe top and threads of jar. Seal. Process in boiling water bath for 10 minutes to complete seal.

Photograph for this recipe below.

BERRY JAM

    4 c. crushed berries
    3 to 3 2/3 c. sugar
    1/4 tsp. salt

Examine berries for stems, insects, mashed or moldy ones. Rinse under cool running water. Drain, crush and measure berries into kettle. Stir in sugar and salt. Cook over low heat until juice runs freely, then boil rapidly. Cook, stirring frequently, until jam thickens.

Skim off foam quickly. Pour hot jam to 1/8 inch of top of jar. Wipe top and threads of jar; seal. Process in boiling water bath for 10 minutes to complete seal. All varieties of blackberries, blueberries, raspberries or strawberries may be used.

Photograph for this recipe below.

CUCUMBER JAM

    4 lg. cucumbers
    4 c. sugar
    1/3 c. lemon juice
    2 tbsp. lemon rind
    1 bottle Certo
    Green food coloring

Peel and remove seeds from cucumbers; chop or grind finely. Place 2 cups, packed, cucumber pulp in large kettle. Add sugar, lemon juice and rind; mix well. Place over high heat; bring to a rolling boil. Boil hard for 1 minute, stirring constantly. Remove from heat; skim off pulp and foam. Add Certo; boil hard for 2 minutes. Remove from heat; stir in a few drops of green food coloring. Pour into hot sterilized jars; seal with paraffin. Yield: Five 8-ounce jars.

Randolph Gregory
Cheshire Grange, No. 131
Keene, New Hampshire

GRAPE JAM

    Grapes
    Sugar

Crush grapes in saucepan; cook for several minutes or until tender. Force through a sieve. Measure 2 cups pulp; place in saucepan. Bring to a boil. Add 3 cups sugar; return to a boil, stirring constantly. Pour into hot sterilized jars; seal. Process pints and quarts in boiling water bath for 10 minutes.

Mrs. Leland Faidley
Sugar Grove Grange, No. 2044
Colfax, Iowa

QUICK AND EASY NO-COOK
STRAWBERRY JAM

    1 3/4 c. crushed fresh strawberries
    4 c. sugar
    2 tbsp. lemon juice
    1/2 bottle Certo

Mix strawberries with sugar thoroughly; let stand for 10 minutes. Combine lemon juice with Certo; add to strawberry mixture. Stir for 3 minutes. Ladle into scalded 8-ounce jars or plastic containers; cover immediately. Let stand at room temperature for 24 hours to set. Place desired amount in refrigerator; freeze remaining jam for future use. One box Sure-Jell may be used instead of Certo. Yield: 5 cups.

Mrs. R. B. Clocker
Barberton Grange, No. 571
Vancouver, Washington

★★★

HEAVENLY JAM

2 oranges
1 lemon
6 peaches
6 pears
6 apples
Sugar
2 c. canned pineapple (opt.)

Grind oranges and lemon through food chopper. Place in kettle. Cover with cold water; let stand overnight. Boil until soft. Peel, core and dice peaches, pears and apples; add to orange mixture. Measure fruit mixture; add equal amount of sugar. Add pineapple. Boil for 20 to 30 minutes or until thick. Ladle into hot sterilized jars; seal. Process in simmering water bath for 10 to 15 minutes. Yield: 4 to 5 pints.

Wilma Coate
Troutlake Grange, No. 210
White Salmon, Washington

GOLDEN RHUBARB JAM
(Recipe 40 years old)

5 c. diced rhubarb
5 c. sugar
1 lb. orange candy slices

Combine all ingredients in large saucepan; let stand until sugar is almost dissolved. Bring to a boil, stirring constantly; cook, stirring, for about 10 minutes or until mixture thickens. Pour into hot, sterilized jars; cover at once with thin layer of melted paraffin. Cool; add another layer of melted paraffin. Yield: 4 pints.

Lydia Swope
Wingston Grange

INDIANA RHUBARB JAM

12 c. chopped rhubarb
8 c. sugar
1 6-oz. package strawberry gelatin

Mix rhubarb and sugar in kettle; let stand overnight. Bring to a boil; cook until rhubarb is soft. Remove from heat; stir in gelatin until dissolved. Place in sterilized jars or plastic containers; cover. Store in refrigerator or freezer.

Mrs. Roy Stephenson
Auburn Community Grange, No. 2418
Auburn, Indiana

RHUBARB-ORANGE JAM
(Recipe over 40 years old)

2 1/2 lb. rhubarb
3 c. sugar
1/2 c. water
Grated rind and juice of 2 oranges

Wash rhubarb; cut into small pieces. Place in kettle. Add sugar and water. Add grated rind and orange juice; mix well. Bring to a boil; cook for 30 minutes, stirring occasionally. Pour into sterilized 6-ounce jelly glasses; cover with melted paraffin. Add 8 ounces seeded raisins, 1/4 teaspoon cloves and 1/2 teaspoon cinnamon for marmalade, if desired. Yield: Six 6-ounce glasses.

Mrs. Clinton Walton
Upper Rogue Grange, No. 825
Center Point, Oregon

RHUBARB-PINEAPPLE JAM

5 c. cut-up rhubarb
4 c. sugar
1 c. crushed pineapple
1 6-oz. box strawberry gelatin

Combine rhubarb, sugar and pineapple in saucepan; boil for 10 minutes, stirring frequently. Remove from heat. Add gelatin; stir until dissolved. Let cool; pour in hot sterilized jelly glasses. Seal with paraffin.

Mrs. Ola Gildersleeve
Sonora Grange
Grinnell, Iowa
Mrs. Donald K. Peck
Litchfield Grange, No. 107
Litchfield, Connecticut

RHUBARB-STRAWBERRY JAM

6 c. finely chopped rhubarb
6 c. sugar
2 3-oz. boxes strawberry gelatin

Mix rhubarb and sugar in kettle; let stand until juice drains. Bring to a boil; boil for 10 minutes. Remove from heat; stir in gelatin until dissolved. Pour into sterilized jelly glasses; cover with melted paraffin.

Mrs. John Cannon
Marshall Grange, No. 1840
Washington Court House, Ohio

SPICED BLUEBERRY JAM

2 lb. blueberries
7 c. sugar
1 tsp. cinnamon
1 tsp. cloves
1 tsp. allspice
1/2 bottle Certo

Combine blueberries and sugar in saucepan; bring to a boil, stirring constantly. Boil for 20 minutes, stirring frequently. Add cinnamon, cloves and allspice; return to a boil. Stir in Certo; boil for 1 minute longer. Pack in hot, sterilized jars; seal. Process pints and quarts in boiling water bath for 10 minutes.

Mrs. Catherine Sebastian
Preston City Grange, No. 110

STRAWBERRY-CHERRY JAM

2 1/2 to 3 c. Bing cherries, pitted
2 c. tart red cherries
2 to 3 c. sliced strawberries
3 1/2 c. sugar
1/4 c. lemon juice
1/4 tsp. almond extract

Combine cherries, strawberries and sugar in kettle; cook over low heat, shaking pan until sugar is dissolved. Increase heat; boil for 10 minutes, stirring occasionally. Add lemon juice and almond extract; boil until jelly sheets from spoon. Stir and skim for 5 minutes. Pour into hot sterilized jars; seal. Process in simmering water bath for 10 to 15 minutes. Yield: 3 pints.

Mrs. Howard Miller
Hall of Fame Grange, No. 2003
Bonner Springs, Kansas

PEACH JAM

3 lb. firm ripe peaches
7 c. sugar
1/4 c. lemon juice
1 bottle fruit pectin

Wash and peel peaches. Remove and discard pits. Cut peaches into fourths. Place 3 or 4 pieces in blender container. Blender-chop until processed; empty into kettle. Repeat until all peaches are processed. Add sugar and lemon juice. Bring to a rolling boil; boil over high heat for 10 minutes. Add pectin; boil for 1 minute. Remove from heat; stir and skim for 5 minutes. Pour into sterilized jars; place lids and rings on jars. Process in boiling water bath for 10 minutes to complete seal.

Photograph for this recipe above.

BURGUNDY WINE JELLY

2 c. Burgundy
3 c. sugar
1/2 bottle liquid fruit pectin

Combine Burgundy and sugar in the top of a double boiler; blend well. Heat over boiling water, stirring constantly, for about 5 minutes or until sugar is dissolved. Remove from heat; add pectin. Stir until blended. Let stand for several minutes; skim off foam with metal spoon. Pour into hot, sterilized jars; seal with paraffin. Yield: Five 6-oz. jars.

Peggy Rogers
Price's Fork Grange, No. 786
Blacksburg, Virginia

SPICED PEACH JAM

2 qt. skinned sliced peaches
6 c. sugar
1 tsp. whole cloves
1/2 tsp. whole allspice
1 stick cinnamon

Place peaches in Dutch oven; mash slightly. Add sugar; mix well. Let stand overnight. Tie spices together in cheesecloth; add to peach mixture. Cook in 300-degree oven, stirring occasionally, until a bit jells when dropped on a cool saucer. Remove spice bag. Ladle into hot sterilized jars; seal. Process in boiling water bath for 10 minutes.

Barbara Catron
Fair Harbor Grange, No. 1129
Allyn, Washington

FRESH APPLE JELLY

Tart firm apples
3 c. sugar

Select sound, richly flavored apples with about 1/4 of them underripe. Wash apples carefully. Cut out and discard stem, blossom ends and bruised spots. Do not pare or core. Slice thinly crosswise; place in kettle. Press down lightly. Add cold water to about 1/8 inch of top of apples. Cover kettle; place over high heat. Bring to a boil. Reduce heat; simmer for 20 to 30 minutes or until apples are soft. Turn apples and juice into dampened jelly bag or square of cotton flannel tied over top of deep bowl. Let drip. Combine 4 cups juice and sugar in kettle. Place over high heat. Stir until sugar dissolves. Boil rapidly to jelling point. Remove from heat. Skim off foam quickly; pour jelly to about 1/8 inch of top of jelly jar. Wipe top and threads of jar. Seal. Process in boiling water bath for 10 minutes to complete seal.

Photograph for this recipe on page 253.

★ ★

CLOVE TOMATO JAM

    4 lb. fresh tomatoes
    1 1/4 tsp. whole cloves
    1/4 tsp. whole allspice
    4 c. sugar
    1/2 c. seedless raisins, coarsely chopped
    1/4 c. lemon juice
    2 tsp. salt

Drop tomatoes into boiling water for 2 minutes or until skins can be easily peeled. Remove stems and skins with the tip of sharp knife. Dice tomatoes; place in large saucepan. Tie cloves and allspice in cheesecloth bag; add to tomatoes. Add remaining ingredients. Bring to boiling point; reduce heat. Simmer for 1 hour and 30 minutes to 2 hours or until thick, stirring occasionally. Remove cheesecloth bag. Ladle into hot sterilized jars, filling to within 1/2 inch of top. Seal immediately. Process in hot water bath for 10 minutes to complete seal. Yield: 6 half-pint jars.

Photograph for this recipe above.

GRAPE JELLY
(Recipe 45 years old)

    Grapes for 2 c. juice
    3 c. sugar

Remove grape stems and wash. Place in kettle; bring to a boil. Simmer until juice appears. Place in jelly sack; let drip. Do not squeeze or add water. Pour 2 cups juice in kettle; cook for 5 minutes. Add sugar; cook, stirring, until sugar is dissolved. Place in hot sterilized jars; seal. The grape bag may be squeezed but jelly will be cloudy.

Mrs. Irene Meyer
Millbrook Grange, No. 1864
Morton, Illinois

SAGE JELLY

    3 c. apple cider
    1 1/2 tbsp. dried sage or 1/2 c. fresh
        sage leaves
    1 pkg. Sure-Jell
    4 c. sugar

Combine cider and sage in saucepan; heat to scalding. Remove from heat; let stand for 15 minutes. Strain through cloth; return liquid to kettle. Add Sure-Jell; bring to a rolling boil. Stir in sugar; boil for 1 minute. Skim off foam. Pour into hot sterilized jars; seal.

Mrs. Frank Pellett
Sugar Grove Grange, No. 2044
Newton, Iowa

★ ★

SOUR CHERRY JELLY

4 3/4 c. sugar
3 c. cherry juice
1 box powdered pectin
1/2 c. water

Mix sugar and 1 1/4 cups cherry juice in kettle until sugar is dissolved. Add pectin to water slowly; heat almost to boiling point, stirring constantly. Pour pectin mixture into remaining 1 3/4 cups cherry juice; stir until pectin is completely dissolved. Let stand for 15 minutes, stirring occasionally. Add the sugar mixture; stir until mixed. Pour into sterilized jelly glasses; pour melted paraffin over tops to seal. Any other juice may be used in recipe. Yield: 5 1/2 cups.

Mrs. Eldon Howard
Springcreek Grange, No. 951
Reardan, Washington

APRICOT-PINEAPPLE MARMALADE

4 c. ground apricots
1 c. crushed pineapple
7 c. sugar
1 tbsp. cream of tartar

Combine apricots, pineapple and sugar in kettle. Add cream of tartar; mix well. Bring to a boil, stirring frequently; boil for 12 minutes. Skim off foam; pour into hot sterilized jars. Seal. Process in boiling water bath for 15 minutes. Yield: 6 pints.

Cora M. Bitterling
Eagle Point Grange, No. 664
Medford, Oregon

CARROT MARMALADE

1 lb. carrots
1 1/2 lb. sugar
2 lemons
1/2 c. chopped nuts

Clean and scrape carrots; quarter. Cook in small amount of water until soft, then mash. Add sugar, juice of 2 lemons and grated rind of 1 lemon. Cook for 20 minutes, stirring frequently. Add nuts. Pour into hot sterilized jars. Seal. Process in simmering water bath for 10 to 15 minutes.

Arlene Rainey
Jefferson Grange, No. 2019
Sharpsville, Pennsylvania

PEAR MARMALADE

3 qt. ground peeled pears
4 c. sugar
3/4 c. lemon juice
5 drops of desired food coloring (opt.)

Cook pears in own juice for 15 to 20 minutes or until soft, stirring frequently; do not add water. Add sugar and lemon juice; cook until thick, stirring frequently. Stir in food coloring; cook, stirring, for 5 minutes longer. Pour into jelly glasses or small, fancy jars; cover with melted paraffin. May be placed in plastic containers and covered tightly, then frozen. One tablespoon red hots may be used instead of food coloring. Yield: Eight 1/2-pint glasses.

Ruth G. Miller
Waubee Grange, No. 2365
Milford, Indiana

TANGY PEACH MARMALADE

18 peaches, skinned and halved
3 whole oranges, quartered
Rind of 1 orange
8 c. sugar

Grind peaches, oranges and orange rind through food chopper. Place in kettle; add sugar. Cook slowly for 45 minutes. Pour into hot sterilized jars. Process in boiling water bath for 10 to 15 minutes.

Marcia Hunt
Columbia Grange, No. 87
Vancouver, Washington

TASTY PEACH MARMALADE

6 c. peaches, sliced or chopped
1 orange, seeded and minced
4 1/2 c. sugar

Combine all ingredients; let stand for 2 hours. Bring to a boil; cook, stirring frequently, until syrup is thick. Pour into hot sterilized jars; seal. Process in boiling water bath for 10 to 15 minutes.

B. J. Hardersen
Tunxis Grange, No. 13
Bloomfield, Connecticut

ZUCCHINI MARMALADE

2 c. sugar
2 to 2 1/2 c. cubed zucchini
2 oranges, peeled, quartered and sliced
Juice of 1 lg. lemon
1/2 tsp. red food coloring (opt.)

Combine sugar, zucchini and oranges; let stand overnight. Add lemon juice; bring to a boil. Remove from heat; set aside for 24 hours. Bring to a boil again; reduce heat to low. Cook until thickened. Add food coloring, if desired. Stir gently; pack in hot sterilized jars. Place lids and rings on jars. Process in simmering water bath for 10 minutes.

Mrs. Myrna Thomas
French Camp-Lathrop Grange, No. 510
French Camp, California

★ ★

GINGER-PEAR PRESERVES
(Recipe 100 years old)

 4 lb. medium-ripe pears
 7 c. sugar
 2 oz. preserved ginger, chopped
 Grated rind and juice of 2 lemons
 2 c. water

Combine all ingredients in kettle; bring to a boil. Reduce heat; simmer for 4 to 5 hours or until thick and dark, stirring occasionally. Place in sterilized jars; cover with melted paraffin. Yield: 1 1/2 to 2 quarts.

Karen L. Amazeen
Tuftonboro Grange, No. 142
Wolfeboro Falls, New Hampshire

GROUND-CHERRY PRESERVES
(Recipe 60 years old)

 4 c. ground-cherries
 1/2 c. orange or pineapple juice
 3 c. sugar
 1/4 c. lemon juice

Husk and wash ground-cherries; place in large kettle. Add orange juice; bring to a boil. Reduce heat; cover. Simmer for 5 to 10 minutes or until cherries are tender but not broken. Remove cover; add sugar. Bring to boiling point, stirring gently until sugar is dissolved; boil for 10 minutes. Add lemon juice; boil rapidly until jelly sheets from spoon or to desired thickness. Place in sterilized pint or 1/2-pint jars; seal. Process in boiling water bath for 10 minutes. Yield: 2 pints.

Mrs. Paul W. Morton, W.A.C.
Freeport Grange, No. 2337
Freeport, Ohio

PRESERVED ELDERBERRIES

 9 lb. elderberries
 3 lb. sugar
 1 tbsp. ground cinnamon
 1 tbsp. ground cloves
 2 lemons, thinly sliced

Remove ripe elderberries from fruit clusters; wash thoroughly and drain well. Combine elderberries and remaining ingredients in kettle; cook until thickened, stirring often to keep from burning. Pour into hot, sterilized jars; seal. Process in boiling water bath for 10 minutes for pints and 15 minutes for quarts.

Mrs. Jesse Tritten, Wife of State Treas.
Plymouth Grange, No. 389
Plymouth, Michigan

MAXINE'S STRAWBERRY PRESERVES
(Recipe about 50 years old)

 1 qt. strawberries, hulled
 1/2 c. water

 6 c. sugar
 1/2 tsp. powdered alum

Mix strawberries, water and sugar in large saucepan; bring to a boil. Cook for 10 minutes, stirring frequently. Add alum; mix well. Place in sterilized jars or glasses; seal. Process in boiling water bath for 10 minutes.

Mrs. Maxine McClure
Susquehanna Grange
Curwensville, Pennsylvania

OLD-FASHIONED STRAWBERRY PRESERVES
(Recipe 50 years old)

 2 qt. hulled strawberries
 6 c. sugar

Place strawberries in colander or on square of cheesecloth; hold in pan of boiling water for 2 minutes. Drain; place strawberries in kettle. Add 4 cups sugar; bring to a boil. Boil for 3 minutes; cool for 5 minutes. Add remaining 2 cups sugar; bring to a boil. Boil for 8 to 10 minutes. Place in large baking pan; let stand for several hours, shaking occasionally and skimming. Pack in hot, sterilized jelly glasses; cover with paraffin. Cover.

Mrs. Arnold Engstrom
Wife of State Master
Elk River, Minnesota

TOMATO FIGS
(Recipe 100 years old)

 8 lb. small yellow tomatoes
 8 lb. sugar
 Juice and grated rind of 4 lemons
 2 oz. gingerroot, finely cut

Scald tomatoes; plunge in cold water. Remove the skins. Place tomatoes in pan in layers with an equal amount of sugar. Let stand for 24 hours. Drain juice into kettle; boil for 5 minutes. Add tomatoes; boil until clear. Remove tomatoes with slotted spoon; set in the sun to harden. Add lemon juice and rind and gingerroot to syrup; boil until thick. Drop tomatoes into hot sterilized jars; fill to within 1/2 inch from top with boiling syrup. Place caps on jars. Process in simmering water bath for 10 minutes.

Mrs. Thelma Hylton
Price's Fork Grange, No. 786
Blacksburg, Virginia

BRANDIED CHERRIES
(Recipe 100 years old)

 Large sweet cherries
 Sugar
 French brandy

Select cherries that are sound and perfect; remove stems with scissors to within an inch of cherries. Pour

★ ★

1 quart water into preserving kettle; stir in 2 cups sugar. Boil and skim until clear. Scald cherries in sugar water for 3 minutes, but not long enough to break skins. Remove cherries with skimmer; spread on flat dishes to cool. Reserve sugar water. Prepare enough syrup to cover cherries in another kettle, using ratio of 2 cups sugar to 2 cups reserved sugar water. Boil and skim syrup until clear; remove from heat. Cool until cold; mix with equal amount of brandy. Place cherries in wide-mouthed bottles; pour syrup over cherries. Seal tightly. Process in boiling water bath for 10 minutes. Store in cool, dark place.

Diane Hylton
Price's Fork Grange, No. 786
Blacksburg, Virginia

CANDIED GRAPEFRUIT RIND
(Recipe about 75 years old)

Grapefruit rind
2 c. sugar

Cut grapefruit rind into strips; remove most of the white part. Soak rind in pan of cold water for 24 hours; boil in clear water until tender. Mix sugar and 1/2 cup water in saucepan; bring to a boil, stirring until sugar is dissolved. Add rind; cook for 10 minutes. Drain rind; dip in additional sugar.

Gladys Holdridge
Jewett Grange, No. 1534
Windham, New York

CRANBERRY SAUCE
(Recipe 75 years old)

1 lb. cranberries
1 c. water
2 c. sugar

Place cranberries and water in saucepan; bring to a boil. Cook for 5 minutes; press through coarse sieve. Add sugar; stir until dissolved. Pour into dish; cover. Store in refrigerator until served.

Florence Smith
Capital Grange, No. 18
Dover, Delaware

GRAPE JUICE
(Recipe over 75 years old)

1 c. grapes
1 c. sugar

Wash and stem grapes. Place in sterilized quart jar. Add sugar; fill with boiling water. Stir, then seal. Process in boiling water bath for 10 minutes.

Mrs. Frank Pellett
Sugar Grove Grange, No. 2044
Newton, Iowa

EASY CANNED TOMATO JUICE

Tomatoes, cleaned

Cut tomatoes in chunks; place in kettle. Cook until soft. Press through sieve. Let stand overnight; skim water from top. Boil until thick. Pour in sterilized jars. Process in boiling water bath for 15 minutes after coming to a boil.

Garnet Kelley
Mendon Grange
Ruffsdale, Pennsylvania

SPECIAL CANNED TOMATO JUICE
(Recipe 30 years old)

Tomatoes
Salt
Sugar
Liquid pectin

Wash ripe tomatoes; slice without peeling into heavy pan. Add enough water to start tomatoes cooking. Simmer until soft. Press pulp through fine sieve. Measure juice; bring to boiling point. Add 1/4 teaspoon salt, 1/4 teaspoon sugar and 1/2 teaspoon liquid pectin for each cup of juice. Bring to a full boil; remove from heat. Stir occasionally for 10 minutes. Place in hot sterilized jars. Process in boiling water bath for 10 minutes.

Dorothy Tobey
Fair Harbor Grange, No. 1129
Grapeview, Wisconsin

GOLDEN SPICED PEACHES

6 lb. peaches
1 c. water
1 1/2 c. white or cider vinegar
4 c. sugar
2 1/2 tsp. grated orange rind
6 1-in. sticks cinnamon
Whole cloves

Peel peaches. Combine water, vinegar, sugar, orange rind and cinnamon in 3-quart saucepan; cook over medium heat, stirring, until sugar is dissolved. Bring to a boil. Stick 2 cloves each into about 1/3 of the peaches; drop peaches into syrup. Bring to a boil; cook over low heat for about 10 minutes or until peaches are just tender but firm, turning several times with wooden spoon. Remove peaches from syrup; pack tightly in 2 hot sterilized pint jars. Add 1 stick cinnamon to each jar; cover top with waxed paper. Cook and pack remaining peaches in 2 batches. Fill jars with boiling syrup to within 1/4 inch from tops. Remove air bubbles with knife or spatula; place caps on jars. Process in simmering water bath for 10 minutes. Yield: 6 pints.

Dollie Belden, Home Ec. Chm.
Trowbridge Grange, No. 296
Allegan, Michigan

★ ★

MOTHER'S SPICED PEACHES
(Recipe over 100 years old)

    7 lb. firm peaches
    Whole cloves
    1 pt. vinegar
    4 lb. sugar
    2 tbsp. ground cloves
    2 tbsp. cinnamon

Peel peaches. Large peaches may be cut in halves. Stick 2 or 3 cloves in each peach or peach half. Combine vinegar, sugar and spices in heavy kettle. Bring to a boil, stirring until sugar is dissolved; cook for about 10 minutes. Add peaches and simmer until fork-tender. Remove and pack peaches in hot sterilized jars. Boil syrup until dark and thick; pour, boiling, over peaches. Place caps on jars. Process in simmering water for 10 minutes to seal. Store in cool place if spiced peaches are not processed.

Helen T. Lynn
Milford Grange, No. 6
Milford, Delaware

SPICED GRAPES
(Recipe about 85 years old)

    7 lb. grapes
    4 lb. sugar
    1 pt. vinegar
    2 sticks cinnamon
    2 whole allspice
    1 tbsp. mace
    1 tsp. whole cloves

Wash grapes and remove stems. Separate pulp and skins. Place skins in small amount of water in saucepan; boil until tender. Place pulp in small amount of water in another pan; cook until pulp breaks open. Place in coarse sieve; mash to remove seeds. Combine pulp and skins in large kettle; add sugar and vinegar. Tie spices in cloth bag; drop into cooking kettle. Cook, stirring occasionally, until tender and thick. Remove spice bag. Pour liquid and grapes into hot sterilized jars; place lids and rings on jars. Process in simmering water bath for 10 to 15 minutes.

Dorothy A. McCray
Slocum Grange
Narragansett, Rhode Island

SPICED STUFFED DATES

    2 1/2 lb. fresh dates
    1 qt. walnut pieces
    3 1/2 c. sugar
    1/2 c. white syrup
    1 c. white vinegar
    1 1/2 c. water
    1/4 tsp. cinnamon
    Several drops of oil of cloves

Slit dates; remove pits. Fill dates with walnuts. Pack upright in layers in jars with walnut stuffing turned to outside. Combine remaining ingredients in saucepan;

boil for 5 minutes. Pour boiling mixture over dates to 1/2 inch from top. Place caps on jars. Process for 15 minutes in boiling water one inch over tops of jars. Remove; cool and label. Store in dry place. Yield: 8 half-pint jars.

Sophia A. Friel
Thompson Falls Grange, No. 123
Thompson Falls, Montana

SPICED WATERMELON RIND
(Recipe 120 years old)

    Watermelon rind
    Alum
    Sugar
    1 lemon, thinly sliced
    Whole cloves to taste
    1/4 lb. crystallized ginger

Cut rind in desired size. Combine 2 tablespoons alum and 1 quart water to make enough alum to cover rind. Cover rind with alum water in glass or enamel container; let soak for 10 to 15 minutes. Cook over low heat for 10 minutes. Drain; cover with cold water. Let soak for 2 hours. Drain, then dry with paper towels. Weigh rind; combine 1 pound sugar and 1 cup water in large kettle for each pound of rind. Add lemon slices, cloves and ginger. Bring to a boil; cook for 10 minutes. Add rind; cook until rind is clear and crystallized. Spices may be removed, if desired. Pack, boiling, into hot sterilized jars. Pour boiling syrup over rind to within 1/8 inch from tops of jars. Place lids on jars, then screw on rings. Process in boiling water bath for 5 minutes.

Mrs. William Birge
Bethlehem Grange, No. 121
Litchfield, Connecticut

GRAPE CATSUP
(recipe 100 years old)

    5 lb. grapes
    2 c. vinegar
    2 lb. sugar
    1 tbsp. cinnamon
    1 tbsp. cloves
    1/2 tbsp. salt
    Red pepper to taste

Combine grapes and vinegar in kettle; cook until soft. Press through sieve. Combine all ingredients in kettle; boil until thick. Place in sterilized bottles or jars; seal. Process in boiling water bath for 15 minutes.

Mrs. A. I. Morris
Rainbow Valley Grange
Fallbrook, California

HOT AND SWEET TOMATO CATSUP
(Recipe over 40 years old)

    2 gal. thick tomato pulp
    2 med. onions, chopped

★ ★

2 cloves of garlic, minced
2 sweet peppers, chopped
2 hot peppers, chopped
1/2 c. mixed pickling spices, tied in bag
2 c. (packed) brown sugar
1/2 c. salt
1 1/2 tsp. dry mustard
1 tsp. red pepper
1 1/2 tsp. black pepper
2 c. sugar
2 c. vinegar
1/2 c. ground horseradish

Combine first 6 ingredients in kettle; boil rapidly for 30 minutes. Remove spice bag. Add remaining ingredients; boil for 30 minutes longer. Pour into hot sterilized jars or bottles; seal. Process in boiling water bath for 10 minutes.

Mrs. Lester Stem
Medford Grange, No. 188
Westminster, Indiana

REFRIGERATED UNCOOKED TOMATO CATSUP

(Recipe 75 years old)

4 qt. chopped ripe tomatoes
2 tbsp. chopped horseradish
1 tbsp. salt
2 tbsp. mustard seed
1 red pepper, chopped
2 tbsp. chopped onion
3 stalks celery, chopped
2 tbsp. (packed) brown sugar
1/2 c. vinegar
1/2 tsp. pepper
1/2 tsp. cinnamon
Pinch of cloves

Combine tomatoes, horseradish and salt in large glass container; let stand for 1 hour. Drain off excess water on top. Add remaining ingredients; mix well. Place in jars. Store in refrigerator.

Mrs. Ruth Wasson
Millbrook Grange, No. 1864
Brimfield, Illinois

CHILI CLUB

(Recipe 100 years old)

12 lg. tomatoes
1 c. chopped celery
3 lg. onions, sliced
2 c. white vinegar
3 c. sugar
2 tbsp. salt
3 sm. red peppers, sliced thin
3 sm. green peppers, sliced thin

Scald and peel tomatoes; cut in chunks. Place in kettle; add celery, onions, vinegar, sugar and salt. Cook for 1 hour and 30 minutes. Add red and green pep-

pers; cook for 30 minutes or until thick. Pack immediately in hot, sterilized jars; seal. Process in boiling water bath for 10 minutes.

Mrs. Nelson Espenscheid
Wallington Grange
Alton, New York

MOTHER'S CHILI SAUCE

(Recipe 55 years old)

40 to 45 tomatoes, peeled and quartered
4 hot green chilies
4 lg. red bell peppers
9 lg. green bell peppers
6 c. sugar
2 qt. cider vinegar
1 tsp. cloves
6 tbsp. salt
1 tsp. chili powder
1 tsp. cinnamon

Grind first 4 ingredients coarsely; place in kettle. Add remaining ingredients; mix well. Boil, stirring occasionally, for about 3 to 4 hours or until thick. Place in hot, sterilized jars; seal. Process in boiling water bath for 10 minutes. Yield: 21 pints.

Mrs. W. C. Weigele
Homestead Grange, No. 215
Wiggins, Colorado

PRIZEWINNING CHILI SAUCE

(Recipe about 100 years old)

45 lg. tomatoes
1 pt. cider vinegar
15 lg. green peppers
6 lg. onions
2 1/2 c. sugar
2 tbsp. salt
1/2 tsp. pepper
4 tsp. whole allspice
4 tsp. ginger
4 tsp. whole cloves
1 tbsp. mustard seed
1 tbsp. celery seed

Chop tomatoes fine; place in kettle. Boil for about 1 hour. Add vinegar. Grind green peppers and onions through medium-coarse blade of food grinder; add to tomato mixture. Add sugar, salt and pepper. Tie spices in 4 x 6-inch bag; add to tomato mixture. Mix well. Cook to desired thickness. Place in hot, sterilized pint jars; seal. Process in boiling water bath for 10 minutes. Brown sugar, packed, may be substituted for sugar. May be cooked in electric roaster; will not burn. Yield: 15 pints.

Mrs. John W. Rehbehn
State Membership Director
West Liberty, Iowa

★ ★

APPLE CHUTNEY

1 doz. sour apples
3 med. onions
1 lb. seeded raisins
1/4 c. salt
4 c. sugar
3 c. cider vinegar
1 tbsp. mustard seed
1 tbsp. whole cloves
1 tbsp. small dried chili peppers

Pare and core apples; cut into quarters. Place in kettle. Peel onions; slice. Add to apples. Chop raisins fine or grind through food chopper; add to apple mixture. Dissolve salt and sugar in vinegar; pour over apple mixture. Tie mustard seed, cloves and chili peppers in cheesecloth bag; add to apple mixture. Cook over low heat until apples and onions are tender and chutney is rich brown color, stirring occasionally. Remove bag. Pour chutney into sterilized pint jars; seal. Process in boiling water bath for 10 minutes.

Mary T. Hironymous
American River Grange, No. 172
Sacramento, California

GRANDMA'S AUTUMN CHUTNEY

12 tomatoes
12 apples
1 hot pepper
1 bell pepper
2 lg. onions, chopped
2 cloves of garlic, chopped
3/4 c. chopped nuts
1/2 tsp. ground cloves
1/2 tsp. mustard
1/2 tsp. cinnamon
2 tbsp. salt
1 pt. (or less) vinegar
1 c. white sugar
1/2 c. (packed) brown sugar
1/2 c. honey
1/2 box raisins, chopped

Peel and chop tomatoes. Remove cores from apples; chop apples. Discard seeds of hot pepper and bell pepper; chop peppers. Mix all ingredients except raisins in kettle; cook over low heat until thick and clear. Add raisins; cook for 5 minutes longer. Do not overcook. Place in sterilized jars; seal. Process in boiling water bath for 10 minutes. Yield: 6-7 pints.

Mrs. Harold Fahy, C.W.A.
Indian Orchard Grange, No. 1020
Lake Ariel, Pennsylvania

EASY MINCEMEAT
(Recipe 75 years old)

5 bowls of chopped meat
2 bowls of sweet cider or wine
4 bowls of sugar
5 bowls of chopped apples
1 bowl of chopped suet
1 bowl of molasses
2 bowls of raisins
1 bowl of vinegar
1 bowl of candied citron
2 tbsp. cinnamon
1 tbsp. salt
1 tbsp. cloves
3 tbsp. nutmeg

Combine all ingredients in kettle; simmer for 2 hours. Pack into quart jars; seal. Process at 10 pounds pressure for 20 minutes. Use same size bowl to measure all ingredients.

Florence E. Bray
Chetco Grange, No. 765
Harbor, Oregon

GRANDMA DELANEY'S OLD RELIABLE MINCEMEAT
(Recipe 75 to 100 years old)

3 qt. chopped or ground boiled meat
5 qt. chopped apples
1 qt. suet or butter
1 qt. chopped raisins
1 qt. whole raisins
2 qt. white sugar
2 qt. (packed) brown sugar
1 tbsp. cinnamon
1 tbsp. cloves
1 tbsp. salt
1 tbsp. pepper
1 1/2 c. cider vinegar

Combine all ingredients in kettle; mix well. Cook for about 30 minutes, stirring frequently. Pack hot mixture into hot sterilized pint jars, leaving 1-inch head space at tops of jars. Adjust caps. Process at 10 pounds pressure for 60 minutes. Pie cherries or candied cherries may be added to mincemeat for extra color and flavor, if desired.

Helen K. Basche
Eagle Valley Grange, No. 656
Richland, Oregon

GREEN TOMATO MINCEMEAT

1 gal. chopped green tomatoes
1 tbsp. salt
Grated rind and pulp of 1 orange
1 c. chopped suet
3 c. (packed) brown sugar
2 c. seeded raisins
1 c. grape juice or cider
2 c. chopped apples or pears
2 tsp. cinnamon
1 tsp. cloves
1 tsp. nutmeg
1/2 tsp. ginger

Place tomatoes in kettle; sprinkle tomatoes with salt. Let stand for 1 hour. Drain. Cover tomatoes with boil-

★ ★

ing water; let stand for 5 minutes. Drain. Combine tomatoes and remaining ingredients in kettle; cook until thick. Pack into hot sterilized jars; seal. Process in hot water bath for 1 hour. Suet may be omitted from this recipe and butter added at the time mincemeat is used for pies. Process suetless mincemeat for 20 minutes.

Betty Conroy
Mission Grange, No. 767
Riverside, California

BRANDIED VENISON MINCEMEAT
(Recipe over 65 years old)

    5 lb. venison neck meat
    8 lb. apples, pared and chopped
    2 lb. seeded raisins
    2 lb. currants
    1 c. chopped citron
    2 c. cider vinegar
    5 lb. sugar
    1 lb. suet
    Salt to taste
    2 c. mixed orange and lemon peel
    1 c. molasses
    1 tsp. cloves
    1 tbsp. cinnamon
    1 tbsp. allspice
    1/5 brandy

Boil venison in kettle until tender. Lift from broth to cool; reserve broth. Remove all bones from venison; grind coarsely. Combine all ingredients in heavy pot; add reserved broth to cover. Simmer for 1 hour. Stir in brandy. Pack in hot sterilized jars; seal. Process at 10 pounds pressure for 20 minutes or in boiling water bath for 1 hour and 30 minutes. Store in cool dark place; keeps for years. Other venison meat may be used, but neck meat is especially flavorsome.

Neola Kreiss
Pescadero Grange, No. 793
Pescadero, California

OLD-FASHIONED MINCEMEAT

    4 qt. lean beef
    2 tsp. salt
    2 c. finely cut suet or vegetable
        shortening
    9 qt. cubed, peeled tart apples
    2 c. boiled cider
    1 lb. raisins
    1/2 lb. currants
    1/2 c. citron
    1/2 c. candied orange peel
    1/2 c. candied lemon peel
    4 c. sugar
    2 c. dark molasses
    2 qt. sweet cider
    1 tbsp. cinnamon
    1 tsp. nutmeg
    1 tsp. cloves

Place beef in kettle; cover with boiling water. Simmer, covered, until tender, adding 1 teaspoon salt during last part of cooking time. Remove beef from broth; reserve broth. Discard any fat; cut beef in small pieces. Combine beef, 4 cups reserved broth, suet, apples, boiled cider, raisins, currants, citron, orange peel, lemon peel, sugar and molasses in kettle. Cook over low heat for 3 hours, stirring occasionally; add sweet cider for moisture as needed. Stir in remaining salt, cinnamon, nutmeg and cloves; mix well. Pack into hot sterilzed jars; seal. Process at 10 pounds pressure for 30 minutes. Yield: 8 pints.

Mrs. Nelson Espenscheid
Wallington Grange
Alton, New York

DELICIOUS VENISON MINCEMEAT

    2 lb. venison neck meat
    1 lb. suet
    7 lb. apples
    Peel of 1 orange
    Peel of 1 lemon
    1 lb. seeded raisins
    1 lb. seedless raisins
    1 lb. dried currants
    6 c. (packed) brown sugar
    1 tbsp. cinnamon
    1 tbsp. cloves
    1 tbsp. salt
    1/2 c. vinegar
    1/2 c. boiled cider
    1/2 c. molasses
    1/2 c. cold coffee
    1/4 c. lemon juice
    1 can pineapple juice

Boil venison in kettle until tender. Lift from broth; reserve broth. Remove all bones from venison. Grind venison, suet, apples, orange peel and lemon peel together. Combine all ingredients in kettle; stir in 2 cups reserved broth. Heat thoroughly. Pack in hot sterilized jars; seal. Process at 10 pounds pressure for 20 minutes or in boiling water bath for 1 hour and 30 minutes.

Lorna Polasek
Humboldt Grange, No. 501
Eureka, California

PICKLED CHERRIES

    1 qt. fresh firm cherries with stems
    1 tbsp. salt
    1 c. cold vinegar

Wash cherries well; pack in sterilized quart jar. Add salt and vinegar; fill the jar with water. Seal. Let stand for at least 3 weeks before using. Pickled cherries will keep indefinitely stored in a cool, dark place. Serve as a meat accompaniment.

Mrs. Leland Faidley
Sugar Grove Grange, No. 2044
Colfax, Iowa

★★

WATERMELON RIND PICKLES

1 med. watermelon
1/2 c. salt
1 tbsp. whole cloves
1 stick cinnamon
1 lemon, thinly sliced
4 c. sugar
2 c. white vinegar
2 c. water

Trim dark skin and pink flesh from watermelon rind; cut into 1-inch pieces. Dissolve salt in 1 quart cold water in large container; add rind. Add more water to cover rind, if needed. Let stand for 6 hours. Drain; rinse and cover with water in large saucepan. Cook, covered, for about 20 minutes or until just tender. Drain in colander. Tie spices in cheesecloth bag. Combine spices and remaining ingredients in saucepan; simmer for 10 minutes. Add rind; simmer for about 1 hour or until rind is translucent, adding more water if syrup becomes too thick. Remove spice bag. Pack, boiling hot, into sterilized jars, allowing 1/8-inch head space. Seal. Process in boiling water bath for 10 minutes to complete seal.

Photograph for this recipe above.

SWEET FRUIT PICKLES

7 1/2 lb. pears, peaches or apples
4 lb. sugar
2 c. vinegar
Stick of cinnamon or whole cloves

Peel pears, leaving whole with stems intact. Boil sugar, vinegar and cinnamon together in kettle. Add pears; boil until easily pierced with fork. Remove pears; place in hot sterilized jars. Boil syrup; pour over pears to cover. Seal. Process in pints and quarts in boiling water bath for 15 minutes.

Mrs. J. Garrett
Fitchville Grange, No. 2356
New London, Ohio

WATERMELON RIND PICKLES

Watermelon rind
Salt
4 c. sugar
2 c. water
2 c. white vinegar
1/4 tsp. oil of cloves
1/4 tsp. oil of cinnamon
Green food coloring (opt.)

★ ★

Peel rind; remove any pink pulp. Cut rind in small pieces; measure out 2 quarts. Soak in saucepan overnight in salt water to cover, using 2 tablespoons salt per quart of water. Drain; cover with fresh water. Cook until just tender. Boil sugar, water and vinegar together in saucepan; add oil of cloves and oil of cinnamon. Drain rind; add to syrup. Cook until translucent. Stir in food coloring for desired color. Pack into hot sterilized jars; seal. Process in boiling water bath for 10 minutes. The use of oils rather than ground spices keeps the rind light colored.

Nancy Wolfe
Brandywine Grange, No. 348
Brandywine, Maryland

PICKLED PRUNES
(Recipe at least 90 years old)

7 lb. prunes
1/2 stick gingerroot
1 tsp. cloves
2 tsp. allspice
2 tsp. cinnamon
1/2 tsp. mace
8 c. sugar
1 pt. vinegar

Prick prunes all around with fork. Mix spices; place in square of cheesecloth; tie to make a sack. Place sugar, vinegar and spice bag in large kettle; heat until sugar is dissolved. Add prunes; bring to a boil. Pour into crock. Let stand for 24 hours. Drain liquid from prunes; bring liquid to a boil. Pour over prunes; let stand for 24 hours. Repeat for 2 more days. Bring prunes and liquid to a boil on fourth day. Place in jars; seal. Process in boiling water bath for 10 minutes.

Lena Germann
Washington Grange, No. 82
Vancouver, Washington

SWEET PEACH PICKLES
(Recipe about 90 years old)

1 pt. vinegar
8 c. sugar
Whole cloves to taste
Allspice to taste
Stick cinnamon to taste
9 lb. peaches

Mix vinegar, sugar and spices in kettle; bring to a boil. Add peaches; cook until tender. Remove peaches with slotted spoon; place in sterilized jars. Keep draining off syrup as settles to bottoms of jars; pour into kettle of syrup. Boil syrup until almost as thick as honey. Pour over peaches; seal. Process in boiling water bath for 10 minutes.

Mrs. Emmet L. Gaston
Muncy Grange, No. 1204
Lebanon, Tennessee

PICKLED PEACHES

6 2 1/2 to 3-in. sticks cinnamon
1 1 1/2 to 2-in. piece of gingerroot

1 1/2 tbsp. whole cloves
12 c. sugar
Vinegar
Salt
15 lb. firm ripe peaches

Break cinnamon into small pieces; pound gingerroot to crush. Tie spices in piece of thin cloth large enough not to crowd spices. Place sugar, 8 cups vinegar, 1/2 teaspoon salt and spice bag in wide kettle or saucepot; mix well. Bring to a full boil; reduce heat so syrup does not continue cooking but will keep hot. Wash and peel peaches. Freestone peaches may be scalded for 30 seconds to 1 minute to loosen skins, then quickly dipped into cold water. Clingstone peaches need to be peeled with sharp knife. Peaches hold color better if dropped, as peeled, into salt and vinegar water, using 1 tablespoon salt and 1 tablespoon vinegar for each 2 quarts cold water. An ascorbic acid mixture may be used instead of salt and vinegar, if preferred, using 1 teaspoon for each quart water. Bring syrup to boiling point when peaches are ready; add 1 or 2 layers of peaches to syrup. Boil for 4 to 5 minutes; peaches should be thoroughly heated but not cooked. Use slotted spoon to transfer peaches to jars, filling each jar to within 1/2 inch of top. Repeat until all peaches are used. Bring syrup to a full boil; pour over peaches. Syrup should fill jars to within 1/4 inch of top. Remove anything spilled on top or threads of jars. Place dome lids on jars; screw bands tight. Process for 15 minutes in boiling water. May add 1 or 2 pieces of cinnamon to each jar of peach pickles, but it is not advisable to add cloves or allspice as they are likely to cause both strong flavor and darkening. Yield: 6-8 quarts.

Photograph for this recipe below.

★ ★

BEST-EVER BEET PICKLES

3 qt. fresh sm. beets
1 tsp. whole cloves
1 tsp. whole allspice
1 tbsp. broken cinnamon stick
2 c. sugar
2 c. vinegar

Cook beets in kettle in water to cover; cool. Slip skins from beets. Pack into sterilized jars. Place spices in bag; place in saucepan. Add sugar, 2 cups water and vinegar; boil for 10 minutes. Pour over beets; seal. Process in boiling water bath for 30 minutes.

Catherine L. Marolf
Beaver Falls Grange, P. of H. No. 554
Castorland, New York

ARISTOCRATIC PICKLES

1 gal. thinly sliced cucumbers
1 c. salt
3 tbsp. alum
2 tbsp. ginger
1 tbsp. celery seed
1 qt. vinegar
3 c. sugar
1 tbsp. whole cloves
1 tbsp. allspice
1 oz. stick cinnamon

Place cucumbers in large bowl; add salt and 1 gallon boiling water. Let stand in salt water for 6 days; stir each day. Drain pickles on the 6th day. Cover with water. Add alum; boil for 10 minutes. Drain again; cover again with water. Add ginger; boil for 10 minutes. Drain pickles again. Combine celery seed, vinegar, 1 pint water and sugar in large kettle. Tie cloves, allspice and cinnamon in cloth bag; drop in vinegar mixture. Bring to a boil; add pickles. Cook until transparent. Remove spice bag. Pack pickles in hot sterilized jars; pour boiling vinegar mixture over pickles, leaving 1/2-inch headspace. Place caps on jars. Process in boiling water bath for 10 minutes.

Bethel Payne
Middlebury Grange, No. 192
Fredericktown, Ohio

BANANA PICKLES

Cucumbers, peeled and cut lengthwise
3 c. vinegar
1 c. water
2 c. sugar
1 tbsp. salt
1 tbsp. turmeric
1 tsp. celery seed
1 tsp. mustard seed

Pack cucumbers in sterilized pint jars. Combine remaining ingredients; bring to a boil. Pour over cucumbers; seal. Process in simmering water bath for 10 minutes.

Mrs. Rhoda W. Fennell
Marshall Grange
Ford City, Pennsylvania

COMPANY BREAD AND BUTTER PICKLES
(Recipe about 50 years old)

12 peeled cucumbers, sliced
6 onions, sliced
2 green sweet peppers, seeded and sliced
1/2 c. salt
2 1/2 c. (packed) brown sugar
2 1/2 c. white sugar
5 c. vinegar
1 1/2 tsp. turmeric
1 tbsp. mustard seed
1 tbsp. celery seed

Combine cucumbers, onions and peppers; sprinkle with salt. Let stand overnight. Drain well. Combine sugars, vinegar, turmeric, mustard seed and celery seed in kettle; cook for 15 minutes. Add cucumbers, onions and peppers; bring to a boil. Pack in hot sterilized jars; seal. Process in boiling water bath for 10 minutes.

Mrs. Mildred Crumb
Templeton Grange, No. 122
East Templeton, Massachusetts

QUICK BREAD AND BUTTER CUCUMBER PICKLES
(Recipe about 100 years old)

3 or 4 onions, sliced thin
2 qt. thinly sliced cucumbers
2 green peppers, sliced thin
3 tbsp. salt
1 qt. vinegar
4 1/2 c. sugar
1 1/2 tsp. turmeric
1/4 tsp. mustard seed
1/4 tsp. celery seed
1 tsp. whole cloves

Combine onions, cucumbers, peppers and salt; let stand for 3 hours. Combine remaining ingredients in kettle; bring to a boil. Boil for 1 minute. Add cucumber mixture; boil for 10 to 15 minutes. Pack in hot sterilized pint jars; seal. Process in boiling water bath for 10 minutes. One red pepper, for color, may be substituted for 1 green pepper, if desired. Yield: 6 pints.

Mrs. Donald R. Wilkins
Winchester Grange, No. 343
Winchester, Massachusetts

FAVORITE BREAD AND BUTTER PICKLES
(Recipe over 50 years old)

6 qt. cucumbers
12 med. onions
3 lg. green peppers
2 sweet red peppers
1 c. salt
6 c. sugar
1 1/2 qt. cider vinegar

★ ★

2 tsp. turmeric
1 tsp. mustard seed
1 tsp. celery seed
1 can pimento, chopped

Cut cucumbers, onions and peppers in thin slices; place in large crock. Sprinkle salt over top; cover with cold water. Place a weighted plate on top to hold slices under brine. Let stand overnight. Pour out into colander to drain well. Combine sugar, vinegar and spices in large canning kettle; bring to a boil. Add cucumbers, onions and peppers; return to a boil. Stir in pimento. Ladle into hot sterilized jars; seal. Process in boiling water bath for 10 minutes. May be used at once, however flavor and crispness improves after storing for several weeks in a cool place. Yield: 12-15 pints.

Mrs. Vernon R. Maw
Mansfield Grange, No. 883
Mansfield, Washington

CRISP PICKLE SLICES

4 qt. sliced unpeeled med. cucumbers
6 med. white onions, sliced
2 green peppers, sliced
3 cloves of garlic
1/3 c. pickling salt
Cracked ice
5 c. sugar
3 c. cider vinegar
2 tbsp. mustard seed
1 1/2 tsp. turmeric
1 1/2 tsp. celery seed

Combine cucumbers, onions, green peppers, garlic and salt. Cover with cracked ice; mix well. Let mixture stand for 3 hours; drain well. Remove garlic. Combine remaining ingredients; pour over cucumber mixture. Bring to a boil. Pack cucumbers in hot sterilized jars; pour boiling liquid over cucumbers, leaving 1/2-inch headspace. Adjust caps. Process in boiling water bath for 5 minutes. Yield: 8 pints.

Lillian Blouvet
Inavale Grange, No. 1248
Friendship, New York

CUCUMBER-CINNAMON RINGS

15 lg. (about) cucumbers
2 c. dehydrated lime
3 c. vinegar
1 tbsp. alum
1 sm. bottle red food coloring
8 1/3 c. sugar
8 sticks cinnamon
8 whole cloves
1 pkg. red hots

Remove centers from cucumbers. Slice cucumbers; measure 2 gallons. Place cucumbers in stone jar. Mix lime with 8 1/2 quarts water; pour over cucumber rings. Let stand for 24 hours. Drain cucumbers; wash in cold water. Drain. Repeat washing and draining until all lime is removed, then drain well. Place in kettle. Mix 1 cup vinegar, alum and food coloring thoroughly; pour over cucumbers. Add enough water to cover cucumbers; bring to a boil. Reduce heat; simmer for 2 hours. Drain; place cucumbers in the stone jar. Mix remaining 2 cups vinegar, 2 cups water, sugar, cinnamon, cloves and red hots; bring to a boil, stirring until sugar and red hots are dissolved. Pour over cucumbers; let stand for 24 hours. Drain off syrup; bring to a boil. Pour over cucumbers; let stand for 24 hours. Repeat for 1 more day. Drain off syrup; bring to a boil. Pack cucumbers in hot, sterilized jars; cover with hot syrup. Seal jars. Process in boiling water bath for 10 minutes.

Mrs. Christina M. Landis
Dixie Grange, No. 2674
New Lebanon, Ohio

EASY SWEET PICKLE CHIPS

4 lb. 3 to 4-in. cucumbers
Vinegar
3 tbsp. coarse salt
1 tbsp. mustard seed
Sugar
2 1/4 tsp. celery seed
1 tbsp. whole allspice

Wash cucumbers thoroughly; cut into 1/4-inch slices. Combine cucumber slices, 1 quart vinegar, salt, mustard seed and 1/4 cup sugar in large saucepan. Simmer, covered, for 10 minutes. Drain; discard liquid. Place cucumber slices in hot sterilized jars. Mix 3 1/3 cups vinegar, 5 3/4 cups sugar, celery seed and allspice together in saucepan; cook, stirring constantly, until sugar is dissolved and mixture reaches boiling point. Fill jars to 1/8 inch from top; seal at once. Process in boiling water bath for 10 minutes. Yield: 5 pints.

Mrs. Clennen Reed
Watertown Grange, No. 1675
Vincent, Ohio

KOSHER DILL PICKLES

7 qt. cucumbers
Garlic buttons
Dill heads
Slices of red pepper
1 qt. 5% vinegar
3 qt. water
7/8 c. salt
1/2 tsp. alum

Wash cucumbers; soak overnight in cold water. Drain; pack in sterilized quart jars. Place 1/2 garlic button and 2 dill heads in each jar. Add red pepper to taste. Combine vinegar, water, salt and alum; bring to a boil. Pour over cucumbers; seal. Process in boiling water bath for 15 minutes.

Irene Mortensen
Creswell Grange, No. 496
Creswell, Oregon

★★

MILLION DOLLAR PICKLES

2 gal. 1/4-in. thick cucumber slices
2 c. salt
2 tbsp. alum
2 1/2 qt. vinegar
16 c. sugar
1/4 to 1/2 c. mixed spices
Stick cinnamon
Green food coloring

Place cucumber slices in crock. Combine salt and 1 gallon water; pour over cucumbers. Let stand for 7 days. Drain well. Pour 1 gallon boiling water over cucumbers; let stand for 24 hours. Drain well. Mix alum with 1 gallon boiling water. Pour over cucumbers; let stand for 24 hours. Drain well. Combine vinegar, sugar, mixed spices, 1 box stick cinnamon and food coloring in large saucepan; bring to a boil. Pour over cucumbers; let stand for 24 hours. Drain off syrup; bring to a boil and pour back over cucumbers for 4 more days. Drain off syrup into saucepan; bring to a boil. Pack cucumber slices into hot sterilized jars with 1 cinnamon stick in each jar. Pour syrup over cucumbers in jars. Seal. Process in boiling water bath for 10 minutes. Yield: 10-12 pints.

Mrs. P. M. Schandel, Lecturer
Greeley Grange
Kensington, Ohio

EIGHT-DAY PICKLES

2 gal. cucumber chunks
2 c. pure salt
1/4 lb. alum
9 c. vinegar
5 c. sugar
1/4 c. celery seed
1/4 c. white mustard seed
1 tbsp. cloves
1 tbsp. allspice
1 med. onion, sliced

Place cucumber chunks in crock or large glass jar; cover with cold water. Let stand for 24 hours. Drain; add salt. Cover with boiling water. Let stand for 24 hours. Drain. Dissolve alum in about 1 quart boiling water; pour over cucumbers. Add enough boiling water to cover. Let stand for 24 hours. Drain. Add 4 cups vinegar and enough boiling water to cover. Let stand 24 hours. Drain; reheat vinegar solution, then pour over cucumbers. Let stand for 24 hours. Repeat this process for 2 more days. Drain and discard vinegar solution. Pack cucumbers in hot sterilized jars. Combine remaining 5 cups vinegar, sugar, celery seed, mustard seed, cloves, allspice and onion. Bring to a boil; cook until onion is transparent. Remove onion with slotted spoon. Pour vinegar mixture over cucumbers; seal. Process in boiling water bath for 10 minutes. Spices may be placed in bag for easy removal, if desired.

Mrs. Mary Gaines Evans
Munsey Grange, No. 1204
Lebanon, Tennessee

FOURTEEN-DAY SWEET PICKLES
(Recipe 50 years old)

Cucumbers
2 c. salt
1 tbsp. powdered alum
5 pt. boiling vinegar
9 c. sugar
1/2 oz. celery seed
1 oz. cinnamon sticks

Wash cucumbers; drain. Slice cucumbers lengthwise; measure 2 gallons. Place cucumber slices in stone jar. Dissolve salt in 1 gallon boiling water; pour over cucumbers. Cover; weight down. Let stand for 1 week. Drain cucumbers; pour 1 gallon boiling water over cucumbers. Cover; weight down. Let stand for 24 hours. Drain cucumbers. Mix 1 gallon boiling water with alum; pour over cucumbers. Cover; weight down. Let stand for 24 hours. Drain cucumbers; pour 1 gallon boiling water over cucumbers. Cover; weight down. Let stand for 24 hours, then drain. Combine vinegar, 6 cups sugar, celery seed and cinnamon sticks; stir until sugar is dissolved. Pour over cucumbers; let stand for 24 hours. Drain off syrup each day for next 3 days, adding 1 cup sugar each day, reheating and pouring back over cucumbers. Drain pickles; pack in jars. Heat syrup until hot; pour over pickles. Seal jars. Process in boiling water bath for 10 minutes.

Rose L. Albright
Mendon Grange, No. 855
Ruffsdale, Pennsylvania

ICICLE PICKLES
(Recipe 35 years old)

2 gal. cucumbers
2 c. pickling salt
1 tbsp. alum
2 1/2 qt. vinegar
16 c. sugar
3 tbsp. mixed spices

Cut cucumbers lengthwise; place in crock. Mix salt with 1 gallon boiling water; pour over cucumbers. Let stand for 1 week. Drain well. Cover cucumbers with boiling water; let stand for 24 hours. Drain well. Dissolve alum in enough boiling water to cover cucumbers. Pour over cucumbers; let stand for 24 hours. Drain well. Combine vinegar, 4 cups sugar and mixed spices; bring to a boil. Pour over cucumbers; let stand for 24 hours. Pour syrup off into saucepan; stir in 4 cups sugar. Bring to a boil; pour over cucumbers. Repeat 2 more times, using remaining 8 cups sugar. Pour syrup off into saucepan; bring to a boil. Pack cucumber strips into hot sterilized jars; pour syrup into jars. Seal. May be used from crock, if desired.

Caroline Minegar
Trowbridge Grange, No. 296
Allegan, Michigan

Photo page 269 — Recipe on page 236.

Photo page 270 — Recipe on page 80.

★ ★

CLEAR DILL PICKLES

. Dill-sized cucumbers
2 qt. cider vinegar
2 qt. water
1/2 c. coarse canning salt
Dill heads

Wash cucumbers; pack in sterilized jars. Fill jars with boiling water; cover with lid. Let stand for 15 minutes. Combine vinegar, water and salt; bring to a boil. Drain jars; add 1 medium-sized dill head. Fill jars with boiling brine. Seal. Process in boiling water bath for 15 minutes. These pickles are always very clear.

Mrs. Mardell McConnaha
Bloomington Grange, No. 2057
Muscatine, Iowa

MOTHER'S MIXED PICKLES
(Recipe over 50 years old)

24 sm. cucumbers, cut in 1-in. pieces
2 qt. small onions, peeled
2 heads cauliflower, broken in flowerets
2 green peppers, chopped
2 qt. chopped green tomatoes
2 tbsp. salt
3 qt. cider vinegar
2 c. sugar
2 tsp. celery seed
3/4 c. dry mustard
3/4 c. flour
1/4 oz. turmeric

Combine vegetables in kettle; cover with water. Add salt; let stand overnight. Scald in same water; do not boil. Drain thoroughly. Mix remaining ingredients together in saucepan; bring to a boil, stirring constantly. Pour over vegetables; heat thoroughly, stirring carefully. Pack in hot, sterilized jars; seal. Process in boiling water bath for 10 minutes.

Edith Atwell
Manitou Park Grange, No. 430
Woodland Park, Colorado

SWEET MIXED PICKLES

2 qt. small cucumbers
1 c. coarse salt
1 qt. pickling onions
1 qt. small cauliflower pieces
1 tbsp. alum
6 c. white vinegar
8 c. sugar
2 tbsp. celery seed
2 tbsp. whole allspice
3 sticks cinnamon

Cut cucumbers into quarters lengthwise, then in half crosswise. Do not peel. Place in crock; sprinkle with

Photo page 271 —
Recipes on pages 135, 140, and 159.
Photo page 272 — Recipes on pages 26 and 111.

salt. Cover with 2 quarts boiling water. Let stand in cool place for 3 days. Fermentation will not spoil cucumber mixture. Pour off brine into kettle; bring to a boil. Pour back over cucumber mixture; let stand in cool place for 3 days longer. Pour off and discard brine. Rinse cucumbers, onions and cauliflower pieces in cold water; dry thoroughly. Place in crock. Dissolve alum in 1 gallon boiling water. Pour over cucumber mixture; let stand for 6 hours. Drain thoroughly. Combine vinegar, sugar and spices in saucepan; boil until syrupy, stirring frequently. Pour hot syrup over cucumber mixture. Let stand for 2 days longer, pouring off syrup, bringing syrup to a boil, then pouring syrup back over cucumber mixture. Pour off syrup into saucepan; bring to a boil. Pack cucumber mixture into hot, sterilized jars; pour syrup over top. Seal. Process in boiling water bath for 10 minutes. Mixed pickles may be kept in open crock in cool place, if desired.

Audrey Schiffler, Sec.
West Point Grange, No. 208
Wendell, Idaho

PICKLES BY THE QUART

Cucumbers
1 c. vinegar
1 tbsp. salt
1 tsp. powdered alum
2 c. sugar
1 c. water
1 tsp. whole cloves
1 stick cinnamon

Wash cucumbers; slice into quart jar. Combine vinegar, salt and alum; pour over solidly packed cucumbers in jar. Let stand for 6 weeks or longer. Drain; wash well. Place in sterilized jar. Combine sugar, 1 cup water and spices; simmer for 10 minutes. Pour over cucumbers; seal. Process in boiling water bath for 10 minutes.

Mrs. Glenn Harris
Chester Royal Grange, No. 2181
Grinnell, Iowa

MUSTARD STICKS

Cucumbers
3 3/4 c. vinegar
3 c. sugar
3 tbsp. salt
4 1/2 tsp. celery seed
3/4 tsp. mustard seed
4 1/2 tsp. turmeric

Cut large cucumbers into quarters; allow small cucumbers to remain whole. Cover with boiling water; let stand overnight. Combine remaining ingredients in saucepan; bring to a boil. Boil for 5 minutes. Pack cucumbers in hot sterilized jars; cover with vinegar mixture. Seal. Process in hot water bath for 5 to 10 minutes.

Helen Thomas
Gold Hill Grange, No. 534
Gold Hill, Oregon

★ ★

LIME PICKLES

1 gal. cucumbers
1 c. builders lime
1 gal. water
2 qt. vinegar
9 c. sugar
1 tbsp. celery seed
2 tbsp. pickling spice

Cut cucumbers into small chunks. Mix lime and water; pour over cucumbers. Let stand for 24 hours, stirring occasionally. Pour off lime water; rinse until clear. Cover with water; let stand for 3 hours. Drain. Combine vinegar, sugar, celery seed and pickling spices; bring to a boil. Pour over cucumbers; let stand for 24 hours. Bring to a boil; boil for exactly 35 minutes. Pack in hot sterilized jars; seal. Process in boiling water bath for 10 minutes.

Irene Cotton, H.E.C.
Brandon Grange
Brandon, Oregon

LIBERTY PICKLES
(Recipe 135 years old)

1/2 bushel sm. cucumbers
Salt
1 1/2 to 2 tbsp. alum
2 1/2 qt. vinegar
Sugar
2 tbsp. celery seed
1/2 box stick cinnamon

Wash cucumbers; place in 4-gallon stone jar. Cover with boiling brine, using 2 cups salt to 1 gallon water. Let stand for 1 week. Drain; cover with boiling water. Let stand for 24 hours; drain cucumbers. Dissolve alum in 1 gallon boiling water. Pour over cucumbers; add enough boiling water to cover. Let stand for 24 hours; drain. Combine vinegar, 1 1/2 cups sugar, celery seed and cinnamon; bring to a boil, stirring until sugar is dissolved. Pour over cucumbers. Drain; add 1 1/2 cups sugar to syrup. Heat syrup, then pour over pickles. Repeat for 3 days. Place in sterilized quart jars; seal. Process in simmering water bath for 10 minutes.

Dorothy B. Marshall
Windom Grange
Mitchell, Indiana

RIPE CUCUMBER PICKLES
(Recipe over 50 years old)

7 lb. ripe cucumbers
3 lb. sugar
1/2 tsp. oil of cloves
1/2 tsp. oil of cinnamon
1 pt. white vinegar

Peel cucumbers; remove seed. Cut in chunks. Cook cucumbers in boiling salted water until tender or until

transparent. Allow to drain well. Mix remaining ingredients and bring to a full boil. Pour syrup over cucumbers; allow to stand overnight. Drain off syrup; bring to a boil. Pour over cucumbers again; let stand overnight. Bring cucumbers and syrup to a boil. Pack in hot sterilized jars and seal. Process in boiling water bath for 10 minutes.

Randolph Gregory
Cheshire Grange, No. 131
Keene, New Hampshire

SACCHARIN-HORSERADISH PICKLES

Sm. whole cucumbers, washed
1 gal. cider vinegar
1 c. salt
3/4 c. grated horseradish
1 tbsp. saccharin

Pack cucumbers in hot sterilized jars. Combine remaining ingredients; mix well. Taste, then add more saccharin if needed. Bring to a boil; pour in jars over cucumbers. Seal. Process in simmering water bath for 10 minutes to complete seal. May substitute 2 tablespoons pickling spice and 1/2 cup dry mustard for horseradish, if desired.

Clella Reitmyer
Jordan Grange, No. 758
Coalport, Pennsylvania

SACCHARIN-MUSTARD PICKLES
(Recipe about 60 years old)

Sm. cucumbers
1 gal. vinegar
1 c. dry mustard
1 c. salt
2 c. (packed) brown sugar
Pinch of alum
2 tsp. saccharin

Wash cucumbers; pack in sterilized jars. Combine remaining ingredients in saucepan; bring to a boil. Pour over cucumbers; seal. Process in simmering water bath for 10 minutes.

Mrs. Matthew Morvatz, C.W.A.
Perry Township Grange, No. 1945
Carrollton, Ohio

SWEET PICKLES IN A CROCK

Firm 6-in. cucumbers
Brine strong enough to float an egg
Cider vinegar
Sugar
Whole allspice
Whole cloves
Cinnamon bark

Wash cucumbers carefully; pack in crock. Cover with brine; let stand for 3 weeks. Drain, scald and return

★ ★

cucumbers to washed, scalded crock. Cover with vinegar; let stand for 10 days. Drain well; cut cucumbers in pieces. Weigh cucumber pieces. Mix 9 pounds sugar, 2 tablespoons whole allspice, 2 tablespoons whole cloves and 1/2 box cinnamon bark with each 10 pounds cucumber pieces; place in crock. Cover crock with plate; let stand for 3 to 4 weeks. No cooking or sealing necessary. Flavor improves with aging.

Mrs. Bernhardt Seibert
Shiloh Valley Grange
Belleville, Illinois

PICKLED HOT PEPPERS IN TOMATO SAUCE AND OIL

6 to 7 lb. hot peppers
2 6-oz. cans tomato paste
2 c. vinegar
4 c. vegetable oil
2 tsp. salt
1/4 c. sugar

Cut peppers into chunks, as desired. Do not remove seeds. Combine tomato paste, 2 tomato paste cans water, vinegar, oil, salt and sugar in a large kettle; mix well. Add peppers; bring to a boil. Cook for exactly 5 minutes. Remove from heat; pack peppers in hot sterilized jars. Pour in sauce; seal. Process in hot water bath for 20 to 30 minutes. Yield: 8-9 pints.

Iola Stebbins
Sabinsville Grange, No. 989
Sabinsville, Pennsylvania

PICKLED OKRA

6 qt. small whole okra
6 heads dill
6 garlic cloves
1 c. vinegar
2 qt. water
1 c. salt

Pack okra in 6 sterilized jars. Place 1 head of dill and 1 clove of garlic in each jar. Combine vinegar, water and salt; bring to a boil. Pour hot brine over okra; seal. Process in simmering water bath for 5 minutes.

Lola Elder
Sunflower Grange, No. 1826
Kingman, Kansas

SWEET PICKLED BEANS

Young tender green beans
Vinegar
Brown sugar
Whole cloves
Stick cinnamon

Drop beans into boiling water; boil for 4 to 5 minutes or until crisp-tender. Drain well in colander; place in stone jar. Cover with vinegar; let stand for 24 hours. Pour off and measure vinegar. Combine 1 1/2 pounds brown sugar, several cloves and cinnamon sticks with each quart of vinegar; pour in saucepan. Bring to a boil; skim off any foam. Let stand until lukewarm. Pour over beans; let stand for 2 or 3 days. Pour off vinegar mixture into saucepan; bring to a boil. Let cool. Pack beans in hot sterilized jars; pour vinegar mixture over beans. Seal. Process in boiling water bath for 10 minutes.

Ruby A. Malinowski
Mountain Valley Grange, No. 79
Yacolt, Washington

ZUCCHINI PICKLES

7 lb. large zucchini
2 c. slaked lime
9 c. sugar
2 qt. vinegar
2 tbsp. broken stick cinnamon
1 tbsp. (heaping) whole cloves
1 or 2 tsp. celery seed

Peel and remove centers from zucchini; cut into chunks. Dissolve lime in 2 gallons water; add zucchini. Let stand for 24 hours. Drain; wash until water is clear. Combine sugar, vinegar, 2 cups water, cinnamon, cloves and celery seed; bring to a boil. Pour over zucchini. Let stand for 24 hours. Bring to a boil; reduce temperature. Simmer until clear. Pack in hot sterilized jars; seal. Process in simmering water bath for 10 minutes. Green food coloring may be added, if desired.

Mrs. W. L. Yockey
Moscow Grange, No. 236
Moscow, Idaho

CALICO RELISH

4 lg. green peppers
4 lg. red peppers
4 lg. onions
10 med. carrots, scraped
1 1/2 c. sugar
2 tbsp. salt
1 1/2 c. vinegar

Cut green and red peppers into quarters; remove seeds. Peel and quarter onions. Grind carrots, green and red peppers and onions through food chopper, using coarse blade; place in kettle. Cover with boiling water; let stand for 5 minutes. Drain well. Stir in sugar, salt and vinegar; bring to boiling point. Reduce heat; simmer, stirring occasionally, for 5 minutes. Ladle into hot, sterilized jars; seal. Process in boiling water bath for 10 minutes. Cool, then label. Store in cool, dry place. Yield: Eight 1/2-pint jars.

Marcia Hunt
Columbia Grange, No. 87
Vancouver, Washington

★ ★

FRESH CORN RELISH

    8 c. fresh cut corn
    2 c. chopped cabbage
    1 1/2 c. diced celery
    1 1/2 c. chopped seeded green pepper
    1 3/4 c. diced onion
    2 c. cider vinegar
    1/2 c. water
    1/3 c. fresh lemon juice
    1 c. sugar
    2 tbsp. salt
    2 1/2 tsp. whole celery seed
    5 tsp. powdered mustard
    1/8 tsp. ground cayenne pepper
    1 tsp. ground turmeric

Combine first 10 ingredients in large kettle. Boil slowly for 25 minutes, stirring frequently. Add remaining ingredients; cook for 15 minutes longer or until thickened. Place in hot sterilized jars; seal. Process in hot water bath for 10 minutes to complete seals. Yield: 7 half pints.

Photograph for this recipe above.

EASY CORN RELISH

    1 lg. head cabbage
    6 red or green peppers
    6 lg. onions
    Salt
    3 c. cut or scraped corn
    6 tbsp. cornstarch
    1 tbsp. dry mustard
    1 tbsp. turmeric
    1 tsp. celery seed
    5 c. sugar
    2 pt. vinegar

Chop cabbage, peppers and onions; place in kettle. Cover with 1 handful salt; let stand for 1 hour. Drain. Stir in corn and remaining ingredients; bring to a boil. Boil for 15 minutes, stirring constantly. Pack in hot, sterilized jars; seal. Process in boiling water bath for 10 minutes.

Mrs. Austin Rowan
Fawn Grove Grange
Whiteford, Missouri

PIONEER CORN RELISH

    1 doz. medium ears of sweet corn
    2 c. chopped onions
    2 green peppers, chopped
    1 red pepper, chopped
    1 c. chopped cabbage
    2 tbsp. salt
    1/4 tsp. pepper

★ ★

1 1/2 tbsp. dry mustard
1 c. sugar
2 c. vinegar, 5% acidity

Cut corn from cob. Combine with onions, peppers and cabbage in kettle. Add remaining ingredients; bring to boiling point. Reduce heat; simmer for 1 hour, stirring occasionally. Pour into hot, sterilized jars; seal. Process in boiling water bath for 10 minutes.

Mrs. Helen Updike
Aurora Grange, No. 874
Wellsboro, Pennsylvania

TASTY CORN RELISH

2 doz. ears of tender corn
1 head cabbage
6 lg. onions
2 red peppers
2 tbsp. celery seed
2 tbsp. mustard seed
2 1-lb. boxes brown sugar
1 tbsp. salt
2 qt. vinegar

Cut corn off cob. Chop cabbage, onions and peppers. Mix corn, cabbage, onions and peppers in kettle. Add celery seed and mustard seed; stir in sugar, salt and vinegar. Cook until cabbage and corn are tender. Place in hot, sterilized jars immediately; seal. Process in boiling water bath for 10 minutes.

Mrs. Robert Hurley
Mt. Pleasant Grange
Wilmington, Ohio

BEET RELISH

1 qt. cooked ground beets
2 sm. onions, chopped fine
3 red peppers, chopped fine
2 tsp. salt
1/3 c. prepared horseradish
2 c. vinegar
3/4 c. sugar

Mix all ingredients in kettle; bring to a boil. Cook for 15 minutes. Place in hot, sterilized jars; seal. Process in boiling water bath for 10 minutes.

From a Grange Friend

END OF SEASON RELISH
(Recipe 60 years old)

2 qt. chopped green tomatoes
1 qt. chopped ripe tomatoes
3 red sweet peppers, chopped
3 green sweet peppers, chopped
3 bunches celery, chopped
3 lg. onions, chopped
1 head cabbage, chopped
1 lg. cucumber, chopped

1/2 c. salt
6 c. vinegar
4 c. sugar
1 tsp. pepper
1 tsp. mustard

Mix vegetables with salt; let stand overnight. Drain well. Stir in vinegar, sugar, pepper and mustard; cook for about 30 minutes. Pack in hot, sterilized jars; seal. Process in boiling water bath for 10 minutes. Shelled beans and lima beans may be added to vegetables, if desired.

Mrs. Iva Denney
Eno Grange, No. 2080
Bidwell, Ohio

FAMILY GREEN TOMATO RELISH

8 c. chopped green tomatoes
1 1/2 c. chopped onions
1/2 c. chopped red sweet pepper
1/2 c. chopped green sweet pepper
1/2 c. sugar
1 c. light corn syrup
1 1/2 c. vinegar
1 tbsp. salt
1 tbsp. white mustard seed
1/2 tsp. white pepper

Mix tomatoes, onions, red and green peppers, sugar, corn syrup, vinegar, salt, mustard seed and white pepper in kettle. Bring to a boil; reduce heat. Simmer for about 45 minutes or until vegetables are crisp-tender. Place in hot, sterilized jars; seal. Process in boiling water bath for 10 minutes.

Emma A. Ingalls
Eclipse Grange, No. 311
Plaistow, New Hampshire

GREEN TOMATO PICCALILLI
(Recipe at least 50 years old)

2 gal. green tomatoes
12 lg. onions
2 qt. vinegar
4 c. sugar
2 tbsp. dry mustard
2 tbsp. salt
2 tbsp. pepper
1 tbsp. ground cloves
1 tbsp. ground allspice

Wash and grind tomatoes; do not peel. Grind onions. Place tomatoes and onions in kettle. Add remaining ingredients; mix well. Cook until tomatoes and onions are tender. Place in hot, sterilized jars; seal. Process in boiling water bath for 10 minutes. Store for at least 1 month before serving.

Gloria G. Wildgreebe
Cedar Grange, No. 534
Maple Valley, Washington

★ ★

OVERNIGHT GREEN TOMATO RELISH

24 lg. green tomatoes
12 med. onions
3 red peppers
3 green peppers
1 c. salt
6 c. sugar
2 1/2 pt. vinegar
1/2 c. mixed pickling spice

Grind green tomatoes, onions and red and green peppers; mix in kettle. Add salt; mix well. Let stand overnight. Drain well; squeeze out liquid. Mix sugar and vinegar in saucepan. Tie mixed pickling spice in cloth bag; add to vinegar mixture. Bring to a boil over low heat; boil for 20 minutes, stirring frequently. Pour into hot, sterilized jars; seal. Process in boiling water bath for 10 minutes. Yield: 6 pints.

Mrs. Harriett Stevenson
Newark Grange, No. 1004
Heath, Ohio

TANGY GREEN TOMATO RELISH

1 gal. ground cabbage
6 green peppers, ground
1 gal. ground green tomatoes
6 onions, ground
1   4-oz. jar horseradish
1/2 c. salt
2 tbsp. cinnamon
3 tbsp. dry mustard
1 tbsp. turmeric
9 c. sugar
Vinegar

Combine all ingredients in kettle, using enough vinegar to cover. Boil for 15 minutes. Pack in hot, sterilized jars; seal. Process in boiling water bath for 10 minutes.

Geneva Atkinson, D.W.A.
Kansas State Grange
St. Paul, Kansas

INDIA RELISH
(Recipe over 50 years old)

7 lb. green tomatoes
2 lg. onions
8 green peppers
8 red peppers
3 pt. vinegar
3 lb. sugar
1 tbsp. whole cloves
1 tbsp. allspice
3 sticks cinnamon
2 tbsp. salt
1 tbsp. mustard seed
1 tbsp. celery seed

Cut tomatoes in quarters. Peel and quarter onions. Cut peppers in strips; remove membrane and seeds. Force vegetables through food chopper. Place in large kettle; bring to a boil. Cook for 15 minutes, then drain through colander. Combine vinegar, sugar and spices in saucepan; bring to a boil. Cook until thick. Sprinkle salt, mustard seed and celery seed over vegetables. Strain syrup. Pack vegetables in hot sterilized jars; pour boiling syrup over vegetables. Place caps on jars. Process in boiling water bath for 10 minutes.

Margy Rebmann
Scio Grange, No. 923
Scio, Oregon

JAN'S SPECIAL RELISH

6 green tomatoes
12 green peppers
2 sm. hot peppers
6 med. carrots
6 med. onions
1 med. head cabbage
1 med. head cauliflower
3 c. sugar
3 c. vinegar
1 c. water
2 tbsp. salt
1 tbsp. celery seed
1 tbsp. (scant) dillseed

Prepare first 6 ingredients for food grinder. Force all vegetables except cauliflower through coarse blade of food grinder. Break cauliflower in small pieces. Combine sugar, vinegar, water, salt, celery seed and dillseed in large kettle; bring to a boil. Add vegetables; boil for 25 minutes. Pack in hot sterilized jars; place caps on jars. Process in boiling water bath for 5 minutes. Yield: 3 quarts.

Janice Curtis
Tuftonboro Grange, No. 142
Tuftonboro, New Hampshire

NO-COOK VEGETABLE RELISH
(Recipe 35 years old)

8 carrots
12 onions
12 red bell peppers
12 green bell peppers
2 med. heads cabbage
3/4 c. salt
1 1/2 c. vinegar
6 c. sugar
3 tbsp. celery seed
3 tbsp. mustard seed
1/2 tsp. ground red pepper (opt.)

Chop first 5 ingredients; place in kettle. Add salt; let stand for 3 hours. Drain. Add vinegar, sugar, celery seed, mustard seed and red pepper; mix well. Pack in hot, sterilized jars; seal. Process in boiling water bath for 10 minutes. Yield: 4-5 pints.

Mrs. Dorothy Stewart, C.W.A.
Victory Grange
Jackson, Ohio

★ ★

ANN'S PEPPER HASH

12 lg. green or red peppers
1/2 head cabbage
12 lg. onions
1/4 c. salt
2 c. sugar
1 oz. celery seed
2 qt. vinegar

Remove seeds from peppers. Chop cabbage, onions and peppers fine; place in bowl. Cover with boiling water; let stand for 30 minutes. Drain thoroughly. Mix salt, sugar, celery seed and vinegar in kettle; bring to a boil. Add pepper mixture; boil for 20 minutes. Place in hot, sterilized jars; seal. Process in boiling water bath for 10 minutes.

Ann Witherwax
Cortlandville Grange, No. 461
Cortland, New York

HARLEQUIN SAUCE

12 sweet red peppers
12 green peppers
12 lg. onions
2 tbsp. salt
2 c. (packed) light brown sugar
1 qt. vinegar

Chop the peppers and onions coarsely. Pour boiling water over peppers to cover; let stand for 5 minutes. Drain; cover with boiling water. Let stand for 10 minutes. Drain; add onions, salt, sugar and vinegar. Bring to a boil. Cook for 20 minutes. Pack in hot sterilized jars; place caps on jars. Process in boiling water bath for 10 to 15 minutes.

Mrs. Herma Jane Huseby
Lexington Grange, No. 94
Bonner Springs, Kansas

MANGO PEPPER RELISH
(Recipe 70 years old)

6 c. ground unpeeled apples
6 c. ground green tomatoes, drained
4 c. ground mango peppers, drained
4 c. ground cabbage
4 c. ground onions
4 c. vinegar
6 c. sugar
2 tbsp. prepared mustard
2 tbsp. coarse salt
1 tbsp. mixed pickling spice

Combine all ingredients in kettle. Bring to a boil; cook for 1 hour, stirring frequently. Pack into hot sterilized jars; seal. Process in boiling water bath for 15 minutes. Yield: 10-12 pints.

Marcia Moore
Plymouth Grange, No. 856
New Plymouth, Ohio

OVERNIGHT PEPPER HASH
(Recipe about 100 years old)

8 red bell peppers
8 yellow bell peppers
8 green bell peppers
1 doz. onions
2 heads cabbage
1/4 c. celery seed
1/4 c. mustard seed
3 c. sugar
3 pt. vinegar

Chop vegetables; place in bowl. Add enough salted water to cover; let stand overnight. Drain well. Add remaining ingredients; mix well. Place in hot, sterilized jars; seal. Process in boiling water bath for 35 to 45 minutes.

Mrs. E. W. Shobe
Madison Goodwill Grange, No. 2630
Washington Court House, Ohio

RED PEPPER RELISH
(Recipe 50 years old)

12 red bell peppers
12 green bell peppers
3 lg. onions, chopped
1 qt. vinegar
2 c. sugar
1 1/2 tsp. salt

Wash red and green peppers; remove seeds. Chop peppers coarsely; place in bowl. Pour enough boiling water over peppers to cover; let stand for 5 minutes. Drain. Cover with boiling water again; let stand for 10 minutes. Drain; add onions. Mix vinegar, sugar and salt in large saucepan; boil for 5 minutes. Add pepper mixture; boil for 10 minutes longer. Pack in hot, sterilized jars; seal. Process in boiling water bath for 10 minutes.

Ada H. Mason
San Marcos Grange, No. 633
Escondido, California

RHUBARB RELISH
(Recipe 50 years old)

2 qt. finely chopped rhubarb
2 qt. sliced onions
3 1-lb. boxes (or less) brown sugar
1 tbsp. cinnamon
1 tbsp. allspice
2 tsp. pepper
2 tsp. salt
1 1/2 qt. vinegar

Cook rhubarb and onions in kettle for 20 minutes. Add sugar, spices, pepper, salt and vinegar; mix well. Cook for 1 hour or until thick. Place in sterilized jars; seal. Process in boiling water bath for 10 minutes.

Mrs. Iris Hardy
Waverley Grange, No. 361
Belmont, Massachusetts

★★★

Place tomatoes in large container; sprinkle with 1/2 cup salt. Let stand overnight, then drain. Rinse in cold water; drain. Combine vinegar, water, sugar and spices in large kettle; bring to a boil. Boil for 5 minutes. Add tomatoes, onions and peppers. Simmer until all ingredients are tender. Ladle into jars up to 1/2 inch from tops; place caps on jars. Process in boiling water bath for 5 minutes.

Mrs. Elsie Bixby, C.W.A. Chm.
Quinnatisset Grange
Thompson, Connecticut

SWEET SQUASH RELISH

12 c. shredded squash
4 c. chopped onions
2 green peppers, chopped
1 red pepper, chopped
5 tsp. salt
2 1/2 c. vinegar
2 tsp. pickling spice
6 c. sugar

Mix first 5 ingredients in kettle; let stand overnight. Drain. Pour 1 glass cold water over squash mixture; drain again. Mix vinegar and pickling spice in saucepan; boil for about 5 minutes. Strain over sugar; stir until sugar dissolves. Add to squash mixture; mix well. Bring to a boil; reduce heat. Simmer for about 10 minutes. Place in hot, sterilized jars; seal. Process in boiling water bath for 10 minutes. Yield: 7 pints.

Mrs. Willis Lotz
Clear Creek Grange, No. 84
Welch, Oklahoma

TANGY UNCOOKED RELISH

1 lb. ripe tomatoes, chopped
16 sm. white onions, chopped
4 med. green peppers, chopped
2 c. seeded golden raisins
1 tbsp. salt
2 c. canned applesauce
2 tsp. dry mustard
2 c. white vinegar

Combine chopped vegetables, raisins, salt, applesauce and dry mustard in a large bowl; add vinegar. Mix well. Turn into large jar; cover tightly. Refrigerate for 1 week or longer for maximum flavor. Yield: About 2 1/2 quarts relish.

Photograph for this recipe above.

SPICY TOMATO RELISH
(Recipe 80 years old)

2 qt. cut-up ripe tomatoes
2 qt. cut-up green tomatoes
Salt
1 qt. vinegar
1 pt. water
2 lb. sugar
1 tsp. cinnamon
1 tsp. cloves
1 tsp. mustard
1 tsp. celery salt
8 sm. onions, peeled
6 red peppers, cut up
6 green peppers, cut up

TANGY COLESLAW RELISH

4 lb. green cabbage, cut into 1-in. pieces
3 lg. onions, quartered
3 green peppers, cut into chunks
1 red pepper, cut into chunks
2/3 c. salt
2 c. sugar
1 tsp. celery seed
2 c. white vinegar

Place enough cabbage, onion and pepper pieces in blender container to fill 4-cup capacity. Cover with cold water; cover blender. Process at chop for 2 to 3 seconds. Drain well. Repeat until all vegetables are chopped. Place vegetables, salt and cold water to cover in a large bowl; cover. Let stand overnight. Drain well; pack into hot sterilized jars. Combine sugar, celery seed and vinegar in saucepan; bring to a boil. Pour into jars, leaving 1/4-inch headspace; seal. Process in boiling water bath for 10 minutes. Yield: 6 pints.

Mildred Anderson
Jefferson Grange, No. 2019
Mercer, Pennsylvania

★ ★

TOMATO-PEPPER RELISH
(Recipe 50 years old)

6 green tomatoes
6 ripe tomatoes
6 green peppers
6 lg. onions
1 hot pepper
Salt
1 qt. vinegar
2 tbsp. turmeric
1 sm. jar prepared mustard
3/4 c. flour
2 tbsp. prepared horseradish
1 c. sugar

Chop green tomatoes, ripe tomatoes, green peppers, onions and hot pepper; place in kettle. Add 3 tablespoons salt; let stand for 1 hour. Drain well. Mix 1 teaspoon salt with remaining ingredients; stir into tomato mixture. Cook for 10 minutes. Place in hot, sterilized pint jars; seal. Process in boiling water bath for 10 minutes. Yield: 6 pints.

Mrs. John W. Steiger
Golden Triangle Grange, No. 176
Eustis, Florida

UNCOOKED RELISH

1 pt. chopped sweet red peppers
1 pt. chopped sweet green peppers
1 qt. chopped cabbage
1 pt. chopped white onions
2 or 3 hot peppers
5 tbsp. salt
2 tsp. celery seed
4 c. sugar
1 qt. vinegar

Put each vegetable through food chopper, using coarse blade. Drain off and discard liquid if vegetables are covered with liquid. Measure each vegetable after chopping. Mix vegetables with salt; let stand overnight. Drain off as much liquid as possible and discard. Add spices, sugar and vinegar to drained vegetables; mix well. Pack into sterilized jars and seal. Process in boiling water bath for 15 minutes to complete seal.

Mrs. Judy Groeper
Millbrook Grange, No. 1864
Elmwood, Illinois

OVERNIGHT ZUCCHINI RELISH

10 c. ground zucchini
4 c. chopped onion
5 tbsp. salt
2 1/4 c. vinegar
6 c. sugar
1 tsp. nutmeg
1 tsp. turmeric
1 tsp. dry mustard
1/2 tsp. celery seed
1/4 tsp. pepper
2 bell peppers, ground

Mix first 3 ingredients in kettle; let stand overnight. Rinse with cold water; drain. Add remaining ingredients. Bring to a boil; reduce heat. Simmer for 30 minutes. Place in hot, sterilized jars; seal. Process in boiling water bath for 15 minutes. Yield: 8 pints.

Edna M. Tholl
Clearwater Grange, No. 299
Clearwater, Idaho

DELICIOUS ZUCCHINI RELISH

2 qt. ground zucchini
4 med. onions, ground
2 lg. green peppers, ground
1/4 c. salt
2 1/4 c. sugar
2 1/4 c. white vinegar
1/2 tsp. ground cloves
1 tsp. turmeric
1 tsp. dry mustard
1 tsp. celery seed
1 tsp. mustard seed

Mix zucchini, onions and green peppers in kettle. Mix salt with just enough water to dissolve; mix with enough water to cover vegetables. Pour over vegetables; let stand for 3 hours. Drain well. Mix remaining ingredients in kettle. Add zucchini mixture; mix again. Boil for 5 minutes. Place in hot, sterilized jars; seal. Process in boiling water bath for 10 minutes. Yield: 4-5 pints.

Tess Johnson
Bennett Valley Grange, No. 16
Santa Rosa, California

RETA MAE'S ZUCCHINI RELISH

13 c. ground zucchini
4 c. ground onions
1 red bell pepper, ground
1 green bell pepper, ground
2 1/2 tbsp. salt
2 1/2 c. vinegar
5 c. (or less) sugar
1 tsp. dry mustard
2 tsp. celery seed
1/2 tsp. pepper
1 tbsp. cornstarch
1 tsp. turmeric
1 tsp. nutmeg
1 tsp. cinnamon

Mix first 5 ingredients in kettle; let stand overnight. Drain. Rinse with cold water; drain well. Add remaining ingredients; bring to a boil. Cook for 30 minutes; remove from heat. Place in hot, sterilized jars; seal. Process in boiling water bath for 10 minutes. Yield: 8-10 pints.

Mrs. Gordon Tate
Mica Flats Grange, No. 436
Coeur d'Alene, Idaho

★ ★

AMISH SANDWICH SPREAD

  2 red sweet peppers
  2 yellow sweet peppers
  2 green sweet peppers
  6 green tomatoes
  6 cucumbers
  6 carrots
  1/2 c. salt
  1 pt. vinegar
  4 c. sugar
  3/4 c. flour
  1 c. prepared mustard

Grind vegetables; add salt and enough water to cover. Let stand overnight. Drain. Add vinegar and sugar; boil for 25 minutes. Stir in flour and mustard; boil, stirring constantly, for 10 minutes longer. Place in hot sterilized jars; seal. Process for 10 minutes in simmering water bath to complete seal. Yield: About 3 quarts.

Maxine Patterson
Keene Hill Grange, No. 1602
Millersburg, Ohio

OLD-FASHIONED SANDWICH SPREAD

  2 c. drained ground green tomatoes
  2 green sweet peppers, ground
  2 red sweet peppers, ground

  1 tsp. salt
  6 sweet pickles, ground
  1 c. sugar
  2 tbsp. flour
  2 tbsp. prepared mustard
  1/2 c. vinegar
  1 c. sour cream
  2 eggs, well beaten

Mix tomatoes and peppers in kettle; sprinkle with salt. Let stand for several minutes; drain. Add 1/2 cup water. Cook until tender. Add pickles; keep warm. Combine remaining ingredients in saucepan; mix well. Bring to a boil; cook until thick. Stir into hot tomato mixture. Place in hot sterilized jars; seal. Process in simmering water bath for 10 minutes. Store in cool place. Yield: 6 to 8 pints.

Mrs. Mary Lou Willis
Morning Grange, No. 217
Gardner, Kansas

CANNED BEEF

  1 front quarter beef
  Salt

Remove bone from beef; cut beef in 2-inch squares. Fry in small amount of fat until all sides are brown. Place in sterilized quart jars, pressing down firmly to

★ ★

get as much beef in as possible. Add 1 teaspoon salt to each jar; add water if there is not enough liquid. Seal jars; pressure can for 1 hour after steam has reached 15 pounds pressure.

Lois Hicklin
Platte Vally Grange, No. 455
Kersey, Colorado

CORNED BEEF
(Recipe over 100 years old)

1/2 peck coarse salt
100 lb. beef, cut into serving pieces
1/4 lb. saleratus
1/4 lb. saltpeter
1 qt. molasses

Place layer of salt on bottom of pickle tub or crock; add layer of beef. Repeat layers until all salt and beef are used. Let stand overnight. Dissolve saleratus and saltpeter in small amount of warm water; stir in molasses. Pour over beef; add enough water to cover beef. Place board or plate over beef; weight down to keep beef under brine. Let stand for 10 days. Remove beef from brine; wash and drain. Place beef in freezer bags; freeze. Two pounds brown sugar may be substituted for molasses.

Hazel D. Thayer
Middlebury Grange, No. 192
Fredericktown, Ohio

RECIPE FOR CURING HOME-KILLED PORK HAMS
(Recipe about 100 years old)

100 lb. pork hams or sides of bacon
7 lb. salt
1 1/2 lb. brown sugar
3 oz. saltpeter
2 1/2 oz. soda

Place pork hams in 20-gallon crock. Mix remaining ingredients with enough water to dissolve all ingredients; boil and skim until no scum appears. Cool until cold. Pour over hams; add enough water to crock to cover hams. Weight down so that hams are covered at all times. Let hams remain in solution for 6 weeks, adding water, if needed. Drain and dry; cook hams. May be hickory smoked, if desired.

Mrs. Nyle Katz
Fredonia Grange, No. 1713
Marshall, Michigan

HEAD CHEESE
(Recipe about 60 years old)

Pork head
Pork hearts
Pork tails
Pork tongues

Pork feet
Salt and pepper to taste

Trim all meat from pork head; place in kettle. Soak overnight in salted water. Drain. Add hearts, tails, tongues and feet or any other trimmings there is no other use for; cover with water. Cook until meat can easily be separated from bones. Drain off liquor; reserve. Remove meat from bones; chop fine. Return meat to kettle; season with salt and pepper. Cover with reserved liquor; boil for about 15 minutes. Pour into shallow pan. Cover with cheesecloth; weight down. Store in refrigerator. Slice to serve.

Mrs. Wayne Clinesmith
Centerville Grange, No. 1468
Centerville, Kansas

SOUSED PIGS' FEET

Pigs' feet
Weak lime water (opt.)
Salt
Vinegar
Whole peppers
Allspice
Cloves (opt.)
Mace (opt.)

Scald and scrape desired number of pigs' feet; remove covering of toes. Singe toes in hot embers to remove covering, if necessary. Place feet in lime water to whiten, if desired. Wash pigs' feet; place in pot of hot, not boiling, water. Add small amount of salt; simmer, removing scum from liquid as formed, until meat is tender and bones are loosened by fork. Remove pigs' feet from liquid; place in jars or pots, filling 2/3 full. Cover with vinegar; fill jars with liquid in which pigs' feet were cooked. Add desired amount of peppers, allspice, cloves and mace; place cloth, then tightfitting cover over jars. Let stand until soused. Remove feet from vinegar mixture; split in half from top to toe. May be dipped in flour and fried in hot lard until brown or broiled until brown, then buttered, if desired.

Mrs. John J. Yearick
Nittany Grange, No. 334
Mill Hall, Pennsylvania

VERMONT HOMEMADE SAUSAGE
(Recipe over 100 years old)

1/2 tsp. pepper
1 tsp. salt
1 tsp. sage
1 lb. ground pork

Mix all ingredients well. Shape into patties; place in freezer bags. Freeze.

Majorie W. Wilsey
Connecticut River Grange, No. 518
Ascutney, Vermont

★ ★

SUMMER SAUSAGE
(Recipe at least 60 years old)

    25 lb. equal parts beef necks and pork
        shoulders
    10 to 12 oz. salt
    1 oz. ground white pepper
    1/2 oz. white peppercorns
    1/2 oz. black peppercorns
    1/2 oz. saltpeter

Trim excess fat from meat. Pork must be frozen at 0 degrees for 21 days, then thawed. Remove skin and bone from pork shoulders, then cut pork into chunks ready for grinding. Force beef through food grinder, using coarse blade. Combine ground beef and seasonings; set aside in cold place for 36 hours. Force pork through grinder, using medium blade. Grind beef and pork together, alternating equal amounts through the grinder. Grind one more time, then let set overnight in refrigerator. Knead thoroughly, adding a small amount of water to make mixing easier. Knead until mixture becomes gray and is thoroughly mixed. Stuff mixture into casings, using sausage stuffer. Casings may be made from clean muslin sewn in long tube shapes. Store in 25 to 35-degree room for 10 days to 2 weeks or until casings wrinkle slightly when sausage shrinks. Prepare fire with hickory, thorn, apple, black birch or alder logs to create smoke with little flame. Hang sausage over smoke 1 hour per day for 2 weeks, then hang in cool dry place, leaving space between casings.

Pat Iman
Wife of State Master
Victor, Montana

TREDA'S HOMEMADE PORK SAUSAGE

    9 lb. lean ground pork
    1 tbsp. pepper
    2 tbsp. sage
    3 tbsp. salt

Mix all ingredients thoroughly. Shape into patties; place in freezer bags. Freeze.

Treda Krebs, C.W.A. Chm.
Lake Creek Grange, No. 818
Harrisburg, Oregon

QUICK-DRIED VENISON
(Recipe over 100 years old)

    Venison
    Salt
    Coarsely ground pepper

Cut venison into 2 x 8 x 1/4-inch strips; rub each piece well with salt, using 1/2 cup salt to every 15 pounds venison. Sprinkle with pepper; store in earthen jar for about 1 day. Thread on heavy string; hang in sun for about 1 week or until dry.

Mrs. Elgin Bauer
Fredericksburg Grange, No. 1650
Fredericksburg, Texas

PICKLED FISH

    Small carp or other fish
    Salt
    3 c. vinegar
    2 c. water
    2 peppercorns
    20 whole allspice
    3 bay leaves
    1/4 c. (packed) brown sugar
    1/2 c. sugar
    1 tsp. pickling spice
    1 onion, sliced
    3 slices lemon

Clean carp; cut into fillets. Salt well; place in enamel pan. Let stand overnight. Wash carp, then drain; cut into pieces. Mix 2 1/2 teaspoons salt with remaining ingredients except onion and lemon; boil for 5 minutes. Add carp, onion and lemon; boil for 5 minutes. May be canned hot or placed in china or pottery dish and refrigerated until congealed.

Mrs. Glenn Harris
Chester Royal Grange, No. 2181
Grinnell, Iowa

GRANDMA'S SUGARED BEETS
(Recipe 50 years old)

    1 qt. beets
    1 c. sugar
    1 1/2 c. vinegar
    1 tsp. salt

Wash and cook beets with skins on until fork-tender. Let cool. Remove skins and slice. Place beets in saucepan; add sugar, vinegar and salt. Boil for 10 minutes. Remove from heat. Pack in jars; place caps on jars. Process in boiling water bath for 10 minutes.

Mrs. Fred Garrett
Rainsboro Grange, No. 2653
Hillsboro, Ohio

SWEET AND SOUR BEETS

    Fresh beets
    2 c. 90-grain white vinegar
    1 tbsp. plain salt
    1/2 tsp. peppercorns
    1/2 tsp. whole cloves (opt.)
    3 c. sugar

Wash beets thoroughly; boil in water to cover until tender. Peel and cut in halves or quarters. Combine vinegar, 2 cups water, salt, peppercorns, cloves and sugar; bring to a boil. Pack beets in hot sterilized quart jars. Fill with syrup; place caps on jars. Process in boiling water bath for 10 minutes. Yield: 8 pints or 4 quarts.

Mrs. Lydia Feuge
Fredericksburg Grange, No. 1650
Fredericksburg, Texas

★ HORSERADISH ★ ★ ★ ★ ★ ★ ★ ★ ★ ★ ★ ★ ★ ★ ★ ★

CANNED CORN AND LIMA BEANS

Fresh corn
Fresh green lima beans
Salt

Cook corn in boiling water for 5 minutes. Cut from cob; do not scrape. Combine with from 1/2 to equal amount of green lima beans; place in kettle. Bring to boiling point; pour to 1 inch of top of jar. This amount of head space is needed because these vegetables tend to swell while processing. Add 1/2 teaspoon salt to pints; add 1 teaspoon salt to quarts. Add enough water to cover vegetables. Wipe off anything spilled on top or threads of jar. Place dome lid on jar; screw band tight. Process pints for 55 minutes, quarts for 1 hour and 25 minutes at 10 pounds pressure.

Photograph for this recipe on page 285.

CANNED CORN

2 qt. corn kernels
1 qt. water
4 tsp. sugar
4 tsp. salt

Combine all ingredients in large saucepan. Cook for 8 to 10 minutes or until milk is clear. Pack loosely into sterilized pint jars to within 1 1/2 inches from top, adding more liquid if needed. Seal. Process at 10 pounds pressure for 55 minutes.

Mrs. Carrie Pritsch
Bremen Grange, No. 2160
Bremen, Indiana

CANNING TOMATOES
(Recipe 75 years old)

Fully ripe tomatoes
Salt

Dip tomatoes in boiling water for 30 seconds; plunge in cold water. Remove skins; cut out stems. Cut large tomatoes in half. Place in large kettle; bring to a boil over low heat, stirring often to prevent sticking. Cook until soft, but not mushy. Ladle into hot sterilized quart jars up to 1/2 inch from tops of jars; add 1/2 teaspoon salt to each jar. Place caps on jars. Process in boiling water bath for 10 minutes.
Method is Connecticut State Grange Blue Ribbon process.

Mrs. Ruth H. Eisnor
Newington Grange, No. 44
Newington, Connecticut

CANNED STEWED TOMATOES

Red ripe tomatoes
1 med. green pepper
1/2 c. chopped onion

1 c. sliced celery
1 tbsp. sugar
2 tsp. salt

Wash, rinse and drain all vegetables. Scald, core, skin, chop and measure 4 quarts tomatoes. Remove stem and blossom ends from green pepper. Discard seeds; cut green pepper into small pieces. Combine all ingredients in kettle; bring to boiling point. Pour to 1/2 inch of top of jars; wipe off anything spilled on top or threads of jars. Place dome lids on jars; screw bands tight. Process pints 15 minutes, quarts 20 minutes at 10 pounds pressure or 50 minutes in boiling water bath canner. Yield: 6-7 pints.

Photograph for this recipe on page 000.

CANNED VEGETABLE SOUP

18 ears of corn
1/2 bushel tomatoes
6 lg. stalks of celery
6 lg. onions
2 heads cabbage
3 peppers
12 carrots
Salt and pepper to taste

Cut corn from ears. Peel tomatoes. Cut celery in chunks. Peel and cut onions in half. Cut cabbage in wedges; remove core. Cut peppers in strips; remove seeds and membranes. Pare carrots. Force all vegetables except corn through food grinder. Combine corn, ground vegetables, salt and pepper in large kettle; bring to a boil. Cook for 5 minutes. Pour into hot sterilized quart jars; place caps on jars. Process at 10 pounds pressure for 1 hour and 25 minutes.

Helen Slaughter
Charity Grange, No. 1208
Dayton, Ohio

CANNED HORSERADISH

Horseradish roots
1 c. vinegar
1/2 c. sugar

Scrape horseradish roots if rough; use brush to wash thoroughly. Do not peel unless necessary. Roots may be ground in meat grinder or chopped in blender with small amount of the vinegar. Do not add salt. Add sugar and vinegar to chopped horseradish to make desirable consistency. Pack in hot sterilized jars; seal tightly. Store in refrigerator. If root is dug in spring, set crowns of plants back in ground to grow more plants for next year.

Floyd Lacina
Chester Royal Grange, No. 2181
Grinnell, Iowa

★ ★

PRESERVED PUMPKINS

Pumpkin
Sugar
Juice of lemons

Cut pumpkin in half; remove seeds. Pare, then cut pumpkin in slices. Measure; use equal parts pumpkin and sugar. Place slices in deep dish; sprinkle with sugar. Sprinkle lemon juice over pumpkin and sugar, using juice of 1 lemon per pint. Let set for 2 to 3 days, adding 1/2 cup water for every 2 cups sugar. Bring to a boil; cook until pumpkin is tender. Let set for 7 days, then drain syrup into saucepan. Boil until thick, then skim. Pack pumpkin in hot sterilized jars; pour boiling syrup to cover pumpkin up to 1/8 inch from top of jar. Process in simmering water bath for 10 minutes. A small amount of ginger and thinly pared lemon rind may be added to boiling syrup for flavor, if desired.

Gertrude A. Pratt
Nemasket Grange
Bridgewater, Massachusetts

CANNED PEPPERS

Green peppers
1/2 gal. white vinegar
2 lb. sugar
1/4 c. salt
1/2 tsp. salicylic acid
1 pt. corn syrup
Olive oil

Cut peppers in strips or quarters. Cook peppers in boiling water until just tender; drain. Combine vinegar, sugar, salt and salicylic acid in large saucepan; bring to a boil. Pack hot peppers in hot sterilized jars. Pour over peppers. Add 1/2 teaspoon olive oil to each jar. Place caps on jars. Process in boiling water bath for 10 minutes.

Mrs. Donald Robertson, Chm., Women's Act.
Robertsville Grange, No. 1784
Paris, Ohio

RED MANGO PEPPERS

Red mango peppers
3 c. sugar
2 c. vinegar

Wash mango peppers; cut in strips. Remove membrane and seeds; measure enough strips to fill 4 pints. Combine sugar and vinegar in 4-quart saucepan; add mango peppers, being certain that liquid covers peppers. Bring to a boil, then reduce heat; simmer for 10 minutes. Pack in hot sterilized jars; place caps on jars. Process in boiling water bath for 10 minutes. Yield: 3-4 pints. May be used like pimentos in cheese spread.

Mrs. Dan K. Stewart, C.W.A.
Victory Grange
Jackson, Ohio

RED PIMENTOS

4 doz. pimentos
1 qt. white vinegar
3 c. sugar
Salt
Oil

Remove seeds from pimentos; rinse. Cover with cold water; bring to a boil. Drain. Fill hot sterilized jars loosely. Combine vinegar, sugar and 1 quart water in saucepan; bring to a boil. Pour over pimentos. Add 1/2 teaspoon salt and 1 teaspoon oil to each jar. Place caps on jars. Process in boiling water bath for 10 minutes.

Mrs. Howard S. Scott
West Salem Grange
Transfer, Pennsylvania

HOMEMADE SAUERKRAUT

5 lb. cabbage
3 1/2 tbsp. coarse salt

Remove soiled leaves and shred cabbage, including heart which contains sugars which help in the fermentation process. Sprinkle salt over cabbage; mix thoroughly. Pack cabbage mixture into sterilized 1 or 2-quart jars. Press down cabbage until juice covers cabbage. Wipe off rims; place caps on jars loosely. Set jars on enamel trays; place where temperature will not rise over 70 degrees. Remove white scum which collects on tops of jars every day. If additional brine is needed to cover cabbage, fill jars to the top with a weak brine made by dissolving 2 tablespoons coarse salt in 1 quart water. Let ferment for about 10 days or until bubbles stop. Fill jars with boiling hot brine; replace caps. Process in boiling water bath for 30 minutes.

Floyd Lacina
Chester Royal Grange, No. 2181
Grinnell, Iowa

HOW TO MAKE SAUERKRAUT

5 lb. cabbage
3 1/2 tbsp. salt

Shred cabbage fine. Pack alternate layers of cabbage and salt into crock, using a potato masher. Cover with plate sufficiently weighted to keep cabbage under brine. Let cabbage ferment for 10 to 12 days. Cook cabbage for 15 minutes; pack into hot sterilized jars. Seal. Process in boiling water bath for 15 minutes for pints and 20 minutes for quarts. Store in cool, dark, dry place. Sauerkraut can be used directly from crock, if desired.

Mrs. Floyd Kniepkamp
Shiloh Valley Grange
Belleville, Illinois

Metric Conversion Chart

VOLUME

1 tsp.	=	4.9 cc
1 tbsp.	=	14.7 cc
1/3 c.	=	28.9 cc
1/8 c.	=	29.5 cc
1/4 c.	=	59.1 cc
1/2 c.	=	118.3 cc
3/4 c.	=	177.5 cc
1 c.	=	236.7 cc
2 c.	=	473.4 cc
1 fl. oz.	=	29.5 cc
4 oz.	=	118.3 cc
8 oz.	=	236.7 cc

1 pt.	=	473.4 cc
1 qt.	=	.946 liters
1 gal.	=	3.7 liters

CONVERSION FACTORS:

Liters	X	1.056	=	Liquid quarts
Quarts	X	0.946	=	Liters
Liters	X	0.264	=	Gallons
Gallons	X	3.785	=	Liters
Fluid ounces	X	29.563	=	Cubic centimeters
Cubic centimeters	X	0.034	=	Fluid ounces
Cups	X	236.575	=	Cubic centimeters
Tablespoons	X	14.797	=	Cubic centimeters
Teaspoons	X	4.932	=	Cubic centimeters
Bushels	X	0.352	=	Hectoliters
Hectoliters	X	2.837	=	Bushels

WEIGHT

1 dry oz.	=	28.3 Grams
1 lb.	=	.454 Kilograms

CONVERSION FACTORS:

Ounces (Avoir.)	X	28.349	=	Grams
Grams	X	0.035	=	Ounces
Pounds	X	0.454	=	Kilograms
Kilograms	X	2.205	=	Pounds

Equivalent Chart

3 tsp. = 1 tbsp.	16 oz. = 1 lb.	4 c. sifted flour = 1 lb.
2 tbsp. = 1/8 c.	1 oz. = 2 tbsp. fat or liquid	1 lb. butter = 2 c. or 4 sticks
4 tbsp. = 1/4 c.	2 c. fat = 1 lb.	2 pt. = 1 qt.
8 tbsp. = 1/2 c.	2 c. = 1 pt.	1 qt. = 4 c.
16 tbsp. = 1 c.	2 c. sugar = 1 lb.	A Few Grains = Less than 1/8 tsp.
5 tbsp. + 1 tsp. = 1/3 c.	5/8 c. = 1/2 c. + 2 tbsp.	Pinch is as much as can be taken
12 tbsp. = 3/4 c.	7/8 c. = 3/4 c. + 2 tbsp.	between tip of finger and thumb.
4 oz. = 1/2 c.	2 2/3 c. powdered sugar = 1 lb.	Speck = Less than 1/8 tsp.
8 oz. = 1 c.	2 2/3 c. brown sugar = 1 lb.	

WHEN YOU NEED APPROXIMATE MEASUREMENTS . . .

1 lemon makes 3 tablespoons juice
1 lemon makes 1 teaspoon grated peel
1 orange makes 1/3 cup juice
1 orange makes about 2 teaspoons grated peel
1 chopped medium onion makes 1/2 cup pieces
1 pound unshelled walnuts makes 1 1/2 to 1 3/4 cups shelled
1 pound unshelled almonds makes 3/4 to 1 cup shelled
8 to 10 egg whites make 1 cup

12 to 14 egg yolks make 1 cup
1 pound shredded American cheese makes 4 cups
1/4 pound crumbled blue cheese makes 1 cup
1 cup unwhipped cream makes 2 cups whipped
4 ounces (1 to 1 1/4 cups) uncooked macaroni makes 2 1/4 cups cooked
7 ounces spaghetti make 4 cups cooked
4 ounces (1 1/2 to 2 cups) uncooked noodles make 2 cups cooked.

MAKE 1 CUP OF FINE CRUMBS WITH . . .

28 saltine crackers
4 slices bread
14 square graham crackers
22 vanilla wafers

Substitutions

WHEN YOU'RE MISSING AN INGREDIENT . . .

Substitute 1 teaspoon dried herbs for 1 tablespoon fresh herbs.

Add 1/4 teaspoon baking soda and 1/2 cup buttermilk to equal 1 teaspoon baking powder. The buttermilk will replace 1/2 cup of the liquid indicated in the recipe.

Use 3 tablespoons dry cocoa plus 1 tablespoon butter or margarine instead of 1 square (1 ounce) unsweetened chocolate.

Make custard with 1 whole egg rather than 2 egg yolks.

Mix 1/2 cup evaporated milk with 1/2 cup water (or 1 cup reconstituted nonfat dry milk with 1 tablespoon butter) to replace 1 cup whole milk.

Make 1 cup of sour milk by letting stand for 5 minutes 1 tablespoon lemon juice or vinegar plus sweet milk to make 1 cup.

Substitute 1 package (2 teaspoons) active dry yeast for 1 cake compressed yeast.

Add 1 tablespoon instant minced onion, rehydrated, to replace 1 small fresh onion.

Substitute 1 tablespoon prepared mustard for 1 teaspoon dry mustard.

Use 1/8 teaspoon garlic powder instead of 1 small pressed clove of garlic.

Substitute 2 tablespoons of flour for 1 tablespoon of cornstarch to use as a thickening agent.

Mix 1/2 cup tomato sauce with 1/2 cup of water to make 1 cup tomato juice.

Make catsup or chili with 1 cup tomato sauce plus 1/2 cup sugar and 2 tablespoons vinegar.

CAN SIZE CHART

8 oz. can or jar	1 c.	1 lb. 4 oz. or 1 pt. 2 fl. oz. or No. 2 can or jar	2 1/2 c.
10 1/2 oz. can (picnic can)	1 1/4 c.	1 lb. 13 oz. can or jar or No. 2 1/2 can or jar	3 1/2 c.
12 oz. can (vacuum)	1 1/2 c.		
14-16 oz. or No. 300 can	1 1/4 c.	1 qt. 14 fl. oz. or 3 lb. 3 oz. or 46 oz. can	5 3/4 c.
16-17 oz. can or jar or No. 303 can or jar	2 c.	6 1/2 to 7 1/2 lb. or No. 10 can	12-13 c.

SUBSTITUTIONS

1 square *chocolate* (1 ounce) = 3 or 4 tablespoons cocoa plus 1/2 tablespoon fat.

1 tablespoon *cornstarch* (for thickening) = 2 tablespoons flour (approximately).

1 cup sifted *all-purpose flour* = 1 cup plus 2 tablespoons sifted cake flour.

1 cup sifted *cake flour* = 1 cup minus 2 tablespoons sifted all-purpose flour.

1 teaspoon *baking powder* = 1/4 teaspoon baking soda plus 1/2 teaspoon cream of tartar.

1 cup *bottled milk* = 1/2 cup evaporated milk plus 1/2 cup water.

1 cup *sour milk* = 1 cup sweet milk into which 1 tablespoon vinegar or lemon juice has been stirred; or 1 cup buttermilk.

1 cup *sweet milk* = 1 cup sour milk or buttermilk plus 1/2 teaspoon baking soda.

1 cup *canned tomatoes* = about 1 1/3 cups cut-up fresh tomatoes, simmered 10 minutes.

3/4 cup *cracker crumbs* = 1 cup bread crumbs.

1 cup *cream, sour, heavy* = 1/3 cup butter and 2/3 cup milk in any sour milk recipe.

1 cup *cream, sour, thin* = 3 tablespoons butter and 3/4 cup milk in sour milk recipe.

1 cup *molasses* = 1 cup honey.

Calorie Chart

Food Milk, Cream, Cheese	Measure	Food Energy (Calories)
Milk, fluid, whole, 3.5% fat	1 cup	160
Milk, fluid, nonfat (skim)	1 cup	90
Buttermilk, fluid, cultured, made from skim milk	1 cup	90
Cheese, Roquefort type	1 oz.	105
Cheese, Cottage, creamed	12 oz.	360
Cream, half and half	1 cup	325
Cream, heavy	1 cup	840
Custard, baked	1 cup	305
Yoghurt, whole milk	1 cup	150

Eggs (large)

Raw	1 egg	80
Scrambled (milk and fat)	1 egg	110

Meat, Poultry

Bacon	2 sli.	90
Beef, lean and fat	3 oz.	245
Hamburger, regular	3 oz.	245
Steak, broiled, lean and fat	3 oz.	330
Corned beef	3 oz.	185
Chicken, cooked:		
Flesh only, broiled	3 oz.	115
With bone, 1/2 breast, fried	3.3 oz.	155
Chicken, potpie, baked	8 oz.	535
Lamb chop, thick with bone	4.8 oz.	400
Lamb, lean and fat	3 oz.	235
Liver, beef, fried	2 oz.	130
Ham, light cure, lean	3 oz.	245
Ham, boiled, sliced	2 oz.	135
Pork roast, lean and fat	3 oz.	310
Frankfurter, heated	2 oz.	170
Veal cutlet	3 oz.	185
Veal roast	3 oz.	230

Fish

Bluefish, baked with fat	3 oz.	135
Clams, raw, meat only	3 oz.	65
Crab meat, canned	3 oz.	85
Oysters, raw, meat	1 cup	160
Salmon, pink, canned	3 oz.	120
Shrimp, canned, meat	3 oz.	100
Swordfish, broiled with butter	3 oz.	150
Tuna, canned in oil	3 oz.	170

Nuts

Almonds, shelled, whole	1 cup	850
Cashew nuts, roasted	1 cup	785
Peanuts, roasted	1 cup	840
Pecans, halves	1 cup	740
Walnuts, black or native, chopped	1 cup	790

CALORIE CHART

Vegetables & Products

Asparagus, cooked, spears .... 4 sp. 10
Asparagus, canned .... 1 cup 45
Beans, lima, immature, cooked .... 1 cup 190
Beans, snap, green, cooked .... 1 cup 30
Beans, snap, canned, green .... 1 cup 45
Beans, snap, yellow or wax .... 1 cup 30
Beans, sprouted mung, cooked .... 1 cup 35
Beets, cooked .... 2 beets 30
Broccoli, cooked .... 1 stalk 45
Brussels sprouts, cooked .... 1 cup 55
Cabbage, raw, shredded .... 1 cup 15
Cabbage, cooked .... 1 cup 30
Carrots, raw, 5½ by 1 in. 1 20
Carrots, cooked, diced .... 1 cup 45
Cauliflower, cooked, flower buds .... 1 cup 25
Celery, raw, stalk, large .... 1 stalk 5
Corn, cooked, 5 by 1¾-in. ear .... 1 ear 70
Corn, canned .... 1 cup 170
Cucumbers, raw, pared .... 10 oz. 30
Lettuce, Boston type .... 1 head 30
Mushrooms, canned .... 1 cup 40
Onions, mature, raw, 2½ in. 1 40
Peas, green, cooked .... 1 cup 115
Peas, green, canned .... 1 cup 165
Potatoes, medium, baked 1 90
Potatoes, medium, boiled in skin 1 105
Potatoes, mashed, milk added .... 1 cup 125
Potato chips, medium .... 10 chips 115
Sauerkraut, canned .... 1 cup 45
Spinach, cooked .... 1 cup 40
Squash, summer, diced, cooked .... 1 cup 30
Squash, winter, baked, mashed .... 1 cup 130
Sweet potatoes, baked 1 155
Sweet potatoes, candied, 3½ by 2¼ in. 1 295
Tomatoes, raw, medium 1 40
Tomato catsup .... 1 tbsp. 15
Tomato juice, canned .... 1 cup 45

Fruits and Fruit Products

Apples, medium, raw 1 70
Apple juice, bottled or canned .... 1 cup 120
Applesauce, canned, sweetened .... 1 cup 230
Bananas, raw, 6 by 1½ in. 1 100
Blueberries, raw .... 1 cup 85
Cantaloupe, raw, medium .... ½ melon 60
Cranberry sauce, sweetened, canned .... 1 cup 405
Grapefruit, raw, medium, white .... ½ 45
Grapefruit juice, canned, unsweetened .... 1 cup 100
Grapes, raw, American type .... 1 cup 65
Grapejuice, canned .... 1 cup 165
Lemons, raw, medium 1 20
Lemon juice, fresh .... 1 cup 60
Lime juice, fresh .... 1 cup 65
Oranges, raw, 2 5/8-in. diam. 1 65
Orange juice, frozen, undiluted .... 1 can 360
Peaches, raw, whole, medium 1 35
Peaches, canned, halves or sliced .... 1 cup 200
Pears, raw, 3 by 2½ in. 1 100
Pineapple, canned, sliced .... Large sli. 90
Plums, raw, 2-in. diam. 1 25
Prune juice, canned .... 1 cup 200
Raisins, seedless, pkged., ½ oz. .... 1 pkg. 40

CALORIE CHART

Strawberries, raw, capped .... 1 cup 55
Watermelon, raw .... 1 wedge 115

Grain Products

Bagel, egg, 3-in. diam. 1 165
Biscuits, baking powder 1 105
Bran flakes (40 % bran) .... 1 cup 105
Bread, cracked wheat .... 1 loaf 1190
Bread, enriched, French .... 1 loaf 1315
Bread, enriched, Italian .... 1 loaf 1250
Bread, raisin .... 1 loaf 1190
Bread, American, rye .... 1 loaf 1100
Bread, white, enriched .... 1 loaf 1225
Cake, Angel Food .... 1 cake 1645
Cupcakes, small, choc. icing .... 1 cake 130
Cake, Boston cream pie .... 1 piece 210
Cake, pound .... 1 loaf 2430
Crackers, saltines 4 50
Danish Pastry, round piece 1 275
Doughnuts, cake type 1 125
Macaroni, enriched, cooked .... 1 cup 190
Noodles, enriched .... 1 cup 200
Oatmeal, or rolled oats, cooked .... 1 cup 130
Pie, apple, 1/7 of 9-in. pie .... 1 sector 350
Pie, custard, 1/7 of 9-in. pie .... 1 sector 285
Pie, lemon meringue, 1/7 of 9-in. pie .... 1 sector 305
Pie, mince, 1/7 of 9-in. pie .... 1 sector 365
Pie, pumpkin, 1/7 of 9-in. pie .... 1 sector 275
Pizza, cheese, 1/8 of 14-in. diam. .... 1 sector 185
Popcorn, plain .... 1 cup 25
Rolls, home recipe .... 1 roll 120
Spaghetti, enriched, cooked .... 1 cup 155

Fats, Oils

Butter, regular .... ½ cup 810
Lard .... 1 cup 1850
Vegetable fats .... 1 cup 1770
Margarine .... ½ cup 815
Salad Dressing, French, regular .... 1 tbsp. 65
Salad dressing, mayonnaise .... 1 tbsp. 100
Salad dressing, 1,000 island .... 1 tbsp. 80

Sugars, Sweets

Candy, milk chocolate, sweetened .... 1 oz. 145
Candy, plain fudge .... 1 oz. 115
Chocolate syrup, fudge type .... 1 oz. 125
Honey, strained or extracted .... 1 tbsp. 65
Jellies .... 1 tbsp. 50
Sugar, brown .... 1 cup 820
Sugar, granulated .... 1 cup 770

Miscellaneous

Barbecue sauce .... 1 cup 230
Beer .... 12 oz. 150
Alcoholic beverage, 86-proof .... 1½ fl. oz. 105
Cola-type beverage .... 12 fl. oz. 145
Ginger ale .... 12 fl. oz. 115
Soup, cream of chicken .... 1 cup 180
Soup, tomato .... 1 cup 175
Beans with pork .... 1 cup 170
Clam chowder .... 1 cup 80

Source: Home and Garden Bulletin No. 72, U.S. Department of Agriculture

Index

PHOTOGRAPHY CREDITS: Back Cover — United Dairy Industry Association; The North American Blueberry Council; American Dairy Association; United Fresh Fruit and Vegetable Association; Idaho Potato Commission; Knox Gelatine, Inc.; Spanish Green Olive Commission; South African Rock Lobster Service Corporation; National Macaroni Institute; California Strawberry Advisory Board; R. C. Bigelow, Inc.; National Live Stock and Meat Board; Pickle Packers International, Inc.; Spice Islands; The J. M. Smucker Company; Charcoal Briquet Institute; Louisiana Yam Commission; A-W Brands, Inc.; California Raisin Advisory Board; Pineapple Growers Association; Green Giant Company; DIAMOND Walnut Growers, Inc.; Pillsbury Company; Kerr Glass; Ball Corporation; John Oster Manufacturing Company; The American Spice Trade Association; Processed Apples Institute, Inc.; Florida Citrus Commission; Standard Brands Products: Fleischmann's Yeast and Margarine; Best Foods, A Division of CPC International, Inc.

For Your Convenience . . .
Additional copies of NATIONAL GRANGE BICENTENNIAL YEAR COOKBOOK
may be ordered, for $5.00 each copy, from: National Grange Cookbook
1616 H Street N. W.
Washington, D. C. 20006